A
KINGDOM
and a
VILLAGE

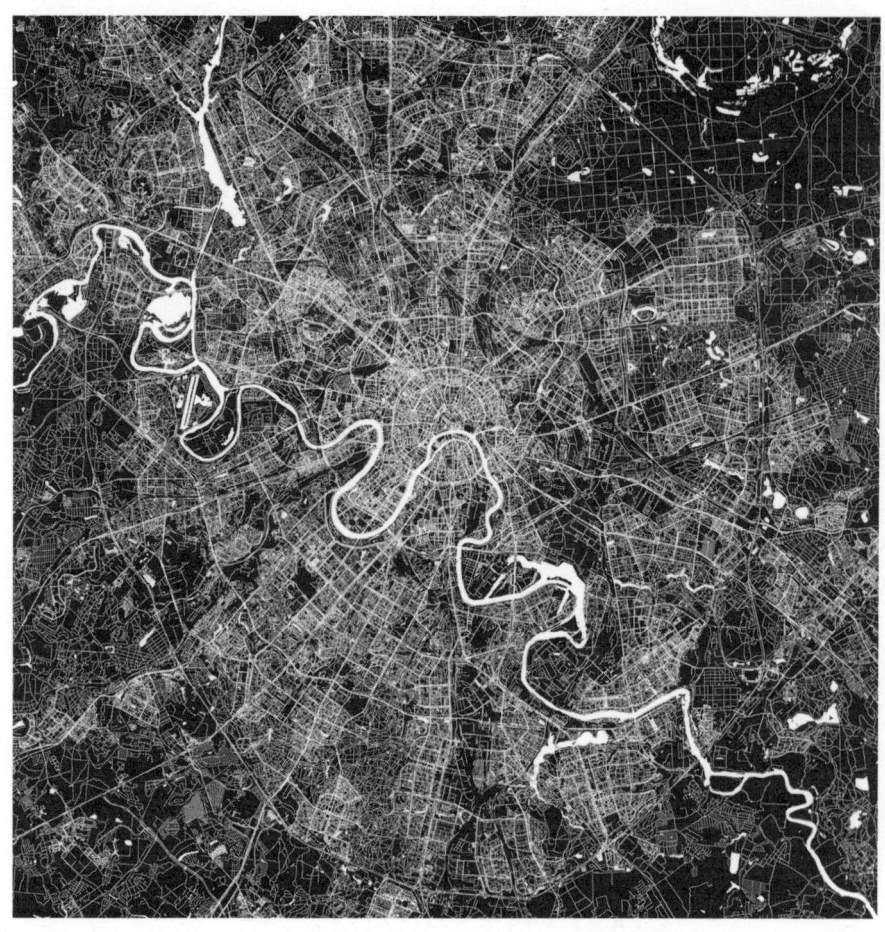

Vector map of Moscow.

A
KINGDOM
and a
VILLAGE

A ONE-THOUSAND-YEAR
HISTORY OF MOSCOW

SIMON MORRISON

THE BODLEY HEAD
LONDON

1 3 5 7 9 10 8 6 4 2

The Bodley Head, an imprint of Vintage, is part of the
Penguin Random House group of companies

Vintage, Penguin Random House UK, One Embassy Gardens,
8 Viaduct Gardens, London SW11 7BW

penguin.co.uk/vintage
global.penguinrandomhouse.com

Penguin
Random House
UK

First published in Great Britain by The Bodley Head in 2026
First published in the United States of America by Alfred A. Knopf in 2026

Copyright © Simon Morrison 2026

The moral right of the author has been asserted

Printed and bound in Great Britain by Clays Ltd, Elcograf S.p.A.

The authorised representative in the EEA is Penguin Random House Ireland,
Morrison Chambers, 32 Nassau Street, Dublin D02 YH68

A CIP catalogue record for this book is available from the British Library

ISBN 9781847926524

Penguin Random House is committed to a sustainable future
for our business, our readers and our planet. This book is made
from Forest Stewardship Council® certified paper.

MIX
Paper | Supporting
responsible forestry
FSC
www.fsc.org
FSC® C018179

For Elizabeth

CONTENTS

PART 3: SOVIET CAPITAL

PART 1

BEFORE RUSSIA

TANYA

Russia (Rossiya) has never been called Russia, not officially. It's been Holy Rus, the Tsardom of Russia, Imperial Russia, Soviet Russia, and the Russian Federation but never just Russia. That place doesn't exist, except in the imagination, in a dreamscape of crime and punishment, war and peace, terror and utopia, Uncle Vanya and Doctor Zhivago.

Moscow stands at the center of a nation comprising eleven percent of the globe's landmass, eleven time zones, and roughly 145 million people—some 13 million of whom live in the capital. Church and state converge in the city, home to the Eastern Orthodox Church and the presidential administration, known colloquially as the Kremlin. Moscow has the power to end the world—a power claimed over centuries to compensate for the real and imagined "grievous bondage" of Russia's history, borrowing a phrase from a revolutionary tune. To thwart invasion, Moscow invaded, again and again, partly defining itself by what it took from elsewhere—from the Polish-Lithuanian Commonwealth and from Kyiv, Ukraine, the Slavic fountainhead. Moscow jealously guards its seized standing. Citizens are surveilled, neighboring territories subjugated, laws manipulated, and independent media organizations exiled.

Nations and their power are always illusions, until they aren't, and

Moscow is an elusive place. Its greatest trick is the "riddle, wrapped in a mystery, inside an enigma" bunkum; the city projects an inscrutable aura but in fact knows itself all too well. On shrill winter nights, Moscow's power is conspicuous, its Orthodox cathedrals and Stalinist high-rises illuminated, though the view dims in the autumn and spring, shrouded in sheets of greige. Isolated between continents, it seems the loneliest of the world's metropolises, unbounded like its aspirations. Had circumstances been different, Moscow might not have been the capital. Or it might not have existed at all.

In trying to understand the city I have studied now for more than two decades, I have sifted through its memories—inevitably along with a few of my own. I've researched the birchbark scratchings that record the oldest layer of Slavic civilization, the history of Russia before Russia in Kyivan Rus, the rise and fall of the Mongol Empire, liturgical chronicles, icons, court documents, military records, music, literature, and more. As I gaze into a distant mirror, I hope to see the present reflected back. "Do you know what this country has been through?" my Moscow friends scoff. It's relatively easy to recall the wars, invasions, pogroms, and prison camps of the last century, harder to resurrect those from centuries ago. Harder still to see the people who have persevered through it all and the culture that preserves civilization, even in deeply uncivil times.

Moscow is hard to love, but I love it. I love it more than other parts of Russia, but I can't say why. Perhaps it's the mirth behind the rudeness, the up-with-life attitude that persists in good times and bad, or the fact that it's completely unfree but seems anarchically unbridled. Nowadays there is less merriment, sunk as Moscow is in a combination of Putin stagnation, the Ukraine war, and the techno-feudalism that is making serfs of us all in a world owned by billionaires pumping propaganda through the black boxes in the palms of our hands. Perhaps that's why I wrote this book: out of nostalgia for pre-oligarch decrepitude, when the world looked at Moscow with pity, and Moscow looked back at the world as if to say: You'll fall apart too, and you won't know how to grieve. Moscow is hardly the oldest place in the world, but it is among the most scarred and experienced.

I first visited in December 1990, on a trip organized by the Slavic

Department of McGill University. It was still the USSR. Border guards entered the plane at Sheremetyevo airport and escorted the twelve of us on the trip into the unlit international terminal. The honeycomb ceiling of brass cylinders hid behind smoke from filterless Soviet cigarettes. A television screen flickered overhead, announcing the arrival of one other flight that evening from Helsinki. A mailbox in the terminal was labeled "for lost documents." That's where any disgruntled citizen could drop a note to the *militsiya* denouncing a traitorous boss or unfaithful lover, ensuring they'd be questioned by police. My visa was stamped at passport control but not my actual passport, so no official trace of the visit was preserved. A student behind me in line blanched with fear. Only later did I learn that he was smuggling thousands of dollars into the USSR to pass to a distant relative. He made it through after our chaperone distracted the inspector by offering him a sealed pack of Marlboros.

We stayed across the street from the massive stone Foreign Affairs building in the (currently) three-star Belgrade Hotel, a place of petty intrigues. The front-desk clerk operated a prostitute ring; peddlers roamed the premises hawking sports jerseys in garbled English while soldiers at the door stared at a television screen tuned to MTV.

Our guide in Moscow, Tanya, was a middle-aged woman who wore thick glasses plucked from a swiveling Optika stand at a Metro station. Like every guide with the foreign tour operator Intourist, she was vaguely affiliated with the secret services (KGB) and so was obliged to fill out reports about her interactions with foreigners that no one read. Tours were all the same: on the jet-lagged first morning, a visit to Red Square and adjacent churches, the depleted GUM department store, the Kremlin treasures, and lunch back in the hotel. Tanya tucked the leftovers—liver and puréed potatoes—in her purse to take home for her cat. The only color in the city could be found in the McDonald's on Pushkin Square with its sky-blue walls and yellow plastic chairs.

"Here is where Chekhov wrote some of his most famous plays, stories, and letters," Tanya narrated as the tour bus passed by the necropolis where Chekhov was interred, not where he wrote anything. We traveled outside Moscow to the enclave of Zagorsk (Sergiyev Posad) to gaze upon gold cupolas and icons of the Mother of God. A girl swaddled in an oversized coat asked to pose for a picture with me, then demanded a dollar. On the trip back to the capital, the bus passed a giant metal statue titled "Worker and Collective Farm Woman," which Tanya explained was cast in 1937 for the Paris World's Fair and hauled back to Moscow to decorate the entrance of an agricultural exhibition.

I went for a walk in the area around my hotel, crossing a cement encirclement into an underpass where Roma huddled. Eventually I found myself on the pitch-black, cobblestone Arbat—one of the oldest streets in Moscow. It sparked my curiosity. As with many street and neighborhood names, the origins of Arbat are unclear. It might come from the Tatar word for cart or caravan, *arba*, I learned later, or the Arabic for suburb, *rabad*. Arbat might even derive from *gorbat* (hunchback), because the road curved in and around streams. An odder explanation links the street name to sorcerers (*koldunï-arbui*) and sacrifices.[1] In September 1475, flames consumed the wooden houses along the road, including the home of Nikifor Basenkov, an aide to Tsar Ivan III, also known as Ivan the Great.[2] Most references to the Arbat in the ancient chronicles are connected to fires, amid mention of invasions and plagues and noble births. Beneath the cobblestones lie layers upon layers of ash and coal. I must have turned down a connecting side street, then several others, shorter and shorter in length. It was difficult to trace the path back through the shadows.

A year after that first trip, I moved to Moscow to learn Russian among people trying to learn English. It was 1991, after the collapse of the Soviet Union and the arrival of no-one-gives-a-damn cynicism. Amid the chaos under Yeltsin, a bleak frontier culture had taken hold. People burned crates in the middle of the road after the market closed; soldiers stripped metal fixtures from the unoccupied institute next door; everyone lined up for the water truck, which drove up around noon. Women sold cabbage pies and pickles out of battered buckets while asking for *den'gi na khram*, donations for the church. Later I learned that this was a scam: Moscow was simply for sale. Anyone older than thirty seemed to be hawking the contents of their apartments on the streets. I didn't understand the point of peddling burned-out lightbulbs until I discovered that people swapped them out at work, sneaking the good ones home.

I lived with obliging Russian graduate students in a tenement on the southwest edge of the city, past the last Metro stop on the red line, the first line ever built. State planning produced octagonal apartment complexes that loomed, nine to seventeen stories high, over patches of park and tiled newsstands. Winter clouds and sleet blurred everything together, but as my eyes adjusted, what seemed dull grew more distinctive. The Russian ambassador to Libya hung out in my room, as did a teenager named Konstantin with an unfortunate stutter and endearing affection for the American rock band Metallica. Yellow roach powder covered the scuffed parquet floors and coated the tongue of Masha the cat, who roamed freely through the complex. When I turned on the light in the communal kitchen, roaches scattered oblivious to the poison. Two ladies staffed the front desk during the day, answering the telephone and laying out mail on the odd occasion it arrived. One had a deathly dull second job as a *dezhurnaya po eskalatoru*, an escalator monitor in the Metro.

I learned to improvise meals from winter vegetables available at the wretched market near the transit hub, and hyperinflation meant that I could subsist on the ruble equivalent of $20 a week. A Nigerian money changer in the dorm next to mine set the exchange rates. Ensconced among piles of bills with Vladimir Lenin's face, he fingered a revolver he claimed to have used just a couple of weeks ago. Across the street, a bread store sold white and rye loaves for the equivalent of a nickel; both sweet Soviet champagne and layer cake were easy to buy. Packs of dogs (former pets) scavenged along the roads and understood traffic lights well enough to avoid getting hit by the double-length buses trundling along Prospekt Vernadskogo.[3] The packs slept in the Metro stations, and sometimes even rode the trains. I once saw a green dog and have since wondered whether it had the same affliction as the blue dogs featured in a *Moscow Times* article a few years back. They had all wandered too close to an abandoned chemical factory.[4]

I continued to puzzle over street names and got lost in etymologies. The word for village, *selo,* is tucked into the word for universe,

Dormitories operated by Moscow State Pedagogical University, 1992.

vselennaya. Sem'ya, family, comes out as "the seven of us." *Zavod,* factory, derives from "behind" and "water," or that which draws from water. The word for bear, *medved,* attaches the word for honey to part of the word for seeker. *Grad* (settlement) and *gorod* (city) and *gora* (mountain) linked in my head once I read that Moscow (*Moskva*) was built on seven hills. The names of the oldest Metro stations also contained micro-histories, so too the faded playbills of the theaters and chipped words at the streetcar stop.

My teachers pretended to teach while I pretended to learn. One of my Canadian classmates lit a cigarette in class; he cruelly pointed out that the rhyming proverb "Ne imey sto rubley, a imey sto druzey" (Better a hundred friends than a hundred rubles) didn't mean much now that a stack of cucumbers cost twice that much. Near the end of my four months there, I received a reminder from McGill that my master's thesis was due, so I spent the rest of my time researching a propagandistic opera by Sergey Prokofiev. The response I received from my teachers when I explained my topic was, in effect, "That old stuff? How boring can you get!"

Soviet life had been a drag, and no path forward for Russia had emerged. Or would. This is another lesson Moscow has for the world: Don't wish for everything to collapse, since what's built on rubble is crooked and unstable. Criminal elements stepped into the void, bringing chaos and reminiscences of the straight, stable life under Leonid Brezhnev. The Swedish-Russian Night Flight club was soon joined by casinos and a bar near the former KGB (current FSB) headquarters called the Hungry Duck, an overcrowded pit filled with sweaty expats hell-bent on a good time. I was a foreigner, and I realized that foreigners were part of the problem: they treated Moscow, and Muscovites, with exploitative contemptuousness. A writer for *Salon* captured the scene at the bar, the men in tracksuits ogling the "maidens of the masses whose lot in Russia, for the past 800 years, has differed in form but remained the same in essence— enslavement to Mongol invaders, serfdom on gentry manors, bondage to blighted kolkhoz and factory and, most recently, exploitation by oligarchs and a corrupt, rudderless state."[5] Judging by the antics of gonzo journalists with multi-entry visas in the 1990s, Moscow was eros unleashed, land of the turbo-charged libido, the urbanized Scythian steppe. Writers for *The Exile,* an expat American newspaper, tried to demonstrate their journalistic credibility by venturing into the provinces to interview striking miners but mostly bragged about their sexual exploits.[6]

I washed dishes in a restaurant serving drunken (bourbon-soaked) beans, bought tickets for a pittance to out-of-tune performances at the Bolshoi Theater, and audited a course at the Moscow Conservatory, though I didn't understand half of what was said. I went camping before it was warm enough to go camping. I finished my thesis. I left and came back, this time to research a dissertation

on aesthetics during the Russian Silver Age at the turn of the twentieth century. I took a room in an apartment building on the northern
outskirts, a fifteen-minute walk along asphalt sidewalks past a Metro
station named Planernaya (or alternately, and with the accent shifted
from the first to the second syllable, Planyornaya, from the French
word for glider, *planeur*).[7] I could have stayed at the conservatory
dorm, but it was so cramped that my friend Galina checked herself
into a women's hospital for a bit of peace. Rent in the apartment was
$200 a month and then nothing, so long as I ran errands for my land-
lady, a middle-aged accountant named Valentina.

She worked for some sort of bank, and her boyfriend pledged
to make good on her threats to a certain Boris Nikolayevich for the
million rubles he owed her after his hair salon went bust (or maybe
never even opened). Hyperinflation didn't bother Valentina, but the
Chechen war, Yeltsin's beet-colored face, and television advertisements for toilet paper did. She invited me to watch classic Soviet films
like *Moscow Doesn't Believe in Tears*, whose title is an ancient proverb
meaning, basically, "You're on your own, kid." No Muscovite would
be so gullible as to assume the government was ever on their side.
Valentina waxed nostalgic about her salad days as a member of the
Communist Party under Brezhnev and doted on her imported Sie-
mens appliances that short-circuited the apartment. Weekends were
spent at her two-story brick dacha, and she flew to Istanbul a couple
of times on shoe-shopping sprees, amassing fifty pairs—enough, she
said, to last the rest of her life. When, as often happened, a Soviet
hero of World War II appeared on television with a chest covered in
medals, I braced for a lecture about how Iosif Stalin had saved the
world. "He did a lot of bad stuff," Valentina reluctantly admitted, but
his security head, Lavrentiy Beria, bore the blame for the murder of
"enemies of the people." She would change the subject by opening
the curtain and gesturing to the apartment complex outside. "Look
what we got built," she said with pride. I stared at the expanse of off-
white rectangles.

Moscow lacked police, basic services, any semblance of a functional government. Crumbled sidewalks were replaced by planks
that covered the sludge that concealed the ancient wood fretwork

that buried the bones of the metropolis and its people. Flea markets sold Soviet kitsch, while imperial antiques disappeared from private collections along with their owners. Nineteenth-century portraits and gilded icons were spirited out the back doors of museums to the West, at the time riding high on its Cold War triumph. Long-buried streams began to leak into basements, and the odor from the *pissoir* in the basement of the Lenin Library rose into the cafeteria and the reading rooms. Ammonia damaged the paper preserving ancient chronicles (*letopisi*) of tales that served the needs of princes and priests at the expense of those beneath them or at their throats. Russian rulers always knew that what was written became the truth, whatever the facts.

I had a library card that allowed me to access books and articles related to my PhD work. Once I'd put in enough time, I was given access to microfilmed documents. Sometimes I was scolded by the stressed staff for ordering too much or expecting the order to be filled on the spot. My naïve impetuousness came back to me a few years ago while sorting through a box of old photographs from my student travels. I found a picture of me standing in front of a bronze statue of Yuri Dolgorukiy, the fabled founder of Moscow. I don't remember who took the picture or the name of the person I'm standing with, just that she was from Siberia.

Today, Moscow is glamorous, unrecognizable from the Russian capital of the desperate 1990s. The gyre of its history, I have learned, often defies the logic of cause and effect. Anything can happen, meaning Karl Marx was wrong: there is no dialectic, no ordered or preordained progression. I have assembled this book with a focus on rulers first and the ruled second, since the latter aren't often recorded during Moscow's first centuries, their lives whirled together under the general heading The People (*Narod*). I move through the centuries chronologically until the era of Peter the Great, then more thematically to consider how Moscow has rebuilt and reimagined itself through the eyes of dreamers and schemers and evildoers. What follows is the history of a great geopolitical power, a story of water and land and fire, nature and people and spirits, hard lessons and harder truths.

1

_____

THE RIVER

To mark the 800th anniversary of Moscow in 1947, the Soviet dictator, Iosif Stalin, ordered a team of archeologists in Kyiv to locate the grave of a prince named Yuri, the supposed founder of Moscow. In 1147, Yuri had reported his presence in a fort on a hill surrounded by a slow-moving river. A dirt and wood barrier failed to thwart determined invaders. It was reinforced and expanded again and again over the centuries, until it became a symbol of sovereign power: the Kremlin, the official seat of the Russian and Soviet governments.

The archeologists' goal was to find Yuri's skull, which would guide the design of a statue of him across from Moscow City Hall. But nothing was found in the Church of the Savior on Berestov where Yuri was thought to have been buried, despite the promises of a plaque inside the chapel claiming "This is where he lies." In 1989, three sarcophagi were found on the grounds along with a beer bottle containing an indecipherable note. One of them, it's been hoped, contains the remains of Yuri, the others one of his sons and one of his wives. DNA tests have been inconclusive.[1]

Nonetheless, the design competition for the statue went forward. The proposal submitted by Vera Mukhina depicted Yuri "in the magnificent ancient clothes of a Russian prince—no chain mail—in a long white cloak trimmed with gold stitching, held with a precious sparkling buckle." He had soft features befitting the prince of a "capital of peace, goodness, art."[2] This design was rejected in favor of another by Sergey Orlov, who made Yuri a true Russian hero and a symbol of the nation's might (his maternal Anglo-Saxon lineage aside). When the monument was belatedly unveiled, on June 6, 1954, one person yelled "Doesn't look like him!" while another insisted "It does!"[3] Communist hardliners argued that a statue of the prince, a feudal exploiter of the peasantry, didn't belong in the middle of Soviet Moscow. They lost the argument.

Yuri girds for battle; his stallion raises a hoof. He is armored and helmeted with a heraldic shield boasting the coat of arms of Moscow: an image of St. George (Yuri's patron saint) slaying a serpent.[4] St. George symbolizes the combined power of the church and the state, which vanquish Russia's enemies while punishing her people for their sins and disloyalty, represented by the serpent. "No matter how terrible the demon might be, power believes, and never doubts, that one day it will manage to defeat the monster and save us all," medievalist Vladimir Sharov explains.[5] Power looks after itself. Power exists for itself.

The prince sits high in his bronze saddle, pulling on his stallion's reins with one of his long arms, pointing downward with the other, as if to say this is where it all began, where the walls went up and the moats were dug and princes, priests, and traders from the Silk Road gathered. Here is the spot near, if not the moment when, Moscow came into being as a fort on a hill along a river.

The river bears the same name as the city: Moscow or, in proper Russian pronunciation, Moskva. It's shallow, murky, and freezes in winter, as do its various tributaries. The Neglinka, its largest tributary, runs underneath the center of Moscow and once served as a defensive moat before being encased in pipes in the eighteenth century. By that time, the Neglinka reeked of human and animal waste and needed to be buried. During severe droughts, the Moskva reluctantly withdrew from its banks and dried up in places. Between 1932 and 1937 an eighty-mile-long canal was dug by prisoners to provide for the city's industrial and domestic water needs. It connected the Moscow neighborhood of Tushino to a network of inland waterways and seas in the north. The alleys in the oldest parts of the city follow the contours of streams that no longer exist, having been rerouted or buried.

The Moskva flows from west to east through Moscow, the surrounding region, Moskovskaya oblast', and a much older city named Smolensk. It eventually merges with the Oka River and then the Volga, the longest river in Europe, spanning well over two thousand miles across boreal forests and desert basins to empty into the Caspian Sea. The Moskva was easily navigable by medieval canoes and sledges, so a ring-fenced settlement arose above a brackish bend. There were long, hard rains and snows, though in nature, as the cliché goes, there's no such thing as bad weather. The forest drowsed in fall and rustled in spring; through the summer, crickets chirped and toads croaked in the marshes, and the meadow across the river hummed. The spirits of the water, wind, and wood had yet to clash with monks and priests and their belief in an almighty God who had made man in his image and granted him dominion over the birds and beasts.

Moscow existed long before Russia but for centuries had no influence, no role in affairs beyond its own wooden walls. The name itself denotes either a boggy place or black, turbid water; it might also, as tourist guides claim, refer to female bears (from the Finno-Ugric words *maska* and *ava*, meaning bear and dam respectively). The Komi language suggests a derivation from *moska*, a cow, and *va*, which means either "river" or "wet." Perhaps the Moskva River was a good spot for breeding cattle? A biblical explanation, popularized in the sixteenth century, claims that Moscow was named after Mosoch, a grandson of Noah who, according to the book of Genesis, succumbed with Noah to the seductions of wine. Mosoch arrived in the Russian lands and named the beautiful site he found overlooking a river after himself and his wife Kva. The combined names of their children became the name of a steep-banked stream, the Yauza. In this fanciful tale, Moscow is more than five thousand years old, but connections to turbid water and cows prove most convincing, because these have a root, *mosk*, in East Slavonic and relate, at heart, to the Russian word for "dank," *promozgliy*.[6]

Statue of Yuri Dolgorukiy across from Moscow City Hall.

The people who traveled and foraged along the river were called, in Old Norse and Old Swedish, *Rus. Russian* of course derives from *Rus,* a word also related to the Finnic *Ruotsi* and the Estonian *Root'si,* referring to Swedes, but the *Rus* were not Russian in the familiar sense.[7] The original Rus seem to have been Scandinavian boatsmen, "the inhabitants of straits between islands."[8] A medieval illustration shows a dozen or so Rus tucked into a pair of sailboats on wheels, having rolled up to the walls of Constantinople from its northern shore.[9] They look happy in their vessel. In winter, when the ice was thick enough, the boatsmen traveled on sledges piled up with goods. They also traveled by land over paths frozen hard as rock.

The origins of the word *Slav,* as in Slavic peoples or Slavic languages, is more obscure. Historians long ago cut the cord between *Slav* and *slave,* an invention of later times. The standard story is that *Slav* was pressed into service as *slave* because so many of the young women sold into bondage came from the East—most notably in 1382, when Asiatic horsemen descended from Genghis Khan sacked

Moscow, flaying and burning thousands of people and dragging away thousands more. Etymological dictionaries also suggest a derivation from a Byzantine Greek word meaning "plunder," which turns the Slavs into marauding pirates. *Slav* also sounds like *slava*, the Russian word for glory. But *slav* and *slava* might simply be homonyms. Linguistically *slav* better relates to *slov*, the Russian for "word." In this conception, the Slavs were tribes who could understand one another, because they spoke the same or similar tongues. And there's more: *Slav/slov* relates to the archaic verb "to hear/listen,"[10] which establishes a neat binary between Slavs and *nemtsi*—literally "the dumb," "those without speech," or inarticulate. *Nemtsi* is a standard medieval word for "foreigners," and in Russian is now the word for Germans.[11] Lastly, there is an appealing correlation between the word *Slav* and the forgotten Indo-European word *slauos*. Who are the Slavs? They are what that word means: people.[12]

The origins of these people are as cloudy as the Moskva itself, and what little is known is suspect. Moscow was a trading route before it became a hodgepodge of hovels and labyrinth of lanes. Pottery fragments reveal the presence or at least the passing-through of hunters and fishers since the Neolithic period, 7000–1700 BCE. Excavations along the Oka suggest the possible presence of East Slavic tribes (the Krivichi and Vyatichi) in the ninth or tenth century CE.[13] Two coins—silver dirhams minted in 862 and 866 in the Iranian city of Merv—also ended up in the bog.[14] Recently unearthed bracelets, pendants, crystals, and beads indicate sophisticated trading activity as far back as 1100, and a lead seal decorated with an image of the Mother of God and the archangel Michael suggests the presence in the area, before 1100, of the Eastern Orthodox Metropolitan of Kyiv.[15] Other artifacts, including "pink slate spindle-whorls, beads and a lead weight from a pair of scales," were not made in Moscow but brought up from Kyiv and as far south as the Black Sea.[16]

Some 550 miles to the south of Moscow, Kyiv was the heart of what would become Kyivan Rus, a loose federation of Eastern Slavic peoples who existed between two empires from the late ninth century to the mid-thirteenth century. The Byzantine Empire stretched down into the Mediterranean, encompassing parts of the Balkans,

Middle East, and northeast Africa. Its imperial center, Constantinople, enjoyed olive trees, a blue-green sea, and bright yellow sunlight. Byzantium was the total opposite of the fur, hide, iron, gray clouds, and smothering snows and frosts of the Rus. This realm has long been credited as the source of the Russian alphabet. The assumption is that Cyrillic came to Kyiv from Bulgaria and Serbia as part of a conscious effort to spread the Christian faith from Byzantium into the Slavic lands. Another argument has the Cyrillic alphabet spreading more naturally, through regular and routine contact between Slavs and Greeks in the Balkans. The alphabet is named after the apostle Cyril, who is believed to have invented (with his brother Methodius) a related alphabet: the Glagolitic, which is less Greek in origin than Eastern.[17] It is more complicated, which might explain why it disappeared from the Slavic world and Cyrillic took hold. The Byzantine Empire also brought the Christian faith, Christian ethics, and literature in Cyrillic to the Slavic world. The language of the Church was quite unlike the language of everyday life—serious, solemn, formal. A "totally untutored East Slav" would have found his own tongue as transmitted by religious texts "strange, in places opaque," as befits the mysteries of faith.[18] Reconstructing the spoken language of the Rus is not possible.

To the north of Kyivan Rus, Scandinavia exerted its political, social, and economic influence. Varangians, adventure-seekers who hired themselves out as mercenaries, confronted the Slavs and other Finnic groups around Novgorod or, as it was originally called, Nevo Gardas.[19] The Varangians did not otherwise establish a presence on the continent but left a larger mark on the Baltic shores, where they influenced the vernacular. *Stor* (large) in Swedish became *storas* (fat) in Lithuanian, and *barn* (child) morphed into *berns*. A sizable percentage of Estonian words are of Scandinavian origin, yet Slavic languages do not show the same influence.[20]

The relationship among these three worlds is as contested as the land itself. Were Scandinavia and Rus merely peripheral to the power of Byzantium? Or did Rus fill the "transit zone" between two competing European influences—the north a realm of brawn and brains, the south one of spirit?[21] Some would elevate the political status of

Scandinavia and claim it defined European culture and politics for a time. The "Slavophile" argument instead emphasizes the mystical-mythical distinctiveness of Slavic lands and their populations, a kind of cult of the black (pagan) earth contra the white (Christian) beliefs imposed on it. This position embraces the primordial spirit world, prehistoric bloodlines, the great cathedral of the forest, and major rivers of Eastern Europe as arteries connecting a body of peoples. Nature was revered, the rhythms of the seasons celebrated. If it did not rain, if the sun did not come out, if blizzards submerged the tracks, if the frost did not relent and the thaw was late, people died.

These civilizations include writers. There survive inscriptions and graffiti in the churches of Rus along with scrapings on parchment (animal skins), wooden tablets, and birch bark.[22] Some very early texts feature Roman and Greek letters in no discernible order, others are in almost indecipherable East Slavonic and Cyrillic scripts.[23] Pre- or proto-Cyrillic scripts have not been found.[24] The tales preserved in the earliest written chronicles are unreliable as fact at a time when the concept of fiction did not yet exist.[25] These complicated but crucial documents sensationalize the good and especially the bad. Tediously copied out by monks and other paid scribes for use in medieval libraries, the chronicles describe princes displacing their brothers and uncles; the gradual, sometimes violent adaptation of a religion in a language few understood, much less spoke; fur, wax, and honey traders; theft; taxation; and—in passing—Prince Yuri. He invited a rival and kinsman to feast at his table in 1147, the year that marks the first recorded mention of a place called Moscow and the river curving through it.

That story is told in the *Primary Chronicle* (or *Tale of Bygone Years, Povest' vremmenïkh let*), a twelfth-century compilation of Norse sagas, melodic tales of heroic deeds, the Bible, and Kyivan historical detritus. It had been attributed to Nestor (1056–1114), a monk of the Caves Monastery in Kyiv, but that ascription has been debunked.[26] A monastic father superior named Sil'vestr claimed that he "wrote" the chronicle in 1116 for his ruler, the Grand Prince of Kyiv, but nothing that old survives.[27] The earliest surviving transpositions, the Laurentian and Hypatian (Ipatiev) codices, date to the fourteenth and fifteenth centuries.[28] Oral Scandinavian tales and a Greek text were also layered in.

Like all such sources, the *Primary Chronicle* is a mirror, not a lens, reflecting the interests of its compilers and their lords and masters. It elaborates the rise of Kyivan Rus as a center of Eastern Orthodoxy, an obvious point of focus for Christian scribes, amid accounts of Eastern Slavs moving south and Western Slavs moving north. The people did not perceive Rus "as a common space, as their Fatherland," during this period, as an article posted on the official Kremlin website has it, and the *Primary Chronicle* does not hint of Moscow being, or even becoming, relevant.[29] It wasn't, so it has no presence in the *Primary Chronicle*. Likewise, little is said about the people of this early era: the nobles, traders, merchants, furriers, tree-choppers, and swamp-drainers (among others). In another gathering of parchment, Moscow is mentioned in passing as an enclave of desperadoes; few lived there when Nestor and Sil'vestr were alive. In the late 1940s, the highly productive, deeply patriotic philologist Dmitri Likhachyov translated the *Primary Chronicle* from East Slavonic and Church Slavonic into modern Russian, then said of his birthplace: "No other country in the world is cloaked in such contradictory myths about its history as is Russia, and no other nation in the world interprets its history as variously as do the Russian people."[30] Even the obscurities of the past seem a point of pride.

Moscow existed before Russia, Kyiv before Moscow. The ancient connections between the two cities cannot be denied, which partly explains Russia's present-day efforts to prevent Ukraine from existing as an independent, European state. But this is not especially new behavior: Similar efforts date from the time of Catherine the Great, who absorbed Ukraine, Siberia, Alaska, and northern California into her empire. Ukraine was part of the Russian Empire until a Marxist named Vladimir Lenin sparked a revolution that turned Ukraine into one of the four original Soviet republics. In the 1930s, Stalin requisitioned harvests to finance his plans for rapid industrialization, causing a famine so terrible that people ate tree bark, and worse.

Ancient Kyiv has been described as a haven for the Rus traveling down from Novgorod, a cold, damp land unfit for most crops.

There they could barter for food and other necessities. In the eleventh century, Kyiv boasted a teeming market along with magnificent cathedrals and religious icons. The settlement was beholden to the Khazars, a semi-nomadic people with trading routes throughout the Crimea, Caucasus, and Kazakhstan. Silver dirhams, medieval Islamic coins buried in sacks in the ground, the Bank of Mother Earth, are evidence of exchanges from points south and east through Kyiv. The Khazars also demanded goods from a local Slavic tribe, the Polyane (related to the word for "field"), who bred cattle, fished, and kept bees. When settlers from Novgorod and Scandinavia arrived in search of better weather and more fertile land, they displaced the Khazars, and Kyiv would become Rus.

The first of the pioneers to arrive from Scandinavia, according to the *Primary Chronicle*, were Rurik and his brothers Sineus and Truvor. After establishing a few trading posts, Sineus and Truvor fell ill and died. Rurik controlled Novgorod until his death in 879. But nothing here is certain.[31] Rurik has been described as a loner and a drifter operating without the assistance of his siblings. And he might have long been a resident of Novgorod, with relatives in the area—not an outsider after all.[32] If nothing else, the story of "brothers acting in partnership" is a hoary historical chestnut (think of Romulus and Remus founding the Roman Empire).[33]

Rurik built up a northern fortress, a "Scandinavian trading emporium of first-class importance," on an island in Lake Ladoga, east of present-day St. Petersburg.[34] He originated the Rurik dynasty, one of two durable ruling families in the entire history of Russia (the other being the Romanovs). His medieval aristocratic descendants all had Scandinavian names: Igor, Ivan, Olga, Oleg. They are, in the annals, the original Rus.

From their trading emporium on Lake Ladoga, the Rus traveled south, encountering the Slavic peoples of the upper and middle Dnieper and the compounds of the Khazars, including a fortified embankment at Kyiv. The Rus also interacted with Bulgars in the east, northern Finno-Ugrian peoples, groups from the Baltics, Hungarians, and Poles, along with the Polovtsï and Pechenegs. Both groups posed mortal threats to the Rus, and their defeat is often cited as proof of Russia's ability to overcome anything. The Pechenegs ate and drank foul things, declined to bathe even when the golden opportunity presented itself, wore helmets and belts, blew horns, and ingested herbs reputed to give them excellent eyesight. Constantinople sought to enlist Hungarians against them, but the Hungarians flinched at fighting the "devil's brats."[35] (A nineteenth-century lawyer, defending a granny who had stolen a teapot worth thirty kopecks, asked the court: "You think she's a threat to society? Imagine dealing with the Pechenegs.")[36] The Khazars might have left Kyiv to the Rus and other Slavs in exchange for their cooperation against the Pechenegs.

An East Slavic tribe called the Drevlyane (from the word for "tree," indicating that these people were forest-dwellers) also interacted with the Kyivan Rus. The Drevlyane lived in partial dugouts protected by unhewn, bark-covered fences. Like all natives of the region, they stayed near the stove in winter hoping that what they had grown and gathered in the summer (right down to the roots) would keep them alive. They had and left little. Excavations of their gravesites have unearthed meager possessions: a single bead, a knife.[37]

According to the *Primary Chronicle*, in 882 Rurik's kinsman Oleg posed as a trader headed to Byzantium just passing through Kyiv. Oleg's soldiers then appeared from behind their sailboat and stabbed to death Kyiv's rulers, Askold and Dir. Oleg seized power as "Grand Prince," demanded gifts from the Slavs, and developed a trading alliance with Constantinople, perhaps to stave off the threat of raids from the Rus, perhaps to keep the Khazars at bay or use the Rus against the Pechenegs.[38] Beyond the *Primary Chronicle*, however, there is no record of Oleg in Kyiv nor even of Askold and Dir.[39]

Oleg had a son, Igor, who became the second Rurik grand prince of Kyiv in 912. He demanded tribute from the Drevlyane in the form of food and drink, first with his mercenaries at his side, then greedily going back for more without his men. The Drevlyane, hoping to be left in peace, did not appreciate this second visit from the bearded, leather-clad ruler in a metal helmet, so put him to death.[40] A Byzantine historian, Leo the Deacon, describes the Drevlyane binding Igor, bending a couple of trees to the ground, attaching the trees to his legs, and releasing the trees back into the air. From one tax collector, the Drevlyane fashioned two.[41]

After Igor's death, his wife Olga, who ruled Rus from 945 to around 962, chose to settle scores. She summoned a group of Drevlyane emissaries to Kyiv, ordering the people of the town to carry their boat through the gates. The ceremonial procession ended with Olga tossing her guests into a ditch and burying them alive. A second group arrived not knowing the fate of the first. She invited them to bathe, then burned down the bathhouse with the emissaries trapped inside. She remained unsatisfied and so laid siege to the Drevlyane for a year before asking that they attend a funeral service for her husband in the town where they had halved him. There was a feast with fermented beverages. The Drevlyane overindulged, and Olga's mercenaries (presumably intoxicated as well) butchered them in the thousands. In exchange for peace, Olga asked the Drevlyane to pay tribute in the form of sparrows and pigeons, three from each household. The Drevlyane obliged. At nightfall, Olga had her soldiers place slivers of sulfur in cloth and fasten these satchels with string to the birds' legs. The bundles were lit. The frightened, flaming birds flew back to their nests, and the entire unhewn town went up in smoke. Those inhabitants fortunate enough to survive were enslaved.[42]

Scandinavian folklore is full of stories like this about avenging widows. Olga's subsequent activities are less fantastical and easier to believe.[43] Most of them concern her romantic exploits in Tsargrad (the East Slavonic name for Constantinople), also her development of trading opportunities for the Rus and interest in making Kyivan Rus Christian.

Her son Svyatoslav fought more than he ruled and lost almost as much land as he gained. He adopted the look of a "nomadic chieftain" on horseback with his scalp shaved (but for a single lock) and a golden earring.[44] He waged war on the semi-nomadic Khazars and their sacral ruler, the qaghan, who lived in a brick palace on the Volga. Svyatoslav and his soldiers eclipsed the Khazars on their own turf in the cities north of Baku on the Khazar (Caspian) Sea. Two Arabic sources describe the Rus gobbling up all the grapes and raisins in the vineyards of the Khazar enclave of Semender in celebration. The Rus also stripped the trees of leaves and stole alms from the poor; valor in battle may also be a myth.[45] Bribed with gold, Svyatoslav did the Byzantine emperor's bidding in thrashing distant relatives of the Bulgars inhabiting the Middle Danube. He met his end against the unwashed Pechenegs near Dristra in northeastern Bulgaria when they ambushed the Rus and turned Svyatoslav's skull into a goblet.

His dominions went to his sons: Yaropolk, Oleg, and Vladimir. Although Yaropolk was awarded Kyiv, he frowned at the size of his holdings and launched a war against his brother Oleg, killing him. Vladimir secluded himself outside his own domain of Novgorod, ceding control of the entire realm to Yaropolk. But not for long: he rallied and returned to power in Novgorod, warning Yaropolk that his time in Kyiv was at an end. The two were also competitors in matrimonial matters: both sought the hand of Princess Rogneda of Polotsk as a way to increase their power. Her father, avoiding the wrath of the belligerent brothers, permitted Rogneda to choose a husband on her own. She preferred Yaropolk, which so angered Vladimir that he brought sword and flame to Polotsk, leveling everything. He assaulted Rogneda in front of her father and brothers before killing them. Then he made her his bride.

Now age twenty, Vladimir decided it was time to take Kyiv. He could not overcome its fortifications so moved to corrupt Yaropolk's ministers. One cooperated—a commander named Blud. The would-be traitor succumbed to second thoughts, however, and advised Yaropolk to flee while also trying to convince him that Vladimir was about as threatening as a tomtit to an eagle. Yet that tomtit seized Kyiv, and Yaropolk scurried from place to place plagued with fear until, exhausted, he surrendered to his brother in hopes of forgiveness. He found none.

Vladimir is a sacred figure in official Russian histories despite the cravings that even this grand tour of mayhem failed to sate. Epic songs about Vladimir (the Fair Sun) tell of nails hammered into skulls, maidens sold into harems for a fraction of the cost of horses, dungeons, and revelries.[46] His achievements on the battlefield, after a slow start, convinced him that his pagan gods favored him. To elicit and express gratitude for their support, he held feasts in their honor and even, according to a Christian chronicler committed to documenting the sins of paganism, presided over the human sacrifice of a Christian boy along with his father. Vladimir built a pantheon at his residence dedicated to Perun, the pagan god of fire, and erected similar shrines in other cities.[47] Paganism was practiced throughout Kyivan Rus in the form of rituals celebrating the seasons and sacrifices to bog-dwelling devils, birds, trees, and even the spirits inhabiting stones.[48] He believed in these rituals even after becoming Christian.

His conversion came after exploring other options and considering the connection between sacred and secular authority. Vladimir dispatched aides called *muzhi* (servitors) to meet with Islamic Bulgars, Catholic Germans, Jewish Khazars, and Orthodox Greeks to learn about their religions. Because he considered himself superior to the pope, he ruled out Catholicism. The Jewish Khazars failed to impress owing to their perceived rootlessness. Islam appealed to Vladimir for permitting multiple marriages, but he enjoyed alcohol too much to consider abstaining. His aides admired Constantinople's resplendent religious services. "We did not know if we were in heaven or on earth," they marveled in the immense interior of the Hagia Sophia. The Greek religion won out.[49]

Access to the divine was a means to an end: Vladimir sought to consolidate his rule. He hungered for power, Byzantine power most of all, and moved to acquire it through Christian marriage. His chosen bride, Princess Anna Porphyrogenita, the daughter of the Byzantine emperor Romanos II, was reluctant to become his sixth wife. (Her last name, meaning "of the purple room," references the special chamber of the palace where she was born after her parents ascended the throne.) To placate her father, Vladimir promised to deliver the city of Kherson (Sebastopol) in Crimea to him. The siege lasted months, and Vladimir anticipated defeat before learning the location of the water lines into the city and stopping them up. He demanded that Anna arrive before he converted to Christianity. The emperor, in turn, demanded he convert before she was sent. Vladimir agreed to be baptized so long as Anna was on her way.[50] The *Primary Chron-*

icle adds the symbolic detail that Vladimir lost his eyesight before his conversion, only to recover it afterward.

Marriage seemingly bettered him. He laid down his weapons, liberated his concubines, and began to preach and practice goodness. In Kyiv he had the statue of his old idol, Perun, stripped of its gold and silver gilding to expose the wood underneath. Then, in 988 or 989, he ordered the entire population baptized. "Whoever does not turn up at the river tomorrow, be he rich, poor, lowly or slave, he shall be my enemy!" he declared, granting himself supreme authority.[51] To mark the baptism of Rus, the mint in Constantinople issued gold coins with Vladimir's likeness.

The residents of Kyiv complied, Christians having long been in their midst. Byzantine architects and masons built four churches in the city. Monasteries were established and a metropolitan (Feofilakt) named. Bishops were then placed in four other sees in Rus, including Novgorod.[52] Historian Andrzej Poppe has argued, controversially yet convincingly, that the Kyivan Church was not independent at first. Instead, it was a metropolitanate under the patriarchate of Constantinople.[53] Whatever the official structure, new parishioners who had otherwise lived in harmony with the spirit world were frightened by priests threatening hell and damnation. True, the river spirit was a dangerous seductress—her emerald-green tresses lured men into the deep—but the house spirit, the *domovoy* in the glowing recesses of the giant clay stove, was benevolent and genuinely useful: sewing, sweeping, healing the sick, even keeping the scarier forest spirits outside. After priests started chasing the *domoviye* away, chores piled up. Some people rebelled against the arrival of Orthodoxy by fleeing to the forests.

Paganism hung on for centuries, continuing to explain the cold and heat, the movement of the sun and the stars, even blending with Christian ritual. Sorcerers, witches, and wizards prepared aphrodisiacs in Novgorod and exposed food-hoarders during a time of famine while priests preached of sin and redemption. Tasked with finding out whether rumors about "well-to-do women" stockpiling food and furs were true, the sorcerers "cut open their backs at the shoulderblades and by magic extracted from their bodies corn or fish, and they killed many women, and expropriated their possessions."[54] A dual faith still exists in Russia, as the popular holiday Maslenitsa attests. Celebrated at the end of winter in the week before Lent, it is on the one hand Christian, on the other chock-full of pagan elements, including the burning of a giant straw doll.

When Vladimir died in 1015, in his mid to late fifties, his eleven sons turned against one another in their desire for power. The Rurik dynasty cleaved into three rival branches named after the three sons who eliminated the others before trying to eliminate one another. Kyiv's position declined, and competing principalities acquired strength. The sequence of events is bedeviling but alluring enough to have inspired a present-day boardgame called Rurik: Dawn of Kiev. Among the pieces are daggers, clubs, crossbows, and a *lodya* (a light open boat carved from a single tree) laden with logs, fish, bearskins, honey, and beeswax. The game pits Vladimir's sons and their advisors against one another in contest to secure the southern Rurik stronghold. Everyone schemes, but the winner is determined by chance.

The harshest of the Ruriks battling for Kyiv was Svyatopolk, nicknamed "the accursed" in the sagas for how he came into the world and what he did as part of it. His paternity is in question, but he seems to have been the son of a Byzantine nun whom Vladimir had "made pregnant."[55] Installed in Turov (Belarus) at age eight and soon thereafter married to the daughter of the Polish ruler, Svyatopolk conspired with his wife to depose his father, who discovered the plan and imprisoned him. After Vladimir's death, Svyatopolk claimed control of Kyiv. The people rightly resisted him, however, and he suspected three of his brothers—Boris of Rostov, Gleb of Murom, and Svyatoslav of the Drevlyane—of trying to depose him.[56] Boris was supposedly hunted down and knifed either inside his tent or outside while relieving himself. Then Gleb was killed by Svyatopolk's cook. Svyatoslav met his end trying to escape his accursed brother. None of the three resisted death, according to the account produced by Nestor and other anonymous tales, because death, even unjust death, was an obligation, a duty.[57] There is a coda to the tale that turns it into a play of holy communion with a deep bias against Svyatopolk.[58] Supposedly, Gleb's body was discarded among logs only to reappear, miraculously, beside Boris's.[59]

Svyatopolk's older brother Yaroslav was the grand prince of Novgorod during that city's golden years, which are celebrated in a cycle of epic songs about a merchant who, thanks to the sea king, strikes it rich by catching a fish with golden fins.[60] One popular version of the tale (turned into a lavish opera by composer Nikolay Rimsky-Korsakov) features a Varangian visitor to Novgorod, who describes the fearful crags of his homeland from which his bones were formed, the mists that give him thought, the clutch of sharp arrows and fine swords, and his pagan god Odin.[61] To defend Novgorod against his brother, Yaroslav assembled a massive fighting force of Novgorodians and Varangians on the banks of the Dnieper. After an exhausting standoff, Yaroslav's soldiers crossed the river in a final surge. "The wrath of Yaroslav" overwhelmed Svyatopolk, who swung into the saddle and rode to Poland, literally losing his father's crown on the way.[62]

Syvatopolk regrouped and returned to Kyiv with Poles at his side. He attacked Novgorod again, and this time he triumphed, though the celebration was brief. "A devil came upon him and his bones were softened; he couldn't ride a horse, and was borne on a stretcher," the *Primary Chronicle* reports.[63] Svyatopolk died terrified and feverish. A foul odor rose from his grave. Yaroslav still had to contend with yet another brother, Mstislav, for control of Kyiv. Their conflict lasted years only to end in wearied détente. Yaroslav kept Kyiv and Novgorod along with the territories of the west, while Mstislav ruled the settlement of Chernigov and lands to the east.

Mstislav died after a hunting trip accident in 1036. Since he did not have a son, Yaroslav was left in control of his holdings—a treacherous but rich territory stretching from the Black Sea to the Baltic and from the Oka River to the Carpathian Mountains. He forged connections with dynasties in Europe by arranging for his three sons to marry foreign princesses. One of his sisters ended up with a Polish king, and he dispatched his daughters to courts as far away as France. Before his death in 1054 at age seventy-six, he appointed local, "Russian" bishops in Kyiv, which complicated his relationship with Constantinople. He sanctified Boris and Gleb, built cathedrals, had service books translated into the local language, and represented himself as a person of learning: "wise," according to his nickname. He revered St. George, after whom he was baptized, and started the trend of having an image of the dragon slayer on his seal.[64] The coins of Yaroslav's realm feature a trident, depicting either the holy trinity or a falcon and cross—the future national symbol of Ukraine.

Despite the fighting, by the end of the twelfth century the population of Kyiv expanded to somewhere between forty and fifty thousand, a populace comparable to London and Paris at the time. The grand prince lived in a wooden compound called a *dvor*. Outside his compound were churches and the dwellings of jewelers, potters, carpenters, tool and weapon fashioners, and glassmakers; merchants distributed these local goods and finer products brought from Constantinople and the Middle East. He and his kin relied on a network of blood relatives and advisors called boyars. These were clansmen of warrior caste who managed the territories overseen by the prince. The circle of boyars went by the name *druzhina*, similar to the Russian word for friend, *drug*. Later the *druzhina* was renamed the *duma*, referring to an advisory council or parliament. Everyone had their place: servants, officials, and the soldiers in the prince's army. *Kholopï* (slaves), *smerdï* (unfree peasants), and *zakupï* (peasants who could attain freedom by settling a feudal loan) occupied the lower tiers with the laborers who mucked the stalls and rang the bells.

For Yaroslav and the other grand princes of Kyivan Rus, power rested in the right to collect various tributes (taxes) from the population and to impose fines for malfeasance. Payment went to a debt collector in the form of goods or *grivnas*, a term denoting a metallic weight, usually silver, though at this time beads, hides, livestock, and humans were also accepted as payment. Coins, mostly produced elsewhere, circulated. Some of the laws at the time—and their associated penalties—are recorded in a collection of decrees titled *Russian Truth* (*Russkaya Pravda*). It exists in copies of different lengths from different eras; the earliest, *Yaroslav's Truth* (*Pravda Yaroslava*), dates from around 1017, *The Truth of Yaroslav's Sons* (*Pravda Yaroslavichey*) from 1054 or so. A longer version lists the cost of revenge killings: 40 *grivnas*. Maiming someone with a sword or goblet set the assailant back a dozen *grivnas*, cutting off a finger, only three. Property damage, horse and cattle theft, and profanation made the list. Physical punishment often substituted for fines. A *kholop* named Dudika, charged with blaspheming a bishop, couldn't pay and so had his nose and hands chopped off. Sorcerers lost tongues, fingers, and other extremities for practicing their craft.[65]

Financial transactions seem to have been recorded on birch bark, along with everyday problems and worries. More birch bark is preserved north of Kyivan Rus than south, given the nature of the soil. The richest cache comes from Novgorod, which would rival Moscow until the grand princes of Moscow destroyed it and its way of life. Novgorod was the site of one of the earliest schools in Rus, founded in 1030, and the population was more literate than elsewhere. Evidence comes from the chronicle of the St. Sophia Cathedral, where the children of churchmen were taught books as part of Christianity's fierce battle against pagan belief.[66] The clay under the city has preserved the skins of animals and trees alike. Birch bark was cut into segments, scraped, boiled, written upon, then rolled up. Archeologists mistook the rolls as "fishermen's floats" before noting that some preserved words.[67] To date, about twelve hundred birchbark letters have been unearthed, dating from 1025 to the end of the twelfth century.[68] Most are from Novgorod and the neighboring fortification of Staraya Russa. Four are from Moscow but dated much later.

Most of the birchbark letters, discovered buried up to twenty-five feet beneath streets once paved by logs, come from the houses of boyars and merchants. Many record financial transactions but some preserve timeless sentiments. A six- or seven-year-old boy named Omfim, evidently bored copying out the alphabet at a school run by the church, drew a picture of himself as a warrior defeating a monster.[69] Mikita asked his girlfriend Anna to marry him: "I want you, and you me," and there's a witness who will back him up.[70] A birchbark love letter from a woman to a man has also been recovered: "[I have written] to you three times. What is it you hold against me, that you did not come to see me this Sunday? I regarded you as I would my own brother. Did I really offend you by that which I sent to you?"[71] It continues like this for several more lines, a letter written by an unidentified person with identifiable feelings, of whom there is no knowledge beyond what she etched with bone or iron stylus into the inner layer of bark more than a thousand years ago.

Before his death, Yaroslav apportioned princedoms to his sons. Izyaslav, the eldest, received Kyiv and Novgorod, the biggest prizes. He built the Kyiv Monastery of the Caves, now a UNESCO World Heritage Site, and participated in the writing of the *Russian Truth*. Svyatoslav, the second oldest son, installed himself in Chernigov; Vsevolod, the third son, received Pereyaslavl. Two other sons died before reaching adulthood, so their holdings, including the towns of Smolensk and Vladimir, went to the others. The "triumvirate of the sons of Yaroslav" together suppressed their cousins and nephews, ousted non-Rus tribes from their lands, and subjugated peasants. The trio had their hands full, however, with the wilder members of the Polovtsï, a Turkic tribe described as blond, blue-eyed, and fair-skinned. The Polovtsï had pushed their closest rivals, the notorious Pechenegs, out of the way to open a trading corridor from the steppe to the Black Sea. From there, they began to interfere with affairs of the Rus. The Polovtsï suppressed Pereyaslav, ushering in a war with the Rus that lasted more than 170 years.

A revolt against the grand prince Izyaslav forced him to flee to his wife's cousin in Poland. He regrouped, rounded up the Kyivans who had rebelled, and cut out their eyes (and other parts). He then went after the city of Polotsk, whose ruler had casually taken his place in Kyiv while he was with his wife's cousin in Poland. Izyaslav died in battle with two other princes (both relatives) in 1078. Svyatoslav lost his life to "the cutting of a sore" at the end of 1076, suggesting that an attempt to remove a tumor failed.[72] Vsevolod was left to rule Kyiv from 1078 to 1093. He fought without success, and so deputized his son, Vsevolod II Monomakh, to do the fighting for him.

Vsevolod II retained his last name from his mother, a close relative of the Byzantine emperor Constantine Monomachos.[73] He preached peace and good deeds while also, in a famous testament, touting his accomplishments on the battlefield. His pacifism came only after considerable soul-searching. "My campaigns were in all eighty-three; the other smaller ones I do not remember," Monomakh recalled late in life. "I concluded nineteen treaties of peace with the Polovtsï, took prisoners more than a hundred of their chief princes and let them go free," he confessed, "and I had more than two hundred put to death and drowned in the rivers."[74] After the drownings, Monomakh assumed control of Kyiv with the support of the townspeople but, like his predecessors, feared usurpation. He strategically positioned his oldest son from his second marriage, Yuri, likely born sometime between 1095 and 1100, to secure his rule.[75] Monomakh seated Yuri as a boy in the principality encompassing the towns of Rostov, Suzdal, and Vladimir. He also arranged Yuri's first marriage to a preteen Polovets, a blond maiden of nomadic warrior descent, in hopes of preventing the Polovtsï from turning against the Rurik princes who had savaged them. Thanks to their union, Yuri secured conditional support from her people.

Ultimately Yuri went on to have at least fifteen children of his own, with two wives. Little is known of his second wife, Helena, beyond her escape after Yuri's death from Kyiv to Constantinople, her birthplace. Their marriage would have made sense for a prince seeking to rule Kyiv and points farther south, like Tmutarakan (Crimea), where trade with Constantinople was all important. Perhaps he imagined a son or grandson becoming the next emperor of the Second Rome. Had he married someone local, a girl born in Kyiv (or Suzdal), her family would have merged with the Rurikovichi and claimed a stake in dynastic successions. Marrying someone who did not speak the language and did not have relatives in the region avoided this problem.

The lore surrounding Yuri was elaborated in the first half of the eighteenth century, when Vasiliy Tatishchev took on the task of translating and annotating the *Primary Chronicle,* the Laurentian and Hypatian Codices, and several other historical sources, including documents from outside Kyivan Rus. History was not yet a discipline bound to fact, and Tatishchev, an imperial statesman and governor, wanted most of all to be a great storyteller. His tale of the founding of Moscow involves lust, murder, suspiciously learned academic commentaries, and mistakes in transcription.[76] Tatishchev has Yuri bedding a cornucopia of concubines and exercising all-conquering ambition. A representative sample, involving a Suzdal governor named Stepan Kuchko:

> Though Yuri had a Princess worthy of love, and though he loved her, he also often visited various young ladies from among his subjects, and enjoyed himself more with them than with the Princess: he would spend night after night out horseback riding[77] and drinking. . . . Among all his lovers, the wife of Kuchko, the governor of Suzdal, had the most powerful hold on him, and he did everything for her as she wished. But when Yuri went to Torzhok, Kuchko did not go with him. He could no longer stand being mocked by his inferiors, nor could he denounce them to Yuri, since he knew they spoke the truth, but he was incensed on behalf of the Princess. So he went off to his own estate, taking his wife along; there he put her under lock and key and began to plan his defection to the court of Izyaslav of Kyiv. But when Yuri heard that Kuchko's wife had been imprisoned, he abandoned his armies, leaving no further instructions, and traveled, accompanied by a small coterie, in great haste and rage to the Moskva River, where Kuchko lived. There, without investigating anything, he swiftly murdered Kuchko, and married Kuchko's daughter off to his own son Andrey. He liked the spot so very much, however, that he established a walled settlement and stayed there and kept building it up until Andrey's wedding.[78]

When his father died in 1125, Yuri secured Suzdal at the center of a fortified latticework of fourteen towns. Wheat passed through from north to south, which allowed Yuri to influence affairs in the northern settlement of Novgorod while he plotted ruling Kyiv in the south. His desire to extend his reach later earned him the nickname Yuri the Long Arm (or the Far-Reaching One, Dolgorukiy). One of his fingers poked into a plot of land on the Moskva River.

By the middle of the twelfth century, Kyivan Rus had begun to disintegrate. The rulers of Kyiv could no longer install their protégés where they liked, and when one ruler angered another, a third would seize the advantage. The line of succession begun by Vsevolod, Yuri's grandfather, fought against two begun by his brothers. Yuri twice captured Kyiv and twice expelled Izyaslav II, prince of Kursk, Polotsk, Turov and Pinsk, Volhynia, Pereyaslavl, and Peresopnytsia and three times the grand prince of Kyiv (from 1146 to 1149, for a few months in 1150, and from 1151 to 1154). Fighting between fathers and sons, and among first, second, and third cousins, further confused the situation, pitting everyone against everyone for ancestral lands, fortifications, and trading routes. Uncles battling nephews is a theme, with uncles triumphing most often.

In 1147 Yuri sent an invitation, presumably written on calf- or sheepskin decorated with laces and personal stamps, to his kinsman and rival Svyatoslav. It read: "Come see me in Moscow, brother."[79] The "brother" was a distant cousin from a different branch of the Rurik dynasty based in Chernigov, and Yuri wanted to celebrate their respective conquests.[80] Yuri had strengthened his hand in the north, and Svyatoslav had strengthened his hand in the middle of Kyivan Rus. Izyaslav II was boxed in down south.

Defeating Yuri, Izyaslav II decided, would remove one of two threats to his rule—the other being the Church. Izyaslav II had assembled the bishops of Kyiv to elect a metropolitan without Constantinople's permission, violating canonical law. For his part, Yuri felt that Izyaslav II had to go and emerged triumphant for a time. On August 27, 1149, Yuri achieved his dream of living among the golden domes of Kyiv. He lasted there until September of 1150, then retreated to his stronghold in Suzdal after Izyaslav II confronted him again—this time with Poles, Hungarians, and even Czechs at his side. Yuri made it back to Kyiv only after Izyaslav II's death in 1154.

Meanwhile, to secure the settlement of Moscow, in 1156 he ordered additional wooden fortifications built, leaving his son Andrey to supervise their construction along the moat. The Moskva ran along one side of the roughly triangular shape of the Kremlin, and the moat (the Neglinka) along another. The third side abutted present-day Red Square. Excavating the basement of the Soviet Palace of Congresses on the Kremlin grounds in the late 1950s exposed the remains of a rampart twenty-three feet high and forty-eight feet thick at the base. The rampart was held in place by hooked-together logs and topped by a thick wooden fence. Thus, Moscow was transformed into a strategic frontier town, a tax-collecting checkpoint defending Suzdal and the surrounding lands from Chernigov, Smolensk, Ryazan, and Novgorod—all linked by the Moskva River and its tributaries. Horsemen constantly rode past the bog, jingling and jangling in their saddles. In 1176, an army from Ryazan doubled back and attacked. A sword from the battle was discovered by archeologists in the remains of a defensive ravine on the Kremlin plateau. It is inscribed "ETCELIN ME FECIT" (Etcelin made me), indicating manufacture in the German Rhineland between 1130 and 1170.[81] Yuri did not witness the attack. Andrey fled to Vladimir, and there built the Church of the Veil. It stands in beautiful isolation, the white walls and gold dome lifting visitors heavenward.

The townspeople of Kyiv never supported Yuri and resisted paying the tributes he demanded to support his campaigns. On May 10, 1157, Yuri feasted in Kyiv with guards all around and wolfhounds padding through the hall. He grabbed slabs of herb-crusted meat from a platter; red juice ran from his mouth into his beard. That evening, complaining of terrible stomach pain, he took to his bed. Five days later, he was dead, presumably from poisoning plotted by his foes. The townspeople robbed his house and those of a kinsman. The unrest spread to other places controlled by Kyiv, including Suzdal, whose residents were stripped of everything they had. Yuri was entombed next to his father, but his grave was ransacked. And so, as Soviet archeologists discovered, the tomb is empty. Extant portraits come from Kyivan Rus medieval warrior templates rather than any true likeness. Yuri's sobriquet, Far-Reaching, is posthumous.

Under the Rurik rulers, Kyivan Rus was a trading network with an imported religion, pagan tradition, and multi-ethnic population. Power was local, familial, personal. In a distant future unimaginable to Yuri, the people of an inhospitable land would form an empire reaching across Eastern Europe, including the Slavic countries of Belarus, Poland, Ukraine, Bosnia, Serbia, Macedonia, and Montenegro, Central Asia, and the Far East. Yuri had nothing to do with that, but his statue stands at what became the center of its center: Moscow.

2

ASH

For THOUSANDS of years, the Mongols and their herds moved back and forth across Eurasia, never alone, never together, under the cope of heaven and mantle of the tales their ancestors told. Allegiances based on the changing seasons and shifting grasslands coalesced into an immense empire of the steppe, a realm without edge that reached into Rus. In the summer of 1240, the Mongols attacked Kyiv—an event long feared but shocking nonetheless. Kyiv was the richest Rurik holding, the Slavic wellhead; other attacks had come from the east, but none so calamitous. Kyiv collapsed. "Amid the bushes, thickets, and thorns," wrote the sixteenth-century French explorer and Franciscan priest André Thevet, "are the ruins and fragments of buildings and palaces that once belonged to kings and princes."[1]

In the historical sources, the Mongols are interchangeably referred to as Tatars, or Mongol-Tatars, or Tatar-Mongols, as if the names didn't matter.[2] But they did. The Tatars were ethnically distinct from the Mongols but enrolled in Mongol armies; they were part of the Mongol Empire, also known as the Golden Horde. The languages of the two groups were slightly different, as were their spiritual affiliations: the Tatars became Muslim, while the Mongols eventually embraced Buddhism. The Muslim population of the Republic of Tatarstan, part of the present-day Russian Federation, points to the

Mongol Empire as a noble, proud part of its past, as do other Muslim populations in Russia and former republics of the Soviet Union.

The Mongols (and the Tatars) attacked in crisscrossing formations on the hoof and deployed catapults capable of hurling balls of flame the distance of a bowshot. Gifted with acute eyesight, their warriors could target human prey miles distant across the flat Eurasian plain. Everything in their campaigns was impressively planned, from the deployment of advance scouts to the use of human shields to the transport and selling of slaves and collection of tribute. At its height, the empire covered more than nine million square miles, sixteen percent of the earth's landmass, and encompassed a quarter of the world's population. Eventually, however, the places the Mongols raided built better defenses and organized nastier resistance, which caused the overgrown empire to weaken, break up, cave in on itself. Russia inherited the remains, including the Mongols' sophisticated communications network—an equestrian messenger service known as the *ortoo,* or *yam* in Russian. Moscow still has streets named Yamskaya. These were part of an outer-wall neighborhood where coachmen (*yamshchiki*) once kept their horses on their plots of land. Clerks recorded the names and numbers of travelers and the payments for runs.[3] To walk from this area to the Kremlin takes about forty-five minutes, but the coachmen's pony express could get there in ten.

The Mongols both attracted and appalled those who wrote about them. Tales of their carnivorism are legion in medieval chronicles and travelogues.[4] Simon of Saint-Quentin, a Dominican friar, joined a mission to Persia in the 1240s to protest the Mongol killing of Christians and was almost dispatched himself. His castigation of the Mongols as "full of continuous sin," indiscriminately copulating and addicted to sodomy, is as inaccurate as it is unhinged.[5] Matthew of Paris's 1259 *Chronica Majora* includes a painting of Mongols beheading their captives, roasting them on a spit, and chomping on their legs like drumsticks.[6] Giovanni da Pian del Carpine's *Historia Mongalorum* imagines the Mongols dining on one another, sacrificing "every tenth man of the company" to stave off starvation in northern

China.[7] In truth, the Mongols more often ate small, steppe-dwelling animals: rabbits, rats, sousliks, and marmots. Carpine denies that they ate "mise [mice] with long tails, nor any kinde of mise with short tailes," or at least he didn't see them doing so, though he notes "puddings" made from horses and hogs; the former tasted better.[8] In the hot summer, the Mongols drank fermented mare's milk; in the winter, "excellent drinks" of boiled rice, milk, and honey.[9] Matthew adds "frogs, dogs, and snakes" to the bill of fare, along with berries and root vegetables (poorer folk ate less meat than richer people, as was true of most cultures).[10] At the ruler's court, honored guests stuffed themselves with roasted lamb, mutton, and horsemeat while enjoying wrestling matches, foot races, and shooting contests. On the barren, blustery steppe, where firewood was scarce, horsemen ate raw meat softened under their saddles. The bond with their horses was such that steppe nobility were sometimes buried beside or atop their bridled companions. Complete horse skeletons and stuffed horse heads have been recovered from burial mounds.[11]

Accounts of their physical appearance are no less lurid. A Persian poet described the Mongols as having "rotting graves" for nostrils, lice-covered chests, matted hair, lusterless tans, and skin "as rough-grained as shagreen leather, fit only to be converted into shoes."[12] An Armenian chronicler added buffalo-sized heads, snouts, and bowed, hog-sized legs.[13] Carpine's account is considerably kinder: slender waists, broad faces, high cheekbones, small eyes, beards, tonsures, and long bangs at the back which were braided and draped around the ears. Portraits bear him out, though most Mongol portraits are of horses, not humans. Franciscan missionary Guillaume de Rubrouck (1220–93) notes that the women, too, shaved their heads. "These gentlewomen are exceeding fat"—this was a compliment—"and the lesser their noses be, the fairer they are esteemed: they daube our [over] their sweet faces with grease too shamefully: and they neuer lie in bed for their trauel [trial] of childbirth."[14]

A Mongolian source called *The Secret History of the Mongols* celebrates the establishment of the Mongol Empire after centuries of domination by other groups. It dates from sometime around 1240 and survives in the Mongol language as translated into Chinese characters. Linguists have long puzzled over the text's syntax, symbolism, and (like everything else written about the Mongols) wild fabrications. Mainstream histories combine generous quotations from the *Secret History* with the travelogues of missionaries and adventurers; Marco Polo's *Book of the Marvels of the World,* and a cluster of Persian histories detailing the life and times of Genghis Khan, whose name is translated as "Universal" or "Oceanic Ruler"—an odd description of the overseer of a landlocked empire.[15] His legacy varies: In China, not to mention Mongolia, he is esteemed, but in Russia, outside the regions near Mongolia, he is portrayed as a ruthless savage.[16] When the empire became too large to function, it was separated into four Mongol-Tatar khanates. The khanate of the Ural-Volga region, responsible for the leveling of Kyiv and the repeated sacking of Moscow, picked up the name Golden Horde, *Zolotaya Orda*—referencing, among other things, the "golden habitation" of the horsemen's ruler.[17]

Genghis was born in 1156 on the Onon River and given the name Temüjin, "made of iron."[18] He had "fiercely issued" from the womb, his mother told him as she put him to bed, with "a black clot of blood in his hand."[19] He lost his father, the chieftain of his tribe, when he was nine. He, his siblings, and their mother were exiled to the steppe, where they struggled to survive on roots, berries, fish, and birds shot with bone-tipped arrows.[20] The abduction of Temüjin's first wife by three Merkit tribesmen sent Temüjin along "the paths of the elk" into the mountains for spiritual counsel, after which he secured her rescue by reducing anyone "of the Merkid 'bone'" to dust (or, as the *Secret History* has it, "dung").[21] Temüjin claimed animals (wolves, ravens, and falcons) as his counsel, along with a shaman "reputed to be in the habit of ascending to heaven on a dapple-gray horse and conversing with spirits."[22] When the shaman challenged his authority, Temüjin scraped out his insides. Later, he sought advice and spiritual justification for his actions from Taoist magicians, Tibetan lamas, and Nestorian priests.

Temüjin conducted raids against Naiman, Khmag, and Keraite tribesmen before taking on the Mongol-Tatars. Temüjin's grassland cavalries wore iron-plated hide and armed themselves with bows and arrows (bundled, notched, bone- and metal-tipped, sometimes dipped in poison), sabers with thirty-inch blades, hatchets, iron maces, flails, hooks, and nooses. Apparently, Temüjin exterminated males taller than the height of a cart axle.[23]

After defeating his former brother-in-arms Jamukha, his principal foe, Temüjin exercised flexible control of the entire Mongol-Tatar expanse. In 1206, his allies and the remnants of his rivals assembled on the Onon River, genuflected, and endorsed the expansion of his rule as Genghis Khan. His lieutenants pushed south, north, and west, supposedly followed by caravans of round felt tents with wicker roofs and bases, graced with pictures of birds and beasts and filled with furs and carpets.[24] These were loaded onto wagons pulled by teams of oxen. Everyone heard the armies coming, but when inhabitants of Nishapur first heard the noise in 1221, they had decided— fatally, it turned out—not to surrender in advance. After sacking the Silk Road city, the Mongols stacked up the skulls of the dead at the gates.[25]

Invitations to meet with Genghis could not be ignored. In 1219, a Taoist patriarch said to be more than three hundred years old received a summons: Genghis wanted to know the secret of his longevity.[26] Was it medicinal? Magical? To reach the khan, the patriarch, Ch'iu Ch'u-chi, traveled from Peking through southern Mongolia to Samarkand in Central Asia to Qunduz in northern Afghanistan. Each time he thought he had reached the khan, the khan had moved on. Their eventual first meeting left Genghis disappointed—the patriarch was merely old, not ancient, and knocking on death's door. Still, the khan liked his company and made him part of his entourage. The patriarch advised the khan to "respect human life," "stop killing," and abstain from sex along with other fleshly indulgences. Thus Ch'iu Ch'u-chi spared northern China from plunder and his followers from servitude.[27]

In 1227, Genghis was suddenly felled by a bolt of lightning. In his honor, "splendid horses" and forty finely adorned maidens were sacrificed to fulfill his wishes in the next world.[28] He planned an afterlife of pleasures commensurate with his life on earth: after marrying several times and enjoying the company of concubines, he left behind an unknown number of descendants. In 2003, an Oxford University geneticist estimated that "1 in 200 men worldwide" may be directly or indirectly related to the khan.[29]

Such is the lore, chipped away at by archeologists, ethnographers, and historians who have dismantled the myth that the Mongols under Genghis and his successors were natural-born barbarians who roamed uncharted open spaces because they could not imagine staying put.[30] In truth, the armies traveled along known routes among established centers; settlements grew as pastoralism declined. "Steppe" and "urban" cultures contrasted, as did the oral laws (*yāsā*) and culture of Islam. Patterns of travel were affected by changes in terrain, precipitation, and snow cover. After the khan dismantled the Khwarazmian Empire, a Mongol capital was built: Karakorum. It expanded from a modest enclave of yurts to include, after Genghis's death, a palace with an immense central sculpture imported from France called the Silver Tree of Karakorum, from whose branches milk and wine flowed.[31] When the easternmost Mongol capital was relocated first to Xanadu and then to Dadu—the future Beijing—Karakorum became unimportant.

The Golden Horde boasted its own capital: Sarai, or Sarai Batu, founded in the 1240s by Genghis's grandson, Batu Khan, on fertile ground on the lower Volga River, seventy-five miles north of Astrakhan and another sixty from the Caspian Sea. About a century later, it was replaced by another capital, also named Sarai, leading to endless confusion in the sources. *Sarai* became the Russian word for "barn," but the original Sarai was a cultural center as well as a farming, trading, and manufacturing hub. As to what it and other, smaller Mongol cities looked like, the sources suggest broad streets, mosques and minarets, bazaars, dugouts of different sizes, honeycomb residences, and larger houses of air-dried mud brick.[32] Slaves from different places did the building; the architecture varied. Artifacts attest to an affection in aristocratic households for precious metals carved into the shapes of magical animals. Decorated swords and quivers of birch bark, leather, and bone have been unearthed. Archeologists note a supplanting of Chinese with Islamic designs on belt cups and pouches while tracing the expansion of the east–west fur trade. Research has discredited the notion that the Mongols "were culturally so poor that they had no past."[33]

The 1240 siege of Kyiv by the Golden Horde was preceded by three years of campaigns in two phases. The Mongols first entered Rus in the spring of 1223 to suppress not the Rus but the tribe of the Polovtsï. The Mongols had sought to avoid conflict with the princes, but when the princes allied themselves with the Polovtsï, conflict was unavoidable. After defeating the Polovtsï on the Kalka River on May 31, 1223, the Mongols moved to subdue the princes and their boyar-commanded armies.[34] In the northeast, the fighting began in the late fall of 1237 and lasted through the early spring of 1238. Fourteen cities fell in just three months; the attacks were sudden and strange. First, the prosperous Oka River settlement of Ryazan was razed to the ground, then Moscow. The population of each place went from five or six thousand to almost nothing.[35] On December 16, 1237, "foreigners called [Mongol-]Tatars arrived in countless numbers, like grass-fed locusts, into the land of Ryazan." They camped on the river before sending "emissaries to the prince and princeling of Ryazan, a sorceress and two men with her, demanding from them one tenth of everything," a tenth of the people, their herds, and the rest of their belongings. The prince refused and sought help from relatives in other cities against the "foreign pagans," who surrounded and then climbed over the walls of Ryazan on December 21. Then the inevitable gruesomeness: The invaders "killed the prince and princess. And men and women and children, monks and nuns, priests, some by fire, others by sword. And violated nuns and priests' wives and good women and virgins in the presence of their mothers and sisters," the *Novgorod First Chronicle* reports. "God saved the Bishop," but everyone else in the town was punished for "our sins."[36]

Looking back at the account of the sacking of Ryazan, Russian chroniclers decided it needed embellishing. A sixteenth-century retelling called the *Tale of Batu's Capture of Ryazan* is steeped in Russian religious and nationalist dogma and bound to a sense of victimhood. The story begins with the grand prince of Ryazan trying to spare the town by sending his son Fyodor to Batu Khan with gifts of all sorts and sizes. Batu is an edgy host, offering plum wine, promising not to invade so long as he gets his pick of Ryazan's beautiful women for himself. The loveliest of them, he knows, is Fyodor's Byzantine wife Euphrasia. He asks to see her. Fyodor says no, and Batu flies into a rage, inhospitably beheading him and his entire retinue and leaving the corpses in a field for wild animals to devour. Euphrasia commits suicide at the news, jumping out of a window with a baby in her arms. The grand prince raises a massive force against Batu and defeats his bravest knights in a series of battles outside Ryazan. Batu, however, regroups and murders everyone in sight.[37]

Some of Moscow's fighters had been sent to Ryazan to help, but witnessing the complete eradication of the town they "ran off, seeing nothing there."[38] Archeologists have found evidence of panicked evacuation. Jewels were buried and storerooms locked. The defensive wall was demolished. Those who failed to escape Ryazan died. There is evidence of mass graves and, at the base of the excavation site, remnants of an inferno and a thick layer of ash.[39] The missionaries and explorers who tracked the Mongols in Rus describe them taking hostages, conducting reconnaissance operations, and attacking the aristocrats, church people, and crafts-makers with battering rams, flamethrowers, and perhaps even gunpowder.[40] Children heard stories about the Mongols and pretended to battle them, digging forts and shooting arrows at shadows. But that was just pretend; no one knew what to expect, least of all the person nominally in charge of Moscow, the son of the grand prince of Vladimir and a great-grandson of Yuri Dolgorukiy.[41]

Batu's fighters moved along the ice of the Moskva to Moscow, at the time a tree-covered enclave of no more than five thousand. The siege of Moscow happened in the middle of January 1238 with the Mongols climbing from the iced-over river toward the compound on the hill, the future Kremlin, toward the forces arrayed by the commander of Moscow, a man named Filip Nyanka, or Phillip the Tutor. (Whether he was an actual tutor or just descended from one is a mystery unlikely to be solved.) The commander "sat on his horse" as the enemy approached, then "reinforced his head with the sign of the cross," opened the gates of Moscow, and screamed. The Mongols "imagined" a huge army coming at them, even though there wasn't one, and retreated. Batu advanced, "captured [Filip] alive, tore him apart, and scattered the pieces in a field."[42] The commander of Moscow died, the *Primary Chronicle* declares, "for his Orthodox Christian faith."[43] The Mongols torched Moscow's walled wooden palace, churches, and everything else.

The only remaining structures from the 1238 siege are an earth and timber rampart along part of the present-day sixty-eight-acre Kremlin, which now contains four cathedrals and five palaces, green space, presidential and administrative offices, and a lot of locked doors. By the time the Mongols were done, all that remained of Moscow was its name.

The Mongols moved on to Vladimir, a stronghold in the northeast, with Moscow's overseer (the grand prince of Vladimir's son) as their captive. Seeing his pitiful condition and hearing his wails, his brothers begged the Mongols to spare his life and theirs. All were executed. The Mongols loaded their stone-throwers and built up the ground in front of the walls to make climbing over easier. The catapulting began on February 3, 1238, and lasted four days. The grand prince's family, boyars, and common people sought refuge in the Cathedral of the Dormition while the Mongols poured into the city through the golden gates. The Old Church Slavonic account of the events is bracing: "And they ransacked the sacred church of the Theotokos. And the residence of the prince they set on fire. And the monastery of Saint Demetrius, and others, having ransacked, they burned. And regarding the people old and young. The abbots and priests. And deacons. And monks. And nuns. And the blind and lame. And deaf. They excised them all. And the other men and women. And children barefoot and homeless. Dying from the frost, and it was seen then, a great trembling evil, and this multitude was taken as prisoners to their camps."[44]

During the massacre, Grand Prince Yuri II of Vladimir was away; he had ridden to Novgorod and Rostov seeking help against the Mongols from his cousins. But there was no escape. On the banks of the Sit River, the Mongols caught up to him. Another phalanx of Mongols headed east, to the middle Volga, and a third group, led by Batu, moved northwest, to Torzhok. The people of that town appealed to Novgorod for assistance. The request was denied, and Torzhok surrendered. Novgorod itself was spared by a fortuitous spring flood that kept the Mongols at bay. The Golden Horde subsequently departed Rus to quell a series of uprisings on the steppe. Fighting the Polovtsï and two other nomadic groups kept them occupied through the summer of 1238, after which they rode back into Rus, triumphant, with their daggers pointed at Kyiv. Its "majesty and beauty" impressed the Mongols enough to prevent them from destroying it.[45]

Most cities in Rus had perhaps one thousand experienced fighters—an elite retinue of barbed-arrow shooters—along with whatever peasant recruits and paid former foes could be mustered from their huts in the countryside. They had no chance against the ten thousand archers, lancers, and mounts who made up each Golden Horde tumen. The people of Rus had no knowledge of throwing machines and siege warfare before Genghis Khan's kinsmen arrived. The cities did not communicate with one another for their common good; there were no mutual defense agreements or regional command centers. Their fighting forces were but a tenth the size of those of their enemies from the steppe.[46] Kyiv was better equipped than other cities, but still no match for the invaders. It fell to them with stunning speed.

Kyiv was hardly as prominent in Rus as it had been under Yaroslav the Wise, but it was still the largest city by far, with a population of about 45,000, twice that of Novgorod. The princedom had been beset by endless fighting among the Ruriks and suffered the decline of Constantinople, its most important trading partner. Frequent raids by the Polovtsï had also weakened Kyiv to the point that it lost control over its affairs, passing from the general administrative control of the Vladimir-Suzdal appanage to that of the Galitsko-Volinskoye region. The grand prince of Kyiv, Mikhaíl, married the sister of the grand prince of the principality or, from 1253, the kingdom of Galitsko-Volinskoye.

When Batu announced that he planned to pin Kyiv "to his horse's tail," she ran to the grand prince.[47] He hesitated. Batu's emissaries advised Mikhaíl to surrender. Once more he hesitated. Then he had the emissaries killed. Outraged, Batu ordered an attack, which was led by his cousin and a future great khan, Möngke, on November 28, 1240. The horde gathered at the Lach Gates, medieval Kyiv's Polish district, where the trees provided cover. The outer fortifications— a massive semicircular complex of tiered guard stations built of thick logs—came down. The ramparts and inner walls between the districts fell soon after the hand-to-hand combat began. The leader of the resistance took an arrow to the chest. The Church of the Tithes, Kyiv's sacred heart and a burial site for the Ruriks, collapsed when crowds of people rushed into the galleries seeking God's protection. Afterward, an eyewitness "found an innumerable multitude of dead men's skulls and bones lying upon the earth," adding that there "scarce remain 200 houses, the inhabitants whereof being kept in extreme bondage" by the Mongol occupiers.[48]

Centuries later, when Imperial Russian and Soviet archeologists excavated parts of the upper and lowland districts of Kyiv, they found the remains of ancient log-frame and mud-walled dwellings and evidence, from 1240, of a terror-stricken flight into the countryside. Pinpointing exact dates proves impossible, complicated by mislabeling, theft, and other forms of mischief, but ceramics from the time of the Mongol invasion are distinct. The dirt beneath the modern streets of Kyiv in the aristocratic neighborhoods, the citadel, and the lower trading district, or *podol*, conceals chains, dishes, keys, knives with bone and wooden handles, molds, needles, pans, riding equipment, scythes, thimbles, iron weapons, amber, and copper crosses. One of the dugouts, the residence of an artisan, contained a bronze lamp, a silver moon, the scorched spine and ribs of a cat, and the remains of a child wearing three glass bracelets. A jug full of beads was dropped as someone fled; several people died when the tunnel they were digging by hand collapsed on them. The skeletons of two children—sisters, seemingly—were found huddled together in a stove; their hiding place from the Mongols became their grave. Floor tiles from the Church of the Tithes, sections of columns, fragments of frescoes, and sarcophagi lay deep in the ground. The remnants of a well (perhaps for storing treasures), piles of bones from a mass grave, and an earlier pagan burial ground have also been identified. Deep at the bottom of another pit, beneath coal and ash, researchers discovered a box of silver and gold jewelry. One of Kyiv's elite families owned a silver-gilded coin from Venice with the likeness of Duke Enrico Dandolo, who participated in the sacking of Constantinople in 1204. A big pot with a spoon in it belonged to an artisan named Maxim. He was making porridge when Kyivan Rus came to an end.[49]

News from Rus reached Europe before the Mongols themselves did. They slayed Czechs, Poles, and Hungarians before unexpectedly pulling back to the steppe in the spring of 1242. Had Batu Khan continued his campaign, Mongolian might have become the language of international commerce. Instead, he chose to develop his headquarters in Sarai on the Volga, minding the lands of Rus from afar.

The arrangement was straightforward. The Ruriks could stay in power if they paid for the privilege. Batu tallied the number of people in Rus, taxed them, and demanded obeisance from the princes in strategic matters. To keep them in line, he sanctioned occasional acts of terror. The clever and more ruthless Ruriks exploited the Mongols as well. Such is the case of the prince of Novgorod, Alexander Nevsky (1220/21–63), whose life was celebrated in a late thirteenth-century manuscript probably authored by Kirill II, the metropolitan of Kyiv.[50] Nevsky lacked the means to defend the realm from the Golden Horde, but he beat back existential threats from Scandinavia, the Baltics, and Europe—a signal that perhaps one day the even more existential threat from the east would be extinguished. But that never happened. True, by the fifteenth century the Mongols were beginning to fade from view, but Rus and Russia never recovered from the experience. The memories remain, and tales of Nevsky are both sources of national pride and useful government propaganda assuring all that Russia will never suffer such humiliation or abuse again. Nevsky is the "heavenly patron" of the current FSB, the successor to the KGB, and revered as the symbolic "warrior-ruler" of the state.[51] The 2022 Russian invasion of Ukraine has been likened to Nevsky's battles against the "collective West." What is the "collective West"? According to the Kremlin today, it is "the Teutonic Order, Sweden, the [Polish-Lithuanian] Commonwealth, Napoleon's empire, the Third Reich, and NATO."[52]

Nevsky biographies often begin with a bleak description of thirteenth-century Rus besieged from all directions. In the east, the Golden Horde placed principalities under its yoke. Swedish and German Crusaders moved into Rus on colonizing drives, but Nevsky and his superb archers (*streltsi*) prevailed in a couple of skirmishes with the Swedes, then in a brief tussle with Teutonic warriors on Lake Chud. Nevsky always prayed to God for help in his battles, but also, in the manipulated sources, asked for divine retribution against anyone who dared to violate Rus's sacred borders.[53] Nevsky probably fought against the Swedes not on the frozen surface of the lake—as a 1938 Soviet film shows—but on the banks and marshes, taking advantage of the fact that his archers, crossbow shooters, and horsemen could handle the cold. They wore frost nails (cleats) on their feet, so had an easier time navigating the crusted-over bog than the Teutonic defenders of European Christendom.[54] That Nevsky triumphed with help from Batu Khan's emissaries is excluded from accounts, and the rest of his interactions with the Mongols is downplayed. Also downplayed is the exchange he had with Pope Innocent IV, who offered Nevsky the support of the Teutonic Knights. Nevsky had a strategic choice to make between the Catholics and the "pagans" of the steppe. He chose the latter. Focusing his energies more on the east than the west spared Rus a potentially fatal setback.[55]

In 1263, Nevsky and one of his brothers traveled to Sarai. The trip was hazardous, and the families of the travelers had just modest odds of seeing them again. Nothing of this place survives, save a replica of sorts built as a set for a lavish 2012 Russian movie called *The Horde* that has since become a tourist attraction.[56] Nevsky ventured even farther to Karakorum, the cosmopolitan stronghold of the entire Mongol-Tatar empire and the long-haul destination of diplomats, merchants, and supplicants like the Ruriks. Nothing remains of Karakorum today except for the stone turtle that once marked the entrance. Nevsky left no description of how he made the trip through this obscure and still little-traveled part of the world. Accounts from others who made it through the Celestial Mountains during Nevsky's time are fragmentary and confused. No wonder:

filthy, hungry, dreaming of baths and honey-cake, they must have felt like they would never arrive at their destination or make it back home. The 3,800-mile ride took well over a year, long enough to make the reason for the trip moot.

Nevsky paid court to the khan in a humiliating effort to convince the Mongols not to attack Rostov. He succeeded, but then took sick with a boiling fever and died on the way back. He spent his final hours in the town of "Small Town" (Gorodets), with just enough time left to him to take his monastic vows, thereby reinforcing his image as a defender of the Russian Orthodox Church against threats from all sides. Nevsky was buried in a white-stone sarcophagus in an arcosolium (catacomb) in Vladimir.[57]

After Nevsky's death, control of Moscow passed, in confusing fashion, to his youngest son, Daniil, who was just two years old in 1263.[58] Thus began a period when no single actor in the northern lands had sufficient power to dominate. Daniil was named after the family saint of the Moscow princes, Daniil the Stylite, who lived in Constantinople during the fifth century. His biographical profile is exemplary. This holy man spent most of his life atop a column—standing there from dawn to dusk or until he collapsed—praying, preaching, curing the ill, exorcising demons, refusing food, water, and shelter.[59] The foundation of the column trembled during fierce storms that lashed Daniil's naked body and coated him in ash and ice. He died on his perch in an iron pen the Byzantine emperor built for him out of pity for his divinely inspired suffering. Mourners climbed the ladder to find him crumpled into the smallest shape possible, knees pressed against his chest and feet gnawed to the bone by pests.[60]

The saint's feast day is December 11, which suggests that Daniil of Moscow was born either in November or December of 1261. Adulthood in the medieval era began at age twelve: in Daniil's case, 1273. He is not listed in the sources as an independent prince before 1282, leaving it unclear who was minding the compound while he was growing up. The best guess is his uncle, Yaroslav, who made his home in Tver, about a hundred miles northwest of Moscow.[61] Tver, like Moscow, was constructed on a bog and populated first by traders from the north and then by refugees from the south, where the Mongols concentrated their raids.

Daniil is said to have been brave, wise, relatively diplomatic, kind to the poor, and supported by his people.[62] He later fought against the boyars and the prince of Ryazan, but his legacy is otherwise benign, the previous thirty or so years of his rule having been largely peaceable. Revenue from the trade and craft settlements along the Moscow waterways—blacksmith shops, tanneries, and jewelry and pottery enterprises—funded the construction of a beautiful white stone church like those in Vladimir-Suzdal at the time.[63] Daniil founded a cloister in his holy ancestor's name (Danilov monastïr') on the right bank of the Moskva River and, in his final years, like his father, took monastic vows.[64]

He married Mariya Glebovna of Beloozero in 1261, who gave him nine sons between 1281 and 1294 plus one daughter in 1298. The family relied on two boyar families, the Byakonts and the Velyaminovs, for backing. From the latter came the Moscow *tïsyachnik/ tïsyatskiy*, the regent who oversaw the fighting forces, or militia, and other functions within the civic structure, from summertime construction to trade to the levying of fines. The word *tïsyachnik* relates to *tïsyacha*, thousand, which gives a rough sense of the number of people running the affairs in Moscow and places like it, as least at the start. In Novgorod, which subordinated the power of the prince to the city council (*veche*), the *tïsyachnik* was elected along with the mayor (*posadnik*). Not so, however, in places with strong aristocratic power. There the position of *tïsyachnik* belonged to the more influential, senior boyar families. With the consolidation of Moscow as its own princedom, the role of the *tïsyachnik* declined, and the position would be abolished in a move that strengthened the power of the prince at the expense of anything resembling an electoral process.[65]

For much of Daniil's reign in Moscow, his older brothers Dmitri (ruling in Pereyaslavl and its environs) and Andrey (in Gorodets) were at each other's throats, squaring off with assistance from rival Mongol forces. Daniil was forced to enter these hostilities in 1293, when the Mongols returned to Moscow. The drama between the brothers and their boyars and militias was staged within a modest area of present-day Russia, a subsection of the Golden Ring of towns and regions surrounding the capital. It involved a diverse cast of characters, like the Mongol leader Nogay, a *tyomnik* (dark presence) who gained control of a broad swath of Golden Horde terrain and took the illegitimate daughter of the Byzantine emperor Michael VIII Palaeologus as his bride.[66] Fighting unfolded in the towns of Vladimir-Suzdal and Pereyaslavl (present-day Pereslavl-Zalessky). Tver was also involved, though it is not part of the Golden Ring. So, too, Novgorod, at a distance from Tver about the same as Tver's from Moscow, and in the same northwest direction. The towns and the villages in between would be repeatedly overrun, leaving the people with next to nothing, "weeping and sobbing."[67]

Daniil was the first of the Moscow Ruriks to gather neighboring principalities as allies against the Mongols, which allowed Moscow to annex these realms. When Daniil (or perhaps one of his sons) incorporated the neighboring enclave of Kolomna, the entire length of the Moskva River came under Moscow's control. Moscow acquired a bigger presence—big enough, after Daniil's death—to be disinhibited, indulging aggressive impulses. For no known reason, his sons went after the town of Mozhaysk, captured it, and imprisoned the local ruler, Svyatoslav. Mozhaysk became the first part of a future Moscow kingdom: the Tsardom of Muscovy.

The "skirmishes," as the chronicles called them, brought Daniil's life to an end on March 5, 1303, at age forty-one. According to Rurik traditions of succession, Daniil's sons would not have become anything more than minor players, but the Mongols disrupted the pattern. The Daniilovichi took control of places the invaders had leveled. Although it has been argued that Moscow "seized" the Rurik throne on the way to becoming a great power, it remained a quiet place save for those times when the Mongols burst through the green black forest.[68] Some of the raids were bloodless, a few dozen horsemen stocking up on supplies, others the opposite as residents became carrion, buildings became ash, all became nothing but tears reportedly shed by statues of saints on the anniversary of such calamities.

Daniil's successors tried to ease fears about the Mongols by assembling defensive stone walls around the compound. Of course, people outside the compound were left even more fearful, so another set of fortifications went up around present-day Red Square and a market center called Kitai-gorod—an ambiguous name of uncertain origin.[69] Archeologists started scrutinizing the layers of char too late to determine what Moscow was like during Daniil's lifetime, much less earlier.[70] Excavations inside and around the Kremlin were spoiled by the building of the Metro system and related state-mandated construction projects, so Moscow (represented as the center of Slavic civilization) has only a tenuous grasp on its history before the fifteenth century. The capital of Russia today was, for centuries, insignificant and peripheral, a dot on a map of the unknown. But the Slavs of the east came to recognize that they had something in common—an external threat, not just the menace of each appanage to the others. In its face, a distinct outlook, sense of being, and a new culture emerged.

3

PLAGUE

As they told bitter tales of deprivation and martyrdom, of plundered treasures, reckless deeds, and marauding clans, hardship brought the people of Rus together. Those who shared these stories formed communities of shared experiences—real or imagined. The people, to paraphrase the French philosopher and political theorist Ernest Renan, had "many things in common," but also had "forgotten many things."[1] Much has been forgotten about Moscow before the twelfth century, and nearly nothing had been recorded, but the storytellers, the authors of the chronicles, insisted that Moscow—not Kyiv—was the sacred heart of Slavic civilization, the cosmopolitan node of settlements along trading routes of water, forest, and plain where the Slavs of the east encountered Finns, Greeks, Hungarians, Persians, Swedes, Tatars, Baltic groups, Pechenegs, Polovtsï, and the Slavs of the west.

Power (*vlast'*) didn't find a home in Moscow until a couple of rulers named Ivan arrived. Before then, in the thirteenth and fourteenth centuries, power belonged to the Tatars of the Golden Horde, who brought discord to the scattered principalities of Rus—along with some benefits. The favor shown by the khan to the ruling family of Moscow increased its reach, and profits from the east–west trading network developed by the Golden Horde funded the Eastern Orthodox Church.[2] Trees were felled and sharpened, stones hauled up the hill from the Moskva, and clay applied to walls by famished, disfigured laborers. Inside the Detinets, as the Kreml' (the Kremlin) was first called, the cathedrals and residences of the rich assumed a look of permanence and divine favor.[3]

The sons of Daniil of Moscow, especially Yuri, lived well under the Golden Horde. The rulers of Tver did not. Though Tver entered the fourteenth century in a position of strength—Mikhaíl secured the position of grand prince from the Sarai Khan Tokhta and profited for a decade as a tax collector for the Golden Horde— strategic blunders and unpreventable mishaps reduced Tver to what it is now: a stopover town, neither big nor small, with a decent college, a Goat Museum, and a lot of bridges. About 400,000 people live there; Moscow, two hours away by car, has over thirty times that number.

Tver's decline began in 1313, when Tokhta's nephew, Sultan Giyas al-Din Mohammed Öz Beg, became the khan. He married off his sister, Konchatka, to Yuri, the prince of Moscow, in 1317. The marriage was advantageous for Yuri, who was granted permission to expand his holdings by conquering Tver. Obviously, the grand prince of Tver, Mikhaíl, wasn't a part of this plan. He kidnapped the khan's sister as a bargaining chip to keep Yuri out of Tver, but the plan failed when the poor girl died of fright.[4] Yuri took the long trip to Sarai to report that he no longer had a wife and the khan had lost a sister. The khan hauled Mikhaíl before his court to explain himself and chained him up in a tent with stone blocks around his neck. Mikhaíl's *zhitiya* (hagiography) says that he spent his last days reading the Psalms. The khan left the task of killing Mikhaíl to Yuri, who cut out his heart as a souvenir. The corpse rotted in a stable before being sent back to Tver. In 1320, Mikhaíl was laid to rest in the Transfiguration Monastery.[5]

Yuri would himself be murdered, and then his murderer would be murdered. It took eight years, until 1328, for Moscow to subdue Tver. By then, Yuri's brother Ivan I was ruling Moscow, and he was, from the khan's perspective, excellent at his job: a pliable lapdog who ensured the efficient payment of tribute.[6] Ivan acquired a nickname, Kalita, which meant "purse," the sort that merchants wore around their waists. The Russian word for money, *denga*, then *den'gi*, derives from *dangs,* silver coins circulated by the Golden Horde. These replaced the glass beads, slate discs, and pelts used in older times for small transactions; silver bars remained the standard for larger sums. Coins issued by Moscow and other princedoms reflected the realities of life under the Golden Horde: One depicts a man with a sword and a poleaxe with the words "Grand Prince Dmitri [Donskoi]" encircling the image; the other side features a patterned frame and an Arabic inscription reading "Long live supreme ruler Öz Beg Khan."[7]

Kalita also translates as "moneybag," suggesting that Ivan squeezed a lot of *dangs* out of the principalities he controlled. Land was collateral for loans the princes of Rus took out to settle their debts to the Golden Horde, and Ivan was an efficient collector. He skimmed the proceeds to purchase land for himself and, in 1339, invested in a wall of thick oak logs to protect his compound.[8] The earliest Russian histories of his rule suggest that he did some good. He gave to the poor, made northern Rus safe for European traders by chasing out "Tatar thieves," freed slaves, and generally presided over a "happy time."[9] Recent histories assert the opposite: he didn't care about his subjects.[10] Both versions have something in common. Refugees, including the metropolitan of the Orthodox Church in Rus, flooded into Ivan's realm seeking safety and stability, which he provided.

The metropolitan, Maximos, reportedly fled Kyiv to avoid death at the hands of the Tatars, who tore through Kyiv in 1299. But the Tatars weren't anywhere near Kyiv in 1299, and the metropolitan's move involved months of planning in consultation with Constantinople.[11] He didn't simply skip town, destination unknown. Maximos settled in Vladimir in 1300 and spent most of his time preventing rival princes from killing one another. After his death in 1305, an abbot named Peter (Pyotr) from Ukraine became metropolitan. Being caught in the power struggle between the khan and the local rulers of Rus was not something Peter's previous life of silent monastic labor had prepared him for.[12] But he did as God ordained, donning the mantle of metropolitan, presiding over the See, tending to the flock, traveling to Sarai, and occasionally letting his opinion on political matters be known. Three of his epistles survive. Two remind priests of their duties; the other encourages priests who have succumbed, or might succumb, to blasphemous temptation to retreat to the monasteries of the hinterlands.[13] Moscow's first great building, a cathedral honoring the Dormition (the "falling asleep" of the Mother of God before angels carried her heavenward), was built on land granted to Peter from Prince Ivan I.

In August 1326, the foundation of the Cathedral of the Dormition was laid on the site of a wooden church dating back to the time of Yuri Dolgorukiy. The cult of the Theotokos, which the Dormition cathedral celebrated, represents the Mother of God as a fierce protector of cities. It was good and right to claim her for Moscow, a new religious capital. Metropolitan Peter is said to have prepared a tomb for himself in the cathedral's walls before traveling to Sarai to meet with the khan on a peacekeeping mission. The trip back was long and miserable, sapping Peter's strength. He died in Moscow that December. The "Legend of the Death of Metropolitan Peter," compiled after Peter's death by a bishop from Rostov, follows the trail of miracles that led to his canonization as a saint. He (or rather his relics) removed tumors, cured a boy who was unable to speak and whose hands were "rooted" to his chest, gave a blind slave girl the gift of sight, and restored movement to the limbs of a woman who had been paralyzed for two years.[14]

Ivan I Kalita wanted Moscow to look as good as Tver, and perhaps even Vladimir, so emptied his treasury to finance the construction of four more churches. The first, the Church of St. John of the Ladder (of Divine Ascent), was built over the summer of 1329 and presumably celebrated the subduing of Tver. The next, completed in the fall of 1329, was dedicated to the Apostle Peter, the metropolitan's namesake. The cult of the apostle tells of his escape from the prison. An angel appeared, his chains fell off, the doors opened, and the angel led him out. This is a resurrection story of sorts, so building a church in the apostle's name speaks to Moscow's survival and revival after the years of strife with the House of Tver.[15] Next came Spas na boru, the Church of Our Savior in the Forest, which replaced an earlier wooden church dating from the childhood of Daniil of Moscow. The last church built by Ivan, the Church of the Archangel, was completed in 1333. Ivan would be buried in its crypt, as would numerous other princes and tsars, almost up to the time of Peter the Great.

There was less wood in Moscow's sacred spaces than stone, thus greater protection from fire. But its force could not be avoided. Stoves burned day and night in the city, and embers blew through open windows not covered with shutters, horn panes, or oiled skins into houses, then from yard to yard. Dropped candles, lightning strikes, tree clearings, piles of straw and dung, and huts crowded close together—all could spark disaster. The first catastrophic blaze, on May 3, 1331, tore through the Kremlin. Four years later another fire swept through the streets. The chronicles mention it in passing, treating it as a routine inconvenience rather than the cause of death and destruction. A third blaze, on June 13, 1337, destroyed eighteen churches inside and outside the Kremlin, and several private chapels. And on May 31, 1343, all Moscow caught fire, consuming the prince's compound, boyars' residences, workshops, storehouses, and pens before torrential rains dissolved everything else.[16]

Worse was the plague, which arrived in Moscow in 1352, having coursed through the continent. Christians blamed Muslims for the sickness, Muslims blamed Christians, Christians and Muslims blamed Jews and pagans. Traders spread reports of wine and wool as the source, but surely the supernatural was at work, people believed. It had happened before. The ancient Varangian town of Polotsk (in northern Belarus) has in its lore a horrible night in 1092 when anyone leaving their house succumbed to ulcers inflicted by a demon. The afflicted began riding through the town during the day, infecting everyone and anyone. Residents referred to them as the living dead. Perhaps the demons had returned.[17] Notions of time didn't depend on linear progressions; instead, the future is a product of the past, so what happened will happen again. As the Bible says, the "last will be first and the first last."[18]

The pestilence immortalized as the Black Plague passed from fleas buried in the fur of rats into the bloodstreams of the horses and horsemen of the Golden Horde. People caught it by being bitten, inhaling the bacteria, or otherwise absorbing the contagion through their skin. Caravans, cargo holds, land, sea: The fleas traveled around the world, and with them the bacillus called *Yersinia pestis,* which blocked the digestive systems of the rat fleas as it multiplied, causing the fleas to starve, thus to bite and bite again, then to disgorge the bacillus into the bloodstreams of its victims.[19] Fever, chills, diarrhea, rashes, inflammation of the lymph nodes, boils, organ failure, gangrene, hysteria, and seizures ensued. On average, it took just two days for a person to die from the disease, as the Tatars learned before the Slavs did.

A greater commitment to cleanliness would have helped, of course, but over time something of the opposite occurred. The medieval was a smelly epoch but not terribly so, because foul odors caused fear. The expression "ill wind" stems from the widely held belief that disease-bearing spirits lurked in foul air. The smell of armpits, bad teeth, intestinal plumbing, tallow, and smoke from hearths was unavoidable so generally unnoticed. Moscow had its own distinct aromas, from the rivers and apple trees, broom "spirits" (the fragrance of birch twigs), dust, wet fur, the first snow of autumn (a smell so melon-sweet that the city's future regents forbade clearing the streets), wildflowers, lilacs, berries, boiled cabbage (a wintertime staple), liquid spirits, onions, garlic (chewed raw), dung, slop.[20] The markets were pungent; goods imported from the Silk Road made them smell better, or at least, for long-distance travelers, more agreeably like home. Moscow's rivers and streams allowed everyone to bathe. Recurrences of the plague, however, made people fear pretty much everything: rain, eating fish, naps. The Rus, like the Tatars, began to avoid bathing—at least in water—for fear of opening their pores to possible infection.[21]

A conservative estimate suggests that, in the second half of the fourteenth century, Rus lost a quarter of its people.[22] The decimation of the populace left crops and animals untended, increasing the need for slave labor. The ruling houses were wiped out as well, meaning more power was held in fewer hands. The consolidation of land under central control became easier, at least until the Tatars took notice.

The Tatars managed to turn the plague to their advantage even as they suffered from it. Such is the tale told by Gabriele de' Mussi (ca. 1280–ca. 1356), who recorded what he heard about the horrendous happenings in Kaffa (now Feodosiya, Ukraine), a cosmopolitan port town on the Black Sea administered by the republic of Genoa but beholden to the Golden Horde, which charged a three percent tax on goods sold through the port. Tensions flared between the Genoese and the Tatars over the slave trade. First in 1343 and then in 1345, the Tatars attacked Kaffa and trampled across another Italian trading enclave, the town of Tana in the Don River delta. The conflict would have persisted even longer, but the Tatars started dropping dead by the thousands. Corpses rotted in the sun. The commander ordered a retreat from Kaffa, but not before engaging in a horrifically ingenious act of biological warfare. The Tatars loaded the corpses of their fallen comrades onto catapults and lobbed them over Kaffa's fortifications, hoping, in de' Mussi's description, "that the intolerable stench would kill everyone inside. What seemed like mountains of dead were thrown into the city, and the Christians could not hide or flee or escape from them, although they dumped as many of the bodies as they could in the sea. And soon the rotting corpses tainted the air and poisoned the water supply, and the stench was so overwhelming that hardly one in several thousand was in a position to flee the remains."[23] De' Mussi describes the plague ships full of infected sailors and cargo that traveled from Kaffa to Venice and were allowed to dock until the dockworkers started dying. He also writes about his own experience of the disease at home in Piacenza, where his duties as a notary included signing death certificates.

When the sickness reached middle Europe, people looked heavenward for an explanation. King Philip VI of France heard from his medical advisors that the 1345 conjunction of the planets Saturn, Jupiter, and Mars "under the moist sign of Aquarius" was the cause, as well as noxious vapors emitting from earthquakes.[24] The Italian humanist Giovanni Boccaccio attributed it, more conventionally, to "God in His just wrath by way of retribution for our iniquities."[25] He made this claim in *The Decameron* (1353), a collection of fables about a group of friends from Florence who escape the plague in the countryside, entertaining one another with tales of frisky monks, obtuse priests, a princess's forbidden love for a commoner and her father's rather excessive affection for her. Everyone is titillated by the bawdier anecdotes, including the servants, whom the friends over-hear frolicking in the kitchen. Boccaccio, who lost several friends to the plague, wrote in Italian vernacular prose instead of scholarly Latin verse to describe a looser, freer world where the old codes of etiquette and mores no longer applied.

In Rus, where few could read, much less write, the feudal order stood fast. Far from spurring a rebirth of philosophical thought and new forms of literature, the plague in Rus reduced the ranks of the elite, gutted the urban labor force, and curtailed education. The Black Death, for Rus, strengthened superstitions and increased reli-gious prohibitions. Monks made parchment into Bibles and hagiog-raphies, not subversive fiction directed at the church and the ruling elite.[26] When the boyars of Pskov began coughing up blood, their impulse was to hand over everything they owned—land, villages, lakes, and fisheries—to the churches and monasteries in hopes of forgiveness for their sins and perpetual prayers for their souls after death. Then they fled, leaving poor and helpless people behind. Tatishchev describes "bodies in counts of 20, 30, and 50 piling up for placement in single graves in the churches . . . and more were left unburied, and there was great weeping and sobbing among all of the people seeing each other dying and knowing the same thing awaited them."[27]

The plague, "God's righteous judgement," spread from Pskov to Novgorod and on to Moscow. The grand prince, Ivan I Kalita's son Simeon, feared the worst for his ruling house and so prepared his last will and testament. "And lo," he wrote, "I write this to you so that the memory of our parents and of us may not die, and so that the candle may not go out."[28] The candle went out: Simeon was felled by the plague in 1353, as were both of his sons and one of his two brothers. The metropolitan also died. All this happened in a single week.

Simeon's brother Ivan II, nicknamed "the fair" for his honey-colored hair, was also tagged "the meek" for his lack of ruthlessness. He lost more land than he acquired during his seven years in power while his courtiers bickered. His second-in-command was found mysteriously "murdered on the square, at matins, and some said this was carried out either through the counsel of the grand boyars or by someone else, in secret."[29] The killing might have been planned by the Velyaminovs, one of the fiercest boyar clans, but exactly who was responsible will never be known.[30] Gawkers gathered round the corpse in the central square as the bells were rung for the matins service just before dawn on February 3, 1357. Ivan II died two years later at age thirty-three.

His heir, Dmitri Ivanovich, better known as Dmitri Donskoi, assumed power at age nine, relying for counsel on the metropolitan, Alexei, whose father was a boyar of the Byatkonts clan, the archenemy of the Velyaminovs.[31] Donskoi was also mentored by Moscow's hegumen (monastic head), Sergey (Sergius) of Radonezh, who supported Donskoi in the campaigns he launched and policies he pursued but also encouraged him to keep his cool: better to bribe a foe than to cut off his head. Donskoi, however, wanted to be a hero. He had fallen asleep as a child to stories about Alexander Nevsky, Daniil of Moscow, Prince Vladimir of Kyiv, Monomakh, and the passion-bearers Boris and Gleb. The Rurik bloodline fortified him.

The dry, hot months always brought fires, but in 1365, a year of drought and unbearable heat spawned an inferno straight out of Dante that turned most everything into ash. "The heavens made a sign," one of the chronicles recounts, "and the sun turned blood red and blacked out. And the haze lasted for half the summer. And the heat and fire were great, forest and marsh and field burned, rivers dried up and everyone felt fear and horror and immense sorrow."[32] Stoked by fierce winds, the fires spread from one side of Moscow, through the Kremlin, to the other, following the line of development along the river. The first church to flare up gave the catastrophe its name: the Great "All Saints" Fire. Nature was not to blame, the priests declared; rather, the people's sins, their "darkness," had caused the drought that created the spark that ignited straw roofs and everything else.[33] The stone churches of the Kremlin survived, but the residences of the prince, boyars, and regent (*tïsyachnik*), along with the books and charters inside, did not.

The destruction convinced Donskoi to invest in fireproofing. The

Kremlin was to be encircled by white walls, high stone towers, and arched gates. The task involved some 3,500 workers and a comparable number of horses and carts. Peasant laborers and slaves hauled slabs of limestone up the hill from sledges on the frozen river, pulled them in carts across a field of snow-covered ash, and stacked them on top of one another. "Spitting and cursing" in their epic toil, they gave Moscow a striking new appearance; some buildings were even painted.[34] The limestone helped keep the Kremlin intact after 1367, despite subsequent droughts and fires. From his newly fortified seat of power, Donskoi "began to accomplish many things" and forced "all the Russian princes to do his will."[35]

Details of Donskoi's reign are preserved in twenty-one letters on paper and parchment, discovered in Moscow during the building of sled runs from the Kremlin down to the river in 1843. One letter describes Donskoi's resettlement policies around 1363. The land was unpopulated, and yet moving around it was oppressively bureaucratic, requiring just the right document. The papers Donskoi gave to Yevsevka, "a commoner from Torzhok who is moving to my domain of Kostroma," exempted him "from paying duties, taxes, and levies for *yam* [use of posthouses], *tamga* [border customs], trade transactions, weight collection, river [travel by water], bones [people traveling with him], docks, guest yards [inns], or anything else." All Yevsevka needed to do was pay the grand prince "five martens a year" for permission to live in Moscow.[36] Not that he could do whatever he wanted: "I have ordered the *tisyachnik* to keep an eye on him," Donskoi wrote. "And if Yevsevka, having presented this letter, still has money taken from him, I will punish that person."[37] Moscow and Novgorod quarreled over Torzhok, an outpost near Tver. Donskoi's 1363 letter implies strict controls on the movement of "bones" among rival domains, but also, in Yevsevka's case, an incentive to resettle. The chronicles describe Donskoi overcoming those rivalries to strengthen Moscow's position in the north.[38]

Donskoi faced threats from the west and the east: from Algirdas, the Lithuanian ruler, who twice burned down the *posad*, the merchants' area outside of the Kremlin, and from a Mongol-Tatar emir named Mamai—an agent of chaos lampooned in the old Russian expression "your place is so messy it's as though Mamai's been here." Donskoi arranged a truce of sorts with Algirdas and took the fight to Mamai in a pair of famous battles. One took place along the Vozha River, and another on a field, Kulikovo, located near the Don River, which gave Grand Prince Dmitri his moniker Donskoi. He adopted the clever ruse of dressing up one of his commanders in his princely clothes, and then, after Mamai began attacking the wrong person, charging him from behind. His achievement at Kulikovo is memorialized in a remarkable number of historical sources as well as patriotic narratives from ancient times to the present.[39] Donskoi's name graces a nuclear submarine (the largest in the world), a Moscow boulevard as well as a transit station, and an ill-fated warship in the Russian Imperial Navy.[40]

But Russian accounts of Donskoi's life are selective.[41] According to Mongol-Tatar histories, he failed to protect Moscow. While the reckless Mamai was harassing Donskoi and other Rus princes, a nastier warrior named Timur, or Timur the Lame after a fall from a horse left him partially paralyzed, was building minarets from the skulls of his victims for fun. (Timurid structures influenced the design of the Taj Mahal.[42]) His other delights included chess, and he is said to have invented a gameboard of 112 squares, with giraffes, camels, elephants, war engines, viziers, and shahs as figurines.[43] He established a base in Samarkand, present-day Uzbekistan. Tall for his time at five feet, eight inches, Timur aspired to be a giant among men by restoring the empire of Genghis Khan, from whom he said he was descended. He sought to reunite the khanates and Sarai under his control by conquering territory from India and Korea to the Caspian Sea and the Mediterranean.

Seeking to neutralize Mamai, Timur aligned himself with another Mongol-Tatar emir named Tokhtamïsh. With Timur's backing and encouragement from the princes of Suzdal, Tokhtamïsh attacked Moscow in August 1382. Donskoi had lost his best soldiers to the Tatars at Kulikovo and had no forces to defend the city. He fled, as did the metropolitan and the boyars and everyone else with a cart and a horse. Those left behind prayed, fornicated, emptied their masters' cellars of honey, silver, and wine, stumbled drunk through the streets, and hollered at the Tatars standing on the other side of the walls. A ragtag militia shot arrows at the invaders, poured boiling water on them, hurled rocks, and shot crossbows and cannons.

The arrows ran out, as did the water. Tokhtamïsh persuaded Moscow's defenders to open the gates, claiming that his quarrel was with Donskoi alone. But once his men were in, he led a deranged slaughter. According to the *Tale of the Invasion of Tokhtamïsh*, a narrative assembled long after the fact, some 24,000 people (most of Moscow's population) died in "a fourfold destruction: first by the sword, second by the fire, third by the water, and fourth by all of them." The Tatars broke down the doors of the churches, flogged the priests, beat the abbots, smashed the altars, and stripped the icons of their gold, silver, pearls, and precious stones then broke their frames and ground them into the dirt. The "expensive vestments" of the priests disappeared along with the grand prince's "hidden" treasure. The teller of this gruesome tale runs out of nouns recounting the "grief," "horror," "sorrow," "weeping," "wailing," and the feelings of "destitution," "shame," and "humiliation." The saga concludes with a bit of sociopathic burlesque: Moscow "was the greatest of the cities, a wonderful city, full of people and bustling, with numerous lords and all manner of riches" until that moment. "In the single hour it took to capture, plunder, and torch it, everything changed. Nothing could be seen but bare earth and smoking ruins and piles of corpses, and the holy churches stood ravaged, as if orphaned, as if widowed."[44]

Tokhtamïsh allowed Donskoi to retain his title as grand prince of Moscow so long as he submitted to Sarai and paid tribute on time. Donskoi brought Moscow back to life before he died, on May 19, 1389, his body and mind utterly exhausted. He was interred beside his grandfather, Ivan I Kalita, and left behind a wife, Eudoxia, who survived him by eighteen years.[45]

Where he had been motivated by a sense of mission, she seemed driven by obligation. Raised in Nizhny Novgorod as daughter of the grand prince of Suzdal, she is said to have lived in service to her name, which means, like the Latin *prudentia,* "good judgment." Likely educated by a monastic elder, Eudoxia had two possible paths in life: managing a household, living in comfortable quarters in gowns sewn

Defense of Moscow from the Troops of Khan Tokhtamïsh. Miniature from
the *Litsevoy letopisnïy svod (Illustrated Chronicle Compilation,* 1568–76).
Tokhtamïsh (1350–1406) attacked Moscow in 1382 because the grand prince,
Dmitri Donskoi, refused to pay tribute.

with jewels; or becoming a nun in a monastic cell, sleeping on a cot
or a mat on the ground, engaged in prayer and contemplation beside
other women without saying a word to them for months at a time,
if ever. Had the choice been presented to her, she might well have
chosen the latter. But Eudoxia didn't have a choice. Her marriage to
Donskoi at age thirteen took place in Kolomna, as Moscow was ravaged by the fire of 1365.

She was in Moscow at the time of Tokhtamïsh's siege and escaped
with an infant in arms (one of at least twelve children she had with
her husband). After Donskoi's death and Moscow's rebuilding,
Eudoxia inherited thirty-one parcels (*volosti*) of land and settlements. She wore chains under her clothes as a form of penance and
encouraged the building of stone churches and convents, including
the Nativity Church (attached to the princely residence) and the
Ascension Convent near the Spasskaya (Savior) tower of the Kremlin.[46] The Trinity Chronicle, which Eudoxia might have had a role in

copying, describes the construction and decoration of churches in Moscow, the gathering of talented fresco painters, and the shrines brought to Rus from Byzantium. The chronicle notes the births and deaths of Eudoxia's relatives and the passing of her daughter Maria in Lithuania, a loss so terrible that she arranged for the body to be brought back to Moscow for burial in the Nativity Church. Eudoxia's sons were instructed to "live in love and peace among themselves," not allowing "the strong to offend the weak."[47]

Just weeks before her own death in July 1407, Eudoxia was tonsured. The priest conducting the sacrament blessed her with the name Euphrosyne, perhaps after Euphrosyne of Suzdal (d. 1250), whose prayers had spared her convent from destruction by Batu Khan. The "Legend of the Grand Princess Eudoxia" tells of the miracles that occurred after she took tonsure, including the curing of a blind man who touched her sleeve and wiped his eyes. Of her relics, fragments of a belt embossed with images of the twelve major feasts of the Orthodox rite survive—nothing else.

Eudoxia was both the subject and keeper of icons, eternal objects of eternal beauty, faith made physical. Faith overcomes, transcends, and protects against the horrors of human behavior and the bleakness of the landscape. The icon, as an image of that faith, serves as a window on and mirror of the soul, as well as an access point to another world. These objects possess real power. Legend claims that, in 1395, heeding dictates from above, Eudoxia had an icon of the Mother of God transferred from Vladimir to Moscow to protect the city, its metropolitan, governor, boyars, merchants, and everyone else from the Golden Horde. Another version of the same tale has the metropolitan, not Eudoxia, bringing the icon to Moscow for a mass prayer; still another, a legend built into a legend, has Donskoi leading a battle with the icon held aloft alongside his banner; and yet another has the icon going nowhere at all—it remained in Vladimir.[48] The icon shows the Christ Child nestled against Mary's cheek. Her eyes are directed neither at him nor at the viewer. The image combines profile and frontal views, surmounting linear perspective. The icon is of a particular type, known as "Eleusa," and exudes tenderness in a golden glow.[49] Mary's face is darker than the child's, soot having been added to the olive-colored pigment as a symbol of experience. The design of the icon and its materials indicate Byzantine origin. From Constantinople, the icon is thought to have been sent in 1131 to the Devichy (Maiden) Monastery outside of Kyiv. One of Yuri Dolgorukiy's sons brought it north. A priceless religious artifact, it is now preserved in a house church that is part of Moscow's Tretyakov Gallery.

Hundreds of icons were made in Rus, but just thirty or so survive from the first wave of Golden Horde attacks. Robberies and invasions through the centuries as well as the animus of Marxist-Leninists in the Soviet era destroyed the heritage. Some icons were ill-made and thus painted over, repeatedly, the boiled linseed oil used as resin on the original images turning black from candle smoke and soot.[50] These are fragile objects made of cloth, mosaic tile, gold leaf, black metal, berries, birch, butternut, egg, sumac, wild mint, mustard greens, and other dye plants gathered in the woods, stuffed in skin bags, and brought to the village or town priest to decorate the church. Often the scenes were narrative with a central panel depicting a saint surrounded by scenes of his posthumous miracles and episodes from folklore. Fantastic palaces, magical animals, and stouter, shorter people appear behind the ethereal, tall, thin dramatis personae of the famous icons created in Novgorod and Moscow. These images made of cypress or pinewood and cloth and tempera (a mixture of natural pigment, egg yolk, and rye beer) capture the immaterial, the spirit of a saint or Christ or Mary. To look at an icon, within the darkness of a stone church lit by candles made from beet root or tallow, is to see past the past and to perceive the interior, the essence of time, the soul, and the soil.

Like the chronicles, icons place one layer of time atop another and assimilate spiritual symbols. Icons of Christ, the Theotokos, and popular saints have telltale colors: green for the force of life; red for suffering and resurrection; white for purity; blue for celestial bliss. Brown expresses transience; black the grave, death, and the abyss.[51] Silver, gold, and other expensive metals are used to embellish figures encased in physical form but free of defects, undergoing transformation. The challenge for the iconographer is (quoting a member of the Holy Synod of the Patriarchate of Moscow) "to render, as far as possible and to as great an extent as possible, those spiritual qualities whereby the person depicted acquired the Kingdom of Heaven."[52] For this reason, icons are often referred to as portals to heaven, giving the viewer access to another dimension.

Over time, Rus developed its own distinctive iconic style. Rather than gold or silver occupying the entire space, for example, Russian icons use white or yellow ochre pigment as the background. In *Crucifixion,* an icon from fourteenth-century Byzantium, the background is rendered in gold and blends with the halo of Christ, whose body is well-defined, fleshed-out through the careful mixing of pigments. In the *Miracle of Saint George and the Dragon,* an icon from Rus a century later, the saint appears in a red mantle on a black horse against a yellow background that mimics gold gilding, the quality of light. The body is given much less volume. The flatness and the sharp, angular positioning are distinct to Rus, the eastern representation of the dragon reflecting the Rus perception of the Tatars. George's heroic dragon-slaying is itself an addition to a Greek and Latin cult that had him enduring seven years of torture for declaring his belief in Christ. He was said to have been beaten, his limbs chopped up and crushed, molten lead poured from trachea into esophagus, nails hammered into his skull and on and on. He died three times before reaching, after three resurrections, heaven.[53] His resilience became a source of miracles. The tale is a metaphor for anxieties about decay and death, the cycles of nature, and in the Russian context the suffering of the people. There is no amount of hardship that cannot be endured.

Whereas Moscow suffered the worst of the Mongol-Tatar raids through Rus, Novgorod was spared and indeed flourished as a cultural center, producing illuminated manuscripts with pictures of animals, plants, and, in one instance, a creature with two humps, a long neck and floppy ears: The benighted artist had tried to draw a camel without ever having seen one.[54] Novgorod was also a center for making icons, so too was Pskov, Novgorod's ecclesiastical subordinate. Doubtless the most celebrated icon-maker of the period, Theophanes the Greek (Feofan Grek, ca. 1340–ca. 1410), trained in

Constantinople before relocating to Novgorod then, at the end of the fourteenth century, to Moscow. Theophanes's icon of the Mother of God holding the Christ Child in her arms is said to have been presented to "Prince Dmitri Donskoi" as protection on the eve of his battle against the Tatars in 1380. Its attribution is much in doubt, and the image likely dates from much later, considering its materials and evident, intense emotion.[55] Another icon, *The Transfiguration of Christ*, was certainly made by Theophanes, as revealed by the shift in monochrome expression into a palette both natural (earth tones) and supernatural (blue and precious gold leaf). Christ stands atop a mountain, flanked by the prophets Elijah on the left and Moses on the right. Below him are his apostles, from left to right: Peter, looking up in awe; John, crouched with his hand holding his chin in bewilderment at Christ's transfiguration; and James, looking away with his eyes covered, unable to confront the miracle. Their robes are illuminated in a metallic blue-gold sheen, emphasizing their proximity to the supernatural. Small black fissures in the wood denote a frightening abyss.

Theophanes's student Andrey Rublyov (ca. 1360–ca. 1428) is credited with elevating the icon into a supreme art form blending the mortal and immaterial. He is the subject of a 1966 film by Andrey Tarkovsky. In the first scene, an artisan fashions a hot air balloon out of stitched-together hides. It rises above the river, glides over rowers, and settles into the marsh in a beautiful, euphoric tableau. The film explores life outside the walls of Moscow, along the water, in huts and barns. Onions and apples are staples, rain and cold have spoiled the grain. Naked men bearing bright torches fan out over a river to escort a burning effigy into a crude boat. The Tatar invasion and the debates between Theophanes and Rublyov lead to scenes inside the Kremlin and the Cathedral of the Dormition. The grand prince and his retinue are seldom seen; the grand princess's *terem,* the secluded upper-floor rooms or tower where she spent the bulk of her days, is never shown. A laborer spends the night standing in a lake to avoid wolves. Guards bash the head of a buffoon against a tree trunk and smash his zither. A blond pagan woman offers herself to Tatars for a horse blanket after fighting off dogs for a scrap of meat. Snow falls through an open ceiling; a massive bell is forged from molten metal poured into a mold of clay and timber in a pit and hauled up by dozens of men pulling on ropes. Commoners live amid waste; boyars put them to the wheel. Still, they strive and try to catch a glimpse of something greater. The film is shot in black and white until the epilogue, when Rublyov's icons radiate from the screen in a burst of brilliance.

His most renowned icon, an image of the Holy Trinity, references a tale in the book of Genesis called "Abraham's Hospitality." Angels representing the Father, Son, and Holy Spirit visit Abraham with the news that his wife will bear a son. The harmonious color scheme and the fluid outlines suggest both the unity of God and a silent communion of God's three aspects. The figures look at one another, not at or beyond the viewer, and the Holy Spirit focuses on the center, where a chalice with a calf's head, symbol of Christ's sacrifice and devotion, rests on the table. Minimal details—Abraham's house in the background on the left and the Oak of Mamre—invoke the book of Genesis. Rublyov's icon is sparser, more abstract, and thus more universal than others of the Trinity.[56]

Artists who made icons would begin their work in prayer. Those prayers were then made manifest in images either empathetic or judgmental. Both qualities exist in Christ Pantocrator, Christ the "all-powerful," but neither consolation nor comfort is offered in the eyes of Christ, the Mother of God, or their saints to people living in fear of fire and ice. The church—itself an icon of religion—became a bedrock to the princes and boyars in the Kremlin for the foundation of the state. In the fourteenth century, there was no state, but its later formation came with tremendous risks, especially when rulers started aligning themselves with God. For what was given to Rus by God, God could take away.

4

THIRD ROME

I n 1404, a monk from Mount Athos named Lazar built a mechanical clock in the Kremlin, the first such clock in Russia. He was paid 150 rubles (15 kilograms of silver), a colossal sum that kept him fed for years. The clock hung in a tower at the grand prince's palace and marked time using gears, springs, and levers. "No man strikes it," a sixteenth-century chronicle reports, but "by man's cunning," it "somehow wondrously strangely" moved by itself. The chronicle includes a drawing of Lazar as an old man with a long gray beard, showing the clock to Grand Prince Vasiliy and two of his vassals. Three weights—two small, one large—hang below the clockface, where the names of the hours are indicated using Cyrillic letters (A—1; B—2; Г—3; Д—4; . . . AI—11; BI—12). The hammer atop the clockface struck a bell mounted beside it. The clock did not have hands, so it seems that the dial rotated counterclockwise on the hour.[1]

Although the grand prince liked his clock, the mechanical measurement of time was perceived, like astrology and other forms of divination, as the devil's doing. Clocks spoiled a natural rhythm. Time had long been marked by candles, shadows, hourglasses, and fallible human bell ringers who worked only during the day when the movement of the sun through the sky could be observed. Bells announced the morning, evening, religious services, and holidays.

Time was fluid: It slowed down at dusk, when the loss of light lulled people to sleep, sped up at dawn, and faded quickly into memory.

The chronicles decided what should and should not belong to time. Since the sorrows defining the origins of Russia—the Mongol-Tatar domination of Rus, the beginning of Lithuanian domination, the unsavory specifics of Moscow's conquest of surrounding towns—didn't seem appropriate to remember, much less commemorate, and scribes let them be forgotten. Case in point is the fraught relationship between Vasiliy and Vytautas, a Lithuanian grand duke who possessed land extending from the Black Sea to the Baltic. He ruled Kyivan Rus and Ruthenia from the island castle in a lake where he had been born, enjoying the entertainments of trumpeters, pipers, jesters, and dwarfs.

Vasiliy took refuge in Vytautas's home after fleeing Moscow during a Tatar raid, leaving his people behind to fend for themselves. There, in decadent surroundings, he encountered the Duke's daughter Sophia. He courted her, and the two were engaged in 1385; six years later, they married in Moscow. Relations soured, however, when Vytautas decided that Novgorod and Pskov should belong to his realm, not Vasiliy's. The conflict between father-in-law and son-in-law lasted from 1406 to 1408.[2]

In 1425, the title of grand prince passed from Vasiliy to his ten-year-old son, Vasiliy II, with Sophia as regent. Power seems to have swung back and forth between Vasiliy II's branch of the Moscow house and other family rivals. Vasiliy II's uncle, Yuri, made the hazardous trek to Sarai in hopes of receiving the patent to Moscow from the Golden Horde khan, Ulug Mehmed, but the trip proved a waste of time. The khan awarded the patent to Vasiliy II after meeting with him about a potential "consolidation" of the principality of Moscow, the Golden Horde, and Lithuania.[3]

Once installed as ruler, Vasiliy II moved ahead with the wedding already arranged for him by his mother. He was prevented from marrying his first choice of bride, the granddaughter of a boyar who had fallen into disgrace, and instead took the hand of Princess Mariya Borovskaya, daughter of the prince of Serpukhov, Borovsk, and Maloyaroslavets, and granddaughter of diplomat Fyodor Kobïlin (also known, perhaps for his independent spirit, as Fyodor Koshka, "the Cat," and a distant ancestor of the Romanovs).[4] The wedding took place in Moscow on February 8, 1433. Guests included the resentful uncle Yuri and two cousins from Galich. The older cousin, also named Vasiliy, turned up wearing a belt decorated with gold coins and precious stones. Had he dressed less ostentatiously, he might have been able to enjoy the mounds of salted fish and jugs of honey wine offered to guests. Bloodshed among branches of the family might also have been avoided.[5]

For three generations, the belt had been a symbol of power in Moscow. Sophia believed it belonged there as an heirloom passed down to her from Eudoxia and Donskoi. "It was she," after all, "who arranged the marriages, she who made the political alliances, and she who—backed by the khan—pursued her son's claim to the throne," historian C. K. Woodworth explains. For complex reasons, it ended up around the waist of Vasiliy, the cousin from Galich, who had married Vasiliy II's original choice of bride, the granddaughter of the disgraced boyar. Sophia tore it off him at the wedding, a "disconcertingly strange" action that brought the Galich and Moscow principalities into conflict.[6] The chronicles record subsequent mayhem: kidnapping, murder, and blinding—a punishment for treason popularized by the henchmen of Byzantium.[7]

The boyar was the first to lose his eyes. Second was the belt-wearer himself, who, like his father, had tussled with Vasiliy II for years. A peace was reached but did not hold. In 1436, the grand prince captured his cousin and ordered his servants to scoop out one of his eyes, leaving him with a squint (*kosoy*) for the remaining twelve years of his life, which were probably spent imprisoned underground. The third blinding was Vasiliy II's own, an act of revenge carried out by the younger cousin, Dmitri Shemyaka, a wreck of an individual with a vicious streak.[8]

Hostilities between Shemyaka and Vasiliy II began in 1445, when militias led by Ulug Mehmed's sons defeated Moscow's forces in a battle at Suzdal. Vasiliy II was captured and maimed, his fingers sliced off, and Shemyaka assumed the throne. The fingerless grand prince managed to secure his release from the khan in exchange for jewels and other riches. The khan then equipped him with "five hundred Tatars" for the ride back to Moscow.[9] It was hardly a happy homecoming: a fire stoked by intense winds in drought conditions burned everything to blackness. The bells of the city rang ceaselessly, their clappers swinging madly back and forth in the firestorm.[10] Those who escaped camped outside of the city until the fire extinguished itself, then returned to the charred outlines of houses and streets, a persistent odor, and ash that stained clothes and boots. Even the grand princess, Mariya, was left homeless, so relocated to Rostov.

Shemyaka withdrew to Uglich but, "devilishness filling his head," spread gossip among the nobles, boyars, and enemies of Christian Rus. He claimed that Vasiliy II was planning to surrender all Rus to the khan for personal gain—a lie.[11] On February 12, 1446, while Vasiliy II was on a pilgrimage to the Trinity Lavra of St. Sergius with his sons, his opponents rode into the Moscow Kremlin, reinstalled Shemyaka as ruler, and imprisoned Vasiliy II's wife and mother. Shemyaka's accomplices found Vasiliy II hiding among the tombstones of a church and hauled him back to Moscow chained to a sleigh. Shemyaka contemplated killing Vasiliy II outright but decided that doing so might cause further strife among the Russian princes and once more provoke the khan's intervention. He instead held a trial of sorts, interrogating Vasiliy II about his treasonous relationship with the Tatars and accusing him of loving "the [Turkic] language of the infidel" more than his own.[12] On Shemyaka's order, thugs entered the room where the grand prince was being held; they pressed him to the floor with a board on his chest while a stableman named Beresten brandished a knife and began slashing his face. Vasiliy II passed out in a pool of his own blood, sightless and disfigured.[13]

Shemyaka exiled Vasiliy II to Uglich and then, fearing an uprising among the grand prince's supporters, offered him an appanage in Vologda. Vasiliy II's wife followed. Once Vasiliy II regained his strength and powers of persuasion, princes and boyars flocked to his banner, as did the hierarchs of the church, who reproached Shemyaka and threatened him with excommunication. Supporters plotted to free Vasiliy II from Uglich (although Vasiliy II had already freed himself) and began to gather fighters for him against Shem-yaka, who withdrew to Novgorod. There he met his end on July 17, 1453, after his cook, acting on behalf of Vasiliy II's agents, added a poisonous herb (the leaves or root of a plant called monkshood) to his chicken dinner.[14] Vasiliy II received the news with delight—"immodest glee"—during a church service.[15]

Back in control, Vasiliy II (*Tyomnïy,* "the Blind" or "the Dark") filled Moscow with fighters who withstood another Tatar attack in 1451. To bolster his authority as *gosudar* (sovereign), a term taken from the Greek *despotes,* Vasiliy II dispossessed those princes still holding lands in the principality.[16] He tightened his grip on Suzdal and the Vyatka River, menaced Pskov, and eliminated those nobles who allied with Shemyaka. The republic of Novgorod remained independent, siding with the Galich princes against Moscow during the civil war and aligning itself politically and culturally with Vilno, the Lithuanian capital.

The alignment would not last long, however, because Moscow intervened in the affairs of Novgorod and Pskov. Had these cities and Vilno cemented their relationship, Russia might have ended up looking, behaving, and believing very differently over the centuries to come.[17] Much of the political and religious persecution that abet-ted the centralization of the state might have been avoided.[18]

Through his reign, and even in exile, Vasiliy II cultivated the sup-port of the church and Metropolitan Jonah, the first "Metropolitan of Kyiv and All Rus" appointed without the approval of the Ecu-menical Patriarch of Constantinople, where, owing to Ottoman penetration, the Greek Mother Church was in peril. The previous metropolitan, Isidor the Apostate, had been seated in Moscow by the Byzantine emperor in 1437, at age fifty-two. He was tasked with finding common ground between the Eastern Orthodox and Roman Catholic Churches with the aim of protecting Constantinople from the Turks. Just five months after arriving in Moscow, Isidor traveled with a delegation of theologians to Ferrara, Italy, in hopes of recon-ciling the churches. Subjects to be debated included "the suffrages of the living faithful," the Son as well as the Father as the origin of the Holy Spirit, the existence of purgatory (the Greeks and the Latins agreed that lesser sinners dwelled in a middle realm between heaven and hell but disagreed about how these souls reached salvation), the status of the pope, and the use of yeast in Communion bread.[19]

Grand Prince Vasiliy II reacted with horror to the new East-West agreement, and after Isidor, returning to Moscow with a Latin cross, acknowledged the authority of the pope rather than the patriarch in 1439, Vasiliy II confined him to the Chudov monastery. Castigated by the council of Russian ecclesiastics, Isidor might have been burned at the stake; instead, he was left in a cold, damp cell to rot, tormented by parasites. Eventually he escaped, with help, to Lithuania, Poland, and then to Italy, where the pope named him a cardinal to reward his efforts on behalf of unification. His mission continued: Isidor was dispatched to Constantinople, with gold florins and soldiers, to help defend the city against the Ottomans. After the fall of Constantinople in 1453, the Turks went after him. Isidor somehow survived—slipping out of sight after swapping clothes with a corpse—and made it to the Vatican, where, in his late sixties, he retired.[20]

Isidor's replacement, Jonah, was tonsured at age twelve, then lived and worked as a baker in the Simonov monastery in Moscow before ministering in the Ryazan and Murom dioceses. Vasiliy II recommended Jonah to Constantinople for the position of metropolitan in 1431, but the war between Moscow and Galich intervened. Jonah would become embroiled in this conflict, threatening "God's punishment" on those allies of Shemyaka guilty of "treachery and recklessness" and "taking advantage of murder."[21] In 1443, after Isidor was imprisoned for apostasy, Vasiliy II chose Jonah again as metropolitan, signaling the need to defend Orthodoxy from Catholic infiltration. He wrote a letter to the Byzantine emperor requesting permission to consecrate Jonah in Moscow for expediency and security. The roads were treacherous; it took ages to reach Constantinople, and the Turkish threat loomed. Vasiliy II did not receive a response, so in 1438 the bishops of Moscow consecrated Jonah on their own. The "widowhood" of the Russian See was the principal justification for this move along with "dissensions between the lords of Rus and the Caesars of Tsargrad [Constantinople]." Addressing his flock ("ye, my children"), Jonah claimed "the will of the auto-crat," the grand prince, as pretext for his promotion.[22] The Russian church had become autocephalous, almost by chance, a monumental but frightening development interpreted by Moscow as divine will.[23] God punished the Greek church, and Constantinople, for backsliding into Latinism.

The grand prince guaranteed the metropolitan's protection and in so doing asserted spiritual primacy over the Orthodox faithful of Rus as well as the territories under Lithuanian control, a setup that extended to the Dnieper basin and Kyiv. The arrangement did not last. In 1458, the king of Poland organized the installation of a different metropolitan in the Lithuanian lands, while Moscow remained the Orthodox platform.[24] The "hagiographical chronicle-histories," the art, and the ceremonies of the church now had Moscow—not Constantinople or Kyiv—as a locus.[25]

Meantime, the Golden Horde vanished. Ulug Mehmet seized power in Sarai after killing Tokhtamïsh's sons but was then ushered out of power himself. Infighting broke the Golden Horde into smaller khanates across the Urals in Siberia, on the Black Sea in Crimea, and in Astrakhan on the Volga. Ulug Mehmet bested the competition by building alliances with Lithuania and the Ottomans. After withdrawing from Sarai, he established a fourth khanate in Kazan. An enchanting city with a bewitching past, Kazan is represented in tourist guides as a utopian cultural and religious crossroads, a small fur-trading outpost that became a fortress and kingdom and symbol of imperial conquest, a place where marauding horsemen morphed into reliable trading partners and allies of Rus, forgetting Islam to become a Christian See on the Volga.[26] The reality is altogether nastier. Raiders from Kazan besieged Moscow and allied cities like Ryazan, looting them for treasure and slaves for markets in Persia while demanding payment of tribute. Then the reverse: Moscow attacked Kazan. Becoming a state required butchering the recalci-trant and extracting resources from the conquered in the service of power—*vlast'*—claimed as a divine mandate.

Vasiliy II's last consequential move, made half a dozen years before the end of his rough and gruff existence, was naming his eldest son as heir. Father-son dynastic successions would no longer be contested, and the rulers of Moscow would no longer need the blessing of the Horde to enact them.[27] Ivan III ran the affairs of court on behalf of his sightless father, who in his final years was more a symbol of power than an active force. Vasiliy II died of "sukhotnaya bolest," tuberculosis, a scourge ascribed to evil spirits. The Resurrection Chronicle claims that the infections that appeared outside of his lungs were treated by cauterization, burning of the skin, which led to gangrene.[28]

Russian fairy tales often describe characters named Ivan who, aided by magical forces, battle monsters and bring peace to the land. People emerge from their hiding places to greet their ruler in celebration. But Ivan is also a monster: the peace, happiness, and order he brings is but an illusion, a spell. It will be shattered, and the people's affection will turn to fear. The formation of the state perpetuated the spell—as did invasions, civil strife, and natural disasters. In the sixteenth century, the spell turned Rus into the Tsardom of Muscovy, which became the Russian Empire, the Soviet Union, and the Russian Federation of today.

Ivan III began that long process. He held power for an impressive forty-three years, from 1462 to 1505, during which time the affairs of court became affairs of state. Most of his existence involved expanding the realm and bolstering Moscow as its center. Details are scarce, but it seems he first captured Novgorod.[29] After that realm was confiscated, Tver was surrounded and forced to capitulate to Moscow, followed by Pskov and Ryazan, and lastly the territory of the Orthodox faithful held by Lithuania. First cities fell, and then towns and villages, after which the independent holdings of rival princedoms ended up, with shocking speed, in Ivan's hands. He also took control of monasteries and churches and their administrations. He imprisoned and executed his rivals and arranged for the transfer of "ancestral" territorial "rights" to the Moscow state.[30] Ivan III's offspring, boyars, advisors, and their families settled on this land, partitioned into service estates that maintained a significant fighting force.[31]

The distance between Moscow and Novgorod is 300 miles as the crow flies. A horse in good condition can travel up to 40 miles a day on even terrain. Ivan III's princedom bordered the Republic of Novgorod less than 100 miles from Novgorod proper, allowing him to strike with relative ease, if provoked. He was provoked in 1470. That year, Ivan III was informed that Marfa Boretskaya, the widow of Novgorod's elected mayor (*posadnik*) and an immensely rich landowner, had been agitating for closer relations between Novgorod and Lithuania in hopes of restraining Moscow. There are stories and plays about her life portraying her as the heroic leader of a doomed resistance, though there is no clear sense of her actual role, if any, in poking the bear. She might have been set up by the apostate metropolitan of Novgorod, Pimen, who supported a merger of the Orthodox and Catholic faiths. Boretskaya's possessions included slaves, anywhere from 300 to 1,300 villages to the north and south, and interrelated grain-growing, salt-boiling, and linen-spinning operations. She had her hands full as a prominent Novgorod matriarch and, perhaps for this reason alone, would end up in chains, as would other members of her bloodline. After her estate was confiscated, she was either exiled or took tonsure. The sole contemporary description of her political activities, produced by monks, is didactic and represents her as a force of evil, the devil's accomplice. She was so frightful, historians Gail Lenhoff and Janet Martin propose, as to stoke a fear of women among the monks of Rus and keep them celibate.[32]

The other traitors, from Moscow's perspective, were Novgorod's Lithuania-leaning boyars and the "flags" (fighting units) they commanded, badly, against Ivan III's forces. Before hostilities began, he sent a delegation into Novgorod with an ultimatum addressed to the "people of Novgorod," whose land, animals, and possessions he considered his own. They were part of his Rurik heritage, which extended back before the time of his grandfathers and great-grandfathers to the baptism of Rus and even before that to the Scandinavian traders who traveled from the Baltic down to the Caspian. "We own you and favor you and protect you from everything, but we are willed to execute you, if you do not regard us as you did in the old days,"

Ivan III declared.[33] Novgorod's priests recommended accommodation, listening to the grand prince as if to God, but Novgorod's elite balked, which made conflict inevitable.

The archbishop of Novgorod advised restraint, telling his men to fight not the Muscovites but the soldiers from Pskov allied with them. (Their banners revealed who was who.) Ivan III advised the opposite: dispersal, lancing, and gratuitous flogging. He had far fewer soldiers than his opponent but trained and equipped them better, using close formations, thick armor with lance rests, long lances with metal rings, swords, knives, and crossbow barrages ahead of horse attacks. The battle on the Shelon River lasted two hours on a mid-July morning. Up to 12,000 Novgorodians were killed, with 2,000 more taken prisoner in the post-battle mop-up. Ivan III's commanders then moved toward Novgorod itself, looting and burning with malice. The carnage ended with the elite begging for their lives and opening their purses. Ivan III fined the city 16,000 silver rubles to recoup the costs of ransacking it.[34]

Formally taking over Novgorod and its population of some forty thousand would mean governing it, which Ivan III lacked the bureaucrats and institutions to do.[35] He first tried enforcing peace through repression, ordering periodic roundups. He monitored the *veche,* the popular assembly responsible for law and order, and formed alliances with Novgorod's elite and senior boyars. Some of them called him their "sovereign." The fragile peace unraveled after Ivan III arranged a meeting with the *veche* to discuss the city's future as Moscow's satellite. The *veche* demurred: "And you, sir, we beat on your forehead, so that you keep us as in the old days, with only the vow of alliance."[36] But the offer to return to the prior status quo had expired. Ivan III commanded another siege of the city. He dismantled Novgorod's administration and, in a symbolic act, had his horsemen pull down the bell that brought the *veche* into session, carting it back to Moscow along with sacks of gold and silver, gems and pearls.[37] Ivan III assumed control as an autocrat with unlimited power, unconstrained by laws.[38] Thus despotism arrived in Rus.

Violence came from the top, from the "tsar" (caesar), as Ivan III came to refer to himself. He rejected "king," which had been suggested by a foreign diplomat, and instead opted for a title that affirmed his ancestral ties to the land. The double-headed eagle, associated with a branch of the Byzantine ruling family, appeared in his seal.[39] It represents the emperor's (tsar's) control of sacred and secular life as well as of lands to the east and west. Ivan III executed pagans, Muslims, and heretics. Consolidating his power, the autocrat went after "rootless cosmopolitans," meaning Jews from abroad, and he used their presence in Rus as pretext for a purge of the Church. He confiscated land given to the Church by dying lords in exchange for prayers for their souls, ousting the priests.

Information about the scandal called the "heresy of the Judaizers" comes from abbot Iosif of Volokolamsk (1439/40–1515), who wrote a primer of Orthodox thought called *Prosvetitel'* (*The Enlightener*). Iosif targeted a scholar from Kyiv, Zacharias de Ghisolfi, whose translations of Hebrew texts had supposedly "seduced" two Novgorod priests and convinced them to reject "the Virgin birth, the Resurrection and the Trinity"; to embrace the Law of Moses; and to blaspheme icons, among other affronts to Orthodoxy. Iosif decried Ivan III's decision to invite the priests to Moscow, where others also converted, including Ivan III's *dyak* (secretary) for foreign affairs. Gossip spread about the Judaizers of the Moscow court dabbling in the black arts, astrology, astronomy, and "fables." An inquisition and trials followed in Moscow and Novgorod. Those convicted of heresy were either flogged or burned at the stake. An Italian Jewish doctor was killed, though not for anything heretical: he had failed to prevent the death of the tsar's eldest son from illness.[40] The episode seems paradoxical given the prominence of Jews in Ivan III's court, including Khozi Kokos (Turkic for "Blue-Eyed Pilgrim"), who served as liaison between Ivan III and the Crimean khanate in the 1470s during a time of fragile peace.

Although the Tatars were significantly weakened, Ivan III continued to flatter the Crimean khan, Mengli Giray, gifting him piles of sables and bags of coins and ensuring that his emissaries paid a special form of obeisance to the khan called *chelobit'ye:* bowing so low that their foreheads touched the ground (kowtowing). Other, more humiliating acts of deference, like dropping to the knees and licking up the drops of mare's milk that happened to fall from the khan's goblet onto his horse's coat, disappeared, as did Ivan III's tolerance for diplomatic speeches. His second wife recommended feigning illness to avoid listening to the droning litanies.[41]

Besides the Tatars of Crimea and Kazan, Ivan III had to contend with an aggressive, overambitious remnant of the Golden Horde on the steppe. It was led by Ahmed bin Küchük after he ousted his brother and proclaimed himself sole legitimate heir to the khans of Sarai. He hoped to subdue Ivan III, so dallied with King Casimir IV of Poland-Lithuania. Ahmed demanded Moscow's complete submission and bristled at Ivan III's refusal to pay tribute. After eight years, Ahmed came to Rus to collect, moving his cavalry into Rus from the south. Ivan III's scouts raised the alarm; cities were evacuated, and Moscow's gold and silver reserves were stashed in the city of Beloozero to the north. In the autumn of 1480, Ahmed reached the Ugra River, about 150 miles southwest of Moscow, confident that he would be joined there by Lithuanian fighters. Ivan III's soldiers arrayed themselves on the opposite bank of the river. Some projectiles were lobbed across the water, falling short of their targets; the two armies repositioned. Nothing of consequence happened besides the weather turning cold and the horses eating through all the local grass. After several weeks, it became clear that the Lithuanians weren't going to turn up. Ahmed ended the standoff. A chronicle compiled in Kazan claims that he immediately returned home, having received word that his base camp near Sarai had been raided by Ivan III's Crimean allies. Other sources have Ahmed plundering a dozen or so Lithuanian settlements as payback for Casimir IV's betrayal with nary a thought of returning home. Ahmed met his end a few months later when still another group of Tatars, from Sibir, ambushed him on the Donets River.[42]

Ivan III had bigger plans—not of his own but fashioned by the Byzantine princess Sophia (originally Zoya) Palaiologina, his second wife. The niece of the last Byzantine emperor, Constantine XI Palaiologos, Sophia and her brothers fled after the Ottoman conquest from Morea (Peloponnese) to Rome with their father. The family brought their most precious possessions, including the skull of St. Andrew, in a casket. As heirs to the Byzantine emperor, Sophia and her siblings lived in a splendid mini-court of their own, with servants, doctors, and horses at their disposal, language and mathematics teachers, and priests who raised them as Catholic, despite their having been baptized Orthodox. The Vatican considered her an asset and tried to control her life: where she traveled, what she read, who she married. When word reached Italy in the late 1460s that Ivan III's first wife had died, Pope Paul II (successor to Pius II) suggested that Sophia wed the tsar in hopes of extending the influence of Catholicism and perhaps even uniting the Catholic and Orthodox Churches. Envoys traveled to Moscow with the proposal and a painting of Sophia.

Portraiture was unknown to Rus, and the image of Sophia surprised those who saw it. Presumably it represented Sophia more flatteringly than did the Italian poet Luigi Pulci. A wicked satirist, he scurrilously described her as obese, greasy-faced, garishly attired, and ill-mannered, speaking only in Greek. After seeing her in Rome, Pulci told his patron, Lorenzo de' Medici, that he "dreamed every night of mountains of butter and fat, tallow and *panelli* [oil-soaked mashed seeds] and everything off-putting."[43] Others recalled Sophia more charitably, with emphasis on her intellect, not her appearance; a 2016 Russian television series imagined her to be both stunningly beautiful and cleverly resourceful.[44] After consulting with the metropolitan, his mother, and his senior boyars, Ivan III agreed to the marriage; he was indifferent to Sophia's conversion to Catholicism. The nuptial rites were conducted in Rome in his absence when Sophia was seventeen. The papacy provided a dowry, which included 4,000 ducats from the Medicis that had been earmarked to support war against the Ottomans. The funds were distributed, at the order of the pope, to the new "queen of Russia, for certain costs that she will have in connection with her travel to Russia and for other expenses."[45] Among the gifts she brought to Moscow was a family heirloom from Morea: the double-headed eagle coat of arms.

On June 24, 1472, Sophia traveled in a grand entourage that made numerous stops, including Siena and Lübeck and, after eleven days aboard ship on the Baltic, Reval (Tallinn) and Dorpat (Tartu). From there, she journeyed to Pskov. The reception was enthusiastic until the head of her delegation, Cardinal Bonumbre of Ajaccio, dressed in a scarlet robe with a Latin crucifix, failed to venerate the icons in the Orthodox cathedral, scandalizing the locals. Sophia restored decorum by upbraiding him. Mead flowed, the boyars paid homage to Sophia with gifts, and she promised to assist them in their dealings with her husband.[46] She arrived in Moscow in November after more than five months in transit. It was snowing; she entered the rustic court of the Kremlin wearing white. There was a second wedding, this time with Ivan III present, after which the polyglot, polymath Sophia converted back to Orthodoxy. Rather than remain sequestered in her quarters, she began to exert influence in internal and external political matters.

Moscow must have disappointed her. The city may have been newly powerful, but it looked nothing of the sort. The home of the Church was a godforsaken place. A firsthand account of the look and feel of Moscow around 1476 comes from Ambrogio Contarini, a diplomat from Venice who condescended to the foreigners he encountered in their own lands. Traveling through Rus, Contarini and his entourage slept rough in the forest and on the ice, crossed rivers on rafts tied to horses' tails, and when provisions ran out, subsided on cider and "a little honey in the combs" given to them by peasants. In Moscow, Contarini stayed in a "small and unpleasant" room and received an audience with Ivan III, then a handsome thirty-five-year-old, who chastised the Italians for fraternizing with the Tatars. Contarini was detained in Moscow until his priest could arrange payment from Venice to cover debts to several Russian and Tatar moneylenders.

While waiting for the "ransom," as it were, Contarini wrote up his impressions of Moscow on the cusp of its transformation during Ivan III's ambitious final years. For Europeans, the people of Moscow held the same exotic status as Persians, the Golden Horde, the Crimean khanate, and the Ottoman Sublime Porte. Muscovites were beautiful but coarse; their religion was rigid, anathema to the kind of liberal thought that allowed education to develop in Catholic Europe. Contarini counted five hundred horsemen defending Moscow from

Tatar invasion. He describes sleds and boats carved from tree trunks so massive as to hold nine or ten horses; the superabundance of "peltries" for sale; and the diet of grain, flesh, mead, nuts, melons, and wild apples (no other fruits). In November, those selling livestock, game, birds, hay, and wood congregated in bazaars erected on the already ice-covered Moskva, less exposed to wind than the buildings lining it on both sides. The animals, Contarini adds, were "frozen whole," as hard as marble "and it is curious to see so many skinned cows standing upright on their feet." For wintertime amusement, the locals, a "handsome" but "brutal" group, raced horses along the river. "Sometimes, also, a neck is broken."

> They have a pope [metropolitan] of their own, appointed by the sovereign, and hold ours in little esteem, saying that we are doomed to perdition. They boast of being great drunkards, and despise those who are not. They have no wine of any kind, but drink a beverage made of honey and the leaves of the hop, which is certainly not a bad drink, especially when old. The sovereign, however, will not grant permission to everyone to make it; for, if they had that permission, they would be constantly intoxicated, and would murder each other like brutes. Their custom is to remain from morning till midday in the bazaars and to spend the remainder of the day in the taverns in eating and drinking. After midday you cannot obtain any service of them whatever.[47]

Obviously, he didn't believe the locals deserved his company, and nothing of their spiritual lives made an impression.

In response to Contarini's report, Ivan III resolved to make Moscow look the part of the capital of a state. He sent an ambassador, Semyon Tolbuzin, to Italy in search of talented Italian and Greek engineers and builders. For an impressive sum, he acquired the services of Contarini's associate Aristotele Fioravanti, a municipal engineer from Bologna. Fioravanti came with the recommendation of the theologian Basilios Bessarion, who had educated Sophia Palaiologina in Rome. Dazzlingly skilled, Fioravanti was much sought after. He lifted and installed bells, built bridges, restored ditches, shored up defenses, relocated and righted swaying towers (though some still fell down), designed beautiful copperware, and improved the processes through which giant-sized bricks were cast and baked and mortar mixed. Fioravanti had worked for the Sforza family in Milan and the Hungarian king, Matthias Corvinus. In February 1473, he went to Rome, either to relocate the monumental Sarcophagus of Constantia or to build the Sisto Bridge. There he was arrested for circulating counterfeit coins in Bologna bearing his likeness. Matthias Corvinus had given him permission to mint the coins and intervened to release him from prison and save his life. Fioravanti was left unemployed and in debt over an investment in a mill. Seeking work elsewhere, he considered an invitation from the Ottoman sultan to build a palace for him in Constantinople. He decided instead to accept Tolbuzin's invitation to Moscow, arriving there in March 1475 with his son and a ten-year-old apprentice, Pietro (Petrushka). Ivan III hired him for his building skills and for his talents as a munitions manufacturer. From the metalworks he operated in the Kremlin, Fioravanti produced the falconets (small mobile cannons) and larger mortars that allowed Ivan III to pummel and bring the Republic of Novgorod to heel in 1479. Fioravanti also enabled the grand prince's campaigns against the cities of Kazan and Tver in the 1480s.[48]

Fioravanti gained an understanding of ecclesiastical architecture in Rus and its deficiencies: the shallow foundations, the thin mortar, the haphazard, partial brickwork imported from abroad or produced in small batches by potters, the eclectic jumble of churches, monastic cells, and crooked, mud-covered paths between priests' and princes' residences. Given his obsession with precision and proportion, the disorder must have left his eyes aching. He opened a brick factory in a peasant compound, Kalitniki; there his perspiring laborers produced, day and night, the tens of thousands of bricks needed to build a capital. In the heart of the Kremlin, Fioravanti was tasked with the transformation of the Assumption Cathedral into a symbol of "early Greek piety" relocated to Rus.[49] The cathedral had burned to the ground in the summer of 1470. Ivan III had first tried to resurrect it with his own architects, in imitation of the Assumption Cathedral in Vladimir. The lot was cleared, the crypts emptied, the sacred remains of Metropolitan Jonah relocated, the foundations laid, and stone walls assembled. But Moscow's builders erred in their measurements; a wall collapsed, pulverizing everything at its base. Ivan III turned to Fioravanti for salvation, and he delivered, designing a majestic cathedral of five domes and five apses atop massive slabs of white stone and giant bricks on a limestone base. Its airiness, clean lines, and feeling of surrender to the divine were so enviable that Ivan III refused the request of the rectors of Bologna to allow Fioravanti to return home. In winter 1483, he arrested Fioravanti for trying to leave and confiscated his possessions. Fioravanti rehabilitated himself and returned to work. Before his death in 1486 in Moscow, he supplied the names of other Italian architects and engineers who would continue his work.

Thus, the Swiss-born architect and sculptor Pietro Antonio Solari was brought in.[50] He was in his forties, and did not make it to fifty, dying either from malaria (the curse of Moscow's springtime swampiness) or from the harsh chill in 1493 after three invaluable years in Ivan III's service. Solari helped realize the brick walls and six of the Kremlin towers. He also collaborated with another architect, Marco Ruffo, to complete the ensemble that included Ivan III's chambers and the Palace of Facets, a reception hall with an exterior finish of sharp-edged (faceted) white stone squares and windows of high double-lanced arches characteristic of Lombard architecture.[51] A single central pillar held up the vault and a roof covered in gold leaf. The gold is gone but the rest of the palace survives, decorated with murals of biblical scenes.

The palace was dwarfed by the churches and by a larger, grand palace. Their roofs all rise above the top of the Kremlin walls, whose heights change depending on the terrain, from three times the height of an average person to twelvefold. The thicker summits hold battle platforms and swallowtail battlements with V-shaped notches. Through them, Moscow's *streltsï* (now with firearms) aimed their weapons.[52]

Underground, the Kremlin's denizens prowled a catacomb dating back to at least the fourteenth century and Dmitri Donskoi. Those given a coveted glimpse of the subterranean network and its unchanging conditions have identified water intake tunnels, a subterranean listening post used to detect enemy diggers, treasure vaults, crypts, and storage spaces for basic goods.[53] The space included pits for prisoners nicknamed "stone sacks," and chambers where, according to nineteenth-century Muscovite storytellers, suspected criminals were force-fed salt in hot spaces, beaten with burning candles, and stretched on the rack.[54]

One of the oldest spaces housed trunks of books and documents in Greek taken from Constantinople to Rome and then, with Latin manuscripts added, to Moscow by Sophia Palaiologina as part of her dowry. To prevent the books from being consumed by fire, Sophia had them buried. Ivan III's successor invited a monk, Maximos the Greek, to catalog and translate the collection. Nothing is known to survive of this library, despite the heroic efforts of a Soviet archeologist most active in the 1930s, Ignaty Stelletsky, to locate it, but belief in its existence, somewhere under the Terem Palace, persists. The problem is that some of the tunnels have collapsed over the centuries, or been filled in, leading, in the pitch-black, to dead ends.[55] Moreover, the tunnels can no longer be accessed: what lies beneath the Kremlin is classified information.

Each of the Kremlin towers has a tale to tell, and all but two have names. The tallest at 80 meters (262 feet) is currently star-topped and almost six times the height of the shortest at 13.5 meters (44 feet), though the latter isn't part of the Kremlin walls, having been built as part of an entrance bridge.[56] There's an "alarm" tower (Nabatskaya) and a tower named after a boyar (Bersen-Beklemishev) who lived beside it. The oldest of the towers lining the Moskva River is called the Secret (Taynitskaya) Tower. It had a well in its base and an escape route to the water. The Kremlin could be accessed on foot across wooden drawbridges and through the entrance gates of the Frolovskaya and Nikolskaya towers. Frolovskaya refers to the Kremlin's former Church of Frol and Lavr (Florus and Laurus). The tower was renamed Spasskaya, after an icon of the savior hanging above the entrance on the inside, and it has been topped with several clocks. Nikolskaya is the name of a Greek monastery. These are the big towers on the east side, which once led from a shantytown into the Kremlin. For security reasons, Ivan III cleared the area closest to the fortifications. The openness of the resulting square made it seem "beautiful," "wonderful," which modern Russian renders as *krasivaya, prekrasnaya,* related to the Russian word for red, *krasnaya.* An etymological dictionary of the Russian language notes the "secondary relationship" of redness to beauty, to something adorned or painted up.[57] There has never been anything obviously red about the square save for Soviet banners and, for a time, the carpet on a staircase leading into the Palace of Facets. Thus, Red Square is properly Beautiful Square.

After Solari, two other Italian masters were hired, both named Aloisio and so confused in the sources. The older of them, Aloisio da Carcano, must have established himself in Milan, since he was invited to Moscow at the special request of envoys sent there. He and his team completed the Kremlin fortifications; after that Aloisio designed, in Milanese style, the grand prince's residence and the Borovitskaya tower. [58] Between 1505 and 1509 the younger Aloisio realized the Cathedral of the Archangel Michael, a reconstruction and reimagining of another cathedral dating back to Ivan Kalita's time, but with elements borrowed from Venetian palaces of the era.[59] Like the Assumption Cathedral, the Archangel Cathedral has five domes, the tallest in the middle representing Christ and the others the evangelists Matthew, Mark, Luke, and John. The younger Aloisio helped the older Aloisio finish the grand prince's residence, the precursor to the Grand Kremlin Palace built between 1837 and 1849.

One or the other Aloisio engineered the brick-lined moat that separated the Kremlin from Red Square. The moat dates from after Ivan III's death, in the early years of the rule of Vasiliy III, who hoped to prevent infidels from burrowing like chipmunks under the Kremlin walls or pulling weapons up close. (Armor made swimming across the moat impossible.) Red Square probably had a drain or a trench before the moat was dug. When it was done, it adjoined the corner towers of the Kremlin; it was either supplied by the Moskva River and drained into the Neglinka through pipes or serviced by reservoirs. It smelled; pond scum accumulated on the sides and the surface. Supposedly during the reign of Ivan the Terrible, the middle of the moat, the current location of Lenin's tomb, was drained and turned into a lions' pit. (The big cats were gifted to Muscovy by Mary I of England.) Under a subsequent ruler, Tsar Alexei, the pit housed an elephant donated by the Persian shah Abbas II. The elephant died from gastrointestinal illness and frostbite.[60] In 1812, the moat was drained and turned into a garden as part of the post–Napoleonic War restoration of the ruined Russian capital. The lone present-day trace of the moat is a public toilet to the left of the Spasskaya tower, down two flights of stairs.

The people, too, were hemmed in. Historian Catherine Merridale describes the Kremlin becoming an island as well as a labyrinth, one set of walls enclosing another enclosing another. For the rulers, no amount of protection from the ruled and from the enemies of them all was enough. Kitai-gorod, the neighborhood that included the marketplace of Red Square, was also sealed up, with monastic cells on the inside and prison cells on the outside.[61]

But Moscow had arrived—in clouds of dust, to the sound of trees being cut down, with the smell of Fioravanti's brick stove, and thanks to the perspiration of thousands of laborers enlisted to build a capital. It morphed in the imagination of chroniclers from the real to the fantastic, though, in truth, even after the great buildings were completed, fires, fighting, and the seasons reduced Moscow's visual impact. Future rulers would commit themselves to making the actual place ever more like the imagined one. By enhancing the skyline and gilding the spires, they affirmed Moscow's status as a seat of power and summit of faith, the place of salvation whose foes would be condemned to eternal torment.

Measuring time remained controversial, and not just because clocks began to be built in Moscow.[62] From the time of Kyivan Rus through the reign of Vasiliy II, both September 1 and March 1 marked the beginning of the New Year, with March 1 the start of the growing season and September 1 the date when decrees and other official notices took effect. The Orthodox Church also began the New Year in September. In 1492, March 1 was dropped for what appear to be superstitious reasons. The Byzantine Empire used a calendar that dated creation to 5,508 years before the birth of Christ;

the world was expected to end 7,000 years after creation—in 1492. So strong was the belief in this prophecy that, on September 1, 1477, the mother of Ivan III, Mariya, sent the massive sum of 495 rubles (enough to purchase five hundred horses) to the Kirillo-Belozersky monastery with specific instructions for the monks to pray for the Moscow princes for fifteen years, that is, until September 1, 1492. Life slowed down in 1491; fewer things were made, and the number of traders dwindled. Then 1492 arrived and all was fine, a relief to everyone and justification for something that Church officials, for whom superstition was anathema, had said: Neither Christ nor the saints claimed that the world would end on a specific day. The year 7000 is not mentioned in the Book of Revelation. Instead, the Holy Bible declared the opposite: "But about that day or hour no one knows, not even the angels in heaven, nor the Son, but only the Father."[63]

Since nothing apocalyptic happened on September 1, 1492, the Church decreed that the New Year should begin on that day alone. The March 1 crop-planting celebration fell away. This religious decision was complemented by a political one. By taking Sophia Palaiologina as his second wife, and by approving the installation of September 1 as the new New Year two decades later, Ivan III announced to the realm that, after the fall of Byzantium, Moscow remained the one true Orthodox state.

An abbot from Pskov named Philotheus took the idea further in the wake of a different prediction. A clerk had brought to his attention an astrological foretelling of a great flood in 1524, included in a German almanac in the possession of Ivan III's physician. The translation had fallen into the clerk's hands, and at the end of 1523, just months before the predicted flood, he asked Philotheus for clarification. In an epistle that ranks among the most important documents in Russian history, Philotheus countered that the stars do not determine the fates of people and places; rather, divine will does. To shore up the point, he recounts a story in the Book of Revelation about a woman pursued by a red dragon with seven heads. The beast's tail pulls stars down from the heavens and it spews a torrent of water from its mouth, which the woman, "clothed in the sun, and the moon under her feet, and a baby in her arms," escapes by fleeing into the desert. The woman is the Christian kingdom, deluged by unbelievers. The original kingdom, Rome, had drowned in apostasy, as had Constantinople. Moscow was alone, and Moscow stood firm as the third Rome ("and a fourth will not be," Philotheus cautioned).[64] The Orthodox Church and the tsars depended on one another for survival, and for salvation from the demons pressing in from all sides.

IVAN IV

T SAR IVAN IV is best known as Ivan the Terrible (Ivan Groznïy). "Dreadful" is another translation of his posthumous nickname.[1] European traders told stories about his butchery that made their patrons gag, but most of the violence was in their imaginations, and they generally overlooked Ivan's achievements. The best-known accounts of his rule are biased and contradict one another.[2] Three come from men who had been his prisoners, though he found uses for them at his court and allowed them some freedom of movement. The fourth was recorded by Andrey Kurbsky, an accomplished field commander who defected from Ivan's realm in 1564.

All had obvious reasons to loathe the tsar and fixated, in their recollections, on bleakly comedic moments in his rule, like the time he poured soup over the head of a jester too rude for his taste. (Hearing that the jester had died from the scalding, the tsar snorted, "To hell with him! He made no attempt to recover!")[3] In Kurbsky's case, authenticity is an issue: the letters he exchanged with Ivan have been deemed "fake," a "mystification" produced by a later writer with an encyclopedic knowledge of folktales, Greek theologians, the chronicles, and the hierarchies within the court. The author of the purported fabrication has not been identified (a couple of names have been floated, unconvincingly).[4]

Russian historians of later times decided that Ivan's image needed softening and gave the grossest of his deeds a psychological pretext. Ivan needed to be terrible to eliminate the traitors who had knives out for him and to repress the Mongol-Tatars who had suppressed all Rus. His brashest orders—the forced relocation of entire populations from their ancestral lands—served to concentrate power in his hands. In truth, the tsar seems to have been quick to anger, but anger, like wrath, meant something different then than it does now—more like disgruntlement.[5] Reading between the lines in the chronicles, travelogues, and other sources, historians have imagined "Magna Carta–like" and "English Parliament–like moments" in his long rule.[6] Ivan commissioned histories, approved the operation of a printing press (a typesetting operation) in Moscow, and memorized the psalter; he also had a professional poisoner in his retinue.[7] Such, at times, has been Russia's tragedy: barbarism in the service of civilization.

Born on August 25, 1530, Ivan nominally became grand prince and head of the ruling branch of the Rurik dynasty at age three, following the death of his father, Vasiliy III, from hunting injuries. Ivan's uncles wanted the tsardom for themselves, but his mother, Elena Glinskaya, got rid of them, ensuring that power remained with her, even though her side of the family wasn't Rurik. She died five years later—perhaps from poisoning, as rumored—leaving Ivan at the mercy of the boyar clans he reviled as treacherous embezzlers.[8] He was confined to his rooms in the Kremlin by the powerful Shuisky faction, who distributed privileges among themselves before dying or getting killed off. On the sickening side of things, Ivan tortured small animals, throwing them to the ground from the tops of towers and, as a teen, galloped through the squares and markets of Moscow beating and robbing people for sport.[9] He had few friends; his younger brother was deaf and mute. Ivan learned to speak Tatar, perhaps from the children of courtiers, and learned to read, though he probably didn't deign to write, instead dictating his missives to scribes. The longest of them highlights the "countless sore sufferings" he endured in his youth. "Many a time did I eat late, not in accordance with my will."[10]

We don't really know what he looked like. An envoy from the Holy

Roman Empire described the tsar as tall, stout, and energetic at age forty-six, with a long, thick, curly black beard. "His eyes have been described both as small and as large," according to an excellent if equivocating biographer; "they were light-colored, bright, and flickered rapidly from place to place." Paintings from later times give him thick lips, fleshy ears, a high forehead, a receding hairline (or no hair at all), and the "eagle nose" of his grandmother Sophia Palaiologina. His remains, exhumed from the Cathedral of the Archangel in 1963, suggest a person standing nearly five-foot-ten at around 190 pounds, statuesque for the time.[11] The examination also revealed a skeletal deformation stemming from scrofula, a form of tuberculosis that he contracted as a child. Ivan the Terrible suffered boils as a boy and chronic back pain as an adult.[12]

Then there is his personality—one of the first in Russian history ever to be described in detail. Calmness eluded him. He easily lost his cool, spittle flying from his mouth as he shrilly raged. He had a caustic sense of humor. Having been condemned by Kurbsky as a sadist, he castigated his rival for "barking like a dog," "belching forth serpent's venom," and plotting "wicked, houndish" schemes against him. Referring to other people, or matters more abstract, Ivan relied on gentler metaphors: "a lone swallow does not make for spring-time," nor did "a lonely line a geometrician" or a "single sail a sea," he said, quoting the Greek theologian Gregory of Naziansus.[13] Ivan cared deeply about his dynastic origins and treated the rank and file of his court like dirt—likening his personal guards, the men doing battle for him against the tribal aristocracy, to dung beetles. Ivan's God, the God of the Old Testament, was a fearsome score-settler, subjecting "anyone and everyone" to "divine" violence.[14] The tsar memorized sermons, sang in the churches surrounding his rooms, composed hymns, and observed monastic hours, sleeping for no more than three hours between prayers.[15] He soaked up folklore, the sagas of rebellion and superstition and magical critters told to him by "three old blind men" who "followed each other at his bedside."[16] The tales are still told today, with Tsar Ivan himself as a character.

His coronation on January 16, 1547, was performed by the metropolitan, Macarius (Makariy), with Ivan the first tsar to be thus crowned. He was named grand prince of Vladimir, Novgorod, and Moscow, stitching together the three princedoms that had dominated Rus after the sacking of Kyiv, and "Tsar of All Russia," a place of unfixed borders where diverse elements battled one another: humans and animals, men and women, Christianity and paganism. The coronation lasted hours, with blessings, Bible readings, hymns and prayers, the ringing of frost-covered bells, and splendid regalia, including the Cap of Monomakh, the bejeweled cross of the Life-Giving Tree, a thick gold chain from Byzantium, a scepter, and a metal shoulder piece called a *barma*.[17] Candles and incense enchanted the rooms of the palace and the Dormition Cathedral, transforming January's steel gray cloud into glitter. It was a sober occasion of strict etiquette, lacking the merriment of Golden Horde ceremonies: Ivan would not be tossed, like a khan, into the air from a rug.[18] Ascending twelve steps onto a platform covered in purple cloth in the middle of the cathedral, Ivan affirmed his faith, reading poems of repentance and renouncing the hooliganism and maiden-chasing of his early teens.[19] Ivan needed the Church to reinforce his standing, and the Church needed him.[20] Metropolitan Macarius prayed for the defeat of the "barbarian tongues," Tatars and other outsiders, and asked Ivan to cast a "merciful eye on the obedient," including his boyars and nobles, their children, and other "Christ-loving" people.[21] That he had no intention of doing so became apparent immediately. Ivan skipped a tutorial with a court priest in order to put to death a rival and three boyars.

The coronation concluded with Ivan processing to the Church of the Archangel to pray at the tombs of his ancestors. His brother Yuri sprinkled silver and gold coins on the carpet in front of him as he walked, reaching three times into a sack held by his uncle.[22] This event has morphed in historical imagination. In Sergey Eisenstein's 1944 film about Ivan's reign, grinning courtiers pour the coins onto the tsar's head from giant bowls. Later in the film, soldiers are seen dropping coins onto a plate before heading into battle, to be reclaimed if they survive—a simple means of counting the dead. Eisenstein suffuses his film with more provocative dualities, suggesting, for example, that Ivan the Terrible was bisexual and his court queer.[23]

On February 3, 1547, less than a month after his coronation, Ivan married for the first time. He wanted to be with a woman who spoke his language, as opposed to a bride from outside of "all Russia," as he had few companions and wanted to have someone to talk to.[24] And so, as had been the case for his father, a bride show was arranged: the boyars and princes of the towns of the tsardom brought forth a dozen trembling beauties for inspection, as at a cattle auction. Boyar politics were integral to the choice of Anastasia Zakharina-Yuryeva as his bride. Ivan likely knew her father, who had been present at the reading of Vasiliy III's will. She was close to Ivan's age (born between 1530 and 1532), a tall, fetching girl with long dark hair, high cheekbones, pale skin, scarlet lips, and a soul-piercing stare. Her father's name was Roman, and her brother's children adopted Romanov as their surname.[25] Anastasia's marriage to Ivan the Terrible facilitated the rise of the Romanovs, who would replace the Rurik lineage as the second great dynasty in Russian history.

Their first child, Anna, born two years into the marriage, lived just a year. The second, Dmitri, also died as an infant, having been dropped by accident into a river by a nurse during a pilgrimage.[26] (Pity the nurse.) Their next two children, Ivan and Fyodor, beat the odds by reaching adulthood. Anastasia died on August 7, 1560, age twenty-nine, five days after Crimean Tatars attacked Moscow. Sickly, her body weakened by difficult pregnancies, she departed Moscow for Kolomenskoye, the settlement where her husband had been born (during a lightning storm, according to legend) and there quietly died. Ivan trailed her funeral bier in a state of abjection, weeping and wailing. The population grieved with him, and rumors spread: She had not been brought to sacred places; she had been exposed to demons. Her exhumed remains showed faint traces of arsenic, though not enough to indicate poisoning and perhaps coming from the cosmetics she used. Still, questions linger.[27]

The metropolitan recommended an immediate second marriage. "Are you going to bewail your lost wife forever?" a priest asked him, and Ivan heeded the advice.[28] Ivan's envoys fanned out in search of a bride, eventually returning to Moscow with the daughter of Temryuk, the khan of Kabarda. Ivan had never seen her before, but that was a trifling matter: An alliance with an opponent of the Crimean Tatars was the aim of the union. Her birthname was Kucheney, but she took the name Maria at the Russian court. Her marriage to Ivan was cause for a cacophonous celebration; the din of hundreds of church bells made conversation in Moscow impossible. She lasted with Ivan for nine years, dying at age twenty-three or twenty-four after a long trip. The mourning period was "hypocritical," according to Karamzin's History of the Russian State, since, unlike Anastasia, Maria was disliked. She was just as "terrible" as her husband, and even he had cause to fear her. She doled out perks to her relatives, danced and drank and summoned spirits, and was just too exotic (despite learning Russian, joining hunts, and attending bear fights and other Kremlin entertainments). Karamzin imagines Ivan using her death as pretext for the "reprisals and executions" he conceived in "dreadful solitude" at a retreat outside Moscow.[29] The child Maria had with the tsar lived for just two months, the rumored victim of foul play or a witch's curse. His next wife, Marfa Sobakina, died a virgin less than three weeks after her wedding. According to an ambassador from the Holy Roman Empire, Daniel Prinz von Buchau, the tsar suspected that Marfa had died after "imbibing some sort of potion sent to her by her mother through a courtier (with the help of this drink she, perhaps, wanted to become fertile)." Ivan worked out his grief by putting away "both the mother and the courtier."[30]

The next two sopranos in his nuptial chorus, Anna Koltovskaya and Anna Vasil'chikova, were both tonsured soon after their marriage. Ivan came into conflict with their families and decided he couldn't stand the sight of them. The first Anna outlived her marriage by fifty-three years and used her status as tsarina to "further the fortunes" of her cloister, the Convent of the Presentation of the Virgin in the Temple.[31] The second Anna, "gifted with the most beautiful appearance," died soon after her tonsure. As befitted her station, she was laid to rest in an exquisite headdress fashioned with silk and gold symbolizing the tree of life and a shroud of scarlet damask with ornaments denoting royal power.[32]

Ivan's next wife, Vasilisa Melent'yeva, is an enigma. She was not from a noble line and might not have married the tsar at all. Instead, Melent'yeva might have been a mistress or a woman he raped and abandoned. The last of Ivan's wives, Mariya Nagaya, was chosen from a "public gathering of females" and charged with "assuage[ing] the melancholy that had mounted because of things that had gone badly for him."[33] The aristocratic maidens tramped around in the mud, and his gaze fell on the slender, ash-blonde Nagaya. When Ivan announced her as his choice, she fainted from fear (her father attributed her loss of consciousness to happiness). The wedding was an intimate affair. Nagaya gave birth to a son, Dmitri, in 1582, and Ivan died in 1584. Her presence in the Kremlin thereafter became *neudobno,* inconvenient. She and her baby, her brothers, and her retinue were sent to their appanage in Uglich.[34]

Most of the information about Ivan's wives and what happened to them went up in smoke, as did the records of Ivan's childhood and his father's rule. The worst of the fires, the Great Fire of Moscow, started by chance—arbitrarily. On June 21, 1547, an old woman lit a candle in the church of the Exaltation of the Cross Monastery. It blew over in a gust of wind, starting a fire that spread along a trading conduit. From there the wind pushed the flames into Kitai-gorod and the neighborhood it had absorbed within its walls. This area had once been the home of the craft-makers and merchants ousted from the Kremlin to make rooms for churches and the royal court. All of it dissolved into ash as the hellish tempest intensified. Ivan's stone rooms "cracked and fell apart" after the gunpowder tower exploded. "Iron parts and implements glowed crimson with heat," one account reports, and "copper melted." The inferno moved along the Tverskaya, the road leading northwest from Moscow to the town of Tver, and the curved lanes and alleys—all "under clouds of thick smoke." It traversed the Neglinka, which curved from a bog in the north of Moscow down to the Kremlin, ravaging the cannon yard and collapsing churches in the neighborhood on the river's right bank. The metropolitan "remained in the Cathedral of the Dormition, praying, even though he was almost unable to breathe because of the smoke. Someone forced him to leave, and people wanted to lower him from a secret passage to the riverbank on a rope—but he fell, was severely injured, and was taken to Novospassky Monastery, barely alive." The winds died down too late, after there was nothing left to burn along the jumbled roads. Some areas, including Zaryadye, "behind the markets" on Red Square, were spared because they had burned earlier in the year, during the hot, dry spring. The ground smoldered for days. "People with their hair burned off, their faces blackened by the soot, wandered like shadows among the horrors of the vast decimated desert: they went looking for their children, parents, whatever was left of their home—and howled like animals when they found nothing."[35]

The fire killed 1,700 men, women, and children. There was an uprising, a hunt for scapegoats, and accusations of witchcraft directed against the despised Glinsky family, relatives of Ivan the Terrible. Word spread of his "sorceress" grandmother, Anna, summoning the inferno by cutting the hearts out of corpses and soaking them in water. Flying through the white night as a magpie, she supposedly sprinkled her devilish brew onto the wooden rooftops of the city.[36] Five days later, in front of the horrified metropolitan, the mob stoned one of the tsar's uncles, Yuri, to death and dragged his corpse into Red Square. The crowd rounded up members of the gentry (*deti boyarskiye*), beat and killed them and their servants, ransacked their homes, and stole their livestock. The tsar, his family, and boyars fled to the hilltop village of Voroblyovo, where they had a perfect view of Moscow's incineration. It was God's wrath, Ivan's childhood tutor Sil'vestr admonished, and God had mercifully spared the teenage tsar. The tsar publicly expressed contrition for the disaster, then placated the mob by pledging his own hunt for villains.

There would be other fires, smaller and larger, caused by the weather or human accident, fueled by houses built of pine and spruce beams and roofs of planks and sod. A foreign diplomat at Ivan's court reported seeing three or four blazes at a time, with axe-wielding watchmen rushing to chop down the house closest to the flames in hopes of slowing the spread. Stone buildings came with iron shutters that prevented flames from entering through the windows, but wooden structures were exposed inside and out, top to bottom. Ivan instructed Muscovites to keep barrels of water in their yards and on their roofs. In July and August, houses were often pounded with hailstones the size of "apples from the forest" (crab apples), causing further damage.[37] Each year hundreds, sometimes thousands of people lost their homes. The barrels of water didn't help combat the larger fires. The solution, for those with enough coins to spend or goods to barter, was instant replacement. A forest market opened at the edge of Moscow at noon each day (even on religious holidays) where walls and roofs could be purchased and even delivered.[38] Nothing was permanent or meant to last. Houses were assembled in a couple of days, allowing time for the builders to hit the *kabak* (tavern) and down a tankard or two of mead.

For permanence there was the Church and the governing structure Ivan fashioned in imitation of the Church, with servants ranked like angels. The *Tisyatskaya kniga* (*Thousand Book*) lists his best, most important courtiers along with their genealogies and the amount of land they received for their service as diplomats and members of the *Zemskiy sobor*, the council of the land (feudal estates). Ivan also took advice from the boyars' duma, which had a pseudo-parliamentary function in the *Gosudarev dvor*, the Sovereign's Court. Certain ranks, like *okol'nichiye*, were vaguely defined. The term suggests nearness, being close to or around (*okolo*) something, but it might come as well from *sokol*, meaning falcon, perhaps indicating the ascension of falconers through the ranks to become the equivalent of lords in waiting. Ivan also employed *udochki* (catchpoles or debt collectors) and masters of the revels, armorers, butlers, hunters, nurserymen, larder-fillers, and dozens of *d'yaki* (clerks).

Some of the titles are misleading since, by Ivan's time, the people called armorer no longer made armor (just like, in the English context, people with the surname Miller no longer mill). The *konyushiy*, or master of the horse, looked after more than just the horses and their stables. Ivan placed the master of the horse above all the other

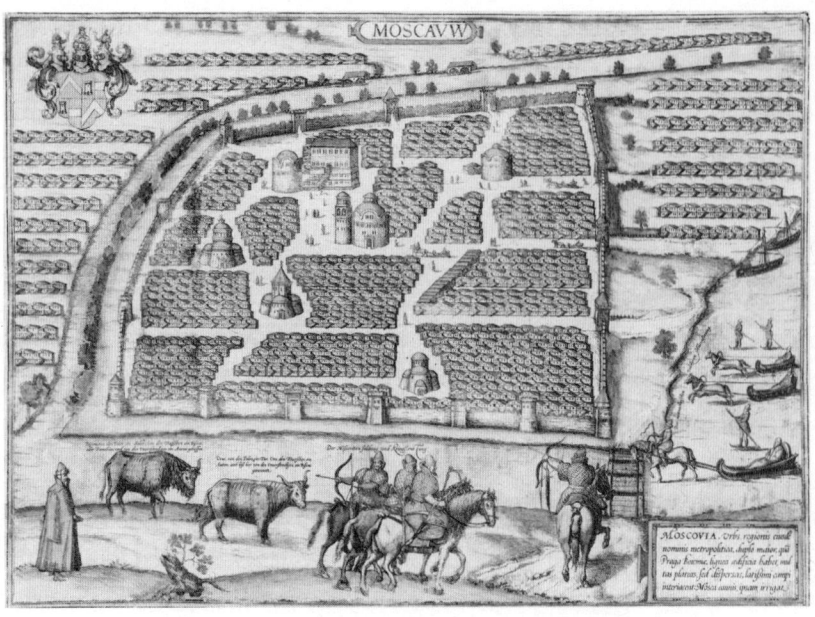

Map of Moscow by Georg Braun (1541–1622) and Frans Hogenberg
(ca. 1540–90), published in Cologne in 1575 in the multivolume atlas
Civitates Orbis Terrarum (The World of Cities). The Latin cartouche reads,
in Barry Ruderman's translation: "Moscow, capital of the eponymous region,
twice as large as Prague in Bohemia, has wooden buildings, many streets,
but scattered, with wide spaces in between them. The Moskva irrigates the
city." Because Moscow lacked "walls, moats or ramparts," Braun notes that
"the streets are closed with barriers at several places; when night falls,
a strong guard is placed there, so that no one can pass through at night after
a certain hour."

boyar ranks. He was responsible for the entire court: from financing the sovereign's domain to equipping his soldiers. The title, equal
to that of co-ruler, was held by another infamous sovereign, Boris
Godunov, before he became tsar. Second in importance was the
postel'nichiy, the tsar's personal attendant. He accompanied the ruler
on official trips, tended to his well-being, went to the bathhouse with
him, and either slept in the same room as him or in one adjacent to it.
The *postel'nichiy* kept the tsar's bedmakers and dressers under close
watch. Another individual of high rank, the *dvoretskiy,* looked after
the civil affairs of the Church, acted as judge, and managed the court
budget. The *dvoretskiy* likewise oversaw the sovereign's meal pre-
parers, who in turn oversaw the table-setters and goblet-fillers. The

manager of the tsar's weapons was assigned a title, as was the keeper of the state seal; these were Ivan's most trusted confidants. Teachers, hunters, and the lower-level servant who handed Ivan's stirrup to him when he went out riding were all ranked. The world beyond the Kremlin—Moscow proper—and the other cities and towns of Muscovy had ranked service groups of their own and select nobles (*dvoryane vïbornïye*) came to the capital from the regions.[39] The word "guest" (*gost'*) in Russian designated a merchant from elsewhere, as opposed to the local hawkers and peddlers of goods.

In Kitai-gorod, Ivan operated a print yard (Pechatnïy dvor) that typeset the liturgy. The scribes of the church despised the printers, who forced them to flee for their lives to Lithuania. An English ambassador claimed that arsonists set the print yard on fire at night; "the press and letters [were] quite burnt up," which "the clergy men" had prayed would happen.[40] Ivan oversaw the gathering together of hagiographies and apocrypha, a dynastic history, a guide to legal proceedings called the *Sudebnik,* and the 9,745 folios and 17,774 images in the *Litsevoy letopisnïy svod* or *Illustrated Chronicle Compilation.* He would not have thought of history in linear terms. The past recurs, the sun and the seasons advised him, such that the past is at once the present and the future.

His rule also marked the appearance, or reappearance, of the *Domostroy,* or *Household Book,* a Russian version of the kind of good home and garden manuals that appeared elsewhere in Europe for the well-to-do, literate people who lived in compounds comprising main and service buildings, gardens and orchards, surrounded by high fences with servants and slaves. The title and contents reflect the metamorphosis of the concept of a home (*dom*) as a sanctuary into the home as an economic structure (*o-stroy*). Neither the author(s) nor the readership of the *Household Book* is known; it seems to have been compiled between the late fifteenth and mid-sixteenth centuries and embellished by the archpriest Sil'vestr. It provides some general information about the lives of Muscovites. Mothers did not dote on their children because half their children died and childhood ended early. Some clay toys survive, along with lullabies and descriptions of education. People lived on top of one another in close quarters, never alone, except for those in monasteries or on the run. The diet of Muscovites was fruits and vegetables with some fish; meat was a luxury. The *Household Book* contains various recipes for mead, baked turnip pie, and candied fruits. Chairs were in short supply, glass nonexistent. In large residences and small, heat came from a single clay stove that could be slept on top of; houses had a special corner reserved for icons and other sacred objects. Buildings were given locks.

For the elite, cleanliness was encouraged. They were to show unconditional submission to the Church, tsar, and head of household. The guiding principle is that a tidy residence determines, and represents, a tidy heart and soul: "pickled mushrooms and clean straw [reflect] the soul as clearly as acts of charity," as the introduction to the English translation reads.[41] Scrubbed fingernails meant cleanliness inside the body.

The *Household Book*, then, details a patriarchal ideal that might have been a product of, or accompaniment to, the structural reforms introduced by Ivan at his Select Council, *Izbrannaya rada*, in the "good" first part of his reign. The system needed to make room for courtiers from newly acquired lands and for functionaries who owed their existences to the tsar, as opposed to the princes and boyars whose estates were inherited. Ivan's reforms included, at their boldest, the confiscation of hereditary lands and their redistribution among his people. He made numerous enemies and imagined countless more. He dealt with them first by sealing himself off in a state within the state, then by having his henchmen liquidate them. That happened during the "bad" second part of his reign.[42]

Like his predecessors in the Kremlin, Ivan feared the Tatars. In 1547–48 and 1549–50 campaigns against the khanate of Kazan on the Volga River were unsuccessful. But Ivan took Kazan on his third try, in 1552, then captured the khanate of Astrakhan in 1556. Ivan pushed on toward the open seas, hoping to secure ports controlled by Crusaders: the Knights of the Livonian Order, a branch of the Teutonic Order transplanted from the German-speaking lands to the northeast. Fantasies of lightning-fast conquests turned into years-long slogs and abject failures. Livonia was allied with Lithuania, and

Lithuania had merged with Poland, a major power Ivan could not hope to defeat, especially with Sweden on Poland's side.

Darkness descended. He withdrew to the hunting lodge of Alexandrovskaya Sloboda (settlement) northeast of Moscow and announced his abdication in a pair of letters, the first sent to the metropolitan and boyars, full of rage about the traitors and embezzlers in the court and the protection some received from traitors and embezzlers in the Church. The other letter, read aloud on Red Square, was meant to reassure the people that he had no issue with them.[43] The people were not convinced.

No one replaced him. Fearing chaos, the elite clans summoned him back to Moscow. The Nikon chronicle claims that the sobbing citizens of Moscow threw themselves at the metropolitan, asking, "Who will have mercy on us, deliver us from foreign presence?" "When the wolves see sheep but not the shepherd, and the wolves snatch the sheep, what will save them?"[44] Ivan agreed to return on one condition: that he could create a safe, pure space for himself, swept clean of traitors and saboteurs. He had a list of enemies that only lengthened as his paranoia deepened. Ivan feared his boyars and the clans aligned with him and his forebears, as well as the boyars of the metropolitan and the boyars of the princes in the countryside. He wondered about his meal-preparers and quill-pushers, even the peasants pulled from the fields to work in the kitchen.

Seeking protection, he built the *oprichnina*. The word means "the widow's land," but for Ivan it was a private court, a cordoned-off space that he alone controlled. It housed a special guard unit, the *oprichniki*, typically seen as forebears of the secret police of Russia's future: Stalin's NKVD, Brezhnev's KGB, Putin's FSB. The ranks of the *oprichniki* swelled from 1,000 to 5,500, and their duties expanded from protecting the ruler to protecting the realm of Holy Rus from threat. Theirs became an apocalyptic battle against hedonism with salvation at stake.[45] Between 1564 and 1572, then, Muscovy was two places: one aligning God and tsar and the chosen people, and the other a sparser place of crisscrossing "infidels and heretics."[46] The Orthodox Church and the security services were conjoined from that moment forward to the present day.[47]

Most members lived in the present-day Arbat neighborhood around the site of the present-day Lenin (Russian State) Library, abutting the *ostozh'ye,* a meadowland where horses grazed and hay was stacked.[48] Their compound encompassed a cluster of fenced-in courtyards and huts; its stronghold was a renovated palace once occupied by Ivan's brother-in-law, Prince Mikhaíl Cherkassky.[49] Productive enterprises and lavish estates were gradually placed under *oprichnina* administration, along with important trade routes and the English Russia Company.[50] Ivan relocated clerks, servants, treasurers, cooks, bakers, and kennel-minders from their domiciles along the river to the new structures. He left the rest of the administration and the non-sacralized land, the *zemshchina,* under the control of the boyars' duma.[51]

The account of Ivan's reign assembled by the Livonian captives Johann Taube and Elert Kruse describes a small number of the *oprichniki* coming from boyar clans. Others were the lowest of the low, the dregs of the tsardom. Outsiders, too, joined the ranks, including Heinrich von Staden, a semi-literate lansquenet who profited from the robbing, despite condemning it to his patron, the Holy Roman Emperor, and encouraging the invasion of Muscovy.[52] Emboldened by the tsar, the *oprichniki* became ever more sadistic, rolling their male victims around naked in the snow before killing them and forcing women, also naked, to chase after clucking chickens on the streets before raping and murdering them. Taube and Kruse describe Ivan conducting macabre experiments on his innocent captives. His henchmen removed tongues, sliced through noses, and mutilated genitalia.[53] To ensure economic hardship in the *zemshchina,* the *oprichniki* plugged up water wells with body parts, burned crops, and drained fishponds.

During this time, Ivan began feuding with the metropolitan, Filipp, who, based on his conduct, refused to bless him. "The stones under your feet, if they were living souls, would complain about you, yell at you and judge you," Filipp scolded.[54] Ivan put him on trial, and witnesses appeared out of nowhere to accuse the metropolitan of corruption, black magic, and assorted acts of perversion. This was a man who had spent most of his life praying, baking, and milling.[55]

Ivan had once trusted him to cleanse the duma of treacherous evil, but on November, 8, 1568, after conducting a service in the Dormition Cathedral, Filipp was stripped of his episcopal vestments, beaten in the face with his cross and chains, put in sackcloth, and hauled to the Epiphany Monastery on a sledge. His feet were compressed into stocks and his head and torso bound in thick chains. He lasted for just over a year in this pitiable state, having accepted his fate at the hands of a "heartless man" of "feigned reference." The merciless jailor was *oprichnik* Grigory Skuratov, whose activities had previously involved raiding the homes of disgraced nobles, keeping the loot for himself and handing the land to the tsar, then kidnapping their daughters. Skuratov was a small man (*malïy*) who liked to say, or have his victims say, "I beg you," *molyu tya*. That explains his nickname, Malyuta. Most of the time he had others do his dirty work, but on December 23, 1569, according to Filipp's hagiography, Skuratov personally "smothered" him "with a pillow" in his cell.[56]

The *oprichniki* were a pious order in self-sacrificing service of the Christian king of a Holy Land, attacking the tsar's enemies with bared fangs and sweeping everything treasonous out of Russia. Ivan modeled the appropriate behavior by wearing a cilice and rousing himself to worship at midnight. They dressed in monastic black and carried "a dog's head on the neck of their horses and a broom on a whip-handle."[57] There is enough agreement in the sources to indicate that actual dogs' heads hung around the horses' necks, their eyes rolled back and teeth bared. The heads belonged to the snarling hounds circling boyar estates; they had to be slain before the doors to the estates were cudgeled down. Still, the exact number of *oprichniki* traveling with the heads is unknown.[58] Their oath of allegiance prohibited them from fraternizing with anyone but their own kind, and even then they kept mostly silent. Disobedience meant landing on the enemies' list and the loss of "any hope of eternal salvation."[59] The horrors are too great and too frequently noted in the sources to be dismissed as fabrications.

Novgorod, Moscow's alter ego and the city that could have been the capital of a much different Russia, went through the worst in the first two months of 1570. The *oprichniki* destroyed everything. There

was no obvious reason for the attack, since Novgorod had been sub-
dued by the tsar's predecessors and posed no threat. Treason, corruption, and conspiratorial collusions directed against Ivan have
been floated as explanations. Perhaps the archbishop of Novgorod,
Pimen, had been seeking to place Novgorod under Lithuanian-Polish
protection, which might explain Ivan's highly theatrical humiliation
of the churchman. After the Cathedral of St. Sophia was ransacked
and Pimen stripped of his title and belongings, Ivan "married" him
to a mare. The archbishop was forced to ride the mare backward, legs
tied together under the animal's stomach, blowing on bagpipes and
plucking a zither like a minstrel.[60]

For the invaders, murder was not sufficient; there had to be mayhem on the streets of Novgorod, "five whole weeks" of "insane hell"
that left scores dead.[61] The earliest description of the nightmare
comes from a Pomeranian imprisoned at the court of Ivan, Albert
Schlichting. Never letting a foreign "guest" go to waste, Ivan enlisted
him as a translator and servant of his Belgian doctor. Schlichting
overheard (or said he overheard) things about boyars in Novgorod
being bayonetted in pens, crowds of people drowning in the Vol-
khov River after the ice onto which they had been herded collapsed
beneath their weight, nobles tied to sleds sent in opposite directions,
a merchant thrown into the freezing waters and then, for variety's
sake, immersed in boiling water for failing to reveal the location of
his treasure and predicting the tsar's bad end (the demons he had
seen at the bottom of the river would come calling for Ivan's soul).
Some of those banished from Novgorod returned; desperate to find
food, they resorted to cannibalism. Even Ivan was disgusted.

Schlichting's account, written before and after his escape from
Moscow, is echoed by churchmen and diplomats (none of whom
were eyewitnesses) with additional details provided by a Lithuanian
who had traveled to Novgorod in the service of a Muscovite nobleman. He described nobles "roasted" in stoves and the river "swollen
with corpses."[62] (Kurbsky provides a variation: a monk cooked in a
frying pan after having pins inserted under his fingernails. "And in
such torments he died.")[63] The cannibalism tale recurs, coupled with
stories of abducted virgins, looted churches, drained fishponds, and

burned crops. English emissary Jerome Horsey claimed "the most bloody and cruelest massacre that ever was heard of in any age." Ivan put away people "young and old, burned all their household stuff, merchandises, and warehouses of wax, flax, tallow, hides, salt, wines, cloth, and silks, set all on fire, with wax and tallow melted down the kennels in the streets, together with the blood of seven hundred thousand [!] men, women, and children, slain and murdered, so that with the blood that ran into the river, and of all other living creatures and cattle, their dead carcasses did stop as it were the stream of the river Volga [Volkhov], being cast therein." Horsey grossly expands the story of the archbishop's humiliation to document the wrath Ivan inflicted upon monasteries for the "horrible sins, extortion, bribery, and excess usury," not to mention "gluttony, idleness, and sodomy, and worse, if worse, with beasts."[64] Witches were burned, and "big fat friars" set upon by famished wild bears for entertainment.

Quite a story, which ends back in Moscow with the abrupt end to the *oprichnina* and the *oprichniki.* The men riding around with dogs' heads and broomsticks failed to protect Moscow from the southern khan, whose forces overran the city in 1571, burned down a quarter of the houses (there were about 40,000 at the time), and carted off blondes to be auctioned in slave markets in Kaffa.[65] The moral? Attacking is easier than defending, bullies are cowards, and what Ivan considered to be Moscow's best defense was no defense at all.

The tsar had only himself to blame, but continued to blame others— for the wars, the tax policies, even the drought that "turned rye to crumpled grass" and brought rogues, beggars, and what an English diplomat, Giles Fletcher, called "counterfeit crippells" to his residence.[66] Ivan's guards "knockt in the heads" of the swindlers and sent the true sufferers to the monasteries "to be relieved."[67] On July 25, 1572, Ivan oversaw the killing of suspected traitors from Novgorod, the Kremlin, and the disbanded *oprichnina* in a sunken patch of Kitaigorod. Musketeers hammered stakes in the ground and suspended beams between them, a weird sight that caused the locals to flee. Ivan summoned them back to witness his housecleaning. Dressed in black on horseback, axe in hand, he commanded the execution of a treasurer, a printer, and dozens of bedraggled Muscovite noblemen. Hearing their shrieks, he forgave about half of them, putting them on surety bond with his nobles. The rest, including those who had confessed under torture, were strung up.

The death of Ivan Vistovatov, one of the tsar's longtime advisors and the rough equivalent of a foreign minister, was the most horrible. Accused of colluding against the tsar with the king of Poland, the Ottoman sultan, and the Crimean khan—charges he didn't understand and rejected as impudent slander—he was hoisted naked to the beam for the merriment of the tsar's loyalist horsemen, who galloped around him, reaching out their swords to cut off his nose, an ear, and his penis. The tsar was displeased: Vistovatov had bled to death too fast. He raged at the rider who had sliced through his genitals, promising him a similar fate. (The rider later died of the plague instead.)[68] Vistovatov's body rotted in the sun for a while before being tossed into the pit and covered over. "There was great silence in Moscow," according to a chronicle.[69]

Then, as before, Moscow began to revive and to rebuild with better defenses, including the moat that separated the Kremlin wall from Red Square. Ivan left no explanation for the cadavers, the marriages, the hatred of Novgorod. He also left no explanation for his decision to decorate his realm with a building that gloriously, euphorically defied the ugliness of its history. It came into being slowly, piece by piece. The original wooden structure was scrubbed, painted, and transformed into one of most astonishing constructions in the world: the Cathedral of the Intercession by the Moat, also known as St. Basil's Cathedral, the onion-domed church on the square across from the clock tower.

The church became the symbol of Moscow and eventually of all Russia. Nicknamed "Jerusalem," St. Basil's seems to float above the square owing to a curve in the land leading down to the river. It looks bigger from a distance than up close, and the play of colors makes the domes look like burning candles. From above, God's own perspective, it is the shape of a perfectly symmetrical star. The dynamic layering of the structure—the contrast between the angular crosses and the orbs beneath them—reflects advances in design and blends

Greek and Italian influences. It also gives evidence of building in stages. St. Basil's Cathedral began in 1553 as a single small chapel of wood or stone. In 1554, it was expanded into a network of eight chapels (one circled by seven) and in 1555 into a network of nine (one circled by eight).[70] The chapels were connected by narrow corridors and a hidden staircase discovered during a Soviet-era refurbishment. The basement concealed a treasury. Four chapels in the circle are named for patriarchs and saints whose feast days align with dates in the battle of Kazan, which the cathedral celebrated "in gratitude to the Virgin."[71] The Intercession chapel in the center also commemorates Ivan's "storming of Kazan" in 1552. Another chapel celebrates the "Entrance of the Lord into Jerusalem" and is associated with Ivan's triumphant return to Moscow after the Kazan siege. Moscow, like Jerusalem, was the "Kingdom to Come." The Trinity chapel is associated with heaven, and the Intercession chapel with earth.[72] The inclusion of the two other chapels, named after Saints Nicholas and Varlaam, has no clear explanation. There are two more besides: the chapel of St. John, added in 1672 to preserve his miracle-working relics, and of St. Basil, which dates from 1588.

Basil (Vasiliy) was born in a village near Moscow. His parents loved him but were too poor to look after him. Bullied as a child for his odd mannerisms and strange noises, he left home at age sixteen to apprentice with a shoemaker. When a bread-seller asked for a pair of boots to get him through the winter's snowy mud, Basil began to cry, explaining that he had foreseen the man's death: The boots needed only to last for two short days. Basil's visions persisted; he entered the Church but soon left after the Holy Spirit instructed him to reject the rituals of the Church and seek an immediate communion with God. He tromped the lusty, dirty streets of Kitai-gorod in all seasons, sleeping in a tower, repulsively clad, burdened by chains wrapped around his neck and torso, a "fool for Christ" with knobby joints and bruised, blistered skin. How much of the behavior of holy fools was innate and how much intentional can never be known. Basil was ridiculed, even beaten, but also became renowned for sensing what others could not. He appeared at births and deaths, seeing the grave in the cradle. In the perception of holy fools, time was a wheel, going round and round. Every aspect of life happened at once, such that parsing time into past, present, and future was merely a trick played by the flesh on the spirit. Thus, Basil didn't think of his prophecies as such; instead, he simply sifted through the layers of time. According to canonized legend, Basil saw Russia as part of Constantinople and Kyiv, just as Ivan's Muscovy could be seen as part of Stalin's great empire across a sixth of the globe.

Basil lingered in markets, spilling kvass and overturning trays of pastries made with foul ingredients. He smashed an image of the Virgin Mary, Mother of God, declaring it the devil's work because the surface pigment concealed a picture of a ghoul. Basil saved a drunkard from an evil tavern keeper by chasing the devil out of his drink. The fleeing devil must have been a strange sight, although no stranger than the image of Basil kissing and babbling at the corners of one house and throwing rocks at another. If "drunkenness and dancing and blasphemies, as well as other loathsome and vile deeds" were happening inside, his hagiographer explained, then the corners should be kissed because the angels expelled from their house were sitting there "despondently weeping." If, on the contrary, the house belonged to "devout keepers of the fast," then the devils clinging on the outside needed to be driven away "lest they cause the righteous to stumble."[73]

Basil used cleverness to punish deceit. In one anecdote, thieves tried to steal a warm fur coat given to him by a boyar in the depths of winter. One planned to play dead while another asked Basil for the coat as a donation for the burial. Basil knew that he was being tricked but offered the coat nonetheless. He then went into a trance and started singing a song about cunning fox-fur coats out-cunning cunning people. The thief who'd been playing dead died.

Basil predicted the June 1547 fire of Moscow. The day before the blaze broke out in the Exaltation of the Cross Monastery, he had been seen silently praying there, tears running down his face, foreseeing the cataclysm, urging people to protect the towers and walls. He is said to have prevented another fire from destroying Novgorod. The tsar had invited him to the Kremlin on the sovereign's name day and given him a goblet of wine as a treat. Basil dumped the wine out of a window. Another goblet was filled, and it too ended up in the street, angering the tsar, until Basil explained to him that he had used the wine to extinguish a fire in Novgorod at that very hour. Ivan sent a messenger to find out what was happening there. The messenger confirmed that the fire raging through the streets had suddenly gone out; a naked man had been seen pouring water onto the flames.[74]

Basil died at age eighty-eight, having spent seventy-two years as a holy fool, famished, parched, his mortal body always at extreme risk. Ivan helped transport his resin-sealed coffin to its burial place. With the departure of his soul, the city "was filled with fragrance."[75] In 1577, Basil was interred on the grounds of the cathedral that now bears his name. Following his canonization in 1588, the chapel containing his relics was added to the rest of the ensemble. The shrine atop his grave has not survived save for an image of Basil made of satin and silk with gold thread.

Lore has it that after the construction of St. Basil's, Ivan blinded its architects to prevent their designing anything else as beautiful. The tale is told, and retold, in the travelogues of Adam Olearius (1634), Konrad van Klenk (1675), and Bernard Tanner (1678).[76] The identities of those architects, named Barma (which in this context might mean "mumbler") and Postnik (otherwise referenced as Ivan Postnik and Postnik Yavkovlev), are disputed. Barma is first mentioned in a hagiography of the late sixteenth century before appearing in various chronicles: In one, he and Postnik morph into a single person. Postnik is thought to have begun the cathedral before leaving for Kazan, leaving the bulk of the work to Barma, though he supposedly returned to Moscow in 1588, eyesight intact.[77]

By then, Ivan was four years dead. He collapsed while playing chess with his advisor Bodgan Belsky. The king piece kept toppling over. Then the tsar himself fell. There are other descriptions of his passing, and the usual Muscovite rumors of malfeasance. Lutheran pastor Pavel Oderborn, who never met Ivan or set foot in Moscow but managed to publish a Latin-language account of his rule in 1585, imagined the tyrant's final days in prose lifted from accounts of the final disease of King Herod, the archetypal evil king. Ivan despised Lutheranism, and the pastor, living in Riga, engaged in a religious polemic against him.[78]

Ivan "had such strength of body and robustness of limbs that he looked as if he could endure for many days anything that even an uninterrupted disease could throw at him," Oderborn begins:

> But by the power of God the affliction settled on him so power-fully that he gave up on the hope of the cures of medicine and with his mind in upheaval he dragged out his life in misery; for many days he didn't speak to anyone, or take food, or utter speech, but seemed as if struck dumb.
>
> The disease finally settled on him so powerfully that, with his intestines and guts putrefying, his very privates were tortured, infected with the foulest stink by the animals which are wont to be born in rotting bodies. And so when, among most bitter tortures of mind and body, he had prolonged with food and drink his accursed and cruel breath, almost before he could have thought it he came, with his mind in turmoil, to the fatal hour and last finishing line; but he was carried off by a manner of death that was in no way common.
>
> When he had said this [his final words], he fell into the third period of lethargy, and not long afterwards he breathed out his spirit with a groan and wretched bellowing; the abscesses which had occupied his privates immediately burst and filled the whole building with such a stink from the pus gushing out that the bystanders, not wishing to be infected by the disease-bearing putrefaction, took to their heels, abandoned him, and fled in different directions. He died on the 28th day.[79]

The tsar might have deliriously called out for his son, the heir apparent, but the young man was dead. Ivan IV had murdered the intended Ivan V three years before, on November 19, 1581. The son had come to his wife Elena's defense after the tsar had clipped her ears and whacked her with his metal staff for dressing immodestly in her quarters, covering her pregnant body with one garment

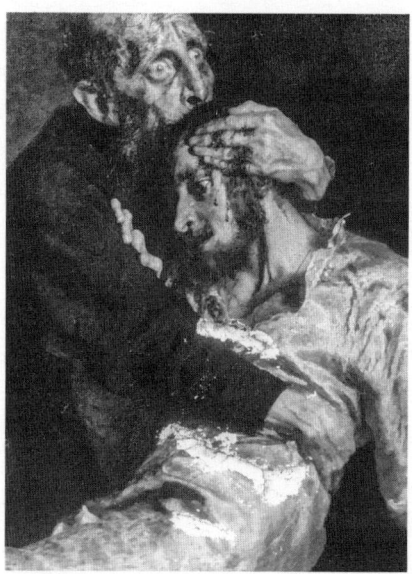

Fragment of Ilya Repin's 1885 painting of a grief-stricken, madness-engulfed Ivan the Terrible holding the son he has just struck dead. Nationalists have disputed the accuracy of the murder, and the painting has been vandalized on three occasions, most recently in 2018 by an inebriated visitor to the State Tretyakov Gallery.

rather than the required three. Elena miscarried the next day. The son raged at his father, reminding him of his mistreatment of other wives, and the father, losing control, cracked open his skull with the same staff.[80] The terrible killing is immortalized in a famous painting by Ilya Repin of 1883–85. The tsar kneels wild-eyed in horror as he tries to stanch the flow of blood from his son's temple. The furniture is overturned, the carpet bunched up.

Ivan's other son from Anastasia, Fyodor, proved ineffective as a ruler. Feeble-minded, he was nicknamed the bell ringer after his favorite activity. Fyodor did not want power, and power did not want him. The Rurik line came to an end.

6

PRETENDERS

THROUGH THE YEARS 1462 to 1584, from the start of the reign of Ivan III to the end of the reign of Ivan the Terrible, Moscow became bureaucratic. The chancelleries, or *prikazï,* of the Kremlin oversaw the courts, taxation, agriculture, the guards, and police. The Posol'skiy prikaz was the Foreign Affairs Chancellery; the Razboynïy prikaz dealt with brigands. For the Church, there was a Monastïrskiy prikaz. The high-ranking bureaucrats, or *d'yaki,* who ran the chancelleries exercised their powers zealously, oppressing commoners who, for obvious reasons, didn't want the fruits of their labor taxed and confiscated. "I have seen them sometimes when they have laid open their commodities . . . to look still behind them and towards every door: as men in some fear, that looked to be set upon and surprised by some enemy," Giles Fletcher reported back to England of the plight of peasants and laborers, adding that the people living on crown lands resented funding wars and other "grand undertakings."[1] Through such undertakings, Moscow evolved into a "fiscal-military state" overseen by a divine ruler.[2]

Still, the rulers died wholly human. Ivan III perished from excessive drinking and a brain disease that led to him losing sight in one eye and the use of one hand. At the other end of the century his grandson Ivan the Terrible gave up the ghost after flipping over a chessboard.[3] Paranoid and unstable, he anticipated a grand come-uppance for his marauding, so issued a decree in his final years to bolster Moscow's defenses. He imagined building an external net-work of walls and towers, gates and locks such that his grandfather could only dream of. The *d'yaki* went to work raising funds from the Orthodox Church and its monasteries, Russian and foreign mer-chant corporations, and commoners.

In the sixteenth century, the Kremlin contained the tsar's quar-ters, including the tsarina's upper floor *terem,* the metropolitan's pal-ace, chancelleries, and a hospice. Red Square bustled with "men and women, slaves and idlers," the commotion enhanced by icon-sellers, cobblers, saddlers, hatters, prostitutes (seen holding turquoise rings in their mouths), and a set of stalls called the "lice market," an out-door barber shop. The ground was whisker-carpeted and pleas-ant to walk on barefoot.[4] Beyond Red Square, Kitai-gorod housed additional chancelleries, a printing plant, and residences for traders (*gostï*), foreign travelers, and commercial-diplomatic types. English-men, Poles, and Spaniards occupied large stone structures.

South of the Moskva was an unattractive district called Strele-tskaya sloboda. It dated back to Ivan III and was protected around the edges by a log and dirt barrier.[5] The name refers to the *streltsï,* who made the area their home. Excavations in the 1990s revealed where they lived and some of their belongings: hinges, blades, locks, spurs, toys, and "trash pits."[6] Those *streltsï* stationed in Moscow behaved badly enough for a code of conduct to be imposed on them. It specified "no hurting of other people, no robbing," and no frat-ernizing with "wizards and witches."[7] The code also prohibited the men from drinking on the job, though that happened, as an etching of an 1682 *streltsï* uprising makes clear: their faces are puffy, their eyes heavy-lidded, as if they'd prepared for battle by raiding the wine cellars of disgraced boyars. Streletskaya sloboda picked up a nick-name, *naleyki*—a combination of "pour me a little more" and "keep the glass full." The glasses were filled even on fast days, an insult to the Church. An Italian diplomat, Antonio Possevino, noticed, unpleas-antly, that the *streltsï* were a rather gassy bunch, and investigated their diet: beer and mead and "a kind of aquavit, which [the musketeers] commonly drink at meals for the prevention of flatulence, to which their diet—raw meat, onions, and cabbage—renders them prone."[8]

The massive building project Ivan the Terrible initiated was called Tsar-gorod, also known as Bel-gorod (from the word for white, belïy).[9] Combined, the two Russian names translate as "The Tsar's White City." Completed between 1585 and 1593, Tsar-gorod enveloped greater Moscow from the north, west, and east—a semicircular fortification network, some six miles long, that generally followed the contours of a preexisting rampart. (The Moskva River was the southern barrier.) Beyond that, for about nine miles, Moscow was protected by another barrier called Skorodom. The name refers to a forest market where prefab parts of houses could be bought, though some sources claim that it refers to the haste with which the logs of coniferous trees were pulled by horses to the site, then split into planks and assembled by carpenters. Skorodom was the Home Depot of its day. A miniature from 1591 shows a contented-looking brigade of carpenters wearing tunics and hats with earflaps, mallets in their hands, assembling an octagonal platform. Cannons poke through holes in the walls at odd angles—a cheerfully robust defense some "three spears in height."[10] In the seventeenth century the carpenters were replaced by diggers, and the Skorodom barrier by zemlyanoy val, a dirt wall or mound that went around Moscow on both sides of the Moskva. The land beyond it was quiet, free of people. These days the fortification line is called the Garden Ring Road, which doesn't have any gardens. It's a six-lane highway and tunnel complex that's impossible to cross by foot or bicycle without getting flattened.

The designer of Tsar-gorod was Fyodor Kon' of Smolensk.[11] His birth and death dates are unknown, and how he became a master architect for church and state is a mystery "shrouded in a haze of romantic legends" and "poetic fiction."[12] Tsar-gorod was the largest construction project in Moscow to date, and Kon' was overseen by the Chancellery (Prikaz) of Stone Works. He mobilized laborers and masons to smash stone in the quarries of Myachkovo, transport the slabs by horse and wagon to Moscow, mix lime powder and

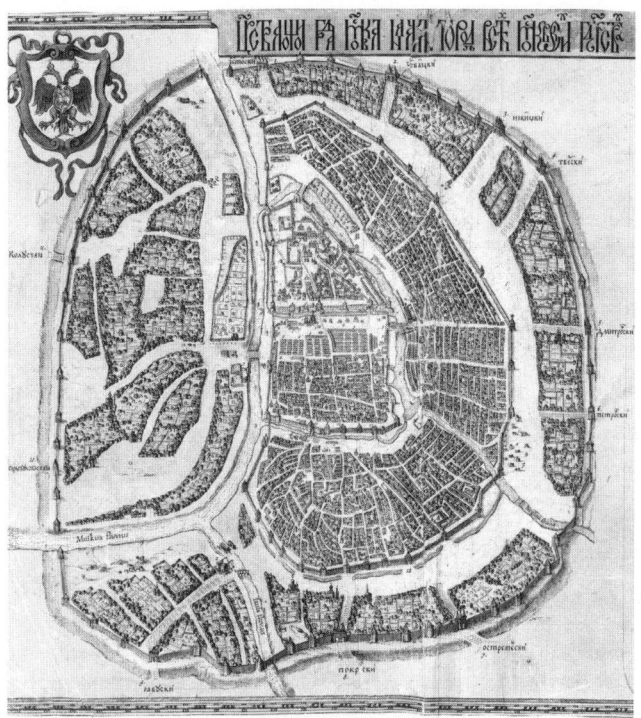

Map of 1613 Moscow by Dutch cartographer Hessel Gerritsz (ca. 1581–1632), perhaps based on a survey commissioned by Boris Godunov. The map identifies the landmarks and properties in the center, Kremlenagrad, together with those in Kitai-gorod, Tsar-gorod, and Skorodom (which included "the grand duke's garden," where flowers, vegetables, and fruit were grown for consumption in the Kremlin; "bathhouses"; and "lumber markets"). The map also shows Streletskaya sloboda and the land most open to attack in the south. The city's gates are identified in shorthand Cyrillic, a rarity in Dutch mapmaking. The map's ornate title reads: "Reigning settlement of Moscow, the main settlement of all Muscovite states."

water for plaster, dig out clay for bricks and fire them in the city's kilns. "At Moscow our grandfathers, fathers, and we, your orphans, made bricks in the brickyards, made the Tsar's White City," one of the laborers tried to explain.[13] Exposed sections of Tsar-gorod had rectangular towers of up to four stories in height with sloped bases through which cannons pointed downward through "loopholes." This feature made Tsar-gorod "cleverer" than the walls of Antioch, Constantinople, or Aleppo—at least according to a religious chronicler in the know, Paul of Aleppo.[14] The bases of the towers included furnaces, storerooms, and combat chambers. Staircases led from the bases to the vaulted rooms of the first, second, and third tiers and the hipped roofs.

Tsar-gorod was an impressive sight. Moss coated the bases of the walls; the tops were scrubbed bright white; the corner towers were decorated with banners and flags. Sadly, nothing survives today save the names of the towers, which now belong to squares, and a strip of the foundation preserved in an "archeological park" near Pokrovsky Square.[15] The fortifications were replaced by fashionable boulevards—the "gardens" that gave the Garden Ring Road its name—and the bricks recycled in an orphanage and Moscow's government building. There's no record of the tolls collected there, nor evidence of fighting or invasions.

Tsar-gorod protected a neighborhood of the elite and their families (the people for whom the *Household Book* was intended) together with the residences of cloth-makers, metalworkers, and the tsar's stable keepers. The area included a large garden, a corn market, horse market, and hay market each separated from the others by log-lined roads. The alleys, lanes, and side streets of present-day Moscow are still named for the things once made there, from armor to kettles to plates. (The Soviets kept up the habit in the command economy of the twentieth century, naming the bread stores "Bread" and the polyethylene kitchenware outlet "Plastic.") Blacksmiths sweated through their clothes on Blacksmiths' Street: Kuznetskaya. Wooden bridges spanned the Neglinka with the largest named for the blacksmiths, Kuznetskiy most. Lined with mills, forges, and baths, the river supplied a network of interconnected ponds.

Tsar-gorod had twenty-seven or twenty-eight towers: the maps are inconsistent. Tver (Tverskiye vorota) was the first one built, followed by Nikita (Nikitskiye vorota) tower to the southwest and Petrov (Petrovskiye vorota) to the southeast. Arbat (Arbatskiye vorota) came after them, then the tower "on the pipe" that guided the Neglinka under the Tsar-gorod fortification. This tower and several others were "blind," meaning no one kept watch from them. The entrances were of different sorts: archways with iron gates raised and lowered into place, iron-clad doors (or multiple sets of them),

L-shaped tunnels, side entrances. The Neglinka washed around the feet of two stone bulls before disappearing underground in anticipation of its "reclusive future."[16] In later centuries, the river would be rerouted and completely hidden from view, except when foul steam billowed up through Moscow's grates or when the underground cesspools, which were never cleaned, overflowed after heavy rains. At such times, glop surged into shops and houses, reminding their appalled residents of the bones and blood and cursed dankness beneath their feet. The river was cleaner and brighter in the seventeenth century, and when it reappeared after its brief concealment on the other side of the "pipe" wall, it fed into a fishpond that extended to a bog.[17]

The defenses were much needed. After Ivan the Terrible's death, Moscow and the commonwealth of Russia entered a period known as the "Time of Troubles" or *Smutnoye vremya.* Most histories have the *Smuta* beginning with the coronation of Boris Godunov in 1598 and petering out with the election of the first Romanov tsar, Mikhaíl, in 1613. In between these two events, in 1605, a pretender to the throne passed through the Nikita tower and set up court for himself. He was a polarizing figure. For some in Moscow, he was a savior. For others, he was a scourge, the Russia-annihilating spawn of Satan. Theologians attributed the *Smuta* to Russia's loss of bearings: God had abandoned the people, rich and poor, to their sins. It's the simplest of explanations for the most complicated of events.

Nikolay Karamzin, the official court historian of Tsar Alexander I, contextualized the *Smuta* in his *History of the Russian State,* which then inspired the poet Alexander Pushkin to write a play. He in turn inspired the composer Modest Mussorgsky, whose opera *Boris Godunov* in two versions (1869 and 1874) is a staple of the repertoire, the second grittier and scarier than the first as a meditation on the relationship of the people to power. There is a Tsar, and a Pretender, and a person styling himself as Tsar, and the Crowd; power moves among them. There is also a fictional "old monk chronicler" named Pimen, and another monk named Varlaam, who sings a merry ditty on the border between Muscovy and Lithuania about an un-merry event: Ivan the Terrible's siege of Kazan.[18] Mussorgsky comes close to declaring Russia a floundering civilization, but his opera, a magnificent achievement of that civilization, undercuts that idea. The ending of the second version is especially potent: a holy fool, Nikolka the Iron-Cap, wanders a forest clearing with a village burning in the distance, singing about the moon and a kitten's mew and Russia's pitiless place in the cosmos.[19] The opera ends on a dissonance, a musical question mark. Mussorgky, like Pushkin and Karamzin, ponders the question of recurrence: Is time a loop, are the old stories the same as the new ones? Do people have agency or do events happen outside of their conscious intending?

Ivan the Terrible exercised agency, but his "short, squat, swollen," and uncomplicated son did not, even as he played the part of tsar for fourteen years from 1584 to 1598.[20] He had no preparation for governing and led a simple, deeply pious life in the Kremlin: waking at four, dressing and washing, receiving the cross clerk who brought the icon of the saint to be celebrated that day, going to church for the matins service, returning to his quarters to consider the requests of boyars, then attending mass, dining, sleeping, and rising for the vespers service.[21] Fyodor left the bulk of state affairs to a group of regents, including Boris Godunov, as his father had arranged before his death. Fyodor's limitations were common knowledge in Moscow—the Kremlin spewed gossip—and efforts to remove him were the talk of the town. "There was some tumult and uproar among some of the nobility and commonality, which, notwithstanding, was quickly pacified," the English emissary Jerome Horsey said of a botched coup attempt by Ivan the Terrible's bodyguard and chess partner Bogdan Belsky, "throughout all the city of Moscow was great watch and ward, with soldiers and gunners; good orders established, and officers placed to subdue the tumulters and maintain quietness."[22]

Boris emerged as the power behind the throne, an improbable development considering his unremarkable beginnings. His relatives claimed heroic origins, a lineage back to a prince (*murza*) of the Golden Horde who entered the service of the first of the rulers named Ivan. But within the context of Kremlin power politics, his family was nondescript. Boris came from a boyar clan of small means based in Kostroma.[23] His father was a "low-ranking provincial gentry cavalryman," who earned a nickname, "Crooked," after he mangled his nose, or a limb, falling from a horse.[24] Nothing about his mother is known except for her name: Stepanida, tonsured as Sandulia. He became part of Ivan the Terrible's court through an uncle, Dmitri, who had been recruited into the *oprichnina*. Boris himself became an *oprichnik*, then a boyar, and finally achieved the position of *konyushiy*, Master of the Horse, in charge of the entire court apparatus. Gifts were lavished on him as the man in charge. Horsey brought him pipe organs and harpsichords, and "thousands of people resorted and steyed about the palace to heer" the "lowd and musicall sound thereof."[25] The other crucial factor in Boris's ascent was his sister Irina, who, according to Horsey, liked the music-making most of all and kept it going—a reminder that happiness existed even in times of strife, and that there were many more days of contented sweet sounds than nights of worry. Fyodor did not understand the music but chose Irina as his bride. She went to mass with him, two hours a day, and assisted in his reverent pastime of commissioning monasteries. Boris married another type of person: Mariya Skuratova, the daughter of the *oprichnik* enforcer Malyuta Skuratov. The sins of her father made her a villain at court. A grain buyer and diplomat from Holland demonized her as a reincarnation of Queen Semiramis of Assyria and harsher than Boris.[26]

There were three other influencers, among them Ivan Shuisky, a prince of the Suzdal line purportedly descended from Alexander Nevsky; Ivan Mstislavsky, a senior boyar and second cousin of the tsar; and Nikita Romanovich Zakharin-Yuryev, the head of the Romanov clan and Fyodor's uncle.[27] Nikita fell sick just a few months into Fyodor's reign and withdrew to his residence in Kitaigorod. Before he died, he had Boris promise that his family would be looked after. Shuisky profited as aide to the tsar, then overreached by plotting a coup of his own, abetted by several boyars, the metropolitan, and Moscow's merchants, which added to the "tumult and uproar" in the streets until a snowstorm chased everyone home. Mstislavsky also overreached. He imagined his sister replacing Irina

Godunova as Fyodor's wife, which did not go over well with Fyodor or, presumably, Irina.[28]

The scheming unnerved Boris, who bribed Horsey to take "secret messages" to England requesting asylum should he need it. He remained in Moscow and in Russia thanks to the confidence placed in him, with his sister's help, by Fyodor. The tsar granted Boris license to settle scores, and he banished the malefactors of the court to the villages before going after the chief threat, Shuisky, whom he forced into monkhood and "discreetly" murdered. (Boris left the dirty work up to a bailiff, who asphyxiated Shuisky "with smoke from burning hay and stubble [the straw left after scything]."){[29]} The metropolitan was exiled north of Novgorod and replaced by a Boris loyalist, Iov, who became, on Boris's initiative, the first Patriarch of Russia. The lesser threat, Mstislavsky, was also "thrust into a friary."[30] There he would have been able to resume his pastime under Ivan the Terrible: book collecting and the writing of "secret chronicles."[31]

Before his coronation, Boris solidified the rules that bound peasants to the land in Russia, turning peasants into serfs, *krepostnïye krest'yane,* a name that refers to a binding contract, a bill of sale.[32] Serfdom was not Russia's invention but an age-old form of exploitation adopted from France. Under Ivan the Terrible, freedom of movement had been limited by law, and Boris shrank it even further. He abolished the privilege of St. George's Day, a harvest festival when peasants were allowed to relocate to more fertile land or in search of a better arrangement with a landowner, even both. Removing the privilege did not exactly endear those mucking out stalls and scything in the sun to the tsar. Serfs paid taxes with coins—the days of payment in goods and labor had ended—to their communes, bypassing the landowner who paid taxes of his own based on the value of his assets. They paid tiny amounts, less than a ruble a year, to a tax collector. Not all peasants became serfs. Those who worked their own land, *chernososhnïye krest'yane,* or for the Church occupied a separate category.

Serfs were not "talking tools" who could be replaced or disposed of by their owners.[33] They were not slaves. Baptism granted serfs the status of religious subjects always recognized as human beings.

Slaves did not have such status, having surrendered it as debtors or having it taken from them as captives, and the rules concerning the keeping of slaves were much harsher than those dealing with serfs. Unlike slaves, serfs could not be killed by their masters on a whim, nor could they be bought and sold to others—though, to be sure, landowners found ways around this latter rule when convenient for them. An elaborate set of laws called the *Sobornoye ulozheniye,* from 1649, brought an end to even the limited freedom of movement that serfs had enjoyed. Harboring runaway serfs became a punishable crime, as did unauthorized travel abroad, riding a horse over a foe, making moonshine, running a brothel, stealing a horse, and, less seriously, disrespecting one's parents, stealing apples, and scooping out someone else's bees. The punishments were of an eye-for-an-eye quality; the penalty for burying someone alive, for example, was burial alive.[34]

Despite Boris's efforts, tax revenues continued to decline, forcing him to add people who had not previously been taxed to the rolls.[35] None of it would matter, as Boris discovered after Fyodor's death on January 7, 1598. Fyodor's wife, Irina, served a mere nine days as ruler. Talk came and went of a strategic second marriage to a Habsburg, as certain boyars preferred, but Irina took the veil and said goodbye to the world instead.[36] She entered the Novodevichiy (New Maidens) Convent about half a mile from Moscow along the river, leaving the question of her husband's successor to the *Zemskiy sobor.* The selection of a new autocrat was God's will, she informed the delegation of priests and nobles who trekked to the convent for her recommendation, then added that the *sobor* was free to interpret God's will by putting her brother Boris on the throne. On March 15 (not the Ides of March on the Orthodox calendar, but a portentous date nonetheless), the *sobor* issued a document, the Affirmation Charter of 1598, describing how and why Boris was elected tsar. It asserts, falsely, that he was Ivan the Terrible's preferred successor to Fyodor. The charter also made Boris the people's choice. It includes some five hundred signatures, from priests to merchants to the people looking after the tsar's tents while traveling.[37]

Some of the people demurred. An owl—a creature that cannot

see the light of God—flew into a church across from the Kremlin, a bad omen. There had been another possible heir to Fyodor, but he had died at age eight in 1598. Tongues wagged about Boris's involvement in his death, even though, according to the Orthodox Church, the boy was ineligible for the throne. He was the product of Ivan the Terrible's 1581 marriage to Mariya Nagaya, which the church did not sanction. (Three marriages were the limit in Orthodoxy; this marriage was the sixth or seventh.) Nagaya argued for her son Dmitri to become tsar instead of Fyodor, and then for Dmitri to be named as Fyodor's successor. Her meddling resulted in her and her family's forced relocation to Uglich, a town northeast of Moscow on the Volga River. There the scheming continued.

The recent history of Uglich may be nondescript (the Soviets turned it into a watchmaking center and maintained a hydroelectric plant there), but its ancient past is colorful, and not just because of Boris, Mariya, and Dmitri. For centuries, Uglich was the seat of a tiny princedom independent of Moscow. In 1328 it was purchased by the grand prince of Moscow, Ivan Kalita, as a strategic outpost. It was overrun by foreign fighters—Tatars, chiefly, but also Lithuanians—and embroiled in Ivan the Terrible's campaign against Kazan. Residents floated a fortress down the river to help with the battle.

Dmitri lived with his mother in a small court at the center of Uglich. He was a strange child who shared his father's ghoulishness. He "delighted (they say) to see sheep and other cattle killed and to look on their throats while they are bleeding (which commonly children are afraid to behold), and to beat geese and hens with a staff till he see them lie dead."[38] The simplest explanation of his own death has Dmitri suffering an epileptic seizure—blamed at the time on an excess of black bile—while playing a tossing game (comparable to mumblety-peg) with a stake. Dmitri either fell on top of the stake or, less likely, stuck it into his own throat during a spasm. His mother walloped his nanny for allowing the tragedy to happen. Tsar Fyodor approved an investigation, headed by the Patriarch of Moscow and All Russia, Iov, and including a member of the Shuisky clan. The extant partial report is a mess of contradictions, out-of-order pages, recycled stock phrases, and indications of tampering. Dmitri's relatives claimed foul play while simultaneously acknowledging the illness.[39]

Dmitri's death was announced by the biggest, heaviest bell in Uglich. The mayor of the town, Mikhaíl Bityagovsky, tried to silence it but the ringer—the sexton of the Cathedral of the Transfiguration— locked himself in the tower and kept banging away at it. The people of Uglich considered Dmitri their ruling prince and believed Maria when she told them that he had been murdered by Kremlin agents under Boris's direction. He had the power to organize the killing and the need and the will to do it, she insisted. There was a rebellion. Bityagovsky, his son, and several others were hung. Boris used his authority to put down the uprising, punishing everyone and every-thing involved, including the bell. He had it dragged into the town square, where a blacksmith burned off its cross, cut out its tongue (clapper), and removed one of its ears (hangers). The bell was scourged with a dozen lashes and sent to Siberia along with all the other rebels, who hauled the bell through bogs and frost for an entire year. The trip ended in the outpost of Pelim, just across from the Ural Mountains. There the rebels built a prison for themselves and served out their sentences.

The bell traveled farther east to Tobolsk, where it was locked up in a cell and inscribed with a description of its crime. In time it was repaired and hoisted to the top of a cathedral to ring the canonical hours and act as a fire alarm. The people of Uglich asked for the bell back, but the governor of Tobolsk refused to return it, claiming that it had been banished to Siberia for life. After a protracted legal pro-cess and much petitioning, Tsar Alexander III pardoned the bell in 1892, three hundred years after its exile. A commission from Uglich accompanied its trip back home on a Volga steamboat. The bell is now a museum exhibit.[40]

With Fyodor and Dmitri dead, Boris became tsar.[41] He took the throne on September 1, 1598. His title as Great Lord, Great Prince, and Tsar, and the name of his son (another Fyodor) as tsarevich were inscribed in golden rings around the top of the Ivan the Great Bell Tower of the Kremlin, to which Boris added two tiers, increasing its height to 270 feet. Then a pit was dug for the building of a furnace and the molding and pouring of a bell of "a weight that had not yet been"—more than 78,000 pounds.[42] It was fashioned on Boris's command by Andrey Chokhov, who loved making big things. In 1586 he forged the colossally impractical Tsar's Cannon—fun for tourists to gawk at but used just once—and several battering rams named after magical animals. The bell was also impractical. Too heavy to be hoisted up the tower, it instead hung in a short, stout belfry beside the base. Two dozen ringers pulled ropes on either side of the clapper. Others had to position themselves inside the belfry to keep the clapper moving back and forth rather than side to side, which would have caused the belfry to collapse. They lost their hearing.[43]

Thus Boris broadcast his power to friend and foe alike, so long as the ringers kept pulling the ropes. Before taking the crown, he assembled his decked-out soldiers at a camp south of Moscow on the Oka River. There he conveyed a message to a diplomat from the Crimean khanate that he was a tsar not to be trifled with. Another achievement on the international front involved the return to Russia of land that Ivan the Terrible had surrendered to Sweden. On the day Boris took the crown, barrels of mead and beer were placed on the city streets for everyone to have their fill.

Three times a week, Boris met with the heads of his chancelleries at seven in the morning and received supplicants, petitioners, and advertisers from the provinces on other days.[44] He had a beautiful daughter, Ksenia, and dangled the possibility of marrying her to a Swede, or a Habsburg prince, or a Dane—all for diplomatic leverage. The marriage to the Swede fell apart because he was too much of a lout for Boris's taste, immodestly bringing his mistress to Moscow and generally making a terrible impression.

The journal of the Danish ambassador to Moscow, Axel Gyldenstierne, relates the pitiful details of the attempted marriage of the Danish prince Hans (Johan of Schleswig-Holstein) to Ksenia.[45] Hans and his entourage were escorted to Moscow by bailiffs who lent them horses and looked after tolls. Housing was offered, but it was dreadful—the rooms suffocatingly overheated, lacking furniture and food and the utensils to go along with it—so the Danes opted to sleep in tents by the river. Later, they learned that the occupants of the buildings had been doing everything in their power to keep the disease-bearing insect and rodent population down by fumigating rooms and burning beds.

The Danes were then installed in a vast courtyard near the Kremlin, forbidden to roam around Moscow lest they see something unpleasant. Hans expressed an interest in seeing his prospective bride, but Church custom forbade it. He was reassured that Ksenia was comely, with dark hair and eyes and a porcelain complexion along with a gift for languages.

The date of the wedding was to be fixed after Boris completed a pilgrimage to the Trinity Lavra of St. Sergius. The trip lasted from October 6 to 17, 1602. Meantime, infection spread through the diplomatic compound. When Hans fell sick on October 15, the head of the apothecary, Boris's second cousin Semyon, did the exact opposite of what he should have done. He declined to treat Hans, not even to order baths or herbs or anything helpful, and instead connived to steal his cash and jewels. He was delighted to see Hans stricken, because he was against the wedding, knowing that it would limit his influence in the Kremlin.

Boris returned to Moscow to pray for—and attempt to pay for—a miracle. He donated to monasteries and ordered alms to be given to the poor in hopes of divine favor. Hans slipped in and out of consciousness, his hands and feet turning ice-cold. Boris visited on October 27, berating the doctors for their ineffectiveness and threatening, through an interpreter, to impale them. He offered to relocate Hans to the Kremlin and hold the wedding as soon as Hans convalesced, but it was too late. When conscious, Hans wept from pain and self-pity, telling his people that God was punishing him for traveling to a non-Christian land. Boris sought a last-minute intervention from a healer—a witch—but on the evening of October 28, Hans died. He never met Ksenia, and she never married.

Boris had ruled sternly but sagely, to the satisfaction of the boyars' duma, but his luck was turning along with the weather.[46] It rained cats and dogs throughout the summer of 1601, and then, when it came time to harvest, frost hit. Snow fell in September, two months early. Efforts to sow winter grain failed; nothing rose from the ground in the spring because it had been too cold for the seeds to germinate. The meteorological weirdness has been ascribed to a cooling trend called the Little Ice Age but also attributed to the February–March 1600 eruption of the Huaynaputina volcano in southern Peru, which happened at the same time as another, even larger eruption in the Aleutian Islands.[47] The entire planet was affected, in all directions. There was flooding in Sweden, late wine harvests in Burgundy, and an Easter blizzard in England. Manila galleons made the crossing from Mexico to the Philippines in record time owing to an increase in wind speeds.

The Great Famine in Russia lasted from 1601 to 1603. First honey disappeared, then vegetables, then cereal crops. The price of rye increased by sixfold in the first year of the famine and three times that in the second year. High prices led to hoarding. The tsar accepted responsibility for his people's earthly affairs and tried to feel their pain and ease their suffering. (The patriarch, in contrast, did not. Wicked gossip spread about him refusing to sell his own grain stores in anticipation of prices rising. He still refused even after the food had gone rancid.) According to the Piskarev Chronicle of 1645, a medley of sources about the Time of Troubles, Boris also opened homeless shelters: "And in Moscow, three almshouses were built: at [the Church of] the Prophet Moses on Tverskaya [Moscow's central avenue] there was an almshouse, and in it were poor laymen; and an almshouse across from the Cannon Yard, for nuns; and an almshouse at Kulishki [east of Kitai-gorod], for poor women."[48] Laborers caravanned into the city asking to work for food. Boris enlisted them in a social welfare project, cutting and pulling slabs of stone into the Kremlin to remake Ivan the Terrible's wooden quarters.[49] He also put them to work on the fortifications. Boris imported grain from the growing regions of his commonwealth to Moscow to distribute to the poor. Some of the bread went to swindlers dressed in rags like beggars, who sold it to desperate families for profit. Dutch trader Isaac Massa, a reasonably reliable eyewitness to Boris's reign, claims that "bread was ordered baked at a standard weight, and sold at a fixed price. But to evade the regulations, the bakers made their wares heavier by adding a half measure of water. Thus, the evil was worse than before."[50] Those with food stuffed themselves sick for fear of it disappearing.

The desperation increased. People ate horses, cats, dogs, fungi, grass, and bark, which poisoned them. "There were even mothers who ate their children," Massa adds for shock effect.[51] A French soldier recruited into Boris's service as cavalry commander, Captain Jacques Margeret, seconded the claim ("to see a wife kill her husband or a mother her children in order to eat them—these were ordinary enough occurrences") then added the tale of a wood seller being strangled for food by "four women, neighbors, abandoned by their husbands," who admitted to killing the peasant.[52] Babies were abandoned to wolves on the roads into Moscow. Those who died on the streets inside the city were collected and placed in shrouds for eventual burial in mass graves. "Unfortunates who had merely fainted" ended up thrown in the ditches "like tufts of wool in a basket."[53] Anywhere from a hundred to a hundred and twenty thousand people ended up in these graves, over which roads and factories and apartments were later built.[54]

The famine ended in 1604, but before then a mysterious individual claiming to be the escaped Dmitri, miraculously spared execution, or perhaps resurrected, appeared in Poland. It's assumed that this figure—variously known as the Pretender, the False Dmitri, and the First False Dmitri (he had imitators)—fled his monastic order and ended up in Poland in the service of a prince (Adam Wiśniowiecki) and a king (Sigismund III) seeking to increase Polish power, magnates interested in Russia's riches, and Jesuits seeking to Catholicize the place. The Pretender agreed to marry Marina Mniszech, the daughter of the principal Polish financier of his efforts; attracted exiles from Moscow to his banner; and crossed the Lithuanian border into Russia intent on taking power from Boris. He picked up additional followers, villagers, peasants, and Cossack fighters who blamed Boris for the years of famine.[55]

Kepler's supernova appeared in the sky, an event that likely influenced the people who ferried Dmitri's army across the Dnieper

River. As the supernova grew bright enough to be seen throughout the day, Boris asked a female soothsayer to explain its meaning. She told him, contemptuously, that he had a competitor for the throne.[56]

Boris rose against the Pretender, but the resistance splintered.[57] The turning point came near the settlement of Kromï. Forces aligned with the Pretender encouraged soldiers loyal to Moscow's elite, if not Boris himself, to defect. Then, shockingly, word reached the encampment that the tsar had died. The stress of his existence had become unbearable, his mind was too staggered, and he suffered a stroke. (Massa adds the wrinkle that the stroke might have been self-inflicted, alleging that Boris took poison after a huge meal and a gathering of the patriarch and bishops for his tonsure. "He said he was close to death, and scarcely had these birds of evil omen changed their prayers and accomplished their office when the tsar gave up his soul at three o'clock in the afternoon."[58]) Boris's son Fyodor II took power for a few months. The Piskarev Chronicle describes his coronation with grim understatement: "Some came to kiss the cross, while others, turning hostile, did not kiss the cross."[59] The tide had turned against the Godunovs.

The Pretender's delegation arrived in Moscow on June 20, 1605, backed by swelling throngs cheering him as the "true son" of Ivan the Terrible and Russia's "rising sun."[60] His luxuriously attired personal guard was led by the mercenary Jacques Margeret, who had once been in Boris's service.[61] Margeret ingratiated himself with Dmitri after being pardoned for his earlier actions as the commander of Boris's foreign troops. Like other soldiers of fortune, Margeret was loyal to himself and himself alone. He wanted to survive and benefit from a steady salary and some of the spoils of victory. Dmitri respected Margeret's battlefield valor and implementation of "new Dutch tactics—linear formations behind barricades—for the delivery of mass firepower in battle."[62]

Fyodor didn't last long. He was strangled. The Pretender's supporters entered the Kremlin on a looting spree, discovered the liquor and wine casks, guzzled "from their hats," then committed the foul deed.[63] Fyodor was strong, and it took at least four of them to overpower him. Killing his mother and uncle was simpler. False Dmitri I became, for ten months, Tsar Dmitri, and expected to be treated as such by the people of Moscow, ordering them to place their trust and faith in him as the "born sovereign," which he wasn't.[64]

Knowledge of his reign is slight, since the relevant documents were ordered destroyed by Vasiliy, next to take the crown, a member of the Shuisky clan. Dmitri reunited with his "mother," Mariya Nagaya, who legitimized his rule by claiming for her own benefit that, yes, he was indeed her resurrected son. Dmitri acted like a person of the people, friendlier to the nobles than Boris had been, but he also showed himself an outsider in the ceremonial aspects of his governance and his architectural choices. (His Polish-style palace, built where Boris's had stood, was done up with brocades and canopies of gold and silver, plush velvet walls, green fireplaces with silver grills, and crimson window curtains. Even the nails holding the place together were dipped in gold.)[65] Dmitri deftly handled the boyars and the Church, with the notable exception of the future patriarch, Hermogenes, who refused to endorse his marriage to a Catholic. The drum-banging, trumpet-blowing, dancing, drinking, and impertinence of the Polish hussar "guests" of Moscow before, during, and after Dmitri and Marina's defiantly Catholic wedding outraged the court's conservatives, as did the gifts Dmitri lavished on his friends—horses, furs, golden basins, necklaces, and glasses.[66] It would have rankled the inner circle that Dmitri kept Boris's daughter Ksenia as a concubine in the months before the wedding, before depositing her in a convent.

Marina was reviled for her personality ("adventurism," "passion for luxury and prodigality"), looks ("thick lips, denoting pride and vengefulness, a stretched-out visage widening at the bottom, too long a nose, thin black hair, a frail body and a diminutive stature"), and peculiarly Polish pursuits.[67] The sacks of herbs and tightly clasped books she had brought from home implied sorcery, a pastime she shared with Dmitri, who "paid excessive attention to medicine." Lore transformed Marina Mniszech into Marinka the Witch. She would be accused—two murdered husbands and one murdered child later—of placing a curse on the Romanovs. None of the rulers, she allegedly promised, would die of natural causes.[68]

Claims of Dmitri's competency and enlightened approach to governing must be weighed against his considerable errors of judgment. He reneged on his promise to provide Poland part of Russia's western upland. He did not secure the favor of Muscovite noble families with fighters at their disposal and ignored their threats to his rule. And he effectively threw his life away by assuming he could control Vasiliy Shuisky, which was impossible.[69] Shuisky wanted power for himself, and in the first days of Dmitri's rule openly plotted to have the new tsar killed. He was arrested, and after a trial, a smirking confession, and sentencing, the chopping block was readied. But for unclear reasons, Dmitri decided to commute Shuisky's sentence and instead send him into exile. Even that didn't happen. Someone–perhaps Dmitri's mother, perhaps an advisor–convinced Dmitri to pardon Shuisky, who then remained at court and resumed his intrigues against the tsar.[70]

The Pretender-turned-Tsar met his end on May 27, 1606. The alarm bell rang in the palace; Shuisky's henchmen confronted Dmitri's bodyguards. (Jacques Margeret was sick in bed that night and away from his post.)[71] Dmitri bellowed a warning to his wife and her ladies-in-waiting before squeezing himself through a window to escape. He broke his ribs and a leg in the fall. Musketeers fired at the assassins and tried to move the tsar to safety. The assassins instead pounced on the tsar and ran him through.[72] Marina Mniszhek might have been executed, too, but in exchange for abandoning the title of tsarina, she was freed from prison and sent away from Moscow in a caravan with some four hundred other Poles and all their belongings. She made it back to Poland after a year and a half in Yaroslav. Those foreigners who remained in Moscow suffered "cruel destruction," according to the Russian-born Englishman James Freese, who said he witnessed it firsthand. The Polish, German, and Hungarian cavalrymen in Pretender Dmitri's service were "massacred, and their houses rifled; their wives and children exposed to misery, and very many of them cruelly butchered by the rude multitude within the City of Moscow: which inhumane act caused a Sea of blood to have its current through many of the streets within the said City."[73]

And so there was another tsar, the nefarious Shuisky, modestly supported at first and then despised by everyone, including Margeret, who resigned from his post as soon as he could do so safely.[74] Shuisky claimed that he was the boyars' choice as ruler because he was of Rurik descent and a Suzdal prince.[75] But his reign was a protracted nightmare haunted by the past. His antagonists believed, or willed themselves to believe, that False Dmitri I, whom Shuisky worked so hard to exterminate, was the actual son of Ivan the Terrible and a legitimate ruler—not an imposter at all.

Shuisky's solution was to open a tomb in Uglich and prove that the real Dmitri lay there dead. The effort was futile. As Massa recounts, the remains had decomposed beyond recognition in the years since the boy's demise. Dmitri's tomb emitted nothing but an odor; there were no bones to be found. So Shuisky, not to mention the Orthodox Church, had a problem: Without physical proof of False Dmitri I's deceit, Muscovites would remain loyal to him and forever distrustful of Shuisky (much as they had been of Boris). There was a pause, and then an act of everlasting evil. Needing to bring the relics of the dead child, St. Dmitri, to Moscow, a fresh corpse was made available for veneration. Another child was killed. A delegation traveled from Moscow to Uglich to retrieve the coffin, and the people of Moscow followed. "I did the same myself," Massa notes, "as I was curious to see how this would end." The delegation bore the coffin into the Archangel Cathedral as the bells of Moscow's churches pealed; bishops went into the streets to describe the lame beginning to walk, while the blind could see and deaf hear. Massa sought to get into the Archangel to witness the miracles for himself. Instead, he witnessed "a sick man, or one who passed for such," brought into the church "to be restored to health." The smoke of the incense caused him to collapse and die, an event that the "charlatans" attributed to the old man's "faltered" faith.

"Thus did the Muscovites, sightless already, become even blinder," Massa concluded.[76] Subsequent events, however, indicate that the people were unimpressed by the miracles. Tsar Vasiliy was almost toppled for the charade. The body of the first False Dmitri, whoever he was and wherever he came from, was sent to hell in an elaborate hazing. First his corpse was dragged through a crowd, with a "minstrel's bagpipe" in his mouth.[77] Then the mutilated "sorcerer" was cremated in a movable siege tower painted with devils.[78] The anonymous child sainted in Dmitri's name found no greater peace. In 1812, French troops occupied the Kremlin and emptied the shrine to St. Dmitri, scattering the relics. The sin that produced those relics, committed by church and state, has never been acknowledged.[79]

Shuisky clung to power until July 1610, facing revolt after revolt, one led by a runaway serf, Ivan Bolotnikov, from the southeast, others instigated by princes, boyars, and even merchants. Margeret recalls a black comic episode in which Shuisky voiced his frustration with the efforts to oust him: "I am tired of such plots," he told a crowd of petitioners outside the Kremlin. "Sometimes you want to murder me, sometimes it is the nobles and even the foreigners [you're after]."[80] The bizarre appearance in the summer of 1607 of a second False Dmitri—a laborer, priest's son, or Cossack masquerading as the escaped False Dmitri I—fueled the crisis.[81] "There started a rebellion in the northern and Ukrainian cities," the Piskarev Chronicle reports, "where they said that Tsar Dmitri was alive, he'd fled, the defrocked monk was there, he hadn't been killed. And from those places, other scoundrels started calling themselves Tsar Dmitri as punishment for the sins of all Orthodox Christians."[82] There would be a bizarre second, then an even stranger third, fourth, and fifth self-styled Dmitri, each attracting the gullible and dispossessed to their cause and then, as narcissistic cult leaders are wont to do, reneging on their promises of food, salaries, and salvation.[83] Agents from the Polish-Lithuanian Commonwealth kept track of their activities and encouraged their activation for the sake of keeping Moscow unstable.

False Dmitri II established a base of operations in the town of Tushino in 1608 and harassed Moscow for two years with "ill-assorted" supporters from Poland, "malcontents" from within Russia, Cossacks, German mercenaries-for-hire, and a group of boyars, some from the Romanov clan.[84] (In one of the most vexing episodes of the entire *Smuta,* Marina Mniszech, wife of the first False Dmitri, opportunistically recognized the second False Dmitri as her husband.) To temper his influence, and those of other troublemakers draining resources and sapping whatever semblance of authority he possessed, Shuisky reached out to the Swedish king, Karl IX, for support. In exchange for a fortress, a couple of towns, and a pledge to leave Livonia alone, Shuisky received three thousand mercenaries (most of them non-Swedish) who ousted False Dmitri II from Tushino and fragmented his forces.[85] There was nothing benevolent about Karl IX's support, however. He was a cousin of the Polish king and the two of them were at each other's throats (while also both dealing with disquiet and unrest at home). The Swedes and Poles fought at Klushino, near Smolensk, at the end of 1609. The Swedes lost badly enough for Swedish soldiers to defect to the Polish side, and the Poles used them against the Russians. That event was the beginning of the end of Vasiliy's reign. According to James Freese, Shuisky had "exasperated the spirits of the Nobility against him" and "alienated" everyone else.[86]

The end of the end came when False Dmitri II's forces allied with the Poles against Moscow. Shuisky was deposed, sent to a monastery, then shipped with two of his brothers to Warsaw, where they were held in a small, dark cottage. A group of seven senior boyars filled the void in Moscow for a few months, then accepted an alliance with King Sigismund III. Fearing Russia's collapse, seeing the unrest on Moscow's streets, and worrying that another ghost from Uglich might seize power, the boyars invited several thousand soldiers under the control of Polish commander Stanisław Żółkiewski to watch the gates and man a Kremlin garrison.[87] The invitation marked the return of Jacques Margeret to Moscow, now in Poland's service, as part of an "elite brigade" of 950 foreigners buried deep inside the Kremlin, paid from the "dwindling treasury," technically protecting the seven boyars, but effectively looking after King Sigismund III's interests.[88]

The Polish monarch now had the chance to achieve his dream, "sparked by religious zeal," of installing "a pro-Polish, Catholic regime" in Moscow.[89] That ruler, a pretender of another sort, was his own son, Władysław, who was fourteen years old at the time. His nominal ascension to power is seen by most Russian historians, taking their cue from the *New Chronicle* of 1630, "almost as the visitation of a transcendental evil."[90] But Władysław had no real power and never actually set foot in Moscow. His father pulled the strings on the occupation, as did his envoy Żółkiewski and the harsher, crueler man who replaced him as Polish military overseer of Moscow, Alexander Gosiewski.

King Sigismund III's involvement in Moscow's affairs was not especially popular in Poland. He faced resistance from Polish magnates for his overreach, and he lacked the means to finance his effort to absorb westernmost Russia into the commonwealth. Without food and fuel, his soldiers lost morale. Looting sprees hardly endeared them to Muscovites, who were also deeply offended by the Poles' disrespect of their religious customs. Locals reminded the newcomers that the Eastern Orthodox Tsardom of Muscovy was hardly the Grand Duchy of Lithuania, amenable to absorption into the Polish Catholic space. Their unhappiness with the Polish guests (and the boyars who had extended the invitation) exploded when it became clear that Sigismund III had no intention of sanctioning his son's conversion to Orthodoxy as Russian tsar, as Żółkiewski had pledged would happen. It was a double cross of a deeply underhanded monarch indulging the fantasy that the Catholic and Orthodox Churches would somehow reunite, something that had been attempted in Florence back in 1439 with sorrowful results.

Gosiewski tried to keep his forces in line, first with words, which failed, and then by culling the ranks. A drunken, "heretical" Polish gunner by the name of Bliński pelted the icon of the Virgin Mary on the Sretensky Gate, which he and his *rota* had been assigned to guard. The boyars complained to Gosiewski, and Gosiewski ordered Bliński's execution for all to see. His hands were cut off and nailed to the gate, and the rest of him was tossed onto a pile of wood and set on fire. The boyars brought another complaint to Gosiewski, "that some Pole had shot at the cross on the top of a church tower with an arrow getting stuck in the dome." A nobleman's daughter came forth to accuse a Pole of violating her. He was given the death penalty, but a Polish officer named Bobowski suggested that the guilty party instead be punished according to Moscow law, with a beating in the street, which saved his life.[91]

For a while, the attacks on the Kremlin were rebuffed by Captain

Margeret's "elite harquebusiers."[92] The Polish side had gunpowder, the Russian side had knives—it was no contest. Still, the people with the knives kept coming, leaving Gosiewski and his advisors tussling with the conundrum of how much repression was too much. He prohibited the Orthodox celebration of Palm Sunday to keep people off the streets.[93] Then he imprisoned the patriarch, Hermogenes, who wasted away in his cell. Word of the high priest's martyrdom, and Gosiewski's attacks in general on the Orthodox faith, spread around. Soon the hunt was on for anyone with a Polish name and the "cursed Moscow traitors" who had collaborated with them.[94] Two organized rebellions took hold.

The Poles and their foreign allies held the advantage over the rebels so long as the liberators were at odds with one another (the Cossack factions of the rebellion intrigued against the gentry contingent) and they could keep themselves supplied through forays into the countryside.[95] With the fortifications under their control, Margeret's brigade could creep along the tops of the walls from the Kremlin to Kitai-gorod, Tsar-gorod, and back again. One of the ghastlier incidents happened in October 1610 at the "Tower of Seven Peaks" where the Tsar-gorod wall turned inland from the Moskva on the western side. The cannons were aimed at an area called the Crimean Ford, where Tatar horsemen had launched their raids. (Even before it was finished, the twelve-story spiked tower convinced a Crimean khan, Ğazı II Giray, not to cross the Moskva and invade.) The Poles in the tower, some three hundred in all, held off the Russians until a defector informed the rebels that the Poles had stashed explosives in the lowest tier. The rebels lobbed burning arrows through a slot in the wall, causing the entire tower to go up in flames. Those Poles who scaled down the sides of the tower on ropes to escape the flames were speared by bayonets.[96]

Another tower, on a bend in the Moskva just south of the Kremlin, also played a role in the conflict, this time to the Poles' advantage. The tower was called Chertol'ye (Chertol'skiye vorota), which highly suggestive legend translates as "devil's hole." It stood where the Great Fire of 1365 had started, after a candle or icon lamp fell over and set ablaze the pile of huts between the ravine and the Kremlin. That inferno was supposedly the revenge of the pagan god Perun on Holy Rus.[97] In March 1611, Muscovites mobilized for an assault on the Polish-Lithuanian garrison after erecting barricades, blocking off streets with sleds piled high with wood, and digging trenches close to the Kremlin in a "triangle bounded by the great white wall," while also arraying cannons on the opposite side of the Moskva. Margeret, monitoring the maneuvers from his perch in the garrison, noticed that the rebels had forgotten to secure the Chertol'ye entrance and thus protect their rear flank. He led his men from the garrison through the Kremlin's Secret (Taynitskaya) Tower, moved along the still-frozen ice of the Moskva to the "devil's expanse," and attacked the Muscovites from behind. Conrad Bussow, another soldier of fortune on the Polish side, boasted of the horrors inflicted. "Having levelled the Chertol'ye [tower] to the ground, our soldiers also went over to the other bank of the Moskva and there set fire to the redoubts and all the houses they could reach. No war cries or bells could help the Muscovites. Our soldiers were aided by wind and fire, for wherever the Muscovites fled they were followed by the wind and the flames, and it was plain that the Lord God wished to punish them for their bloody murders, perfidy, avarice, and Epicurean sodomy."[98] The target of Bussow's calumny is Shuisky, whom he had once served but turned against.

Gosiewski ordered entire swaths of Moscow reduced to "dung and ashes," something he had also done, using firebombs, to the city of Smolensk.[99] The first liberation movement ended with wives and children fleeing barefoot. Bussow recovered his moral compass to condemn his comrades' "degeneracy, whoring, and godless living" and the piles of "bacon, butter, [and] cheese" left to spoil in the burned-out basements. He decried the "arrogant" shooting of "pearls as big as peas or beans out of their muskets at the Russians" and the Polish officers who "gambled away at cards the children of prominent boyars." Foot soldiers and dead-enders stole "clothing, linen, pewter, brass, copper, and utensils, which they dug out of cellars and ditches and could have sold for more money, they left behind, taking only velvet, silk, gold coins, precious stones, and pearls. In church they stripped the saints of their silver vestments embroidered with gold thread, their stoles and the collars so richly ornamented with precious stones and jewels. Many Polish soldiers obtained ten, fifteen, or twenty-five pounds of silver torn from the idols, and those who set out in bloodstained muddy clothes returned to the fortress in costly garments."[100]

About fifteen hundred Poles and their allies remained in their garrison supported by reinforcements. They held hundreds of Muscovites prisoner and kept on the lookout for rebels entering the city from other parts. They were bored, hungry, and angry that their salaries consisted of baubles pulled from crowns and scepters instead of easily convertible gold coins. Discipline disintegrated in the garrison. Margeret, who was paid in "small gold crosses," departed what was left of Moscow for Warsaw, then left Sigismund III's service altogether, nauseated by the king's religious zealotry.[101] He was wise to exit the scene when he did. Poland's domination of Moscow ended in August 1612 thanks to a second liberation movement led by a vendor from Nizhny Novgorod named Kuzma Minin and Dmitri Pozharsky, a minor prince close to the throne during Godunov's reign.[102] Minin and Pozharsky's improbable collaboration ended the *Smuta* and a period of inaction, ineptitude, and "insane silence" on the part of Russia's "natural leaders."[103]

Ideologues, nationalists, tsars, and Russian Federation presidents love the tale of this couple, the hero of the peasant-worker "folk" who crowdfunded a rebellion (taxing the people of Nizhny Novgorod and convincing the people of other Volga towns to empty their purses for him, then using the proceeds to purchase weapons and pay soldiers), and the highborn representative of the "state" who despised the seven boyars for capitulating to King Sigismund III. Eighteenth-century historian Vasiliy Tatishchev gilds his fanciful description of Minin's rabble-rousing with an extravagant declaration of patriotism: "I'm prepared to surrender everything to my name, all I have, every last thing and more to this cause, my home, my wife and children, I'm willing to give it all up in service and aid of the fatherland. I'd prefer to see my entire family die in abject poverty than to witness the fatherland befouled and possessed by thieves."[104] But the embellishment of the tale began as soon as the *Smuta* ended, with the "author" of the Piskarev Chronicle describing Minin as an unprepossessing sort—and a "pagan"—who, like Robin Hood, took from the rich and gave to the "poor ruined folk" who had fled Moscow. Funds went as well to Pozharsky, the upper crust's choice to lead the rebellion.[105]

Painters, filmmakers, and composers loved them too. In 1811, the serf composer Stepan Degtyarev (1766–1813), sometimes called Russia's Haydn, produced a pleasant, solemn oratorio about Minin and Pozharsky. It was performed on Red Square in 1818 at the unveiling of a bronze statue of the hero liberators (still standing but cracked despite restoration efforts).[106] The singers and chorus embody freedom, love, sacrifice, patriotism, and a just "holy" war (the concept is expressed by the cellarer Avraamiy, the devoted nephew of a monastic scribe). Minin appeals to the people; Pozharsky, still recovering from a gunshot in the hand from a previous battle with the Poles in Kitai-gorod, agrees to lead the militia into battle, represented by march strains and preceded by choral prayers. The music rises heavenward, promising utopian triumph. The librettist Nikolay Gorchakov departs from the historical sources in the oratorio's third, final part. After defeating the Poles, Pozharsky relinquishes his command, claiming he does not need its "flattery."[107] The records indicate the opposite.

Pozharsky mobilized his men for the march into Moscow at the end of July 1612. The fighting on the streets was fierce for a few days, then sputtered; the battered, tattered Poles had no reserves and nothing to eat but one another, as described by a Kyivan merchant, Bozhko Balïka, who had reached Moscow with a caravan. His awful account is typical of other stories of the *Smuta,* which in later, better times titillated audiences both in Russia and the West. To call it apocryphal, however, is to discredit other eyewitness accounts that document comparable misfortunes. The merchant references the fierce Polish leader Jan Piotr Sapieha, nicknamed Pan Hetman, "Mr. General," and Mikołaj Struś, who was Gosiewski's replacement as commander of the Polish-Lithuanian garrison.

It snowed heavily on October 16, coating the grass and roots, everything. The hunger was unimaginable. We chewed on tugs and girths [from horse harnesses], belts and scabbards, icy bones and carrion. In Kitai-gorod near the Epiphany Church where the Greeks go, Suprun [another merchant] and I found several books of parchment and ate them with hay.... They paid for mice in gold; Pan Raczyński forked over eight coins for a cat, and Pan Budiłow's chief deputy coughed up fifteen for a dog.[108]

Thus ended a string of crises that historians struggle to understand. It's been safer, maybe saner, to focus on the family dramas and bureaucratic intriguing behind the violence. Other than Tsar Fyodor and his mother and uncle, no one was killed in the initial surrender of Moscow to the Pretender. Several people died from drinking in the cellars of disgraced boyars or arguing over booty, but that was it. The clapper swung back and forth for a few years, one self-proclaimed savior replacing another, then the belfry collapsed. The *Smuta* ended as it could only end: in mayhem.

King Sigismund III's reinforcements didn't make it to Moscow, giving the second liberation movement the opportunity to build barricades and station fighters across the Moskva from the Kremlin and on both sides of the Neglinka. By mid-October, after three weeks of shelling, Pozharsky and Minin's militia had expelled the Poles from Kitai-gorod and their garrison.[109] The triumph wasn't immediate: the Poles held the new patriarch, numerous dignitaries, and boyars captive as bargaining chips and were slow to commit to prisoner swaps and returned none of the loot found under the floorboards of merchants' and traders' houses.[110] Rather than surrendering power after his triumph, Pozharsky increased it. He presided over Moscow until the election of Mikhaíl Romanov as tsar—another contentious process, given the now adult Władysław's stubborn attempts to claim power in Moscow as Muscovy's other tsar—and then ran the police department (chancellery). Minin became a member of the boyars' duma. Soon, their heroism was forgotten along with the idea that when the Russian people are united, when "love is all around," as Pozharsky's bride sings in Degtyarev's oratorio, Russia is undefeatable. Despite their honorable and indispensable service to Moscow, Minin and Pozharsky ended up being "ignored, shoved aside, humiliated" by members of the new regime.[111]

On July 21, 1613, Mikhaíl Romanov took the throne. Memories of the *Smuta* fueled Russian animosity toward the Polish-Lithuanian Commonwealth, which weakened through the century and eventually dissolved, to Russia's great advantage. Despite the best efforts of the Romanovs to blame everything on Boris Godunov and the first False Dmitri, the Time of Troubles never quite ended. The Romanovs relocated the capital of Russia to an outpost on the Gulf of Finland named St. Petersburg and expanded the empire to include all the places outside that posed a threat to the inside, but even then the memories persisted, haunting all the future rulers of Russia— tsars and Communist Party bosses, presidents and dictators alike. The events of 1598 to 1613 lie beneath Russia's response to the Napoleonic invasion, the Second World War, the end of Communism, and even NATO's incursions into Eastern Europe some four centuries later.

SECOND CITY

7

FOREIGNERS

IN 1820, ALEXANDER PUSHKIN published *Ruslan and Lyudmila*, a mock epic about "days of yore" and souls "sold to the devil."[1] He tells of a prince rescuing his princess from a sorcerer, an enchanted garden, and the severed head of the sorcerer's brother. The hero isn't especially heroic, but he claims to be and that's the role he's in. The tale is an exotic, erotic adventure filled with stock characters who fail to fulfill their aims but, thanks to Pushkin's poetic magic, are glorified all the same. Such is Russia as defined in the chronicles and hagiographies. Half the time, the heroes don't know who their enemies are; the rest of the time they turn tail, leaving the protection of the fortress to the damsels in distress. And as bad as things get, those heroes seem happy—for the sake of adventure—to make them worse.

The histories of Russia's first major dynasty, the Rurik, overflow with these types of characters. Other than perhaps the paranoid and barbarous Ivan IV, it is difficult to imagine the rulers as real people. Each is reduced to the role, much like characters in fairy tales. Those roles may change as one tale is exchanged for another, but the characters themselves remain familiar, even predictable. More is known about how the Romanovs, the second major dynasty, beginning in the seventeenth century, thought and felt; they emerge from the sources as full-blooded and hotheaded. While living self-indulgent

lives of glittering balls and sumptuous tailoring, they built and maintained an empire.

In between was the "Polish" first False Dmitri. Moscow had been
a sedate place (though not for the reasons it is sedate today: increasing enforcement of public nuisance laws).[2] Culture had belonged to
the Church and the sacred sphere: icons, illustrated manuscripts,
monophonic chant. Moscow had no theaters, concert halls, galleries, or salons—just mummers and the occasional itinerant acrobat
and puppeteer. These performers, known in Russian as *skomorokhi*,
were popular in the taverns but disliked by the authorities for their
untidiness.[3] The noise began with Dmitri—not from fighting but
from entertainment, including, during his brief time in power, a
thing called music. For his coronation in 1605, and then for his marriage, Dmitri put on several parties that shocked and offended the
guardians of Orthodox Church tradition. The musicians he brought
from abroad jubilantly blew trumpets and shawms (a relative of the
oboe) and beat drums in and around the Kremlin. His bride, Marina
Mniszech, became tsarina to the sounds of polyphonic singing in
Latin, the language of the Catholic Church, far, far removed from
the Old Church Slavonic of the Orthodox tradition. This singing
was accompanied by violins and the organ—dozens of performers
in all.[4] Nothing of the sort had ever been heard before in Moscow,
where music had long consisted of bells and fanfares and the occasional modest harpsichord recital.

The Romanovs imagined Europe's secular culture, science, engineering, and civic institutions as models for transforming Russia.
The Eurasian landmass and its population needed enlightening:
Euclidean coherence, logical trains of thought, less talk of the soul
and more positivism. Change would come, but the developments
faced such stiff resistance in Moscow that another Russian capital
would need to be built to accommodate them. Meantime, the first
Romanov ruler, Mikhaíl, took the scepter and crown in the Kremlin happy to be alive and hoping to stay that way. The revolutionary
transformation of church and state was not top of mind. He needed
to rebuild Moscow.

The Romanov dynasty almost didn't happen, or it happened by

accident, at least according to an 1836 opera by Mikhaíl Glinka. Set in 1613, *A Life for the Tsar* finds the Poles patrolling the woods near Moscow, where the newly elected ruler is hiding in a monastery. They encounter a logger and demand to know the tsar's location; the logger leads them in the other direction, deeper and deeper into the dark, cold forest, where he is presumably killed by frost-bitten Poles for his duplicity. There's a kernel of truth in this telling. Mikhaíl was in fact difficult to find when he was elected tsar, a benign, banal consensus choice as ruler pushed into power at just sixteen years old by the *Zemskiy sobor*, which "intervened" to impose some order in Moscow after the parade of pretenders.[5] It took a month to track him down in a monastery near Kostroma. Told of his ascension, he burst into tears—of sadness or happiness or even teenage angst, no one knows.

Installing him in the ruined Kremlin was one thing, keeping him there another. He needed protection, experienced aides, and both of his parents giving him advice. Mikhaíl took his mother's counsel but chiefly followed the commands of his father, Patriarch Filaret, who had been held in gentle captivity in Poland until being liberated in 1619. (Several border towns were ceded to Poland in exchange for his release.) Filaret's return to Moscow was supposed to be triumphant, but the burned-out capital couldn't mount much of a celebration. Mikhaíl was relieved to have his father home, so he would no longer be pushed around by simpler figures. Filaret became, in effect, the ruler of Muscovy and the Orthodox Church. Documents co-signed by Tsar Mikhaíl and the "great sovereign" Filaret allowed the latter to run the government and the Church until his death in 1633. Only then did Tsar Mikhaíl's own reign begin. Filaret made Muscovy a much more suspicious and cynical place than it had been before the Smuta. He erased all connection to the first False Dmitri, who had treated him well, and told terrible stories about the Poles during the Time of Troubles. Anyone caught saying anything positive about the Pretender, he announced, was subject to severe punishment.

The second False Dmitri and his backers had leveled a huge part of the Moscow region, stalling the economy for a generation. Doors were missing, roofs damaged, floors covered in ash and dust. In 1634, the German ambassador Adam Olearius, passing through Moscow on a mission to bring Persian silk through the tsar's realm to Baltic markets, found out that there were some forty thousand ruined sites in Moscow. It was as if the fire of 1611 had just happened.[6] Stone, brick, lumber had disappeared; anything useful cost more than anyone could afford. Olearius was shocked by the amount he was charged in transit fees to pass through Muscovy by the impoverished government and had to send members of his team back to his employer, the Duke of Holstein-Gottorf, for additional funds.[7] The tsar tried to increase revenue wherever and however he could, but taxes were difficult to raise in the absence of people willing and able to pay them.[8]

A mapmaker in Olearius's delegation produced a bird's-eye view of Moscow showing buildings jumbled together amid broad lanes, galloping horses, and even scuffling children. Blackened roofs define the neighborhood where, according to the map's legend, "9,000 foreigners live, but the Tatars almost ruined."[9] The map shows the tsar's and the patriarch's residences, the Kremlin churches, the icon market, the prison, and "Hôtel de Ville" (City Hall) in Kitai-gorod. The Moskva and Neglinka Rivers lead the eye to the markets in Tsar-gorod and Skorodom, where fish, flour, and "grain for brewing beer" are sold. The map shows the past as well as the present. The former location of the Muscovy Company is given, so too a burial ground for foreigners and the place "where the Patriarch blesses the water on Epiphany"—in the snow and ice of January. From the distance, Olearius noted, Moscow's golden cupolas resembled Jerusalem. Inside, it was more like the cramped town of Bethlehem.[10]

The blight was a portent: evil spirits needed to be excised. The new Romanov regime focused on rooting out the remaining first and second False Dmitri supporters and hunting down anyone, foreign or domestic, suggesting they might have been genuine. Eliminating the resistance was the priority. Only then could Moscow be remade.

To secure the dynasty, Mikhaíl needed a spouse. His first bride, the daughter of a boyar, fell ill right after the wedding then coughed for three and a half months after. When she died, rumors imagined that she was punished for having been cruel to another boyar's daughter Mikhaíl might have chosen in her place. The rival had reportedly been poisoned, with her "bouts of vomiting" cited as proof of infertility. Thus, it was decided that Mikhaíl couldn't marry her. The might-have-been bride was exiled to Verkhoturye in the Ural Mountains, but the patriarch intervened and allowed her to live in Nizhny Novgorod, closer to Moscow. She hoped to reunite with Mikhaíl after the death of his first wife, but by then he had chosen a sturdier partner—or rather, one had been chosen for him by his mother.[11]

Mikhaíl's second marriage, to Eudoxia Streshneva, followed fast on the heels of the first, at the start of 1626. By that time the debris had been cleared from the Kremlin and some of the roofs repaired. The rebuilding buried the Byzantine-Italian architectural designs of the past beneath a Russian-designed royal residence, new and restored churches, and the extension of the Spasskaya (Savior) tower with a belfry and a clock—the first of three versions of the emblematic Kremlin chimes. (The offensive carvings of "naked human figures" were soon removed.)[12] Wedding celebrations spread over four days, longer than before, revealing an intentional effort to legitimate and cement Romanov rule through ceremony. Moscow had an unspeakably difficult past and so the government declined to speak of it, instead embracing a new founding. History seems to begin with the Romanovs, Mikhaíl's coronation, and his second marriage, celebrated by speeches and prayers that assured audiences past, present, and future that the throne had been restored to a rightful king by God. Voices of doom defined the beginning of his reign; by the end of it, life had returned to the streets.

Eudoxia bore ten children, cementing the reign of the Romanovs.[13] But when two boys, a newborn and a five-year-old, both died in 1639, worries swarmed the Kremlin about the tsar and tsarina's other son, the eight-year-old Alexei. He survived, so the line continued. Still, the two deaths left Eudoxia bereft and isolated. Something seemed afoul, and suspicions fell on the people with whom the tsarina had regular contact—from those who rode to work from Moscow's diverse neighborhoods to her ladies-in-waiting who lived alongside her. An aide to the tsar remembered a case, at the end of the previous year, involving one of the dressmakers, Dar'ya (Dashka) Lamanova, a "needlewoman" of the court. She'd been investigated for sprinkling ashes along the corridor near Eudoxia, and though cleared of witchcraft at the time, the death of two royal children reopened the case. Dar'ya was detained and compelled to explain herself anew. At first, she admitted to sprinkling the ashes and then, under threat of torture, confessed that she had indeed been spending time with a witch across the Moskva from the Kremlin. The witch, Nast'ya, was rounded up, shackled, and beaten to extract her side of the story, which squared with Dar'ya's. Both women insisted that the magic ashes were not meant to harm either the tsarina or the tsar, merely to earn them favor. To save her skin, Nast'ya gave up the name of another witch, who named three others, and soon an entire coven was exposed—just one more example of the witch trials that gripped West and East in the seventeenth century. Dar'ya was exiled with her husband to Siberia, and Nast'ya died in prison. Nothing was discovered about the cause of death of Eudoxia's two children. Ultimately, Tsar Mikhaíl's son safely became the next ruler of Russia, but fears of needles, pinpricks, and witches' curses linger in one of the most glorious artistic creations in Russian history: Marius Petipa and Peter Tchaikovsky's ballet *The Sleeping Beauty* (1890). The heroine, of course, falls victim to a spindle.

While tasked with locating and eradicating Poles and Swedes hiding in the forests of Muscovy, Mikhaíl tried to keep the peace. It wasn't easy. An administrator in the Posol'skiy prikaz, the Foreign Affairs Chancellery, sought to stoke Swedish anger at Poland to Russia's advantage at the same time his peer sought the opposite—détente—and the tsar's embittered father, Filaret, sought revenge against the Poles for having imprisoned him. Had Muscovy been solvent, had Russia's soldiers been properly equipped, trained, and motivated to fight, and had foreign mercenaries been available, Mikhaíl's rule might have been different. But because he didn't have those assets, he focused on restoration, not expansion. Mikhaíl enlisted foreign tradesmen to remake Moscow, and so, because these people stayed in the city and in some instances married and had families with Muscovites, Mikhaíl began a process of Europeanization that is often exclusively credited to a ruler at the other end of the seventeenth century: Peter the Great.[14]

Mikhaíl also expanded social services, at least for those living in and around the Kremlin. The complexes containing the chancelleries expanded to include the Aptekarskiy prikaz (Apothecary), which was founded in 1621. It served the tsar's family, his inner circle, and the boyars, often preparing reports on causes of death, treatments, medicines, and the medical or magical properties of roots and herbs.[15] Doctors came to Moscow from across Europe. Each received an estate of up to forty serfs and a living allowance of four barrels of honey and four barrels of beer a month along with firewood and 150 rubles for "fresh food."[16] The guards of the Aptekarskiy prikaz kept close tabs on the doctors, concerned that one of the outsiders might poison the tsar. Nothing of the sort was ever contemplated, but the paranoia persisted. (A misplaced paranoia: the enemies of the tsars were local, not foreign, including rival princes, resentful, disdainful boyars, and the peasant-workers on whose backs the tsars had created their wealth.) Mikhaíl's successor brought in a German doctor, Andreas Engelhardt, who was as much an occultist and astrologist as a practicing physician. His medicine bag contained exotic animal products, including, for the treatment of constipation, kidney stones, and for inflammation, crabs' eyes.[17]

The monasteries and churches had their own healers; the rest of the population was left to treat illness and disease with traditional folk remedies and the medicinal plants sold by grocers. Herbalists collected plants from special botanical gardens lining the Neglinka. Plants were dried, pulverized, and blended for the treatment of anything from headaches to indigestion, cramps, childbirth and menstrual pain, melancholia, and even the plague. The medicines were kept under lock and key and tested "on the bodies of the apothecaries and physicians themselves before they were administered to the imperial patients."[18] One of the laboratories processing these potions and tinctures survives as part of the Shchusev Museum of Architecture in Moscow's Arbat neighborhood.

When Mikhaíl began to suffer a combination of distress (related to his failure to secure a husband for his eldest daughter), "scurvy," and "dropsy," his caregivers tried to treat him with "Rhenish wine laced with various herbs and roots to act as a mild purgative" while also limiting the sovereign's access to food.[19] Mikhaíl passed out in church, folded himself into bed, and gave up the ghost in the summer of 1645.

The throne passed without challenge to his son Alexei, who faced an immediate crisis. The Kremlin desperately needed to increase revenue, so Alexei's closest advisor recommended a fourfold increase in the tax on salt. The new rate was rescinded after people rioted in the streets and several lower-level bureaucrats (not the advisor who suggested the tax in the first place) were arrested in a show of solidarity with the public. Alexei then went after the rioters, along with suspected arsonists, highway brigands, and sheep rustlers masquerading as minstrels.[20]

Another, much graver crisis that has never been forgotten in Moscow centered on a series of reforms that the archbishop of the Annunciation Church, the tsar's confessor, sought to enact as a member of the Circle of Zealots of Piety (*Kruzhok revniteley blagochestiya*), a group of reformist agitators demanding a purification of the liturgical books and a crackdown on drunkenness as well as the sinful singing and dancing that came with it.[21] The new patriarch, Nikon, joined their cause. He championed the idea of bringing the Russian Orthodox Church into alignment with the Greek Orthodox Church, which, he believed, had preserved more of the ancient Byzantine rituals than had Muscovy. Nikon was entirely wrong about the Greek liturgical books preserving a more ancient rite—they had changed a lot—but his reasoning, and Tsar Alexei's, was that Moscow, as the Third Rome, was obligated to save the Greek Church and all Orthodox people from the oppression of the Muslim Turks inhabiting Constantinople. Nikon assembled a group of grammarians and chant teachers to compile a list of changes to the Russian Orthodox books, which he then forced into effect. Greek practice was to become Russian practice, right down to the number of fingers (three) used for making the sign of the cross.

Paul of Aleppo, son of the Patriarch of Antioch and one of the suppliers of liturgical books of the Eastern Orthodox and Byzantine Churches to Moscow, recalled Nikon's actions during a sermon that lasted from three in the afternoon until ten at night in a freezing church. He demanded "some old and some new" icons brought to him. Nikon "cut out the eyes" on the icons painted in the German and Polish manner, smashed them on the floor, and demanded them burned. Tsar Alexei was shaken but being "pious and God-fearing" could do nothing to prevent the destruction beyond suggesting, in a nervous whisper, that the icons be buried—not burned. "This icon is from the house of a nobleman of such and such, the son of such and such," Nikon added in a dark tone. The bells rang and the service finally ended; the fatigued faithful had stood for seven hours on a metal floor in "bitter cold and penetrating damp." Paul and the other visitors from Antioch took a sleigh back to their monastic lodgings, but no sooner had they sat down to eat, "half-dead from fatigue," than the bells rang for the vespers service.[22]

Nikon faced resistance from a group called the Old Believers (or, more precisely, the Old Ritualists, *Staroobryadtsi*), who preferred the religion as practiced by their Russian ancestors. Had he been more diplomatic, or flexible, or lived less sumptuously in the rooms and halls that he had built for himself—detractors highlighted his affection for gold and silver stitching, goose down bedding, fur carpets, and artisan breads and pies brought piping hot to him by his personal baker—he might have avoided a confrontation.[23] Instead, he repudiated the Old Believers for their unwillingness to return to what he considered to be the purest ritual and they considered a foreign contamination. He also blamed them for the *Smuta*, arguing that the crises of the era resulted from the Church losing its way. Nikon persecuted the Old Believers for challenging his authority, but despite his and his successors' efforts to liquidate them, they survived in the hinterlands and never ceased castigating Nikon for Hellenizing the Church. Those who escaped the gibbet preserved religious traditions that the official Church and the Romanov tsars marginalized as they did paganism.

The proverb "god provided the priest, the devil the buffoon" sums up the attitude of the tsar and the patriarch to the *skomorokhi* and to all other entertainers, even those who performed good deeds, like bringing laughter to the infirm and the bereaved. Singing songs with "dirty words," the arbiters of morality believed, did to angels what smoke did to bees: frightened them away and welcomed demons to the table.[24] Alexei preferred falconry and the occasional recitation of religious verses to frolicking, though a famous line in his falcon-hunting manual, "time for business, an hour for fun," affirmed that leisure, in moderation, was good for the soul. In 1648, he wrote a letter to a warlord in Belgorod declaring his intention to "right morals and abolish superstition." The tone is harsh: Alexei promises the knout to singers and dancers, riddle-makers, spell-casters, quack healers, and anyone involved in pagan rituals (midnight bathing under a new moon, for example, or pouring wax into water seeking to divine the future from the resulting shape). The *skomorokhi* themselves were exiled "in disgrace," while the patriarch focused on the threat closer to home.[25] In 1653, he "ordered the seizure of musical instruments in the houses; once, five wagon loads were sent across the Moskva River and burned there."[26]

The situation was not as stern as these sources suggest. Nikon didn't succeed in banning music, and Alexei would come around to tolerating it, if not exactly enjoying it. Small harps and mandolin-like instruments could still be heard in the houses of the damned, and for every musician chased out of town another arrived, complementing the singing deacons of the tsar's court and the musical storytellers heard around Moscow. Not every song the minstrels sang was bawdy. The era witnessed the elaboration of a type of choral singing from either Poland or Lithuania, the *kant*, a transitional genre that bridged the realms of *peniye* (sacred singing) and *muzikiya* (pagan instrumental music), and became sufficiently festive to include cannons, bells, and fireworks, the distant inspiration for Tchaikovsky's *1812 Overture*.

While Alexei supported Nikon's efforts to cleanse the Church and the culture, he was more concerned with the present than the past. His gaze fell on Ukraine, then overseen by the Kingdom of Poland. Cossacks living along the banks of the Dnieper in present-day central Ukraine had been seeking independence from the

Polish-Lithuanian Commonwealth, so they appealed to Alexei for protection in exchange for their allegiance to Muscovy. In 1654, Alexei led his fighters into the fray and managed to win back the land Muscovy had forfeited to the commonwealth during the *Smuta*. Once Sweden became involved, a development known in Polish history as "the Deluge," Poland was forced into a humiliating truce with its neighbors.[27] Fighting extended from 1654 to 1667. During these years the plague returned to Moscow, and the crisis in the Church deepened. Taxes continued to rise, as did crime—mostly minor acts of mischief like stealing wood and scaring horses; a secret investigative office was established to root out treason.[28] With Alexei busy fighting Poland for control of Ukraine, the overzealous Nikon served as de facto tsar. He finally fell out of favor with Alexei, for reasons that have never been fully explained—perhaps because he believed that the Church should operate independently of the government, or perhaps because he had become, like the church books, corrupt.[29] Nikon lost his position in 1668.

Meanwhile, the rebuilding of Moscow continued. Alexei ordered able-bodied stonemasons, bricklayers, and potters to Moscow to repair the city's churches, palaces, and the dilapidated defensive walls—threatening to imprison the spouses and children of anyone refusing to leave their current places of employment to heed the call of the capital.[30] Not all the labor was necessarily essential: The pious Alexei hypocritically built a decadent palace for himself on an attractive bend of the Moskva where rulers as far back as Ivan the Great had summered.[31] The treasury authorized payment to a peasant named Ilyanka Ofseyev to transport 100,000 and then 1,100,000 bricks from the factory in Strogino, northwest of Moscow, to Kolomenskoye in the southwest, where the palace's foundation was laid after a prayer service in the spring of 1667. An artel of carpenters, blacksmiths, locksmiths, carvers, and gilders descended on the site under the supervision of the head of the tsar's fusiliers and the clerks staffing the Privy Chancellery (Prikaz taynïkh del). Simon Ushakov, an icon-maker and easel painter whose sensuous style caught the eye of Patriarch Nikon, and the engraver Bogdan Saltanov, who was dispatched to Moscow from Persia, added bright, fresh color to palace fittings.[32] By the time of Alexei's death, the palace had expanded into an asymmetrical layout of 270 chambers and 26 towers connected by a maze of corridors. The hierarchies in the sovereign's family found reflection in the room sizes. The most-used arch included a pair of roaring mechanical lions with glowing eyes. The Romanovs had arrived; the palace "shocked the imagination."[33]

The painting of secular pictures of the tsar and his family, to capture what Ushakov called "the life of the memory . . . providing immortality in praise and glory and an incentive to the living to emulate," took hold.[34] And the period witnessed the opening of the first theater in Moscow. Established in the 1670s, the elite (not public) playhouse was reserved for the tsar, higher-ranking members of the court, and their wives, who were separated from the men and enjoyed but partial views of performances. The theater moved around from the residence of the tsar's deceased father-in-law, Ilya Miloslavsky, to the upper floor of the apothecary and, beyond the Kremlin, to a building in the district of Preobrazhenskoye, a former village outside the northeastern fortifications.[35] The Miloslavsky residence, housing several women of the court, became known as the *Poteshniy dvorets*, the Amusement Palace. It had an unamusing future as the home of Iosif Stalin and the site of his second wife's suicide. The performance space (calling it a stage would be a stretch) was carpeted and curtained, illuminated by candles and reflectors. The performers were Germans who had settled in Moscow along with merchants from the Polish-Lithuanian Commonwealth.

The first performance on February 16, 1672, was a mélange of skits and dances meant to divert an audience of one. Thanks to his second marriage, Tsar Alexei was now in his second youth and a bit dissolute, putting aside governing for more than just falconry: he kicked back to enjoy fireworks, bearbaiting, and a foreign talent show featuring, among other oddities, a blundering, flatulent stage clown named Pickle Herring.[36] An artist from Hamburg, Peter Engels, painted backcloths when he wasn't busy decorating Moscow's churches and palaces in the Kremlin Armory.[37] The Hamburg newspaper *Nordischer Mercurius* (Nordic Mercury) reported the atypical happenings in the Kremlin, which included a ballet of sorts and passing mention of the tsar's fear of trickster fiddlers corrupting souls.[38]

The operation grew for three years, then ended. In its final season, a dozen different plays were mounted in Preobrazhenskoye. A tutor to the tsar's children, Simeon Polotsky, was enlisted as playwright. He produced a play about King Nebuchadnezzar, who cast three boys into a blazing furnace for their refusal to worship a false idol. His script had its origins in the *Service of the Furnace*, performed annually before Christmas in Moscow and other ecclesiastical centers in Russia. In the source biblical narrative from the book of Daniel, King Nebuchadnezzar sees the three boys dancing inside the furnace with the angel. The performance for the tsar included *skomorokhi* in the role of ruffian accomplices of the King. They had been banned from the public square but were sanctioned for the tsar's private entertainment.[39]

Alexei's sudden death in 1676, at forty-five years old, put an end to the private theater. Church conservatives carped about Alexei living an extravagant life inside palace walls while the wrath of God loomed on the frontier. His Amusement Palace seemed a shocking intrusion into the hearts and minds of the faithful and a betrayal of his faith; it was even considered the cause of his premature demise.[40]

The *Smuta*, the beginning of the Romanov dynasty, the nascent impulse to Europeanize, the influx and fear of foreigners, the fracturing of the Church, the first theater—Moscow had changed politically, religiously, and culturally. Some of these changes had been anticipated, but the greatest of all, Moscow's replacement as the Russian capital, could not have been foreseen. Surely such a thing was impossible, yet the impossible happened. Now Russia was dominated by two places: new and old. The new, St. Petersburg, accommodated the "modernizing" influence of the European Enlightenment and indeed was intentionally designed for it. The old, Moscow, resisted Europe—and still does. As the center of Slavophile culture, it considers itself the real home of Russia, the essence. From a Slavophile standpoint, however, the real home of Russia is not in Russia at all but Ukraine and Kyiv.[41]

The capital moved to St. Petersburg in 1712 at the behest of Peter the Great, the grandson of the first Romanov ruler and the most notable of all eighteen. (He officially founded St. Petersburg in 1703 and relocated his family and aides there in 1710.) He was baffled by the realm he inherited, so much so that he rejected the customs and rituals of Muscovy even as the broader population clung to them. He learned the hard way that some of the boyars, all the Old Believers, and most of the *streltsï* were his enemies. Peter hid from them as a child and tried to escape them as an adult. He ran off to Europe, exploring the shipyards, the academies and schools, and the political systems. Although he rejected Moscow, he brought public theater to the city, after which came public opera, ballet, and a homegrown literature that grappled with themes of power and violence while drawing on the chronicles, folklore, paganism, and even the trauma of the *Smuta.* The door to secular culture opened without the support of the Church, which resisted anything to do with Peter the Great's Europeanization of Muscovy.

His rise to power was an accident of good timing and good, or at least adequate, genes—he was healthier than his rivals and had his wits about him. Tsar Alexei had fathered sons with each of his two wives. Fyodor, the eldest surviving son of his first wife, succeeded his father but died of scurvy just five years into his reign and did not produce an heir. The absence of an obvious successor to Fyodor brought the families of Alexei's two wives into conflict. Peter was the first child of Alexei's second wife, thus a threat to the ambitions of his first wife's family to place the younger son on the throne as Ivan V. He enjoyed the support of a boyar named Ivan Khovansky but was almost as sickly as Fyodor and so was declared unfit for rule. The problem was discussed by senior boyars in the palace chambers, and they decided, with the patriarch's blessing, that the next tsar should be Peter.

Khovansky disagreed, and in May of 1682, he organized an uprising that placed him in charge of Moscow's *streltsï.* There were about twenty thousand of these musketeer guardsmen distributed into garrisons of several hundred each. Most lived with their families in wooden compounds south of the Moskva, and they received this housing along with coats and boots, grain, and weapons in lieu of salaries. When they weren't at their posts, they traded and operated businesses. The reasons for the uprising are multiple: Khovansky's antipathy toward Alexei's second wife and bond with the family of his first wife; low morale among the *streltsï* and the theft of income they made from trading; incitement from inside the Kremlin. Rumors spread that Ivan V had been murdered to promote Peter, though these proved false. Clashes on the streets led to a full-blown riot and a storming of the Kremlin, the lynching of antagonistic boyars, and the impalement of two of Peter's relatives right in front of him— a horror that haunted him on his deathbed.[42] A truce of sorts was reached when Ivan V and Peter were named co-rulers with their sister (Peter's half sister) Sophia, the educated, intelligent daughter of Alexei's first wife, as regent. She became de facto ruler, forming a court of her own.

Sophia had a comfortable but "static" upbringing in the *terem*, dressed in furs and satin and gowns of gorgeous reds and purples and colors in-between that the Russian language of the seventeenth century expanded to describe. She and her siblings played with dolls and painted toys, became expert at chess, prayed and went to church, and laughed at the antics of the male and female dwarves tasked with entertaining them in the Kremlin. Sophia read thick religious poetry that even priests found heavy going. She learned Polish but did not travel to Poland, or anywhere else besides the churches and monasteries in and around Moscow. As regent, Sophia maintained a balance among competing factions and kept feuding cousins at arm's length. The cult that developed around Peter in his glory years devalued his sister's achievements, reducing her to a toxic presence in the Kremlin, so power-drunk as to plot his murder. Her rise to power was abetted by a boyar she took as a lover, according to one novelistic account, while another, contradicting the first, claimed "she had none of the physical charms to seduce men to her cause." As ever, fiction here fills a void: Sophia's life was not documented save for references to her deeply pious education and her championing of some of the social and political reforms that historians would credit to Peter. Meantime the half-witted Ivan V busied himself with occasional ceremonial duties, the most he could do, and Peter indulged his hobbies. He learned about soldiering and became obsessed with ships and all things nautical.[43]

A skilled power-player, Sophia remained in charge past the age— sixteen—that Peter might have assumed the throne. She focused on foreign affairs: Russia's relationship with the Ottoman Empire, the Polish-Lithuanian Commonwealth, and the Swedish king, Charles XII. On April 26, 1686, in Moscow, after long and tedious negotiations, an "Eternal Peace" agreement was signed by Russian and Polish-Lithuanian envoys. Poland gave up control of Kyiv and the east side of the Dnieper River to Moscow for 146,000 rubles in compensation. Moscow, in turn, pledged to protect Poland against the Crimean Tatars. The first part of the deal was a triumph for Sophia, the second part a disaster that hastened the end of her rule. By taking the fight to the Tatars, Russia entered a long-term war with the Ottoman Empire. Nevertheless, her supporters, hoping to keep her in charge, considered both boys unfit to govern. There was talk about her extending her rule, but her detractors condemned her for the failure of the campaign against the Crimean Tatars, while also carping about her lavish spending and immodesties.

Throughout Sophia's regency, Peter lived with his mother outside of Moscow in Preobrazhenskoye. On August 6, 1689, he heard "rumors unsafe to be uttered," about an assassination attempt. Patrick Gordon, a Scottish general in the Russian service, reported that, on the next day,

> the tempest broke. At midnight, tidings reached the Tsar Peter that the Strelitzes and soldiers of the guard had received orders from the Kremlin to march upon Preobrazhenskoye, and to put certain persons to death. He instantly sprang from his bed, and without waiting to pull on his boots, ran to the stables, and flinging himself upon a horse, galloped to the nearest wood. Here he remained till his clothes were brought him, when, accompanied by a few attendants, he renewed his flight, and riding in hot haste, reached the monastery of Troitzka [the Holy Trinity], about forty miles from the capital, by six o'clock in the morning. Throwing

himself upon a bed, he burst into tears, and telling what had happened, besought the protection and help of the abbot.[44]

The crisis lasted four days, during which time Sophia gradually lost her base of support and control of Moscow. The patriarch joined Peter in the monastery and several *streltsï* units switched to his side, which allowed him to march into Moscow to claim power. The first known diary (*dnevnik*) from Russia includes a confession of sorts from three boys who had kissed the cross in front of an image of Nicholas the Wonderworker and accepted a bribe of 200 rubles to do an "evil deed": backing Ivan Khovansky in his bid for power during Sophia's regency. Besides rubles, Khovansky promised the boys rights and privileges in the Russian trading market, which, because they were so poor, seemed like an excellent arrangement to them. Sophia grew suspicious of Khovansky after receiving reports from regular Muscovites concerned for the safety of Peter and Ivan V. She advised the three boys to hide outside of Moscow. Fear of torture, or worse, kept them from revealing their names. They identified themselves differently: "One of us has a black wart on his right shoulder, another has a scar across his thigh on his right leg, and we'll give the name of the other later, because he has no such markings."[45]

Sophia ended up in the Novodevichiy Convent, a fortunate fate, given that Peter could have broken her on the wheel. Instead, her life remained much like it had been before her regency. She kept her nurse and her suite of chambermaids and seamstresses, and frequently received deliveries of "bread, fish, honey, beer, vodka, and other victuals."[46] Her siblings visited her, and she learned about Peter's travels as tsar, the agreements he signed, the battles he won and lost, and the scores he settled at home with his enemies—chiefly the *streltsï*. He kicked them out of Moscow, banishing them to Russia's farthest reaches, and replaced them in the capital with better-equipped fighters commanded by foreigners. Still, Sophia retained supporters among the *streltsï* and, in 1698, fell under suspicion for conspiring with them against Peter. The secretary of the Austrian ambassador in Moscow at the time, Johann Korb, heard rumors about Sophia communicating with the rebels with notes tucked inside loaves of bread.

"And that loaf of which they meant to make the bread of death to so many innocent people, led to their own richly deserved ruin," Korb comments. Though intrigue swirled around Sophia, Peter spared her, but not her musketeer favorites, whose frozen corpses hung outside her tower windows through the winter, "so near that Sophia might with ease touch them." It was the coda to his systematic elimination of the guardsmen who had so long threatened his power, and whom he replaced in two phases: first with the regiments and a security apparatus he set up in Preobrazhenskoye, then with foreign-trained fighters. When spring came and buzzards started gathering, Peter ordered the bodies buried and the heads displayed on stakes. Sophia, Korb claims, took "the religious habit" out of remorse, "in order to pass to a better life."[47]

Korb must have been terrified seeing these horrors in person, but he doesn't much express it. In his description of his ambassadorial duties, he lingers on the details of the suffering. The focus in most other accounts of Peter's reign falls on his improbable achievements: the blow he dealt to the Turks; the fight he took to the Swedes; the founding of St. Petersburg; the transformation of the Russian governmental structure; the first newspaper (though it was actually just a newsletter, and limited to celebrating his achievements).[48] The events Korb highlights are downplayed in the official histories of the Romanov era, along with Peter's impulsiveness and the mess of half-realized plans he left behind when he died. The playacting of his youth lasted well into his adulthood, with his circle of advisors and confidants brought into his fantasy world and forced to cavort with him in Falstaffian fashion. Reality was defined by the people of the court of Preobrazhenskoye, where he was raised, and the "foreign settlement" of Moscow, which he visited frequently, and which soured him on the traditions of old Rus. He behaved like a stranger in his place of birth.

The name of this area of Moscow is sometimes translated as the German settlement, or Nemetskaya sloboda, and not just because Germans made up part of the population. *Nemetskaya* distantly derives from *nemoy,* "mute," meaning the people in Moscow who could not speak Russian. Foreign craftsmen had been a presence in Moscow since the fifteenth century. Some had been brought to Moscow as prisoners and could not leave their dwellings; others came of their own free will. Ivan the Terrible allowed them to settle in the wetlands between the Yauza River to the east and south and a creek called Kukuy to the west. Instead of paying them, he allowed them to operate distilleries, which made them rich. Tsar Alexei had ordered those foreigners unwilling to convert to Orthodoxy to relocate their residences to a plot of fertile, well-irrigated land northeast of Moscow on the road to Preobrazhenskoye. According to a 1665 census, the New Foreign Settlement, as it became known, grew to around two hundred courtyards and included Lutheran and Catholic churches and several factories. Who was living with whom, adults and children, is recorded, along with their professions, religions ("of catholic faith," "Jewish"), and ranks ("lieutenant," "corporal"). Nimble-fingered lacemakers gravitated toward tailors and gold-thread embroiderers; metalworkers resided with one another, so too clockmakers and jewelers. A bell founder from Nuremberg named Hans Falk lived near the Swedish glassmaker Julius Koet, who kept Moscow's first laboratories stocked with flasks.[49] And Andrey Vinius, the son of the Dutch metallurgist brought to Russia by Tsar Mikhaíl, lived near them. He made himself indispensable in Peter's government, translating Dutch and German newspapers, running the foreign mail service (operating between Riga and Moscow), then administering the pharmacies, and then the Siberian copper and saltpeter mining operations. He seems to have worked hard, though not hard or efficiently enough to please Peter, who accused him of incompetence and confiscated his properties, serfs included.[50] Johann-Gottfried Gregorius opened a pharmacy on a street that picked up the name Aptekarskiy pereulok (Apothecary Lane).[51]

By the time Peter reached the throne, the area had become an oasis of comfort and cleanliness, with straight, cobbled streets, lampposts, gardens, and tidy houses with flower beds. On Sunday after church, people played music and danced. Peter liked what he saw; he wanted all of Moscow to be like the neighborhood. He met two of his closest advisors in the New Foreign Settlement, and took Anna

Mons, the eighteen-year-old daughter of a German wine merchant, as a mistress. He had all but forgotten his marriage to the fair of face but old-fashioned girl his mother had chosen for him, Praskovya (Eudoxia) Lopukhina, who bore him three children then spent her later years in a convent, at Peter's order.

Peter, like his predecessors, brought foreign talent to Moscow. In 1699, a short, skinny, fourteen-year-old castrato singer named Filippo Balatri was sent (loaned) to Moscow with his parents' consent by the Grand Duke of Tuscany. In exchange, the duke, who had a perverse "passion" for exotic flesh, was gifted two children from the North Caucasus.[52] Balatri lasted two years bouncing around Moscow, first living in the Kremlin and then, tired of being called a Catholic "dog" by the court pages, relocated to the residence of a prominent boyar, spending afternoons in the women's quarters learning to embroider.[53] Though his diaries are lost, he wrote up a couple of accounts of his adventures in the East, including a trip along the Volga River to Astrakhan, where he sang for a khan, Ayuki. "Soldiers fought over the mutton bones tossed from the khan's pavilion," he recalled of the encounter, and a servant boy "licked the plates clean between courses." Balastri saw the bodies of rebellious *streltsï* hanging from posts at the entrances to Moscow and assumed they were Catholic martyrs. His anecdotes and images include the widow of a carpenter describing her husband as a good man "who only beat her when he was drunk and only drank on Sundays"; a laundress who lived in a single room in the New Foreign Settlement with her husband, a cradle, a dog and a cat, and a couple of chickens; mothers using cow horns with sponges stuck in the ends as baby bottles; and the "low-class people" of Kitai-gorod fingering the pearls of his ballroom attire "with hands greasy from the pastries they were eating." In general, he liked the people he met, calling them "agile, active, sturdy, affectionate, and although quick to anger, just as quickly appeased." The tsar, Balatri remembers, dumbfounded the shut-in noblewomen of Moscow by telling them, essentially, to get a life. Peter encouraged them to socialize with the "heretics" of the New Foreign Settlement and to "learn how to sew shirts, coifs, bodices, and cuffs; to cut and curl their hair, and put on powder; to squeeze, beat, starch, press, flail, [and] shave" as Europeans did. Balatri sang Italian arias but also learned Russian songs. He took a liking to Peter's "angelic" mistress, and she to him, and so was invited to spend evenings with her and the tsar in her father's "magnificently decorated" residence, which still stands in Moscow, though it is in terrible condition, having been converted into a warehouse for a factory (now closed) at the Baumanskaya Metro station.[54] It is hard to imagine that the building had once dominated a splendid courtyard with space for dozens of carriages to roll up for candlelit balls, with a windmill and orchards and gardens behind it. Somewhere inside the crumbling walls, the Russian emperor once accompanied a teenage Italian castrato on the harpsichord.

Peter also encouraged members of his court to travel to Europe for their edification. For a land-based people who did not, as a rule, cross borders, the exchange was unprecedented. He also took himself abroad, announcing a European diplomatic mission headed by three ambassadors tasked with building a coalition against the Turks. From March 1697 to July 1698, Peter traveled with the group not as tsar but as the captain of the Preobrazhensky regiment, leaving his formal title behind so that he could pursue his personal interests incognito. In truth he stood out like a sore thumb and everyone knew who he was.

Leaving was a dangerous thing to do. Peter entrusted the running of the government to a cousin, an uncle, the Scotsman Patrick Gordon, and the head of a secret police force he had set up for self-protection, Prince Fyodor Romodanovsky. Gordon had long been one of Peter's companions and in his memoirs recalled evenings with the tsar featuring fireworks—"a five-pound rocket went wrong, and carried off the head of a boyar"—and a hangover so severe as to cause "violent vomiting and diarrhea" for four hours.[55] Gordon was partly responsible for the strategy that secured Peter's first military victory: the capture of the Turkish coastal fortress of Azov in 1696 using groups of Cossack fighters, ramparts, and ships filled with gunpowder sent burning toward Turkish boats.[56] The end of the battle is recounted by the diplomat Zelyabuzhsky in his diary: "And on the 19th [of July], that is, on the day of Christ's resurrection [Sunday] . . .

Azov's inhabitants surrendered the banners, cannons, gunpowder reserves and all the other supplies in the city to the commander of our large regiment. They and their wives and children were freed and released down the Don River to the Kagalnik River in 18 longboats."[57] Capturing the fortress convinced Peter that Muscovy's security and prosperity depended on seafaring fleets, not the small riverboats of the past. The henchman Romodanovsky was an even more trusted associate. He served as Peter's bodyguard and enforcer, rooting out threats to the tsar. He and Gordon kept suspicious watch over each other and Peter's ambitious relatives during the tsar's travels.

Peter brooked no dissent, and his secret police made life deeply unpleasant. Steal a coin and face severe punishment. Korb expressed an interest in the details not dissimilar to the incunabula about Dracula, especially stories about impaling Turks. "The torture that was applied was on unexampled inhumanity," Korb writes of an interrogation of rebels happening in a "pleasant neighborhood" of Moscow. "Scourged most savagely with the cat [o' nine tails], if that had not the effect of breaking stubborn their stubborn silence, fire was applied to their backs, all gory and streaming, in order that, by slowly roasting the skin and tender flesh, the sharp pangs might penetrate through the very marrow of their bones, to the utmost power of painful sensation. These tortures were applied alternately, over and over again."[58] He and other foreigners knew about the tortures because Peter boasted of them, inviting diplomats to take in his "spectacles of suffering."[59]

In Riga, then under Swedish control, Peter asked to inspect the fortifications of the governing fortress but was refused, an insult that he never forgot to Sweden's regret, because it turned his attention from the Ottomans to Sweden and convinced him of the need to gain access to the Baltic Sea coast. From there, his entourage of 250 people, including four dwarves, six pages, doctors, soldiers, and trumpeters, traveled to Mitava (Jelgava), the capital of a princedom called Courland, and on to Konigsberg, where Peter inspected weapons and concluded a trade agreement. Holland gave him an education in his cardinal obsession: ships. The ruler of Russia apprenticed as a carpenter at the Linsta Rogge shipyard in Zaandam, living in the small wooden house of a blacksmith that the Dutch immediately turned into a museum, and then worked at one of the wharves operated in Amsterdam by the Dutch East India Company, fixing pumps, mending sails, climbing up rigging and perching on crosstrees. He studied windmills, roamed botanical gardens, and, at Amsterdam's Anatomical Theater, observed autopsies. (To enhance his entertainment, he supposedly forced one of his courtiers to bite into the flesh of a corpse.)[60] In his later years, Peter bought a collection of anatomical "art" for what became Russia's first public museum. It included reptiles in flasks, embalmed tissue and organ samples from animals and humans, and, shockingly, "the exposed brain of a decapitated child, his face perfectly preserved in a jar; the severed arm of a child, dressed up in lace sleeve, holding an eye socket or an enlarged bladder."[61] He collected freaks of nature, and was viewed as one. The newspaper *Post Boy* reported boys in Zaandam throwing rocks at the strange man in the blacksmith's house. The authorities subsequently announced severe punishments for anyone mistreating the visiting Muscovites.[62] In England in 1698, as a guest of the king living in a house overlooking the Thames, Peter continued his education in shipbuilding, studied frigates and sloops, glimpsed a session of the British House of Lords through a window, and attended the theater, which he had no prior knowledge of and struggled to understand.

Europeans attributed his oddities to his Russianness. Russians attributed his oddities to his Europeanness. His love life was a protracted scandal; he pretend-adopted peasant customs and a rustic look, developing a taste for cabbage soup and *kvas* (a drink made from fermented black bread); he insisted that his closest aides drink to excess like he did, *za kompaniyu,* for solidarity's sake; and he avoided the fussier ceremonies of tsardom like the plague. The devil had him in his clutches. He never wore the pectoral cross all Muscovite rulers had worn before him. The patriarch warned him that (Catholic) Patrick Gordon was a danger to the Russian Orthodox Church. He ignored the patriarch.

Most of the portraits of him are fanciful, suggesting a man of noble grace and bearing, groomed, buttoned-up, as polished as the ceremonial dagger around his tight waist, a blaze of glory. A lesser-known portrait has him in battered shoes and a hat (complete with a bullet hole), and socks that he had mended himself. The average Russian male was about five-feet-three at the time, whereas Peter was a giant at six-foot-seven. He slumped, lurched, and, according to a report from London, suffered from "a nervous convulsion which sometimes transformed his countenance, during a few moments, into an object on which it was impossible to look without terror." The affliction was hardly surprising, even for a ruler with his own staff of caregivers. Everyone had some sort of defect; abnormalities were normal. The same reporter described a jester, or "fool," who "jabbered at [the tsar's] feet" and, even more oddly, a "monkey" grinning "at the back of his chair"—all the while making sure that his readers knew that the land Peter ruled had no schools, no bound books, no one who knew more than a smattering of Latin, and no one in the treasury who could count without the aid of "balls strung on wires."[63]

Returning to Moscow from his travels, Peter imagined putting what he had learned into effect, bewildering the nobles, boyars, and secretaries running the chancelleries with talk of transforming the government. But it couldn't be done on the spot; the most he could immediately introduce were the latest methods for punishing and extracting confessions from rebels. So much for the European Enlightenment.[64]

Peter changed the calendar so that years began to be numbered from the birth of Jesus rather than the creation of the world, and the New Year was set on January 1 instead of September 1. (Several calendars were in use in Europe, and the control of time was becoming a tool for the control of people, how and when they paid taxes or celebrated the savior; Peter claimed an interest in bringing Russia into alignment with those other European Christian and Slavic countries "that profess the Eastern Orthodox faith.")[65] He introduced lighter European-style clothing for his subjects, and, after he returned from his European sojourn, made a show of pulling off the gravy-stained sleeves of boyars. Judging from the mannequins that he put up at Moscow's gates, the look he adopted for his subjects was Hungarian and French and meant to replace traditional robes, long coats, and boots.[66] Needing to bring in revenue and hoping to improve hygiene, he imposed a draconian tax on facial hair. Those who wanted to maintain their bushy beards, as God intended them to do, had to pay for the privilege: an annual tax of 60 rubles per person.[67] Few could afford the tax, even among the elite; buying an estate, or a family of serfs, cost less. Despite efforts to fleece peasants a kopeck for passing through the gates of Moscow with their facial hair in perfect integrity, the tax was a failure. Peter had made shaving the norm in 1698, ceremoniously taking a razor to the beards of boyars himself. Seven years later, there were too few beards left among the ruling class to generate significant revenue and chasing after them wasn't worth the effort. For noblemen, bushy beards declined in popularity.[68]

He ordered the construction of a new public theater on Red Square with a stage and "lowering machines" (fly systems).[69] It seems to have been a space for Peter to gaze upon himself, and for his subjects to gaze upon him. When he realized that the playhouse might need some actors, which Moscow did not have, he sent a street entertainer (puppeteer) named Johann Splawski to the frontier to find some. In Poland, Splawski located a small group of comedians and recruited them to perform in the future "Comedy Temple" on Red Square.[70] The comedians had been traveling around in the company of an actor-turned-entrepreneur named Johann Christian Kunst, whose last name means "art." Having heard that Muscovites bullied foreigners, Kunst balked at the idea of going to Moscow until Peter offered him a hefty fee for his services.

Kunst moved to Russia with his wife, Anna, also an actor, and seven other comedians who doubled as costume-makers. Besides performing, Kunst's duties in Moscow included giving acting lessons to the sons of Russian merchants and clerks. He might not have been the most charismatic teacher: of his nineteen initial student actors, the number soon dropped to twelve. He was also responsible for choosing the repertoire, selecting works about heroic triumph that would appeal to Peter.[71] His greatest challenge was the translation of German playscripts into Russian; frankly, he was not up to it. The playscripts, which had earlier been translated from Italian and French into German, were an unidiomatic, semi-coherent mess and translating them from German into Russian made the mess worse. "Merciful devil," for example, became "scab-loving dog."

Construction of the theater was postponed, repeatedly, owing to arguments about its location. It was to have a place of honor in front of the Nikolskaya tower on Red Square, after the initial site—a trash heap—was rejected. The bureaucrats tasked with the project dilly-dallied until their supervisor in the foreign affairs chancellery tore into them, accusing them of sabotaging the project and threatening Peter's wrath: "Are you really so busy? Here we've more to do and more problems but things haven't fallen behind. As you were told, you need to hurry up building the silo [theater] before the Sovereign's arrival."[72] The delays forced Kunst to present his first shows, including one about the tsar's role model Alexander the Great, in the former residence of a Swiss admiral in Peter's service. The audience included the highborn and rank and file, Russians and Germans, men and women (sitting next to one another), diplomats and shopkeepers. Some chose to smoke during the performance, a fire hazard that sparked arguments and fights.[73] For people with "traditional sensibilities," the bad behavior reinforced their belief that theater of any kind was a profanation of God's word and deed.[74]

When Kunst died in February 1703, the Comedy Temple fell into the hands of Otto Fürst, a goldsmith who claimed to know more about the theater than he actually did. He oversaw the completion of the Comedy Temple, which boasted a large, grooved stage, pulleys and levers, storage closets, and an auditorium planned in tiers with benches on the floor, stalls and boxes above. Huts outside served as changing rooms. An orchestra was assembled thanks to the largesse of a German banker, the recruiting efforts of a Russian envoy in Berlin, and musicians from Poland and Holland.[75] The ensemble increased in size and—owing to Peter's affection for drums and trumpets—discord. Admission ranged from a *grivna* (ten kopecks, the price of a cartload of birch firewood) for a box to three kopecks, the cost of a couple dozen eggs, for a bench seat in the back.[76] Attendance spiked when the sovereign turned up: people came to gawk at him and take in the festive atmosphere. On these occasions, the police kept the gates of the Kremlin, Kitai-gorod, and the outer fortifications open later than usual, until 9 p.m., and granted free access to Red Square (the equivalent of congestion fees were usually charged to enter the center of the city). The sovereign unconvincingly urged everyone to enjoy themselves "freely and without fear."[77]

It was forced fun, the performances baffling and strange even as allegories for Peter's aspirations and achievements. And they spilled beyond the walls of the theater into the streets: "the Russian acting pupils without any permission have taken to going out with swords naked in their hands," an observer complained. "They take things from the market stalls without paying for them. And every sort of insult and humiliation are inflicted on merchants and other classes of people."[78] Muscovites stopped buying tickets, and in 1707, when the city was preparing for conflict with Sweden, the Kunst-Fürst theater and surrounding stalls were disassembled. Then everything else that Peter had done ended.

Peter never stopped thinking of his rule as a kind of performance. He playacted the position he occupied until the end, gaming out different scenarios for his empire-in-the-making with his aides, who played along with him because they had to, mindful that he was in charge and could at any moment shun them or, for amusement, douse them in alcohol and set them alight. His greatest performance as tsar took place on a speck of land won from Sweden in the Great Northern War. There he built a fortress named after his patron saint: St. Petersburg. An unpleasant place to live, it became the capital of Imperial Russia. St. Petersburg often flooded, as opposed to Moscow, which burned. To shore it up, Peter enlisted peasants to sink stones into the water.

His biggest achievements—the Senate and the Table of Ranks (which his half brother had begun to set up before him), a police force "in imitation of the French Lieutenant-Général de Police" of Paris, neoclassical palaces and gardens, the Academy of Sciences— are all associated with St. Petersburg.[79] No amount of force could make these things happen in Moscow and so none did happen in Moscow. The European performances and their stock characters moved north, along with the institutions of secular government and the foreign influences. Peter disliked Moscow, and the people he left behind—the traditionalists, the Slavophiles—disliked him back for his adopted foreignness, his affection for secular culture, his place on the wrong side of the schism. But as of 1712, Moscow was no longer the capital and the city fell silent, the noisy body having departed the quiet soul.

EMPRESSES AND THIEVES

W OMEN GOVERNED RUSSIA through most of the eighteenth
century.[1] Empress Anna, Peter the Great's niece, ruled for
ten of those years (1730–40), having survived a brief marriage to
the Prince of Courland (a semi-autonomous part of the Polish-
Lithuanian Commonwealth). The marriage had been negotiated
by Peter the Great to acquire political influence in the area. Nuptial
festivities included boat rides, cannonades, dwarfs jumping out of
pies and dancing on tables, a deluge of wine, and dozens of toasts.
But Anna's groom, Friedrich Wilhelm, started feeling ill with either
a serious cold or pneumonia. He had drunk too much, as usual, and
died from fever on the trip back to Courland.[2] That left Anna in
charge of a realm she resented: it was poor and dull. She was trapped
there for close to twenty years.[3]

Her life changed dramatically in 1730, when she was named
Empress of Russia by St. Petersburg's Supreme Council. The decision stunned relatives and aides alike. How was it that the regent of a
pitiful little duchy outside of Russia, a woman who'd been compro-
mised by her teenage lush of a husband, would now be empress? The
simple answer: the male line of the Romanovs had died out. Anna's
rule faced broad opposition, so she expanded her security operation
to target those who resisted her.[4]

Anna had her woes, including migraines, insomnia, abdominal pains, and an endocrinal disorder that drastically changed her appearance. She gave up horseback riding and hunting and stayed inside. Her doctors hovered over her like hawks, but their potions couldn't do anything about the renal colic that eventually killed her.[5] Anecdote has a guard seeing her ghost at night, "as pale as could be, head drooped and pacing back and forth." Anna saw the ghost herself and tried to confront the shade before it faded from view.[6] Death was nigh, and the terrified empress needed to settle on an heir. She announced that her infant grandnephew Ivan would be her successor and that her lover, Ernst Biron, would serve as Ivan's regent. Anna died on October 17, 1740, believing that she had shifted the line of succession from her uncle's side of the family to her father's.

The line shifted back to Peter the Great just thirteen months later. With Ernst out of the picture (he'd been banished to Siberia), Peter's daughter Elizabeth seized power on November 25, 1741. She made her move with the backing of aristocrats, ambassadors, and disaffected guardsmen of the Preobrazhensky regiment. Armed to the teeth, they stormed the Winter Palace, but no shots were fired and no blood was shed during the coup.[7] Anna's grandnephew, the intended tsar, was dragged from his bed for an audience with Elizabeth. One account has her reassuring the child that he was "not to blame for anything" and taking him back to her residence.[8] But her sympathies didn't last. She confined him and his family in Kholmogorï, a settlement in the Arctic whose name means "corpse hill," and erased all traces of him from the public record.[9]

Elizabeth was proclaimed empress, and most everyone wished her long years. She was Russia's "native daughter," having come from peasant stock on her mother's side. Spirits rose as the snow and ice of winter receded. Elizabeth "renews nature for us," an ode celebrating her coronation reads. She "covers the fields with flowers again."[10]

News of the coup took three days to reach Moscow from St. Petersburg. The courier began his trip in a city of uneven, sloppily laid cobblestones, Italian, French, and Dutch designs, elegant flat façades, serf-dug canals, and fierce winds. Fresh snow slowed the ride. Moscow came into view on Saturday night, November 28, 1741: brightly painted wooden houses crammed together at odd angles, checkpoints, fences, gates, domes, and spires. He halted in front of the Moscow senate building in the Kremlin and unpacked a hundred copies of the manifesto announcing Elizabeth as empress and fifty copies of the oath to be taken in her honor. The next morning, the manifesto was read aloud in the Assumption Cathedral, the last sentence cueing cannons. Arbitrariness—the success of the coup—had become absolute with Elizabeth's ascension. Decorations were hung, and lanterns lit. Long in advance of her actual coronation, high-ranking officials and generals pledged their allegiance to her in chilly cathedrals; the tallies of the newly faithful were sent to the Moscow senate and reported to the governing senate in St. Petersburg.[11] By February 15, 1742, some 80,000 people had pledged to lay down their lives for the new empress.[12]

The coronation festivities extended from April to June. Elizabeth's cortege in Moscow included a dozen carriages, decorated with gold, brocade, and velvet, surrounded by hundreds of horsemen. They passed under a fantastically ornate arch called Beautiful Gate (Krasnïye vorota), built by Peter the Great after the Russian triumph at the Battle of Poltava. The arch had burned down in 1732; Elizabeth's coronation provided reason to rebuild it. She wore a gown of gold and silver thread and donned an imperial crown specially made for her. The archbishop, Ambrosius, prayed for Elizabeth on behalf of the people, asking the Lord to forgive them their "lawlessness" and beseeching her "to open her heart to the poor and afflicted, to instill in her subjects a sense of justice and avoid partiality and bribery."[13]

Like her father, Elizabeth had grown up in an idyllic setting outside of Moscow. The future monarch was bright and sporty, learned to dance and skate, studied Romance languages, and took to the visual arts, including architecture. Her immodesties animated gossipers, and biographers have represented her as lighthearted (meaning unserious), a pampered princess, the fairest of the land and supposedly a little scattered, indecisive except when it came to acquiring dresses and shoes and putting on balls. She barred her ladies-in-waiting from wearing her favorite color of pink, Simon Sebag Montefiore writes, and when a rival dared to pin a pink flower to a lock of hair, Elizabeth cut it out and slapped her. But the evening continued. Elizabeth "often partied until 6 a.m.," Montefiore adds, "sleeping till midday and sending for jewelers and ministers in the middle of the night."[14] Gossip swirled after she took a dazzlingly handsome Ukrainian Cossack, Alexei Razumovsky, as her lover. "When I was at court," one of Elizabeth's footmen recalled, "I saw that Her Majesty was living with Razumovsky, and I often saw that Her Majesty was sitting on Razumovsky's lap."[15] For wagging his tongue, the footman most assuredly lost it.

Elizabeth is reduced to an in-between ruler, an interregnum between Peter I (the Great) and Catherine II (the Great). Even worse, she's seen as the in-between of the in-between. Her ascension followed that of her mother, Catherine I; Peter II; and Anna. Peter III assumed power after her death. Then Catherine the Great claimed the throne, having dispatched (to put it mildly) her husband, Peter III. But to reduce Elizabeth's reign to a historical entr'acte between her parent and her relative doesn't do her justice. She was neither daddy's little girl nor Catherine II's dotty auntie.

Francesco Bartolomeo de Rastrelli's plans called for buildings of unparalleled sumptuousness, as he himself boasted. The rebuilt palace in Tsarskoye Selo, outside of St. Petersburg, is illustrative: "the column capitals, pediments, and window frames, as well as the pillars supporting the balconies, as well as the statues placed on pedestals along the upper balustrade of the palace, had to be gilded," he wrote.[16] Elizabeth also paid for churches, signed off on the refurbishment of Moscow's aristocratic buildings, and commissioned (again from Rastrelli) St. Petersburg's glorious Winter Palace, which replaced the more modest palace used by Empress Anna. According to architectural historian Susan McCaffray, Elizabeth rejected the older building as altogether "inadequate for the reception of foreign ministers and plenipotentiaries," not to mention "the conduct of ceremonies with a grandeur appropriate to our imperial responsibilities."[17] She concludes that "if Peter bequeathed St. Petersburg's skeleton, it was his daughter ... who bestowed upon it a layer of gorgeous flesh."[18]

She embraced the arts. On September 10, 1749, Elizabeth announced that "from now on, there will be music at court every weekday from noon; on Mondays music for dance; on Wednesdays Italian entertainment, and on Tuesdays and Fridays comedies."

Bright sound became the cure for dull days. Elizabeth traveled with horn bands, commissioned cantatas, and presented theatrical comedies and tragedies, masquerades, operas, and ballets. Among them was *Virtue's Refuge* (*Pribezhishche dobrodeteli,* 1759), whose protagonist, symbolizing the arts and sciences, travels hither and thither looking for a patron and finds one not in America or Africa but in Elizabeth's enlightened realm.[19] These entertainments were for the elite. For the masses, the empress organized pyrotechnic demonstrations that tested the imagination of the German "master of fireworks" Jacob von Stählin, who served her throughout her reign. He, along with the polymath scientist and historian Mikhaíl Lomonosov, was tasked with creating a phantasmagoric Russia. The concluding event of the springtime coronation festivities in Moscow, for example, featured illuminated representations of flowing fountains, bursting flowers, and the empress's "entwined initials" suspended in the air.[20]

Meantime, Elizabeth attended to affairs of state, expanding Russian power through the enactment of progressive policies. Her diplomatic corps made peace with Sweden and advanced Russia's interests in the Seven Years' War, nudging France and Great Britain together against Prussia. She bettered education and motivated the establishment in 1755 of Moscow's (and Russia's) first university (now known as M. V. Lomonosov Moscow State University). She raised taxes on salt and alcohol to finance roads, improving commerce in the process. The supposed party girl was also deeply pious, attending services (she preferred singing in the choir to standing for long stretches), making pilgrimages to monasteries like the princes of Muscovy had, and traveling to the holy caves in Kyiv.

Archbishop Ambrosius had argued against Elizabeth's right to the throne but, after the coup, groveled for forgiveness. He received it and retained his post.[21] At Elizabeth's coronation, he read a prayer about forgiveness, asking the Lord, and the new divine ruler, to forgive the people for their lawlessness. But she'd already done so, issuing a decree on December 15, 1741, ahead of her coronation, detailing "the merciful forgiveness of criminals and the suspension of fines, arrears, and [excessive] charges from 1719 to 1730."[22] Part one comprised a single run-on sentence absolving "military, civil, and other officials" convicted of "dishonorable deeds." These deeds go unnamed. Part two freed those exiled or doing hard labor for the "embezzlement and theft of public funds; or for failure to fulfill contractual obligations." Criminals who had served in the naval corps and other divisions of the imperial services could return to their posts in good standing, while "those who, for reasons of old age or health, or because the punishment imposed on them barred them from serving," could go back home, no questions asked. (Serfs, the empress qualified, could return to their "owners.") Elizabeth also absolved the officials in her service who had been caught stealing from the treasury and sentenced to "the most severe torture." Miscreants owing 500 rubles or less to the treasury received a total pardon; the rest were sent "to Siberia with their wives and children without punishment and allowed to earn a living as they please."

Bookkeeping infelicities and the loss of financial records in fires and floods factored into the empress's decision to forgive certain debts, but she also, to placate the peasants, reduced the poll tax on them. Her generosity wouldn't last forever, she made clear. "The effect of this decree applies just to those who, on the day of the decree's signing, have been judged guilty of the above and are obliged to pay bills, taxes, interest, and fines to the treasury. As to those who are charged with comparable crimes in the future and are thus obliged to compensate the treasury for bills and taxes, they must act according to previous decrees, without omission."

Lost in the mix, but of obvious relevance to Moscow's criminal network, is the question of capital punishment. Elizabeth is foregrounded in biographies and academic studies for doing something that rulers throughout Europe lacked the compassion and conscience to do. She ended capital punishment as "a matter of her relationship with her God."[23] On the eve of the coup that brought her to power, the future empress had, according to a report delivered to the English court, "bow[ed] her head to the ground before an image of the Savior, praying in the secrecy of her heart." She subsequently "appeared with a crucifix before her waiting faithful subjects and demanded their oath of loyalty," cautioning that "if any blood were shed, she would not lead them."[24]

On May 7, 1744, Elizabeth ordered the suspension of hangings—a response to the excessive number of them in the provinces—but it remained unclear if this decree amounted to a pause on executions or an end to the practice.[25] "It is perceived that death sentences and political death [public mutilation and banishment] not be carried out on either the guilty or the innocent," the decree reads.[26] Even in the absence of capital punishment, blood was spilled on her watch, since, as historian Elena Marsinova puts it, "the empress . . . did not concern herself at all with the fates of the pardoned convicts, any salvation of their sinful souls or any possible correction. They would all die anyway, whether it be under the blows of the knout or due to backbreaking penal servitude."[27] Irrespective of the empress's prohibition, the severing of hands and inflicting of pain to extract confessions (suspects were forced to run the gauntlet and "hoisted in the strappado on the beam and subjected to the razor-sharp knout") amounted to de facto death sentences.[28] The moratorium in Moscow swelled the prison population, and what had been a progressive move on her part faced stiff resistance in the courts. Capital punishment resumed after she died, but her successor, Catherine the Great, respected Empress Elizabeth's "meritorious act" and exercised extreme forbearance in death penalty cases, permitting execution only to protect the throne and "the national peace."[29]

The government (its collegiums and chancelleries) maintained a robust judicial system, as did the Church (the Most Holy Synod) and the imperial regiments. Under Peter the Great, the police reported to the courts, the courts to the Justice Collegium, and the Justice Collegium to the governing senate. The system was decentralized in 1727, with the courts coming under local and regional control. In the wake of government restructuring, reforms in the services, and economic changes for better and worse, criminal cabals flourished as fugitive soldiers, vagabonds, escaped convicts, and runaway serfs banded together. The system couldn't support the caseload, so a new bureau of investigations (Sïsknoy prikaz) was established. While the police were responsible for catching criminals, the bureau dealt with their sentencing and incarceration.[30]

Such is the setup for the tale of Ivan (Vanka) Osipov (1718–

ca. 1756), who was a real person but also a composite of tales about thieves like him. A nondescript from nowhere, he became a symbol of defiance, living in the moment, thwarting the rules, thumbing his nose at church and state, robbing from the rich and giving to himself. In a world of enemies and allies, patriots and traitors, revolutionaries and counterrevolutionaries, he was none of the above. Vanka did awful, dastardly things to "correct" the rotten hand he'd been dealt at birth, and stories of his exploits found their way into Russian literature, including Pushkin's novel *The Captain's Daughter* and modernist poet Alexei Kruchyonïkh's "crime novel" in verse, "Vanka the Thief and Sonka the Manicurist."[31] Other writers called Vanka an "honest" bandit, stealing in plain sight as opposed to fleecing people out of sight, like unnoble nobles did.[32] Time turned him into an emblematic everyman, hero of all times. A song from the 1930s likens him to a prisoner in the Gulag, where everyone of good conscience ends up: "From Moscow to the boonies, / the southern mountains to the northern seas / a man travels, like Kain, / along an immense route lined by concentration camps."[33] The system is rotten, Vanka preaches through the ages: refuse to be a part of it. To be criminal is to be uncorrupted.

Vanka was born in Rostov district in the village of Ivashevo, population around two hundred, to a serf owned by Alexei Filyatev, the aging, irascible scion of a merchant family who traded throughout Russia and abroad.[34] Filyatev had properties elsewhere, but Ivashevo was his personal fiefdom. It had stables, ponds, orchards, smitheries, and a dozen or so serfs whom he had no interest in freeing or selling. Vanka didn't have much to look forward to in his life: hard work mostly outside, church services, the occasional tipple, possible marriage. In 1733, famine struck the area. Had he stayed he might have starved.[35]

When Vanka turned ten, Filyatev sent him to Moscow to work for his grandson Pyotr, who owned a manor house in the nicest part of Kitai-gorod. The house and its annexes were large enough to accommodate dozens of people: relatives, assorted guests, and a staff whose chores ranged from rubbing down horses to record-keeping.

Neighbors included a retired doctor from Padua, Anton Sevasto, a specialist in epidemics who worked for the imperial court before relocating to Moscow; and Afanasiy Tatishchev, a traveling companion of Peter the Great.[36] Afanasiy's younger brother Alexei became Moscow's chief of police and, in 1746, began reporting to Empress Elizabeth about his efforts to rein in corruption. He would decide the fate of Vanka, Moscow's crime lord.

That would come later. In 1728, Vanka was doing chores in Pyotr Filyatev's house. He lugged slop buckets and had his head smacked when he failed to swish out the chamber pots. He didn't suffer the abuse alone; court cases attest to the master's foul temper and bizarre humiliations of the other souls in his hands. A serf named Marina went through an especially strange ordeal. Filyatev had her arrested for "putting salt in the ground coffee kept in the tin in the kitchen." Marina did so, she said, not to spoil or improve the flavor (taming the bitterness of the beans) but because she was mad at the maid who boiled coffee for the merchant and wanted to see her punished. Filyatev didn't believe her, and he insisted that she be questioned "with passion" (flogged in the stable) and, if need be, "searched" (with hot pokers) in the Bureau of Investigations. The bureau confirmed the poor girl's story—salt went into the coffee because she was mad at the maid—but Filyatev wanted to know if Marina was involved in witchcraft. Perhaps the salt was a spell meant to change Filyatev's behavior for the better, or a curse placed on the salt-mining operations that (along with caravans and fisheries) made Filyatev one of the richest people in Moscow. Marina doubled down on her explanation of the salt incident, refusing to confess to witchcraft. It says something that she was less afraid of the Bureau of Investigations than she was of her bourgeois master.[37]

Vanka reportedly carried out his duties with "zeal" yet "instead of rewards and favors received unbearable beatings."[38] He stole a few plates and some other things left lying around, but he was right to complain about his master's meanness. Four years later, at age fourteen, he'd had enough. He wanted to be free like his friend Pyotr (nicknamed Kamchatka, roughly meaning patterned cloth), who was about five years older. Before stealing for a living, he'd worked for a sailcloth manufacturer, spending his days on the bank of the Yauza River winding ropes and stitching slabs of fabric together. Morale in the plant was low; no one got paid when business slowed, and the workers were abused by the manager. Historian Yevgeny Akelyev describes the case of a sailor named Merkulov who was beaten so much for cursing, stealing, drinking, and complaining about the beatings that he died.[39] Crime was simply easier and safer, so Kamchatka embarked on that path. Vanka sought to be his sidekick, but first he needed to escape his master. Toward midnight,

> after Filatyev and his entire household had gone to bed, Kain [Vanka], as was his custom, undressed and also lay down in his place; however, he did not have sleep on his mind but instead impatiently awaited the hour when everyone would be in a deep sleep. After several minutes, he noticed that his master and the entire household had fallen sound asleep. Rising, he dressed quietly, and, with the utmost caution, entered his master's bedroom, opened the trunk with the aid of tools he had made ready beforehand, extracted from it no trifling amount of money, and, putting on some of his master's clothes, left the house with all haste.[40]

Such is Matvey Komarov's novelized description of what happened. All that's really known is that Vanka emptied his master's treasure chest and met Kamchatka in the street. A note was left on the gate of the house reading, in crudely rhymed doggerel, "Pey vodu kak gus', esh' khleb kak svin'ya, a rabotay chyort, a ne ya" (Drink water like a goose, eat bread like a pig, let the devil work for you, I won't [or: get yourself another devil, this one quits]).[41]

Vanka needed to disguise himself to make it past the sentries who closed off the streets at night. Priests and the police could move around after dark, but no one else could without special permission, and Filyatev would soon be out looking for him. According to Vanka's *Life and Adventures,* he and Kamchatka climbed over the fence into a priest's courtyard, surprising the "person lying in the yard who rang the bell at matins, that is, the church watchman."[42] Kamchatka clocked the guard over the head with a rod, enabling Vanka to sneak into the priest's chamber and put on one of his cloaks and a caftan. Kamchatka dressed like a sexton. The guards at the checkpoints called out to them but let them through.

Vanka sheltered with pickpockets huddling under the arches of All Saints Bridge (the precursor to the Great Stone Bridge spanning the Moskva at the Kremlin). He swiped some vodka for them, and they invited him into their company in language that defies translation. The fossilized folk expressions are one obstacle, the transformation of those expressions into sonorous strangeness (rhymes, puns, and sound gags) another. The grammar can be analyzed, but the true meaning lies in the exchange of code words and thieves' argot (*vorovskaya fenya*). The language amounts to a kind of spell or incantation meant for the thieves alone:

> We've devoured the floor and everything in the middle ourselves, we rent out the stove and the attic, and to those passing over the bridge, we discreetly hand out alms, and you will be a brother, clad in our cloth's caftan [you'll be one of us]! Live here in our house, where there is an abundance of everything: poles [clotheslines?] hung with nakedness and barefooted-ness, and barns standing for [filled with?] hunger and cold. Dust and soot, and nothing even to munch on.[43]

Handing out alms is slang for acquiring and distributing loot, which is what the thieves set out to do in the morning. Vanka tagged along. But he was inexperienced, so was captured in Squire's Row (the cloth market in Kitai-gorod) and taken in chains to his former master. He was tied up near the bear cub (the master's pet) that occupied the yard and told that he'd be going hungry for a while. Fortunately for him, a servant girl snuck him some food and told him a juicy piece of gossip: there'd been a fight in the master's house and a soldier was killed, his body wrapped in a Persian carpet and dumped into a well. With this information, Vanka could now denounce his captor and escape. Eighteenth-century law required people with knowledge of crimes against the state to report them. Anyone who saw something had to say something, and that something consisted of three words: "slovo i delo" (word and deed).[44] Vanka shouted the magic formula within earshot of an officer who passed by the house. Vanka was taken to the Stukalov Monastery, a secret chancellery the police operated just outside of Moscow. He reported the murder, and when a corpse was pulled out of the well, Filyatev was arrested.

Vanka gained his freedom and began his life of crime, though modestly at first. He bonded with the thieves hiding in and around the gorges, ravines, and swamps of Moscow—places known as "sinner's pass," for example, or "terrible ravine."[45] He reconnected with Kamchatka and learned the language of thieves, referring to police as trash (*musor*) and prisons as stone sacks (*kamennïye meshki*), among coarser turns of phrase about genitalia. He became an expert pickpocket, cutting into purses hung from belts with a flick of the wrist. He lived in taverns and dens, now working alone on the streets of Moscow, then partnering with his buddies, to clean the pockets of fairgoers when the booths and tents were the most crowded. Each successful operation was called a "poem," as if it were a lyrical work of art. Vanka would abandon petty chicanery—stealing scarves from bathhouses and silver crosses from churches—for grand theft, bringing to his side a pack of desperado followers enchanted by his catch-me-if-you-can brazenness. A clever judge of character, he profiled his victims and conducted reconnaissance operations using, among other props, a chicken. He'd toss the bird over the fence into a rich landholder's yard then pound the gate demanding access to the yard to catch his property. Chasing the chicken around allowed him to inspect all the doors and locks for the break-in that night.[46]

Vanka's longest poems—his biggest heists—involved travel among cities, river crossings, careful planning, and a team. He murdered a border guard, kidnapped a child, raped a teen, and committed arson in Moscow during the spring of 1748.[47] Far-fetched anecdotes and his folklore-infused autobiographical ramblings suggest a wicked sense of humor. He smeared one of his victims in goo, chased another into a field without his pants on, and tied a third to the shaft of a hay cart before setting it ablaze.[48] Sometimes he'd be arrested and left to imagine a future in the wilds of Siberia. But the police could be bribed, and he would learn which officials liked Rhein wine, downy hats, and

Italian scarves.[49] Vanka could also count on his pal Kamchatka to get him out of jams and even, on one occasion, jail. Kamchatka showed up with a bag of bread rolls, telling the guards that he'd brought them as alms. He passed them out to the prisoners one at a time, making sure to give Vanka the roll with coins and keys tucked inside. Dropping it into Vanka's hand, Kamchatka whispered, "Treka kalach ela, stromïk, sverlyuk straktirila," slang for "Be careful: in the roll there is a key to unlock the chain."[50]

Prison—as a place, concept, and experience—changed in the eighteenth century. The most drastic shift occurred in the years following the Trinity Sunday fire of May 29–30, 1737, one of the worst in the city's history. Some 2,527 households and 486 shops— a quarter of the city center—were reduced to ash. The Kremlin Arsenal burned down—gunpowder and firefighting equipment had unwisely been stored there together. Spasskaya tower lost its clock, the Kremlin churches their domes. The monstrous "Tsar Bell," the product of four furnaces and a team of foundry workers, was ruined. It had been cast on the order of Empress Anna and sat smoldering in a wood-enclosed pit in the central square. Pouring water into the pit caused uneven cooling; the bell cracked. A giant piece fell from it, and to this day tourists visiting Red Square and the Kremlin learn the strange-but-true facts about the largest bell in the world—200 tons, decorated with angels and inscriptions and a life-size image of the empress—which has never been rung.[51]

Unlike other fires, this one was investigated by the government (specifically Moscow's commander in chief, Semyon Saltïkov) and a report submitted to the sovereign (Empress Anna), listing what burned and what remained in the administrative buildings and churches.[52] Determining the cause of the inferno was less important than surveying who might have benefited from the destruction of tax records, censuses, leases, invoices, or lists of souls bought and sold. These documents mattered more than the buildings that housed them for a simple reason: no documents, no government; no government, no Russia. Authority always resided in the act of writing, and when the records disappeared there was chaos. Lives in Russia began and ended, got better or worse, based on the slip of a pen or loss of a document. Perhaps the owner of the village had died, or was killed, or had moved elsewhere—quotidian details, but key to the people on his land and to their fates. What if no record of them survived? Had they ever then existed in the eyes of the government?

The papers mattered, so as soon as the fire bell rang clerks rushed to the chancelleries on a rescue mission. Firefighting resources at this time included hand-operated pumps of different sorts, pressurized water pipes and wells, and "fire extinguishing machines": gunpowder-infused water barrels to be rolled toward the fire and exploded, spraying water all around.[53] Serfs and servants extinguished the flames "in stoic, fatalistic fashion," while officials watched from afar.[54] Excuses for not helping ranged from being in church to being out of town to being too ill to get out of bed.[55]

The fire of 1737 damaged Moscow's jails, killing many of the people inside but, in a few cases, setting them free. The documents defining their crimes had gone up in smoke. Those still incarcerated were kept in different locations in Moscow, and the Bureau of Investigations relocated to a confiscated courtyard south of the river.[56] In 1739, a new barracks complex—the "big prison"—was designed for convenience, not comfort. Built along Moskvoretskaya Street, an L-shaped road that began at the Spasskaya tower of the Kremlin and ended at a bridge, the complex contained a chapel for daily prayer and confessions, a single barracks building for the guards, and five barracks buildings for the prisoners. The barracks were unlocked during the day, allowing the prisoners to wander the grounds under the guard towers. The latrine could be accessed until midnight, after which buckets were set out. A hole in the wall—a pipe—allowed prisoners to collect food and clothing and other donations from relatives, spouses, and "compassionate townspeople." Prisoners also used the pipe to send their clothes out for washing. Packages needed to be inspected to prevent tools, weapons, and alcohol from getting inside (though, because the guards profited handsomely from selling it, booze sloshed around the prison, causing brawls and the inevitable denouncing shouts of "word and deed").[57] The more devoted wives rented rooms around the corner from the prison, providing food and clothing and support to their husbands. For a bribe, some of the noble prisoners could slip away for conjugal visits.

The wardens were themselves prisoners, paid a small stipend for keeping order in the barracks. The older guards kept an eye on the storage rooms, the "belongings of the disgraced," and the key bag. The younger guards dealt with the prisoners themselves, both the lost causes and the noblemen who'd been locked up for financial chicanery. Soldiers stood at the entrances with guns and bayonets. In 1741, a quitrent peasant was enlisted to build guard towers along the fences. He wasn't skilled enough to put roofs on them. "When it rained," the soldiers "suffered considerable hardship from phlegm" without any way to "preserve" their weapons or ammunition from sogginess.[58] A report from October 16, 1745, listed 296 shackled prisoners and 141 unshackled, for a total of 437 in the "glands," meaning cells.[59] Most hadn't been convicted of anything: processing cases took up to six months (except during the coronation of Empress Elizabeth, when the barracks had to be emptied for appearance's sake).

Just a few steps away, in and around the trading rows, Muscovites of different ranks went about their daily affairs. Fish was fried in open pits, and smoke from stoves floated out through windows. Churches stood beside the residences of Peter the Great's entrepreneurial class. A certain "Ivan Ivanov, son of Popodin," lived near the Kremlin walls in a compound of wooden and stone buildings that included taverns. Stoves kept them constantly heated and, as the sergeant of the bureau fretted, "god forbid" if the taverns caught fire and spread to the prisoners.[60] Moscow's first coffeehouse opened in the Greek merchant yard at the St. Nicholas Greek Orthodox Monastery.[61] A book market operated just steps from the barracks wall: "five-meter-tall standing logs dug deep into the ground and pointed at the top, tightly fastened with transverse planks."[62]

Workers passing in and out of Kitai-gorod saw the "terrible faces" of prisoners poking through the windows of the barracks overlooking Moskvoretskaya Street. For merely going about their daily affairs, they'd be hollered at, insulted, and even threatened. The prisoners, several hundred strong, shouted that they couldn't breathe because of the "great stuffiness" resulting from overcrowding.[63] A law had already been passed prohibiting guards from taking prisoners outside to beg for alms "in bundles [in shackled-together groups]," but that didn't prevent them from shouting from their cells. The shopkeepers of Kitai-gorod had no choice but to put up with the abuse, but when influential nobles heard it, relocating the barracks became a pressing issue.[64]

The solution wasn't to hire more clerks and judges but to close the barracks. Clearing the center of the prisoners and their trash also served the empress's redevelopment plan for the Kremlin.[65] So in 1751, another detention center was ordered built on the edge of the city in Kaluga Square. Everyone who had been under guard in the center of Moscow would be moved to the new facility, which could hold two thousand people. The suffering of the prisoners only increased, but at least people outside didn't have to hear it.

The Kaluga Square prison opened in December of 1752. It allowed for the concentrated confinement of prisoners from several institutions, not just the Bureau of Investigations. The senate had been holding prisoners, along with the chancelleries and collegiums and, of course, the police department. Kaluga held them until 1785, when it was replaced by the infamous Butïrskaya prison on the opposite side of town. By then, Vanka was long dead but had become an antihero for all time, immortalized as the "father of Russian corruption."[66]

Shortly after Empress Elizabeth's coronation, Vanka realized he needed to take a different approach. The police were onto him, and he wasn't safe under All Saints Bridge. He hoped to exploit the empress's "merciful forgiveness of criminals" by turning himself in and confessing his crimes. Doing so allowed him to become an informer, so he could work both inside and outside of the bureau as a kind of mole, letting the bigger fish in the criminal pond know that he could keep them out of prison for the right price. He had to juggle a lot of lies, which he managed to do for years.

On December 28, 1741, Vanka brought a dictated confession to the Moscow senate in hopes of pressing it into the hands of Prince Yakov Kropotkin, chief judge of the Bureau of Investigations and arguably the most important person in Moscow. The prince's adjutant looked him up and down and decided that he wasn't worth the prince's time. Vanka was booted from the premises. He tried again, after a drink, announcing to anyone who would listen that he was a person of importance within Moscow's criminal network. In his confession, he claimed that he had rediscovered God and wanted the other fallen angels to be redeemed.[67]

This time, the prince took him to the Bureau of Investigations for additional questioning. Vanka wouldn't have been so gullible as to believe he'd be granted a fresh start as a God-fearing imperial Russian subject. He must have known, as he faced his questioners, that his plan to keep himself out of jail by ratting out others was risky at best. The bureau might decide to keep things simple, threatening him to extract the names of accomplices. But timing was on his side: the April 15, 1742, coronation of Empress Elizabeth was approaching, and Moscow's streets needed to be cleaned up. Catching thieves required the assistance of thieves.

His confession was copied, together with additional information to be used by the judges—three of them, all nobles—in their questioning. Vanka was then announced as "Osipov's son," age twenty-three, who'd "cheated day and night" throughout Moscow.[68] He'd apologized to the empress for his crimes and promised to lead detectives to his accomplices. Those he couldn't name he could identify by sight. The judges took down the information, looked at the clock, and authorized a roundup that night.

The task fell to a small detachment of soldiers and a protocol officer, there to document the arrests. Vanka took them around the packed trading and residential streets to the east of the bureau in Kitai-gorod and the adjoining neighborhood of Zaryadye. The police raided a suspected brothel and the suspected thieves staying inside, though the truth of the place and its inhabitants couldn't be determined. Everyone's stories kept changing. From there, Vanka led the soldiers into the home of a deacon, various hovels lining the Kitai-gorod wall, and several churches that no longer exist, having vanished into Red Square and Vasilyevsky spusk (the descent to the river behind St. Basil's Cathedral). The grounds of the Church of the All-Merciful Savior—in a packed area that included a graveyard, the Kremlin moat, and the prison of the Bureau of Investigations— yielded an impressive harvest of pickpockets. Another raid occurred in an abandoned courtyard between the Kitai-gorod wall and the Kremlin moat. A soldier-turned-swindler named Alexei Ivanov was caught there. He had "a dirty, greasy sheet of paper" listing the runaway sailors and soldiers plus "idle" male and female merchants (hundreds in all) he'd been planning to denounce. The list included Vanka's name. They knew each other.[69]

By the end of the day on December 29, 1741, 61 people had been brought to the Bureau of Investigations for questioning—many more, according to the archival record, than the "37 thieves" Vanka had fingered.[70] The soldiers detained a man who'd stolen the kaftan of the kvass-maker and "a sailor from the sail factory" who'd "nicked the hat and mittens of a passerby." There's also mention of someone who stole bundles of logs from the river "and sold them to differ- ent people."[71] These people weren't exactly hardened criminals. They were poor.

Vanka proved his worth to the Bureau of Investigations by pre- venting pickpockets from swarming shoppers and catching mer- chants with their hands on the scale, even rooting out corruption within the bureau itself. He thought himself indispensable so agi- tated for perks: housing and clothing and cash to buy food and set- tle his debts. In March 1742, he became an official employee of the bureau, and Empress Elizabeth praised his performance during her visit to Moscow in September 1744. Vanka presented himself to the governing senate, which had accompanied the empress on her trip, and boasted of the fine work he had done in rounding up hundreds of thieves. He wanted to do more but claimed to need protection from other unscrupulous informants. The senators granted him this safeguard; he then paraded around Moscow free of fear from above or below. Vanka took a wife, a widow named Arina, and lived in a proper house with her—the days of sleeping in hammocks, shacks, and literal holes in the wall long past. He bought drinks for those he wanted to keep close, feasted with them *v Blinnoy* (at the Pancake House) in the evenings, and gambled with them all over town so they'd turn to him for help covering their losses.[72] He went to church, donated to charities, and at Christmastime, he built a snow mountain for everyone to sled on. Outwardly, for appearance's sake, he was a model citizen.

And yet he was anything but. Vanka took advantage of the government's efforts to quell a mystical religious practice called Christ-Faith. The movement emerged in the upper Volga of Central Russia at the end of the seventeenth century and was soon adopted by peasants and townspeople alike, reaching Moscow within a decade. Its spiritual teachers advocated asceticism: "pray to God at night, don't fornicate, don't go to weddings or christenings, don't drink wine and beer, don't listen to profane songs, don't stare when people fight." Participants gathered in private houses, monastic cells, and rural communes to dance, spin (as the earth does the sun), and sing sacred songs. Some of their services occurred in ice houses that melted in the spring, leaving nothing behind, no sign of their presence. Self-flagellation—the mortification of the flesh—was also practiced, and they referred to their personal churches as boats, weathering the storm of sacrilege around them.

Stay strong, shipbuilders,
Best the storm!
The Holy Spirit is among us.
Fear neither fire nor hurricane!
Our father Christ is with us![73]

Participants attended Orthodox services; thus, they differed from the Old Believers who had broken from the Church in opposition to Patriarch Nikon and Peter the Great. Still, the paranoid official Church, and the paranoid government to which the Church was attached, considered them a threat. The police rounded up these fundamentally good people as schismatics and interrogated them. The first of the two investigative commissions organized against Christ-Faith in Moscow in the 1730s brought in a noblewoman, peasants, merchants, laborers, and some disaffected clergymen. The second commission, launched in 1745, led to the detentions of a princess (Dar'ya Khovanskaya), sailors, a coachman, the inhabitants of alms-houses, and monks—164 people in all.[74]

Vanka participated in, and profited from, the 1745 commission. For an agreed-upon price, he would leave suspected heretics in peace, or, more often, he would leave them in peace after scaring them half to death. Such was the most regrettable experience of a humble shopkeeper named Yeremey Ivanov, who was placed under house arrest for his involvement in Christ-Faith. Meantime his niece was taken to Vanka's compound and "tormented with lashes" in hopes of convincing her to confess to heresy. "Beat her hard," Arina encouraged her husband. The brave girl kept mum, however, and toward morning, Vanka paid a visit to her uncle, letting him know that if he "prayed hard to god" (that is, paid a generous ransom), his niece would be freed. Ivanov did what he had to do. After getting his niece back, he reported the matter to the police. Vanka was arrested. Under interrogation, he admitted to "taking" the girl and locking her up in his personal dungeon for three days. But he denied ever whipping her or stealing from her uncle. He freed his hostage, he explained, after it became clear that she wasn't involved in the religious sect causing all the trouble. The judges didn't believe him and sentenced him to "harshest punishment with the whip and distant exile." But then—in one of those twists in the plot that make the entire thing seem far-fetched—he was pardoned. The reason? The Sïsknoy prikaz still needed his services as informant.[75]

The carnival of horrors would have continued—Vanka even betrayed his pal Kamchatka—had it not been for the empress's visit to Moscow in January 1749. After a member of her entourage, the personal valet of the future Peter III, was assaulted in broad daylight near the Kremlin, Elizabeth ordered the immediate "suppression" of lawlessness and enacted the equivalent of a Good Samaritan law. Anyone witnessing a crime needed to intervene, even if the crime was violent. If they didn't help, they themselves would be arrested and fined—"no exceptions."[76]

Enacting the decree became the job of the police chief, Major

General Alexei Tatishchev. He was someone the empress could count on, having been attached to the Preobrazhensky regiment and securing the confidence of Peter the Great. He served both Catherine I and Empress Anna, who tasked him with all sorts of things: hiring court jesters, organizing fireworks shows, and building, in the especially cold winter of 1739–40, an ice palace filled with ice animals. Empress Elizabeth made Tatishchev her top cop on May 24, 1742, and he reported to her alone. The senate had no control over him, nor did the Bureau of Investigations in Moscow or the Bureau of Secret Investigations in St. Petersburg. Tatishchev used his considerable power to shut down brothels and other "underground public houses." He also, on the plus side, showed a soft spot for families in need, successfully petitioning Elizabeth to provide free medicine to poor mothers and their children.[77]

Tatishchev received a written complaint—it was put right into his hands by the clerk from the local police chief's office—from a retired soldier seeking justice for what had happened to his fifteen-year-old daughter on the night of January 17. The child had been abducted by Vanka for base purposes. That was the end for the thief, his belated disgrace. He was picked up on the road and brought to the bureau for questioning. He admitted that he'd "invited a girl, Agrafena Fyodorva, to take a stroll with him" in secret and claimed that she'd gone out with him willingly. Hiding his face beneath a fur hat, he took her to a tavern operated by a Frenchman, Mark Bodwick, where they "drank grape drinks," white wine with honey.[78] Later, he was forced to admit that he'd assaulted the girl, ignoring her protests. This information came out during an interrogation conducted by Tatishchev himself in the dungeon. Vanka screamed when the cat o' nine tails was brought out to help jog his memory.[79] Hysterical with fear, he begged for mercy and named high-ranking officials who had been his accomplices over the years. The allegations needed to be investigated by an outside agency. The empress approved a special commission to do it.

It took years to clear the decks, to sort out who had corrupted whom, to sign all the documents with all the sentences. Meanwhile, Vanka rotted in his cell, old and sad, his life and lies exposed, his house and belongings confiscated. In March 1756, he was brought before the public for "political execution." He was flogged, his nostrils slit, and the word "thief" (*vor*) burned into his forehead and cheeks.[80] But he wasn't killed.

Instead, he was sentenced to hard labor in Rågervik, a settlement on a Baltic Sea peninsula not far from Revel (Tallinn). The town had once belonged to Sweden but was ceded to Russia during the Great Northern War of the early eighteenth century. Hoping to control the Baltic Sea, Peter the Great had ordered the construction of a fortress and a port in Rågervik with religious dissenters doing the heavy lifting. Rain, hail, wind, and the mind-boggling scope of the project—besides the port and the fortress, an island was to be connected to the peninsula—turned it into an impossible mission, despite Empress Elizabeth's commitment to completing it on her father's behalf.[81] She expanded the labor force with thieves like Vanka. Elizabeth visited Rågervik in 1746 with an entourage that included the future Catherine the Great, who took note of the plight of the prisoners at the end of a general complaint about the lack of amenities: "The soil of this place is rocky, covered with a thick layer of fine cobblestone. . . . We camped and had to walk on this type of ground for days; my feet ached for four months afterward. The convicts who worked on the pier wore wooden shoes, and they did not last more than eighty days."[82]

Vanka lasted more than eighty days, but exactly how many more is a mystery. All that's known is what he says in his *Life and Adventures*, which isn't reliable: "I was sent to Rågervik, or a Baltic port, that is, to the icy waters, and then to a place a little over seven verses [4.6 miles] from Moscow, where I happen to find myself now."[83] One explanation for his survival is offered by Andrey Bolotov, youthful commander of the guards stationed at Rågervik and author of a bleakly hilarious account of the experience. He describes prisoners dropping lice onto his head, boiling up mush from the same trough used by the cattle, and the utter pointlessness of their labor: "breaking up boulders dug up from the local shore, lugging them to the sea, and hurling into the deep water to attempt to build a broad dam from the shore to the island." The immense depth of the sea and the smoothness of the seabed meant that nothing stuck, so no "foundation" for the dam could be "established." "Before a big storm has even fully risen," Bolotov adds, "everything that's been built up over five years is destroyed and carried away in an hour flat," forcing the work to begin again.[84]

Vanka didn't participate. He'd been released from the chain gangs and had left the barracks in search of better shelter. Those convicts with enough money for bribes lived in separate huts under Bolotov's direct supervision. They ate better food and filled their time with writing or dictating their real and imagined adventures.[85]

1812 AND RECONSTRUCTION

RUSSIA BECAME AN EMPIRE after St. Petersburg became its capital. Unlike Moscow, St. Petersburg lacked roots in the black earth. Its architecture belonged in Italy or Spain or France; the borscht wasn't sour enough; the people smiled for no reason. Whereas St. Petersburg looked forward, importing European bureaucracies and entertainers and flirting with the Enlightenment, Moscow—closer to nature, somewhat warmer and much brighter, derided by the northerners as too staid, a pickled conserve of a place—didn't much care what happened at the imperial court. Having stood at the center of Rus, it clung to Slavophile traditions and sulked in the shadows of its antipode, inured to suffering and proud of the violence it had committed against Kyiv and other closer cities. In 1812, Moscow would suffer again and commit fresh violence, repelling Napoleon in what became known as the Great Patriotic War. Had Moscow not withstood the siege, had it not been willing to sacrifice itself in beating back the French, the empire might have collapsed. Instead, Russia survived and continued to expand through avarice and resentment with the goal of growing so big it would be impossible ever again for any enemy to invade and not be swallowed up.

Such was what Napoleon Bonaparte had in mind for the French empire. Before invading Russia, he had fought one battle after another in Europe and the Middle East, going as far as the kingdom of Sardinia and the Egyptian pyramids. He made brilliant as well as bone-headed decisions, retreating from Russia in winter chief among the latter. In the summer of 1812, just before his forty-second birthday, Napoleon led his Grande Armée into Russia, and there his aspirations met their end. He anticipated taking power in Moscow, maybe even St. Petersburg, while also continuing to fight elsewhere. But power had other ideas, and Tsar Alexander I refused to surrender to the self-declared emperor.

The Russians would counter him with three armies, about 250,000 men total. The commander of the largest, Michael Andreas Barclay de Tolly, imagined losses in the short term and success over the long haul. A Livonian (Estonian) of distant Scottish lineage, he rose through the ranks, treated his men well, prohibited hazing, and demonstrated a kind of pragmatic cleverness on the battlefield. His forces—and Prussia's—scratched Napoleon's face in the 1806 Battle of Pułtusk in Poland. Barclay fought the Swedes and became the governor-general of Finland, which the Swedes surrendered to Russia in 1809. Anticipating a multipronged French invasion of Russia, Barclay came up with the "Scythian strategy" of defeat through surrender.[1] The aggressors would be lured from their base of operations into a battle of attrition against endlessly retreating defenders. A drawn-out fight seemed the best option for Russia (as it would be for later Russian commanders) given the empire's huge expanse, the shakiness of Russia's finances, and the size of its ill-trained fighting forces. The officers, too, proved a problem: some of them were foreign, didn't understand much Russian, and didn't know what they were fighting for.

Among the rank and file were Russians, Belarusians, and Ukrainians pressed into service from the fields and the steppes. Most were peasants and serfs, around twenty years old, conscripted either against their owner's wishes or with his eager consent, because they'd been troublemakers on the estates. The literate among them came from the priesthood; the best fighters were the sons of veterans. Their poverty, faith, and shared experiences bonded them. Heads shaved, each conscript was assigned to an artel that grew food and stitched clothing and instilled love for God and tsar in equal measure. They went into battle with icons around their necks and, in the opinion of one of Alexander I's cousins, accepted their "unavoidable fate more than is the case with the peoples of other countries who are compulsorily conscripted."[2] For those who delayed the "unavoidable fate" of death, there was no returning to their plows: service contracts lasted twenty-five years, since the government didn't want former serfs going back to their families to cause unrest with exciting stories of the wider world. For the wives and children left behind in the villages, the future was bleak.[3]

Tsar Alexander I appointed Barclay minister of war in 1810. Two years later, in June 1812, Napoleon crossed into Russia, and the "Scythian war" commenced. The French blew through one fortification line after another, plunging ever deeper into Russian territory. Barclay and his officers scattered their armies, gathered them, and scattered them again. One retreat was followed by another, leaving behind a vast wasteland of overturned carts and dead or dying horses and men. Eventually, Barclay's soldiers began to doubt his judgment and question his orders. What was the end goal? There didn't seem to be one, and the soldiers "nicknamed their commander-in-chief 'Nothing but Chatter' (Boltay da Tol'ko), a pun on Barclay de Tolly."[4] The tsar reassigned him—giving him command of united Russian and Prussian forces outside of Russia—and appointed sixty-five-year-old Mikhaíl Kutuzov as commander in his place. Kutuzov was a seasoned professional with tremendous charisma. He had led the St. Petersburg and Moscow militias before taking charge of the entire campaign against Napoleon. Then the backbiting and nay-saying began. It was said that Kutuzov wasn't fit for the task; he was past his prime. He couldn't get out of bed; he was heavy and sloth-like, unable at times to lift a pen, never mind conduct field reconnaissance.

Historian Dominic Lieven has argued that Kutuzov's historical reputation was grossly inflated by Tolstoy, who in War and Peace turned the commander into a "Russian patriotic icon." In the twentieth century, Soviet propagandists "raised him to the level of a military genius," better at moving men and equipment around than

Napoleon. "Of course, all this is nonsense," Lieven deadpans, "but it is important not to react too far in the opposite direction, by ignoring Kutuzov's talents," charisma, and experience.[5] His greatest asset might have been his surname, which is about as ancient as one can get in the Slavic context, referencing that pre-Russian time when people's physical attributes became their name. A "kutuz" is "a pillow on which lace is woven" or pulled into a knot. Men of abundant carriage—barrel-chested heading toward obese, of low center of gravity, hard to dislodge—were described as *kutuz*. And in Turkic, the name means "hot-tempered." There are famous Kutuzovs in the ancient chronicles and the "genealogical books of Novgorod, Pskov, Ryazan, and Tver provinces."[6] It is a deeply Slavic, meaning deeply Orthodox name, associated with a man destined to cleanse Rus of Gallic contaminants.

Kutuzov could pull off the maneuver that Barclay, a Romanov loyalist from outside Russia, would have been lynched for even proposing, much less attempting. Kutuzov decided to abandon Moscow to the French and prepare instead to fight in the fields as winter approached. Kutuzov relocated his forces south (southeast and then southwest) to the village of Tarutino—87,000 of them, compared to the 120,000 soldiers controlled by Napoleon. The Russian soldiers were given sheepskin coats for the weather to come; they built bathhouses for themselves and, as Kutuzov insisted, attended religious services on Sundays. Then they ambushed the French, killing three thousand of the soldiers fighting under the command of Napoleon's most trusted officer, Joachim Murat, and scattering the rest like frightened deer.[7] It was a comparatively small battle but one of major importance, because the Russians seized control of the supply routes and communications lines that Napoleon needed to maintain his occupation of Moscow. He had no choice but to retreat with the Russians on his tail.

Kutuzov's thinking was called into question at the time and continues to be even today. When exactly did he decide to pull his forces from Moscow? And was it worth it? The most recent, deeply controversial theory about his thinking was that he was not thinking at all, at least not as he had in his youth. He was an old soldier with a damaged brain. A bullet had entered the left temple of Kutuzov's head back in 1774, during a Russo-Turkish war. Kutuzov recovered but complained of strabismus, misalignment of the eyes. In 1788 during the Russian siege of Turkish-held Ochakov (Ochakiv, Ukraine), a second bullet passed through his skull and might have killed him were it not for the brilliant surgeon Jean Massot, a Frenchman serving the Russian forces. Kutuzov experienced dizziness, headaches, and occasional sharp pain in the right eye (often covered by a black patch) for the rest of his days. He often felt listless; his aides thought him depressed. The current assessment, based on the surgeon's surviving records and published in the American journal *Neurological Focus*, is that damage to the frontal lobe of his brain made precise decision-making impossible for him.[8] The assumption is that surrendering Moscow to the French was an irrational act, completed after plans had been made for the city's defense.

Napoleon also acted irrationally, and no one has claimed wounds to the head as an excuse. He defeated himself by overextending his troops in an inhospitable environment. Despite demonstrating brilliance on the battlefields of Europe and commanding a massive fighting machine with experienced officers at the top as well as hundreds of thousands of replenishable recruits at the bottom, he could not conquer Russia. Had he made it from Moscow to St. Petersburg, replaced the tsar, and announced the emancipation of the serfs, the curve of Russian history would have been very different. But nothing of the sort happened. Fire won the Battle of Smolensk, and the Battle of Borodino devolved into hand-to-hand combat in a field surrounded by forests and swamps. The French won, but the Russians came out looking close to invincible. In Moscow, emptied of its inhabitants, Napoleon stepped into a trap. He had no inkling of Kutuzov's maneuvers until it was too late; his access to roads, the countryside, and the fall harvest was impeded. Supplies ran low. Marauding Cossacks harassed the French encampments at night and captured and tortured rogue soldiers caught foraging for food or decent clothing. When Napoleon's aides second-guessed his thinking, he fatefully declared, "The wine has been poured, it has to be drunk."[9] He lasted in Moscow from September 2 to October 10, on the Julian calendar.

The governor-general of Moscow, Fyodor Rostopchin, was left in the dark about Kutuzov's decision to abandon Moscow, and perhaps for good reason. Rostopchin's lack of administrative experience didn't exactly inspire trust. He fancied himself a country squire, not a big-city mayor, and rather than leadership or vision he brought a mess of biases to the job. He heaped scorn on Moscow's "bloviating" aristocrats, and the "depraved men and scoundrels, underpaid, and despised," staffing the police department. He hated Moscow's restaurants, which, he believed, served nothing but "debauchery . . . music, billiards, Gypsies, buffets, and girls, and there is drink, gambling, and disease for everyone from peasants to officers."[10] Possessing "the soul of a despot," Rostopchin ruled Moscow accordingly.[11] On his first days on the job, in June 1812, he ordered prayer services for himself, banned smoking on the streets, and raided casinos. He aligned himself with the rabble, even telling the tsar that peasants made the best police officers, and he routinely posted "friendly messages" to the public about quality-of-life issues in a "rustic," "fairytale style."[12]

Rostopchin complained to the tsar about Kutuzov leaving Moscow—"he's lost his mind"—but he found purpose in the decision.[13] Now he alone would be the hero; now he had the chance to cleanse Moscow of the foreign elements that had corrupted the old way of life. His xenophobia was well known, and now, to his morbid delight, the French devil was on the very doorstep. In a semi-autobiographical collection of pamphlets from just before the invasion called "Oh, the French!" (Okh, frantsuzï!) Rostopchin lampooned the French Revolution as a "riot in a mental hospital" and Napoleon as a "rogue."[14] He echoed the Holy Synod in denouncing Napoleon as the Antichrist intent on wrecking the Orthodox faith. Friends recalled him using a bust of Napoleon as a chamber pot.

The first order of business was to get average Muscovites—not the snobs in the salons—to join him in laughing at the French. Rostopchin distributed caricatures of Napoleon on the streets and encouraged the public to wipe their derrieres with them. Besides laughter, the cartoons were meant to stoke ethnic nationalist hatred, as were the bulletins he published in *Moscow News* (*Moskovskiye vedomosti*) and put in the hands of priests, the police, and town criers. These are full of rhymes, folksy arcana, and threats, as this August 9, 1812, bulletin bears out:

> Thank God, all is fine and calm here in Moscow! Bread isn't getting more expensive, and meat is getting cheaper. Everyone wants the same thing, to beat the bastards, and that'll happen. Let's pray to God, equip our soldiers, and send them into the ranks. Don't be afraid of anything: we're under a storm cloud; let's blow it away. Once everything makes it through the mill, we'll have flour. But beware of one thing: drunkards and fools; they stagger around with their ears flapping open and take others by surprise. Some think Napoleon has good intentions even as he flays them alive. He promises everything but nothing comes of it. He promises soldiers field marshalships, the poor he promises mountains of gold, the people, freedom. He gets them by their hair, puts them in a vice, and sends them to their deaths, gets them killed either there or here. And for this reason I ask, if one of our people, or one of the foreigners among us, begins to praise him and promise him this or that, then no matter who he is, grab him by the hair and send him to jail.
>
> Lord, Heavenly Tsar! Prolong the days of our pious earthly tsar! Prolong Your grace to Orthodox Russia, prolong the courage of your Christ-loving warriors, prolong the loyalty and love for the Fatherland of the Orthodox Russian people! Direct the steps of the soldiers to the destruction of our enemies, enlighten and strengthen them with the power of the Life-Giving Cross, that protects their brows; and with this sign we will triumph.[15]

Moscow would survive the French, the bulletins proclaimed, so long as everyone stayed calm, put down the bottle, and kept an eye out for traitors. Rostopchin echoed the tsar's appeal to the Holy Synod and commanded the faithful to take up "arms and shield" to preserve "the faith of the fathers."[16] The locals joined him in harassing foreigners and anyone speaking foreign languages on the streets. Rostopchin convinced thousands to join a popular militia after shoving Moscow's French residents onto barges bound for Nizhny Novgorod. The relocation was for their own protection, he claimed. Soon Jewish tavern owners became a target, and Rostopchin sought the expulsion of Moscow's Freemasons for imagined acts of subversion. Secret societies, he decided, posed a threat to the state, since "impeccable" people didn't need to keep secrets.[17]

Smolensk had fallen and the French were nearing Moscow. Rostopchin, however, wasn't going to evacuate until he had to, and he would do it on his own terms: once all other options had been exhausted, like dropping bombs on the roads into Moscow from massive hot air balloons. (He even hosted a German inventor promising to make this dream a reality.)[18] On August 17, Rostopchin belatedly ordered the evacuation of the wounded and the sick—a special concern of his—only to find out that there weren't enough carts and horses to get all of them to safety.[19] His attention then turned to securing the arsenal, government records, the treasures of the sacristy (the room where the patriarch prepared his sermons), and the art and icons in the cathedrals. He wanted to neutralize Moscow's heaviest weapons, the Kremlin cannons, and confronted the challenge of relocating ninety thousand firearms (including a thousand hunting guns purchased by the authorities at a fair) and fifty thousand sabers, broadswords, and cutlasses. (The numbers are approximate; Rostopchin was shocked to discover that the contents of the arsenal had never been inventoried.) He filled barges with guns and gunpowder, but several ran aground or got stuck and had to be detonated.[20]

Sabers went to the Cossacks; functional firearms were sent to Russian soldiers outside of the city along with guns in need of repair. Near the end of August, weapons began to be distributed to the public, in delicate fashion. Having trivialized the French threat, now he somehow had to avoid fear and panic. On his request, the metropolitan held a calming prayer service, after which everyone gathered, made the sign of the cross, and selected a weapon from the Kremlin arsenal for their personal protection.

The general exodus increased after the battle near the village of Borodino on August 26, 1812. Napoleon was running low on soldiers and funds, although the latter problem was easier to solve than the former (through the counterfeiting of Russian banknotes or French assignats).[21] Wealthier Russians locked up their manor houses and headed into the fields. Carriages clogged the roads, laden with human goods (cooks, maids, nurses, footmen, and jesters) as well as furniture and décor. Carts carried merchants, tradesmen, and their families along with deserters disguised as women and wounded soldiers. Those unable to move were left to their fates. "Moscow was shaken with horror," a noblewoman recalled of her decision to flee.[22] The governor-general bid her farewell with withering sarcasm: "I am in fact glad that noble ladies and merchant wives are leaving Moscow so they can feel safe." The result will be "less panic, less gossip."[23] But of course panic and gossip spread, and even his closest allies evacuated. Rostopchin would too, escaping to Vladimir on September 2, three days after his wife and children had left. The poor and infirm had no choice but to shelter in churches and hope to escape the worst.

The French entered Moscow on September 2, 1812, after exchanging grapeshot and cannonballs with the surrounding Russian positions. Napoleon imagined a grander entrance, with flags and bugles and curious onlookers, but he didn't get it—a predicament neatly, if misleadingly, summarized by Pushkin in his novel-in-verse *Eugene Onegin* (chapter 7.37):

> And here's Petrovsky Castle, hoary
> Amid its park. In somber dress
> It wears with pride its recent glory:
> Napoleon, drunk with fresh success,
> Awaited here, in vain, surrender—
> For kneeling Moscow's hand to tender
> The ancient Kremlin's hallowed keys.
> But Moscow never bent her knees,
> Nor bowed her head in subjugation;
> No welcome feast did she prepare
> The restless hero waiting there—

But lit instead a conflagration.
From here he watched, immersed in thought,
The awesome blaze my Moscow wrought.[24]

Napoleon made it to "Petrovsky Castle," better known as the Petrovsky Travel Palace, on a beautiful August afternoon. It was built by Catherine the Great and served as the last rest stop on trips from St. Petersburg to Moscow. (It isn't that far from the palace to the Kremlin, about a two-hour walk down present-day Leningradsky Prospekt to Belarus train station, then straight onto Tverskaya past Mayakovsky and Pushkin Squares.) Sunlight dappled church domes; bees buzzed; agitation surrendered to drowsy calm. The French emperor's soldiers forgot, for a moment, their saddle sores, imagining the comforts of the aristocratic homes they would soon occupy. Their leader looked through his telescope expecting a delegation of "boyars" to hand over the "keys" to the Kremlin. He had no clue where exactly he was or even what epoch he was in: boyars as a political force hadn't existed since Peter the Great.

Napoleon sent word to Paris that Moscow had fallen. But no Russian official deigned to meet with him, and his patience began to wear thin—rather comedically. He ordered scouts into Moscow to find who was in charge; hearing that no one was in charge, he told them to round up whatever boyars they could find. Eventually, some bedraggled Muscovites turned up, not to escort him into the city but to complain about Napoleon's soldiers stealing from them. The final laugh line—in historical retrospect—has to do with the name of the hill on which Napoleon was parked: Poklonnaya (Sloped). Its alternate, folkloric name is Bow Down Hill (related to *poklon*, or bow), the place where, in the Rurik era, foreigners made this physical act of submission to Moscow's ruler. Knowing the meaning behind the name might have alerted Napoleon to the fact he wasn't going to be given keys, or salt and bread, or a letter from the tsar, or any kind of power anytime soon.[25] Doubtless he fumed; doubtless, too, the image of him proudly and inertly standing on the hill is false. He rode around the palace and the surrounding village, crossed the dilapidated bridge across the Moskva River, then turned around and rode back. He decided he needed to fix the bridge. His face reddened, he ranted and raved, and then, his frustration peaking, Napoleon acted. His soldiers entered Moscow in three columns, crossing the Moskva at Sparrow Hills, at Fili, and through the district (former village) of Dorogomilovo. The city was deserted and desolate. Moscow had a population of roughly 270,000 before the invasion; fewer than 10,000 had stayed behind to witness its occupation. Napoleon set up quarters in the Kremlin without fanfare. In his novel *War and Peace,* Leo Tolstoy imagined the foreign emperor's bewilderment and disappointment in a single sentence: "The *coup de théâtre* had not come off."[26]

As the Grande Armée entered, Russian soldiers exited. The groups rode past one another, the officers saluting and communicating in "a friendly manner," even dismounting now and then to exchange souvenirs. Inside Moscow proper, the French encountered servants, assorted ne'er-do-wells, empty stores, and trash. Tolstoy has one of his characters fantasizing about assassinating Napoleon, but no such plot awaited the French emperor. His soldiers, though, had their hands full at the Kremlin. A group of armed Muscovites clashed with them at the Trinity (Troitskaya) tower. The event is habitually interpreted as a heroic example of self-sacrifice for the homeland. Accounts conflict, however, and Russian historians have winnowed out the fiction over time to make the event more tragic— or, in Vladimir Zemtsov's assessment, "pathetic"—than heroic. The French directed cannonballs at the tower gates, broke them down, and shot the nameless Russian patriots point-blank. Some sources describe the "last defenders of the Kremlin" as "a drunken crowd of urban scum" with savage impulses: "There was a crowd of armed Muscovites" in the towers, according to one account from a bandaged-up officer from Naples (a French client state during this period) that was passed to a Russian chronicler. After surprising the invaders with gunfire and wounding several of them, the Muscovites cheered and rushed forward. "A big strong man rushed at the Neapolitan, stabbed him in the leg with a bayonet, then pulled him off his horse by the leg, lay down on him and began to bite his face." The

Neapolitan's men tried to pull the attacker off, "but it was impossible, so the attacker hacked him to death on the spot." He "smelled of vodka," the Neapolitan added, with disgust.[27]

Official Russian descriptions of the Napoleonic invasion insist that the French did all the looting, running amok through the mansions of merchants and the estates of the nobles as the remnants of Moscow's population looked on. Historian Mariya Pavlova finds that the plundering began even before the French rode in: Moscow's destitute took advantage of the crisis to relieve the rich of their gold, silver, and lace.[28] The French continued the effort, as would any occupying army after a long campaign, ordering Russians at gunpoint to help them cart everything from flour and sugar to sofas and chandeliers to the dugouts, grottoes, and pavilions that they made their homes. They parked English armchairs on Persian carpets in the middle of the streets. The French officer Eugene Labeaume recalled his comrades living "in terrible bad weather in the middle of a field, exposed to the elements, but also dining on porcelain plates and drinking from silver cups and generally having luxuries that could only be imagined among the richest of the rich in comfortable environments." There was no respect for religion: the French turned churches into barracks and desecrated icons. Historian Alexander Martin notes that defecation became a tool of war: "Accounts by nobles report that enemy soldiers defecated in churches and threw icons into latrines. Nobles wrote that in upper-class homes, Napoleon's men broke what they could not steal—furniture was smashed, mirrors shattered, books ripped apart—and defecated in the refined interiors. Even officers used ballrooms, libraries, and the like as latrines."[29]

Then the fires began, lit by the Russians, by the French, and by God. The flames spread quickly, ravaging block after block of wooden buildings, engulfing a hospital (the French seem to have been specifically responsible for this blaze, along with another at the Vdoviy dom, or Widow's House, charitable organization), and forcing people across cart-jammed bridges past shredded, discarded uniforms, garbage, and feces toward the river's edge. Voices of the doomed mingled with the echoes of prayer and discordant singing. When the fire threatened his quarters in the Kremlin, Napoleon gathered his precious *articles de toilette* and left. He and his commanders took in the spectacle of Moscow's self-immolation from Petrovsky Travel Palace. Then, on September 8, Napoleon sent a letter to Alexander I claiming that he had no role whatsoever in the fire and outrageously blaming the tsar for his being in Moscow in the first place: "There is no more beautiful, proud city of Moscow: Rostopchin set fire to it," Napoleon announced. "I started a war against your Majesty without anger: one note from you before or after the last battles would stop my procession. . . . If your Majesty keeps some more of those past feelings, you will favorably receive this letter. Nevertheless, you can only be grateful to me for being aware of what is happening in Moscow. By this, my dear sir, my brother, I pray to God that he will guard your Majesty and shore under his holy and dignified protection."[30]

The fire ran its course over three days, and the September weather brightened. Napoleon returned to the Kremlin, instructing his officers, in between card games and reports from the field, to re-establish order on the streets. It wasn't easy. He had an artist in his retinue, a product of Stuttgart with the polyglot name Christian Wilhelm von Faber du Fauer, who drew a picture of the scene with this caption:

> Here and there groups of unfortunate inhabitants could be seen wandering in the grim labyrinth, hoping to discover some part of their home that had escaped destruction or to dig up some miserable food to prolong their unhappy existence. Our troops were everywhere, hoping to discover some trophy and, like children, satisfy their greed with some bauble, only to discard it as soon as they came across some other novelty.[31]

Napoleon appointed a municipal commander, Antoine Durosnel, whose gendarmes enforced a curfew. The occupation had four aims, none achieved: strengthening Moscow's defenses against Russians; rounding up robbers; bringing dispossessed Russians over to the French side; and offering peace proposals to the tsar. The French soldiers were undisciplined, seen smoking and drinking and mucking about before and after inspections. One or two trumpets blared, snare drums rattled, and Napoleon himself arrived on a white horse. The soldiers briefly smartened up. Napoleon gave them a quick, bored glance, ignored their salutation, then released them. The occupation settled into a routine. Millers returned to their mills, washer-women to their washing, while French officers forced Russians to cook and clean for them.

Theatrical life also resumed, after a fashion, with the performance of French comedies and Russian dances in a pleasant serf theater on an unburned street. The texts were tweaked in honor of Napoleon and the depleted Grand Armée. The performers were local French actors who dressed in clothes nicked from mansions and churches. Morale was low, the performances uneven. These included Marivaux's *Le Jeu de l'amour et du hasard* (*The Game of Love and Chance*); Pierre Cérou's *L'Amant autour et Valet* (*The Lover, Author and Valet*); and Jean-François Regnard's *Le Distrait* (*The Absent-Minded Gentleman*), whose protagonist manages to forget his own wedding.[32] Napoleon didn't turn up; he had other things to do. The audience swilled wine stolen from estate cellars and smoked "tobacco from Hungarian pipes with small stems," indifferent to the performances except during patriotic speeches when they bellowed, on cue, "*Vive l'empereur! Vive la France! Vive l'armée française!*"[33]

The wine and tobacco disappeared after a couple of weeks. Meat also vanished, then flour, oats, and other staples. The occupiers roamed the ashes "as pale as shades," enfeebled and emaciated, "searching for food and clothing but finding nothing, wrapping themselves in horse blankets and torn coats," with "either peasants' hats or women's thick, torn scarfs" covering their heads. "It was like a masquerade," a Russian recalled of the French getups.[34] Nothing remained of the belief in liberating conquest that had borne them into Moscow, a place they could not fathom and much less subdue.

Napoleon ordered a retreat, though not before trying to blow up the Kremlin. He also wanted to do away with Novodevichiy (New Maidens) Convent, which he mistook for a fortress. The foul deed was entrusted to the rearguard marshal Édouard Mortier, who rounded up Russians in the street and forced them to dig holes under the wall and churches of the Kremlin. But rain, or perhaps heroic Cossacks, snuffed out the wicks leading to barrels of gunpowder, and nuns diluted the barrels of gunpowder stashed in the crypt. (The French had positioned a barrel of liquor at the entrance to fuel an inferno; the nuns emptied it out.) There were five explosions. The "water-lifting" tower (Vodovzvodnaya); the first unnamed tower; the Corner Arsenal (Arsenal'naya Uglovaya); and Petrovskaya towers all collapsed; two others, Nikolskaya and Borovitskaya, suffered severe damage, and the Ivan the Great bell tower lost its belfry. Novodevichiy survived.

Following this fiasco, the French pulled out. Battered soldiers skittered along litter-strewn, stench-filled streets in twos and threes to their formation points, minds benumbed, stomachs bloated from starvation. The fates of those who didn't make it out varied: a few who had tended to sick Russian babies at the start of the occupation or otherwise demonstrated a human touch were given shelter in cellars. Most were killed on the spot or tortured to death, their corpses left to rot in the streets in the late autumn sun. Mobs (what has been politely called a "popular militia" of serfs, peasants, and assorted unpaid volunteers) awaited the retreating soldiers in the forests, seeking revenge for the burning, the looting, the desecration of churches, the butchering of livestock. Tools of iron and wood gouged out eyes and vital organs.

The withdrawal continued into December. The newspaper *Moskovskiye vedomosti* kept Muscovites apprised of Napoleon's retreat and the Russian attacks on his forces. The road to Vilna was littered with bodies, both people and horses; the French emperor was down to less than a "tenth" of the "various warriors" he had brought into Russia.[35] The temperature fell. Subzero winds put out campfires; ammunition ran out; carts fell apart; frozen corpses were cannibalized. Napoleon survived to regroup and even claimed victory for his Russian campaign, but his command had disintegrated. His European allies became his foes and Russia's friends; serial defeats forced him to abdicate. The French monarchy was restored. No longer a romantic hero, Napoleon was exiled to the island of St. Helena,

The Fire of Moscow, September 1812, by Johann Christian Oldendorp
(1772–1844).

where at least the climate was more forgiving. His time had ended;
he wrote his memoirs.

Rostopchin returned to Moscow on October 24 to confront nothing—
or rather, nothingness itself. The streets in the center were missing, and
four out of every five buildings on Tverskaya had burned to beneath
the ground. (Rostopchin's residence escaped destruction, barely.) The
neighborhoods of Kitai-gorod, Prechistenka, Yakimanka, and Sretenka
surrounding the Kremlin were gone. The outskirts where the French
had stationed themselves remained intact because Napoleon's soldiers
had been put to work dousing flames, again and again and again until
they themselves feared immolation. Statistics indicate that just 28.6
percent of Moscow's housing stock survived the fire. Of 387 government and municipal buildings, half still stood; of 8,771 private
buildings, only a quarter; and merely 1,368 (16%) of the city's 8,521
stone and wooden shops. Peasants from outside Moscow had joined

the French in ransacking manor houses. There was no way to restore law and order, impossible for police to ascertain who had stolen what from whom.[36]

The Kremlin remained save for the fallen towers and collapsed walls. The arsenal, the Palace of Facets, and senate building all suffered damage, as did the plundered monasteries. The moat overflowed with debris. Perhaps for obvious reasons, the French left the Catholic Church in Moscow alone. The abbot was amazed, however, that during the occupation he "didn't see even the shadow of Napoleon. He didn't visit our church and probably didn't even think to. Four or five officers from old French families attended services; two or three confessed. During the occupation, up to 12,000 of them died, but I buried only one officer and a servant of General Grushi according to the rites of the church. All others, officers and soldiers, were buried by their comrades in nearby gardens. There is not even a shadow of belief in an afterlife in them."[37] St. Basil's Cathedral survived along with the muncipal government (Duma) building.

Also spared was the Moscow Imperial Foundling Home, established in 1763 on the embankment close to where the Yauza joins the Moskva. The dowager empress, mother of Catherine the Great's successor, Pavel, oversaw the orphanage and funneled profits from a trio of banks into its operations. Its raison d'être: nurturing and protecting abandoned or surrendered children through their teen years, treasuring them, filling their minds with purpose and hearts with love, and forming from them an enlightened class of honest toilers. The architecture was neoclassical, the education rigorous, and the ideal—reversing the fate of the outcast—unassailable.

Before Napoleon arrived, the dowager empress ordered the children evacuated to Kazan. Rostopchin procured enough carts for 333 wards (143 boys and 190 girls) to head east along with their teachers, hospital patients, and 52 women from another caregiving institution, the Moscow Widow's House, where several hundred women and children lived under the loving care of the Sisters of Mercy. About 350 children were left behind, and a handful joined the fight against the French.

During the occupation of Moscow, the orphanage was managed

by a retired general, Ivan Tutolmin. He would later boast about his heroism during the siege, claiming to have driven cattle from burned farmyards into the orphanage to provide milk for infants. He hid the six cows in question from the gendarmes "with incredible difficulty in the gardens and cellar."[38] When it came to helping patients in hospitals and children trapped in schools, Tutolmin proved ineffective, but he did what he could for his charges. He kept the larders full and removed the wooden fences from the grounds of the orphanage to protect the building from fire. Even so, the stables, barn, and *apteka* burned to the ground while the window frames in the inner courtyard smoldered. Terrified ten-year-olds doused sparks round the clock. Napoleon assured Tutolmin that the orphanage would not be looted, but some French soldiers could not be restrained. A French-speaking guard was posted at the entrance; signs implored potential looters to consider that infants and children—the poorest of the poor—sheltered inside.

Napoleon checked in on the children himself and seemed to have had a soft spot for them, but Tutolmin rightly feared for their well-being after disease swept through the debilitated French forces. And when Napoleon left with those of his men who could travel, hundreds of sick and wounded Frenchmen remained at the Foundling Home. Rostopchin returned to discover the compound in a foul state: gaping windows, doors hanging from their hinges, dung and bones underfoot. The children were shell-shocked and sick, having heard the explosions in the Kremlin and been exposed for weeks to the stench of corpses floating in the river from which they drank infected water.[39] The returning Russians cleared the orphanage of French stragglers, and it resumed operation—a patriotic survivor, defenseless save for its defense of civility.

Rostopchin tried to impose law and order on Moscow but overreached, turning the treatment of Russians suspected of treason into gruesome spectacle. He made an exception for those officials who had been forced, for survival's sake, to work for the French.[40] In an episode immortalized by Tolstoy, just before the French invasion a translator named Mikhaílo Vereshchagin, "the son of a merchant of the Moscow second guild, educated by foreigners and corrupted by tavern conversations," was arrested for treason. He had translated one of Napoleon's proclamations into Russian, and on July 3, 1812, Rostopchin publicly denounced him in one of his bulletins.[41] The senate reviewed the case and, taking account of the status of his father, sentenced Vereshchagin to twenty-five lashes of the whip and exile to Nerchinsk, a fort in the far east of Russia.[42] That wasn't sufficient for Rostopchin, who brought the young man before the public in chains. "His emaciated young face, with a hopeless expression, disfigured by the shaven head, was lowered," Tolstoy writes of the confrontation between Rostopchin (allegorized as Pontius Pilate) and Vereshchagin (Christ).[43] The crowd stared at him in silence. Rostopchin turned pale, jaw trembling, sweat beading his brow as he insisted, fiercely, that the traitor be put to death. A soldier struck him in the head with the handle of his saber. Vereshchagin yelped. That act of violence unleashed the crowd, and Vereshchagin died under their feet.

In recounting this incident, Tolstoy highlights the hypocrisy of Rostopchin's "social philosophies" and their potential for evil.[44] "He was a traitor and a turncoat," Tolstoy imagines Rostopchin thinking of the murdered translator. "I couldn't let him go unpunished, and besides, *je faisais d'une pierre deux coups*; for the sake of calm I gave the people a victim and I punished a villain."[45] This terrible deed was followed by others; it seems that Rostopchin relished them, feverish with rage, and then, after satisfying his bloodlust, rode off in his carriage as gentle as a lamb. The tsar, however, didn't approve. In November, after Napoleon's expulsion from Moscow, Alexander I admonished Rostopchin for his cruelty:

> I would have been completely satisfied with the character of your actions in such difficult circumstances were it not for the Vereshchagin affair, or, better said, its conclusion. I am too truthful to speak to you in any other language than that of complete openness. His execution was pointless, and in no circumstance should have been resolved in such a manner. Hanging him, shooting him—would have been much better.[46]

In 1814, Rostopchin was relieved of his post. He hadn't been the hero he wanted to be, and everyone hated him: the tsar, the court, the newspapers, returning Muscovites gobsmacked by their incinerated city. He fled from Holy Rus to Europe, which he had spent most of his life insulting. In Carlsbad, he was treated for a myriad of ailments, including hemorrhoids, spontaneous bile leaks, and asthma. (His life had been stressful.) Then he visited Frankfurt, London, and his *bête noire*, Paris, to talk about his experiences. For a while, he felt welcome in the French capital, listening to the chitchat on the streets with mild amusement and deciding that the French at home were better than the French on the march. Then, perhaps predictably, he soured on them. "They seem kind at first, then become burdensome and finally disgusting."[47]

He thought about retiring in Europe but thought again. Rostopchin died back in Moscow in 1826, having published a book titled *Pravda o Moskovskom pozhare* (*The Truth About the Moscow Fire*), in which he energetically denied his obvious involvement in the catastrophe. No, he insisted, he hadn't kept firecrackers in his house to light his stove, and if firecrackers or other detonators had been found there in his absence, as a French doctor claimed, they must have been planted by others who had pinched them from estates preparing for "holiday celebrations." Nor was the fire caused by the "quack" hot-air balloon technician "Schmidt." Rostopchin denounced his antagonists for spinning the tale of the "ball" to mock the Russians, when in fact the French had used one themselves, in the 1815 Battle of Fleurus.[48]

The loss of Moscow was Russia's gain insofar as the disaster awakened intense feelings of patriotism throughout the Russian-speaking lands. This was Rostopchin's baleful achievement as much as Kutuzov's. The almost-erased city became a place to identify with and be proud of, and the story of its intentional/unintentional self-sacrifice continues to be told by the government up to the present day. Russia benefited from British subsidies to settle its massive wartime debts. According to an 1815 report to the tsar, the fighting in Russia from 1812 to 1813 drained 157 million rubles from the treasury.[49] This figure seems low, however, and excludes the cost of rebuilding. Fixing the finances meant sharp reductions in spending, higher taxes, and the privatization of government estates.[50]

Alexander I made this newfound pride manifest by clearing the debris, interring the bodies, and transforming Moscow into something that it had never been before: orderly, landscaped, public-minded, still Russian but also imperial. From the ashes, a new Moscow would arise. The tsar convened a reconstruction commission with two subcommissions: one responsible for land development, the other for architecture. William Hastie, a Scottish architect working in Russia, took the reins. He tabled a plan that linked Moscow's radial circles to squares—three series of them reaching through the fortifications and gates—such that the city would incorporate thirty-six new neighborhoods. The oldest trade streets would be paralleled by new ones, creating, for example, an upper and lower Tverskaya. But Hastie hadn't properly considered the Kremlin, Moscow's spiritual center, in his plans. The error was unforgivable.

The commission then enlisted the neoclassical architect Osip Bové (Beauvais) to lead the reconstruction effort. Of Russified Italian and German background, he was given the name Giuseppe at birth (1784) although everyone in his hometown of Moscow called him Osip (Iosif). His parents hoped he would work in design, the same profession as his distinguished relatives, and enrolled him in an architectural school. Bové became an expert on the Kremlin, restoring walls and, at twenty-two, rebuilding the Vodovzvodnaya tower that, five years later, Napoleon detonated. During the war, Bové served alongside Tolstoy's father, Nikolay. When he returned from the fields to Moscow in 1813, gazing at the devastation, Bové began to rebuild Moscow in conversation with the past while reimagining its future.

How to remove the narrow streets and the jumble of styles defining the estates? Traditionalists resisted him, but Bové had a mandate. The commission's first order of business was to define the "number of stories, dimensions, and color scheme of the buildings" under construction and determine "façade designs." The government provided 5 million rubles in subsidies to residents seeking to rebuild their homes and another 1.5 million rubles to level and repair streets—a fraction of the cost of the damage. Private residences in the center would be at once "classical" and "intimate." Bové restored half of them and added 623 new ones made of stone. He built roofs of wood instead of iron, presumably to save costs but inviting yet another inferno. Muscovites living along *zemlyanoy val* were asked to "plant gardens the entire length of the fronts of their houses along the ravine, so that over time the entire span would be lined with foliage."[51] European stores appeared. Parks and promenades opened.

Muscovites of means could propose reconstruction projects so long as their plans resonated with what Bové had in mind. When he rebuffed them, nefarious gossip spread about his personal life.[52] The noble class shunned him but couldn't remove him from his post. Alexander Griboyedov's great drama in verse, *Woe from Wit* (*Gore ot uma*, 1823), captured Bové's predicament in this snatch of dialogue between the chatterers and naysayers frequenting the salons:

Pavel Famusov (a conservative family man, concluding a speech about Moscow's traditions):
Moscow is a city that is—sui generis.

Colonel Sergey Sergeyevich Skalozub:
We owe the fire, in my view,
a city greatly beautified.

Famusov:
Don't remind me—such a pity! Sidewalks,
streets, and houses—everything is new.

Alexander Chatsky (a youthful idealist):
New houses, but old prejudices linger.[53]

When Bové cleared Red Square of debris and grime, he suffered a storm of ridicule from the families of merchants who considered it their right to trade there. He beat them back, emptying the square of businesses in favor of an enclosed shopping arcade opposite the Kremlin—the prototype of present-day GUM (Gosudarstvennïy universal'nïy magazin, the State Department Store). He also drained the moat, laid paving stones, and erected a monument to Minin and Pozharsky, the unlikely heroes of the early seventeenth-century *Smuta* turned into symbols of eternal resistance. The Soviets would relocate the monument to the back of the square, in front of St. Basil's, to allow for athletic demonstrations, parades, and weapons displays.

Along with the moat, Bové eliminated the Neglinka. Sort of. He encased the stream in a pipe more than two miles long—a humiliating fate for the city's aquatic lifeline—and turned the former flood plain along the western walls of the Kremlin into a garden with winding paths and "turf, linden, birch, rowan, and other trees and shrubs." The garden was designed and redesigned, and the name was changed from Kremlin Garden to Alexander Garden (Aleksandrovskiy sad). The main entrance is a polished black iron gate decorated with scenes of Napoleon's defeat. An Italian grotto called "The Ruins" was built into the Kremlin wall in the middle of the garden and includes four massive columns symbolizing Moscow's resilience. The stones inside came from buildings destroyed in the 1812 fire.[54]

Meantime, Bové and other members of the redevelopment team picked up on Hastie's idea of linking Moscow's concentric rings to a network of squares. These included, in the center, Manege Square, a parade ground dominated by a rectangular building in a muscular Doric style with a suspended roof—an impressive feat of engineering for the time. It's been used for all sorts of things: concerts, flower shows, art and food exhibits. In 1817, a regiment of two thousand soldiers crammed into the space to mark the fifth-year anniversary of Napoleon's retreat. The tsar traveled to Moscow for the celebration.[55] The square closest to Manege became the home of the Bolshoi Theater, which Bové built over three years between 1821 and 1824.[56] He collaborated at the start of this project with Andrey Mikhaylov, a professor of the academy of arts and the winner of the design competition for the space. There had been another opera and ballet theater at this location that included markets on the first floor, but it caught fire in 1805 and was razed to the ground save for a single wall. (The blaze started in the cloakroom, just before a performance of a

comic opera about a mermaid, *Lesta, or the Dnepr Water Nymph.*)
Bové reconceived the theater without the markets, turning it into a
majestic edifice of limestone columns, and a portico topped with the
quadriga driven by Apollo. Another smaller theater for plays went up
on the right side of the Bolshoi from the front.

Bové is also the original designer of the Triumphal Arch
(Triumfal'naya arka), an architectural riposte to the Arc de Triomphe in Paris, which had been built in celebration of Napoleon's triumph at Austerlitz. The wooden arch erected in 1814 had rotted in
the rain and snow, so Bové fashioned a brick and ashlar ensemble
(arch, guardhouses, and decorative fencing) on a square marking the
entrance to Moscow from St. Petersburg where the Belarus railroad
station stands today. Designing the square delayed the building of the
arch, which opened on September 20, 1834, after five years of financial setbacks and municipal dithering. Bové just missed the opening:
he had died two months before, at age forty-nine. The metropolitan
blanched at the inclusion of mythological gods in the molding and
refused to bless it. The arch patriotically, if sacrilegiously, stood on
Tverskaya zastava for 102 years, far into the Soviet era, but it jammed
up traffic on what had become the link between Gorky Street (Tverskaya) and the highway to Leningrad (St. Petersburg). Mossovet
(the Moscow Council of Workers' Deputies) had the arch and the
guardhouses pulled down, slab by slab, and the decorative elements
and inscriptions interred in a museum.

Legend claims that these objects would have stayed in the museum
were it not for cosmonaut Yuri Gagarin, who highlighted the importance of historical preservation in a speech delivered to the Central
Committee of the Komsomol (All-Union Leninist Youth Communist League) on December 27, 1965. "In my opinion," the hero of the
Soviet space program told the assembly, "we're still not cultivating
sufficient respect for our heroic past, we seldom think about preserving monuments. In Moscow, the Arc de Triomphe of 1812 was taken
away and hasn't been restored; the Cathedral of Christ the Savior,
built with money raised throughout the country in honor of the victory over Napoleon, was destroyed. Has the name of this monument
eclipsed its patriotic essence? I could continue the list of victims of

the barbaric attitude towards the monuments of the past. Unfortunately, there are many such examples." In reality, the decision to restore the monument (not the cathedral) had already been made by the Council of Ministers of the USSR on December 10, 1965. Gagarin was just making the decision public.[57]

The arch was put back up on an avenue named after Kutuzov. Another location of historical significance with the best view of central Moscow was rejected for logistical reasons. This was Sloped Hill, where Napoleon had waited in vain for a delegation of Muscovites to welcome him into the Kremlin as co-ruler of the Russian Empire. The restorers did their homework; they consulted Bové's designs in the archive and recreated the patriotic carvings and moldings and ironwork of the original structure. But that structure had a problem: it didn't stand out in a neighborhood of brown brick buildings under gray skies. Mossovet couldn't do anything about the skies, but the land was flattened, roads expanded, and an underpass dug to give the arch prominence. Now it is part of Ploshchad' Pobedï, Victory Square, and the park and museum complex built in the 1990s merges the defeat of Napoleon with the defeat of the Nazis and other achievements. The symbolism is diverse and disorienting, beginning with the arch, where a figure from classical antiquity, Nike, shares real estate with Roman warriors wearing Russian chain mail. "The horror and doom of the enemies is contrasted with the firm confidence and boundless determination of the Russian soldiers—the liberators of Moscow," Alexander Smirnov, author of a jingoistic book about 1812, writes of the designs on the arch.[58] In the center of the park stands an obelisk of St. George cutting a serpent's throat, slaying Russia's enemies.

GRAND THEATER

Two later Russian rulers earned the epithet "Great": Peter I and Catherine II. Their greatness comes from their outsized ambitions, including the occupation of territories with hostile populations: Peter founded the Russian Empire, which Catherine II expanded. Empires diversify and dilute populations, so Russia became less ethnically Russian, the land Russia seized—to the distress of its native inhabitants—more so.

Catherine II was overall the sunnier, more liberal sovereign, owing to her interest in education and culture as well as her occasional tolerance for divergent opinions. During her thirty-four-year reign, from 1762 to 1796, she was serious about civilizing a place she disliked: Moscow. "Never has a people held before its eyes more objects of fanaticism, such as miraculous icons at every step, churches, priests, convents, pilgrims, beggars, thieves, useless servants in the houses," she remarked. "What houses, what disorder there is in the houses, where the lots are immense and the courtyards are filthy swamps."[1] Peter had been born and raised in Moscow, but Catherine II, of combined Prussian and Swedish descent, didn't understand (or want to understand) Muscovites. The abattoirs and tanneries, the yowling guard dogs, the ice crusts, mud puddles, and rats, the muttering inwardness of bureaucrats and their scruffy beards—everything put her off. What most visitors considered fetching—the multicolored wooden buildings tended by modest, humble souls—were, she decided, the hovels of dotards. Moscow's more curious street names bolstered her biases. Lazy Lane was named after an area of the city without shopping arcades, where people bought goods from carts; Crooked Knee was a road bent out of shape; Wench-ville (Bab'yegorodskiy) perhaps recalled a legend about brave Moscow women beheading Mongol invaders, but more likely referenced the hanging cast-iron hammers (wenches) used to drive piles into the bog. And then there was Buzz Street (ulitsa Zhu-zha), tribute to the insects swarming above a branch of the Moskva named Buzz River.[2]

Catherine II wanted to remake Moscow—and rural Russia—in the image of her cosmopolitan court in St. Petersburg: enlightened locales with a European aura about them. Neither would cooperate. Her golden age of aristocratic refinement was also a time of arbitrary favoritism. Lie down a sycophantic servant, get up owning a thousand serfs and slabs of land. Former loyalists began to second-guess Catherine's vision of civilization and her ability to impose Enlightenment values on the former capital.[3] Still, she persisted. On March 17, 1776, she granted Moscow's provincial prosecutor, Pyotr Urusov, exclusive rights to mount shows for public audiences. In return, Urusov was required to donate proceeds to the Imperial Foundling Home (the state orphanage) and build a stone theater with a moat. It's often thought that Catherine II's largesse reflected her personal creative interests. She wrote plays and opera libretti, several of which have been translated, including *Oh, These Times!* (1772) and *The Siberian Shaman* (1786). Their plots indicate the empress's impatience with the anarchic mysticism and arcane beliefs of the people she ruled— and, in the best eighteenth-century fashion, she was willing to wield satire rather than the knout.[4] But beyond making people laugh, and perhaps less fearful, she wanted to improve Moscow's standing in the empire and in the world. Place culture in a polished space, and it would attract power. Build a theater in Moscow of finest materials, and the city could aspire to something, temper itself, acquire a loftiness that all the fighting and violence had done nothing to cultivate.

Urusov needed a partner and found one in the traveling illusionist and entrepreneur Michael Maddox, who had come to Moscow from St. Petersburg, where he had tutored the future Tsar Pavel (Catherine II's eventual successor) in mathematics and, when the boy's diligence faltered, taught him magic tricks. On August 31, 1776, Urusov and Maddox signed a contract in the presence of the police, then began organizing Sunday concerts and fireworks spectaculars on the outskirts of the city and light entertainments in an annex of Count Roman Vorontsov's estate. When Vorontsov's theater, little more than a wooden shed, burned down, Urusov surrendered his share of the enterprise to Maddox.[5]

They had already acquired a parcel of land for a new theater on Petrovka, an ancient street named after Pyotr, the transplanted metropolitan of Kyiv, just behind the present-day location of the Bolshoi Theater. Maddox took out loans that he couldn't repay, faced death threats, and took out more loans, burying himself in debt for decades. The theater was built in five months for 130,000 rubles and opened on December 30, 1780. Like the Vienna Opera House and Kärntnertortheater, the Petrovsky, with its sloped plank roof, didn't exactly grace the skyline, but it was an impressive site. Only the neoclassical Senate Palace in the Kremlin and the Pashkov House, the first public museum in Moscow, could compete with its design.

Five doors on Petrovka opened onto three stone and two wooden staircases, which led to the auditorium with a stall, three tiers of boxes, and a gallery. Later, a rotunda with stucco garlands and a mezzanine covered with planks would be added. During intermission, patrons could visit the buffet, where cold appetizers were served by a French chef. Officials, merchants, and students scrunched together on benches on the floor; nobles occupied the loges, and commoners the uppermost stalls. There was a ladies' powder room, but no specific place for men to relieve themselves. Wax and tallow candles illuminated the theater, giving off a meaty smell that mixed cordially with the musk worn by the patrons. Mirrors amplified the stage light, as did handheld torches serving as spotlights. The basement of the rotunda included pantries for props and workshops for a tailor and carpenter, plus a larger space for musicians. Even those who could read music sometimes learned their parts by heart, helping Maddox save on paper, ink, and scribes.

The paved area in the front where carriages pulled up needed fencing off from the streets and alleys. A high wall separated the back of the theater and its water well from the surrounding buildings. Maddox lived in one of them; another presumably served as a stable and carriage house. The more magnificent houses nearby belonged to aristocrats. Maddox's performers settled in a residence down the street built for them not far from a drinking house called Petrovskoye kruzhalo, where they ate pretzels and drank aniseed vodka.

Maddox staged all kinds of entertainments, from comic operas, ballets, and masquerades to Shakespearean tragedies in first-class translations. He was proud of the circus and freak shows he had produced back in England, so equipped his theater with trap doors, mirrors, and mechanical contrivances to depict miracles and disasters. But not even the most dazzling of effects could keep Maddox's enterprise afloat. He clashed with the censors and lost his most talented actors to St. Petersburg's Imperial Theaters. He also had to compete with the serf troupes and orchestras belonging to Moscow's elite, fig-

Bolshoi Theater, 2017.

ures like Count Nikolay Sheremetyev, who staged luxurious opera and ballet performances at their estates outside of Moscow without charging visitors. As the competition grew, Maddox slipped into the burlesque. Pandering failed to expand his audience and merely confirmed the fears of old merchant families and pious townspeople already wary of the theater as corrupting public morality.

By 1794, Maddox was having trouble meeting payroll and found himself begging his stars to accept, instead of a salary, the chance to perform whatever and whenever they liked and keep a significant percentage of the proceeds. The arrangement he made along these lines with Pyotr Plavilshchikov, a pudgy, doe-eyed tragedian committed to representing the plights of the lower ranks, was advertised in the newspaper *Moskovskiye vedomosti* on December 13, 1794. "The performance is a benefit for Mr. Plavilshchikov, who receives no payment from the theater" and asks for "the indulgence of the esteemed public" in "flattering his hope" by attending.[6] He performed then quit, leaving town with the conductor of the orchestra. Maddox sought to increase receipts by staging *Pygmalion,* an Ovid-derived melodrama about a sculptor who, having renounced the pleasures of the flesh, falls in love with one of his own creations. (The goddess Venus takes pity on him and brings the statue to life.) The 1794 and 1796 performances of this drama, to sweet music by the Bohemian violinist Georg Benda, succeeded, but most productions of the period flopped.

The crisis deepened toward the end of Catherine II's reign and during the first years of her daughter-in-law's rise to power as wife of Tsar Pavel. Receiving news of the struggling theater, the empress consort, Mariya, dispatched an agent to report on the Petrovsky.[7] The emissary, Nikolay Maslov, wrote back three weeks later, on November 28, 1799, with a long list of calamities. The Petrovsky had been penniless for at least three years, and Maddox had nothing in the coffers, no one to sweep the stage and bait the mousetraps, no coal to stoke or wood to burn, no costumes for the pirates of the Aegean and their Greek women captives. The theater changed performances so frequently that actors failed to properly learn their roles; their costumes were often unkempt, and sometimes the performers wore their street frocks. Moreover, the theater and dressing rooms were so frightfully cold that the performers often fell ill. "The management, all the while," Maslov lamented, "rebukes them harshly."[8]

Mariya expressed genuine surprise that the hard up actors had not taken matters into their own hands and staged a hostile takeover. Maddox pledged to repair the theater and offered to heat it in advance of performances, but the entire theatrical enterprise had fallen to pieces, and no one from the Moscow aristocratic establishment wanted to clean up the mess. In 1802, Maddox sent a long letter to Mariya, now the dowager empress, in hopes that the Imperial Foundling Home would assume his debts, allowing him to retire with his pride intact after a quarter century of service to Russian culture. An audit revealed that both the theater and the orphanage were awash in red ink, so Mariya ordered the liquidation of Maddox's estate.

His merchant creditors campaigned to prosecute him and wrote to Nikolay Sherementyev for help. The language of the complaint, dated July 4, 1803, is fantastically ornate, stuffed with proverbs, Ryazan dialect, and biblical portends. The Old Believer merchants sought to reclaim the 90,000 rubles they were owed and hoped for Sherementyev's assistance in imprisoning Maddox, since he had played them for fools, "spinning around like a snake and a toad" to avoid his obligations and leaving them "as helpless as crawfish in a shallow" when it came time to collect.[9] Worse, he had made fun of their thick beards. The 90,000 rubles Maddox owed to them—on top of the 250,000 he owed to the governing board of the orphanage— could not be squeezed from Maddox's candle and firewood suppliers, who were also victims of his brazen cunning, and obviously couldn't be wrung out of the orphans in the troupe.

The merchants wanted Maddox to molder in prison until he opened his purse. But, financially speaking, Maddox was as "naked as a falcon," and because he still had the backing of the crown, he could not be locked up.[10] Their desire for revenge as well as repayment betrayed their ignorance of the perks of aristocratic quae pro quibus. Maddox knew that having connected the budget of his theater to the orphanage shielded him from arrest. He would "dive to the bottom of hell" with the 90,000 rubles they had lent him, leaving their children with "no meat for their soup."[11]

On Sunday, October 8, 1805, the Petrovsky Theater burned down save for its stone encasement. It seemed that the Day of Judgment had at last arrived for Maddox. The antisemitic press denounced him as a "typical sort of Jew," which he wasn't, and there was talk of eviction.[12] The dowager empress intervened to let him keep his house instead of giving it to his actors. For a time, he roamed the streets of Moscow in his crimson cloak, then retired to the dacha and garden that he had bought years before, at the height of his powers, in the village of Popovka southwest of Moscow. He died there on September 27, 1822, at age seventy-five, the father of six sons and six daughters who would scatter themselves across the empire.

The 1805 fire left Moscow's artists scrambling to find work performing on estates and in public gardens; theatrical life was once again concentrated in the homes of the nobility. The largest theaters exploited the talents of hundreds of serfs to stage operas, ballets, and divertissements by foreign (Italian) stage designers. Only in the spring of 1808 did the actors and dancers of Moscow find a new home in a domed wooden theater on "crooked-cornered, many-angled Arbat Square"; this theater was designed by Italian architect Karl (Carlo) Rossi, the son of a renowned ballerina, Gertruda Rossi–Le Picq, on order of Tsar Alexander I.[13] The new theater didn't survive the Napoleonic invasion, however, and our contemporary understanding of it comes from novels and short stories. In *War and Peace*, Tolstoy includes a scene at Rossi's theater. Seventeen-year-old Natasha Rostova, just humiliated by her fiancé's father and sister, goes to the opera accompanied by the socially ambitious and sexually attractive Hélène. At first, the opera fails to impress, but Natasha, wanting to lose herself in fantasies, falls under its spell. "She did not remember who she was and where she was and what was happening before her. She looked and thought, and the strangest thoughts flashed through her head unexpectedly, without connection. Now the thought came to her of jumping up to the footlights and singing the aria the actress was singing, then she wanted to touch a little old man who was sitting not far away with her fan, then to lean over to Hélène and tickle

230 . A KINGDOM AND A VILLAGE

her."[14] The opera itself is not named but is generally assumed to be an anachronistic mixture of Meyerbeer's *Robert le diable* and Gounod's *Faust*. Music, for Tolstoy, was a diabolical seduction, so too were dance and theater. In the fantastical story "Postmark: Moscow," Sigizmund Krzhizhanovsky imagines the ghosts of theatergoers like Natasha and Hélène still debating the qualities of this or that actress. The stage in his tale was but a slate of "flat stones over which, as though finishing some long and tedious crowd scene, people keep rushing and rushing—while one strangely lingering spectator still refuses to leave his bronze seat in the front row."[15]

Between 1821 and 1825, the final years of the reign of Tsar Alexander I, a new public theater in Moscow was constructed under the administrative umbrella of the St. Petersburg imperial court.[16] It rose from the craggy gorge where the old Maddox theater had once stood yet was meant to represent a clean break from the past and reflect post-Napoleonic nationalist ambitions. Despite the patriotic turn in the arts, however, the spacious new theater, like the performances within, depended on continental European models like Milan's Teatro alla Scala and Paris's Salle Le Peletier. As a symbol of a city making a new start, a city of the future rather than the past, the theater needed to be bigger, grander than those in France and Italy, standing above if not apart from them. Thus, Imperial Russia's orientation to—yet projected dominance of—the West was captured in marble and plaster.

The impetus to build the theater came from Dmitri Golitsïn, who replaced the disgraced immolator Fyodor Rostopchin as governor-general of Moscow. A basic neoclassical design was approved in 1819, but no specific plans were inked until the summer of 1820, when four members of the Imperial Academy of the Arts put their heads together. The lead planner was Andrey Mikhaylov, a senior professor of architecture, who worked alongside three other members of the academy, including his brother. The first draft was subject to revision, and the budget exceeded what Golitsïn was prepared to approve on behalf of the court. The extravagant plan needed to be scaled back. Throughout his career, Mikhaylov, who also designed the hospital where Fyodor Dostoevsky was born in 1821, saw numerous building projects either canceled or completed by others, the Bolshoi Theater included. The court indulged him with commissions but recognized his limitations.

The architect in charge of Moscow's post-Napoleonic reconstruction, Osip Bové, modified the design with the approval of both Golitsïn and the administration of the Imperial Theaters in St. Petersburg. Bové exercised restraint, eliminating the nineteenth-century version of a shopping center that Mikhaylov had envisioned for the first floor and lowering the flat roof. He did everything he could to control costs, including contracting the masons himself and transporting stone bases to the site on his own expense. It was also his idea to salvage whatever he could from the detritus of the old Maddox theater. But as the Imperial Theaters directorate had predicted, costs still ran well over budget, from the 960,000 rubles allotted by the treasury to the colossal sum of 2,000,000 rubles.

Construction lasted more than four years. In July 1820, the first of the ditches was dug and the first of the thousands of pine logs of the foundation hammered into place on ulitsa Petrovka. (Estimates of the number of logs pounded into the ground range from 2,100 to more than 4,000.) Construction involved hundreds of laborers in the winters, even more in the summers. It did not end until December 1824, and then just barely. The zodiac-embossed curtain and scrims were completed later, and, because of the budget overrun, both Mikhaylov and Bové had to sacrifice the 8,000-ruble imported chandeliers intended to hang in the side rooms, replacing them with illuminations of papier-mâché and tin fashioned by local craftspeople. Bové also had to forgo the giant mirror that he had hoped to hang in front of the curtain, allowing audience members to gaze at themselves; the mere thought of it terrified the directorate, as much for its radicalism as its cost.

The finished building was nonetheless luxurious, with the loges facing the stage drenched in crimson velvet, gold fringe, and braids, and the open boxes on each side suspended from cast-iron brackets. Columns on pedestals framed the galleries, supporting the arabesque-decorated ceiling, from which a massive crystal chandelier was raised and lowered by pulley. Oil lamps provided lighting, along with two parallel rows of candles fronting the loges. The side rooms had enough space to host chamber concerts by touring foreign musicians. The entrance was graced with a portico and led to a grand central staircase and ample reception rooms. Five massive semicircular windows provided light for the auditorium and the stage on each side of the theater. Ten paired columns supported the gable at the back. Since it was bigger than Maddox's operation, it was called the Bolshoi—meaning "Grand"—Petrovsky Theater. Over time, the reference to Petrovsky was dropped. The space in front, Theater Square, was graced with a public garden and later a fountain. The ravine and pond that had once been on the site were filled with rock and soil hauled from demolished bastions in Kitay-gorod. Theater Square came to include a smaller theater for dramas, the Malïy, also designed by Bové.

Both the inside and outside of the Bolshoi inspired, and were inspired by, national pride. *Moskovskiye vedomosti* redundantly heaped praise on the theater as a triumphant symbol of triumphant Moscow, now primed to join the ranks of the great world cities.

> The swiftness and grandeur of certain recent events in Russia have astonished our contemporaries and will be perceived as nothing less than miracles in distant posterity. . . . Our fatherland draws closer to the great European powers with each achievement. Such a thought arises within the soul of the patriot at the appearance of the Bolshoi Petrovsky Theater, whose walls have risen, like a phoenix, in new splendor and magnificence from the ruins. For how long in this place has the eye been exposed to the foul heaps, the remains of horrendous disaster, and the ear to the thumping of the worker's hammer? And now to capture the delighted gaze is a splendid building, an edifice of enchanting taste in height, immensity, and noble simplicity, coupled with elegance, stateliness, and ease. And now the inner walls receive the thunder of the muses; positive inspiration for humanity! Such is the magnitude, in spirit and deed, of Russia's government.[17]

Unlike Maddox's catch-as-catch-can operation, the grand space was conceived from the start as a cathedral to the performing arts, with the mercantile middle classes and inhabitants of the Table of Ranks sitting contentedly beside one another. (An enlightened society is a harmonious one, Catherine II believed.) Even Russophobe Europeans were impressed, and articles about the Bolshoi, accompanied by lavish illustrations of its interior, flowed east to west. "Travelers who visit Russia expecting to find a people just emerging from barbarism are often astonished to find themselves in scenes of Parisian elegance and refinement," the *Illustrated London News* explained. The theater gave Western culture and civilization a new home in Moscow. Although the Bolshoi was slow to adapt to new technologies—gas lighting was not installed until 1836—the "orchestra and chorus were strong," making the theater "a favorite place of resort of the Russian nobility, who usually wear their stars and ribbons at the opera."[18]

The Bolshoi opened on January 6, 1825, with an invitation to artists who had left Moscow for Europe to return home now that they had a place to perform. The benediction was followed by an allegorical prologue featuring Apollo and his muses. "A soothsayer from a mythological world" predicted the nation's future, the glories to come. The opening rhapsodized the immensity of the Russian Empire, the terrain it occupied from Poland to the Caspian Sea, from "the mists of Finland" to the "cloud ridges" of the "formidable Caucasus." Bové, the hero of the moment (Mikhaylov was all but forgotten), basked in a chorus of well-earned bravos. Following the 6 p.m. performance, the theater hosted its first masquerade. Attendees needed to mind their manners, drinking modestly and dressing fetchingly, which meant leaving any "indecent masks" at home.[19]

The Bolshoi Petrovsky didn't last long: It burned down on March 11, 1853, just like its predecessor. Blame fell on the fire watcher, who sounded the alarm too late (it was a sunrise blaze) to summon the firefighters from their compound. They were ill-equipped, with undersized water tanks pulled by sluggish nags, and mishap prone, tangling themselves up in their tethers. The firefighters had been patrons of the theater themselves, escaping on damp days to take in a show or even serve as extras. An eyewitness recalled seeing a fire crew on stage in a devil-themed melodrama. As fate would have it, a major fire broke out along Tverskaya during the performance, and the "devils" rushed out of the theater to the site, leaping in and out of the flames, pikes in hand, covered in red makeup with red helmets and tails—an apocalyptic fever dream come to life.[20]

The fire might have spread across the city. "Had there been more wind at the time, had there not been snow lying deep on the ground and the roofs of the houses, the catastrophe would have been inevitable," the *Illustrated London News* reported.[21] Eighteenth-century costumes were lost in the blaze, along with decorations, an archive of financial and personnel documents, music scores, and rare instruments. Meticulous official reports chronicle the loss of floors, ceilings, lamps, and sofas; the collapse of the roof; even the crumpling of the boiler-room pumps in the heat.[22] They also pinpoint the exact locations of theater employees from seven in the morning until noon and incorporate the testimonies of seventeen boys and twenty-three girls who had been taking dance and music classes inside. The cause of the fire was never conclusively determined, though none of the eyewitness accounts indicate arson. It apparently began in a tool room located on the right side of the stage beneath the staircase leading to the women's restrooms. A technician reported that he used it to store stage materials and warm clothes. Actors on stage first saw sparks and smoke, then felt a massive explosion that shook the ground like an earthquake. (Neither fuel nor explosives were stored in the theater.) Flames overwhelmed the water tanks; the boiling water released huge plumes of scalding steam. The smoke cleared after three days, exposing the foundations and subterranean corridors atop the Neglinka. The part of the Bolshoi Petrovsky that still stood could not be saved, and vegetation eventually encased the remains over the summer as the power of nature reclaimed the temple of culture.

That might have been the end had the religious theaterphobes of Moscow had a say in the matter.[23] But the people in charge of the institution were in St. Petersburg, and the Bolshoi existed at the pleasure of the court and the directorate of the Imperial Theaters. The Bolshoi was rebuilt in time for the 1856 coronation of Tsar Alexander II in Cathedral Square in the Kremlin, and this is the theater (oft-renovated) of today. Its opening was integral not only to the coronation festivities but indeed to Russian imperial ambitions.

The budget and design of the new Bolshoi bore the imprint of political and cultural aspirations to raise the empire from its lowest point since Napoleon. The Crimean War, waged between 1853 and 1856, ended in a humiliating defeat for Tsar Nicholas I. Disputes in Bethlehem and Jerusalem had prompted Russia to march into present-day Romania and threaten the Ottoman Empire. With France and Britain aligned against Russia, a front opened on the Crimean Peninsula near Sevastopol. The city fell to the European and Ottoman allies, forcing Russia to sue for peace. The loss of life and treasure was staggering, and the defeat is still described in apocalyptic terms in Russia, echoing, four hundred years on, the Fall of Constantinople and destruction of Orthodox Byzantium. Muslims and European Christians had united against Russia and would, in the opinion of diplomat Fyodor Tyutchev continue to do so until, he warned, Russia was no more. "For a long time now, there have been two forces in Europe, revolution and Russia. . . . Between them no negotiations, no treaties are possible; the existence of one is equivalent to the death of the other!"[24] Tyutchev had in mind what Catherine II had feared: the disease of revolution spreading to Russia and ending the empire. Soon, the Romanovs would learn that there was no cure. Socialist revolutionaries, including Friedrich Engels, celebrated Russia's defeat in the Crimean War because "the Slavic barbarians are natural counterrevolutionaries," opposed to democratic processes, clinging to their feudal pasts and hereditary dynasties.[25]

The Romanovs hardly considered themselves barbarians, of course. Slavophiles, nationalists, anarchists, the enemies of the regime in Russia, Ukraine, and the Caucasus—these were barbarians, absolutely, but the government had culled them into submission. From the outside, the Imperial Court seemed preposterously overextended, its treatment of subjects unreasonable. The response to such disdain? Defiance in a symbolic assertion of magisterial might. The newly rebuilt Bolshoi served the Romanovs, who frolicked in super-sumptuous surroundings, lavished huge sums on jewel-studded velvets, embroidered panels, ceremonial sabers, and diadem-like headdresses, held the splashiest balls since Louis XIV occupied Versailles, and projected greatness even when events outside their chambers and their theaters threatened their overthrow. Fabulousness and ingloriousness: that was the Bolshoi in the second half of the nineteenth century, an emblem of the Romanov era, an outrageous imposition of opulence on the black earth of the steppe.

The new theater opened to the public on August 20, 1856, just ahead of the coronation, with a staging of Vincenzo Bellini's opera *I Puritani*. Reviewers ignored the opera since the theater itself was the real show, from its expansive façades to its intricate floor mosaics and the mélange of "floral ornaments, rocailles, cartouches, meshes, rosettes and plaits" in the tiers.[26] The accomplished architect who received the commission to rebuild the theater, Alberto Cavos, corrected the problem that had brought the original to ruin: steep stairs that served as smoke shafts in front of large doors that sucked in oxygen. He reimagined the hall in a "Byzantine-Renaissance style," with entrance columns of milky white limestone, loges of crimson velvet, and foyers full of fitted mirrors and grisaille squares.[27] The seats were padded with horsehair and coconut matting—the latest in comfort for merchant derrieres. Gold leaf overlaid papier-mâché moldings in the auditorium. Ingredients for the gilding included clay, egg, and vodka. Paintbrushes were fashioned from the fine hair of squirrels' tails, which was excellent material for the application of thick, rich color.

Ten days after the public opening, the Bolshoi mounted an exclusive gala performance of Donizetti's *L'elisir d'amore* (*The Elixir of Love*), the operatic equivalent of a glass of champagne served with oysters. A reporter in the audience that evening, William Howard Russell, described the event in a small-font, long-feature piece for *The Times* of London. He loved the pale and delicate sea-green interiors, the orange- and fuchsia-perfumed side rooms, and the sparkling arrays of candles that proved too dazzling, in their aggregate, for sensitive eyes. He gushed about the diadems donned by noble ladies in the loges, the discipline exhibited by the officers of the parterre, including their perfectly harmonized cheers when the tsar and tsarina arrived at 8:30 p.m., and the exotic distinctiveness of the Turks, Georgians, and others in attendance from across Eurasia. They were all a part of the ever-expanding Russian Empire, a realm with coasts on the Pacific and Arctic Oceans as well as the Baltic, Black, and Caspian Seas. Russell wanted to go on, but he was past the word limit for his article and could only mention the "lovely young Moldovan, married to a Russian prince, who has just been sent off to the Caucasus" and the brass in the front rows: "Generals and Admirals, Privy Councilors, Officers of State, Chamberlains, and personages of the Court. Behind these are similar officers, mingled together with members of the foreign missions, and the strangers who were invited to be present."[28] The parterre resembled the richest flower beds thanks to patrons uniformed in white and gold, blue and silver, crimson, black, and scarlet. Magnificence defined the center of Moscow, while tattered hardship persisted in the provinces and beyond.

The theater didn't invest much in local talent until Pyotr Tchaikovsky established himself. The operas of other now-familiar Russian composers—including Mikhaíl Glinka, Modest Mussorgsky, and Nikolay Rimsky-Korsakov—only reached the grand imperial stage after intense lobbying, since the Imperial Theater's administration under Alexander II preferred Italian, French, and German works, in that order, to the sartorial, isolated Silk Road fare generated by Slavic nationalists.

Tchaikovsky cut his teeth writing music for a historical exhibition and the marriage of Alexander II's son to the Danish princess Dagmar. The Romanovs had chosen German wives for themselves since the era of Peter the Great, ensuring a strong German presence at the court and in Russian society more broadly. His first opera, *The Voyevoda,* a decorative bricolage of old Rus ambience, was premiered at the Bolshoi on January 30, 1869. It's about a rotten-to-the-core provincial governor (*voyevoda*) who takes two women of distinct ages and social positions as his mistresses. When he's away, he locks the women in his tower chamber. Their lovers hatch a plan to rescue them by getting the governor's guards drunk, but they are captured. Fanfares announce the arrival of a new governor, and the couples are freed. Such was Tchaikovsky's representation of social justice. The premiere was delayed because the chorus was outsourced to a visiting Italian opera company; the soloists didn't properly prepare, and the dancers didn't show up. "Everyone happily worked together to ensure as bad a performance as possible," the newspaper *Golos* (*Voice*) summarized.[29] Later, Tchaikovsky took on Ivan the Terrible in an opera called *The Oprichnik,* which premiered in St. Petersburg and reached the Moscow stage on May 4, 1875. It had a hard time making it past the theatrical censors because, the censors complained, it was less about Ivan's "indomitable despotism and brutal manifestations of the will" than the tsar's sexual appetites.[30] The opera was a success, despite critics grousing that the music didn't sound menacing and oppressive enough. The "freedom goes too far," one reviewer quipped—a sentence that could serve as a conservative motto for the later nineteenth-century Russian experience.[31]

In 1856, the year of his coronation, Alexander II informed the upper ranks that servitude *à la russe* had to end. "The existing conditions of owning souls cannot remain unchanged," he declared. "It is better to begin eliminating serfdom from above than to wait until it begins to eliminate itself from below."[32] The tsar left it to the serf owners to determine how serfdom should end—a clever means, he thought, of escaping blame for the inevitable furor. Innumerable committees met to figure out how to make a profit from the end of profiteering in human lives. Clerks wrote up plans in elaborate script, and the tsar forged a cumbersome compromise. The final proclamation and statute filled an entire book. The basic points: serfs would be freed and allowed to own land purchased from their former owners. Marriage became a matter of personal choice. Freed serfs could vote, set up businesses, and take their complaints to court. At least on paper.

The promised liberation ultimately benefited the liberators, who made vast sums selling their land at inflated prices to their former forced laborers. The statute allowed the gentry to hold on to the best parts of their estates for themselves, selling the least fertile, rockiest acreage to the serfs. Tilling barren soil left them with little to eat and nothing to sell, so repaying mortgages proved impossible. The debt—owed four-fifths to the state bank and one-fifth to the original landowners—passed from parents to children to the children's children, never to be settled.

Though technically emancipated, the serfs remained trapped in the same places they had always been. Emancipation regulators dispatched to villages ensured the timely collection of taxes and enforced the existing social order. The government feared uprisings, sought to prevent a migration crisis, and had little respect for the worker-peasant domain. The masses had revolted before, often in fact, so emancipation was less an attempt to liberate than to regulate, to maintain an oppressive peace and keep the sheep, metaphorically speaking, in the fold. Ending serfdom was an autocrat's solution— that is, no solution at all. The privileged remained privileged, and the underclasses remained under their control.

The benefits of the reforms were modest at best: economic stimulus, increase in banking activities, and incremental improvements in the lives of women, children, and non-elite sectors. In the end, no one was satisfied. Progressive Europeanists wanted additional changes while conservative Slavophiles wanted them all rolled back to protect the feudal order and the old way of life. From the outside, the Russian Empire still seemed barbaric, the court no less rotten than the provincial governor of Tchaikovsky's first opera.

Freedom certainly went too far for Alexander II, who was assassinated on March 1, 1881, by a member of the anti-autocratic cabal known as People's Will. He had survived several attempts on his life, but this time, in St. Petersburg, two explosives were lobbed at him; the second landed at his feet as he emerged from his carriage, shredding his legs and mashing his stomach. There would be no more reforms, however limited.

His burly, ginger-bearded son, Alexander III, took power and tacked, as he felt he had to, in an illiberal, reactionary direction, undoing the policies of his father and re-embracing the trinity of orthodoxy, autocracy, and nationality advanced by his grandfather, Tsar Nicholas I. Alexander III was by all accounts somewhat slow-witted and tedious, the keeper of diaries chockablock with misspellings and grammatical fumbles. Unable to secure the confidence of his advisors, he turned to an old teacher, Konstantin Pobedonostsev, for advice. The guidance provided was extreme. Pobedonostsev was an ultra-nationalist who encouraged political executions, pogroms, and forced resettlement campaigns.

Alexander III professed a love for ballet and opera and indirectly appealed to Tchaikovsky for the favor of a suite of coronation pieces. These included a cantata about the city of Moscow that set words by a poet favored by the court, Apollon Maykov. The score goes back in time, to the city's start, evoking the sounds of nature—the chittering critters in the bog from which Moscow emerged. The singers next list the places where the Mongols laid siege. The ensemble comes together to proclaim that Moscow will bring together the principalities of Rus against all enemies. In the fourth movement, the idea of Moscow as the Third Rome is introduced in heroic recitation (though the opposite, liturgical chant, might seem more appropriate). Alexander III is addressed near the end:

> Now you are for all Eastern countries
> Like the star of Bethlehem that rose up
> Over the sacred stone of our Moscow!

> God loved you and chose you
> to strap on the sword of Constantine
> and be crowned with the Cap of Monomakh.

"Constantine" is Byzantine emperor Constantine XI Palaiologos. In 1834, the Ottoman ambassador to the Russian imperial court had given Tsar Nicholas I a jewel-encrusted sword that supposedly once belonged to Palaiologos. It served as proof of Constantinople's *translatio imperii* (passing of the torch) to Moscow. The Cap or Crown of Monomakh is another such Byzantine artifact.

Also to celebrate Alexander III's ascension, the Bolshoi staged an allegorical ballet by Marius Petipa, *Night and Day* (*Noch' i den'*), about renewal. The Queen of the Night, Evening Star, comets, planets, ferns, swan-maids, mermaids, and dryads join hands in the first half, then the Queen of the Day cavorts with the Morning Star, birds, butterflies, bees, and flies. A parade of the diverse people of the Russian Empire passes by—Finns and Georgians, Poles, Don Cossacks, and Siberian shamans, each greeting the dawn as a symbol of the coronation. Mother Russia enters as a plump matron in the middle of the friendship-of-the-peoples round dance. Even by the standards of grand theater, it was an outsized spectacle, combining ballet, parade, and circus with soldiers in review.[33]

Alexander III defined himself as a ruler reclaiming the distant past of the Rurik princes and the past before that. (In this regard, the cantata was more to his taste than *Night and Day*, but his family liked it so he ordered an encore performance just for them.) Alexander III ruled an empire, but he wanted its heart—Russia—to be for Russians alone. Thus the heart of the heart, Moscow, needed to be cleansed as well. He spent more time in Moscow than in St. Petersburg, and encouraged by his wife, Dagmar of Denmark (crowned Mariya Fyodorovna), developed an ardent loathing of Germans that morphed into xenophobia—Peter's Europeanization and Catherine's imposed imperialism be damned. Alexander III's unexpected death from nephritis at age forty-nine meant that he didn't fulfill his ethnic nationalist agenda, though he did manage, on the cultural front, to shift the repertoire of the imperial theaters to favor Russian works.

The festivities for the ascension of Nicholas II included, in keeping with tradition, a banquet for the dignitaries and a massive outdoor feast for the people, plus concerts, fireworks, and performances at the Bolshoi Theater. Moscow now had a small power station that illuminated hundreds of twinkling lights around the theater and the Kremlin but left areas beyond the center in the dark.[34] Then, disaster. More than half a million people headed to Khodïnskoye field through the night of May 18, 1896, for a "distribution of treats": sausages, pretzels, gingerbread, and other goodies. The occasion was the coronation of Alexander III's successor, Tsar Nicholas II, and the "people's feast" came out of the coronation budget. The distribution from the gift kiosks, which lasted "for twenty minutes to an hour," according to historian Tatyana Sinitsïna, prompted "a stampede that caused fatalities"—1,389 of them in all, with another 1,301 people injured from falling into a ditch adjacent to the kiosks.[35] The bodies weren't taken away until well into the evening. Nicholas II responded bureaucratically, ordering inquiries; he didn't personally visit the site of the tragedy or speak of the impoverishment that had driven the population of Moscow to a field for a government handout.[36] Mean-spirited courtiers assailed Moscow itself for the stampede. It was a "stupid city," "a city in name only," the director of the Moscow Imperial Theaters huffed. "In reality it's just a big dog park."[37]

That was the beginning of Nicholas II's reign and a bad omen of what was to come. Tchaikovsky didn't witness the fall of the ruling family during the First World War, though he seems to have anticipated it. In 1890, three years before his death from cholera morbus, he composed an opera set in the time of Catherine the Great that portended exactly what was happening: the end of the Romanovs. Titled *The Queen of Spades* and based on a tale by Pushkin, it includes a small scene about the empress, although custom—and the law—forbade her divine personage from being represented on the stage. It's the midpoint of her reign. A dance begins, the crowd rushes up for a glimpse of her, but she's had it with everything and everyone—empire, subjects, past, future. She turns her back, swishes her fabulously expensive gown, and leaves the stage.

ZARYADYE

I N 1927, a book titled *Vanished Moscow* went on sale for 85 kopecks—about the cost of two cartons of eggs.[1] The author, Ivan Belousov, had experienced the end of autocracy, the beginning of communism, promises of liberty, and threats of tyranny, but he didn't write about that. His friends landed in tsarist prisons for their political activities, but he didn't write about them. Nor was he interested in sharing his personal life, what happened to him versus what he thought would happen; he says nothing about his marriage to a merchant's daughter, the children they raised, the transformative time he spent in Kyiv, or his rise to renown as a poet, folklorist, and Ukrainian-language translator after health problems forced him to give up his profession as a tailor.[2]

Instead, he told stories about the inhabitants of a tired world experiencing its gradual, then sudden, disappearance in a book of unemotional irresolution. Belousov grew up among people who didn't know how to read or write. Getting a chicken into a pot, delousing bedding, confessing in the local parish, keeping illness at bay—such was (according to Belousov's subtitle) "the day-to-day existence of small artisans, office clerks, traders, townspeople, and minor merchants." He wrote about his neighborhood of Zaryadye.

He was born on November 27, 1863, beneath a slate rooftop in a home nestled within a latticework of streets and lanes located (according to the name) "behind [to the south of] the trading rows." Zaryadye included small businesses, guesthouses, and tenements that had been expanded to accommodate separate entrances from outside staircases. Entire families scrunched together in small rooms.[3]

The north–south lanes followed ancient ravines down to a waterfront flooded by the Moskva in spring.[4] Water was collected and removed depending on the needs of the residents and the seasons. The timber-paved, east–west street running parallel to the river bore the name Mokrinskiy (Water Street). It offered access to the river through a gate. Earlier, Mokrinskiy was known as Great Street. The lovely road on the northern edge of the neighborhood, Varvarka, boasted the ancestral Romanov residence along with a pink and white church from 1514 honoring the Holy Great Martyr Barbara, adopted patron of miners, weaponeers, and traders. Varvarka was also once called Varskaya, meaning "the place where they cook" (*varyat*).[5] Why? No one remembers. Some buildings on the street still bear pockmarks from bullets fired during the 1917 Revolution. The Old English Court in Zaryadye is preserved along with the onetime tax collector's yard and the Church of the Conception of Anna, located in a corner of the neighborhood. The synagogue remains, though it's been much rebuilt. The street where Belousov grew up, Irininskaya, was renamed in 1922 to honor Friedrich Engels, co-author with Karl Marx of the *Communist Manifesto*.

Belousov's father's tailoring shop sat in the corner of a plaster-covered building close to the embankment. As a child, Ivan slept on a bench beside the ironing table. During the day, he ran around barefoot with other kids in the neighborhood, watched how sweets were made in the confectionaries, and played catch-the-thief games with his father's revolver, a gift from the building's owner that his father never loaded. The games ended after the assassination of Tsar Alexander II in 1881, when, fearing arrest as a potential insurrectionist, his father surrendered the gun and its leather holster to the police.[6]

When he turned eight, Ivan learned how to read. His mother was illiterate; there wasn't a single book in his home. But if Ivan could read, then he could help with the bookkeeping. The police made everyone subscribe to *Vedomosti moskovskoy gorodskoy politsii,* the police bulletin, so his father pored through that, first page to last, even perusing the advertisements. Sometimes a book of fairy tales would turn up, and Belousov would look at the pictures and ask someone to read to him.[7] The task of a tailor was to sew and iron, he was reminded, not to pretend to be a dashing knight on a magical horse. For instruction in the basics, Belousov ended up with the wife of the sexton at the Church of the Conception of Anna. She had a teaching certificate, administered tests in the presence of parents and relatives, and kept lists of her students' progress in "morality."[8] Belousov learned the Old Church Slavonic alphabet, which so baffled one of the other students (a baker's son) that he threw his primer into the river, never to return to the church again.[9] Belousov left the church as well, enrolling in a general public school operated by the first merchant guild: "Moscow City School No. 1 according to the regulations of 1872." He graduated in 1880 with a grammar book as a gift.[10]

He went to work for his father among other apprentices from Ryazan, who planned to learn the intricacies of thimble and needlework in the ateliers on Irininskaya Street then return home to work as tailors. Each apprentice received a pair of shoes, two pairs of underwear, a shirt, and a pair of trousers from the owner; parents had to provide winter coats. Everyone had a nickname—"pockmarked," "crooked," "hedgehog"—describing what they looked like, where they came from, or a personality tic.[11] Belousov learned the real names of his peers only after they'd been promoted. Card games and practical jokes absorbed idle hours, and he began to write poems on the side, careful to keep his hobby hidden from his father, who thought reading for pleasure was sinful. (When Ivan started publishing, he did so under a range of pseudonyms.) The newbies swept the floors and chopped the wood for the stove that heated the irons, ran errands for the mistresses of the household, and fetched vodka and tobacco for the older men.

Work began at dawn—five or six in the morning. The proprietors roused their charges for a mug of tea at the adjacent *traktir* (tavern) while the apprentices pulled up bedding ("dirty" chintz blankets and "greasy" pillows in pillowcases that "hadn't been washed in years") and cleared the floor of dust and debris.[12] The morning shift ended at noon, when the apprentices assembled at a communal table, carved bread, and ladled cabbage soup along with lard-slathered porridge into rough-hewn bowls. Work ended at four in the afternoon during slower times but otherwise extended into the evening. In the summer the neighborhood quieted down, and the apprentices from the provinces returned home to their villages. Some of them got homesick in winter and snuck back; their fathers thrashed them and sent them back to Moscow. "After dinner we didn't want to sleep," Belousov writes of his evenings off. "Because we had nothing to do, we told each other stories or anecdotes from our lives—mostly of an adventurous or mysterious nature." Tales of crime and punishment frightened him most. Prisoners were hauled from their cells to a public square, their hands screwed to the floorboards of wagons and signs hung around their necks reading—for those who could read—"murderer," "molester," "robber." Before being marched off to Siberia, each endured a brutal gauntlet. They'd be dragged through rows of soldiers who would beat them senseless with splintered slabs of wood. Once the skin on their backs had been suitably pulped, turning from red to purple to black, the soldiers doused them with vinegar—all to the beat of drums.[13]

Such cruelty belonged to the era of Tsar Nicholas I and earlier, not to the civilized late nineteenth century, Belousov claims. Even today, many nineteenth-century prisons still exist, and one of Moscow's more civic-minded walking tours includes them (the tour is advertised as an interesting thing for Muscovites to do on November 6, a "professional holiday" for record keepers in the penal system).[14] In Belousov's time, Taganskaya prison was a workhouse for convicted criminals; later, it housed political prisoners. In 1958 it was emptied, and in 1960 the compound was blown up and replaced by a kindergarten and apartments. The most infamous jail, Butïrka, operated as a transit facility in the imperial era before housing revolutionaries, a rocket designer, several writers, and the founder of the Cheka (Lenin's secret police). Tales of torture and tuberculosis and bizarre escapes are legion, and despite promises to close it, Butïrka operates in its original location as a pre-trial detention facility.[15] Lefortovskaya prison opened in 1881 and was the hub of the Stalinist correctional apparatus. Its library houses rare editions of Pushkin and Leskov. Sailor's Silence (Matrosskaya tishina) prison arose on the site of a sail-making factory and then a neighborhood for retired sailors that Peter the Great insisted on being quietly residential, reserved for pedestrian traffic only. In the late nineteenth century, it was a mixed-gender prison holding a few hundred swindlers. Students who lived in a dorm nearby joked about trading up to a madhouse or the jail.[16]

The ne'er-do-wells of the neighborhood found themselves in the boardinghouses of Khitrovka, a large square close to the Yauza River. If you needed someone with a special skill, legal or illegal, you'd find your man there. These days it's a quaint neighborhood; residents and the historical preservation society have fought developers that want to install an office building and parking garage on the site—a much different kind of grimness than Belousov experienced.[17] In his time, Khitrovka was the filthiest and bawdiest part of Moscow, home to unskilled laborers and fringe folk who lived on soup made from vegetable peelings and disinfected themselves with vodka. Named after Nikolay Khitrovo, a late-eighteenth-century/early-nineteenth-century general who lived and opened a market in the area, Khitrovka was the smelly underbelly of Moscow. Or, to quote the title of a Maxim Gorky play about the thieves, pie-sellers, and streetwalkers occupying the lanes, it was "the lower depths."

The river blanketed Khitrovka in mist, and "in those murky vapors swarmed pale-faced phantoms in ragged and filthy garments," Lev Tarasov (Henri Troyat) fantastically elaborated in his 1903 panorama *Daily Life in Russia Under the Last Tsar.* Toothless matrons with blue faces and yellow fingers hunched over pots of noodles kept warm within their skirts. Inside the shack with a counter that substituted for a tavern, "hideous faces floated in the half-light like jellyfish on the surface of the sea." Men and women alike landed in the snow after bar fights. Five kopecks bought a place to engage in sex or to sleep off the drink—perhaps both. Piles of flesh buried beneath piles of rags filled a room "steeped in a nauseous odor of rotten meat, vermin and human waste." In a stuffy alcove, unemployed actors eked

Khitrovka, early 1900s.

out a living making copies of plays. They toiled through the night, inky pens in their scuffed hands, then dashed hotfoot to the theaters to sell the copies for fifty kopecks each (fewer if the pages got crumpled). Teenage prostitution was rife, and babies surrendered for adoption (or snatched from cribs) were loaned out to panhandling shrews. Should the "sodden and scabby bundle" die in arms, the beggar would "continue to carry it until . . . dark so as not to miss any alms."[18]

A crime reporter named Vladimir Gilyarovsky hung around the neighborhood and learned that it was controlled by a couple of corrupt police officers. Its denizens were runaways from labor camps and "round-trippers," people who had escaped from prison but would soon be heading back. Gilyarovsky spent time in the "Hard Time" tavern with "tomcats" (pimps) and "kittens" (prostitutes); he also encountered wretches with slabs of wood for shoes, "crabs" (people who, for lack of proper attire, stayed in their bunks all day), and "the head of a living man sticking out of a stone wall" (guarding the entrance to a hideaway inside a hideaway).[19]

In September, for the Feast of the Nativity of the Virgin, candles made of tallow or fashioned from turnips would glow while the owners of the buildings and workshops prayed before an icon. They'd then gift their workers a glass of vodka. Any drops remaining in the

The bird market at Trubnaya Square in 1908. The area picked up its name from a "trub," or "pipe," that once controlled the flow of the Neglinka through a Tsar-gorod tower. After the river was encased underground, a market developed where household goods, flowers, and birds were sold. It also hosted boxing matches and the other street entertainments Belousov describes in his memoirs.

glasses were used to snuff the candles. They would then be relit, and wine served along with a motivating word or two about the work to be done in the fall. Everyone got drunk, but not meanly so, and sometimes they remained drunk for three or four days, losing pay for the work missed and the alcohol they'd nicked from the owners who held on to their passports, preventing them from leaving town.[20] For the Feast of the Epiphany, workers cleansed themselves of the sins they'd committed over the year—"going to gypsies," "brawling," "scandalizing"—by plunging into the icy Moskva.[21] During Lent everyone worked their fourteen-hour shifts on empty stomachs, imagining pancakes and betting on who could consume the most with the fewest glasses of kvass to wash them down.[22]

Belousov describes the Jewish merchants who were sometimes part of the fabric of the community and sometimes not. The first arrived from Belarus in the late eighteenth century from the dissolved Polish-Lithuanian Commonwealth. The western Russian region known as the Pale of Settlement, where Jews could live, was formed in 1835 from conquered land. Immediately the Jews fell under suspicion, accused, in classic antisemitic fashion, of "desecrating gold coins" and "oppressing noble merchants" through predatory pricing. Nothing of the sort occurred, at least not on the level described. There were just 69 Jews in Moscow in the late eighteenth century (49 men, 8 women, and 12 children) out of a population of more than 200,000. And just three of them were registered in the first merchant guild; the rest didn't make enough.[23] But they had to leave, and in 1791, they did, on order from the top.

The ban was lifted in 1826. Jewish merchants from Belarus subsequently received permission to travel to Moscow for short stays at a guesthouse in Zaryadye. Cossacks on horseback escorted the travelers to their rooms; the police subsequently monitored their movements, searched their belongings, and ousted those living in the "vast rickety old hive" without permission.[24] The guesthouse belonged to a noble named Pavel Glebov, and it generated an average of 30,000 rubles a year from its occupants. The cash went straight into his pocket until the government forced him to surrender his lease. Then the income went to charity, funding housing and work for girls in need and covering the costs of a few beds in the public hospital. Money also went to an eye clinic (Glebov lost his vision before he died).[25] Despite protests from the Orthodox Church, the authorities eventually allowed Jewish religious services to take place. The opening of a small synagogue in the area was occasioned by the arrival of Jewish soldiers who had fought for the Russian Empire. They had been demobilized from the Moscow garrison and weren't subject to the same limitations on where they could live as the merchants. They chose Zaryadye as their home because it was cheaper than other parts of the city.

In the 1860s, under Tsar Alexander II, hundreds of Jewish families relocated to Moscow. The wealthiest leased large apartments in the center, hired nannies for their children, and shopped in fashionable stores. The poorest lived alongside Belousov in Zaryadye, having escaped ugliness and violence elsewhere, including, Belousov emphasizes, the Pale of Settlement. Some crammed into the galleries atop the fortune-tellers in the "dark, dirty basements." "There wasn't any particular antagonism between adult Russians and the Jewish population of Zaryadye," Belousov insists, but Russian boys never missed the chance to shout a slur when a Jew passed by. They'd yell "S khrenom!" ("Happy Horseradish!" referring to the bitter herbs of the Passover seder) and "P-p-pr-u-u," the pseudonym used by an antisemitic caricaturist covering a trial of Jewish merchants.[26]

Still, the neighborhood generally tolerated Jewish customs and observances. The thatched-roof huts that sprang up during Sukkot festivities caught Belousov's attention along with the *bekishe* (frock coats) and *payot* (sidelocks) of the men, the quiet that would descend in the galleries on Friday evenings, the synagogue, the candle lighting, and what one of the newspapers, *Day*, contemptuously belittled as "blind adherence to ancient customs."[27] Belousov indulged the local gossip about Jewish furriers as cheats, who sew fur from raccoons into Polish beaver skins to make them silkier, less like Polish beavers than beavers from the Far East (Kamchatka).[28]

Those who came to Moscow from elsewhere lived with kinfolk. Losing that connection meant moving from flophouse to flophouse or sleeping rough. Such people, the lowest of the low, were called "gnawers," a reference, it seems, to the bedbugs keeping them company at night.[29] No one had pensions or guarantees of housing: not the Siberians, not the Greeks, not the Jews, not the Russians. Hospitals, like the "houses of diligence" providing work and housing to those most in need, relied on donations. (Moscow's first public hospital, opened in 1763 under Catherine the Great, relied on funds collected at a healing icon in Kitay-gorod.)[30] Belousov had little exposure to Moscow's posher places: sometimes he'd glimpse oil lamps in the salons of great houses in the carriage rides he took with a seasonal worker who had a pleasant horse. Moscow's municipal government (Duma) wasn't far from his home, but it was off-limits to working-men like himself, and there was no going to the Bolshoi Theater. In the finer markets he'd encounter students in blue and gold uniforms. Sometimes he saw actors out and about on holidays like Lent when the theaters were closed. Shrovetide (near Easter) was the happiest celebration. Roadhouses threw open their doors and presented their richest patrons (government ministers) with poems that had been cleared by the censors for distribution on beautiful paper, declaring the end of sadness and exhorting the consumption of the owner's special dishes and gently encouraging generous tips.[31]

Belousov didn't have a village to escape to and didn't often get out of Moscow, save for outdoor festivals in spring. In May he would head north to Mar'yina roshcha (roughly, Mary's Grove), just past the *skorodom* fortification and the present-day Garden Ring Road.[32] There were carousels and swings and pretty girls singing songs. Religious holidays and royal events also lent his life variety. Everything had to be festive on order of the police, everyone's clothes and hair neatened, so he went to the bathhouse to rub himself raw amid women washing their hair with kerosene "to encourage growth" and whitening their faces with almond flour and herbs.[33] The governor-general of Moscow, Vladimir Dolgorukov, presided over these occasions as (according to an imperial directive dated May 29, 1853) "the chief guardian of the inviolable and supreme rights of the autocracy, the functioning of the state, and the exact execution of laws and orders of the government at the highest level in all of its functions in the region entrusted to him."[34] Dolgorukov loved praising the tsar and wearing tsarist medals. He daffily lorded over balls and feasts; he bejeweled his mistress—the ballerina Anna Sobeshchanskaya—until she married someone her own age and escaped his attention. The fairground that sprang up toward spring boasted believe-it-or-not exotica: "a calf with two heads, the mummy of an Egyptian Pharoah, a wild man brought from Africa who ate live pigeons in front of the crowd, a man with an iron stomach drinking turpentine or kerosene and gnawing the glass with his teeth, and much more besides." Amid the cannonades and illuminations, Belousov would often get into minor mischief by turning off lanterns or swiping candle bowls. He also watched boxing matches on the frozen river (the reigning champion was a "tall, pale old-timer . . . his face covered in scars, his teeth knocked out"); cockfights, with feathers and blood flying all over the place; and the nauseating baiting of blinded, defanged bears. Puppet shows featured Petrushka, the saddest sad sack in all of puppetry, who lost his nose to a puppet dog.[35]

After 1874 horse-drawn trams (omnibuses) began trundling around Moscow on fixed routes, so Belousov could leave his neighborhood more easily. Boys tended toll stations and attached extra horses to the trams to climb the hills. When the trams got stuck in the snow the passengers got out and pushed.[36] Introducing electric trams to Moscow's streets meant building power plants—an oft-postponed development that left the city looking more contentedly traditional than other European city centers. Footage of Tverskaya Street from May 1896 shows horse and pedestrian traffic lumbering along while a pair of officers keep an eye on things. A stout man in a chaise tips his hat and disappears into eternity. The men sport beards of different sorts and walk with impressive posture; few women walk along the street.[37]

The rich merchants living south of the Moskva (and south of Zaryadye) had their own horses and stables. This neighborhood, Zamoskvorechye, had houses of pointed roofs that extended as far as the eye could see beyond the revetment. The residents of Zamoskvorechye liked their quiet; it was a tranquil, old-fashioned suburb of jam-makers, bright frosts, lush gardens, and chicken coops. Sons of certain families met daughters from certain other families through matchmakers, and doors were adorned with icons and copper crucifixes. Deeply religious, the merchants made the sign of the cross before leaving home and clattering up to their businesses. Then, in the evening, when trading ended and the shops were locked, the merchants and their workers would again make the sign of the cross, bowing on three sides and heading home. In summer, they crossed the bridge in spacious four-seater cabs; sleighs of similar size transported them in winter. Passengers and drivers alike wore thick raccoon coats against the chill. The most reverent slowed down traffic to stop and pay respects at every church they passed.[38]

Other recollections of the era, by greater and lesser writers, forswear Belousov's anxious nostalgia and instead embrace the ideal of progress. Among the truly rebellious was Alexander Levitov (1835–77), a writer from a religious family who studied to be a theologian in Tambov, south of Moscow. His father, a sexton, opened a school in his home to educate peasant children. "A mottled herd," Levitov recalled, "starving and therefore stealing from everyone everything they could get their hands on; homeless and brutally torn, without good guiding examples and, therefore, already doomed to death in childhood."[39] His father didn't want to pay for teachers so had his own children look after them, "back-breaking labor," according to Levitov's sister. She complained of splitting headaches and "fingers sliced from trimming goose feathers" for use as quills. Levitov enrolled in a seminary, where he was accused, "without trial or investigation, of sneaking women into an apartment, cursing at an overseer and so sentenced to be flogged."[40] Reading foreign books and writing satire didn't improve his reputation. Levitov fled, breaking his mother's heart, and walked penniless first to Moscow then farther north to St. Petersburg, where, in 1855, he entered medical school. For unclear reasons, he was expelled to the town of Vologda, where he took a job as an attendant in the hospital. Lonely and bored, he succumbed to drink. Alcoholism and the anxieties of a vagabond existence became central themes in his prose. People become drunks for several reasons, Levitov writes, though loving their lives was not one of them. He returned to Moscow in 1860, camping for a time under boats on the riverside before finding lodging and, through a neighbor, a job as a periodical editor. He liked—and so wrote—slum literature, tales of people forced to sell their winter coats for sustenance, living in flophouses smelling of cabbage soup, furnace fumes, and soiled bedspreads, all the while fantasizing about a better life.[41]

The old way of life started to vanish in Moscow during the 1860s, swept away by the reforms of Tsar Alexander II and Governor-General Vladimir Dolgorukov. Moscow's municipal government, the Duma, diversified and democratized. The percentage of aristocrats in the assembly declined and the number of artisans and people of humble backgrounds increased. Commercial banks along a street with an English-sounding name, Moskva siti (Moscow City), funneled capital from Europe to St. Petersburg and down to Moscow. Fancy restaurants opened. Manufactured goods filled homes; out went the hand-me-downs and homemade objects. The shopping area destroyed by fire in 1825 gave rise, in 1893, to an enclosed complex called the Upper Trading Rows (Verkhnïye torgovïye ryadï), known since 1921 as GUM, the state department store. It stands on the other side of Red Square from the Kremlin. Other *magaziní* (shops) opened to rival the pie exchange, haberdasheries, and millineries. Medicine improved, as did education and social services. Newspapers reported street-level health regulation infractions—pigeons disguised as partridges in the markets, spoiled milk or flour. A bacteriological station opened in the Faculty of Medicine of Moscow University. Hygiene in the hospitals improved; new hospitals opened.[42]

Corruption in the court and other places of power went unreported, as had always been the case. And, as always, questions about who belonged in the empire and who didn't were debated. In 1867 in St. Petersburg and Moscow, a series of ceremonial meetings took up the question of cooperation among Slavic peoples, Russian hegemony in the Slavic world, and Slavic political unification.[43] The pan-Slavic congress, as it became known, inevitably questioned the place of foreigners in Russian society and of Russians marked as outsiders owing to their religious practice: Jews. The answer to that question—the place of foreigners and supposed outsiders—haunted Belousov and inspired the ending of *Vanished Moscow,* which laments the loss of a people and a place as well as a historical record. Ultimately, progress demanded Belousov's childhood hangouts be bulldozed. In tourist guides, the official end of Zaryadye dates to the 1930s and Iosif Stalin's grand plans for the reconstruction of the Soviet capital. The unofficial end of Zaryadye, its actual end, was the forced expulsion of Jews in 1891 and 1892. The police ousted the Jewish tenants of the neighborhood, forcing some of them back to the Pale of Settlement. Most were ushered onto trains heading out of the empire, no longer Russia's problem.

Tsar Alexander III authorized the ouster as revenge for the assassination of his father, even though the people of Zaryadye had nothing to do with it. Education, trade, and commerce in Russia had all benefited from Jewish expertise, but traditional Muscovites now rejected the Jewish presence. ("Moscow," it's been argued, had "much the same feeling toward the Jews that the Emirs of Bukhara might have—that is, one of contemptuous tolerance in good-humored times, of grim ferocity when the ugly mood is on.")[44] Lies spread to the effect that Governor-General Dolgorukov owed vast sums to Jewish businessmen; to win forgiveness of these debts, he had reportedly allowed their relatives to settle in Moscow. Word of the imagined quid pro quo reached the court in St. Petersburg. Dolgorukov was said to have been sacked in disgrace in 1891.[45] The truth is simpler. He lost his post because he was too old, or too unwilling, to conduct "a crusade upon Israel."[46]

His position temporarily went to an official with family roots in Ukraine and Greece, Apostol Kostanda, and then to Grand Prince Sergey Romanov, the brother of Tsar Alexander III. He was altogether unlike Dolgorukov. Unfriendly by nature, he didn't receive petitioners and conducted his affairs with "dry formality."[47] He arrived in Moscow committed to a dark deed. He was supported in his plans by the chief prosecutor of the Most Holy Synod, Konstantin Pobedonostev, who, on behalf of his Orthodox faithful, urged harsh treatment of Jews. Pobedonostev longed for the days before Russia had become European, before the establishment of the Pale of Settlement, before even the founding of St. Petersburg. Pobedonostev is credited with an apocalyptic statement: "One third [of Russia's Jews] will die out, one third will be evicted, one third will disappear without a trace into the surrounding population."[48] The new governor-general didn't exactly need Pobedonostev's encouragement: he held intense antisemitic opinions of his own, and in briefly considering transferring the royal court from St. Petersburg back to Moscow, he resolved, in the name of his brother the tsar, to clear Moscow of undesirable elements.

The newspaper *Moscow Leaflet* heeded the dog whistle with page after page of anonymous nastiness ("Moscow is flooded with Jews," "Jews have seized everything in Moscow," and so forth).[49] Similar screeds appeared in the right-wing press of St. Petersburg, including a celebratory report of a new Slavophile society promising "never to have any dealings with Jews." Its "membership fees will go towards the fight against Jewish exploitation, providing, in sum, benefits or credits to fellow members who, by necessity or accident, fell into the hands of the Jews. . . . Great news!"[50] This announcement was preceded, in the "Happy New Year" edition of *Petersburg Leaflet,* by a fulmination on the "Jewish question" that begins with a quotation from Dostoevsky: "Drive nature out of the door and it will fly in at the window." This phrase, the anonymous author insists, "applies perfectly to the Jews" and the eternally futile efforts of the Moscow police to keep the "vagabond," passport-less "sons of Israel" from sneaking across the border of the Pale of Settlement into Moscow.[51]

By law, the Jewish population didn't have the right of permanent residence in Moscow, but bribes to the police, the right-wing press alleged, had allowed the community to prosper at the expense of non-Jewish businesses. The tension between the Russian guild and Jewish guild merchant communities is at the heart of Samuel Vermel's eyewitness account of the events of 1891–92. Vermel was a leader of the Jewish community, a respected doctor, and a bitterly ironic writer. He commences his account by noting that Russian businessmen tended to conduct their affairs "slowly and gently, unhurriedly, praying to God." They sat on their sacks of gold and were set in their ways. They couldn't countenance the "Sturm und Drang" of the "lively, active, fussy, and nervous Jew" who threatened their profits.[52]

On March 28, 1891, the eve of Passover, the tsar signed an ambiguous order protecting Moscow from "semites" and other suddenly illegal immigrants. Alexander III instructed the Minister of Internal Affairs (and through him Grand Prince Sergey Romanov) to "prohibit Jewish mechanics, distillers, brewers, craftsmen, and artisans in general from relocating from the Jewish Pale of Settlement and other areas of the empire to Moscow and its region." The second part of the order was less ambiguous; it authorized the removal of Jews in the "above-mentioned" categories. The newspapers published these words, and panic ensued in Zaryadye. The rest of Moscow remained calm.[53]

The foreign press reported the panic while the Russian press kept mum for reasons of censorship, allowing everything to happen quietly, cloaked in secrecy. The monthly Russian Jewish journal *Sunrise,* which had fought against government antisemitism, was forced to suspend operations in March of 1891, and the large St. Petersburg newspaper *Novosti* was also shut down for half a year for publishing articles sympathetic to the Jews.[54] There were calls to protest, but these came from far away. A book published in 1892 by the Russian Free Press of London under the title *Yevrey k yevreyam*, or *A Jew to Jews*, highlighted the tsar's antisemitism and the violence he had already unleashed:

> Alexander III's ferocious cruelty, brought to bear on tens of thousands of Jewish citizens living outside the Pale, can only be compared to the ferocious cruelty with which he represses any sign of free thinking and independent social life. The reign of Alexander III is a perpetual St. Bartholomew's night [day] massacre for anyone of thought and conscience in Rus, and nothing quite illuminates this night like the inquisitors' bonfires.[55]

Teenagers hollered a humiliating equivalent of "bon voyage" to Jews moving through Moscow's streets, and teachers asked their Jewish pupils (especially those lagging in their studies) when exactly they were leaving.[56] The rich merchants living across the river from Zaryadye "giggled into their fists" at the expulsion of their competitors and the opportunity to create monopolies in the textile industry.[57]

Moscow's Jewish population was diverse. It included conservatives and progressives, Hasidic, Litvak (Lithuanian), and Karaite sects brought together by Rabbi Solomon Minor. A graduate of the Rabbinical School in Vilna (Vilnius) and member of the Haskalah (Enlightenment) movement, he served as the rabbi of Minsk before assuming the position in Moscow. He gave sermons in Russian, published a collection of lectures on morality, taught and argued with Tolstoy about principles of nonviolence, and, with another rabbi, founded a school for the Jewish orphans of soldiers.[58] Financing came from the leading banker and philanthropist Lazar Polyakov, who recommended naming it after the "good" tsar, Alexander II, in recognition of his having relaxed the sanctions on Jewish life, allowing the Jewish population of Moscow to expand and rabbinical courts to operate.

For bravely protesting the expulsion, the rabbi was himself expelled. Then, as further punishment, the synagogue near Khitrovka (ulitsa Solyanka), which began as a modest prayer house in a residential complex, was closed—another loss to a frightened community. Getting permission to build the synagogue in 1887 had been an ordeal; each foundation stone and flake of paint seemed to require a permit. The government demanded that the facility be redesigned, reduced in size. Its dome went up, then in March of 1888, on protest from Pobedonostev, its dome came down. Before the synagogue was even consecrated, the merchants, artisans, and bankers who had financed it were given an ultimatum: either sell it or turn it into a public space. The Torah scrolls were removed along with the Star of David and the replica of the tablets of Moses. The building became a school, then an orphanage, only again serving as a synagogue in 1906. Architect Roman Klein restored the interiors with a golden mosaic of Lebanese cedars wrapped in grapevines and a blue dome with stars.[59] The synagogue survived the Soviet era on the original site, with the façade last restored in 2016 and a café called Bagel operating on the premises.

Before Dolgorukov's dismissal and departure for Nice, France (to treat his ailing heart; he would die in Paris on June 19, 1891), preparations for the expulsion—"preliminary experiments"—began.[60] These campaigns of harassment excluded merchants belonging to the first guild, dentists and apothecaries, degree holders, and "cantonists," the underage sons of conscripts who had fought in the Crimean War. The police instead focused on unskilled workers, whose documents could easily be discredited, found to have the wrong date or signature somewhere. Shopkeepers advertising their wares without the imprimatur of the censor were also rooted out. Targeted next were those registered as artisans but who had retired or never, in fact, practiced their craft. Kostanda, who replaced Dolgorukov, reassured the community that they'd "still be eating matzah in Moscow," but the expulsion orders were soon to expand. Some in Zaryadye, recognizing that their right of residency had been arbitrarily dissolved, expelled themselves. They relocated to the Pale, to Moscow's outskirts, and to Mar'yina roshcha. Residents there did not want to accept the "unlawful" Jews in their neighborhood, however, and called upon the local police chief to oust them.[61] "Refuge" was found in "the cemeteries lying just outside the town." And when "the mocking daylight came, it gilded pictures of anguish and horror," like that of a woman found dead beside her dead child, "to which she had given birth during the dreadful night."[62]

The operation became more efficiently impersonal under Grand Prince Sergey Romanov and his right-hand man, Vladimir Istomin, for whom issuing an order to leave to "an extra Jew, an additional Jewish family, from Moscow was, as it were, his civic duty."[63] Those artisans, teachers, and other "honest workers" who had been in Moscow for under three years and didn't have a family had a maximum of six months to leave. Those who had been in Moscow for six years or less and had a family were given nine months. Older people with large families and businesses with several employees had a year.[64] The physical work fell to the new chief of police, Alexander Vlasovsky, who came to Moscow from Riga, where he had earned a reputation for harshness and oddball behavior. Vermel calls him "a rude and cruel" man, "foreign to feelings of pity and compassion in general and hating Jews organically."[65] He assumed his position in January 1892 and made an "impression" on his boss, Sergey Romanov, for his "efficient, smart, energetic" approach to his duties.[66] Vlasovsky did some good among the bad, putting up streetlamps in the better parts of town, improving firefighting, fining cabbies for cursing, clearing snow before the thaw. He also battled corruption, though this came at the expense of the targeted population—rewarding, for example, five rubles to a police officer who refused to accept a bribe of one ruble from a Jew caught living in Moscow without permission.

Also at the forefront of the campaign was the mayor of Moscow, Nikolay Alekseyev. He was of ancient Muscovite lineage and served as the people's elected representative to Moscow's governor-general. Alekseyev was an energetic, highly cultured official who counted Tchaikovsky among his friends. The municipal government was stacked with members of merchant dynasties at this time, which contributed to the animosity against the Jewish community and Alekseyev's "support of the government policy as pertaining to the nationalism question."[67] His initiatives included, in no particular order, fixing cracked pipes and improving sewage treatment; allocating funds for museums and establishing scholarships; directing and keeping the books for the Imperial Russian Musical Society; donating to schools and hospitals; carousing with the police chief; harassing the Jewish banker Polyakov; and overseeing a relocation of the kosher meat-processing plant outside of Moscow.[68] Alekseyev also provided 300,000 rubles from his own pocket toward the construction of Moscow's first psychiatric facility—as reward for which he was shot in the stomach by a madman (whispered to be a hired assassin) in his government office, dying at age forty.[69]

Vlasovsky likewise met a bad end, though few pitied him. Having overseen the expulsion, he was in extremely good standing with the governor-general and Tsar Alexander III—an esteem he lost four years later after well more than a thousand people died in Khodïnskoye field during the coronation festivities for Alexander's successor. Investigators identified Vlasovsky as the "real culprit" for the casualties caused by the stampede since he should have had his officers "level the canals" and fill "the holes" in the field that had been left after exhibition buildings were dismantled. Ultimately, incompetence, summarized in the archival records as "internal conflicts within the governing elite of Moscow," precipitated the sorrow.[70]

Vlasovsky was chased out of Moscow. He retired in St. Petersburg and there fell sick "with some kind of disease, for which he was treated with subcutaneous injections from a fashionable and popular healer," only to die of blood poisoning.[71]

By then, Zaryadye, as Belousov had known it, had vanished. Throughout 1891–92, bailiffs assigned the Jewish families in the neighborhood deadlines for leaving, sometimes with an extension of a month or two based on personal circumstances. People who had lived in the city for up to four decades or more had to sell their "pathetic junk" for next to nothing, a ruble or two, and if they didn't have time to do that, transit prisons filled with highwaymen and housebreakers awaited.[72] The Moscow correspondent of London's *Daily News* smuggled out an account of "a convoy about to be dispatched at a certain time from the prison" (he doesn't say which one). "Some wore their own clothes, and some the convict's dress with the yellow diamond on the back."[73]

The chronicles of the expulsion narrate foiled escape attempts. One newspaperman fortunate enough to be sheltered by his Russian employer hid in the closet when the police entered the building and waited for the all-clear signal when they left.[74] In mid-September 1892, the Jewish "mood" painter Isaak Levitan was given the order to leave Moscow for Boldino, which caused a protracted scandal. He had long been a fixture in salons and was patronized by the Romanovs. Petitions and protests from his allies and the promise of international embarrassment allowed him to return to Moscow in mid-December, but he never recovered from the ordeal.[75] Still, he was an exception. Even the occasional intervention of the metropolitan of Moscow couldn't prevent the ousting of other prominent figures. Vermel recounts an anecdote about a Jewish electrician hired to wire the governor-general's mansion:

> The work was carried out beautifully and successfully. When the grand prince inspected the electrician's progress, the latter took the opportunity to advocate for himself. "Your Imperial Highness," he said, turning around, "I don't know if I will be able to finish the job."—"And why not?"—"I'm a Jew, and I have to leave Moscow." The grand prince was initially embarrassed, then blurted out, "Well, hurry up then," and quickly left the hall.[76]

A handful converted, becoming Lutheran Christians. The pastor of the Lutheran church in Moscow accepted them without fuss (converting to the Orthodox faith was anathema to Jews for essential doctrinal reasons).

Tears meant nothing. Parents packed up their children, collecting tickets and the trifling allowance raised by a relief committee that had liaised with committees in other countries for assistance in resettling the populace. Jews relocated to Ukraine and Poland, tried purchasing land in Ottoman-controlled Palestine, or traveled from Brest Station to Berlin, Hamburg, Antwerp, and London, pleading for passage to the United States.[77] The American government seemed to accept the tsar's denial of the expulsion, and the plight of Moscow's Jewish population was soon overshadowed by the need to accommodate peasants fleeing a fierce drought in the Volga provinces.[78] Meantime Russian Jews were accused of bringing cholera, the illness that killed the composer Tchaikovsky, to the United States. "These people are offensive enough at best," the *New York Times* said of the Jews (and Hungarians) seeking refuge. "Under the present circumstances, they are a positive menace to the health of the country."[79] Tales of the expulsion from Moscow were soon rivaled by tales of expulsion from New York. "On their journey West some little hope sustains them, but on their return they are sunk in despair, physically and mentally in ruins. One man lately was in a state piteous to witness. He would scarcely speak—and when it did it was with tears. He wanted to go back to Russia to his miserable home and to his five children."[80]

Families ordered to leave in January 1892 had to contend with the harshest freeze Moscow had seen in years, with temperatures dipping below minus 30 Celsius. Frozen conductors pushed frozen children, their parents, the sick, and the infirm into train carriages without seats until they could hold no more, leaving hundreds of others on the ice-covered platform of a single track with their bundles of bundles. Vlasovsky obliged some of them with a deferment; they could leave in spring. When the thaw came, the evictions resumed, and those who missed their assigned train ended up roaming the streets without their baggage, "settling down on benches on the boulevards for the night with the other sad and humiliated 'illegals.'"[81]

By July 14, 1892, it was over—the benches cleared, the flats in Zaryadye boarded up, the keeper of the Jewish cemetery dismissed because he wasn't needed. Last to go were the soldiers. According to the census, 5,319 Jews resided in Moscow in 1871 and 15,085 in 1882.[82] According to Vermel, that number had tripled to 45,000 or so by 1891. The census of 1897 indicates that 38,000 Jews were expelled with 8,095 remaining in Moscow.[83]

The economy suffered. The ruble lost value, and Russian securities on the exchange in Paris tanked after financier Alphonse James Rothschild pulled the plug on a massive loan to Russia.[84] But life went on for Grand Prince Sergey Romanov. The governor-general traveled the city in plush carriages and conducted his affairs in state rooms and theater loges, clinking crystal and indulging mindless chitchat about the weather. December 27, 1892, was marked by a minor source of irritation. That afternoon, he found in his mail "a libelous book on the expulsion of Jews from Moscow. The author didn't spare me, *c'est hideux* [and it's disgusting]." The American journalist Harold Frederic, author of the offending tome, was based in London reporting for the *New York Times* and had visited Russia. The governor-general is savaged, in the chapter titled "The Appointment of Serge," as a "hollow-eyed, narrow-browed man of thirty-five, everywhere throughout the European courts known to be the least intelligent and respectable Romanov since the time of Paul." To prepare for the arrival of "this obscene simpleton" in Moscow, "the Cossacks and police" carried out their "famous midnight descent upon the poor Jewish quarter." As to Moscow, it was "an Arabian Night's dream of a metropolis" with a "burly, swart, round-headed, heavy-jowled barbarian [Alekseyev]" as mayor. Moscow, the rant concludes, "conveys to eye and mind alike the impression of being lost on the map—of having strayed a thousand miles or so westward out of its reckoning."[85]

Today just a segment of the serf-built Kitai-gorod wall that wrapped around Zaryadye survives, along with the embankment stonework and the great old street of Varvarka that bordered Zaryadye to the north. Little else. Photographs from the 1940s propagandistically underscore the contrast of the sadly dull, gray past and the bright present. The images capture falling-down buildings, carts, clotheslines, and "tattered" people.[86] In the 1960s, buildings in Zaryadye came down to create the road leading to a giant hotel—the 3,182-room Rossiya, one of Nikita Khrushchev's projects. The hotel opened in 1967 and lasted four decades before being detonated in favor of nothing. Now the site boasts a park of flashy high-tech attractions nicknamed "Putin's paradise." There are domes, underground recesses, jogging paths and hundreds of CCTV cameras. It's "convenient and modern," as Putin says Moscow should be. If you don't think that people can be free here, the "totalitarian panopticon" provides proof.[87] "Putin's paradise" erased the erasures, carting away the rubble atop the rubble atop the rubble of the ancient neighborhood.

It's always a struggle to remember—much less commemorate, without celebrating—Moscow's past. In 2012, the multimedia Jewish Museum and Tolerance Center opened in a renovated depot near the Mar'yina roshcha Metro station. The Russian government backstopped its development.[88] I visited in 2019 and noted the effort to avoid sensitive topics, including, in the words of one of the content creators, the "men and women of Jewish origin [who] held senior leadership posts until the mid-1930s in elite Bolshevik politics, the command economy, cultural and intellectual hierarchies, and the regime's notorious secret police (known as the Cheka and NKVD)."[89] Better no exhibit—emptiness—than an offensive one. Poverty never looked so good: no holes in the fabrics on the neatly coiffed mannequins, no cracks and chips in the bricks in the walls. The museum offers a sterile, sharp-angled gloss on the pogroms in the Russian Empire between 1881–84 and 1903–06.

The first wave of repressions followed the assassination of Tsar Alexander II, according to a white-lettered placard, and the second the 1905 Revolution (also known as the "Bloody Sunday" uprising)—though the museum insists that the pogroms occurred chiefly in Ukraine. Another placard broadcasts that the "Russian Jewry" emerged from "the medieval community of Poland—self-governing, traditionally religious, and isolated from the rest of society." That distortion is followed by the claim that "hundreds" of Imperial Russian laws "restricted Jewish education," travel, and opportunities for employment, which "led millions to emigrate in search of a better life." Of violence against Jews: not much is said. No less unpleasant is the assertion that "for those staying in Russia, new Jewish movements such as [Socialist-]Zionism and Bundism held the promise of an alternate." Although Jewish groups sided, for safety's sake, with the Bolsheviks, accusations of blood libel proliferated. The NKVD rounded up prominent Jewish intellectuals, executing some, sending the rest to the Gulag.[90]

Wind effects, sprinkles of rain, and simulated locusts viewed through 3D glasses relate events in the Old Testament. Visitors can interact with deceased writers in a virtual version of Odessa; touching a Torah in the interactive synagogue cues a cantor to chant. Installations include Hebrew parchment scrolls, phylacteries, and documents from the Jewish studio theater (the Habima dramatic society) that operated in the back of the Moscow Arts Theater in the first years of Soviet power. Films and photographs document Hitler's atrocities. As for Zaryadye, nothing. An employee of the museum assured me that the Jewish Museum and Tolerance Center has no information whatsoever on Belousov's neighborhood and the disappearance of the people who lived there.[91]

12

MYSTICS OF THE ARBAT

THE ARBAT, a crossroads approaching the Kremlin, emerged as a trading strip and occasional battle zone—home, depending on the epoch, to coiners and musketeers. Gentrification in the nineteenth century transformed the neighborhood into a nest of gentlefolk, to quote the title of Ivan Turgenev's 1859 novel about congenially flawed elites. The who's who of Moscow lived there: the Volkonsky and Trubetskoy clans as well as eminent actors, dancers, musicians, and writers. An oft-renovated building from the seventeenth century houses the Praga (Prague) restaurant, where Tolstoy read from his novel *Resurrection* and the cast of Chekhov's play *The Seagull* celebrated its premiere. At the other end of the street, House 26, stands the illustrious Vakhtangov Theater, founded by the director Yevgeny Vakhtangov in 1921, just a year before his death from cancer. House 37 is fronted by a graffiti-covered wall dedicated to Viktor Tsoi and his iconic Soviet rock band Kino (Cinema). The street also boasts a bronze sculpture of Pushkin and his bride, Natalya Goncharova, across from the apartment where the couple set up house for a few contented months after their wedding.

The Soviets resented the past so wanted it gone. They razed the churches and cafés and replaced the tram lines with trolleybuses. In 1963, state planners built a multi-lane thoroughfare knitting together several streets that pass Arbat Square then reaches across the river to the new housing complexes in the west. Initial plans named the road New Arbat, but it was renamed Constitution and, before it opened, renamed again as Kalininsky Prospekt after the Soviet statesman Mikhaíl Kalinin. Four office towers went up on the southern side of the road and five apartment blocks on the northern side. The office buildings look like open books or, as the designers intended, "sails," rising twenty-five floors from a connecting glass and metal-clad stylobate.[1] Most of the apartments went to Central Committee VIPs and generals who enjoyed a five-minute commute from their apartments through the underpass to their offices. These prefabricated steel-frame buildings of poured concrete and plastic paneling offered great views for those who didn't mind the illuminations across the street (controllers programmed the office lights to spell CCCP during holidays) or, lower down, dust from a road crowded with Ladas and other Soviet cars, though traffic wasn't that bad and the gasoline unleaded.

New Arbat blotted out ancient courtyards along with the homes of the *oprichniki* and their kennels (a disappeared trapezoid called *Sobach'ya ploshadka,* or Dog Playground), the hen yard (*kurya noshka*) beside a church built for musketeer parishioners, and estates built after 1812. The Soviet thoroughfare boasted the flagship store of the All-Union Gramophone Record Firm of the USSR Ministry of Culture (aka Melodiya), the October movie palace (opened in 1967), Moscow's biggest and most popular bookstore, a massive bread store called simply Bread (Khleb), a banquet hall of two thousand seats serving up butter-stuffed chicken Kyiv, a rotating globe celebrating the comfort and speed of the airline Aeroflot, and the friskiest burlesques in Eastern Europe. New Arbat survived the 1990s blight of casinos and strip clubs. It is now decorated with benches and trees and oversized swing sets.

The original Arbat—Old Arbat—survived the troubled twentieth century mostly intact. Leaves and snow piled up all around, "reluctantly and rarely cleared." A special French school operated in the area, No. 12, where Soviet children immersed themselves in the language of Gautier, Mérimée, and the disappeared Romanov dynasty. The streets were spectral at night; the old "whitish lanterns lit only themselves; the light did not even reach their base."[2]

In the mid-1980s, the building façades were painted pastel, benches and lanterns were bolted down, and cobblestone replaced the asphalt that had replaced cobblestone. Residents were relocated. One of them, a beloved Georgian-Armenian bard named Bulat Okudzhava, lamented the street becoming the equivalent of a Potemkin village, a set of pretend houses like those built by Prince Grigory Potemkin along the route of Catherine the Great's inspection tour of the Crimea in 1787. "I wouldn't want to live here now," Okudzhava lamented, wondering "is it even possible to live among theatrical façades?"[3] Better the 1960s, when the police enforced curfews and singers like him were discouraged from performing, than the fake antique feel.

The artifice wasn't intentional, at least not according to architect Alexei Gutnov, a paradoxical figure from a paradoxical family (his father was an agent of the Communist International, his mother a medieval historian). He worked on the totalitarian Palace of Soviets project but also wanted to make Moscow more pedestrian friendly, though his ideas were often rejected by Soviet high command. The Research and Design Institute for the General Plan of the city of Moscow endorsed his plans for the Arbat, but Gutnov butted heads with modernist architects like Igor Pokrovsky, who had spent years building Soviet embassies in Africa and avoided "tinkering with old junk" like the Arbat neighborhood. Pokrovsky didn't like pastel paints, preferring black, white, and shades of gray. He talked of "placing bulldozers on each side of the street, following these bulldozers to the end of the street" and filling the resulting emptiness with "spacious, gleaming" buildings.[4] He contributed to the building of modernist apartment towers and office buildings on Kalininsky Prospekt and took great pride in the result—despite public disgust over the demolishing of ancient lanes and squares. His unsentimental plans for the Arbat were rejected by Gutnov and other architects like Iosif Loveyko, a distinguished People's Architect of the USSR with a love of marble. He affectionately remembered the Arbat of the 1920s, especially the cellar café in House 9. "When I was 15 years old," he recalled, "I was in this 'cellar' and Mayakovsky and Pasternak arguing with each other right in front of me. Do it—turn it into a pedestrian street!"[5]

The budget for a redesign didn't fall into place until after the 1980 Moscow Olympics, and logistics proved tricky. Because the buildings along the street had sunk into the soil over time, people descended two or three steps to enter the buildings; thus, the street needed to be lowered and stone plinths refashioned. More funding would have to be procured for restoring the foundations, laying sewer and water lines, and rewiring the street once the tangle of overhead lines came down. Laying paving stones required special expertise. Moscow's street workers knew everything about asphalt and cement but nothing about decorative roadwork, so older people who knew something about older roads were brought in. After the Committee for the Protection of Monuments approved the historical restoration work, Gutnov's team figured out the "color passport" for each of the façades after grimacing at the generic yellow spray paint initially applied. The painters were given natural colors and proper paintbrushes. Their skills made a huge difference; when they were finished the street shimmered.[6]

The gleam bothered another architect named Mikhaíl Kakushkin, who had urged a more considered approach. He saw the project as an opportunity—perhaps the only one—to penetrate deep into the history of the area, restoring depth and texture to the buildings, recovering disappeared courtyards, and expanding efforts beyond the Arbat into the alleys where, centuries before, people lived in houses decorated with pictures of animals and stars and other pagan symbols. Mysterious objects discovered during the excavations, beneath layers of char, included a note reading "Look under Vasya's oak tree." There's no oak tree to be found, though perhaps, in the basement beneath the basement where the tree once stood, Vasya's friend had hidden a silver dish or icon frame.[7] Kakushkin was assigned the restoration of House 44, a jewel of the eighteenth century that had belonged to a distant relative of Turgenev and the grandmother of another eminent writer, Fyodor Tyutchev. The building collapsed during the fire of 1812 but was resurrected in 1837. Pushkin frequented House 44, as did members of the anti-tsarist underground. Kakushkin imagined putting in a restaurant featuring traditional Russian cuisine cooked on a peasant stove.[8] A Hard Rock Café ended up in the building, though it closed in October 2022 in response to Russia's invasion of Ukraine.

Other historical streets have been reconfigured, some turned into high-end shopping arcades covered by barrel roofs. None retains the magic of the Arbat of the 1860s under Tsar Alexander II, which became the hub of a progressive movement that welcomed people of diverse ranks, backgrounds, and identities. The 1860s expanded educational opportunities for girls and women of all social classes— developments that predated similar liberal reforms in England and France. Culture in Moscow became, for a couple of decades at least, broadly feminist.[9] And in the salons of the wealthiest women of the Arbat neighborhood, the artists of the Silver Age—so called, after the Golden Age of Pushkin—gathered at the turn of the century, an era like no other in expanding Moscow's cultural offerings.

The Symbolists, as most of the artists of the Silver Age were known, chafed against reality. They were interested in the imagination, transience, and substances like fire—less for the ruin it so often brought to Moscow than its metaphoric associations with transformation, purification, passion, and the divine. They tried, in literature and music, to bridge the divide between known and unknown, past and future. Their spiritual quests ranged through the occult, Indian religious philosophy, and Russian Orthodox ritual before the time of Peter the Great. Of course, bad things happen when one plays with fire, and the Symbolists harmed one another in their efforts to fuse life and art. "Some of their creative energies and intimate experiences sparked their creativity," the poet-aesthetician Vladislav Khodasevich remembered, "but some instead leaked into everyday living, much as a live wire leaks electricity when insufficiently insulated."[10] Khodasevich admired elements of Symbolism—the privileging of

272 · A KINGDOM AND A VILLAGE

feeling over thought, the discrediting of secular positivism—but decried the recklessness of the leading mystics.

Their place in the grand sweep seems small, though there is a connection to the prophets of the past, the holy fools and mediums and wizards who had their own ideas of Russia, of Moscow, and of life itself, whatever the claims of the people in charge. The Symbolists, as visionaries, charted an alternate path, but didn't get far in transforming their illusions and delusions into reality. Their Russia is the place that might have been, a place that exists in dreams so perhaps stays safest there. Other visionaries, like Vladimir Lenin, succeeded (at least partly) in turning dreams of a Russia that didn't exist into reality.[11]

Among the Symbolists on the Arbat were Andrey Belïy, a resident of House 55, and Marina Tsvetayeva, who once lived at No. 53, as had Pushkin and Goncharova and Tchaikovsky's younger brother Anatole. The poet Alexander Blok rented space a couple doors down from Belïy in Arbat No. 51.[12] Blok straddled both sides of the Revolution, producing a play stuffed with religious symbolism called *The Rose and the Cross* and a poetic masterpiece about the Revolution, *The Twelve,* wherein Russia is brought through a blizzard by a savior who might be the Second Coming or the Antichrist. Composer and pianist Alexander Scriabin spent his experimental final years a few steps from the Vakhtangov Theater between Old and New Arbat on Bolshoy Nikolopeskovskiy pereulok. He rented the second floor of a mansion from a professor of philology who lived on the first floor. The street is named for the non-extant Church of St. Nicholas on the Sands, where in 1493 a forgetful priest went home without blowing out the candles lit by his parishioners, an act whose consequences generated the expression "Ot kopeyechnoy svechi Moskva sgorela [a kopeck candle burned Moscow down]." And it did so again and again and again, according to Sigizmund Krzhizhanovsky, a writer of the fantastic who lived in a tiny room on the Arbat in the 1920s. "Past residents of Moscow were professional *pogoreltsï* [people who have lost everything in a fire]," he lamented. "They lived from fire to fire: they built to please not so much themselves as the kopeck candle."[13]

Fires didn't threaten essential human existence, according to the Symbolists. Reason did, enlightened reason, because it alienated people from nature and from one another. Reason had also replaced feeling as provider of knowledge. Thus, the gulf between the secular intelligentsia and the peasant faithful is a recurrent theme in Symbolist literature. In a public lecture from October 1892 called "On the Causes of the Decline and on the New Trends in Contemporary Russian Literature," Dmitri Merezhkovsky declared war on the supposedly "indestructible dam" fashioned by empirical sciences in favor of those mystical practices accessing "the boundless and dark ocean that lies beyond the boundaries of our knowledge." Unification through faith is a goal, and Merezhkovsky draws in the faith of the peasant—the hot flame by the icon in the coldest of nights—and extols an art that "snatches the soul from life and just as quickly bears it away." He has tough things to say about critics who belittle his reveries as "vague chirpings," as insignificant as "nutshells dancing on the top of Niagara Falls." They just didn't get it. Symbolism was neither frivolous nor a fad but "a return to the ancient and eternal, to the never dying."[14]

The Symbolists turned against life (understood as sensory realism) by eschewing representation. Instead, they embraced art that altered perception, that defied the here and now and illuminated the path into a metaphysical beyond. Belïy became the leader of this pursuit only to abandon it, becoming what the keeper of his archive, Monika Spivak, calls a "man of scandal."[15] The saint self-consciously shape-shifted into a sinner, and what began as a progressive movement seeking liberation dissolved into its decadent, self-indulgent, often nihilistic opposite. Born Boris Bugaev, Andrey Belïy was a pale, thin child whose mother kept him home most of the time out of fear that he would contract a fatal disease. She also feared him becoming like his father, Nikolay, a professor of mathematics and physics at Moscow University. She wanted Boris/Andrey to go into the humanities, as opposed to entering the "boring and repellent" world of his father. (Nikolay Bugaev was in truth a highly charismatic individual who founded the Moscow school of function theory and was also active in the Moscow Psychological Society.) Boris/Andrey was bullied at school for his long hair and effeminate look, so avoided his classmates, preferring to read adventure stories and draw. Defying his mother but pleasing his father, he graduated from Moscow University with honors in natural sciences.[16]

He also studied history and language, befriending Mikhaíl Solovyov, whose brother, religious philosopher Vladimir Solovyov, wrote about all sorts of things: art, love, law, his visions of the Divine Sophia, the potential invasion of Russia from the East, unification of the Christian churches, materialism and the Antichrist, the deficit of beauty in the world. He anticipated Russia's "non-violent" spiritual "transfiguration"—as opposed to the "violent transformation" actually on the horizon.[17] Mikhaíl lived on the second floor of Bugaev's building with his wife, Olga, a painter. Their living room became a salon for the artists of the Silver Age and a hotbed of debate about everything from the status of the Church and the meaning of icons to the anticipated political apocalypse in Russia. In a long, complicated, semi-autobiographical poem called "First Encounter" (Pervoye svidaniye, 1921), Belïy recalled his time in the apartment:

> Mikhal Sergeich turns to me
> From his bisque-colored chair;
> His pince-nez glass has come alive,
> Awash with brilliant sparks;
> Arraying questions like a fan,
> Puffing his amber chibouk,—
> He'd let out streams of smoke
> And flash his light-blue eyes at me;
> And with the incense of unique beliefs
> He'd fumigate my every question;
> And, having stirred the atmosphere,
> He'd poke his nose into his smoke-puffs,
> Placing one leg upon the other,
> And flicking off his ashes . . .
> He is—a hand outstretched to God
> Through gentle blizzard winds![18]

Besides writing about himself, Belïy also wrote about Moscow in a four-part fever dream of an epic named for the city.[19] It's a tough read, filled with nonsense sounds, neologisms, slang, archaic expressions from ancient dictionaries, and foreign words in ternary meter, but the descriptions of the Arbat harness the magic of the moment. "Scattered all over" the neighborhood, he writes, were "churches from various eras, medium, tall, and some small, with gold leaf and plain; out from under a layer of windblown, thick grime peeked the green, red, flat, low, and high roofs of houses, large houses, small houses, some dressed with glazed tile, others stuccoed, or simply in tattered materials, types long forgotten, reposed under trees, some rebuilt, some with columns, some not, and some balconied, faced with acanthus, caryatids supported each cornice and balcony; triangle gables on houses, large houses, small houses on Wildhowling, Snuffsneezer, and First, Second, Third, and Fifth, and Fourth, Sixth and Seventh Rottentooth Alleys."[20] In summer, the Arbat becomes a "rotten dump" of "dry fish and no rain; the stones bake; the rotten courtyards reek," the "fumes of asphalt rise above the brew of human bodies." A theater stands in a "wretched, stunted garden"; the audience "spits seeds, peels oranges, under the illusion of an acacia tree with leaves turned gray in the grime under the heavenly canopy: the city sky is filled with dust."[21] Belïy's Moscow still smells like the *Smuta:* the trash from the Godunov mansions has never been carted away. It's also deeply paranoid, a mystification of a police state. Everyone feels that they are being spied on, the eyes of others drilling into their backs, all of Moscow watching itself. People's gazes are generated by fear, and people's fears are generated by gazes. The mind is its own panopticon, consciousness and unconsciousness monitoring each other, as does the real and unreal, the dream world and waking existence.[22]

This is a late project, conceived in Belïy's final years, but no more or less esoteric than the writing he produced throughout his career. His prose, like his poetry, didn't exactly fly off the shelves; a lot of it went unpublished or ended up in small-circulation journals with astrological and mythological names like *Libra* (*Vesï*) and *Golden Fleece* (*Zolotoye runo*). He and his Symbolist colleagues—friends and foes—benefited from a network of patrons seeking to elevate themselves through art. Those with the greatest heft included Margarita Morozova, née Mamontova, a fetching aesthete who won (and survived) the excessive affections of the debauchees of the Silver Age. Her father had squandered his fortune gambling, but at age eighteen she married into fantastic wealth and moved into a columned mansion on Smolensk Boulevard with a courtyard, fountain, Egyptian sphinxes, and a large staff, including a cook, chef, coachman, doorman, electrician (the mansion had its own power plant), handyman, sommelier, and even a watchmaker. Morozova frequented the theater, collected art, and hosted balls for hundreds of guests. Food was ordered in from the Hermitage restaurant, the ladies were given "beautiful cockades made of ribbons of all colors," and a Romanian orchestra accompanied cotillions and mazurkas.[23]

Alas, the high life had its lows. Her eccentric industrialist-entrepreneur husband, Mikhaíl Morozov, was reckless and abusive; he almost killed her in a boating accident on the Volga. She tried to avoid his presence when he drank but he drank constantly, and Morozova was glad to see the end of him in 1903. (He died of nephritis, aggravated by a diet of vodka, steak tartare, and cayenne pepper. "It was terrible to watch," she said of his dietary habits.)[24] Widowhood suited her. She had a strong activist streak and, after 1905, hosted meetings of radical Orthodox organizations like the Christian Brotherhood of Struggle, which wanted the Church to separate itself from the autocracy and lead "the struggle for a new social order and bright future."[25] In 1902, she met the composer Scriabin through the director of the Moscow Conservatory, and their friendship blossomed after Scriabin offered to give her free piano and music theory lessons.[26] Morozova loved hearing him play and, unlike the composer's first wife, Vera, indulged his fantasies. Scriabin recommended books on philosophy and psychology to her while confiding "the most intimate and tiniest details of his life." "Sometimes, even if it was raining or windy and cold, we'd go for long walks along the boulevards," she recalled. "After a while it seemed like we weren't walking at all but borne on the wings of some kind of new life."[27]

Belïy, however, considered Scriabin a poseur, a charlatan who latched on to fashionable religious and philosophical ideas then mapped them onto his music. Morozova never stopped believing in the composer, however, nor did the great intellectual force behind the entire "mystic" Symbolist enterprise, Vyacheslav Ivanov, who explained the intent behind the music better than Scriabin himself ever could.

Scriabin and Ivanov had similar interests and common experiences. Both were born and educated in Moscow. (Ivanov grew up near the zoo, Scriabin in Khitrovka.) Both lost a parent in early childhood and found comfort as well as inspiration from traveling abroad. After studies at the First Moscow Classical Gymnasium and the Faculty of History and Philology at Moscow University, Ivanov relocated to Berlin. He then embarked on an extensive museum tour of Europe, sustaining himself as a translator, lecturer, and writer. He immersed himself in ruins, paleography, farming in ancient Rome (the subject of his dissertation, written in Latin), Apollo, Dionysius, Friedrich Nietzsche's *The Birth of Tragedy Out of the Spirit of Music*, Orthodoxy, paganism, the dithyramb, ancient and modern Greek, religious rites, art and life, the real and the more real. Ivanov's perception of the ancient world was not that of sunlit white columns but cauldrons of passions.

He liked Scriabin for the reasons Beliy didn't. The composer was excitable, often speaking without pause, one thought tacked on to the next, but also enchantingly childlike, once mulling what kind of music fish might like.[28] Scriabin accumulated ailments, including damage to his right hand from over-practice, and relied on traditional cures, like kumiss, the fermented mare's milk imbibed by the Mongols for its medicinal properties.[29] He attended the Second International Philosophical Congress in Geneva, took interest in Helena Blavatsky's theosophical writings, and read the Symbolists, especially Ivanov's writings about ancient Greek theater and bacchic revelries.

Before his mystic immersion, the short piano pieces Scriabin composed sounded like Chopin: emotional, ruminative, gentle on the ear. His First Symphony derives from Wagner and, in the choral finale, from Beethoven's setting of the "Ode to Joy." Ambition exceeded technique, and reviewers pounced. "My god, such unnatural harmonies, and how much pretentious, dilettantish music there is in it!"[30] Scriabin began to wonder if what the Symbolists said about music might be true: Could it provide access to the beyond, enacting what was hitherto only represented? Was it a tool for eschatological revelation?

His later works set new precedents. Critics reached for trippy metaphors trying to get their heads around them. His *Poem of Ecstasy* was described in a Henry Miller novel as "a bath of ice, cocaine, and rainbows."[31] The sequel, *Prometheus: The Poem of Fire,* imagined the white light of death as rebirth. It premiered in 1911 in Moscow's Assembly of the Nobility, a social club near the Bolshoi Theater that included space for concerts and glittering balls. (Pushkin describes the space in *Eugene Onegin,* as does Tolstoy in *War and Peace.*) Several rows were occupied by trade workers. Some booed before the conductor Serge Koussevitzky lifted his baton; others booed after he put it down. But the composer's supporters cheered. In creating a tone poem about Prometheus, Scriabin himself became Prometheus, a demiurge offering wisdom to the masses—along with a fair dose of hallucinogens in sound.[32]

The music, the poems, the paintings—cultural historians look at this time in Russia's history and in Moscow's with wonder. Certainly it was ornate, especially compared with the asphalt and cement to follow. The task of art, the Symbolists taught, was to move us higher rather than lower in the cosmic ranking, to make us more godlike and divine than beastly. But baser instincts prevailed, and the compact civilization that the Symbolists built for themselves in Moscow collapsed. Their art became primal, the superhuman replaced by the subhuman. And eventually a real primal force, Bolshevism, ended their movement. The Revolution chased some of the Symbolists out of Russia. The rest, to survive, found modest places for themselves in Soviet publishing houses or proletarian arts organizations, tricking themselves into believing that some sort of spiritual transformation had taken place. The hedonism continued, as did the quest for the stars, but Marxism-Leninism had nothing in common with mystic Symbolism.

Today the Arbat is a destination for cultural tourists. Buses shuttle guests to former manor houses turned mannered museums, including the former homes of Pushkin, Chekhov, and Glinka. One of the children who grew up in an apartment facing the Scriabin Museum remembered "eerie sounds coming from the lower floor of the museum—you couldn't call those sharp, loud, and long sounds music—and multi-colored flashes." Maybe some of its Symbolist energy endured. Everything behind the window "sparkled yellow and purple."[33] Alas, it wasn't the spark of the supernatural. In 1965, the first floor of the building was converted from a communal apartment into an electronic music studio that, the museum reports, "gradually faded away" in the 1970s.[34] Management passed from the Museum of the History and Reconstruction of Moscow to the Glinka Central State Museum of Musical Culture under the USSR Ministry of Culture. In 1984, the longtime director and "priestess" of the museum, Tatyana Shaborkina, retired after forty-six years of service to Scriabin's music. She nurtured creative thought inside the museum when such thought was prohibited on the street, and defended Scriabin against Soviet ideologues seeking, as in the case of Belïy, to expel him from cultural memory. That meant arguing, passionately if unconvincingly, that Scriabin's mystical sounds were less idiosyncratic and experimental than a harbinger of revolution as defined by Marx and Lenin.[35] Shaborkina kept the museum going during World War II, when the archive had to be evacuated and the museum was damaged by the shock wave from the bomb that hit the Vakhtangov Theater.[36] Moscow was under siege, trenches were being dug, and average citizens were putting out fires on rooftops, and Shaborkina was simultaneously patching up the walls of the museum and hosting Scriabin lectures and concerts in Scriabin's six-room apartment (until 1941, one of those rooms had been occupied by the composer's aunt). The walls had to be patched up again in the 1960s during the construction of New Arbat. Steam hammers operated just steps from the museum and cracked the foundations of the buildings throughout the neighborhood. Shaborkina successfully appealed to UNESCO and other cultural preservation organizations for support.[37]

With her passing, the museum lost its esotericism. The experimental music performances on the first floor ended, despite the efforts of Moscow's composers to keep them going.[38] Today, all that remains of Scriabin's magnificent color-light fantasies is a plywood circle with (mostly) red and purple lightbulbs and a set of switches. The museum has amped up its offerings to the public, including "night in the museum" events sponsored by Moscow's Department of Culture and assorted virtual exhibits. Although Scriabin didn't grow up in the building, lectures on his childhood are offered there to kids ages five to eight, who can amble over to the Museum of Illusions for bigger fun and then have their pictures taken in front of a pair of statues of Nikolay Gogol: one "happy," with grinning lions adorning the lampposts, another "sad."[39]

The structures that preserve the legacies of the mystics of the Arbat affirm, on the one hand, Russia's outsized contribution to world culture. They also, on the other hand, represent dreams that ended in great sorrow, in revolution and war, after Beliy and Scriabin had passed into an unreachable realm.

PART 3

SOVIET CAPITAL

REVOLUTIONARIES AND COUNTERREVOLUTIONARIES

IN MOSCOW in 1922, a woman who was just learning to write completed a homework assignment called "My Childhood." Her mother died when she was four months old, she says at the start, and her father squandered her inheritance on booze. Her grandmother placed her in an orphanage somewhere, then she boarded in a convent before "fighting" destroyed it. After working for a miller in a village, she eventually made it to Moscow with a bundle on her back. That, she said, was her experience of the Russian Revolution: personal chaos caused by political upheaval. "It was hard for me."[1]

The author of "My Childhood" joined a "political education circle" in Moscow. She found out that the Russian Revolution began not in 1917 but in 1905, and in different places. One of them was Biliki, Ukraine, a little settlement without passenger rail service, where a handsome priest named Georgy Gapon grew up. He claimed in his memoir that he was converted to the revolutionary cause in his youth, inspired by a dream about hounds attacking a gentle giant and tearing apart the flesh with their razor-sharp teeth. The giant, he explains, is Russia, and the keeper of the hounds the cruel tsar. The giant has two sons: a soldier who joins the hounds in the attack until the giant smashes his weapon, and a peasant, "a burly, powerful, good-natured figure, handsome in his simplicity, but fettered

284 · A KINGDOM AND A VILLAGE

and chained to the plough," who laments not being able to help his father.[2]

Growing up, Gapon read Tolstoy and wondered why the Russian Orthodox Church didn't advocate for fairness and justice for those doing the hardest work in the direst circumstances. He knew from his soft-hearted father, a village elder humiliated by government officers, that the local council (the zemstvo) lacked any real power, which was held by St. Petersburg and its bureaucracies. From his hardened, deeply religious mother, Gapon learned the lives of the saints and all the tricks the devil tried to play on them. He attended the lower ecclesiastical school in Poltava and became a priest, although his experience was troubled: other priests accused him of stealing from their congregations. Gapon found happiness in marriage to the daughter of a merchant who, like him, believed that "the essence of religion" resided "not in its outward forms but in its inner spirit—not in any ceremonies, but in love for one's neighbor."[3]

Gapon and his wife had two children and then, after just four years together, his wife died. He recalled her ghost visiting him in a dream and waking up to a curtain of flames in his bedroom. The icon in the corner glowed ruby red. He had another dream about being hunted by the figure of fate, a force telling him that he would soon cross the line between life and death. Seeking purpose, Gapon decided to relocate to St. Petersburg. He passed the entrance exams to the upper ecclesiastical school and began to meet, as part of his mission work, with prisoners, orphans, and guttersnipes—the wastrels of the imperial capital's slums. He also met with steel-plant employees. His charisma attracted a following of thousands, and he became the workers' trusted advocate. Recognizing his influence, the Okhrana (secret police of the Russian Empire) sought out his help in separating the organizers of the labor movements from those in their midst who would dismantle the government. Gapon lectured to workers and organized discussion groups, charities, concert outings, and diversions for children; meanwhile, he reported to the Okhrana.

Russia's defeat in the Russo-Japanese War (1904–5) caused widespread unrest. The tsar boasted about the empire's naval might and insisted on the sacrifices everyone needed to make to fund the war machine, only to be humiliated in the Far East. Strikes in weapons plants spread to other factories and spilled into the streets of major cities, including the imperial capital.[4] On January 5, 1905, Gapon brought a petition to the Winter Palace demanding (among other things) eight-hour shifts and paid overtime, a raise from 60 kopecks a day to 100 for men and 40 to 75 for women, freedom of speech, workers' rights committees, reinstatement of dismissed and imprisoned workers, and grade-school education financed by the state.[5] Union representatives in Moscow also wrote petitions making the case for universal suffrage. Gapon pledged to support the tsar; nothing in his petition posed a threat. No matter how miserable the workers were, they would still lay down their lives for the sovereign. The minister of finance advised Nicholas II to ignore the petition, so he did. Four days later, on the morning of January 9, tens of thousands of men, women, and children marched toward the Winter Palace demanding fuel and food. They sang while carrying icons and crosses. Cavalrymen pushed forward, ordering the converging streams to disperse. As the crowd continued to push forward, artillerymen opened fire. The icons and crosses didn't protect anyone.

"Day of Terror in Czar's Capital, Troops Slay Women with Children and Men," the front page of the *New York Times* blared in the aftermath of the massacre, adding that Gapon, the "idol" of the protesters, "miraculously escaped a volley which laid low half a hundred persons" during the "unspeakable horror."[6] Unrest and civil disobedience spread throughout Russia; more strikes happened in a single month than during the entire previous decade combined, involving bakers, bankers, plumbers, and even the police.[7]

Moscow had its own 1905 rebellion. It began in Zamoskvorechye, a neighborhood across the Moskva River to the south. There stood the residences of merchants (the early to bed, early to rise types highlighted by Ivan Belousov in his iconic memoir), factories, and barracks (vestiges of the soldiers' garrisons of old Rus). Munitions plants and heavier industrial operations lined two roads, Yakimanskaya and Pyatnitskaya, both named after churches.

Pyatnitskaya was the home of a large publishing house owned and operated by Ivan Sïtin. He came from peasant stock but had married into wealth and used his father-in-law's resources to open a small printing press. He aggressively acquired properties and machines to expand this business as Russia's largest publisher, producing maps, diaries, calendars, catalogues, caricatures that could be used as home decorations, the magazine *Vokrug sveta* (*Around the World*), the newspaper *Russkoye Slovo* (*Russian Word*), and mass editions of the Grimm Brothers, Leskov, Turgenev, and Tolstoy.[8] By 1917 he was operating stores in Moscow and fourteen other cities. His business grew so fast that he employed contract workers on top of the men and boys (no women) on his regular payroll. At the end of July 1905, workers hit the bricks in hopes of being paid not just for the letters they set but also for the punctuation. Sïtin refused to budge on the question of pay for punctuation, offering instead to reduce shifts from nine hours to eight.[9]

This "arcane orthographic revolt" morphed into a larger strike involving workers from other industries.[10] In December, a large-scale rebellion, thousands strong, erupted. The barracks of Zamoskvorechye were flashpoints, so too the dormitories in the Lefortovo, Basmannïy, and Rogozhskiy districts to the east. Lefortovo was a hub of civilian manufacturing, including the Moscow railroad carriage workshop, while Basmannïy, a former German settlement, housed technical schools, a manometer plant, and the crucial Kursk railroad hub, which received coal from Tula. Rogozhskiy, an Old Believer settlement that maintained a printing press and a school, produced ceramics, porcelain, and mirrors. The Moscow metallurgical plant operated there, along with a government wine-house and the "Kristall" vodka plant. Historian Diane Koenker notes that the former eastern village of Preobrazhenskoye, "where young Peter I [the Great] was said to have built the first Russian fleet," had become "an area of factories, taverns, and low wooden buildings that housed workers, their families, and an occasional cow or pig."[11]

The Moskva River formed a horseshoe around another working-class neighborhood in the south. Its name, Khamovniki, refers to the coarse hemp clothing (*kham*) that used to be manufactured there for laborers. (From *kham* comes the Russian word for coarse or unmannerly behavior, *khamstvo*.) Elegant residences and attractions these days are plentiful: galleries, the Pushkin Museum, Luzhniki Stadium, the Cathedral of Christ the Savior, and the historic "Maiden's Field" medical campus. For nineteen years, 1882–1901, Tolstoy occupied a modest wooden house in this neighborhood; it's now a lovingly preserved museum. The writer's interactions with (observations of) the toiling *muzhiki* of Khamovniki inspired a lecture called "On the Census in Moscow," in which Tolstoy, who helped administer the census, urged members of the elite like himself to atone for their greed by giving to the poor and helping to cauterize "all the wounds of society, the wounds of poverty, of vice, of ignorance."[12]

This lofty ideal didn't exactly coincide with the demands of the workers, nor with the desires of teachers, clerks, or domestic servants—much less the louts rebelling for rebellion's sake, putting state power to the test. On December 7, 1905, diverse factions—the Moscow Council (Soviet) of Workers' Deputies and representatives of the railroad and the post and telegraph unions—called for a general strike at high noon. People rushed to stock up on supplies and filled buckets with water, even though, the Moscow Council promised, the water would not be turned off. Gas, too, would keep flowing, "because otherwise water and resin in the gasholders would freeze, causing pipes to burst in the frozen soil, something that couldn't be fixed until spring." Hospitals, pharmacies, and essential workers in the chancelleries were spared as targets, but not the transit system. The first sign of trouble came on the Kursk railroad line when the strikers started pelting a passenger train with debris, chasing all who had tried to get off back on. The electric trams stopped working, as did all the newspapers (the typesetters couldn't work without power). Still, the Moscow Council fulfilled its promise of putting out a newspaper of its own, *Izvestiya* [of the Moscow Council of Workers' Deputies]. It was published by Sïtin's firm, which had an independent power supply. (Not that Sïtin had a choice: the strikers held him hostage as the newspaper was being set.) Students left their desks; the stock market crashed, and there was a run on the banks that employees didn't know how to handle. The solution? Join the strike. "Tonight in the absence of power the theaters and clubs were closed," the St. Petersburg newspaper *Novoye vremya* (*New*

Times) reported. "The streets are empty."[13] The imperial court was stunned to learn that Muscovites had mobilized against the stagnant status quo.

For one day, the mood was positive, even buoyant, and the first rallies mostly ended peacefully. The next day Moscow's governor-general appeared to promise a restoration of order; that didn't happen, but members of the "Federal Council," the professional revolutionaries seeking to turn the strike into an armed uprising, were rounded up. "I'd been jailed in Tsarist Russia many times," one of those professional revolutionaries recalled,

> but I had never felt such severe mental stress before, especially in the first weeks of imprisonment. I was plagued by the thought that, with our ridiculous arrest, we had unwittingly let down the party organization and the Moscow Council of Workers' Deputies. Of course, it wasn't difficult to replace us, but still, our withdrawal from the ranks right at the start of the general battle couldn't help but introduce some disorganization into the leadership of the strike and uprising.[14]

There was calm after the arrests, according to a telephone report from Moscow to St. Petersburg, but then, in an ominous sign, the phones went down.[15] The armed uprising was now in the hands of the "disorganized" leadership of the Moscow Council. Meantime, the second issue of *Izvestiya* rolled off Sïtin's press, along with copies of Marx's *Communist Manifesto* and, for contrast's sake, a book of panegyrics to Tsar Nicholas II.[16] Political rallies were held on Strastnaya (Pushkin) Square and a small patch of green with fountains called Aquarium Garden. The crowds spilled onto the streets, marching "in all directions with red flags," while "Cossacks and dragoons" tried to disperse them, cracking whips over their heads.[17] The government locked the Kremlin gates and iced them over to keep the rebels out. The rebels adopted the same tactic against the police, using old fences and other pieces of junk to build barricades, wrapping them in wire pulled from trams, packing them with snow, and

The 1905 Revolution.

then dousing them with water to form a hard shell.[18] Shrapnel and buckshot flew into crowds from behind these makeshift barricades.

It took several long days for the government to reclaim the streets using soldiers from Moscow's garrison and reinforcements from the capital; the Semyonovskiy regiment departed St. Petersburg in mid-December after a prayer service and parade.[19] Meantime, *Novoye vremya* reported that the rebellion had dissolved into a directionless, purposeless morass—perhaps because the rebels had "tired themselves out," their "uprising having fizzled," or perhaps because "a new tactic" with heavier weapons was in the offing. During the lull, however, something terrible had happened back at Sïtin's publishing house, the source of all the trouble.

> Up to 600 vigilantes barricaded themselves [inside]. Most of them were typesetters, armed with revolvers, bombs and a special kind of rapid-fire device called a machine gun. To subdue the vigilantes, [troops] surrounded the building with all three types of weapons. The vigilantes started shooting from the building and threw three bombs. Artillerymen launched grenades. Recognizing the hopelessness of their situation, the vigilantes set

fire to the building, intending to take advantage of the commotion by escaping. They did. Almost all of them escaped through Monetchikovskiy pereulok [Minters' Lane] as the building burned inside out, leaving just the walls standing. The fire killed many people, the families and children of the workers living in the building as well as bystanders from the neighborhood. The troops besieging the building suffered injuries; some were killed. During the day, the artillerymen shelled several private houses, from which shots were fired and bombs thrown. All these houses suffered significant damage.[20]

The strike took a turn. The government issued a shoot-to-kill order, and the rebels responded with acts of barbarism. On December 15, according to *Novoye vremya*, "a group of revolutionaries had entered the apartment of Alexander Voyloshnikov [head of the Moskovskaya sïsknaya politsiya, the bureau of investigations], dragged him into the yard and, not heeding the prayers of his children, shot him."[21] The person pulling the trigger was a twenty-four-year-old "born rebel" and self-described "cop killer" named Vladimir Mazurin.[22] By the time troops arrived from St. Petersburg to clear the streets once and for all (or so it was thought), 1,059 people had been killed, including 137 women and 86 children. Troop losses were smaller: 28 killed and 78 wounded. Thirty-six police officers died.[23]

The centers of resistance included a furniture plant owned by Nikolay Shmit (Schmidt), a socialist who not only joined the rebellion but also housed and financed rebels, purchased weapons for them, and transformed his plant into a bomb-making operation. Shmit was eventually arrested and, because he refused to reveal where the weapons were stored, his furniture factory was destroyed by artillery fire. Shmit was beaten into confessing and placed in an isolation unit in a prison hospital—a room so small that he couldn't stand up. His schizophrenic neighbors howled, which kept him awake at all hours. Whether a warden killed him or he committed suicide (exsanguination from slicing himself with glass) is uncertain.[24]

The uprising ended, bitterly, at *Tryokhgornaya manufaktura*, the oldest textile operation in Moscow. The complex included a hospital, a school, an arts and crafts space, and even a playhouse. Workers and their families learned to read; steeped in Marx and socialist thought, they distributed leaflets in support of the rebellion. The chemical workshop then became a weapons lab. Since the owner, Nikolay Prokhorov, had been fundamentally decent to his employees, they didn't turn against him, although, on December 20, 1905, he became their de facto hostage in a final confrontation with authorities. By this point, calm had returned to other parts of the city. Traffic had picked up, and the stores were filled with people seeking "to reward themselves for the days of abstinence and terror," *Novoye vremya* deadpanned. (The news from Moscow, never on the front page of this courtly newspaper, fell from the top to the bottom of page 2.) The workers of *Tryokhgornaya manufaktura* hung on for a few more days. "Holed up inside, ringed by soldiers," the radicalized cotton weavers and calico printers refused to surrender, despite "numerous people getting killed in the shelling and shooting and destruction."[25]

Photographs by Vladimir Shukhov, an engineer who had obtained a camera at the world's fair in Paris, capture the before and after: The hopeful crowds, the speeches, then, a couple of weeks later, the overturned trams and *drozhkies,* smoking buildings, idle horses, pedestrians with their heads down in the middle of making the cross, grimacing soldiers from the Semyonovskiy regiment, the zoo entrance, and Shukhov's own trim shadow crossing the lens. People opened their windows and headed outside. The newspapers *Russkiy listok* and *Moskovskiye vedomosti* reappeared; banks cashed checks. It was a bigger event than the uprising in St. Petersburg, but because the 1917 Revolution began in St. Petersburg (or Petrograd as it was renamed in 1914 in response to anti-German sentiment), the events of 1905 have been overshadowed. Both revolts were rehearsals of sorts for the events of February and October 1917. Both were sources of pride for the Bolsheviks and other socialist organizations, despite their having little to do with it. As 1905 passed into 1906, it seemed that the crisis had passed. The rebels with the bombs had been jailed or killed, and strikers had returned to work. The forced calm might have lasted had it not been for the First World War and the ineptitude of the tsar, exquisitely gifted at making bad situations worse.

In 1906, Nicholas II blessed the establishment of a representative parliament that would approve laws. (His other option was a permanent state of emergency and the surrender of government operations to generals.) But the new state Duma Nicholas II allowed to convene was a ruse, an act of deception; it had no power. Control of the budget remained with the court, and the tsar could still issue decrees that no one could question. Just one of its two houses, the lower one, comprised elected officials, and Nicholas II could dissolve the Duma whenever he liked, as he did in 1906 and 1907 in rejection of the parliamentarians' demands for reforms.

Another ruse involved urban labor groups: unions, cooperatives, social welfare groups, and charities. The tsar permitted them to operate so long as they didn't do anything. By 1912, Moscow had 153 workers' cooperatives, brought together under the auspices of the Moscow Union of Consumer Societies. The police kept them under surveillance lest the taboo subject of strikes came up during their meetings. The tsarist system sealed itself off from the restless masses, refusing to accept any input from the outside. The groups had little ability to improve the lives of their workers beyond sharing resources and organizing educational activities.[26]

Nicholas II clung to power for another decade, through Russia's entry into the First World War but not its exit. Russia's declaration of war had much less to do with an assassination in Sarajevo than with German industrial imperialism, French decline, and the disintegration of the Ottoman Empire. It also had a pan-Slavic element. Central Europe sought to deprive Serbia of its conquests in the Balkans—something Russia, with its centuries-old patronage of the Serbs, could not permit to happen. But the tsar, his government, and his armed forces were ill-prepared. The planned reorganization and modernization of Russia's and Ukraine's military districts had not been completed. Bureaucratic indecision and infighting during the summer of 1914 (the periods of "pre-mobilization," "private mobilization," and "general mobilization" for war) caused bewilderment and chaos. Russian steelworks didn't have the equipment for weapons production; the railroad network didn't reach far enough to carry troops to the Eastern Front, much less over the Carpathian Mountains. The soldiers' courage and zeal didn't help them when their cartridges ran out. According to one of their commanders, Anton Denikin, "the armies of the Southwestern Front crossed the Carpathians" in December of 1914, "in severe frosts, snow blizzards, on steep, icy mountain slopes," a superhuman effort that resulted in devastating defeat. The following spring, in the Subcarpathian town of Przemyśl, Denikin's "Iron Division" found itself powerless against German mortar attacks. "We could not respond, there was nothing. . . . Our exhausted regimes repelled one attack after another with bayonets or shooting at point-blank range . . . I felt despair and a sense of absurd helplessness."[27]

Defeated people scapegoat others. Russians of German heritage were bullied on the streets while rumors of treasonous aristocrats spread. Even as socialist factions went from backing the war to calling for peace, the Bolshevik leader, Vladimir Ilyich Lenin, anticipated a positive outcome: the fall of the Romanovs. Ending "tsarist-monarchist chauvinism," he declared, would cease the centuries-long repression of "Poland, Ukraine and a number of peoples of Russia" through the incitement of "national hatred" on behalf of a "barbaric government."[28] The dynasty ended, but not the war. In fact, Lenin inherited it.

The pseudo-parliamentary democracy that emerged after 1905 lasted until February 1917 (or March according to the Gregorian calendar) when female textile workers took to the streets on International Women's Day (February 23/March 8) to protest the war, the bread lines, and workplace abuse. The crowds swelled; Nicholas II abdicated. Why? The colossal number of deaths in the war, the accelerating labor unrest, the inability of the police to police and soldiers to soldier, the hooligans, the anarchists, the escaped prisoners: Russia had become ungovernable, and Nicholas II was told as much by the aides who helped make the mess. Nothing was happening, he deluded himself, even as Petrograd began to glow from fires in the streets and sailors and soldiers in Kronstadt, the island fortress that protected the imperial capital, rebelled.

The abdication and resignation of the tsar's ministers defined the first phase of the revolution, the positive one, producing feelings of liberation and excited debate. A provisional government took shape. It comprised members of the former Duma and shared power with a council, or soviet, of deputies representing the interests of the pro-letariat. Both entities had armed forces at their disposal. Perhaps no one was in charge, no one needed to work or go to school, and noth-ing cost anything anymore: food, transport, utilities—everything was free, at least until everything ran out and chaos ensued. The rest of Russia learned of the events in Petrograd through the telegraph network operated by the railroads. The commander of Moscow was advised by his superior in Petrograd to ensure sufficient food sup-plies to prevent a general strike.

The next day, February 28, there was a general strike. Factories ground to a halt; workers occupied police stations and freed prison-ers. Moscow formed a soviet in parallel to the formation of the Petro-grad Soviet. Soldiers from the massive Moscow garrison defected, as did Cossacks and cadets. The provisional government appointed a commissioner for Moscow. Even in the wearing of red ribbons in support of the revolution, as China Miéville irreverently writes of the events of 1917, there was "class differentiation." The better-dressed wore ribbons the size of tablecloths; the poor harangued them for their stinginess. "Share [the ribbons] out among us. We've got equal-ity and fraternity now."[29]

Nature contributed to the tumult. On May 8–9, 1917, a freak bliz-zard swept through Moscow, dumping enough snow on the streets to make it look like February, when the revolution had begun. "A hurricane of snow swept over Moscow before flying south, tearing off roofs, pulling down telegraph poles, knocking people and beasts off their feet," the newspaper *Moskovskiye vedomosti* reported. "The destructive path of this elusive anarchist is as follows: striking the area to the south, flying like a fury into Kyiv and causing innumera-ble disasters to the fields, gardens, and vegetable patches there. What a surprise for us malnourished people!"[30] Tolstoy's twelve-year-old granddaughter Tanya remembered the storm and the preceding upheaval in her diary, touching on the abdication of Tsar Nicholas II amid mention of the provisional government and the personal consequences of the blizzard. She was living outside of Moscow in Yasnaya Polyana in 1917:

> March 3: Today we're all terribly anxious because the entire newspaper is dedicated to the appointment of the new government.... It would be good if it were all for the better, and yet I feel sorry for the old tsar. All the old ministers have been arrested and new good ones appointed. All political criminals have been released.

> April 28: We were planning to live in Ovsyannikogo [near Kursk] in the summer but now I think we won't because there are various hooligans from the factory running around there and lots of riots in Russia now. Our violets are blooming, the cuckoo calling and the nightingale singing, and I'm sitting at home with a cough. Yesterday was a wonderful day, 10–15 degrees [Celsius] in the shade. Mom gave me a very cute white chicken, "Lyubochka."

> May 9: Yesterday and today have been terrible days. 2 degrees below zero and snow piled two and a half feet tall. There's wind, snow, and something incredible is happening in the yard. Two of our chickens have died, and the worst is that one of them is the queen [the best egg-layer]. I'm terribly afraid that the animals will die because no one has any hay, and everyone was counting on grass, which, of course, is now impossible to get.[31]

Industrial production fell. Fuel shortages disrupted food supplies, and the flow of taxes into the budget slowed then stopped. Hyperinflation brought the financial system to the edge of collapse. In Moscow, time was turned back to conserve power: classes began and ended an hour earlier, while it was still light. Bath houses were ordered closed for three days a week (a development that affected much of the population of Moscow).[32] Electric advertising was prohibited, and the use of power in homes severely limited, causing the cost of candles to spike. Those who wasted power were fined, even jailed. *Moskovskiye vedomosti* advised people to curtail their telephone conversations, since even the phone lines consumed power and life was too serious for idle chatter. Fashionable ladies made do with cheaper fabrics and short wide skirts known as "wartime crinolines." Moscow's police investigated the theft of a drive belt from a printing house and found it in a shoe shop, where it had been turned into soles.[33]

The dry law of 1914 remained in place, and with it the usual plusses and minuses of the curtailment of alcohol production and removal of wine and beer from businesses (excluding pharmacies and certain upper-class restaurants). Public drunkenness decreased, productivity slightly increased, domestic violence declined, and mothers had more cash to spend on their children now that fathers weren't wasting their wages on booze. Moonshine production, the secret consumption of homemade mash, cocaine and morphine use, and the imbibement of poisonous alcohol surrogates like cologne increased. "Denatured alcohol" (ethanol), meant to be used for cleaning or medical purposes, continued to be sold in wine shops. Purchasing it meant obtaining a book of tickets from the regulator. That didn't stop people from obtaining denatured alcohol on the sly and turning it into a potable potion by filtering it through "hot black bread with the crust cut off," boiling it up with lemon rinds or a combination of "clovers, cinnamon, and onions" to remove the toxins, the bad smell, and the bitter taste. Reserve soldiers rioted over the prohibition, but it remained in place through the war—right up to 1920.[34]

Outsiders looking in concluded that the provisional government would fall and that its second prime minister, a committed socialist named Alexander Kerensky, would lose his post, though what would happen afterward—the restoration of the tsarist system, perhaps, or dictatorship—was a question mark. No one expected Lenin to come out on top.

His real last name was Ulyanov, and he grew up in Simbirsk on the Volga River. (Oddly enough, so did Kerensky.) His parents were teachers, and he himself studied hard and earned good grades, then, as a law student in Kazan, became involved in student politics. That got him expelled, and his applications for readmission were rebuffed. His radicalization as a Marxist followed the death of his older brother, Alexander, who was arrested and executed in St. Petersburg for his involvement in an assassination plot against Tsar Alexander III. Lenin also moved to St. Petersburg, embedding in underground political circles that brought him into contact with revolutionaries in Europe. His work on a Marxist newspaper resulted in his imprisonment for a year and exile to eastern Siberia for three more. He wasn't allowed to work during his exile—he spent his time reading and writing—but the government provided him with an allowance that covered food and rent for a wooden house owned by the widow of a grain merchant.[35]

He settled on Lenin (after the Lena River in Siberia) as his new surname in 1902. By then he was living in Europe, and wouldn't return to Russia until 1905, and then only briefly. He spent most of the revolution as a political exile in Zurich, living with his politically like-minded spouse Nadya (Nadezhda Krupskaya), in a "small and stuffy" house owned by a Zurich cobbler.[36] He would return for good in 1917. On March 21 and 22, 1917, his "letter from afar" was published in the Petrograd newspaper *Pravda* as abridged by the editors. One of them was a returned exile from Siberia named Iosif Stalin.

Lenin benefited from German financing in his quest to light the spark of the revolution, which obviously also served German interests in defeating Russia.[37] Foreign investment explains how he and his cluster of revolutionaries paid for their train rides, how the Soviets and the Red Guards established themselves throughout Russia, and how they financed the daily printing of 85,000 copies of *Pravda*, not to mention the making and distribution of pamphlets and posters bolstering the Bolshevik cause.[38] Lenin returned to Russia on a small train under German guard from Zurich through Frankfurt and Berland up to Stralsun. Then Lenin crossed by barge into Sweden and boarded another train for the circuit around the Gulf of Bothnia into Finland and Russia.

Lenin thought bluntly and clearly. There was to be no intermediate, bourgeois phase in the transformation of Russia into a socialist state. He believed in the inevitable, dialectical-materialist triumph of socialism over all other forms of political thought while promising justice to the presumed victims of the rotten, decadent, autocratic system. But he had no power beyond his rhetoric and his title as chairman of the Bolshevik faction of the socialist democratic movement. For all his take-no-prisoners commitment as an ideologue, he wasn't an especially compelling presence. Descriptions of him raging at the cosmos in "peasant meter" from the balcony of an art nouveau mansion (occupied by the Bolsheviks after its ballerina owner fled) are exaggerated. He delivered intelligent, sarcastic, and surprisingly self-effacing lectures in an accented Russian that betrayed his time away. He didn't roll his r's, owing to a small speech impediment, and his intonation was flat, as best one can tell from the sixteen speeches recorded at a firm outside of Moscow between 1919 and 1921.[39] Lenin's talent as an orator resided in the empathetic chords he struck with disaffected workers, disgruntled soldiers, and the dispossessed. The table of ranks had to go, he insisted. Banks needed to be merged, and land wrested from its lords and placed under state control. Power, for once, would be placed in the hands of the people. There would be bread, land, and peace. The proletariat would extract their pound of flesh from their former oppressors. That last promise—payback—was kept, but not the others.

Nothing would have come out of any of his talks and publications had it not been for Prime Minister Kerensky's failures. He was a lawyer by training and a solid actor. He sought to please, shined on the podium, joined a committee aiding the families of those killed during the 1905 uprising, advocated for minors, and denounced antisemitism.[40] But his prosecution of the war was a disaster. Crises on the streets deepened. Had he had a better grip on Petrograd, he might have had Lenin arrested when he arrived at the Finland Station on the night of April 3, 1917. Instead, Lenin was greeted by a marching band playing "La Marseillaise" and a hopeful throng of workers, sailors, and members of the Bolshevik party he had been leading from afar. He stood on a car in the square outside the station and delivered an overzealous speech about global proletarian revolution. The people who greeted him had smaller, local concerns. Either he hadn't read the room correctly or he didn't care.

More speeches followed. Rhetorically, the government and the revolutionaries pointed pistols at one another, but no one fired. The First All-Russian Congress of the Soviet lasted in Petrograd for an exhausting three weeks, June 3–22. Almost 1,100 delegates attended from local and regional councils. On this occasion, the Mensheviks (supporting the provisional government) outnumbered Lenin's Bolsheviks (against it) by more than two to one. Lenin expressed his disdain for the government and demanded its immediate dismantling. Finding little favor among his comrades, he took his least moderate ideas to the streets and energized the protest movement. Soldiers poured into Petrograd to defend the government, shooting hundreds, and, with the police, hustling workers back to their posts lest their mutinous brains get bashed in. Kerensky ordered the arrest of the entire Bolshevik leadership. Lenin, the person most responsible for the crackdown, fled. Of all the weird events in the revolution—true, half-true, and fictional—Lenin's grand escape tops the list. He hid in the attic of a barn for a few days and, when it seemed like he might be nabbed, moved into a hut made of twigs and straw in a field near a lake. There's now a museum in that field, and it's weirder yet, featuring a replica of the hut and its adjacent haystack along with Lenin's teapot, stool, and pages from the book that he started writing there, *State and Revolution*. For exercise, Lenin went swimming in the lake, despite the mosquitos.[41]

Back in Petrograd, Kerensky miscalculated. The commander in chief of the imperial armed forces, Lavr Kornilov, ordered a troop division into Petrograd to maintain order and to drive the Bolsheviks out. He recognized the threat Lenin posed even in his absence. Kerensky, however, misinterpreted Kornilov's intentions as an attempt to seize power for himself and so declared him a rebel and a traitor. Had the two of them trusted each other, Lenin might have been stopped. Instead, when he returned to the fray, Lenin appealed to the soldiers and workers of Petrograd to save the revolution, national and global. Railroad workers dismantled rolling stock, and thousands signed up for the detachments to defend the Bolsheviks from the advancing troop division. Kornilov's supposed attempted coup failed, and he was stripped of his titles and imprisoned. The person in charge of the troop division killed himself.

Then, in October, Lenin took command of a militia called the Red Guards. On the 24th, the militia seized control of the bridges, telephone system, and railroads. The provisional government retained control of the Winter Palace and the adjacent General Staff headquarters. The Second All-Russian Congress of the Soviet was scheduled for the morning of October 25, but the opening was delayed until 10:40 in the evening owing to arguing among socialist factions and reports of fighting at the Winter Palace. By 3 a.m. the fighting was over; Lenin's forces had taken control, allowing him to declare the end of the provisional government and a new government of and for the people in the Community Party councils that the Bolsheviks would soon control in full. "Remember that now *you yourselves* are running the state," he informed "the population" in *Pravda*. "No one will help you unless you unite and take *all the affairs* of the state into *your own* hands. *Your* Soviets are now bodies of state power, legislative, decision-making bodies."[42]

The Mensheviks were told, by Leon Trotsky, that their time was up. Soon they'd be rotting in "the *svalka*—town dump—of history."[43] Meantime, Kerensky fled north in hopes of staging a counterrevolution, though, in the end, neither the Whites (the monarchist and capitalist forces) nor the Reds (the Bolsheviks) wanted anything to do with him. Soviet historians and Socialist Realist artists caricatured him as a yellow-bellied liar who capitulated to the Germans and escaped the Winter Palace wearing a woman's dress.[44] There is as much truth in that as there is in Lenin masterminding the revolution from Bolshevik headquarters, as opposed to hiding in a hay hut until the moment was right.

Moscow's October was more violent than Petrograd's, since in Moscow junior officers, cadets, and students were willing and able to defend the provisional government against the Red Guards, even after the provisional government had ceased to exist. Nikita Okunev, an agent with a steamship company, kept a journal of the revolution and the October *Smuta* (his word):

> Appeals from the two governments in the streets: Kerensky's and Lenin's. Each speaks of the illegality of the other. Such is the predicament of the submissive son of the fatherland! Whom does he obey? The Kremlin yesterday was surrounded by Bolshevik soldiers, but later the cadets and Cossacks arrived and ringed themselves around the chain of Bolsheviks, who were, it's being said, themselves surrounded by different Bolsheviks. . . . Moscow has of course been put under martial law, or, I would say "bilateral martial law." The city isn't fighting the city's troops and the city's troops aren't fighting the city's people. Rather, the city's troops are fighting themselves.[45]

The fiasco was caused by the commander of Moscow's government troops, Konstantin Ryabtsev, who had appealed to Petrograd for reinforcements while also negotiating with the armed forces controlled by the Bolsheviks under the soviets. The Bolsheviks arrested him as he was trying to skip town "disguised as a peasant," according to gleeful reporting in *Pravda*.[46] Fighting for control of the Kremlin was fierce, passing from the control of the Bolsheviks to the cadets and back again depending on who rotated gun cylinders the fastest.

Writer Konstantin Paustovsky described his experience at his apartment on the boulevard close to Nikita Gates:

> The machine-gun was answered by rifle fire. A bullet flew in through my window and straight into a portrait of Chekhov on the wall. The bullet hit Chekhov in the chest and tore a hole in his white pique waistcoat. I later found the portrait buried under a heap of plaster. The crossfire crackled like burning brushwood. Bullets clattered on the metal rooftops. My landlord, an elderly widowed architect, called out to me to join him in some back

rooms facing the courtyard. Two little girls and their old nanny were sitting on the floor. The woman had wrapped them up from head to toe in a thick shawl.

"We're safe here," said the landlord. "It's not likely the bullets can pierce the interior walls." "Papa are the Germans attacking Moscow?" the older girl asked from under her shawl. "No, there aren't any Germans." "But then who's shooting?" "Be quiet!" her father snapped.[47]

Prose of this sort didn't come naturally to Paustovsky. He wasn't much interested in dramatic events, privileging instead a kind of concentrated uneventfulness—writing about restful slumber, the outdoors, and random encounters with strangers. When Paustovsky mentions the damaged portrait of Chekhov falling off the wall, he's alluding, gently, to the end of an era and a superfluous, purposeless aristocracy. In his autobiography, he mentions going to hear Lenin speak in a barracks but seems more interested in the damp and cold, the thick smell of tobacco in the dim light, a soldier joking about getting the clap, and a photograph of another soldier's bride than in anything the leader of the revolution had to say. "I had trouble hearing him," Paustovsky admits.[48]

Okunev's recollection of the revolution in Moscow is, by contrast, a panorama—of the fires and smoke and blown-out windows of the hotels and theaters, with a quip about the telephone building surviving because it had been built by Swedes, not Russians. As to the Kremlin: "people write about all the acts of destruction through history, the fires, the executions, and God bless them!" But what he saw with his own eyes seemed worse. He hoped that "the terrible scenes would awaken the conscience of those who rebelled against their brothers" and prevent their repetition. He witnesses the burial of "more than 400 people on Red Square without church rites.... May God rest them and have pity on those who weep and grieve for them!"[49]

Lenin didn't consolidate power immediately. Like his nemesis Kerensky, he supported the election of a constituent assembly, but when the Bolsheviks lost, Lenin decided that representative government wasn't such a good idea after all. No sooner did the assembly convene in January 1918 than he put an end to it, outlawing all political parties except his own. This decisive move put him in charge, but of what? Russia's institutions—factories, farms, banks, lines of communication—had collapsed. Swaths of Russian territory had been surrendered in advance of the armistice with the Central Empires, signed on December 15, 1917. The end of the Great War coincided with the start of a civil war.[50]

As the Germans advanced on Petrograd, Lenin, his wife, his guards, his inner Bolshevik circle, and Stalin relocated to Moscow on another secretive train ride, this time along a dangerous stretch of the tracks. Other trains followed at regular intervals, transporting office workers, their supervisors, and their families, "as well as enormous quantities of furniture and equipment, literally 'down to the kitchen sink.' "[51] Few thought that the relocation was permanent, but it turned out to be just that, ironically fulfilling "the Slavophiles' timeless dream of returning the capital to Moscow," in the words of Lenin's accomplice Grigory Zinoviev, chairman of the Communist International.[52]

In March 1918, the makeshift government took over the gilded offices and apartments of the Kremlin, which a pro-Bolshevik militia had confiscated in November 1917 from imperial government officials. They also crowded into the opulent Metropole and National Hotels as well as mansions that had been sequestered first by anarchists, a political force much feared by Lenin, before being re-sequestered by the Bolsheviks. "The filth was indescribable," a British agent, Bruce Lockhart, said of one of the mansions after the routing of the anarchists. "Broken bottles littered the floors, the magnificent ceilings were perforated with bullet-holes. Wine stains and human excrement blotched the Aubusson carpets. Priceless pictures had been slashed to strips."[53]

The hapless Tsar Nicholas II was still alive, but not for much longer. His journal entries in 1917 make for chilling reading in their blandness. He and his family had been placed under house arrest in Tsarskoye Selo before being moved to the governor's mansion in Tobolsk, Siberia. He rates novels and church services and talks about the weather. The news from Petrograd was a little too cryptic for him to understand. Another member of the ruling class, the tsar's youngest brother, Mikhaíl, declined the offer to succeed him.

On the night of July 16, 1918, he and the tsarina, their son and four daughters, their cook, doctor, valet, and their pet spaniel were led into the cellar of a merchant's house in Ekaterinburg, followed by the firing squad. Bullets careened off the chests of the girls, who had stitched diamonds into their clothes for safekeeping. Bayonets and rifle butts finished the job. The corpses were loaded onto a truck and driven into a forest, stripped naked, doused in acid to disguise their identities, soaked in gasoline, lit on fire, and buried in a shallow grave. Lenin learned of the killing in his Kremlin office, marking the report "Received. Lenin."[54]

Thus ended the imperial era. Thus ended, too, the hopes of the revolution. There would be famine, civil war, and an economic implosion that no decree, scheme, or aesthetic could prevent—save for a brief period of free-market reforms that Lenin's successor, Stalin, derided as an obstacle to the pursuit of communist utopia. Meanwhile, the dictatorship of the proletariat surrendered to the dictatorship of the security apparatus, Lenin's serpentine *Chrez-vïchaynaya komissiya* (*Extraordinary Commission*), the Cheka.

As before, violence belonged to the state. As before, Moscow's streets fell silent. And as before, there was little food or fuel.

The Cheka began operating on December 7, 1917, from the head-quarters of a former insurance firm on Lubyanka Square. Its mandate exceeded that of the secret chancelleries under the tsars in the search for enemies of the Bolsheviks. Some of these were former allies, including Mariya Spiridonova, a cult figure in the annals of the revolution thanks to her terroristic attacks on tsarist officials in defense of the rights of peasants.[55] After she shot a sadistic tsarist official in Tambov, she was jailed and exiled to Siberia. The press coverage of the case was sensational; she became a hero of the resistance and the face of the Left Socialist Revolutionaries (SRs). The 1917 Revolution liberated her, but she denounced Lenin when he requisitioned food and fuel from the peasants and demanded land concessions. During a Congress of Soviets at the Bolshoi Theater, she accused him, to his face, of betraying the revolution.[56] Her involvement in the assassination of Wilhelm Mirbach, the German ambassador to Soviet Russia, landed her back in prison and branded her a foe of the revolution she had once advocated. Lenin used the assassination to suppress the Left-SR threat to the Bolsheviks more broadly.[57]

The Cheka uncovered grand conspiracies by the Right SRs in May 1918, by an organization called the "Union for the Defense of the Motherland and Freedom" at the end of that same month, by allies of "the fiendish demagogue" Spiridonova in July.[58] Monasteries were turned into prisons, and martial law was extended. Lenin introduced his New Economic Policy in hopes of preventing Russia's bankruptcy, but speculators took advantage. Anxiousness turned into listlessness. Okunev wrote only intermittently during this period, and he wouldn't complete his record of the revolution and civil war until the end of his life. Terrible things happened to him: his son went to work for the Cheka; his wife committed suicide. He spent more time in churches than he used to and listed himself in nostalgic reveries. He explained how to heat a room without heat, how to make rations last, noted the sight of a dead horse on Lubyanka Square, and casually mentioned Russia going bankrupt. He shook his head at the squandering of precious resources on revolutionary marches and parades while remarking that the Bolsheviks' destruction of the symbols of Imperial Russia imitated the Orthodox Church's destruction of pagan idols.[59] The Bolsheviks seized culture for themselves, erasing the culture of the past. Cardboard factories produced posters and placards that turned political demonstrations into stations-of-the-cross processionals along Moscow's streets, with Marxist ideologues replacing priests. The revolution in the arts—the transformative energies of Constructivism and Futurism—outlasted the revolution on the streets, distorting the historical perception of how Moscow, and Russia, became Soviet. It wasn't a transcendent process, or some sort of dialectical synthesis. The revolution was a series of mistakes—some amusing, most serious—taken advantage of by a ruthless politician, Lenin, who found himself presiding over a catastrophe of his own making.

The revolution was marketed, globally, as a grandiose popular uprising. But the proletarians of the world didn't unite as Lenin envisioned. Instead, the conflicts he stoked in Russia, Eastern Europe, the Caucasus, and Eurasia transformed a sixth of the planet's landmass into an entity called the Union of Soviet Socialist Republics.[60] Moscow, meantime, became the capital of the Russian Socialist Federative Soviet Republic, with municipal matters handled by the Moscow Council of Workers and Red Army Deputies (*Moskovskiy sovet rabochikh i krasnoarmeyskikh deputatov,* or MSRiKD). Funding for this body came from the state treasury—200 million rubles to "meet urgent expenses" in January and February of 1919, for example—as approved by the Council of People's Commissars and People's Commissariat of Internal Affairs (NKVD).[61]

According to a rather utopian-looking *skhema* from 1919, MSRiKD was organized like Moscow itself, with rings and a star in the middle denoting the "central administrative department." The ring connecting the tips of the star shows the municipal government's subdepartments: "audit," "training," "criminal investigation," "trade and manufacture,"

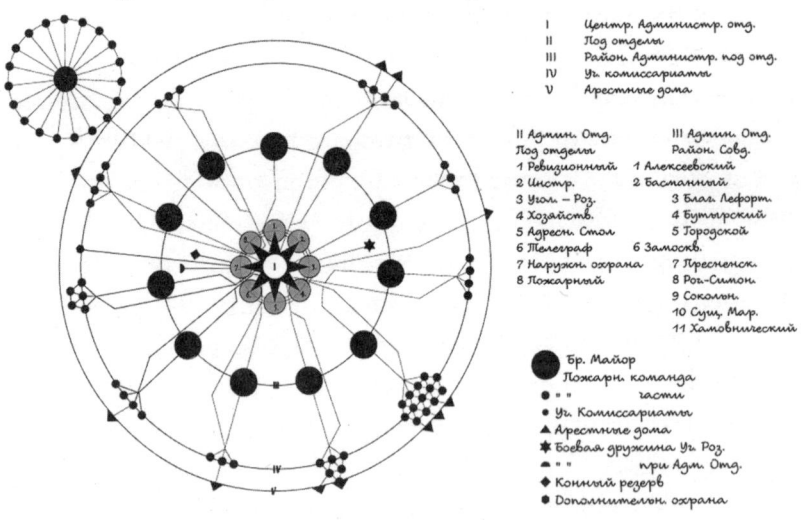

Organizational chart of the Moscow Council of Workers and Red Army Deputies (1919).

"address desk" (issuing certificates of residence but also serving as a general information bureau), "post and telegraph" (communications), "external security," and "fire." This ring is enclosed by another representing Moscow's eleven districts: Alekseyevskiy; Basmannïy; Blagushe-Lefortovskiy; Butïrskiy; Gorodskoy; Zamoskvoretskiy; Presnenskiy; Rogozhsko-Simonovskiy; Sokol'nicheskiy; Sushchyovsko-Mar'inskiy; Khamovnicheskiy.[62] The next ring moving outward names the municipal bureaucracies: the people's commissariats (equivalent to chancelleries or ministries) of enlightenment (education); communications (the postal and telegraph services); trade and manufacture; finance; social welfare; labor; healthcare; internal affairs (the local NKVD); agriculture, state control (accounting and auditing), food, and armed services. The outermost ring designates "arrest houses"—these are identified by triangles and accompanied by stars that mark the "combat squads" of the criminal investigation apparatus.[63]

The Great October Socialist Revolution consigned the tsarist era to the dustbin of history, then threw itself away as well. It ended with the formation of a government that kept the streets quiet by keeping ever greater numbers of people in prison. Overcrowding forced the arrest houses to mix common criminals with political prisoners. Thousands of the latter were killed.[64] The further the descent into darkness, the brighter the political rhetoric about the free, just, and open world to come, about how, soon, neither prisons nor the secret police—the Cheka—would be needed anymore.

The other detention facilities in Moscow were also crowded and commingled counterrevolutionaries with (according to the police blotters) arsonists, horse thieves, and people charged with assaulting officers on patrol.[65] The prisons operating out of former mansions, monasteries, and factories had different names—jail, labor house, camp.[66] One occupied the 1918 headquarters of the party of Left Socialist Revolutionaries–Internationalists, which aligned itself with the Bolsheviks; another camp was set up in a brickmaking operation that had once been owned by the Russian-Belgian entrepreneur Alfred Gasha. The "Gasha Concentration and Production Camp No. 1 of the Main Directorate of Public Works," as it became known, provided the model for other camps in Moscow. Prisoners were put to work to cure themselves of the disease that caused them to take the wrong path in life. (The revolution had technically removed the social causes of their lawlessness, making mental and physical illness the culprit.) Rather than rotting in prison with nothing to do, prisoners should feel that they too had the right to work.

Who were the people enjoying this equality? The first camps in Moscow housed, through the First World War, prisoners of war. Later the population diversified to include idlers, saboteurs, and common criminals like Konstantin Gordeyev, a twenty-three-year-old Muscovite twice arrested in 1921–22 for trafficking in contraband, locked up in Butïrskaya, then interrogated at the Interregional Criminal Investigation Department, where it was decided, "based on his convictions and criminal history and in order to preserve public safety," to relocate him to a camp in Arkhangelsk.[67] The Political Red Cross, which provided aid to POWs before and after 1917, generated list after list of Moscow's prisons, their detainees, "and their services," meaning the goods produced in their workshops. Included are the names of immigrants and foreign fighters detained in Petrograd and transported to Moscow between 1918 and 1922. The collapse of the tsarist system left diplomats of neutral nations in a precarious situation, desperate to liaise with the commissar for foreign affairs, Leon Trotsky, trying to salvage their investments in Russia, and mobilizing to bring their people—immigrants working as cheesemakers, teachers, and governesses—back home.[68] Edgar Kamp, age thirty-four, was arrested on June 2, 1918, at the Swedish mission, where he'd been working as a courier. Like his arrested boss, the head of the mission's passport division, he'd been interrogated twice and diagnosed as "neurotic." On March 22–23, 1919, the Cheka carried out an "ambush inside the Polish Committee" in Moscow and arrested everyone in sight: the elderly, the infirm, and former prisoners who had come to collect food to take back to their former cellmates.[69]

The makeup of the prison population changed—slower than one might assume—from revolutionaries to counterrevolutionaries, including Princess Tatyana Kurakina, who was arrested by the Cheka in Kyiv in 1919 as an accomplice of the Whites and moved from one makeshift prison camp to another before landing in

Novinskaya Women's Prison. After two years of insults and physical abuse, she was released and, with the help of a fake marriage certificate, managed to escape Soviet Russia for Italy, where she wrote a caustic account of her post-1917 experiences.[70] Kurakina remembers the man who drove her to the prison through the "dirty, disgusting streets of the worker-peasant capital" and handed her a package of quality cigarettes, saying, "Oh, I feel sorry for you, lady; I'd prefer to take you home, not to prison. Well to hell with them, those Bolsheviks. How long will God put up with them?"[71] The pampered princess couldn't abide the squalor inside the jail. She got up early to bathe by herself and spent as much time as she could in the library to rid herself of the laughter, dancing, fighting, and cursing in her cell. Kurakina had never encountered lesbians before and reacted to their presence with horror. Likewise the prostitutes and cocaine addicts. "For all the ignorance, darkness, and rudeness of the Russian people, there were certain vices they had no idea about in the past," she wrote.[72] Kurakina feared the worst from the doctor when she took sick, but he treated her kindly, since he came from the "old regime" and loathed the Bolsheviks, not that he could say so aloud.[73]

Culture under the Bolsheviks belonged to everyone, so music and theater happened on the street, in factories, in hospitals, and at Novinskaya. A model for this form of Marxist-Leninist cultural enlightenment was the prison operated by the Bolsheviks in another part of the Moscow Gulag system: the Ivanovo Convent, located just west of Kitai-gorod.[74] What might seem like the ultimate in atheistic sacrilege—turning a sacred space into a jail and an institute for the study of criminality and crime—had precedent: the convent had always been used for prisoners, including Dar'ya Saltïkova, a "perverted landowner" condemned to the convent's dungeon for life under Catherine the Great.[75] (Saltïkova's evils supposedly included slamming serfs into walls, burning them, and pulling their hair out.) The Bolsheviks made the convent part of their prison system in 1919; the parishioners who had called the convent home were now replaced by shackled counterrevolutionaries.

That fall, the counterrevolutionaries stepped out of their shackles and began to put on performances with the blessing of the Commissariat for Enlightenment, since, for the Bolsheviks, having prisoners perform serious plays, learn to read, attend lectures on socialism contra capitalism, and even sing and dance in cabarets would make them better people—Soviet people. Camp life was a kind of purgatory between old and new. Redemption was possible, at least in the showcase facilities like Ivanovo and Novitskaya. The cultural activities included, on April 22, 1922, a foreign offering: a three-act play by the Danish writer Sophus Michaëlis called *A Marriage in Revolution* (1905).[76] The performers came to Novinskaya from another Moscow prison for women, Novo-Peskovskiy, opened in a building that had once belonged to the furniture manufacturer Shmit. It is the current address of the British embassy.[77]

Presumably *A Marriage in Revolution* was seen by the unidentified author of "My Childhood." She was one of the women held in Novitskaya, though how and why she ended up there cannot be determined in the absence of a name. Perhaps the Bolsheviks arrested her for living with God, or because of something her grandmother had done as a member of the *Basmanniy sovet*. Perhaps that brittle relative dropped her off at the prison just to get rid of her. The strangest of all possibilities: the author of "My Childhood" wasn't a prisoner at all but a guard in training. Those people, too, needed to learn to read and write.

Most of the prisons in Moscow closed after the civil war but opened elsewhere. Conditions in those that remained seemed to improve, though the reports on conditions—written in stilted semiliterate prose—can't be trusted. It is an unpleasant truth that the better future promised by the Bolsheviks meant better prison conditions.[78] Moscow's penal system between 1917 and 1923 has elements in common with the forced labor camp system that came afterward, in the most desolate parts of the land of the Soviets. The name of that system was the Gulag.

14

STALINISM

L ENIN DIED, mentally and physically enfeebled, on January 24, 1924, his revolution a travesty. The Bolsheviks were just another band of invaders, worse in their insistence on occupation than the Mongol-Tatars, with Lenin another pretender. The land lacked the institutions, factories, and fungible currency for wealth to be redistributed from the bourgeoisie to the proletariat, as Karl Marx had envisioned. But the invaders insisted on staying, and the masses were re-enserfed. Neither socialism nor communism arrived. Dictatorship did, masquerading as totalitarianism, one folded inside the other.

The Bolsheviks suppressed religion and mysticism, the Church and the Symbolists, condemning official and unofficial spiritual practices as cults. But Bolshevism was itself a cult, and Lenin its first leader. His corpse was embalmed (freezing was ruled out) then placed in a glass sarcophagus in a mausoleum on Red Square. Embalming specialists have maintained the mummy for more than a hundred years now, and it looks ever better with age. In 1925, Lenin's brain was sent for autopsy—not a common practice for famous people in Russia but, with the establishment of a brain institute in Moscow, a newly popular one. A small slice was sent to Oskar Vogt of the Kaiser Wilhelm Institute of Berlin, the world's expert on gray matter. Was there a scientific means of proving Lenin's genius? According to the initial results, the "pyramidal cells" in Lenin's cerebral cortex demonstrated a capacity for highly organized thought, even after he suffered his first stroke.[1] In 1928, however, Vogt started using photographs of the slice in his lectures in Berlin and likening Lenin's brain to those of "criminals" as well as people suffering mental disabilities.[2] Meantime, the rest of the brain deteriorated in a vat in Moscow, so it was transferred to a guarded facility. It was subject, in the years ahead, to additional analyses by Russian scientists who, having compared Lenin's brain to that of the poet Vladimir Mayakovsky among others, affirmed its superior neurovascular structure.

Lenin did not name a successor and had serious doubts about Stalin, who did not consolidate power until the end of the 1920s. At the height of his rule, close to two hundred million people fell under his control. The principal instrument of that power was the NKVD, described by a prisoner as "the master of life and death of every citizen of the Soviet Union," the "chief builder of the state in every conceivable way," with a "virtual monopoly of exploitation, mostly by means of slave [serf] labor."[3] The NKVD had an enormous infrastructure, including a school in Moscow (on the grounds of the Ivanovo convent) offering lectures to agents-in-training on the history of incarceration from the era of Peter the Great to the present, the function and structure of Soviet prison camps, the criminal system within the criminal system of those camps, and prosaic matters like mail censorship, sanitation, tuberculosis prevention, and transportation. "The Gulag," the syllabus reads, "is not an economic resource, but an organ of the NKVD called upon during the transition from capitalism to communism to protect the dictatorship of the proletariat and the socialist construction carried out by it from encroachments by class-hostile elements and violations by de-classed elements [former landowners, for example] and unstable elements among the working people." Under Stalin, everyone labored for the cause, and that labor was meant to be beneficial—enlightening. "The obligation of socially useful labor for all citizens, proclaimed in 1936 by the Stalinist Constitution, also applies to persons deprived of liberty who are capable of work." In 1946, a lecture was added which focused on events in the Gulag during the war. Agents learned about groups within the system that were "preparing acts of sabotage, spreading defeatist fascist agitprop among prisoners, and the increase in banditry and other crimes." Of course, these hostile elements required "liquidation."[4]

Stalin transformed Moscow, now the capital of Russia and the Soviet Union, into a map of his obsessions, embossing it with hammers and sickles but also repurposing symbols from the past, some of them religious. The curves of Cyrillic lettering were rasped to fit the geometric ideals of constructivist style. Buildings went up at breakneck speed, but these were not places individual people could call home. Life in the USSR focused on groups: Pioneers, the Komsomol (Communist Youth League), the All-Union Communist Party of Bolsheviks, trade and professional unions, collective farms, work brigades, and labor camps. To accommodate parades and marches and machines, streets were widened and smoothed.[5]

Urbanization and industrialization increased the need for recreational space, so in 1932 an exhibition space was turned into a park named after the writer Maxim Gorky. The advertised amusements included roller-coaster rides and motorcycle races. In official rhetoric, life was happier. Some thought ruefully back to all that had happened in the wake of the revolution, all that was lost, but legions of fresh-faced youth embraced the revolution as an opportunity. No longer exploited, harassed, and alienated from their labor, they would see themselves reflected in the new world they fashioned from the wreckage of the old. Hope and optimism filled their hearts, and though they could never forgive their oppressors, they could reeducate those products of the past to honor what Bolshevism had forged. Progressive youth would supplant the representatives of the feudal order, the descendants of boyars and priests.

Stalin fashioned himself as the savior of the Russian people but expected them to pay tribute. He created a world where children denounced their parents and landed in orphanages as reward for their service to the state. Their mothers and fathers were arrested, interrogated, convicted, and put on trains to mining operations in the far north or east. Prisoners built their own prisons, sleeping under the Arctic sky in "a steady 40 degrees Celsius below zero," boiling flour in water as the only food.[6] Terror became overwhelming, then routine: in 1937 and 1938, there were more than 1.5 million arrests and more than 650,000 executions.[7] Stalin falsified reality and then falsified the falsehoods, so much so that prisoners in the Gulag system sent him birthday greetings and his secret service agencies started turning against one another. That was after he had purged his own support system, gutted his diplomatic corps, decimated the upper ranks of the Communist Party, and culled the leadership of the Red Army.

There is no easy explanation for the cascading waves of terror. Stalin seems not to have been psychotic, but his actions point to such a condition. Historians of the period tried to identify what prompted the compiling of the increasingly arbitrary arrest lists. Ultimately, thousands upon thousands of people were arrested in Moscow alone. Ideology itself might be the true cause of the terror—or raw power. Those spared indulged the fiction, propagated in the newspapers *Pravda* and *Izvestiya*, that the violence was justified. The alternative was impossible to contemplate, even as acquaintances, neighbors, friends, and relatives disappeared. One thing seems certain: the Stalinist commitment to going the distance in service to the purest form of communist ideology.

To promulgate his power, Stalin turned to censors, agitational propagandists, and cultural representatives. The three groups overlapped and aligned in the realm of photography. The most notable Soviet photographers had started out as abstract painters and textile designers predisposed to de- and re-constructing events rather than mirroring them. Their photographs crafted thesis-antithesis oppositions meant for the viewer to synthesize, multiple-angled montages, and unusual perspectives (the bird's-eye views used in Alexander Rodchenko's 1928 *At the Telephone* and *Gathering for a Demonstration,* for example). Photographers responded to the first Five-Year Plan for economic development by creating superimposed representations of Lenin, loudspeakers, hydroelectric lines, and marching Pioneers with banners held aloft—a collage celebrating Soviet progress. Rather than hunger, the images informed the illiterate, there was teeming abundance; instead of isolation, there were bustling lines of communication. Representations of the past required adjusting to

Posters of Lazar Kaganovich, Stalin, and Nikita Khrushchev put up by the Moscow Communist Party organization on the Yauza Embankment, November 7, 1935. The illuminated sign reads "Long live October."

suit the present, so images were cropped, clipped, airbrushed, blackened, and whited out. The present, too, posed problems. Re-touchers smoothed Stalin's pockmarked face and placed him beside Lenin in fabricated scenes. High-ranking officials starring in the show trials of the late 1930s were eerily erased from photographs. Trash disappeared from pictures of Moscow, replaced by flower beds.[8]

After Stalin turned against Nikolay Yezhov, the People's Commissar of Internal Affairs and impresario of the purges of 1936, he too disappeared from a photograph with Stalin along a Moscow canal. In another image from 1926, Stalin appears with three of his closest allies: Nikolay Antipov, Sergey Kirov, and Nikolay Shvernik. Three reproductions later, Stalin stands alone in a decluttered landscape. Some of the alterations are artful, others crude and sometimes confessional, preserving ghostly traces of the excisions. The infelicities are meant to be noticed as demonstrations of arbitrary power. There you are, walking in your trench coat beside the Great Leader and Teacher. Until you aren't.

Periodicals documenting the transformation of the Soviet capital and the republics in its grasp relied on similar tricks. A lavish monthly called *USSR in Construction* (*SSSR na stroike*, 1930–49) showcased industrial development and, in the September 1931 issue, feted the renovation of Moscow from its tsarist "big village" days into a socialist metropolis. It was published in multiple languages by an editorial collective that included Gorky. The socialist-realist novelist Valentin Katayev published in the large-format pages, which included illustrations by utopian designer El Lissitzky. Works by the writer Isaac Babel also appeared, though he would be arrested in 1939 and subsequently blotted and cropped out of Soviet history.

"During the years of war and intervention," the September 1931 editorial reads, "Moscow's urban economy was quickly destroyed. Its restoration, which began only in 1921, has now ended. But it was not just a restoration. The face of Moscow has changed beyond recognition over the years. Moscow today is the capital of a socialist country with a population of three million; it is the largest industrial center, providing 13% of the country's total industrial production. The Moscow of today and tomorrow is no longer the calico Moscow of the past, but a metal Moscow."[9]

The magazine specialized in before-and-after makeovers, tucking church spires out of sight or confining them to the margins of the sepia images while casting Lenin's shadow over five-story barracks buildings. The Imperial Foundling Home is pictured, though it's now a "Palace of Labor." Lenin's mausoleum, made of red and black granite panels affixed to concrete, recalls both an Egyptian pyramid and an Aztec tomb. (Gwendolyn Leick describes it as "a curiously Babylonian-looking building, recalling a ziggurat in its stepped outline and the recesses and niches of mud-brick temples.")[10] Designed by Alexei Shchuchev, it replaced a wooden shelter that had been hammered together and painted in haste during the hard frost of January 1924 and a sturdier edifice with a dais erected three months later. The magazine shows street sweepers tending to the bridges and lanes just after dawn, and street-cleaning machines kicking into action in the evening, prying dust from stones with water jets. Workers recline on wooden beach chairs in the park, still wearing their uniforms, and children play in a solarium. In what seems to have been an editorial misstep, the back cover shows a rather morose-looking group of kids in knitted hats and scarves behind a banner reading "proud of the launch of the [AMO] plant."

A new meatpacking plant opened, horses were replaced by buses, and the shacks where the brick stoves had served as bed and table morphed into a dining room beside a "bathroom the likes of which a worker in the tsarist era couldn't have dreamed." Nor could a Soviet worker dream of such a bathroom, though the magazine wanted its Russian, English, French, German, and (after 1938) Spanish readers to believe otherwise. "Workers have been relocated to the former residences of nobles," page 22 reports. "Here is one such residence on Moscow's Bread Lane [Khlebnïy pereulok]," an elite building notable for its stone staircases, iron-reinforced ceilings, and oak floors (renovated, it remains one of the most beautiful and exclusive residences in Moscow's Arbat neighborhood). The magazine extols the success of its socialist transformation: "Before the revolution, the English consul [R. H. Bruce] Lockhart, General Vasiliyev, and other aces and rentiers lived here. Bubentsov, a carpenter and shock worker at the Geophysical plant who lurked in basements, has been a resident of this house since 1920." Lockhart's residence on the fifth floor was left vacant after he was arrested.

The Bolsheviks confiscated the building from a Moscow merchant, Adolf Gutwein, and assigned its apartments to high-ranking officials, cultural and scientific luminaries.[11] One of these was the psychiatrist Pyotr Gannushkin, a specialist in acute paranoia who defined the revolution, subversively, as a "traumatic epidemic." He was accused of using "reactionary theory to fight the pace of socialist construction." To save his skin, he published an article in the journal *Revolution and Culture* (*Revolutsiya i kul'tura*), "On Preserving the Health of Party Activists" (Ob okhrane zdorov'ya partaktiva), praising the stamina and extraordinary mental health of Communist functionaries. He subsequently spent time treating patients who imagined themselves to be reincarnations of the last tsar or Lenin; he also tended to members of the secret police afflicted by madness.[12] Surely their stress was job-related. His colleagues confronted similar cases of "superhuman horrors," "grief," "increased psychoses and neuroses," and, owing to the shortage of food, "the emaciation of the intelligentsia" who made things worse for themselves by drinking an astonishing "40 cups of tea" a day.[13]

Thus, picture-perfect propaganda appeared in the magazines while carefully edited photographs documented the disappearance of suspected traitors to the Soviet cause. One of those expunged was theater director Vsevolod Meyerhold, whose productions bested those of his peers in concept and performance and whose fate was shocking even by the shocking standards of his time. Exactly why he was executed remains uncertain.

Meyerhold was of Russian-German heritage, the eighth son of a merchant of the second guild from Penza.[14] Born as Karl, he Russified his name to Vsevolod and converted to the Orthodox faith in 1895. Meyerhold's talent landed him a position in the Moscow Art Theater as a student of Konstantin Stanislavsky, and from there he worked in experimental theater studios before securing a position, in the years before the revolution, with the prestigious Imperial Theaters. In 1917 he committed to supporting the Bolshevik cause as a representative of the intelligentsia. In 1920, he became the head of the theater division of Glavpolitprosvet, the government's political education, or "enlightenment," committee. Meyerhold became a committed agitational propagandist, although his subsequent innovations in physical theater (biomechanics) would affront the conservative culture of Stalin's era. The general director of the Bolshoi, a Communist ideologue named Elena Malinovskaya, half seriously recommended putting Meyerhold in an asylum.

In 1921, the forty-eight-year-old Meyerhold divorced his wife and took up with a twenty-eight-year-old student named Zinaída Reich (Raykh), who had worked for the People's Commissariat of Enlightenment before becoming interested in acting. The couple flourished in the late 1920s, and Meyerhold became the driving force in the entire "Theatrical October" enterprise. He maintained his own troupe, a threadbare operation that toured in Europe and received enthusiastic reviews. The director returned to Moscow hoping to build a large theater for himself, but on August 26, 1937, the project was discredited in an article in *Izvestiya* written by Yakov Kornfeld, a conservative architect specializing in clubs for workers and palaces of culture. He blamed Meyerhold for everything wrong with theater across the USSR: actors, equipment, architecture, audiences. Meyerhold had supposedly departed from realism into an alienating formalism. In the theater he was building on Mayakovsky Square, "The actor will perform as if in a circus, alternately addressing one or another group of spectators, and then those behind him won't be able to hear anything and will only see his back . . . dramatic action—facial expressions, gestures, words—will inevitably be weakened."

Meyerhold was accused of having lost his ability to communicate with audiences, indulging abstract concepts at the expense of everything bright and beautiful. Whither heroism, the sacrifice of the individual to the collective? "Before it's too late, we need to change Meyerhold's theater project," Kornfeld insisted. "The building must fully meet the requirements of theatrical realism."[15] Shortly after his screed appeared in the newspaper of the Presidium of the Supreme Soviet, Platon Kerzhentsev, chair of the all-powerful Committee on Arts Affairs, published an article called "Someone Else's Theater" in the newspaper of the Central Committee of the Communist Party. He zeroes in on the supposed fact that just one of the 700 theaters operating in the Soviet Union had failed to put on a production marking the twentieth anniversary of the Great October Socialist Revolution.

That theater belonged to Meyerhold, who seemed unable to shed the "mysticism, symbolism, and God-seeking stupefaction" of the past. The Committee on Arts Affairs instructed him to fall in line, get with the ideological program, and stage plays about the Soviet experience. The director responded by adapting Nikolay Ostrovsky's 1936 novel *How the Steel Was Tempered* (*Kak zakalyalas' stal'*). It's a tale of overcoming: growing up in rags during the waning years of the tsarist era, then finding purpose with the Bolsheviks. The hero, Pavka Korchagin, loses his vision along with the use of one of his hands and both of his legs but nonetheless works in construction, tempering railroads as he himself has been tempered by revolution. It's about hard times, sure, but the individual and the epoch create each other; there's more to life than the pursuit of comfort. Meyerhold made it all seem "depressing," in Kerzhentsev's opinion, so it was pulled from the repertoire after its second official viewing. Meyerhold missed the big picture of the triumph of history over nature, turning the dream of socialist self-realization into a nightmare of suffering and disability. "Does Soviet art, do Soviet audiences, need such a theater?" Kerzhentsev asked. The answer was obvious.[16]

Thus ended Meyerhold's career. He was left with no income and no clear route to regain political favor. A few days after the article was published, he gathered his company together and tried to put on a brave face, telling the two hundred or so people in attendance that the criticism was fair and just. Beating himself with Kerzhentsev's whip, he pleaded guilty as charged for his failure to uphold the ideals of Socialist Realism. But he felt deeply betrayed by accusations from colleagues that he had resisted "comradely" advice, "sacrific[ed] the resources of the theater for his own family's interest," and treated the entire operation like an "appanage principality" of ancient Rus.[17] "I'm traumatized—not from the guidance coming from the Party and the government," he explained, "but from some of your statements." Meyerhold resumed his self-flagellation. "Still, I can't escape the facts, I get what I deserve. . . . I'm in a state of the greatest loneliness."[18]

On June 19, 1939, Lavrentiy Beria, who replaced Yezhov as head of the NKVD, authorized Meyerhold's arrest. The now sixty-five-year-old director was picked up in Leningrad, shipped to Moscow, and locked in Butïrskaya prison. He wrote a long letter to the highest-ranking official he knew personally, the Soviet foreign minister Vyacheslav Molotov, describing the interrogations that had forced him to confess to fictitious crimes against the state. The letter was written in sections, over several weeks, since paper (if the scraps can be called that) was given to him just once every ten days. His heels, legs, and back were beaten. "In the intervals between these actions, the investigator threatened: 'If you don't sign the protocols, we will beat you again, leaving your head intact—so that you can think—and your right hand—so that you have something to sign.'" So he confessed but begged Molotov to intervene: "Do you really believe that I'm a traitor to the motherland (an enemy of the peo-

ple), that I'm a spy, a member of a right-wing Trotskyite organization, a counter-revolutionary who carried out Trotskyism in my art,
and that I (intentionally!) sought to undermine the foundations of
Soviet art?"[19]

Meyerhold admitted to the "shortcoming" of trying to make
his theatrical productions provocative and "original," and that this
approach had led to him being accused of "formalism," which in the
eyes of the regime was equivalent to "Trotskyism," meaning that
which dares to challenge Stalinism.[20] He mentions other artists
tarred with a contra-revolutionary brush, including poet and novelist Boris Pasternak, who was spared arrest at the last minute and
survived Stalin to write *Doctor Zhivago*, a taboo novel that circulated
secretly in the USSR in the years following its completion in 1955.
The prose dared to be free in its background references to a half
century of trauma, and its publication in the West in 1957 made the
writer's life miserable. He barely escaped arrest, though some of his
Russian readers did not. "In the 70s," Pasternak's niece Ann recalls,
"I met a Russian who told me, rather sourly, that he'd served six years
in the camps for possessing a *samizdat* chunk of *Doctor Zhivago*. Ten
pages of blurry carbon copy. 'Oh dear,' I said; 'I hope it was worth it.'
'Worth it! A chapter of nature description?' "[21]

Meanwhile, on the night of July 14–15, 1939, Meyerhold's second wife, Zinaída Reich, was murdered in what was described in the
press as a burglary gone horribly wrong. In fact, she had protested as
NKVD agents searched her apartment for incriminating materials.[22]
Neighbors in the building heard but did not respond to her screams,
and she was found enucleated. Had she been the victim of a jewelry
theft, she might have been given an official burial, and her neighbors
would not have been sent north to the labor camps. It is unknown
whether Meyerhold knew about her death before his own. On February 2, 1940, Meyerhold was shot.

Before Stalin's reign of terror, the government had tolerated experi-
mentation in the arts, allowing directors like Meyerhold, writers like
Pasternak, and composers like Dmitri Shostakovich considerable
freedom in representing the conversion of the old world into the

new. But on January 17, 1936, on the eve of the purges, the Committee on Arts Affairs (Komitet po delam iskusstv) was established by decree of the Central Committee and Council of People's Commissars (Sovnarkom) of the USSR.[23] Kerzhentsev, a career propagandist, became its chairman. Theater was Kerzhentsev's priority—he was an occasional playwright—but he also had it in for leading composers, including Shostakovich, whose music needed tempering, and so too did his personality. Shostakovich wasn't respectful enough, and he could be downright sarcastic. "Today," he wrote to his pal Ivan Sollertinsky in November 1935, "I had the enormous happiness of attending the concluding session of the congress of Stakhanovites [shock workers]. I saw comrades Stalin, Molotov, Kaganovich, Voroshilov, Ordzhonikidze, Kalinin, Kossior, Mikoyan, Postïshev, Chubar, Andreyev, and Zhdanov. I listened to the introduction of comrades Stalin, Voroshilov, and Shvernik. I was captivated by Voroshilov's speech, but after hearing Stalin I couldn't hold myself back and shouted 'Hurrah' with the entire hall and applauded without end. You will read his historic speech in the newspapers, so I won't expound on it here." It was, he concluded, "the happiest day of my life: I saw and heard Stalin."[24]

The regime decided to shut Shostakovich up, which meant shutting down performances of the ballet *The Bright Stream* (*Svetlïy ruchey*). Its scenario pits people from the city against country workers on the "Bright Stream" collective farm while endearing cottage-dwelling retirees who have seen and done it all take full measure of the changes around them. The urban visitors bring red Communist banners to decorate the farm, but the peasants prove indifferent, even hostile, to the Communist court just as they had been to the imperial court. They need re-education. They receive it.

In advance of the premiere at the Bolshoi on November 30, 1935, machinists from a suburban Moscow plant (SVARZ) specializing in the manufacture of trolleybuses were invited to a rehearsal, as were ball-bearing makers and a group from a plant (DINAMO) that produced locomotive engines. This might not have been the ideal audience for a preview of a ballet about life on a collective farm, but the industrial workers enjoyed themselves, despite being baffled by the intrigues of the second act. Later, during the actual run at the Bolshoi, "a group of Don Cossacks" took in the show, having won dancing and singing contests in their local collective farms for the privilege of being "shown the wonders of the Soviet capital."[25] Whether these were actual farmers remains unknown, and in fact most of those forced onto Stalin's collective farms lacked basic skills, which resulted, as Stalin's aides predicted it would, in disaster. Besides attending the ballet, the Don Cossack "farmers" took a ride on the Moscow Metro, the first line of which had just been completed; went to the circus, planetarium, and zoo; visited the state stores for manicures, coats, and boots; and bought gifts for people back home. Their expenses were paid by the general director, Vladimir Ivanovich Mutnïkh, from the Bolshoi account. His guests sent him a thank-you note printed in big letters in crayon, ending with a plea: "We would ask you personally, Vladimir Ivanovich, when comrade Stalin next comes to the Bolshoi Theater, to tell him that we, the collective farmers of Veshensk, will never forget December 3, 1935, when we saw on that happy day our dearest friend, our great leader comrade Stalin."[26]

Mutnïkh enthusiastically supported the production of *Bright Stream*, but, as Shostakovich told Sollertinsky, Mutnïkh's assistant Boris Arkanov worried about its lack of seriousness, meaning Shostakovich's lack of seriousness. Given that Sollertinsky himself found much to dislike in *The Bright Stream*, Shostakovich felt the need to ask his friend's forgiveness. He described the ballet as his personal Waterloo, a "shameful failing," adding that he would not object to its cancellation.[27]

When the noose tightened on artistic expression under Stalin, the twenty-nine-year-old Shostakovich was turned into just that—a shameful failure—in front of his colleagues, both those who nurtured his precocious talent and those who resented him for it. Other proletarian musicians reproached him for spreading himself too thin in composing for film, young people's theater, ballet, and opera. After his foes started insinuating about anti-Soviet tendencies, his support network shrank. In January and February 1936, Shostakovich was the subject of two damning reviews (not editorials, as is often claimed) published in *Pravda*. They appeared after the successful run of *The Bright Stream* at the Bolshoi, including a performance on December 21, 1935, Stalin's fifty-sixth birthday. The despot had taken in an earlier performance from his concrete-reinforced loge, and he had not, it seems, disapproved of what he saw—at least not at first. Things turned sour, however, when Shostakovich's opera *Lady Macbeth of Mtsensk* (*Ledi Makbet Mtsenskogo uyezda*) was accepted for production at the Bolshoi Theater affiliate (a theater of just over 2,100 seats at the time; it is now used, with fewer seats, for musicals and operettas). Stalin attended that show as well, along with Molotov and two other aides: Anastas Mikoyan, a Politburo member who introduced canned foods, corn flakes, and corn on the cob to the Soviet Union; and the ideologue and propagandist Andrey Zhdanov, who played the piano and fancied himself an expert on composition. The four men didn't stay until the end.

Lady Macbeth is based on an 1865 story by Nikolay Leskov, as adapted by Shostakovich and Alexander Preys, with whom he had also collaborated on his first opera *The Nose,* based on a Gogol satire of tsarist bureaucracy and the Table of Ranks. The story is one of several that sinks Shakespearean plots into the mire of provincial Russia (as Turgenev did a couple of times). It's grim fodder, documenting the transformation of a beaten-down housewife into a murderer after her repeated molestation. Shostakovich composed the music between October 14, 1930, and December 17, 1932, then organized partial and complete run-throughs for colleagues and performers in Leningrad, Moscow, and Sverdlovsk.[28] He dedicated it to his wife, Nina Varzar, a student physicist who would rise to impressive prominence, contributing to articles published through the USSR Academy of Science "on the existence of unstable charged particles of hyperprotonic mass," "the mass spectrum of charged cosmic ray particles," and other topics reflecting her expertise in spectrometry.[29] Space was her place, as opposed to the political realities consuming her husband.

Stalin could choose between two different productions of *Lady Macbeth* that were running simultaneously in Moscow. The one he didn't attend was tamer than the one he did. It took place up the road from the Bolshoi at the Nemirovich-Danchenko Theater. The production was claustrophobic, tightly choreographed, and focused on interiors of low ceilings, heavy furniture, handmade wallpaper, dark rugs, bricks, mortar, a shovel, a cane, dirty frocks, and intense stares. The final scene, when the murderous anti-heroine Katerina marches to Siberia to serve her sentence of hard labor, bunched up the characters in bedraggled derangement, some looking menacing, others injured and hopeless.[30] The guards stand behind them, amid poplar trees. The show Stalin did see, on the Bolshoi's second stage, went for the jugular. Much of the action unfolds in front of Katerina's rickety wooden house, with the sloped floors and exterior staircase collapsed into a platform for the final scene (eight rather than nine in this version).[31] The prison guards assembled on the tilted platform while the prisoners themselves crammed close to the edge of the stage. A photograph shows Katerina leaning out of the window in distress, watching her bushy-bearded father-in-law (Boris) whipping her tidily attired lover (Sergey) with a knotted rope in the yard beside an apple tree. A filth-covered figure called the "shabby peasant" looks on in horror.

The *Pravda* denunciations of Shostakovich's upbeat ballet and downbeat opera were unsigned, signaling that they received top-level approval. It's now known that they came from the typewriter of an opportunistic journalist named David Zaslavsky, a former Bundist (member of Jewish socialist political movement) eager to demonstrate fealty to the Party and to Stalin.[32] Shostakovich had met him and perhaps learned of Zaslavsky's efforts to wreck his career.

The denunciation of *Lady Macbeth* appeared in the January 28, 1936, issue of *Pravda* under the bruising title "Muddle Instead of Music" (Sumbur vmesto muzïki). Zaslavsky savagely mocked Shostakovich's desire to titillate the "perverted tastes of bourgeois audiences with twitching, bawling, neurasthenic music." The opera assaulted the listener with "a stream of sounds that is—by design— inharmonious and chaotic. And "'love,'" Zaslavsky added, "is smeared all over the opera in the most vulgar manner." There are no love scenes, and the circus-like music of the rape scene of act 1 is musically linked to the score's other episodes of brutality, something

Zaslavsky didn't bother mentioning. "This is a meaningless game that might turn out very badly," he warned.[33]

The denunciation of *The Bright Stream* followed on February 6 under the equally bruising title "Balletic Falsehood" (Baletnaya fal'sh'). It targeted the choreographer, Fyodor Lopukhov, as much as Shostakovich, with dire consequences for the choreographer's career. It also signaled trouble ahead for Mutnïkh, who had appointed Lopukhov to the position of artistic director of the Bolshoi ballet. "A serious theme demands a serious attitude, great and conscientious work," Zaslavsky advised, and that attitude was lacking in *The Bright Stream*.[34]

Shostakovich reached out to Stalin, through Kerzhentsev, for advice on how to mend his ways.[35] He had been targeted by the system Stalin built and by the people Stalin put in place for ideological re-education and had to find a way to rehabilitate himself. As Shostakovich wrote to Sollertinsky on February 29, 1936: "Desperately sitting at home. I'm expecting a call."[36] But the summons to Stalin's office didn't come.

For Stalin, "Muddle Instead of Music" served its intended purpose. "Yes, I remember the article in *Pravda*. It gave the correct policy."[37] These words were transcribed by the cinema affairs official Boris Shumyatsky, who met with Stalin to discuss the tasks ahead for Soviet culture. Shumyatsky affirmed Stalin's opinion that "Shostakovich, like most composers, can write good realistic music, provided, however, that they're led."[38] "That's the nail," Stalin replied, before opining at length on the subject in a virtual paraphrase of "Muddle Instead of Music." He concluded: "Nobody is keeping track, nobody is giving composers and conductors specific requirements for mass art. The Arts Committee should adopt the *Pravda* article as a program for music. Otherwise the result will be bad."[39]

The program was adopted. The journal of the Union of Soviet Composers, *Sovetskaya muzïka,* scrambled to reprint Zaslavsky's articles. Everyone had read them, but reprinting them heightened the stakes, spurring a call to action. The Union called a general meeting; resolutions and reactions from assorted musicians and critics in Moscow and Leningrad were published, speeches transcribed, and the source of the formalist poison that had so infected Shostako-vich investigated. There were even attacks on him as a person, like this gem from writer Yuri Olesha published in the newspaper of the Union of Soviet Writers:

> He's very gifted, but very detached and withdrawn. It can be seen in everything. In his gait. In the way he smokes. In the elevation of his shoulders. Someone said that Shostakovich is our Mozart. Externally, genius can manifest itself in a couple of ways: in Mozart's radiance, or in Shostakovich's disdainful isolation. This disdain for the "rabble" gives rise to specific features of Shostako-vich's music—those ambiguities, the quirks that only he needs and which belittle us.[40]

Olesha rode high in late 1920s, having penned a successful short novel that was turned into a play called *Envy / A Conspiracy of Feelings* (*Zavist' / Zagovor chuvst*) about the director of the Soviet Food Indus-try Trust who dreams of self-peeling potatoes, among other wonders of streamlined production. He fends off the anti-Communist losers plotting his downfall. Olesha is credited with coining a phrase used by Stalin to describe Soviet writers: "engineers of the human soul." In the mid-1930s, Olesha would experience a less radical version of what Shostakovich did as he struggled to adapt to official artistic criteria. While critiqued for his unempathetic style, he was never outcast or deprived of income for it. Still, he surrendered the satire, black humor, and imaginative wildness of his youth. Olesha's career ended batheti-cally: he became a soccer reporter.[41]

The simple but vexing problem for artists living under Stalin was that no one knew the rules. They thought they were complying only to be told they weren't and that they needed to be taught a lesson, sent like dogs back to their packs with hurt paws. Another, more abstract problem for the artists was the nature of totalitarianism. Authoritarian regimes repress people for what they do, insisting on conformity and compliance. Totalitarian regimes repress people for who they are: obstacles on the path to paradise.

Meyerhold wasn't given the chance to redeem himself, but

Shostakovich was, perhaps because Stalin loved music too much to eliminate his top talent, perhaps because he conformed so smartly, churning out agitprop of the most appealing sort. When the Song and Dance Ensemble of the NKVD was established in the fall of 1939, Shostakovich hastened to join the collective, providing light patriotic music for the merriment of jack-booted agents.[42] Doubtless Shostakovich could not refuse the commission to write the music, and it must have taken him but a few minutes to whip it together— much as he had been whipped together. But what about his music for the 1949 film *Padeniye Berlina* (*The Fall of Berlin*)? Did he need to fulfill the commission for this appalling contribution to the Stalinist cult of personality?

He did, because in 1948, he was lambasted again by the regime for the listener-alienating "formalism" of his nonpolitical works: the instrumental compositions that didn't tell stories of heroic Soviet derring-do, the modernist sounds that Zhdanov likened to "power drills" and "musical gas chambers."[43] Such was his life under Stalin. He was free to compose what he wanted until he wasn't until he was again. The churn paused only during the war years, 1941–45, when he distinguished himself as a sincere musical patriot and joined the nomenklatura, adding political work to his creative work.[44] His Seventh Symphony is a musical fortress moving from a belittling representation of the invading Nazis to ultimate triumph. Shostakovich completed it while in evacuation in Kuybïshev (Samara). Conditions there weren't great but better than in the city of his birth, St. Petersburg (Leningrad), which the Nazis blockaded for 872 days, causing mass starvation.

Stalin was warned of Hitler's plans from diverse sources, including German turncoats, a Soviet intelligence agent in Japan, and Winston Churchill.[45] But he dismissed the reports as a ploy by Great Britain meant to provoke him into attacking Germany. The trap had been set in August 1939, when Molotov and his German counterpart, Joachim von Ribbentrop, signed a non-aggression pact dividing Poland between the Third Reich and the Soviet Union. Subsequent negotiations in the Kremlin that September resulted in a "Secret

Additional Protocol" that clarified the two dictatorships' spheres of influence—although just how the documents were fashioned is a riddle. Molotov was new in the job of foreign minister and swamped with other duties, while Ribbentrop's, Stalin's, and Hitler's roles in the process shifted.[46] Historian Philip Decker has written about the setting for the meetings, noting that, as Ribbentrop mounted the stairs of the Grand Kremlin Palace, he would have seen a painting by Ilya Repin titled *The Reception of Volost Elders*. It depicts Tsar Alexander III meeting various religious figures and representatives of the peasantry. The painting had been taken down by the Bolsheviks after the revolution, but Stalin pulled it out of storage. Tsarist history had returned to Russia, a change that Ribbentrop and his entourage interpreted as a sign that Stalinist expansionist aggression had peaked.[47]

On December 18, 1940, Hitler issued Directive 21, the spur for the Third Reich's invasion of the Soviet Union. "The German Wehrmacht," Hitler declared, "must be prepared *to crush Soviet Russia in a quick campaign* (Operation Barbarossa) even before the conclusion of the war against England."[48] At 4:15 a.m. in Moscow on June 22, 1941, three million German soldiers and three thousand tanks opened fire on Soviet outposts, poured across the border, and conducted multiple air raids targeting cities in the south, north, and west. Berlin notified the world of the attack five hours before Moscow did. Molotov got on the radio at 12:15 p.m. to denounce the apocalyptic treacherousness of the Nazis.[49] Directives rained down from the Communist Party and Sovnarkom apparatus onto the heads of the numbed masses. Moscow's air defenses lurched into combat readiness, and bomb shelters opened. The Moscow garrison enforced a 10:45 p.m. curfew and locked down the city between midnight and 4 a.m.[50] Male plant workers sent to the front were replaced by the women who had been working in back offices. The agitprop division of the Central Committee pivoted from extolling Stalin's leadership to producing anti-Nazi posters and organizing rallies. The Patriarchal Locum Tenens Metropolitan of Moscow and Kolomna (Sergius) encouraged Russians to defend Russia's sacred borders and surrender their souls to the fight.[51] Patriotic films of the distant and recent

330 · A KINGDOM AND A VILLAGE

past—*A Soldier Walked from the Front, Alexander Nevsky, Chapayev, If Tomorrow Is War,* and *Red Devils*—ran in the cinemas along with hastily made newsreels about surviving air raids, poison gas, and fire-bombs.[52] Blackout curtains were hawked on the streets.

The Germans advanced to within two hundred miles of Mos-cow and prepared an offensive named Operation Typhoon. Stalin remained in the Kremlin while high-level officials and other state assets evacuated to Kuybïshev and points farther southeast. In July, German reconnaissance flights over Moscow began, causing panic. Acts of anarchic hooliganism became commonplace as Muscovites weighed the plusses and minuses of life under Nazi, as opposed to Soviet, domination. The Church did what state media could not do: declared the war against the Nazis a fight for global civilization. Patriotism won out over nihilism, and a "volunteer" people's militia, a serious fighting force of 140,000, emerged.[53]

Those able-bodied people who did not heed the call to join the militia, or escaped being sent to the front, became members of the labor front (*trudfront*) tasked with digging sniper trenches, tank traps, and shelters, gathering scrap metal and donations, harvesting crops, and keeping watch on apartment rooftops during nighttime raids. As hundreds of small, crude firebombs fell from the sky, resi-dents donned asbestos gloves and scrambled across the rooftops to hurl them to the street, where neighbors extinguished them with sand or water. Footage survives of women in gas masks shoveling the flaming projectiles into buckets, their heroism embellished with tales of kids racing to be the first to put out the fire in the courtyards.[54]

The bombardment intensified in July 1941. On the worst night of the blitz, two hundred planes dropped huge explosive bombs in half-hour waves for five hours. The order to take cover was relayed through speakers on the sides of buildings. Sovinformbyuro (Soviet information bureau) radio announcer Yuri Levitan issued direc-tives on behalf of the government in a funereal monotone. Between 11 p.m. and midnight, thousands of people, mostly women and chil-dren, headed underground, bringing enough clothing and bedding to keep them warm through the night in the stations and tunnels of the new Metro system. Tougher Muscovites opted to stand on the roofs, where many were killed by blast waves and falling debris.[55]

During the first winter under siege, Muscovites hacked away at the frozen earth with pickaxes and shovels to slow Hitler's advance. Two lines of fortifications were dug once the soil thawed in the summer, another in October before the next winter freeze. Roads were jammed with metal spikes and textile factories re-outfitted for parachute and uniform production. "Enthusiasts" proved better trench diggers than soldiers and collective farmers, but the Komsomol outdid them all, while also providing books, musical instruments, and chess sets to entertain members of the militia.[56] Stalin ordered factories dismantled and put onto trains to be reassembled outside the strike zone, but when the trains broke down, parts of the factories ended up in the wrong place. The Red October chocolate factory on the river island across from the Kremlin produced rations for the front as well as high caffeine "Kola" bars to keep Soviet pilots and submariners awake. "Commercial" stores, which sold higher-priced, better-made goods than the cooperatives, closed. The stores lining Gorky Street (renamed Tverskaya) were ransacked, and crowds formed well before opening at the farmers' markets, ready to buy anything that turned up. Milk and tobacco were sold at obscene prices, ten times the usual cost, then resold by speculators and double-dealers on the side. The price of butter increased a hundredfold. Meat disappeared altogether. The government chaotically reintroduced ration cards, as it had periodically since 1917, monitoring the distribution of everything from salt to stockings. In the absence of antibiotics, residents resorted to ineffectual folk remedies thought to kill TB germs, including lemon juice mixed with honey and salt, along with crushed eggshells to combat hypocalcemia. Mossovet ordered younger children evacuated with a parent into the countryside, but the process of preparing boarding schools was slow. Most children (about 55,000 in grades one to six) remained in Moscow.[57]

There was a stranger priority: the Politburo of the Central Committee endorsed a resolution of the Council of People's Commissars ensuring the evacuation of Lenin's mummy from Moscow to Tyumen, where it stayed until 1945.[58] Lenin's tomb was camouflaged as a regular house, and pictures of other houses and trees were painted onto Red Square to misdirect warplanes. The domes of the Kremlin churches were also disguised, and the river filled with decoys. Barges set off from the piers of the southern port of Moscow with art collections and precious books.[59]

The theaters and parks continued to operate. Leading artists of the Bolshoi Theater opera stars sang on the radio; broadcasters read letters from the front, union houses held lectures on "propaganda afternoons," and university classes met. The symphony opened its twenty-first season at the Tchaikovsky Concert Hall even as musicians joined frontline concert brigades and performed in hospitals. A trio of circus performers headed out of town to entertain Red Army units, then inexplicably abandoned their saxophones and accordion at the edge of a forest. One of them "suffered a mental shock" and "disappeared forever."[60] At the Moscow State Art Institute, at the initiative of an honored professor, students designed anti-Nazi posters of "Cannibal Hitler and His Bastards."[61] Athletes demonstrated defensive water sports by swimming in clothes while holding a rifle, walking across logs, tossing grenades from boats.[62]

The government warned that any pro-Nazi nihilists spreading false rumors about the war would be punished. The police evicted nonresidents (people lacking an official permit to be in the capital), socially undesirable types, and anyone caught with items that should have been requisitioned or were considered illegal, including bicycles, motorcycles, narcotics, two-way radios, typewriters, even carrier pigeons.

Sovinformbyuro, a Moscow office of about eighty people established by the Central Committee and Council of People's Commissars just three days after the start of the war, stressed the positive of the Soviet war effort amid hair-raising accounts of German acts of barbarism: public hangings in the central squares of Soviet cities, mutilation of corpses, and the use of children for target practice for machine-gunners.[63] The newspaper *Moscow Bolshevik* printed accounts of Nazi blunders, including an impossible report of Hitler's car crashing into the Moskva River.[64] The "labor feats" of the rear also received colorful coverage, lest the reader think that scientific research and sports had ground to a halt.

As to actual news for the people under attack, that came from state radio. The broadcasts were intermittent. Either the signal went dead or was interrupted by a metronomic ticking sound followed by an air raid bulletin. Muscovites knew little about the condition of the city beyond their neighborhoods, even less about the progress of the war elsewhere, and feared asking their neighbors what they might know. Details about the blockade of Leningrad and the battles in Kursk and Stalingrad arrived in piecemeal fashion.

The battle for Moscow ended in December 1941. Soldiers defending the approaches to Moscow were taught to ski, sliding into attack mode, and the Moscow Air Defense District launched hydrogen balloons that looked like "huge silver fish." These floated high enough to disrupt Luftwaffe aircraft and force them out of bombing range. The balloons were effective so long as they remained tethered to the ground, and one poor soldier, Dmitri Veligura, found himself spiraling aloft when the cable he was guiding snapped. (Andrey Tarkovsky's film *Andrey Rublyov* moves this episode to the fifteenth century.) Veligura soared higher and higher along with the balloon on a minus-38-degree night. He couldn't let go without falling to his death and had to try pulling himself up the rope to the gas valve. He reached it an hour later, and he was able to release enough gas to land the balloon intact. His comrades found him half-dead in a field—hands and faced scratched and severely frostbitten, clothing in tatters—but he had saved both himself and a valuable piece of equipment.[65] This event can't have happened as described, but, like countless other apocryphal stories, it enriched nationalist lore.

Hundreds of thousands of people sacrificed themselves to defend Mother Russia from the infidels. In 1941 alone, according to official statistics, "partisan detachments and fighter-sabotage groups of the Moscow region eliminated 6,809 [German] soldiers and 350 officers, 5 aircraft, 64 tanks and armored cars, 48 artillery pieces, 751 trucks and 96 passenger and staff vehicles, 265 carts, 34 bases and ammunition depots and fuel. 5 trains were derailed, 35 bridges blown up, and 6 command posts destroyed. Communication lines were severed in

1,043 locations. 306 machine guns, 1,415 rifles and other pieces of equipment were either destroyed or captured."[66] The numbers don't capture what the Red Army accomplished.

Like Napoleon, Hitler lost his bet on the Russian weather—temperatures dropped to a record cold of minus 43 Celsius in the winter of 1941–42—and moved too far too fast to the east, mistakenly assuming that he could re-arm his troops and refuel tanks and planes using the Soviet railroads, despite their having different gauges than those in Europe. With the end of the German attacks on Moscow in 1942, the Soviet phase of the war, which was by no means the end, had at least pivoted, and those upper-level officials who had been evacuated to Kuybïshev began to trickle back into the city. Checkpoints remained in place along the perimeter and services continued to be sporadic, but residents no longer had to keep the blinds drawn.

Moscow marked the end of the Second World War with a parade on Red Square, a tribute to the people's heroism. Anniversaries of the war after 1945 were solemn events, not the pageants of the present day.

On March 5, 1953, Stalin died of a stroke. A commission for organizing the funeral was immediately formed on order of the Presidium of the Central Committee, with Nikita Khrushchev chairing.[67] Stalin's brain was removed for analysis and his body put on public display for three days in the Hall of Columns of the House of Unions, site of the show trials. The doors opened at 6 a.m. and closed at 2 a.m., twenty hours later. Muscovites moved past, an endless stream of coats and hats. Dozens of cameramen captured material for a film that was never released—though, in 2019, the Ukrainian filmmaker Sergey Loznitsa assembled 95 minutes of the footage under the title *State Funeral*. There are no scenes of hysteria in his edit, no stampedes, despite confusion—blamed on the commandant of Moscow—over the timing of the March 6 move of the body to the Hall of Columns. Some of the mourners are teary, but most stoic, concealing unguessable feelings.

After the mourning period concluded, Stalin's corpse was interred beside Lenin in the Red Square mausoleum. In 1961, upon recon-

"Last Address" plaques attached to the façade of an apartment building in central Moscow, listing the victims of the Stalinist purges, their occupations, dates of arrest, execution, and rehabilitation. The square holes symbolize the destruction of photographs. The "Last Address" project was initiated in 2014 by journalist and political activist Sergey Parkhomenko and the Foundation for the Perpetuation of the Memory of Victims of Political Repression. Critics argue that the plaques are mounted haphazardly without consulting relatives or researching the pretext for the arrests—some of the victims might have been collaborators. Dmitri Kuzmin, the grandson of a repressed officer of the Red Army, has complained that the plaques make older parts of Moscow and other Russian cities "look like cemeteries."

sideration of his legacy, it was relocated about three hundred feet away, to a necropolis in front of a Kremlin wall holding the remains of lesser revolutionaries. Stalin and Lenin remain three hundred feet apart to the present day.

In his final years, Stalin had retreated into paranoid, dissatisfied isolation, leaving the empire in paralysis, unable to provide for its people and protect itself but committed to the projection of all-conquering might. With the eight-hundredth anniversary of Moscow's founding (1947) in mind, Stalin signed off on the construction of seven (initially eight) high-rises in Russian baroque style to circle the city's center in rough consonance with the shape of the Kremlin towers. The cornerstones were laid on September 7, 1947, at 1 p.m., one hour after the base of the monument to Yuri Dolgorukiy was erected. The Soviet press hyped the past-meets-present symbolism: "The spirit of the nation passed before us in that hour: the distant past of Rus, the warrior on his horse, in his helmet and chain mail, pointing down with his hand: 'Moscow is here'—and gigantic high-rise buildings fashioned with the latest technology for the people of the socialist world, for the builders of communism, for new people."[68] The proportions and silhouettes of the new buildings had to be "original, their architectural and artistic composition linked to the historical architecture of the city and the silhouette of the future Palace of Soviets." (Between the Nazis and Stalin, little of the historical architecture remained.) Plans included one 32-floor building, two 26-floor buildings, and five 16-floor buildings, all mixed-use, all meant to be finished in five years, by 1952.[69] After the plans were passed from the Central Committee to Mossovet, everything changed: architects, locations, heights (by a floor or two), shapes, cladding, purposes, timelines, weights, even the number and types of workers (professional, Komsomol, prisoner) on-site.

The architecture and cityscape of central Moscow remain Stalinist. The average tourist sees the past Stalin allowed preserved, and even what's new under Putin still reflects his maximalist impulses. In between the two, during the half century between 1950 and 2000, Russia sank massive sums into soldiers, weapons, and its satellite Soviet Socialist Republics—not the city. Nikita Khrushchev built the Rossiya Hotel in the 1960s and added a congress hall to the Kremlin complex; his successor, Leonid Brezhnev, authorized new facilities for the Olympic Games in 1980, recognizing that the USSR lagged the West in everything from telecommunications to international airports. Sheremetyevo-2 (now Terminal F) was commissioned from a West German firm, while French and Russian architects designed the semicircular Cosmos Hotel for visiting dignitaries.[70] The massive stadium that hosted the opening and closing ceremonies predated the games; it was quickly built in 1955–56 in a low-lying area of Moscow called Luzhniki, or "Meadows," after several thousand people had been relocated and the eighteenth-century Church of the Tikhvin Icon of the Mother of God demolished.

Khrushchev and Brezhnev wanted Muscovites to move out of barracks and communal housing into carbon-copy apartment complexes described in popular songs like Yuri Saulsky's chipper "We're Moving into Our New Home." The Soviet '60s and '70s still evoke nostalgia for its simpler, better, cleaner pleasures—dachas, family readings, social clubs, ad-free television—and the optimistic brightness, light humor, and romantic dreaminess captured in classic Soviet movies. The world was not gentle and chaste, of course, but these are the decades people prefer to remember given all that had happened before and would after. Under Yuri Andropov, Konstantin Chernenko, and Mikhaíl Gorbachev, Moscow declined, though never approaching the blight of American cities—poor or rich.

Those mid-level artists, lesser sons of the people, fortunate enough to have survived both the purges and the war, returned to Socialist Realism, as the official artistic doctrine of the Soviet period was called. Elites like Shostakovich, who lived long past Stalin, hoped for an end to the agitprop and had to settle for its mere softening. Shostakovich addressed what he and Russia and the USSR had gone through in explicit terms in his Thirteenth Symphony (1962), which sets poems about the deaths of Jews in a ravine outside of Kyiv, shortages in the stores, and fear. Toward the end of his life, the composer produced a series of works that rejected ideological directness for enigmatic emptiness. Didacticism was a fraught concept that Shostakovich, in the years before his death in 1975, repudiated. Because by then he was able to express what he wanted in his music, he ended up expressing nothing at all—save for the desire to turn back the clock to his childhood, to a time before Meyerhold was executed and he was denounced, and perhaps even before then, as though he were wishing he'd never been born at all.

The cultural response to Stalinism has been counterintuitive in trying to reverse events. Nothing can get better, so perhaps the past can be fixed. Let Novgorod be the capital. Spare the Pretender assassination. Give the Provisional Government a second chance. Let

Stalin meet his end before Lenin's death and allow a moderate to take the helm. Might this unfortunate civilization be given another chance? The question keeps getting asked. *Doctor Zhivago* hints at this urge to revisit and revise, as does Anatoliy Rïbakov's *Children of the Arbat* (*Deti Arbata*), which was published in 1987 but drafted much earlier, circulating in clandestine copies (*samizdat*) before becoming a blockbuster. It's about Bohemian types who'd done well in the 1920s only to find themselves trapped in the Stalinist darkness. Old Bolsheviks are repressed or consigned to irrelevance in irrelevant jobs while young Bolsheviks find themselves unmoored by the purges. The protagonist, an upstanding *komsomolets* named Sasha Pankratov, is sent to Siberia for an innocent joke published in a student newspaper; his antipode, Yuri, joins the NKVD, hoping to rise through the ranks, but begins to hate himself. "Before, he'd look forward to the interrogation with impatience and expectancy," the narrator relates, "but now he did so with secret terror."[71] Bring the two characters together and elements of the author's biography emerge: Rïbakov himself went to Siberia, where he served the regime and distinguished himself in the war as a tank commander. After the collapse of the Soviet Union, preparing to move to the United States, Rïbakov boasted of the "literary bomb" he'd hurled at Stalin and the deluge of letters he received from "former repressed people" and the relatives of executed "enemies of the people."[72] Their anguished tales helped him to produce the two sequels to *Children of the Arbat: Fear* and *Dust and Ashes*.[73]

Rïbakov died in 1998. His final interview, published in the journal *Friendship of the Peoples* (*Druzhba narodov*), is full of nostalgia for Lenin's time, not Stalin's, because at least Lenin recognized devastation as devastation, rather than adding further devastation to it. The civil war was over, the economy in a shambles. Free-market elements needed to be brought back to Moscow to fill the stores and put an end to the humiliations of the ration-card system. Lenin introduced the changes in 1923 and, almost instantly,

> the devastation ended. Yes, there were dissatisfied people among the communists, shouting: this is a return to capitalism, there

were even cases of suicide. But Lenin wasn't afraid.... Food cards were cancelled. Private stores opened on the Arbat. We had everything. In Hunter's Row they were chopping meat again. At the Smolensk market they sold all sorts of food and what not! Milkmaids went from house to house with their cans, men hawked potatoes, greens.... The nation, destroyed during seven years of war by whites, reds, and greens, whatever you want to call them, recovered in a matter of months, it was restored and rose up.

But it all went bad, and the only people resisting were Russia's artists, at terrible risk, until they could resist no more. "And can literature change anything?," Rïbakov plaintively wonders. "In the land of Pushkin and Tolstoy, Stalin appeared; in the land of Goethe and Schiller, Hitler arose."

THE METRO

MUCH OF THE MOSCOW METRO dates from the Soviet era. It's a world unto itself: a subway system, museum, nuclear bomb shelter, center for innovation, and experiment in urban design. There are 294 stations on fifteen lines and counting, but anyone can navigate the system, designed by geniuses for use by regular people.

Constructivist lettering, orb-shaped chandeliers, semi-precious stone from the Urals, murals of revolutionaries and collective farmers decorate the vestibules and platforms of the stations willed into existence as part of Stalin's economic development plans in the 1930s and 1940s. By contrast, plainness characterizes the stations constructed in the 1960s and 1970s under Nikita Khrushchev and Leonid Brezhnev. But compared to systems in Europe and certainly the United States, even these stations are shinily impressive, no tiles ever allowed to dull or fall to the floor or stains to spread (dampness isn't much of an issue in the system). The newest stations, popping up on the periphery faster than the maps can mark them, are modernist, futurist, supremacist, QR-coded, and glowingly spacious. Abstracted plants, mathematical equations, and chemical formulae feature prominently on their wall décor. Dostoevsky station, named after the novelist Fyodor, features murals of *Crime and Punishment* and the nihilistic, revolution-themed novel *The Devils*. When it opened, in 2010, psychologists feared it becoming a "suicide mecca,"

October station on the Ring Line, which opened as Kaluga station on January 1, 1950. It was renamed on June 6, 1961, to avoid confusion with another Kaluga station on a different line.

but no one yet has jumped onto the tracks.[1] The Metro was intended for a classless society, but Moscow nowadays is extremely stratified. For students, shift workers, concertgoers, soccer lovers, retirees making some extra rubles delivering packages for DHL, and indigents alike the Metro is indispensable, while the affluent opt out for inconvenience's sake, preferring traffic jams to public conveyance.

Nothing beats the Ring Line for getting around the city, and it comes with a silly origin story. Stalin supposedly put his coffee cup on the blueprints, leaving behind a brown stain that the architects interpreted as an order: the system would have a coffee-colored ring line. It's a variant of a tsarist-era anecdote about building the train line between St. Petersburg and Moscow. A slip of the pen made it seem as if Tsar Nicholas I wanted to include a bend in the line, and so, rather than questioning the autocrat about his intentions, engineers included the curve, adding a half hour to the trip.[2]

The distribution of housing and manufacturing facilities by the State Planning Committee (Gosplan) meant that some people lived at one end of the Metro system but worked at the other end, a commute of up to three hours a day by Metro and connecting bus. But that's an extreme: commuting takes an average of about 45 minutes per day for most people.[3] Before and after work, passengers drift off to sleep at speeds exceeding fifty miles per hour between stops ten minutes apart at the system's extremes. Whether you travel one stop or one hundred, the undiscounted fare is the same: 75 rubles (as of May 2025, or 91 cents). Stenciled instructions on the windows insist that seats be relinquished to the elderly, infirm, and pregnant. Before capitalism arrived, the wood-paneled cars lacked advertising, save for stickered notices of job openings with the Metro. Female employees benefited from days off for housekeeping and menstrual cycles. Later, stickers appeared marketing office supplies, cold medicine, language and accounting classes, hot-water heaters (since, for a month each year, the steam pipes running into the largest apartment complexes are shut down for maintenance), and forged doctor's notes to get off work. Tallying up all the hours, I guess I've spent about six months of my life on the Metro.

I used to see a stray dog in one of the stations I frequented—a midsize pooch surviving on bread and bologna from the kiosks. He never seemed to board the trains, though others did. In 2001, a passenger inexplicably stabbed a dog to death during rush hour. The ensuing public outrage forced the attacker into hiding and brought other cases of animal abuse to light. Funds were raised for a monument to the dog, titled "Compassion."[4] I started to avoid the station and its monument, walking instead to stantsiya Mayakovskaya. Stalin spoke there during World War II, and it's a must-see for tourists, with rhodonite columns, diorite walls, and, in the rotunda, a mosaic ceiling of a partly cloudy sky with fighter planes and lines taken from two of Vladimir Mayakovsky's poems ("A Cloud in Trousers" [Oblaka v shtanov] and "The Backbone Flute" [Fleyta-pozvonochnik]). I traveled from there to Vodnïy stadion (Water Stadium), on a riverbend where people used to swim and fish. It's the fourth-to-last station on the north end of the Zamoskvoretskaya Line. Built in 1964, Vodnïy stadion is an exercise in the utilitarian plainness Khrushchev demanded of post-Stalinist architecture. The line itself dates from

1938, the worst of all times in Soviet history, marking the start of the third Five-Year Plan, which was focused on armaments production.

My hours on the Metro increased when I moved south to stantsiya Domodedovskaya. It felt like an interstellar distance from the Russian State Archive of Literature and Art, where I spent my days huddled in the microfilm room. During the Covid epidemic, the station was renamed DomaDedovskaya, which translates as "[keep] grandpa at home." A parallel change was made to another southern station that I naïvely used to think was named after someone's grandma, stantsiya Babushkinskaya, but in truth the name refers to a famous Soviet pilot, Mikhaíl Babushkin. Covid prompted its renaming as DomaBabush-kinskaya: "[keep] grandma [or, I guess, that pilot] at home."[5] Besides the hour it took to ride from one end of the line to the other, the challenge of living at grandpa's place was the long walk to the bus that went to the station. I was staying in a 1970s prefab apartment building across from an abandoned skating rink. The narrow elevator broke down before and after work, when people needed it most, and the dented letter boxes went unused save for flyers advertising secondhand goods. The entrance smelled of orange peels, cigarettes, and paint solvent. My unemployed landlord owned a couple of Siamese cats that he cared for so deeply that he kept an anxious journal of their litter-box excursions. I slept in a coffin-sized room adjacent to the kitchen. It had dial-up internet and a bookshelf housing the collected works of Soviet novelist Mikhaíl Sholokhov.

Later, I moved to the north end of the Purple Line, the underworld's busiest. Late one night I emerged from the last car in the last station to witness an obese drunk falling slowly down the escalator, one hard steel step at a time. The Moscow escalators move more quickly than those in systems elsewhere—a point of pride—and because of a quirk in their design, the rubber handrails operate at a different speed than the stairs. This poor sod slipped at the top and bounced four flights to the bottom, landing at my feet with a bone protruding from his arm. I called the station attendant for help. She berated her injured comrade for a few minutes before summoning an ambulance.

Stantsiya Taganskaya.

Underpasses leading into the stations are lined with glass-windowed kiosks (22,000 in all) selling everything from kewpie dolls and condoms to hand-knitted socks and Red Bull. The entrances to the older stations have coffee machines and bakeries so under-ventilated that the bakers themselves get baked. Fashion shows and choral concerts have been held in the system, as have cosplay events and even a funeral wake. On the night of August 24–25, 2007, friends of the recently deceased poet Dmitri Prigov loaded a banquet table onto a car on the Ring Line and dined in memoriam. Surprisingly, the police didn't interfere with the party, allowing it to travel around and around the center of the city until all the food and drink was consumed.[6]

Like the city above, the plan of the Metro looks highly rational on paper: concentric circles, discrete circumferences, hypotrochoids, interlocking triangles. The first time I saw a map I thought of my childhood Spirograph set. The lines are color-coded for tourists and the reading impaired; recorded announcements by women alternate with announcements by men to help orient the blind as to which direction (north or south, east or west, clockwise or coun-terclockwise) they are traveling in. The oldest stretch of track, from the mid-1930s, runs northeast from Crimea Square (named after an ambassadorial court of Crimean Tatars in Moscow) and the Park of Culture (Park kul'turï) to the Palace of Soviets (renamed Kropotkinskaya in 1957, after the geographer, explorer, and theorist of anarchism Pyotr Kropotkin, who was born in the area). The line continues to the Lenin Library and the place that once held Moscow's game market, or Hunters' Row (Okhotnïy ryad). A branch of this 1930s line runs west to east from Smolensk Square to Game Market through Lubyanka station. Originally, this station was named after a mass executioner, Felix Dzerzhinsky, and the bad karma remains. Lubyanka leads to a station honoring first secretary of the Leningrad Regional Party Committee Sergey Kirov, a far more likable character in the Stalinist cosmos, who was shockingly murdered on December 1, 1934.[7] To build stantsiya Kirovskaya, the thirteenth in the original system, a popular tavern was torn down.[8]

From there, trains pass through a station beneath the site of the Beautiful Gate (Krasnïye vorota) built by Peter the Great after his triumph at the battle of Poltava and rebuilt for his daughter Elizabeth's coronation. Stalinist agitprop ensues, including a station named for the Komsomol (All-Union Leninist Young Communist League), the teenagers who "volunteered" to build the Metro. Stantsiya krasnoselskaya is named after a village so lovely the inhabitants dubbed it Beautiful Village (Krasnoye selo). Merchants and goldsmiths lived there in the time of Boris Godunov; they rebelled against Tsar Fyodor (Boris Godunov's son) and joined the campaign of the False Dmitri heading into Moscow. The last stop, Sokol'niki, references Sokol'nich'ya sloboda, the forested settlement where, under Tsar Alexei and the young Peter the Great in the seventeenth century, falconers trained their birds for aristocratic pleasure hunters. The entrance to the station looks like a park pavilion with a stained glass window, a five-pointed star in the ceiling, bas-reliefs of the Metro builders, and, inside the station itself, a majolica panel with a map of Moscow.[9]

The dullest station in central Moscow—I confess this is my opinion—exits onto the least dull place: Theater Square, home of the Bolshoi. The architect, Ivan Fomin, settled into a style called "proletarian classicism" in his final years and wanted the station to feel like being backstage for a performance of the "joyous, liberated art of the peoples of our nation."[10] Before the revolution, Fomin had been a member of the progressive "World of Art" movement, which vibrantly revived ancient Slavic folk fare. His station looks back to that time, but the stone has dulled, and the porcelain figurines of dancing Kazakhs and Uzbeks are almost invisible in the dimness. Fomin was encumbered designing the southern vestibule; he was told that it needed to double as the lobby of a movie palace, which was never built.[11] The other side sold ballet and opera tickets when the station opened; now it sells Metro passes.

Electric Plant station (stantsiya Elektrozavodskaya) does better by its name with rows of round lamps in the ceiling fashioned by the neighborhood bulb-maker. Auto Plant station (stantsiya Avtozavodskaya), by contrast, avoids reference to automobiles, and a close look at the holes in the walls indicates that it once had a different name: ZIS (Zavod imeni Stalina, the Factory Named After Stalin). Stations named after printers and boilers and other types of blue-collar workers are shorn of referents, but Rasskazovka, named after a village and its storytelling settler, has pretend card catalogs for columns.

In the 1950s, Khrushchev repudiated the Stalinist cult of personality, ordering Stalin's name and image scrubbed from the system. The collapse of the Soviet Union in 1991 ushered in another wave of Metro station renaming. The historical names of streets and neighborhoods were reclaimed. Game Market became Station Named After Kaganovich became Game Market became Marx Avenue became Game Market again—a history in rondo form. The station facing the Kremlin walls has changed names five times to date. It came into existence in 1935 as Communist International Street (ulitsa Kominterna). Between 1946 and 1990 the station bore the name of the Bolshevik hero Mikhail Kalinin, and, for three days in November 1990 it was Vozdvizhenka, in reference to the Monastery of the Exhalation of the Holy Cross, which had been torn down in 1934 to allow for the digging of the Metro. (During the excavation, remains of *oprichnina* residences were discovered.) Now, thanks to the work of a post-Soviet Moscow government's "subcommittee on renaming," the station is Alexander Garden, after the park that conceals the Neglinka River.[12]

The heart of the system was and remains Soviet, a gift from the masses to themselves. Its origins, however, are pre-Soviet, and had imperial imaginations been allowed to flourish, the Metro might have been less Socialist Realist and more Fabergé. Fantasies about public conveyance date back to the 1872 Polytechnic Exhibition and the construction of a horse-drawn railroad up and down Moscow's central conduit, Tver Street (ulitsa Tverskaya). Municipal authorities awarded a Belgian joint-stock enterprise a long-term concession to build horse-pulled tram lines in the center. Another exhibition in 1882 introduced the first electric tram, and in 1898 an electric tram line began to operate.[13]

Meanwhile, an engineer and state councilor named Vasiliy Titov argued for digging a tunnel from Kursk railroad station to Mar'yina roshcha through two of the city's most popular squares.[14] The idea was as fantastical as something out of Jules Verne,[15] and no one in Moscow wanted to replicate the just-opened London underground system, where steam engines pulled gas-lit carriages underground. Even though the tunnels had generous ventilation, passengers on the platforms choked on smoke.[16]

Titov's plan also rankled the Russian Orthodox Church. Penetrating the underworld, according to the metropolitan, was a sin. Beneath the earth lay the kingdom of Satan and the realm of the dead.[17] Subsequent proposals kept above ground. In 1901, another engineer pitched building a circular railroad and tunnel system with five lines extending from the ring to a central station (Alexander Garden). This project failed, as did a proposal assembled by a group of American entrepreneurs who obtained permission from a sponsoring bank to explore the streets of Moscow, and the soil beneath them, for a public transit system.[18]

On May 15, 1902, engineers Yevgeny Knorre and Pyotr Balinsky proposed another project to Moscow governor-general Sergey

Romanov. Months passed; nothing happened. Finally, in October, Moscow's Duma gave Balinsky a hearing (Knorre was away). He assembled a colorful presentation, including models and paintings, asking for a budget of 155 million rubles to be raised from the private sector.[19] Balinsky stressed the challenges of modern life: Moscow now boasted a million people and needed to address the new urban issues arising from "apartment life, decentralization, price increases for basic necessities, and increased mortality."[20] Crowding and pollution made public transit crucial. He and Knorre proposed a central station underneath Theater Square and the Bolshoi Theater plus an aboveground station behind St. Basil's Cathedral. Electric trams would run in radial lines from the stations, linking Moscow's center through the long-gone fortification circumferences to the suburbs and regional rail lines. They would move people by day and cargo by night. The Church recoiled at building rail lines near innumerable sacred sites, including the Church of Three Saints at Beautiful Gate. Authorities rejected the plan as a naked land grab that would surrender municipal governance to "unnamed foreign capitalists."[21] Moscow's tram operators objected, likewise horse-drawn carriage operators, industrialists, and environmentalists seeking to protect parks and squares. It was a "farce," the kind of thing that a "high school student" would dream up.[22]

Mocked high and low, Balinsky withdrew, but his partner persisted. In 1912, Knorre and another engineer with the unfortunate surname "Ruin" proposed a three-line subway system so suburban trains could run underground into the center. The entire regional network would be electrified with funding from an English financial group and technology from a German electrical company.[23] The proposal went through several revisions and construction had just started when Russia entered World War I, bringing everything to a stop for years. Transport continued to rely on horses that would get stuck in the mud on washed-out roads, tractors pulling wagons, and steam-driven trams—"samovars on wheels," as Soviet writer Konstantin Pautovsky described them—that pulled candlelit carriages north from the center past Butïrka prison. These trams linked cities to suburban towns to villages in the forests. They whistled "in a child's falsetto," shooting sparks from thick black pipes. When the locomotives panted to a halt at curves in the line, passengers stepped out to smoke so that "the smell of wild cloves, warmed by the sun, filled the carriages."[24]

The population of Moscow during the civil war period fell by almost half: from two million to just over one. Industrialization and the Ukrainian famine reversed the flow, and by 1925 Moscow's population matched and then surpassed the pre-1917 number, reaching three and a half million by 1932, with a huge able-bodied labor force. The tram network, horses, and the newer buses and autos in the capital could not keep up. Slogans appeared on the streets—"Give us a metro!"[25]—signaling the beginning of the construction of an underground transit system with two branches, asphalt-covered platforms, floor lamps, sculptures, and bas-reliefs. The Bolsheviks abolished talk of the sacred earth. Now the Soviets would tame Mother Nature.

Tentative planning for the Metro began in Moscow's city and regional Communist Party apparatus together with Mossovet and the railroad administration. Soviet agents clandestinely studied the London and Paris transit systems, and a German firm, Siemens-Bauunion, offered technical expertise. Meantime in Moscow, the designers, tasked with doing something that had never been done before, struggled to come up with a plan and squandered funds. In 1930, officers from Rabkrin (the People's Commissariat of the Workers' and Peasants' Inspection) began to arrest those holdovers from the tsarist era who had allegedly sabotaged the project. Fearing for their lives, the remaining designers finished a plan and sent it to the printers. Some of them were also arrested.[26]

Turning the plans into reality and cracking the whip over tens of thousands of laborers fell to Lazar Kaganovich, a onetime cobbler who became "Politburo troubleshooter" in Ukraine before inheriting several "tough assignments" in the rebuilding of Moscow.[27] Through force of will, not to mention plain old force, Kaganovich tackled the region's enormous infrastructure problems, including the deterioration of the tram system.

At first, Kaganovich didn't think that the Metro was such a good idea, nor did some of the experts quoted in the Soviet press in the late spring of 1931. His solution to the transportation problem involved more buses and electric railroads in the suburbs. Stalin, however, wanted a Metro system, and so one was built. George Morgan, an American engineer, offered his services as a tunnel-building expert, while Soviet engineers disguised as laborers traveled to Europe to study and appropriate technology. With Kaganovich in charge, those who objected to the Metro as a "decentralizing" and "anti-social" mode of transport were lampooned as out-of-touch cranks.[28] The head of construction, Pavel Rotert, somehow managed to avoid being snared in the NKVD campaigns against foreign-born Soviets. (He was born in 1880 in Białystok, Poland, once part of the Russian Empire but outside the Soviet sphere.) His second-in-command, Konstantin Finkel, was no less suspect, having worked in Berlin on the transit system. Rotert and Finkel rummaged through the existing plans for the Metro and came up with their own, which the Council of People's Commissars approved on September 13, 1931. At Stalin's insistence, the Metro became a priority for the city and indeed the entire country, an urgent, "shock" construction project.

The people in charge—including Kaganovich, his protégé Nikita Khrushchev, the head of Mossovet Nikolay Bulganin, Rotert, Finkel, and the rest of the Metro Construction administration—confronted huge logistical challenges, everything from narrow roads to a lack of technical expertise to quicksand. Rotert brought in people he knew from the construction of the Dnipro hydroelectric station; some who had been imprisoned by Rabkrin as saboteurs returned to their former posts—albeit traumatized.[29] Material was in such short supply that marble mined from tombstones ended up in the stations. The technology didn't yet exist for the pumps, fans, and relays. Major decisions were left to the last minute. Even after the tunnels were dug (in pairs), it remained unclear whether the system would use island platforms (as in London) or cheaper side platforms (Paris). Islands won for artistic reasons. Another issue was the height of the ceilings: a two-vault design was safer than a three-vault design, but the latter held more visual appeal.[30]

The USSR did not have a single operating escalator, but the Moscow Metro needed them, so the Soviets reached out to companies in Europe (the Otis Elevator Company and the Carl Flohr manufacturing firm) for technical specifics. The effort failed, so the Soviets tried to purchase a working escalator to dismantle and copy. Otis saw the ruse for what it was and demanded twelve times the price, while Carl Flohr complained to the Soviet trade mission in Berlin. In the end, the escalators were built in a piecemeal fashion from purloined plans and parts.[31] This act of industrial espionage was not, of course, acknowledged by Kaganovich's team, nor was it included in the collection of children's stories and poems about the Metro published in 1935. The magic staircase (*lestnitsa-chudesnitsa*) was presented as a purely Soviet invention.[32]

In the end, the Metro was dug by hand by young men and women (75,000 of them at the peak of construction) who knew little about cement pouring, timbering, and rock or soil types. Metro Construction educated them on the fly, but the cement got diluted and the timber rotted. The first construction site flooded, cracking surrounding buildings and shutting down a neighboring factory. A deficit of rolled metal beams meant that logs served as fasteners in the pits. Equipment rusted in the rain; much of the rock and soil was removed from the sites by buckets on cables. The piles accumulated and threatened to collapse; trams carted away the refuse.

The year 1932 came and went with little accomplished, according to the report of an expert commission investigating the geological, electrical, and architectural dimensions of the project. The report, a thousand copies of which were distributed for free, emphasized the words "inadequate" and "insufficient." Environmental research hadn't progressed far enough to pinpoint the location of underground water, determine the feasibility of pumping it beneath the carboniferous limestone, or prevent flooding. The final pages added to the despair by rejecting the proposed lighting design for the cars—side and top brackets—as "incompatible with their style and purpose," and "unhygienic." Dimness enabled dirtiness.[33]

The Central Committee and the Council of People's Commissars told the engineers to spend less time in the office, more time in the pits. Skilled employees received raises and better rations. (In Moscow and Leningrad in the 1930s, basic goods were either rationed or distributed through "closed workers' cooperatives": stores that operated inside of businesses for their employees alone. Economic historian Yelena Osokina, as an expert on this subject, also documents the despair of people forced to barter gold and silver for basic foodstuffs.)[34] Komsomol brigades of adolescents ages fourteen to twenty-three took matters into their own hands when it came to obtaining wood from the port of Arkhangelsk and other sites. Officially, the brigades brought pride and discipline to the Metro while also keeping on the lookout for kulaks (farmers who became wealthy after the abolition of serfdom and who resisted collectivization), Trotskyites, "right opportunists," and other enemies hiding in the holds. A true belief and thirst for adventure motivated the Komsomol, but there are also stories about these young workers becoming disenchanted with hard labor and with a political system that repressed parents and relatives. Uniforms were inadequate, pay meager, black bread rations pitiful. Muscovites with other jobs were mobilized to work on the Metro on their days off, turning central Moscow into a giant anthill of frantic activity.[35]

The pace quickened, chaotically, and the layout of the system kept changing. Kaganovich rejected the design of the entrance of Arbat station after it had been largely built, then rejected its replacement.[36] Mayakovsky station fell a month behind schedule, owing to the clogged stone-cutting process. "The station's interior finishes have to be completed in April," admonished the Communist Party propaganda handlers in the foremen's office. They demanded that "the building managers and director of the marble plant . . . fully provide the site with people and marble."[37]

Incident reports indicate about a hundred injuries per thousand employees, mostly burns and broken bones. The number of deaths is unknown, though rumors spread of staggering losses. The NKVD rounded up the tattlers, but now and again, workers whispered about bodies buried in the walls. A sign in one tunnel read "Confess, Kaganovich, how many people did you kill here?"[38]

Most accidents involved explosions or collapses, often deep underground. Some of the stations began as trenches, others required digging under Moscow's tributaries and layers of sediment. In the absence of metal shields—a later acquisition—the tunnels were secured with wood, rubble stone, and mortar, then coated with scalding bitumen (tar) and glassine. Flu, pneumonia, and rheumatism left workers in bed, as did decompression sickness. Protocol required workers to exit the pressure chambers into lock chambers. It took about half an hour for pressure to be reduced to normal levels and the buildup of nitrogen to clear the blood. When that didn't happen, when the lock chambers malfunctioned or workers left too soon, the nitrogen formed bubbles in the blood and tissue that caused cramps (the bends), paralysis, and severe pain. The most serious accident happened at the excavation site beneath Theater Square. A short circuit sparked a blaze that killed two: a tunnel shield installer and a pylon sinker. Eleven other workers suffered carbon monoxide poisoning. Shutting off the air compressor brought quicksand into the tunnel. A crater formed, and a three-story building collapsed. Kaganovich, Bulganin, and Khrushchev hot-footed to the scene. The NKVD evacuated the neighborhood after arresting four suspected saboteurs.[39]

The workers' accounts of their experiences landed on the desks of agitprop publication editors who turned them into redemption narratives, tales of wastrels of the streets becoming heroic "shock" workers. "My job was to roll back the rock," one of them recalled:

It was tough at first since I wasn't used to physical labor. We filled 5–6 push carts each shift and felt that this was quite a lot. But the old miners we worked with just laughed at us.

We didn't know a damn thing. They'd say to us, "Attach the overhead board" and we'd be standing there like fools not knowing what to do.

But gradually we adapted. I began to fill 8–10 push carts per shift, then broke the record with 20 and by the end even 40 wasn't a challenge for us.[40]

It wasn't a challenge because some of the shifts lasted twenty hours—or even, the *udarniki* boasted, twice as long as that. These "shock workers" led the charge into the excavation sites, joined by

Komsomol members (like the rehabilitated ruffian quoted above), miners from the Donbass, small groups of prisoners, dispossessed kulaks (subsequently dismissed from the project as undesirable elements), and carpenters and metalworkers from Moscow's factories.[41]

Seasonal laborers who traveled to Moscow using the exact opposite of rapid transit—horse and wagon—also contributed to the effort. Metro Construction first screened them for potential disruptors while also encouraging other members of the brigade to root out "socially alien elements" in the ranks: fakers, lazy idlers, kolbasa thieves, and doubt-sowers.[42] The Communist Party ranks, too, required cleansing, and in 1937 it was revealed that "the man sent to explain to the Moscow Metro builders the need for vigilance against enemies turned out to be one himself."[43]

Upon receiving passports and permits, some laborers ate and slept together in their artel, or cooperative association. "They turned the parish into a dorm for us," a carpenter from the provinces recalled, and they gave him and his wife "a nook to the right of the kliros [the choir space]."[44] He built fences and threaded hot scaffolding rods through the tunnels. Most workers lived in barracks on Moscow's outskirts, falling asleep in their clothes and hoarding vegetables in their bedsheets. Over time, the "Party sorcerer" Kaganovich upgraded living conditions. Sanitation improved, curtains went up, educational clubs were formed, films shown, and lectures presented. To work well, the workers learned, they needed to work on themselves.[45]

In 1935, after three years of digging in Satan's domain (as the Church called it), the Metro began to operate along a red-colored line named after the Bolshevik leader Mikhaíl Frunze. Considering the initial slow pace of work at the start and the inadequacies described in the 1933 report, the achievement almost defies comprehension: thirteen stations, 7.2 miles (11.6 kilometers) of track, fourteen trains of four cars each (nine operating at the same time), seventeen entrance halls, fifteen escalators, eleven step-down substations, and more than five hundred factories producing metal, boards, cement, crushed stone, rubble, and gravel.[46] The high-ceilinged, marble and bronze designs of the stations and entrances emerged from a competition held by Mossovet between March 30 and April 9, 1934, as digging was coming to an end. Each station needed to have a distinct look so that even the "illiterate passenger could immediately recognize the station from the window of the subway car."[47]

A 1935 agitprop docudrama dedicated "to the initiator of the construction of the best subway system in the world, the great Stalin!" shows Komsomol workers clinking and clanking beneath the streets of Moscow. The streets are clogged with trolleybuses, cars, horses and drays, and zigzagging pedestrians. The soundtrack shifts from cancan to fanfare to march as the soil is tested, the mine shafts dug, and the shock brigades lowered into the pits with their lanterns and boring equipment. Cut to the halcyon after-work life of the laborers, brought to Moscow from diverse regions of the Soviet Union. Comrade Yusupova, a tunneler in the fifth mine, is seen doing her morning calisthenics, brushing her hair, taking a hot soapy shower, "learning her national songs," and attending a drawing class in a beautiful suburban manor house. (The portrayal is fantasy, not reality: The actual barracks lacked electricity, insulation, basic furniture, and sometimes even mattresses, never mind clean linen. There was little to read and the radios sometimes didn't work. People were stressed and irritable.) Then it's back into the maw: Separate groups of workers grind through the stone toward one another. One of the stations and a gleaming stretch of tunnel are completed, so Stalin gives a speech. Much of the footage came from newsreels about miners in other parts, and the streets of Moscow appear to have been gussied up with props. The images of Muscovites hanging off the sides of the packed streetcars are exaggerated to make a point.[48]

A test train with two cars made it through three stations on October 15, 1934, close to the anniversary of the revolution. In February 1935, a longer train navigated the entire system. The grand opening was set for May 1, but the system began operating on a limited basis months before for delegates to the Seventh Congress of Soviets of the USSR and other special guests, including a newspaper reporter who traveled the stations late into the night, "amid the noise, din, and cheerful conversations, so that all sense of time was lost, so that no one thought that we were merely using a convenient, modern type of urban transport. Instead, it was like an amazing, never-before-experienced carnival in fabulous marble palaces."[49] The reporter couldn't comment on the flaws: the crooked joints, cracked marble slabs, uneven surfaces, and the curtains concealing collapsed walls. Nor are they revealed in the manipulated photographs of the first day. The Metro as a space of fantasy is captured in a painting by Alexander Labas, who made a name for himself romanticizing the wonders of technology. The painting eschews the thick monumental style privileged by the regime for ephemeral airiness, such that the elevators ascend heavenward, one of them—empty of passengers—thinning into silver beams.[50]

The cars had padded seats and milk-colored lighting. Trains ran about three minutes apart, reversing course at the ends of the lines after cleaners swept them out and crisply attired conductors changed shifts. Music blasted on the streets in celebration, and a one-of-a-kind airplane—an eight-engine behemoth named after Maxim Gorky—circled overhead.[51] Khrushchev greeted a workers' parade from the balcony of Mossovet.

Stalin took a couple of rides in April 1935, before the system was fully operational and after 830 million rubles had been spent from the state budget with bridge loans from Moscow's banks when the budget was exhausted.[52] His first trip, at the beginning of the month, was a fiasco. The signaling equipment in the tunnels shut down and the train ground to a halt, leaving the dictator trapped in the abyss. (Imagine the panic on the faces of the Metro's employees.) The failure stemmed from "a change in the temperature and humidity conditions."[53] Stalin's bodyguards were to blame, as they had ordered the ventilation holes in the tunnels sealed to protect against a poison gas attack. When Stalin emerged from the station, he walked to his limousine without saying a word to the group of engineers waiting to greet him.[54]

He decided to take the second ride during a birthday party for his daughter's governess in the Kremlin. Kaganovich was there, and he turned pale at the thought of it. Perhaps it might be better to ride the Metro another day, or at least after midnight when the system was closed to the public? Stalin wasn't afraid of an assassination attempt that night and wanted to go right then and there. The group (which included both Stalin's daughter, Svetlana, and his son, Vasiliy) drove to Crimea Square and descended into a station that "had the smell of damp lime from a house that hadn't yet dried. It was clean and bright" and the platform lightly populated, the governess wrote in her diary.[55] Stalin's bodyguards arrived; the stations down the line were alerted to his presence. Hardly anyone had seen Stalin in the flesh, and the flabbergasted citizenry erupted in cheers. Stalin waited impatiently for the first train car to be decoupled from the rest and security to be arranged. Finally, after a thirty-minute delay, the VIP group made the trip to Game Market, where Stalin disembarked to inspect the escalator and the rest of the station. He would have encountered a space altogether unlike the cramped station of the present day. The northern vestibule consisted of a refurbished manor house, with small lamps in the ceiling and statues of athletes (later a statue of Stalin himself would be added). The southern vestibule occupied the first floor of the hotel and provided access to an entrance hall of vaulted ceilings, tetrahedral columns, stucco molding, and tall floor lamps (chandeliers came later). The station, deep in the ground, was meant to offer passengers the sense of being in a sunlit castle.

It became a mob scene, the public cheering and rushing up to Stalin despite the guards' efforts to hold them back. The governess was almost crushed against one of the columns. Svetlana was terrified, Vasiliy hysterical. A cast-iron lamp was knocked over and the cover smashed. Stalin stayed uncharacteristically cheerful, riding with his children and the governess to the final stop, Sokol'niki, where armored cars were waiting to take them back to the Kremlin. But the Soviet ruler wanted the adventure to continue and insisted on everyone making the return trip to Smolensk station, where no vehicles were waiting for them. After finally making it back to her room and pouring herself a stiff drink, the governess reflected on "the beauty and decorations in the stations." She continued: "One can only bow to the energy and enthusiasm of the youth who have done all this work, and to the leadership bringing about such a mass achievement. Everything was built with lightning speed to brilliant results."[56]

Finally, on May 15, 1935, at 6:45 a.m., all thirteen stations opened to the public. According to the newsreels, the first to purchase a ticket at Sokol'niki was Pyotr Latïshev, a "hero of labor" who worked at the Red Proletarian machine tool plant.[57] In fact, the first rider was a seventy-five-year-old pensioner who had fought in the revolution and, before that, the Russo-Japanese War.

A week before the grand opening, the Communist Party (the Politburo of the Central Committee) and the Soviet government (the Council of People's Commissars) approved the second phase of the Metro. After 1935, the initial self-sacrificing assault on the soil and rock beneath the city became a better-planned attack, involving fewer workers and stronger equipment: jackhammers rather than shovels, electric carts, and closed method of construction. The stations completed between 1938 and 1954, one year after Stalin's death, feature massive central naves and graceful steel columns and, in Revolution Square station from 1938, sculptures both domestic (mom and dad about to take a swim) and defensive (sharpshooters loading their weapons). Legend spread about the artist who decorated Revolution Square station. A colleague warned him that his sculptures had come out misshapen; the Soviet people looked crooked and crumpled, depressed, beaten down, no enthusiasm on their faces. The artist packed his suitcase, assuming that he would be arrested the next day, when Stalin himself would be inspecting the station. But Stalin liked everything about it.[58] To this day passengers rub the bronze snout of a partisan's dog for good luck. Besides statues, mosaics, and plaster bas-reliefs, the designers relied on decorative stone: solid and striped marble, granite, onyx, and rhodonite. Tiling replaced the asphalt on the platforms.

Surveillance of the system increased, and a nest of anti-Communist intriguers was discovered. On November 2, 1937, the chief of the Metro, Adolf Petrikovsky, was arrested—accused by a colleague of participating in an anti-Communist nationalist organization. The NKVD interrogated him, then left him to rot in a cell for ten months. On August 20, 1938, Stalin authorized his execution. His name appeared on a neatly typed list from the NKVD (Yezhov) of 670 "general" members of the population, "former military work-ers," "former workers of the NKVD," and "wives of enemies of the people."[59] Technically, the list had to be assessed by the military collegium of the USSR supreme court, but that was pro forma. The Soviet ruler, touting himself as the best friend of Metro workers—indeed all workers—had authorized Petrikovsky's end. He was shot on September 17, 1938, at the Kommunarka firing range, his corpse thrown into a mass grave. The next chief of the Metro, Vladimir Dneprovsky, lasted in the position just five months and presumably, in the absence of any information about him, suffered the same fate as his predecessor. Hundreds of others heroically involved in build-ing the Metro were repressed—something that happened through all industries through all the Soviet Union. In a 2009 issue called "the truth of the Gulag," the newspaper *Novaya gazeta* decried the continued reverence for Stalin as the builder of the Metro and the absence of a memorial plaque to the "innocently destroyed" people holding the picks and drills.

> In Russia, in almost every family, someone was either shot, or went through the labor camps, or was dispossessed, or deported as a representative of a "bad" people or deprived of voting rights for being the son of a priest or an "exploiter." It's strange to think that our country is inhabited by people who love not themselves and not their relatives, but only the authorities and the state. Peo-ple who are indifferent to the history of their own families and the fate of their neighbors. People who consider themselves the property of the state. People for whom the state replaces God.

And so, *Novaya gazeta* concluded, Russia and its people go around and around in circles, like the trains on the (Inner) Ring Line, the just-completed (Outer) Grand Ring Line, and the aboveground trains of Moscow's Central Circle.[60]

On October 16, 1941, the doors of the Metro didn't open. Save for loudspeaker announcements, governmental operations had ceased:

no police, no streetcars, no subway. The day before, Stalin had issued evacuation orders for the government elite, along with this directive:

> In the event of the appearance of enemy troops at the gates of Moscow, the NKVD—comrades Beria [the director] and Shcherbakov [colonel general]—are to detonate enterprises, warehouses and institutions that cannot be evacuated, as well as all the electrical equipment of the Metro (excluding water supply and sewers).[61]

Mines were laid and transformers removed. Trains headed to the Sokol depot to be used for evacuations on the aboveground lines. Chaos ensued. Assuming that the Germans had arrived, people burned official papers, Party membership cards, and the "detritus of Communism" in building courtyards.[62]

Stalin made the volte-face decision to get the trains rolling again at 2:12 that afternoon. Operations formally resumed at 6:45 p.m., but the match was lit. There were strikes over unpaid wages, fighting in the streets, and arson in the factories. Sausage-makers at the Mikoyan Moscow Meat Processing Plant walked off their jobs on the 17th, taking the sausage with them. The plant's guards and local reservists (members of the NKVD "Destroyer Battalions") restored order and arrested the plant's director. At another plant, employees shouting "Kill the Communists" binged on stolen vodka. Shoe and coat factories were plundered; employees at a milk plant dunked their boss in a barrel of sour cream; students tore up textbooks and ransacked classrooms. Teenage boys beat Russian Jews and carjacked evacuees at the city's exits. Couples split up, taking other lovers. Martial law was imposed on October 19.[63]

In the winter of 1941–42, the Metro operated on a reduced schedule. There were three lines in operation at this time, twenty-one stations, and two depots. German planes blitzed the darkened city and the surrounding regions for months, killing 130 people and injuring 792 others on the night of July 21–22 alone. A bomb collapsed the shallow tunnel between Arbat and Smolensk stations. Damage to water pipes caused the tunnel to flood, trapping passengers inside a train.[64]

In the spring of 1941, municipal authorities had prepared the system for use as a shelter in case of attack. Trains stopped running at 7 p.m., and power to the third rail was switched off. Aboveground, traffic lights were dimmed, factories concealed in tarps, and the glass ceiling of the GUM department store on Red Square smeared black. Militia officers sealed apertures and covered sections of track with plywood. Children and the elderly bedded down either inside the idled trains or on the platforms with mattresses and blankets from home. Everyone else slept in the tunnels. Before the lights-out announcement, people talked quietly, drank tea, read, played cards, knitted, and sometimes even watched films. Kursk station had a reading room.

Construction of the system continued during the war; seven new stations came online while the system's service plants also manufactured bullets. Stalin initiated plans for an alternate tunnel and shelter network colloquially called Metro-2. Its existence might explain the strange arrangement of sections of the track, the presence of unoccupied but for some reason never-demolished buildings in densely populated neighborhoods, and the dishes rattling in the kitchens of apartments where no Metro exists. Perhaps Metro-2 leads out of Moscow to Samara, out to the Urals, to the safest place in the USSR—no one knows for sure.[65] There is also a popular legend about the 1938 Airport (Aeroport) station on the Green Line—that the design came from the plan for a bunker, tipped on its side. The neighborhood once housed the Frunze central airfield, from which, in 1922, Russia's first international flights originated. The terminal building is now the site of a mall and a franchise of the Kazakh Mu-Mu cafeteria chain.

I visited one of these mythical sites, Bunker42, located around the corner from a legitimate Metro station: Tagan, referencing the coppersmiths who used to live in the area. (A *tagan* is a trivet.) In 1985, the Soviet government dismantled the bunker then gutted it.

In 2006, Novick-Service, a private firm, purchased the metal-lined structure for 65 million rubles, turning it into a combination Cold War museum and entertainment complex. Because Bunker42 is operated for profit, it's a catch-all for anyone willing to book the space. Visitors can both survive Armageddon and celebrate their birthdays amid strobe-lit Communist detritus. The signage is in Russian, English, and Chinese, but tours are offered in Russian, English, and Spanish. For promotional purposes, Novick-Service lists the Ministry of Culture, the Russian Union of Travel Industry, Peace Without Borders, and Akadem-Servis as partners.

My guide was a pale-faced man who seemed to live in Bunker42. His voice boomed as he led me down eighteen flights of stairs, beneath Taganskaya, a deposit of limestone, and a dozen or so feet of cement and steel. I could faintly hear trains rumbling overhead. The guide had me watch an agglomeration of footage from the Cold War in the underground theater before entering the bunker itself. He recited statistics about intercontinental ballistic missiles and asked if I'd like to blow up New York City in the simulator. I declined. Finally, I was allowed into the bunker, built in the final years of Stalin's life as an alternate command center for long-range aviation. It consists of four tunnels meant to house up to three thousand people for ninety days. Just one of the tunnels is open to the public; another is permanently flooded. There's a model officer's bedroom and a cutout in the wall meant to look like a mine shaft. I asked about the legend that the bunker's builders were exiled to prevent them from spilling secrets; the guide didn't answer. There was yet another flight of stairs down into a dark corridor where alarms sounded and red lights flashed to simulate a nuclear attack. From there, the guide led me into the canteen, a blend of retro and futuristic galactic imaginings with plush red velvet sofas, rainbow LED lights, and disco balls. TV screens showed music videos from the seventies and eighties.

The Ring Line appeared at the end of the Second World War after eight years of construction and had a dual defensive purpose. It connected the Metro to aboveground train stations alongside underground command posts and secure defense facilities invisible to the eye. It isn't quite a ring. The line follows the aboveground Garden Ring thoroughfare, the descendant of the *skorodom* fortification, then bends north to access Moscow's largest aboveground stations. The architects pursued ideological themes: the triumph of communism, the transformation of nature, the abundance of the land. Reforestation is a theme. Kursk station, from the 1950s, borrowed from the designs of Roman temples and the Macellum of Pompeii in celebrating the Red Army's march to Berlin. It includes a scandalously restored quotation from the Soviet anthem in the vestibule ("Stalin reared us—on loyalty to the people. He inspired us to labor and to heroism"), and the station is saturated with ribbons and garlands. The Urals supplied the stonework, and the Leningrad firm Russian Gems decorated it. Tile came from Kursk, site of a pivotal tank battle.

In the older stations, the ventilation grilles are embossed with wheat sheafs of bronze and pale gold and hammer-and-sickle combos. The latter are ubiquitous in the system but vary in quality: they ring the overhead lighting, are embedded in columns, painted onto the light stands on the escalators. Mismatches are prized. Stout, benign-looking hammers tend to be paired with sickles of razor-sharp teeth. The aboveground station called "Sickle and Hammer" doesn't include sickles and hammers.

Two of the Metro stations and a regional rail station connecting Moscow to the southeast are named after a certain Pavel or (to use the diminutive) Pavelets. Stantsiya Paveletskaya on the Green Line showcases mosaics of miners from the Donbass, bas-reliefs of a girl making hand grenades, Corinthian columns, references to 1812, and hammers and sickles. Three of the mosaics had to be redone because Khrushchev couldn't abide the sight of Stalin's face on the streets, factories, and transit system of Moscow (not to mention paintings, plays, operas, ballets, films, and the mastheads of newspapers).[66] Stalin had been ever-present, then he was nowhere to be seen. Serpukhov station, named after an ancient princedom, opened in 1950, was likewise cleansed of reminders of the Great Terror and the Great Patriotic War, as Soviets named World War II. Stalin's image was cov-

Mayakovsky station as an air raid shelter in 1941.

ered by a mural titled "Morning of the Cosmic Era" with a mother in a work shirt, boots, and swept-up hair cradling her child as he reaches toward a star.

The mishmash of styles reveals bureaucratic bungling when architects disagreed, then split the difference. New Settlement station (stantisya Novoslobodskaya), which opened on the Ring Line in 1952, offers a case in point. Builders Alexei Dushkin and Alexander Strelkov almost came to blows debating whether the entrance to the station should be round and resemble a grotto, as Strelkov wanted, or be perpendicular to the street. Strelkov won, boasting that his design stirred "music to sound in the soul" of the commuter.[67] Novoslobodskaya features stained glass panels and a mosaic dedicated to "world peace" by Pavel Korin, a deeply religious artist. Before the revolution, he had decorated churches with icons and frescoes of angels; during the Soviet era, he submitted to official demands for Socialist Realism in his art but held fast to his spiritual beliefs—working, from 1935 to 1959, on a large-scale painting titled *Disappearing Rus. Requiem.*[68]

The Metro bore Kaganovich's name through phases two, three, and four—right up to 1955. The smaller Leningrad Metro began operating on November 15 of that year, named after the founder of the Soviet Union, Vladimir Ilyich Lenin. Kaganovich found himself embroiled in conflict for his continuing allegiance to Stalin during the new era of de-Stalinization. He kept silent about his role in the Purges. "I loved Stalin, and I loved him because he was a great Marxist. He did much that was not good, and for this we judge him," he hedged.[69] His name was removed from the Metro. The Moscow system would also now be Lenin's. The renaming occurred on November 29, at the instruction of the Presidium of the Supreme Soviet and Moscow's Communist Party operation.[70] In 1957, a power struggle between Khrushchev and Kaganovich resulted in Kaganovich's expulsion from the Politburo. The almighty Metro builder lost his posh flat and ended up in the Urals running a small potash operation until 1961. His wife died; he was ousted from the Party; he expressed remorse for his role in the execution of hundreds of railroad workers. By the time of his quiet death in 1991, age ninety-seven, the Metro had expanded to a thousand percent of its original size.[71]

Artist Olga Velchinskaya has described the Metro as haunted, full of ghosts.[72] The spookiest station, according to a website devoted to such matters, is Falcon (Sokol), built on the site of NKVD executions.[73] And the tunnels have inspired post-apocalyptic fiction. In Dmitri Glukhovsky's book and game series *Metro 2033, 2034,* and *2035,* monsters roam the streets of Moscow; older and newer stations harbor the remnants of human civilization. Governments form: the Hanseatic League of stations on the Ring Line battles the Commonwealth of VDNKh (the Russian acronym for Exhibition of Achievements of the People's Economy). People in the stations live on fungi and fermented beverages while brainwashed children congregate in Victory Park (Park Pobedï) station. A neo-Nazi organization controls the Purple Line. The protagonist of the first part of the series, a nomad named Artyom, seeks shelter in the ghost stations of Metro-2, "the secret, Stalinist, second underground said to contain golden rails and subterranean gods."[74]

Metro-2 exists. Look for it behind the painted steel doors in the regular Metro system. But there are no gods or golden rails there. The tunnels lead to Bunker42, to its replicas, and to nowhere at all.

SWIMMING

RUSSIAN (SLAVIC) FOLKLORE teems with spirits, including the pure souls of ancestors and the impure, unclean souls of those who died unbaptized or before their time.[1] The mythological cosmos includes forest and field spirits, spirits of the land, lakes and water-ways, noon and midnight and seasonal holidays, and also patron spirits of crucial human haunts or livelihoods (hearth, bathhouse, mill, threshing-barn, cattle shed).[2] Central Moscow contains impure spirits and unclean places, including—perhaps surprisingly—the site of a church, which became a public pool, which became a church again. It is a place of sorrow, with an eerie history.

After Napoleon was expelled from Russia in 1812, Tsar Alexander I held a design competition for a new cathedral in Moscow to be named not after a saint or the Mother of God but after Christ himself.[3] The winner was Karl Vitberg, a twenty-eight-year-old graduate of the Imperial Academy of Arts. He had moved from St. Petersburg to Moscow at the invitation of the director of the Imperial post office, an old acquaintance. He decorated the walls surrounding the post office compound with allegorical paintings and fulfilled a commission from Rostopchin to design an album about the Napoleonic War. For the next two years, he studied building design while living in an apartment in the post office alongside accountants, package sorters, and censors who opened and checked through mail from

---

abroad.[4] Vitberg's plans for the cathedral, which passed through several revisions, demonstrate the influence of Masonic mysticism in referencing the Ark of the Covenant and the Masonic altar. The building was to represent the religious and political alliance among Russia, Prussia, and Austria. Tsar Alexander I praised Vitberg for correctly "deducing" what he'd been looking for: "not just another pile of stones, a regular church, but the animation of a religious concept. I didn't think I'd be satisfied," he acknowledged. "I didn't think anyone would be inspired by the project, and so kept my wishes to myself. In the end I evaluated twenty proposals, some of which were very good, yet all quite plain. You, however, have made the stones speak." The conversation became more circumspect when Vitberg admitted that he didn't yet have the skill to build the church but was an enthusiastic learner.

The tsar asked him to explain how he had become interested in architecture, and Vitberg went into exhaustive detail about everything but architecture. He spoke about his childhood in St. Petersburg and a doctor who had attempted to inoculate him against smallpox by injecting him with pustules from an infected patient to build up resistance to the disease. But the "bad stuff" the doctor stuck into his arm "formed a tumor" that required an operation, which in turn forced him to quit the cadet corps and left him with a gaping wound in his side for two years. Once he recovered, he went to a Lutheran boarding school for training in medicine but realized he wasn't "cold-blooded" enough to perform operations. He petitioned for admission into the Imperial Academy of Arts, where he studied historical portraiture. He moved to Moscow after his plans for marriage in St. Petersburg fell apart. The tsar listened for as long as he could to Vitberg's excursions, then clasped him on the shoulder and said, in effect, that he trusted him to build the church but would be keeping an eye on him.[5] The tsar gambled on the ambitious architect-in-training presumably because what Vitberg said to him aligned with his own spiritual leanings, the change in the sovereign's outlook, and rhetoric, after the events of 1812. The defeat of Napoleon was seen through a providential lens; Alexander I was, with other European rulers, the "abundant" beneficiary of Christian "grace."[6]

The cathedral was to be located in Sparrow Hills, the "crown of Moscow," according to the sovereign, at the junction of the two roads the French soldiers had used first to attack the city, then to retreat from it.[7] The cathedral would be carved into the side of the hill and filled with natural light. God stood at the center of the architectural compass with lines scattering in all directions from that center toward an outer ring symbolizing Creation. Three levels would denote earthly existence, the gospels, and the undisturbed peace of eternity. Dozens of bells were to peal through four octaves. Skeletons would be displayed. The lowest level catacombs were to be lined with the long flat bones of Russian soldiers who had died fighting Napoleon. This lower level would "press against the earth on three sides, and only from the east would light enter through massive windows with the image of the Nativity of Christ painted on the glass. The absence of light in the temple and its immersion in the earth corresponds to the idea that our body, belonging more than anything to the earth, receives both life and light from Christ."[8] Columns above were meant to be forged from the iron of confiscated French cannons.

On October 12, 1817, the fifth anniversary of Napoleon's retreat from Moscow, the tsar led a procession from Luzhniki to Sparrow Hills. Alexander I prayed, then descended into a trench to lay the cornerstone for the church, and then left, having placed Moscow's metropolitan and the governor-general in charge of the project. They authorized the purchase of "18,600 souls" as construction workers (the number eventually rose to 23,254).[9] Because the project was religious and under the beneficent gaze of the deity, Vitberg wanted the serfs to volunteer for the project and to agree to their own sale. He promised them humane treatment: no abuse. And he promised to build homes for them at the construction site along with a hospital and a kitchen serving pottage, bread, and boiled meat. The hardest work—the granite-cutting, tree-felling, and canal-digging—happened elsewhere under difficult conditions. People died and disease was rampant, and at a certain point the commission overseeing the project began to complain about the condition of the laborers: Some were missing arms, others had gone blind or run amok, or even lost their minds.[10]

The soil was porous; materials didn't arrive on time; suppliers embezzled funds; rivals schemed against the architect; digging and foundation stalled. The commission demanded an explanation for the problems. Vitberg couldn't sleep for the stress and pressure of it all. He appealed to the tsar for help dealing with his employees and contractors, but the tsar died and his hardline successor, Nicholas I, ordered an investigation of Vitberg himself. The ordeal lasted seven miserable years. Vitberg was asked why he left logs out to rot, why the digging of the canal had been bungled, why shipments never arrived. A million rubles had been pilfered from the construction budget, and Vitberg was blamed. He accepted his fate: exile with other political undesirables to Vyatka (Kirov). There, he befriended the youthful socialist Alexander Herzen, who had been exiled to the provinces in 1835 for a minor censorship offense. "Among these ugly and greasy, small and disgusting faces and scenes, deeds and titles, in this stationary frame and orderly environment, I remember the sad, noble features of an artist crushed by the government with cold and insensitive cruelty," Herzen wrote of Vitberg's misfortunes under Nicholas I. The architect's reputation had been "snatched" from him along with his last "crust of bread."[11]

Eventually, Vitberg received a pension and permission to return to his hometown of St. Petersburg. He secured some commissions, sometimes working without compensation. He died in 1855 after suffering a paralyzing stroke, age sixty-eight. The pit that he had dug on Sparrow Hills was filled in. The souls—that is, the serfs—he had purchased became permanent possessions of the government. The stonework went to build palaces, the planks and unused iron sold at a discount, and the hospital used to treat wounded laborers was torn down.[12]

In 1831, the prolific builder and professor of architecture Konstantin Thon was enlisted to salvage the project. He had experience in Moscow, St. Petersburg, Novgorod, Pskov, Kazan, and Tomsk, and is credited with the Grand Palace of the Kremlin as well as the railway stations at each end of the line connecting Moscow and St. Petersburg. A friend likened him to Pushkin; a foe called him messily derivative and overly ambitious.[13] He worked in an old Russian and Byzantine style endorsed by Nicholas I: no columns, no Masonic mysticism, no pantheistic alliance. The sovereign wanted the Cathedral of Christ the Savior moved to a different location, the Chertol'ye ("devil's hole") ravine close to the Kremlin. Chertol'ye had been the site of the nastiest fighting of the Time of Troubles, so bore obvious symbolic significance. Russia had survived itself, the Poles, and the French; it would overcome the Germans too. Building the cathedral in that place, however, meant moving a beloved convent that had been keeping bad spirits out of Moscow for centuries—or trying to. The abbess refused to leave and chained herself to an oak tree behind the building. When the police cut the chain, she issued a curse: "This place will be empty."

Popular lore expands the curse with the words, "except for a muddy puddle."[14] A worker dismantling the convent soon fell to his death from the roof, cross in hand. A holy fool appeared to predict the expansion of Chertol'ye to absorb "all" of Moscow's devils.[15] The abbess was taken away, her convent moved to a village outside of Moscow.

Construction of the cathedral was approved on April 10, 1832, but work again proceeded slowly. Thon had better managerial skills than Vitberg. He also enjoyed the support of Tsar Nicholas I as well as Moscow's metropolitan, Filaret, who lent his state-aligned nationalist-religious fantasies to the project. But Thon was constantly questioned about costs (for oversized doors and elaborate decorations) and delays. When he got sick and took time off from work, he heard about it from on high.[16] Erecting the largest dome took eight years; the construction scaffolds on the outer walls didn't come down until 1860. Ultimately, construction took forty-six years, from 1837 to 1883, long past the oppressive reign of Nicholas I and just past the reign of his reform-minded son, Alexander II, assassinated on March 1, 1881.

Thon died that same year, age eighty-six, two years before the cathedral's completion. His disciples finished it to a tune of 15 million rubles from the government's coffers.[17] The completed cathedral rose well over a hundred meters from the base to the top of the highest cross, dominating Moscow's modest skyline; the interior floor space measured 2,100 square meters. The largest cupola had a diameter of 30 meters, and the bells in the corner towers weighed 58 metric tons.[18] The western façade depicted Russian soldiers under divine protection, while the eastern and northern façades were dedicated to the saints. The southern façade narrated the events of 1812.

The Cathedral of Christ the Savior was consecrated on May 14, 1883. The next day, thousands of Edison lamps illuminated the Kremlin and Red Square for the coronation of Tsar Alexander III—though nothing could shine brighter than the sovereign himself.[19] The opening festivities included Tchaikovsky's 1812 Overture. When the dignitaries left, the cathedral was left to the clergy and the public, who enjoyed the space somewhat too much—turning the hours before and after services into social gatherings. Friends chatted; mothers nursed; kids ran around touching the icons with grubby hands. In the summer on the river, fishermen cast their lines while others dove from a raft.[20] Having used up the budget on the domes and crosses, the city couldn't afford to improve the neighborhood. In the nearby bathhouses, carpenters and their apprentices took their biweekly baths for five kopecks each (this fee covered the admission, use of a towel, and a bar of soap). Ivan Belousov remembered the cathedral's surroundings: "low dilapidated buildings containing dubious-looking taverns and other types of drinking establishments—brothels for people of suspicious reputation." The neighborhood was called "the Valley of the Wolves" and the faithful "feared going there at night."[21] The Russian Revolution of 1917 severed the relationship between church and state. Priests were repressed. Metropolitan Sergius declared his allegiance to the regime: Christian Socialism could have a home in Russia. "We want to be Orthodox and at the same time to recognize the Soviet Union as our civic Motherland, whose joys and successes are our own joys and successes, and whose failings are our own failings," he wrote in 1927.[22]

Half of Moscow's churches came down in the first years of Soviet power, once their valuables had been confiscated to "provide bread for the hungry."[23] The government, whose threat to seize icons and bells faced resistance from the patriarchate and the common faithful, mounted a press campaign in 1922 to defend its actions. "Refusing to help the starving people under all sorts of hypocritical pretexts and with Jesuitical tricks, the ruling part of the clergy is at the same time engaged in clearly criminal counter-revolutionary agitation against the Soviet regime," Leon Trotsky informed the Politburo of the Communist Party's Central Executive Committee.[24] The Church had been stripped of its legal rights and priests rounded up, but Lenin (and Stalin) also had to deal with parishioners arming themselves with axes and pitchforks to prevent the demolition of the churches that had provided succor throughout their lives. Bells were preserved where bell ringing was permitted, along with religious objects of lesser value, but the faithful nonetheless rebelled. The government's claims that the official church had nothing to do with faith, that the patriarchate had robbed the people to build monuments to serfdom, didn't resonate. St. Basil's Cathedral, with its painted onion domes, survived the Soviet wrecking ball, but the Cathedral of Christ the Savior, "built in honor of the frosts that had forced the French to leave Moscow," did not. Stalin's aides discussed turning it into an anti-religious museum, having also vetted proposals to remove the Kremlin bells and cannons—those seized from Napoleon's forces back in 1812—to cast "useful things" from them.[25] Then on June 5, 1931, the Politburo ordered the razing of the cathedral; a month later the Central Committee echoed the command. Before it came down, its contents were looted, the copper siding peeled off bit by bit, and the gold domes melted down for foreign currency. Some of the wooden icons were turned into chairs. A Moscow schoolteacher bravely sent a letter to the Vatican in Rome asking the pope to address the "barbaric" rumor that the vandalized cathedral was about to be blown up.[26]

Filmmaker and photographer Vladislav Mikosha documented the destruction and wished he hadn't, the event was so depraved, monstrous, and terrifying. In his memoir, he recalls his boss at the newsreel bureau calling him in for "a serious task. The less said about it the better." The boss's index finger jabbed the air. "It's a directive from above!" Mikosha went home in a sullen mood and, breaking his promise of confidentiality, told his mother that he'd been given the secret job of documenting the leveling of the church, day by day, hour by hour, using as much film as needed, no excuses. "If you're joking, I'm not amused," his mother admonished him. She defended the historical and artistic value of the cathedral as a great achievement of the people. "We all donated to it, throughout Rus, the poorest to the richest . . . God forbid!"

The next morning Mikosha and his assistant filled out the paperwork to enter the church's grounds. He was asked to list his relatives, both living and dead, as part of his background check. Preservation experts had rescued some of the art, breaking into fragments what could not be extracted intact. He witnessed soldiers trampling roses and lilacs and laborers throwing statues of the apostles with nooses around their heads into the mud. "Hands, heads, and the wings of angels were torn off, marble bas-reliefs cracked, columns crushed by jackhammers. Golden crosses were dragged from the smaller domes by steel cables with the aid of powerful tractors." Marble tiles ended up on the walls of the Metro.

Mikosha felt sick. He brought the camera to his eye. "I could not imagine that everything I would be filming would cut into my soul, my heart, like a disgustingly rusty blade, and that I would live in torment and bleed with pain long after the church was gone. For the rest of my life." His lens caught the smashing of stained glass, snow blowing through gaps in the walls. "But neither crowbars, nor heavy sledgehammers, nor huge steel chisels could overcome the resistance of the stone." The Cathedral of Christ the Savior, he learned, was made of sandstone slabs filled with molten lead. Cement had not been invented when Thon was alive.[27]

The cathedral refused to fall. Stalin couldn't abide the sight of its skeleton and let it be known that he was disgusted with the impotence of the demolishers. He ordered it blown up. The first set of explosions, on December 5, 1931, shattered the pylons supporting the central section; the second set brought the cathedral's suffering to an end. Those living close to the church described "salvos of rock, marble, and brick" shooting up. "The ice on the river must have cracked: in any case, a loud, lingering boom sounded over the river—and in the courtyard wells. The beacons along the fence flashed on and off, and, after straining to find its voice, the siren began screaming."[28] Mikosha's footage of the explosion shows angels falling. His mother, after hearing the concussive booms, cried long into the night. He suffered nightmares, seeing the church in ruins, over and over, imagining the same for his street, apartment building, and room. He didn't believe in God, he said, but he believed in the cathedral.[29] It's not known what his mother believed.

Late in life, in 1978, the doctrinaire Socialist Realist novelist Valentin Katayev braved mention of the cathedral in a memoir. He had the talent and ambition needed to navigate the militarized culture of the 1930s. Written in stream-of-consciousness style, his memoir alludes to the loss—the arrest, the incarceration—of experimental writers who refused to take the agitprop path he had done with novels for teens like *I Am a Son of the Working People*. Katayev relates his experiences as a soldier in the First World War: the death he had witnessed, the lifelong cough he developed from exposure to phosgene gas. He describes being with his girlfriend in Moscow. The metropolis is empty. He remembers the cathedral, but it's gone, and it seems that he and his lover have also died, like Romeo and Juliet, their souls flown away, their bodies "pressed to one another in eternal sleep on the basalt steps of the dead cathedral, deprived of God."[30] For those wondering how people lived under Stalin, Katayev had a strange answer: vaguely.

The largest church in the world needed to be replaced with something characterizing Soviet power, an even bigger building: a skyscraper. Stalin's accomplice, the future Leningrad Communist Party boss Sergey Kirov, pitched the project in a repetitive speech at the Bolshoi Theater on December 31, 1922: "They say we're wiping the face of the earth clean of the palaces of bankers, landowners, and kings. This is true. We'll put a new palace in their place, a palace for workers and working peasants, we'll gather everything Soviet countries are rich in and put all of our worker-peasant creativity into this monument."[31] Stalin came to embrace the project in the years ahead—increasing the building's (or buildings') height and thickness, adding an illuminated hammer and sickle at the top along with antennas and docks for zeppelins.[32] Once the initial questions and fears about building the palace on the site of the church had been addressed, architectural imaginations went to work.[33]

Several competitions were held for the design. Together with the underground churches of the Metro, the palace would be the crux of the plan for a New Moscow, a "Fourth Rome" with the Central Committee matrix as its Vatican. The drawings are astonishing: the Kremlin is reduced to a bauble, the road leading from Moscow to Tver transformed into a Soviet Elysium Fields lined with administrative buildings leading to the palace. Competitions for the palace were at first closed to the public, then opened to anyone interested in participating. Foreigners submitted their designs, as did people without any architectural training whatsoever, including a twelve-year-old girl. An earnest submission came from the Swiss-French modernist Le Corbusier, who sought to represent "the mechanism of collective life," with "transparent structures," "spaces in dynamic tension," and the roof of the grand hall "suspended on wires from a parabolic arch which would have dominated the skyline of Moscow."[34] A New York City garage builder named Hector Hamilton also sent in a proposal and bizarrely came away with one of the top prizes for a sterile cluster of square buildings; the award was rescinded without explanation.[35] The commission instead went to a dependable, experienced architect from Odessa, Boris Iofan. Moscow had earlier awarded him with a commission for the House of Government, an apartment complex for elites that included hot water, gas, and garbage chutes in the kitchens (a luxury at the time, but also a freeway for cockroaches). Iofan lived in one of the penthouses.[36] His conception of the palace reflected his time in Rome, where he studied ancient classical design, and the United States, where he was dazzled by the construction of Rockefeller Center. Stalin's role in the design of the palace has been exaggerated—questions about the project were low on the agenda of the Politburo, nor did it feature in meetings in Stalin's Kremlin office. Iofan drove the project from the start, and Stalin's August 7, 1932, "selection" of Iofan as the chief architect was rhetorical. Iofan ran all the initial design meetings, he had experience building on swampland, and he had the ears of Stalin's chief aides.[37]

Ambitions grew. Iofan imagined a trapezoidal structure of three grand tiers over a stadium-size assembly hall with a small statue of a liberated worker at the front of the top level. Two other architects, Vladimir Shchuko and his junior partner Vladimir Gelfreikh, developed a rival version that adopted a rectangular design, positioning the statue—now of Lenin—in the middle and raising the height from three tiers to seven (frankly leaving a lot of useless space at the top). The modification was accepted by Stalin, but he vetoed the rectangular design as too much like the photographs of Manhattan skyscrapers he'd seen. The Palace of Soviets was ultimately envisioned as a series of cylinders, the biggest in the middle rising 250 to 300 meters (820 to 984 feet) into the sky. The statue of Lenin was to be 50 to 75 meters (164 to 246 feet) tall and meant to rival the Statue of Liberty.[38]

It was to house 15,000 Communists in the grand hall alone: moving them in and out of the space would of course have been an issue, likewise the amplification of individual voices in debate sessions.[39] The palace would require a dedicated Metro station, but one of the designs on exhibit in Moscow's Historical Museum has buses spiraling through the complex.[40] Another includes a massive parking lot. Party delegates are imagined taking banks of escalators and elevators to their perches, breathing perfectly conditioned air, dining on fine food, and reading the latest issue of *Pravda* in recessed lighting. Designs from the final years of the project's existence have the halls equipped with hydraulically raised and lowered screens capable of showing silent and sound movies and newsreels. Outdoor screens were even considered for public presentations. Some of the later plans include an in-house studio "processing film negatives and phonograms for newsreels of all urgent events taking place at the Palace of Soviets." Multiple copies of the newsreels would be distributed to cinemas.[41]

An article in Moscow's other main paper, *Izvestiya,* brought everything together. It was published in spring of 1934—the second year of Stalin's second Five-Year Plan. The author romanticizes the smell of polycyclic compounds (asphalt) mingling with the odor of damp dirt from the digging of the Metro. Trucks pour cement over the remains of wooden shacks and other vestiges of the "useless," "harmful," and frankly "inconvenient" past. The Soviet capital will no longer suffer dirt roads smelling of livestock. The proletariat happily relocates into residential complexes containing "an array of cultural, medical, cooperative, and social services." It's quieter and cleaner now that factories sit outside the city center. New avenues replace the "dirty old game market" leading past the ten-floor cement buildings of the Moscow Hotel on the edge of Red Square and the headquarters of the Council of People's Commissars. Paved Lenin Lane leads toward the illuminated Palace of Soviets and the bronze statue of Lenin that defines the skyline now that the "shimmering golden dome" of the Cathedral of Christ the Savior is finally gone.[42]

The author leaves out inconvenient details. Building the Palace of Soviets meant developing—and importing, from the West— technologies that didn't yet exist in Moscow. Surrounding factories had to find ways to load segments of columns and beams on trains that could later be assembled, piece by piece, on-site. The entire construction effort, part of Moscow's efforts to shed the recent and distant past, demanded a huge labor force supplied, as in the case of the Metro, by migrant (deported) peasants, the Komsomol, and forced laborers. NKVD detainees became construction workers, though, in a typically perverse twist, their foreman was himself arrested by the NKVD on June 11, 1937. He was hauled off the construction site, then shot for the supposed crime of associating with Stalin's doomed nemesis Nikolay Bukharin.[43]

A few days after the arrest, Iofan delivered the keynote speech at the First All-Union Congress of Soviet Architects. "For the first time in history," he propagandized,

a magnificent palace is being built not for despots, oppressors who enslave the masses, but for a free people. The Palace of Soviets is the greatest of monuments to the brilliant leader of the proletariat, Lenin, a monument to the Stalinist era of the victory of socialism, the embodiment of the Stalinist Constitution. The history of the design of the Palace of Soviets, and the creative work of its architects, attests to the focus, insight, and dedication of the Party and the Government, the Council on Construction as chaired by Comrade Molotov under the direct guidance of Comrade Stalin (Applause).[44]

The applause lasted until 1939, when the palace substructure—the "tons of concrete and steel" poured for the foundation—began to slide into the Moskva.[45] The sticky black bitumen slathered onto the walls of the gargantuan pit couldn't keep the groundwater out. Iofan had failed; foreign experts were consulted for a fix. The rocks formed during the Carboniferous period that had once withstood the weight of glaciers now required reinforcing. Still, the sliding continued.

Meanwhile, pictures of the completed Palace of Soviets were printed in newspapers and on postcards as if to will the vision into reality.[46] The January 1937 issue of the magazine *Moscow Construction* (*Stroitel'stvo Moskvï*) was issued with two different covers. Soviet readers saw Stalin and the Soviet flag superimposed on an image of the palace. Foreign (American) readers saw only the palace and a silhouette of the Kremlin in pastel blue. "Rather than a competition of ideologies," an architectural historian writes, "the journal's American cover conveyed simply a contest in skyscrapers. The Soviet Union was just catching up with the United States."[47]

The catching-up was interrupted. In June 1941, work on the palace came to a halt owing to Hitler's invasion of the Soviet Union. Just seven stories of steel had gone up atop the giant concentric rings of the base. All able-bodied men were needed at the front, in munitions factories, and on the edge of Moscow digging trenches. The steel frame came down. The beams were used to repair bombed-out bridges and develop anti-tank defenses.

Stalin squandered millions of lives to win the war. Moscow prevailed. The site of the Cathedral of Christ the Savior, which became the site of the Palace of Soviets, stood empty. The erasure was erased. It snowed and rained and the hole filled with water, just as the abbess of the Alekseyevsky convent had predicted it would in 1837. Iofan persisted with his project, reconceiving it as a monument to the Soviet triumph over Hitler—much as the cathedral had marked the Russian triumph over Napoleon. He increased, decreased, then increased the size of the building again, but six revisions of the plan came to nothing.[48]

After the war, the Soviet Union defaulted on its debts. Crops failed owing to bad weather; dystrophy spread among hungry children living in communal apartments, sheds, storehouses, and basements. Bolstering industrial output, mining operations, and building nuclear facilities took precedence over the care and feeding of the civilian population, as did the construction—by prisoners of specialized subdivisions of the labor camp system—in Moscow of eight new high-rise buildings, one for each century of the city's existence. The Council of Ministers, the Council on Construction, and the Union of Architects announced another design competition for the palace on Sparrow Hills, where the chronicle of the Cathedral of Christ the Savior began.

Seven of the eight high-rise "sisters" were realized between 1947 and 1957 amid no end of arguments about the number and layout of floors and walls, the inclusion or exclusion of clocks and crowns and spires, and whom, besides privileged apparatchiki, the buildings might accommodate. Their bases were expanded, and floors added to the central sections along with decorative pilasters and pylons. The first of the architectural blockbusters to be completed, in 1952, was the twenty-five-floor Kotelnicheskaya Embankment Building, the last the thirty-four-floor Ukraine Hotel, four years after Stalin's death. Kotelnicheskaya included communal apartments in a side wing but also housed, in the central part, apartments for elites like prima ballerina assoluta Galina Ulanova and poet Yevgeny Yevtushenko. Their residences boasted built-in-radio tuned to state media, telephone and television jacks, hot water, central heating and gas, and direct access to high-speed elevators. Nothing came of the administrative complex intended for the demolished Zaryadye neighborhood.

The largest building, at thirty-six floors, went to Moscow State University. It strikes a majestic pose on the horizon, beautifully illuminated at night just beyond Sparrow Hills. In its initial conception, it had enough space to accommodate "5,250 undergraduates and

The Kotelnicheskaya Embankment Building, designed by Dmitri Chechulin, architect in chief of Moscow under Stalin, opened in 1952.

750 graduate students," along with faculty, academic departments, canteens, libraries, and museums.[49] Construction was chronicled in the newspapers with sentimental pathos: "Prokhor Turuntayev has been part of the biggest construction projects in the country. He was the first steeplejack to put a star on the Kremlin towers. For restoration work during the war he earned an Order of Lenin. He's a natural at his trade, installation, a simple soul who loves to work. He has the look of an ancient Russian knight."[50] No mention was made of the thousands of Gulag prisoners transferred to work at the university construction site, and the decision to use the uppermost floors as housing for those who hadn't been paroled—creating a kind of penthouse labor camp. Guards sealed off the airshafts, staircases, and elevator wells to prevent anyone from sneaking away—though at least twelve managed to escape.[51] The rest of the workers (the paroled

ones) lived in nearby barracks, ate gruel, and went back and forth to the site without escorts. In 1952, one of the workers built a hang glider to escape his prison in the sky. There are different versions as to what happened next. Either "Icarus" made it to the other side of the Moskva River and disappeared forever or he was shot down by the guards. A witness claimed he saw two men flying with homemade wings: one survived, the other did not. The "happy ending" version of the tale finds the escapee having been captured upon landing but then released by Stalin, who couldn't help but admire his bravery.[52]

Stalin's successor, Nikita Khrushchev, had little use for higher education—save for technical institutes—and didn't like the high-rises. In a decree titled "On the Elimination of Excesses in Design Planning and Construction," he denounced his predecessor's affection for baroque monumentalism.[53] Khrushchev also condemned Stalin's latticework of northern prison camps and the entire cult of personality behind his rule. There would be no Palace of Soviets but the complete opposite: unpalatial, prefab apartment complexes of three to five stories with gas stoves and balconies and outlets for radios and televisions. Khrushchev built them on the cheap, promising to replace them with sturdier structures.

Architect Dmitri Chechulin, winner of three Stalin Prizes, who had served in the Red Army during World War II, competed with Iofan for commissions in the new budget-conscious era. Chechulin won. In the late 1940s, he had drawn up plans for two of the Stalinist high-rises: the mixed-use Kotelnicheskaya Embankment Building and the unrealized Zaryadye project. The soil of that ancient neighborhood couldn't support what Chechulin had in mind, but, fifteen years later, he built a gargantuan hotel of 3,182 rooms on the site—the famous Rossiya Hotel, which hosted presidents, prizefighters, and variety shows with synthpop accompaniments.

In 1958, Chechulin received the commission to transform the site of the Palace of Soviets into something useful: a public swimming pool. Water had always been there. First there was a swamp, then a courtyard belonging to the leader of Ivan the Terrible's *oprichniki*; it later became a swamp again. It was emptied so a convent could be built, and when the cathedral replacing the convent was blown up by Stalin, the site became the foundation for the Palace of Soviets. After World War II, the site became a bog—a wetland supplied by rainwater—and now it was to be a pool.

Chechulin published the blueprints in an article in a construction magazine. The opening sentence is a whopper: the pool, he said, wasn't meant to replace the Palace of Soviets, because the Palace of Soviets was going to be built elsewhere, in the southwest of Moscow. The city's government thus gave him the honor of building a park and pool complex and re-asphalting the surrounding roads. No park came into existence, no new roads, and the pool didn't have the feature Chechulin most wanted it to have: dancing fountains. Nor did it operate around the clock and convert into a skating rink in the depths of winter. Chechulin noted the need for speed, putting pressure on Moscow's cement mixers and pipe-installers to fill the void.[54]

The result was the biggest pool in Europe, Stalinist monumentalism made liquid, a place where the souls of "enemies of the people" could congregate, an unclean space. Chechulin drew inspiration from the ancient Roman baths of Caracalla and planned the surface of the bowl to occupy thirteen thousand square meters. Saltwater was meant to flow up from a sea a thousand meters beneath the capital. The ancient reservoir had supposedly been tapped for a meat-processing plant on a street named after a fighter pilot, Viktor Talalikhin, but the water could not be piped into a project of this scale. Drills became clogged with an alloy of lead and tin dating from 1837. Diving deeper would have cost an amount equal to the annual budget of the Moscow Sports Committee. So the digging stopped, and a conventional pool supplied by the city water system was created.[55]

For several months, laborers "chiseled and drilled, bulldozers roared and dump trucks rumbled day and night."[56] On July 16, 1960, the "Moskva" pool opened to fanfare, and more than five million people took a dip that year. The state-run humor magazine *Krokodil* published a cartoon of Chekhov's Three Sisters dashing into the water, waving their towels high in the air and chanting "To Moscow! To Moscow! To Moscow!"[57] The pool's amenities were advertised on a newsreel with a pleasant soundtrack. Pleasure craft float by the "class lux" hotel Ukraine (the second tallest of the Stalinist high-rises, and heavily bugged since it catered to foreigners), Gorky Park, Kutuzovsky Prospekt, and finally the pool itself.[58] The camera pans over strollers in a garden and cars flowing over smooth asphalt before zooming in on three blond boys in pressed shirts and shorts. They're heading to the "artificial island," the "Moskva" pool.

The pool was partitioned for use by all types of swimmers of all ages. Teens could meet there as a cheap after-school activity. The sector reserved for athletes included diving platforms and an eight-lane pool with an underwater entrance. From the top of a pavilion, a nattily dressed crowd watched synchronized swimmers forming flower shapes with their limbs. Through the windows of a passing streetcar, a diver could be seen pirouetting in the air, leaping from the shoulders of a partner into the deepest part of the pool—six meters (later the depth would be reduced by half to avoid drownings).

Swimsuits, fins, masks, and towels are all available for rental. Everyone gets a locker—cut to smiling men soaping themselves up in the shower—and little ones receive beach balls and floaties. There's a snack bar and a sauna and what looks to be a barbeque pit. Medical clearances aren't required; no one, no matter how unkempt, need line up for a pass. The pool does, however, have a nurse's office for injuries. If you can't swim that's fine too: the pool's instructors offer lessons.[59] It's a ruble and a half for a ticket at the Kropotkinskaya Metro Station, less than the cost of breakfast for schoolkids. Families can purchase year-round passes.

The 1960 newsreel showcases the pool's mechanical room, the boilers, filters, and compressors. To prevent contamination, water is constantly refreshed and tested three times a day at an epidemiological station (the camera cuts to a blond lab technician in a bright white coat) to ensure clean and crystal-clear recreation. Antibacterial installations, chlorine, sand filters, and ultraviolet light keep dirt and germs away. There's never been a violation, the administrators boast. The edge of the pool reads "Don't stand on the edge." Marxist revolutionary Che Guevara does just that on his visit to the pool in November 1960.[60]

Moscow Swimming Pool, August 8, 1960. The site was home to a church, then the Palace of Soviets, then the pool. Now a church is there again.

The pool operated from 8 a.m. to midnight year-round, so long as the temperature didn't drop below minus 20 degrees Celsius. The hardiest, most thickly padded Muscovites swam only in the front, enjoying the sensation of ice crusting on their rubber caps. Did the lifeguards wear coats? Did they even show up? Regulars recall that the swimmers were their own lifeguards, and although I heard about municipal authorities permitting the occasional nighttime water disco, with colored lights illuminating the pool, nothing of the sort seems to have occurred. Muscovites who grew up in the 1960s also insist that just as there was no disco, there was no canteen, shashlik, soap in the showers, functioning lockers, and often no lights at night. The pool looked like a huge inkwell after sunset.

At some point, algae formed on the sides and bottom of the pool. A meningitis outbreak prompted jokes about sanitation, and rumors were rife of religious fanatics seeking to avenge the destruction of the Cathedral of Christ the Savior who lurked behind the curtain of vapor and drowned swimmers in the deep end. The rumors derive, crudely, from the rich and poignant Russian lore concerning the behavior of *rusalki,* female water spirits in the depths of lakes and swamps who could sometimes be seen sitting on the shore in tearful sorrow. Some *rusalki* do good—others bad, their "bathing games" a trap, promising "unnatural death."[61] Related tales had "the ghosts of pious old women flying over the waters," making the sign of the cross, "syphilitics and lepers" using the pool, having faked their health certificates, and "a dreadful tale about a boy who went for a swim, and the next day his nose perforated."[62] People cracked their heads slipping on the ice on the concrete shore; lifeguards couldn't see through the mist.

There is no scientific proof of the church's outlines appearing in the mist, and the stories of gangs drowning unsupervised boys are conjectural, though I defer to the recollection of Jana Howlett, who had a pass for the pool in 1967 and befriended one of the guards, Boris Pravdin. She came from England but spoke Russian without an accent, and at the pool people didn't fear talking to her because they assumed she was a local. Boris had been kicked out of university and brought in income forging documents. He showed Jana the pool's "special section," where "all sorts of things went on," black marketeering of goods from abroad and the provision of escorts for Party bureaucrats. "As I remember, the entire racket was run by the pool's director."[63]

One former employee recalled his duties in fantastically exaggerated detail.

> When I was a student in the 1960s at Baumanka [Moscow State Technical University], I worked as a lifeguard at the pool. After class, I went to Kropotkinskaya; they'd pull a diving suit over me and I had to walk along the bottom of the pool for several hours to make sure no one had drowned. And people often drowned there.

When asked how much he was paid, he laughed: "Are you kidding? Nothing. After the shift, we were allowed to swim in the pool for as long as we liked."[64]

The floor was raised a couple of meters to save on water and cut down on the number of mishaps. But the chlorine steam caused another problem: It corroded fences and damaged exhibits at the Museum of Fine Arts across the street, according to the administration—though the same administration had used the pool to wash priceless tapestries with baby soap, sea sponges, vinegar solutions, and vacuum cleaners. That happened in 1986 under police guard, when the pool was closed to the public— briefly during the summer—for maintenance.[65] The museum's complaints to the sports authorities about the corrosive vapors went unanswered. The exhibits were saved by the rising cost of water and electricity, which forced the pool to close in 1991.

The bowl sat empty for three years before it shut for good. Cracks formed in the cement, and the pipeline network corroded. With the spring thaw, a shallow lake formed at the bottom, and children from the neighborhood climbed down to float on makeshift rafts, playing pirates. Dog owners brought their four-legged friends to the pool, where they did their business. "The barbarization of life has reached its limit," the newspaper *Izvestiya* lamented of the desolation; "lanterns are smashed at night, along with everything else."[66]

When dismantling the pool, excavators discovered huge pits clogged with debris and contaminated groundwater. The cathedral had been built on the ground, but streams leaked inside. Laying the foundation of his never-realized Palace of the Soviets, Iofan rerouted the streams back into the Moskva, but then that foundation had been pulled up. Below the bottom, in darkest darkness, Iofan had built something else: a bunker. "The center of the concrete ring concealed a Politburo room, sixty meters beneath the pool," a member of the patriarchate told a reporter in 1999. It was sealed off and forgotten when the pool was built, but "it still had active wiring, and telephones. And there was an inscription on the telephones: 'Remember, comrade, the secrecy of telephone communications is not guaranteed.'"[67]

Not everyone who swam in the pool knew that the cathedral had once stood there, though unresolved histories "haunt" renovated spaces as they do memories.[68] Evidence of the cathedral's existence was airbrushed out of photographs like the pockmarks on Stalin's cheeks, unflattering images of trash on Moscow streets, and the faces of arrested Politburo members. Rebuilding the cathedral in the 1990s meant telling the public, misleadingly, that the pool had once been the holiest site in Russia, as opposed to a cathedral commemorating the expulsion of Napoleon. It was revived "thanks to the intervention of higher powers," officialdom insists: "several religious buildings have been here through the ages, and it is here that people came seeking protection and help."[69] Moscow mayor Yuri Luzhkov explained that the restoration was an act of repentance, and that he had been motivated to do it when a pensioner, "some kind of mystic," turned up at his office with a rare Bible. Her husband had had a vision of the restored cathedral and asked her to present the Bible to the person who had brought the abbess's curse to an end.[70] Luzhkov loved telling this story.

Rebuilding happened quickly between 1994 and 1999, thanks to funds gathered from the precariously financed government, charitable organizations, McDonald's, Coca-Cola, Deutsche Bank, and Kremlin-connected entertainers like the peruke-wearing crooner Iosif Kobzon (whose warbling, Sinatra-esque baritone still echoes in my head from a banquet one of his associates invited me to attend at GUM in 2013). Painted plastic replaced the original bronze inside the church, and, for the domes, "titanium nitrate [was] sprayed over with gold lacquer."[71] Painters added their faces to the murals (something of a tradition in Russian church decoration). Five years later, on December 31, 1999, the first of two consecrations of the reactionary restoration of the cathedral took place. Grand faith had returned to Moscow, though rather hastily, based on pieces of a more reverent past that Soviet power hadn't eliminated.

Moscow's devout don't frequent the rebuilt cathedral. It's illegitimate to them, a profanation built with dirty money. The pool could have been filled with holy water and used for baptism; the church should have been inflatable.[72] There have been scandals, some actual, like Pussy Riot's performance of a "punk prayer" on the solea in 2012:

Virgin Mary, Mother of God, banish Putin, banish Putin,
Virgin Mary, Mother of God, banish him, we pray thee!

Congregations genuflect,
Black robes brag gilt epaulettes,
Freedom's phantom's gone to heaven,
Gay Pride's chained and in detention.[73]

The music was as poor as the poetry, and the performance didn't much shock, since the cathedral has been used as much for corporate shindigs as for services. Perks for the priests include an on-site car wash, and religion takes strange forms in the main hall: A concert of the Soviet "hit parade" was held there on August 2, 2022.

So even churchgoers miss the pool, and even non-swimmers miss seeing clouds of steam rising from the waters in the dead of winter. (I saw them during my first visit to Moscow.) There are several Facebook groups dedicated to Moscow's history, most unhappily contrasting the present with the past and the past of the past. Pictures of the pool always elicit nostalgic comments about golden childhoods: "How I remember it!" Black humor enters the mix for those forced to swim. "I had Phys Ed classes there when I was in medical school," one Facebooker related. "Probably in 1978–79, always in the winter. You'd dive from the shower under a rubber curtain of some sort right into the pool. I shudder remembering my rubber cap shrinking in the cold to the size of a fist and almost popping off. Then the gallop to the Metro in the frost with wet hair. There were no hairdryers, so sniffles and sore throats and off we went to study like fools and it was terrible."[74] Moscow is hot in the summer, and pools much needed. The church that replaced the biggest pool in Europe continues to be derided as a monument to Luzhkov and a bank machine for the Orthodox state-within-the-state. "People of faith—not those who come for Easter services to bless cakes and eggs or, now and then, light candles for their health and peace of mind—don't need churches, priests in robes, choirs, icons, or candles."[75] For three decades, Muscovites swam atop the foundation of the Palace of Soviets, which was also the ruins of a cathedral and the remains of a convent. They swam in chlorinated water above a freshwater stream flowing into the Moskva, above an imagined ancient sea.

NEVERLAND

I REMEMBER MY Soviet tour guide, Tanya, talking unenthusiastically about Russia's rulers as she shepherded our group across Red Square in the winter of 1989. "And now," she said, anticipating the end of Gorbachev's reign, "we have the hero Yeltsin." There are two ways to explain that threshold moment. One would privilege the shocking suddenness: "everything was forever, until it was no more"; the other might see life as a kind of loop, such that everything was forever, until it was no more, until it was again forever.[1]

The second loop option has proved both the most and least comforting. After Stalin's death, the repressions that had held the former kingdoms and colonized states under Russian control eased. His successor, Khrushchev, welcomed a post-Stalinist moment of liberalization known as the Thaw (*Ottepel'*), but the moment passed when Khrushchev was placed under house arrest. Brezhnev then returned to the ideological status quo ante, but the system proved unable, and unwilling, to ease national tensions in the republics—particularly those between Russia and Ukraine.[2] The Soviet Union was over before it was over, doomed by its reliance on enfeebled general secretaries—Brezhnev, Andropov, and Chernenko—who died in 1982, 1984, and 1985, respectively. The USSR didn't collapse so much as stagger to an end, the last European empire to do so. Cynicism bred contempt, especially after the Chernobyl nuclear disaster and Gorbachev's Janus-faced attempts to loosen things up but at the same time maintain some belief in founding doctrine. *Glasnost'* (openness) succeeded; *perestroika* (restructuring) failed, and both led to a botched coup d'état. The reluctant, trembling, hungover vice president of the Soviet Union, Gennady Yanayev, together with seven other hardliners, tried to seize power. However, on Monday, August 19, 1991, Yeltsin, president of the Russian Soviet Federative Socialist Republic, stood on a tank in the late-summer rain and rallied the public to prevent the putsch.[3] If the plot succeeded, he knew that one of the quarter million pairs of handcuffs rush-ordered from a plant in Pskov would snap shut on his wrists.[4] But the coup unraveled before the rain ended, ushering in what Yanayev had hoped to stop: the end of the Soviet Union. Throughout the crisis, state television showed Tchaikovsky's ballet *Swan Lake* on repeat. The final curtain came down, television resumed regular programming, and the teenagers driving the tanks returned to their bases.[5]

Gorbachev was relatively youthful, and under more favorable conditions he might have proved a pivot toward change and an exit out of the loop, but the system was too sclerotic. The USSR hung on for four more months after the attempted putsch, but on Christmas Day 1991, the flag with the hammer and sickle was lowered and the Russian tricolor raised over the Kremlin.

Before becoming the Russian Federation's first president, Boris Yeltsin was a populist fighter—a swaggering tell-it-like-it-is type. His Siberian grandfather had been branded a kulak by Stalin, who put Yeltsin's father, a carpenter, in a labor camp. Raised poor in a barracks near Sverdlovsk, Yeltsin almost flunked out of school and rode the rails around the Soviet Union. He learned several construction trades, joined the Communist Party in 1961, cracked the whip on building projects in Moscow, and inserted himself into the political arena, serving first as RSFSR Duma backbencher, then speaker, and finally president. In 1977 he carried out the Politburo order to tear down the home where the Bolsheviks murdered the last tsar, Nicholas II, and his family. In 1991, he tore down the entire Communist Party apparatus.[6]

The beginning of the end of "communism" (a utopian vision that the Soviet Union never achieved) was dismal. The ruble tanked; the central bank defaulted. "Democracy" meant hyperinflated "free markets," crime-filled streets, contract killings, hostage-takings, pyramid schemes, the implosion of governing institutions, the evaporation of savings, and the ruination of the lives of innocent, loving, infinitely generous people. The capitalist invasion of New Arbat brought garish casinos. Yeltsin offered shares in state enterprises to the average citizen, who sold them for a pittance to oligarchs. Privatizing apartments allowed criminals to pay pensioners for their homes, to be acquired after their deaths, which, in certain extreme instances, the criminals hastened.[7] Such lawlessness explains why a considerable percentage of the Russian population in the 1990s considered the demise of the Union of Soviet Socialist Republics a tragedy, even as people in other parts of the former empire celebrated. No one—no one—misses those years.

Yeltsin survived re-election as Russia was coming undone. When Chechen factions demanded independence, Yeltsin pulverized the Grozny parliament building, prompting terrorist attacks in Moscow. When Yeltsin died in 2007, he left a Gogolian hodgepodge of corrupt anti-corruption and unfree freedoms as his legacy. He had the courage to open up the archives to expose the rot in the system but—being still in the loop, and a product of the loop—added his own name to the files.

To restore order, the FSB (Federal'naya sluzhba bezopasnosti, the Federal Security Service) handpicked Vladimir Putin as the next president. He was the sole candidate who had pledged not to hold Yeltsin answerable for his misdemeanors. The sloe-eyed security service functionary became, for a time, a charismatic, athletic, stabilizing force. The patriarch, Alexei II, blessed his ascent and the restoration of vertical power. In the absence of a Politburo or Central Committee to oversee his actions, Putin had a free hand to execute Chechen rebels and to close casinos. When the oligarch-controlled media criticized his response to the loss of a nuclear submarine, stripping him of his *Übermensch* aura, Putin took the media into his own hands and turned against the oligarchs, liquidating their assets and expelling them from senate building offices. He promoted loyalists from the security services (the FSB and the military intelligence agency) and the police agencies, recentralized the entire law and order apparatus and—according to the exiled political scientist Ekaterina Shulman—has managed to turn Russia into an "empire of fines."[8] The state now disciplines not with prisons but with Kafkaesque administrative harassment.

Putin called the end of the Soviet Union the "greatest geopolitical catastrophe" of the twentieth century.[9] That grievance enfolds a host of others: his hard upbringing as a member of the most Soviet generation (he was born six months before Stalin died); the embarrassing inarticulateness of the Communist Party gerontocracy; the political innocence of Gorbachev; the boycott of the 1980 Moscow Olympics as protest against the Soviet invasion of Afghanistan (though Misha the Bear, the cheerful fuzzy mascot, won the heart of the world all the same). Putin resented that no one had picked up the phone in Moscow when his spy post in Dresden was attacked by protesters on December 5, 1989;[10] resented hyperinflation in the 1990s, which forced him to moonlight as a taxi driver; and resented Ukraine imagining itself as part of Europe rather than as prime Russian real estate. He talks about a path back to greatness and God's plan for the chosen Russian people, which has meant lassoing the liberal press and repressing anyone who would challenge the notion that a strong Russia, a Russia back on the march, is perhaps not the best possible scenario for Muscovites trying to raise a family and live a decent life. Putin started jailing and killing his braver critics, then, appetite whetted, went after influencers and bloggers and canceled the visas of foreign correspondents. In December 2024, he decided to terminate the law rehabilitating those jailed or executed for crimes against the state under Stalin and other Soviet rulers.[11]

I've twice seen Putin speak about culture and Russia's mission to preserve traditional values amid an energetic increase of censorship that includes the doxxing of artists who resist even if only by being who they are.[12] The Federal Service for Supervision of Communications, Information Technology and Mass Media wields a sword against anything LGBTQ+. Oscar Wilde and Stephen King have been yanked from the shelves, so too has an unfinished novel by Dostoevsky about an orphaned girl's relationship with the beautiful daughter of a prince.[13] In 2014, Putin gifted Russians the Sochi Winter Olympics (Misha returned as a plush polar bear) and Crimea, its annexation "the New Year present of their dreams, the island of their childhood."[14] The performance of confiscating the peninsula from Ukraine exceeded anything the opening or closing ceremonies of the games could offer.

That was then, when the president was popular, practicing the right kind of coercion—when oil prices boosted the value of the ruble and financed Moscow's transformation into a showcase capital. Tenements toppled along with crime rates. Swaths of color appeared in the sea of gray. Fashionable new neighborhoods popped up just west of Pushkin and Mayakovsky squares in an enclave called Patriarch's Ponds, where but one pond of the original three remains. Cashmere goats were once bred there, their wool destined for the

Tverskaya Military Parade Rehearsal, May 4, 2015.

Kremlin court, along with fine fish for the patriarch's table. When Peter the Great abolished the patriarchate in 1721, the area reverted to a bog; it wasn't until after the fire of 1812 that the neighborhood was beautified with cobblestone roads and a promenade. The Soviets chopped up the great houses nearby into communal apartments and rechristened the area Pioneer Ponds.[15] Throughout the Cold War, it was laced with intrigue and served as the setting of spy novels and tales of devilry. Now it is a comfortable residential area, expensively, fancily Old European in feel, with cold brew dispensaries, farm-to-table restaurants, and renovated apartments marketed as the "soul of the city" on real estate portals.[16] However, Patriarch's Ponds is not in keeping with the kind of "high-density, high-rise" developments increasingly championed by the current Moscow mayor, Sergey Sobyanin—who, critic Alexei Shchukin points out, isn't exactly trained in architecture. The population is declining, Shchukin adds, and there is no shortage of land, but Sobyanin is following the path of vertical "Asian megacities."[17]

Something similar happened to Gorky Park. "For generations of future communists," the Soviet government told the proletariat back in 1928, "even recreation should be productive." The park boasted a dance hall, a cinema, a "silent corner," and reading rooms where the consciousnesses of dissolute teens would be transformed into reliable cogs of the *partapparat*. H. G. Wells, ever an optimistic futurologist, visited in 1934 and left a note in the visitors' book saying how much he loved it: a place for rebirth, he enthused. Since 2011, the park has been under constant renovation. The rusty recycled rides and shooting ranges with crinkled tin ducks are long gone. So too the gunk atop the boating pond and the sagged fencing around Luna Park. Gorky Park now boasts ping-pong tables, skateboard competitions, *boule lyonnaise,* food trucks, Asian fusion restaurants and French-Italian cafés. Elite consumerism takes the form of a five-star spa, artificial waterfall, and an exclusive pool overlooking the Moskva. Because parks need squirrels, and Gorky Park had none, tassel-eared replacements were imported from southern Siberia with detailed instructions on how to feed them.[18]

Today the population of the greater metropolitan region (the city and satellite towns) exceeds sixteen million well-educated people. Apartments dating from the Stalinist Great Terror in the late 1930s rest atop boutiques selling Prada, while the chicest citizens inhabit condominiums in the "impossible" architectural designs of the 1920s Futurist period. Central Moscow is a theatricalized, *skazochnoye* (fairytale) place. Actual theatrical life is, for connoisseurs with long memories, a shadow of its former self; the shadow lengthens when the theaters are upgraded. The superficial gleam, the bright wrappers covering buildings under renovation, inspire mixed emotions: disappointment, sadness, resentment. The eyes want to see through the artifice to find what was there before.

Russian businesses have replicated and replaced the foreign enterprises that left because of sanctions. Doubtless they will return when the sanctions are lifted, but for now, the government preserves Moscow's capitalist comforts even in the absence of the global brands that Muscovites had long taken for granted. There's a copy of McDonald's named Vkusno—i Tochka (Delicious—Period) and one of Starbucks known as Stars Coffee. The tourist attractions still operate, combining all possible historical figures—pre-imperial, imperial, Soviet—despite the obvious contradictions. A costumed Lenin poses for pictures beside a decked-out boyar. Tsar Nicholas II sometimes joins them, no longer afraid of the Bolshevik firing squad. Near the resplendent Red Square are the refurbished Bolshoi and renovated Hotel Moskva. The hotel's fashionable first floor arcade features a popular midpriced restaurant offering a twenty-first-century version of medieval trading-bazaar fare: plates from Europe, Russia, and Asia. Signs prohibit smoking hookah pipes inside, but patrons partake anyway. The name of the restaurant is Strana kotoroy net, the place that isn't: Neverland. The name suggests desire, illusion, and nostalgia all at once.

In February 2022, Putin invaded Ukraine, partly to keep NATO and the EU away from Russia's borders, partly to indulge his Romanov restoration fantasies and the ideals—nationalist, then pan-Slavic, then Slavic supremacist—that have sometimes ended in disaster. When the "special military operation" failed, and Putin's effort to sell the failure as a triumph likewise faltered, he resorted (as dictators do) to radically increased repressions at home and barbarism on the frontier. "The war is forever," sociologist Grigory Yudin argues, "there are no aims whose fulfillment could end it."[19] Protest the fighting and get sent to the front; ignore the email telling you to report for duty and lose everything. The Russian president used to be good at keeping a balance: manipulating oligarchs into thinking they are manipulating him, keeping the *siloviki* preoccupied with outfoxing one another. But another catastrophe seems nigh—this time with the potential of reducing the globe to nuclear ash. Putin, a student of ultra-nationalist, ultra-Slavophile history, knows that single mistakes, like the accidental tipping over of the kopeck candle, can burn everything down.

His Neverland features a statue of a prince from Kyiv also named Vladimir, who supposedly brought the Christian faith from Constantinople to Moscow. Putin spoke at the statue's unveiling, claiming that his ancient Ukrainian father figure "laid the moral foundation on which our [Russian] lives are still based today. It was this strong moral bearing, solidarity and unity that helped our ancestors to overcome difficulties and win victories for the glory of the fatherland, making it stronger and greater with each generation. . . . Today it is our duty to stand together against contemporary challenges and threats, using our spiritual legacy and our invaluable traditions of unity to go forward and continue our thousand-year history."[20] Going forward might mean going nowhere at all but perpetuating the unbounded rule of the distant and recent past.

Yet somehow the nation is not its government. In 2024, the Georgia-born, self-exiled, London-based Putin critic Boris Akunin (Grigori Chkhartishvili) circulated an excruciating series of interviews with Russian political prisoners. The interviews were conducted over email, through a system called FSIN-*pis'mo* (Federal Penal Service Post), a business farmed out by the government to a private firm. The Kremlin ignored the London samizdat existence of the interviews but authorized online harassment of and prank calls to Akunin. (Thinking he was speaking to Ukrainians, he "sang like a nightingale about Russia needing to be dismembered.")[21] The responses to his questions from the prisoners evince an almost perverse belief that Russia and its political systems are independent of one another. Thus, the Symbolist dream of spiritual renewal persists despite unimaginable material suffering. When asked "What makes you sad?" few of the prisoners stated the obvious: prison. Konstantin Zeltsev, a twenty-year-old convicted of disrupting train schedules and "railway sabotage," answered "lies." Opposition politician Ilya Yashin claimed "meanness and injustice," and Andrey Trofimov, a member of the anti-Putin Freedom of Russia Legion, pointed to the end of the USSR. "The Soviet Union died a natural death (old age has no cure)," he remarked, "but it was still very sad, and at the funeral there were many good things to be said about the deceased." He appended: "I will mourn Russia too (her death will be terrible)."[22] Putin's nemesis Alexei Navalny was interviewed and insisted, as he always did, that no one should be afraid. He remained unbowed even in the foul Arctic Circle prison where, abused, malnourished and, most likely poisoned, he died.

Russia has reductively been called the holy fool among nations, a simpleton speaking the truth, as well as an ideocracy, pursuing ideologies and beliefs that inspired the artists of the Silver Age and their fantasies of transcendence.[23] Moscow's rulers killed in pursuit of an end to all killing; the empire expanded to prevent contraction and curtailed invasion by incorporating invaders into the imperium. Russia cannot be decolonized, taken apart, reduced in size and so humbled, because power of the sort wielded by this state insists on expansion. If the porous borders collapse, then Russia will cease to exist. This process began when Moscow was a small town ruled by brutes. The small town became a big town through the absorption of others, then a regional and imperial capital, then the uncertain metropolis of the present, its ruler looking to the past for the future.

I keep thinking about Vladimir Sharov's fairytale-like novel *The Old Girl*, about a woman in the 1930s who has it all: family, faith in the government, a comfortable apartment with all the conveniences. She loses everything, arbitrarily. Friends stop talking to her; no one picks up the phone when she calls for help. Utterly lost, she searches for a way back to her old life. Then she picks up a book—her own diary—and starts reading it back to front. It's a portal to the past. Time reverses itself in sympathy, and she sparks a trend. The people she knew when she was young join her as apostles longing to reclaim the faith annihilated by the state, returning to the past. They hope she'll look them up, but she leaps over them further back in time to her girlhood, when her faith in God was purest.[24] Perhaps, if the novel were a little longer, she would even find herself dancing around midnight fires, freed from civilization, re-enacting the bacchic rituals closer to the start of it all.

It's fiction, but fiction conspires with fact in the history of Russia and of Moscow as past, present, and future spiral in on one another. The spiral narrows and expands, intensifies and reverberates, one loop added to another. The foundation pits fill in while being dug out. An additional circle of stations is added to the Metro system. The massive church is a heated pool is a church again. The Neglinka flows above- and belowground, flooding Theater Square before and after the Bolshoi Theater is built for the second, third, and fourth time. The melon-sweet snow falls on the Arbat each winter of each year of each decade of each century. Stories of the city and its people resurface to be retold, refashioned, resurrected. The documents might burn, but not the words on them.[25]

Perhaps a reckoning will emerge. Perhaps power might yet burrow under the seven hills surrounding Moscow before it ever came to be, when oarsmen on the river once sought safe harbor for the night. Perhaps death will sit at the stern, not the bow.

ACKNOWLEDGMENTS

Moscow gave me my life's work, which has been rich and full and defined by extremes. I am grateful to everyone I've gotten to know there: archivists, barkeeps, baristas, curators, dancers, diplomats, fixers, guides, historians, musicians, the neighbor next door who hopped between balconies to let me in when I locked myself out, police officers, priests, shopkeepers, writers, Volodya and Natalya, and their cats. My deepest thanks to Princeton University and Stanford University's Hoover Institution for financial backing, and to the scholars who helped me to research and write this book: Maryana Petyaskina, first and foremost, also Caryl Emerson and Chester Dunning, plus Thomas Keenan, Stephen Kotkin, Marina Swoboda, Boris Wolfson, and my brilliant and generous colleagues in Princeton's Slavic and History Departments. I am grateful to Sofia Cipriano and Rachel Glodo for proofreading. My wonderful editor, Emily Cunningham, offered sensitive, discerning, always correct advice on the drafts; I'm honored to have been able to work with her and with her assistant, Tiara Sharma, and the rest of the production team at Knopf. I am indebted, as ever, to Will Lippincott for his counsel, friendship, patience, and trust.

The dedicatee, Elizabeth Bergman, is my life's happiness as is our daughter, Nika. Both are loved more than all the words in all the books.

NOTES

INTRODUCTION

1. Vladimir Mel'nichenko, *Arbat, 9 (fenomen doma v istorii Moskvï arbatskoy)* (Moscow: Stolitsa, 2012), 9–14.

2. *Polnoye sobraniye russkikh letopisey. Tom 12. Letopisnïy sbornik, imenuemïy Patriarsheyu ili Nikonovskoyu letopis'yu*, ed. S. F. Platonov with S. A. Adrianov (St. Petersburg: Tipografiya I. N. Skorokhodova, 1901), 158.

3. Vernadsky Avenue, named after famed geochemist Vladimir Vernadsky (1863–1945).

4. "Blue Dogs Spotted Near Abandoned Factory," *Moscow Times*, February 15, 2021, https://www.themoscowtimes.com/2021/02/12/blue-russian-dogs-spotted-near-abandoned-factory-a72915.

5. Jeffrey Tayler, "A Midsummer Night's Bacchanal in Moscow," *Salon*, July 30, 1998, https://www.salon.com/1998/07/30/feature1_3/.

6. James Verini, "Lost *Exile*," *Vanity Fair*, February 24, 2010, https://www.vanityfair.com/culture/2010/02/exile-201002.

7. The station is associated with a flying club.

CHAPTER 1

1. G. Yu. Ivakin, "Nekropol' tserkvi Spasa na Berestove v Kiyeve i 'pogrebeniye Yuriya Dolgorukogo,'" *Rossiyskaya arkheologiya*, no. 2 (2008): 107–17, esp. 112–13.

2. O. P. Voronova, *V. I. Mukhina* (Moscow: Iskusstvo, 1976), 176. The lone description of Yuri in the historical chronicles is much less flattering: "considerable height, fat, . . . white face, small eyes, a long and crooked big nose, thin beard" (S. A. Golovin, *M. M. Gerasimov: Istoricheskoye naslediye velikogo antropologa* [Blagoveshchensk: BGPU, 2018], 60).

3. A. I. Filyushkin, "Kogda i zachem stali stavit' pamyatniki personazham Drevney Rusi?," *Paleorosiya. Drevnyaya Rus': vo vremeni, v lichnostyakh, v ideyakh* 7 (2017): 386; "Pamyatnik Yuriyu Dolgorukomu," moscowwalks.ru, March 17, 2010, http://moscowwalks.ru/2010/03/17/pamyatnik-yuriyu-dolgorukomu/.

4. Andrzej Poppe, "The Christianization and Ecclesiastical Structure of Kyivan Rus' to 1300," *Harvard Ukrainian Studies* 21, no. 3/4 (December 1997): 349–50.

5. Vladimir Sharov, "Ikona Svyatogo Georgiya Pobedonostsa s kleymami," in *Iskusheniye Revolyutsiyey (Russkaya verkhovnaya vlast')* (Moscow: Arsis, 2009), 96.

6. "Proiskhozhdeniye nazvaniya goroda 'Moskva,'" *Progulki po Moskve,* accessed March 26, 2021, https://liveinmsk.ru/article/proishozdenie-nazvania-moskva.

7. Simon Franklin and Jonathan Shepard, *The Emergence of Rus, 750–1200* (New York: Routledge, 2013), 28.

8. Omeljan Pritsak, "The Origin of Rus'," *Russian Review* 36, no. 3 (July 1977): 250.

9. Oleg Ovsiannikov and Marek Jasinski, "The Two Oldest Shipbuilding Traditions of Kyivan Rus in the Ninth and Tenth Centuries," *Mariner's Mirror* 82, no. 3 (1996): 337. The illustration comes from the *Radziwiłł Chronicle,* a fifteenth-century East Slavonic manuscript copied from a thirteenth-century original.

10. The perception of Slavs as slaves is assessed within different contexts—Slavic, European, Middle Eastern, Ancient, Modern—by Anna Klosowska, "The Etymology of Slave," in Catherine E. Karkov, Anna Klosowska, and Vincent W. J. van Gerven Oei, *Disturbing Times: Medieval Pasts, Reimagined Futures* (Santa Barbara, CA: Punctum Books, 2020), 151–214.

11. My thanks to historian Simon Franklin and linguist Don Ringe for this information, email communications, March 10 and April 3, 2021, respectively.

12. My thanks to linguist Ronald Kim for this information, email communication, April 4, 2021.

13. David B. Miller, "The Many Frontiers of Pre-Mongol Rus'," *Russian History* 19, no. 1/4 (1992): 249.

14. Ivan Zabelin, *Istoriya goroda Moskvï* (Moscow: Tip-litografiya T-va I. N. Kushnerev i Ko., 1905), 5.

15. Nicole Prevost-Logan, "Moscow Reclaims Its Past," *Archeology* 50, no. 4 (July/August 1997): 33; M. G. Rabinovich, "Drevniy tsentr Moskvï," *Voprosï istorii,* no. 3 (1990), http://istorja.ru/articles.html/russia/rabinovich-m-g-drevniy-tsentr-moskvyi-r415/.

16. Franklin and Shepard, *Emergence of Rus,* 336.

17. Ibid., 218. Among the best sources on this subject in English is Alexander M. Schenker, *The Dawn of Slavic: An Introduction to Slavic Philology* (New Haven, CT: Yale University Press, 1995), 165–83. The spoken/written language distinction in Kyivan Rus might or might not fit the definition of diglossia. See A. A. Alekseyev, "Pochemu v Drevney Rusi ne bïlo diglosii," in *Literaturnïy yazïk Drevney Rusi,* ed. A. N. Yel'cheva (Leningrad: Izdatel'stvo Leningradskogo universiteta, 1986), 3–11; and B. A. Uspenskiy, *Kratkiy ocherk istorii russkogo literaturnogo yazïka (XI–XIX vv.)* (Moscow: Gnozis, 1994), 4–8.

18. Franklin and Shepard, *Emergence of Rus,* 220.

19. Zena Harris and Nonna Ryan, "The Inconsistencies of History: Vikings and Rurik," *New Zealand Slavonic Journal* 38 (2004): 119.

20. My thanks to linguist Ilya Magin for this detail, email communication, March 18, 2021.

21. Adam F. Kola, "The Primary Chronicle in Light of World(-)System Theories and Social Constructivism," *Russian History* 44, nos. 2–3 (June 2017): 156.

22. Simon Franklin defines the writing habits of the Rus in *Writing, Society and Culture in Early Rus, c. 950–1300* (Cambridge: Cambridge University Press, 2002), 16–82. Chronicles, decrees, and psalm books are "primary" forms of writing; inscriptions, etchings, and notches on coins, medallions, swords, and tally sticks are "secondary"; graffiti, like the initials scratched onto pots and bricks, is "tertiary."

23. Lyudmila B. Karpenko, "Skazaniye 'O pis'menakh' Chernoriztsa Khrabra kak istochnik izucheniya glagolicheskoy problemï," in *Preslavska knizhovna shkola. Tom 7*, ed. Totyu Totev (Shumen, Bulgaria: Marin Drinov, 2004), 172–82, esp. 178.

24. Franklin, *Writing*, 83–85, 92–93.

25. Barbara W. Tuchman's "law" about perception and reality applies as well to medieval Rus as it does to medieval France, her area of specialty: "The fact of being reported multiplies the apparent extent of any deplorable development by five- to tenfold." (*A Distant Mirror: The Calamitous 14th Century* [New York: Alfred A. Knopf, 1978], xviii).

26. Oleksiy Tolochko, "On 'Nestor the Chronicler,'" *Harvard Ukrainian Studies* 29, no. 1/4 (2007): 31–59. Nestor's name first appears in a late-sixteenth-century copy of the *Primary Chronicle*, but not the copy from which it was made (ibid., 37.) The emotional attachment to his involvement begins with the Russian Empire's official historian Nikolay Karamzin (1766–1826) who declared Nestor "the father of Russian history." "[G]ifted by a curious mind, he listened with attention to the oral legends of ancient times, to the popular historical tales; he saw the monuments, he saw the graves of the princes; he conversed with patricians, with the elders of Kyiv, with travelers, with dwellers of different Rus regions; he read Byzantine chronicles, church notes and thus became the first chronicler of our motherland." (*Istoriya gosudarstva Rossiyskogo*, quoted in ibid., 32).

27. *The Russian Primary Chronicle: Laurentian Text*, ed. and trans. Samuel Hazzard Cross and Olgerd P. Sherbowitz-Wetzor (Cambridge, MA: Mediaeval Academy of America, 1953), 4.

28. The reader might be interested in knowing where these chronicles, created centuries ago in isolated monasteries, are kept. The Academy of Sciences (*Akademiya Nauk*) of the Imperial Russian capital of St. Petersburg maintained oversight of matters related to cultural heritage, including the preservation of ancient historical documents, under the minister of public education Sergey Uvarov (1786–1855). There were no other research institutions in Russia during Uvarov's time, and universities were beginning to be established. The archive of the academy became the home of most of the chronicles, though in the case of the oldest extant version of the *Tale of Bygone Years*, the Laurentian Codex, the situation is somewhat more complicated. Laurence (Lavrentiy), the monk after whom the Codex is named,

is presumed to have worked in a scriptorium in Nizhny Novgorod. He completed the codex in 1377, after which it was transferred to monasteries in Vladimir and Novgorod, where, in 1765, it was copied. This copy ended up in the archive of the academy. The original, in the meantime, was transferred to the governing body (the Holy Synod) of the Orthodox Church in Moscow. In 1811, the codex was presented as a gift to Tsar Alexander I, who placed it in the Russian National Library in St. Petersburg. "Lavrent'yevskaya letopis' 1377 g. Elektronnoye predstavleniye rukopisnogo pamyatnika," Rossiyskoye istoricheskoye obshchestvo, April 9, 2020, https://historyrussia.org/index.php?option=com_content&view=article&layout =edit&id=4199.

29. "Stat'ya Vladimira Putina 'Ob istoricheskom yedinstve russkikh i ukraintsev,'" kremlin.ru, July 12, 2021, http://kremlin.ru/events/president/news/66181.

30. D. S. Likhachev, "Russian Culture in the Modern World," *Russian Social Science Review* 34, no. 1 (1993): 70.

31. The chronicler misread the words of a song, or a Rurik inscription somewhere. The Scandinavian phrase "Rurik sineus truvor" means "Rurik, their houses a trustworthy guardian" or "Rurik and his people, trustworthy guardians." Andrey Chernov, "Proshchaniye s Sineusom i Truvorom," *nestoriana,* September 5, 2017, https:// nestoriana.wordpress.com/2017/09/05/riurik_bez_bratiev/.

32. Harris and Ryan, "Inconsistencies," 123: "According to the Yakimov Chronicle [lost to us but referenced by the eighteenth-century historian Vasiliy Tatishchev], Rurik and his cousins on his mother's side belonged to an ancient ruling Slav dynasty of Novgorod and thus were the grandsons of Gostomysl [a legendary ninth-century ruler of Novgorod]."

33. Franklin and Shepard, *Emergence of Rus,* 39.

34. Ibid., 33.

35. Ibid., 97–98.

36. "V obrashchenii Putina nashli frazu iz vïstupleniya advokata vremen Rossiyskoy imperii," *lenta.ru,* April 8, 2020, https://lenta.ru/news/2020/04/08/speech/.

37. Franklin and Shepard, *Emergence of Rus,* 117.

38. The title of grand prince, which has Byzantine origins, is used by historians to identify the senior and most powerful Rurik prince in each of the Rus principalities, Kyiv first and foremost. According to the chronicles, the first ruler to explicitly adopt the title for himself was one of Yuri Dolgorukiy's sons, Vsevolod the Big Nest ("big family," 1154–1212), who spent his childhood in cosmopolitan surroundings in Constantinople before taking charge of the northern principality of Vladimir-Suzdal. As cities outside of Kyiv increased their might, the title of grand prince was used to designate regional hegemony and seniority. The rulers of Moscow began referring to themselves as grand princes in the later fourteenth century, and as the future Russian capital increased in size and significance, those rulers came to monopolize the title, sometimes adding "of all Rus" to it. See Andrzej Poppe, "Words That Serve the Authority: On the Title of 'Grand Prince' in Kievan Rus," *Acta Poloniae Historica* 60 (1989): 159–84.

39. Franklin and Shepard, *Emergence of Rus,* 107.

40. Barbara Evans Clements, *A History of Women in Russia* (Bloomington: Indiana University Press, 2012), 4, defines the tribute-paying system roughly as follows: "The rural folk of the Rus confederation [Kyivan Rus] were free to run their own lives so long as they paid their taxes. They could even dodge that obligation by relocating to places beyond the reach of the warriors. There were no local landlords adjudicating disputes and managing agriculture, as in Western Europe, because Rus warriors, true to their Viking roots, spent most of their time at war or on trading expeditions. The farmers only saw them or their representatives once a year or so, when they came around to collect taxes, paid mostly in furs and honey. The rest of the time the men in armor left the peasants alone."

41. B. A. Rïbakov, "Vosstaniye drevlyan. Ubiystvo Igorya," Istoriya.RF, accessed May 21, 2025, https://histrf.ru/read/articles/vosstaniie-drievlian-ubiistvo-ighoria-event.

42. *Polnoye sobraniye russkikh letopisey. Tom 2. Ipat'yevskaya letopis'*, ed. A. A. Shakhmatov (St. Petersburg: Tipografiya M. A. Aleksandrova, 1908), 35; *Pamyatniki literaturï Drevney Rusi. XI—nachalo XII veka*, ed. D. S. Likhachyov (Moscow: Khudozhestvennaya literatura, 1978), 74–75.

43. Clements, *A History of Women*, 7.

44. Franklin and Shepard, *Emergence of Rus*, 143.

45. Dan Shapira, "So, Who Were the Khazars?," *Tablet*, January 28, 2021, https://www.tabletmag.com/sections/history/articles/history-detective-shapira-khazars.

46. L. A. Magnus, *The Heroic Ballads of Russia* (New York: E. P. Dutton & Co., 1921), 4, 17–18.

47. Jonathan Shepard, "Marriages Towards the Millennium," in *Byzantinum in the Year 1000*, ed. Paul Magdalino (Leiden and Boston: Brill, 2003), 24.

48. John Fennell, *A History of the Russian Church to 1448* (New York: Longman, 1995), 78.

49. This tale recalls the *Book of the Khazars*, Judah ha-Levi's description of the conversion of the Khazar king to Judaism (after assessing other religions).

50. It is assumed that one of Vladimir's aims in initiating war with Byzantium was to assert Rus dominance in Eastern Europe. Still, Rus and Arabic sources indicate that Vladimir's campaign was also motivated by an agreement to provide assistance to the co-emperors Basil II and Constantine VIII in suppressing a rebellion led by Byzantine general Bardas Phokas, which broke out in 986 (Mikhaíl Psell [Michael Psellos], *Khronografiya. Kratkaya istoriya*, trans. Ya. N. Lyubarskiy [St. Petersburg: Aleteyya, 2003], 95).

51. *Polnoye sobraniye russkikh letopisey. Tom 2*, 72; *Pamyatniki literaturï Drevney Rusi. XI—nachalo XII veka*, 133, 159–60.

52. Fennell, *History of the Russian Church*, 40, 43.

53. Poppe, "Christianization," 338–41.

54. Fennell, *History of the Russian Church*, 82–83. The hoarding story comes from a 1071 entry in the *Primary Chronicle*.

55. Franklin and Shepard, *Emergence of Rus*, 190–91.

56. Ibid., 185.

57. Ibid., 188–89. I make reference to Nestor's *Lesson Concerning the Life and Murder of*

the Blessed Passion-Bearers Boris and Gleb (*Chteniye o zhitii i poglubenii blazhenuyu strastoterpiyu Borisa i Gleba*) and the anonymous *Tale and Passion and Encomium of the Holy Martyrs Boris and Gleb* (*Skazaniye, i strast', i pokhvala, svyatuyu mucheniku Borisa i Gleba*), in D. I. Abramovich, *Zhitiya svyatïkh muchenikov Borisa i Gleba i sluzhbï im* (Petrograd: Tipografiya Imperatorskoy Akademii Nauk, 1916), 1–66.

58. Fennell, *History of the Russian Church*, 11.

59. Alan Timberlake, "The Recovery Narrative of Gleb," *Harvard Ukrainian Studies* 28, nos. 1–4 (2006): 329; Franklin A. Sciacca, "In Imitation of Christ: Boris and Gleb and the Ritual Consecration of the Russian Land," *Slavic Review* 49, no. 2 (Summer 1990): 253–60.

60. "Sadko the rich trader" (*Sadko bogatoy gost'*), included in *Drevniye rossiyskiye Stikhotvoreniya, sobrannïye Kirsheyu Danilovïm* (Moscow: Tipografiya Simyona Selivanovskogo, 1818), 266–74.

61. The "Song of the Varangian Guest" (*Pesnya Varyazhskogo gostya*), from Nikolay Rimsky-Korsakov's 1898 opera-bïlina (epic tale) *Sadko*.

62. Mykola Andrusiak and A. Mykytiak, "Kings of Kyiv and Galicia (On the Occasion of the 700th Anniversary of the Coronation of Danilo Romanovich)," *Slavonic and East European Review* 33, no. 81 (1955): 344.

63. *Polnoye sobraniye russkikh letopisey. Tom 2*, 92; *Pamyatniki literaturï Drevney Rusi. XI—nachalo XII veka*, 159–60.

64. Sharov, "Ikona," 92.

65. Information in this paragraph is from Franklin and Shepard, *Emergence of Rus*, 217–25, 235.

66. A. N. Nasonov, ed., *Novgorodskaya pervaya letopis' starshego i mladshego izvodov* (Moscow and Leningrad: Izdatel'stvo Akademii Nauk SSSR, 1970), 538; *Polnoye sobraniye russkikh letopisey. Tom 5. Pskovskiye i Sofïyskiye letopisi* (St. Petersburg: Eduard Prats, 1851), 136. The earliest known book from Rus, a Gospel lectionary, was fashioned in 1056–57 at the order of the governor of Novgorod. See Simon Franklin, "Dirty Old Books," in *Picturing Russia: Explorations in Visual Culture*, ed. Valerie A. Kivelson and Joan Neuberger (New Haven, CT: Yale University Press, 2008), 12.

67. Information and the quotation in this paragraph are from Franklin, *Writing*, 36–37.

68. Jos Schaeken, "Comments on Birchbark Documents Found in the Twenty-First Century," *Russian Linguistics* 41, no. 2 (2017): 124–25. The corpus (both the birchbark documents and ancient Russian inscriptions on Novgorod and Kyiv churches) is expertly categorized and deciphered by V. L. Yanin, A. A. Zaliznyak, and A. A. Gippius, *Novgorodskiye gramotï na bereste. Iz raskopok 1997–2000 godov* (Moscow: Russkiye slovari, 2004).

69. Gramota No. 203, *Drevnerusskiye berestal'nïye gramotï*, accessed March 12, 2021, http://gramoty.ru/birchbark/document/show/novgorod/203/.

70. Gramota No. 377, *Drevnerusskiye berestal'nïye gramotï*, accessed March 12, 2021, http://gramoty.ru/birchbark/document/show/novgorod/377/.

71. Franklin and Shepard, *Emergence of Rus*, 302.

72. *Pamyatniki literaturï Drevney Rusi. XI–nachalo XII veka*, 210.

73. He is associated with one of the most precious treasures of the Moscow Kremlin

treasury, the Cap or Crown of Monomakh, supposedly given to him by the Byzantine emperor in recognition of his achievements. The emperor Constantine IX Monomachos died in 1055 when Vladimir II Monomakh was two, however, and the oldest pieces of the Cap of Monomakh are from the thirteenth century and of Central Asian Mongol origin. Nancy Shields Kollmann, "The Cap of Monomakh," in *Picturing Russia*, ed. Kivelson and Neuberger, 38–41.

74. *Pamyatniki literaturï Drevney Rusi. XI–nachalo XII veka,* 407.

75. The Hypatian Codex has Yuri's older brother Vyacheslav saying to him, "I am your senior, not by a little but by a lot: I had already grown a beard when you were born." Yuri answered: "You are in the right when you say so. You have been like a father to me." Vyacheslav is thought to have been born in 1083, and would have begun to show a beard around age seventeen, which means Yuri came into the world sometime between 1095 and 1100. He must have born in the spring, because his saint's day falls on April 23 and the rule in Kyivan Rus was that a baby had to be baptized within forty days of birth. V. A. Kuchkin, "Istoricheskiye portretï. Yuriy Dolgorukiy," *Voprosï istorii,* no. 10 (October 1996): 36.

76. Mikhaíl Konstantinovich Yuraslav, "Vengriya i russkiye knyazhestva v XII veke" (Dissertatsiya na soiskaniye uchyonoy stepeni doktora istoricheskikh nauk, Institut rossiyskoy istorii RAN [PhD thesis, Institute of Russian History of the Russian Academy of Sciences], 2017), 78.

77. Another, better respected Russian historian of the imperial era, Nikolay Karamzin (1766–1826), identified a significant mistake in Tatishchev's transcription and embellishment of his sources. It had Yuri playing or hearing music and drinking with his lover. The phrase "na skomoni" in the transcription seemed to refer to a Hungarian musical instrument, but the transcription, Karamzin deduced, should have been "komenom ikh," referencing the horses Hungarians rode in an equestrian tournament in Kyiv in 1151. Tatishchev mapped a detail from a knightly contest in Kyiv onto his tale of Yuri's activities near Suzdal in 1147. Ibid., 79.

78. Vasiliy Nikitich Tatishchev, *Istoriya rossiyskaya s samïkh drevneyshikh vremen. Kniga vtoraya* (Moscow: Imperatorskiy Moskovskiy Universitet, 1773), 300. The tale is elaborated in *Boyarin Kuchka ili Istoricheskaya povest' o knyaze Yurii Dolgorukom i otkuda vzyalas' pervoprestol'naya Moskva* (Moscow: Tovarishchestvo I. D. Sïtina, 1891).

79. *Polnoye sobraniye russkikh letopisey. Tom 2,* 236.

80. V. A. Kuchkin, "Rostovskaya zemlya, Suzdal'skoye i Vladimirskoye knyazhestva v XI–pervoy treti XIII v.," *Rossiyskaya istoriya,* no. 4 (2019): 97–98. Information in the following paragraphs is from Kuchkin, "Istoricheskiye portretï," 51–54.

81. Rabinovich, "Drevniy tsentr."

CHAPTER 2

1. Ye. M. Lunyak, "Batïyevo nashestviye v otobrazhenii frantsuzskikh srednevekovïkh avtorov," *Zolotoordïnskoye obozreniye* 9, no. 1 (2021): 37. Thevet (1502–90) is repeating what he heard from others; he didn't see the destruction himself.

2. The question is taken up by Rafael' Bezertinov, "Kto takiye tatarï i mongolï?," Mezhdunarodnïy Fond Issledovaniya Tengri, April 11, 2015, https://tengrifund.ru/kto-takie-tatary-i-mongoly.html.

3. John Randolph, "Communication and Obligation: The Postal System of the Russian Empire, 1700–1850," in *Information and Empire: Mechanisms of Communication in Russia, 1600–1850,* ed. Simon Franklin and Katherine Bowers (Cambridge, UK: Open Book Publishers, 2017), 158, 161.

4. These accounts are from John Masson Smith, Jr., "Dietary Decadence and Dynastic Decline in the Mongol Empire," *Journal of Asian History* 34, no. 1 (2000): 35–52.

5. Mirko Sardelić, "John of Plano Carpini vs Simon of Saint-Quentin: 13th-Century Emotions in the Eurasian Steppe," *Golden Horde Review* 5, no. 3 (2017): 502.

6. Lunyak, "Batïyevo nashestviye," 30–31.

7. Richard Hakluyt, *The Texts and Versions of John de Plano Carpini and William de Rubruquis* (London: Hakluyt Society, 1903), 115–16. Carpine is also offended by Tibetans for being "wont to eat their own parents" (ibid., 232).

8. Ibid., 192, 194.

9. Ibid., 191.

10. Lunyak, "Batïyevo nashestviye," 31; Smith, "Dietary Decadence," 38.

11. V. A. Ivanov, "Khimerï i mirazhi Zolotoy ordï," *Zolotoordïnskoye obozreniye* 2, no. 1 (2014): 195.

12. Frank McLynn, *Genghis Khan: His Conquests, His Empire, His Legacy* (Boston: Da Capo Press, 2015), 19, Kindle; quoting Amir Khosrow (1253–1324).

13. Ibid.; quoting Grigor Akanc (ca. 1250–1335).

14. Hakluyt, *Texts and Versions,* 196.

15. Atâ-Malek Juvayni (1226–83), *Tārīkh-i Jahān-gushā* (The History of the World Conqueror, 1260); Rashīd al-Dīn (1247–1318), *Jāmiʿ al-tawārīkh* (Compendium of Chronicles, 1316); Serāj-al-Din Jowzjāni (1193–after 1266), *Ṭabaqāt-e nāṣeri* (The Nāṣerean Tables, 1260).

16. Ewa Nowicka-Rusek and Ayur Zhanaev, "The Image of Genghis Khan in Contemporary Buryat Nation Building," *Polish Sociological Review* 187, no. 3 (2014): 382–84.

17. V. V. Tishin, "Yeshcho raz o soderzhanii termina *orda* i kategoriyakh 'Zolotaya Orda,' 'Belaya Orda,' 'Sinyaya Orda,'" *Zolotoordïnskoye obozreniye* 7, no. 2 (2019): 306. Marie Favereau, in *The Horde: How the Mongols Changed the World* (Cambridge, MA: Harvard University Press, 2021), 1–2, 17, Kindle, succinctly explains how the Horde came to be: Genghis Khan's chief heir, Jochi, fell out with his father and lost his priority of access to the throne. After his death, Jochi's sons Batu and Orda relocated to the Ural-Volga region and established their own administration, "ulus Jochi," aka the Golden Horde. Batu controlled the eastern "blue" wing of the Horde, and his brother the western, "white" wing.

18. Soviet ruler Iosif Dzhugashvili's adopted surname, Stalin, means "made of steel," but there's no connection to Temüjin. Stalin was familiar with ancient Georgian and Persian rulers, not Mongols, around the time (1912) he chose the name for himself.

19. *The Secret History of the Mongols,* trans. Francis Woodman Cleaves (Cambridge, MA: Harvard University Press, 1982), 23.

20. Ibid., 18.

21. Ibid., 37, 46–47.

22. René Grousset, *The Empire of the Steppes: A History of Central Asia,* trans. Naomi Walford (New Brunswick, NJ: Rutgers University Press, 1970), 217.

23. Timothy May, *The Mongols* (Leeds, UK: Arc Humanities Press, 2019), 12.

24. Hakluyt, *Texts and Versions,* 188. The plausibility of "the nomadic tent mounted on a cart" is challenged by Michael Genvers and Wayne A. Schlepp, "Felt and 'Tent Carts' in 'The Secret History of the Mongols,'" *Journal of the Royal Asiatic Society* 7, no. 1 (1997): 93–116.

25. McLynn, *Genghis Khan,* 302.

26. Tao-Chung Yao, "Ch'iu Ch'u-chi and Chinggis Khan," *Harvard Journal of Asiatic Studies* 46, no. 1 (June 1986): 201, 206.

27. Ibid., 202, 211–13, 216.

28. Grousset, *Empire of the Steppes,* 248.

29. John Travis, "Genghis Khan's Legacy?," *Science News* 163, no. 6 (February 8, 2003): 91.

30. The following information is from J. M. Rogers, "Recent Archaeological Work on the Golden Horde," *Bulletin of the Asia Institute* 14 (2000): 135–46.

31. Smith, "Dietary Decadence," 42–43.

32. Ivanov, "Khimerï," 198.

33. Rogers, "Recent Archaeological Work," 135.

34. Roman Hautala, "Russian Chronicles on the Submission of the Kyivan Rus' to the Mongol Empire," *Golden Horde Review* 1, no. 1 (2013): 208–9.

35. Apocalyptic descriptions of the Mongol incursions dominate the *Novgorod First Chronicle,* which partly (for ninety-four years) overlaps with the *Primary Chronicle.* The *Novgorod First Chronicle* begins in 1016 and concludes in 1471, in the aftermath of the 1453 capture of the Byzantine capital of Constantinople by the Ottomans, which monastic scribes represented as the end of the world. Arnold A. Lelis, "The View from the Northwest: The Chronicle of Novgorod as the Mirror of Local Experience of Rus' History, 1016–1333," *Russian History* 32, no. 3/4 (Fall/Winter 2005): 389–90.

36. *Polnoye sobraniye russkikh letopisey. Tom 3. Novgorodskaya pervaya letopis' starshego i mladshego izvodov,* ed. A. N. Nasonov (Moscow and Leningrad: Izdatel'stvo Akademii Nauk, 1950), 74–76.

37. Serge A. Zenkovsky, ed., *Medieval Russia's Epics, Chronicles, and Tales* (New York: E. P. Dutton, 1974), 198–207.

38. *Polnoye sobraniye russkikh letopisey. Tom 2. Ipat'yevskaya letopis',* ed. A. A. Shakhmatov (St. Petersburg: Tipografiya M. A. Aleksandrova, 1908), 75.

39. Daniel C. Waugh, "The 'Owl of Misfortune' or the 'Phoenix of Prosperity'? Rethinking the Impact of the Mongols," *Journal of Eurasian Studies* 8, no. 1 (2017): 16–19.

40. Stephen G. Haw, "The Mongol Empire—The First 'Gunpowder' Empire?," *Journal of the Royal Asiatic Society* 23, no. 3 (July 2013): 441–69.

41. Rashīd al-Dīn, *The Successors of Genghis Khan,* trans. John Andrew Boyle (New York: Columbia University Press, 1971), 59.

42. A. D. Gorskiy, "K voprosu ob oborone Moskvï," in *Vostochnaya Yevropa v drevnosti i srednevekov'ye,* ed. L. V. Cherepnin (Moscow: Nauka, 1978), 178; quoting an addition to the late-fifteenth-century *Nikanor Chronicle* in the hand of Johann Paus (1670–1735).

43. Ibid., 176; quoting the Laurentian Codex.

44. Information and quotations in this paragraph and the next are from *Polnoye sobraniye russkikh letopisey. Tom 1. Lavrent'yevskaya letopis',* ed. I. F. Karskiy (Leningrad: Izdatel'stvo Akademii Nauk SSSR, 1926–28), 360–61.

45. *Polnoye sobraniye russkikh letopisey. Tom 2. Gustinskaya letopis',* ed. A. F. Bïchkov (St. Petersburg: Tipografiya Eduarda Pratsa, 1843), 339; John Fennell, *The Crisis of Medieval Russia, 1200–1304* (New York: Routledge, 2014), 82.

46. Fennell, *Crisis,* 84–85.

47. Michael F. Hamm, *Kyiv: A Portrait, 1800–1917* (Princeton, NJ: Princeton University Press, 1993), 5.

48. Hakluyt, *Texts and Versions,* 122.

49. Information in this paragraph and the next is from M. K. Karger, *Drevniy Kiyev: Ocherki po istorii material'noy kul'turï drevnerusskogo goroda. Tom 1* (Moscow and Leningrad: Izdatel'stvo AN SSSR, 1958), 496–508; and Denis Sinor, "The Mongols in the West," *Journal of Asian History* 33, no. 1 (1999): 11.

50. John Fennell, *A History of the Russian Church to 1448* (New York: Longman, 1995), 133.

51. "Pochemu Aleksandr—Nevskiy? On imeyet otnosheniye k Moskve? A k FSB? Stïdnïye voprosï o knyaze, kotoromu mogli postavit' pamyatnik na Lubyanke (no, vidimo, ne postavyat)," Meduza.io, February 27, 2021, https://meduza.io/feature/2021/02/28/pochemu-aleksandr-nevskiy-on-imeet-otnoshenie-k-moskve-a-k-fsb.

52. "V Kremle podgotovili novuyu metodichku o tom, kak propaganda dolzhna rasskazïvat' o voyne," Meduza.io, August 1, 2022, https://meduza.io/feature/2022/08/01/v-kremle-podgotovili-novuyu-metodichku-o-tom-kak-propaganda-dolzhna-rasskazyvat-o-voyne-my-ee-prochitali.

53. D. A. Lyapin, "O chom molilsya Aleksandr Nevskiy: evolyutsiya zhitiynogo syuzheta predïstorii Nevskoy bitvï," *Paleorosiya. Drevnyaya Rus': vo vremeni, v lichnostyakh, v ideyakh,* no. 1 (2020): 121.

54. Donald Ostrowski, "Alexander Nevskii's 'Battle on the Ice': The Creation of a Legend," *Russian History* 33, no. 2/4 (2006): 289–312, esp. 292.

55. Hautala, "Russian Chronicles," 212, 214–15.

56. Rimma Bikmukhametova, "In Russia, 'Horde' Blockbuster Drawing Tatar Objections," Radio Free Europe, September 19, 2012, https://www.rferl.org/a/the-horde-film-tatarstan-stereotypes-russia/24713352.html.

57. He hasn't rested in peace, however; his remains have been relocated several times for political reasons. M. V. Shkarovskiy, "Sud'ba moshchey svyatogo knyazya Aleksandra Nevskogo v XVIII–XX vekakh," *Paleorosiya. Drevnyaya Rus': vo vremeni, v lichnostyakh, v ideyakh,* no. 1 (2020): 247–55.

58. The confusion relates to Nevsky's brother Mikhaíl the Brave, the actual overseer of Moscow. Mikhaíl left behind no heirs, and so Moscow became escheat, falling under the control of Nevsky's appanage Vladimir-Suzdal. Nevsky passed Moscow on to Daniil, his fourth son.

59. His biography is provided in *Three Byzantine Saints: Contemporary Biographies of St. Daniel the Stylite, St. Theodore of Sykeon and St. John the Almsgiver*, ed. and trans. Elizabeth Dawes and Norman H. Baynes (Crestwood, NY: SVS Press, 1977), 7–71.

60. Ibid., 68–69.

61. V. A. Kuchkin, "Pervïy moskovskiy knyaz' Daniil Aleksandrovich," *Otechestvennaya istoriya*, no. 1 (1995): 93.

62. The following information about Daniil of Moscow is from Kuchkin, "Pervïy mos-kovskiy knyaz'," 93–107; and I. Ye. Zabelin, *Istoriya goroda Moskvï: Neizdannïye trudï* (Moscow: Izdatel'stvo im. Sabashnikovïkh, 2004), 29–37.

63. Mikhaíl Ivanovich Il'inskiy, *Opït istoricheskago opisaniya o nachale goroda Moskvï, kak i po kakim prichinam ona osnovalas', kem i kogda prestol velikoknyazheskiy tuda perenesen; i ot chego sey gorod poluchil togda svoye vozvïsheniye* (Moscow: Tipografiya A. Reshetnikova, 1795), 8.

64. The cloister, which also functioned as a citadel, was relocated in 1330, leaving only Daniil's grave on the original site. Through the centuries, the cloister suffered numerous indignities: fire, theft, looting of relics, and, in the Soviet period, removal of eighteen bells. (They were sold to Harvard University.) After the Soviet Union collapsed, the Orthodox Church reclaimed the monastic complex named after Daniil, which now houses the official residence of the patriarch of Moscow. In 2008, after protracted negotiations, the bells came back home.

65. See Mikhaíl Aleksandrovich Nesin, "Novgorodskiye tïsyatskiye v 1410-x-1420-x gg.," *Istoricheskaya i sotsial'no-obrazovatel'naya mïsl'* 6, no. 2 (2014): 129–31.

66. For diplomatic purposes, several natural or adopted daughters of the Byzantine emperor and other members of the imperial clan became Mongol brides. Maria Palaiologina (d. after 1287), another illegitimate daughter of Michael VIII Palaeolo-gus, married into a khanate and founded a church in Constantinople called Panagia Mouchliotissa: The Church of Our Most Holy Lady of the Mongols. My thanks to historian Teresa Shawcross for this information, email communication, July 23, 2021.

67. *Polnoye sobraniye russkikh letopisey. Tom 18. Simeonovskaya letopis'*, ed. A. Ye. Presnyakov (St. Petersburg: Tipografiya M. A. Aleksandrova, 1913), 78; Kuchkin, "Pervïy moskovskiy knyaz'," 96.

68. Favereau, *Horde*, 226.

69. The name is sometimes translated as "Chinatown," but there is nothing Chinese about Kitai-gorod—though perhaps, as one of the contributors to https://ru.wikipedia.org/wiki/Китай-город offers, the eastern fabrics bartered there gave the area a Chinese association. *Kitai*, the website continues, might derive from *kita*, an obsolete word for something braided or bundled, like the stakes used to make fences. In 1535, a stone wall strong enough to support gun carriages was built around the neighborhood; before that it had been defended by a moat and—

perhaps—fencing. Kitai/Kita might also be related to the Turkic word for "fortress" or the Tatar word for "middle," denoting the center of the city. Or, as Igor' Kondrat'yev suggests, it may come from the Latin words *cita urbs*, fast (fast-built) city. *Cita* would have been pronounced *kita* by Italian architects employed in Moscow ("Belïy Tsaryov gorod," Arkhnadzor, March 12, 2008, http://www.archnadzor .ru/2008/03/12/bely-j-tsaryov-gorod/).

70. Soviet ethnographer Pyotr Miller, among others, lamented the deficit of archeological research. "Moscow," Miller wrote in an unpublished article from 1934, "has never been a place where archaeologists have aspired to do their field work, and for the entire rather long life of our various archaeological organizations, of the thousands of expeditions sent each summer to Karelia, Siberia, the Caucasus, Crimea, and other more or less distant places, not one of them went to Moscow. It is as difficult to find an archaeologist in Moscow in the summer as, say, a fresh cucumber in Solovki [far northern Russia] in February." Otdel pis'mennïy istochnikov | Gosudarstvennïy istoricheskiy muzey f. 134, d. 151 [P. N. Miller, "Raskopki v Moskve," 1934 g.].

CHAPTER 3

1. Ernest Rehan, "Qu'est-ce qu'une nation?" (1882), Digithèque de matériaux juridiques et politiques, accessed November 26, 2024, https://mjp.univ-perp.fr/ textes/renan1882.htm.

2. Robert O. Crummey, *The Formation of Muscovy, 1304–1613* (Abingdon, UK: Routledge, 2013), 31, Kindle.

3. Nikolay Mikhaylovich Karamzin, *Istoriya gosudarstva Rossiyskogo. Tom IV* (St. Petersburg: Tipografiya N. Grecha, 1819), 241; Catherine Merridale, *Red Fortress: History and Illusion in the Kremlin* (New York: Metropolitan Books, 2013), 30–31.

4. John Fennell, "Princely Executions in the Horde, 1308–1339," *Forschungen zur Osteuropaischen Geschichte* 38 (1988): 12.

5. "Zhitiye Mikhaíla Yaroslavicha Tverskogo (perevod)," *Drevnerusskaya literatura,* accessed July 26, 2021, http://drevne-rus-lit.niv.ru/drevne-rus-lit/text/zhitie -mihaila-tverskogo/zhitie-mihaila-tverskogo.htm.

6. The Imperial Russian economist Andrey Zablotskiy-Desyatovskiy (1808–81) theorized that the invasion of the Mongol-Tatars destroyed the "clan principle in interprincely relations," because the "tribal calculations of the princes were alien to the khans," who found it more desirable to deal with a single tribute-payer. "By his obsequiousness, one of the poorest and weakest princes, Ivan I of Moscow, achieved in 1330 the title of Grand Prince, which he passed on to his son, and which eventually became associated with the Moscow princely family." Ivan and his descendants enriched themselves through their obeisance, and learned that ancestry was less important than financial, "material" power. Rossiyskiy gosudarstvennïy istoricheskiy arkhiv (RGIA) f. 940, op. 1, d. 296 [A. P. Zablotskiy-Desyatovskiy, "Istoricheskiy ocherk russkikh obshchin ot drevneyshikh vremen do kontsa XVII stoletiya"],

ll. 29–30. This is one of several examples of amateur histories being produced by statesmen at a time when history, like law and economics, was not considered a discipline. Most such texts are schematic and legalistic, and express concern for the state, not people or governance or institutions.

7. P. G. Gaydukov, "Katalog imennïye den'gi velikogo knyazya Dmitriya Ivanovicha Donskogo (1359–1389)," *poludenga.ru,* accessed August 10, 2021, http://www .poludenga.ru/Donskoi/katd.html.

8. Ivan Zabelin, *Domashniy bït russkago naroda v XVI i XVII st. T. 1. Domashniy bït tsarey v XVI i XVII st.* (Moscow: Tovarishchestvo tipografii A. I. Mamontova, 1895), 14. In his will, Ivan itemizes all that he had accumulated and intended to keep in the family. Moscow was to be shared by his sons. He gave his oldest son, Semyon, the towns of Mozhaysk and Kolomna, their *volosts* (peasant districts), and eighteen other settlements and territories, plus "four gold chains, three gold belts, two gold cups with pearls, a gold saucer with pearls and gems, and two large plaques of gold. Of the silverware I give him three dishes." To his second-oldest son, also named Ivan, he willed thirteen territories, nine villages, assorted gold and silver goblets and platters, and a "heart-shaped gold belt." He gave his third son, Andrey, eleven territories, gold cups, a belt with pearls of Italian design, a "khan belt," "two gold charms," and "two small gold ladles." Ivan's daughters got the dregs: necklaces, rings, assorted baubles, a couple of sable pelts.

He also gave his three sons the patrimonial emblem authorizing the collection of border customs along with "quitrents" (a kind of rent paid by peasant house-holds, often in foods like honey) and the duties collected on goods shipped by land and water. Should the Mongols (Tatars) annex any of his holdings, he explained, "then you, my sons and my princess must redistribute the volosts anew without consideration of those the Mongols have confiscated." He willed the silver ingots in his vault to the Church along with his finer clothes. His herds, flocks, the villages he owned, and those held with the metropolitan also went to his sons. Ivan permitted his second wife, Princess Ulyana, to keep the village she had inherited from her father along with one he had recently bought for her. He willed three other villages to the Church in his memory. "Whosoever deviates from what is written in this will is a criminal before God," he concluded. Rossiyskiy gosudarstvennïy arkhiv drevnikh aktov (RGADA) f. 135 (drevlekhranilishche), op. 1, d. 14. The circa 1339 will exists in two versions, the second, slightly longer one is consulted here. Both are reproduced in *Dukhovnïye i dogovornïye gramotï velikikh i udel'nïkh knyazey XIV– XVI vv.,* ed. L. V. Cherepnin (Moscow and Leningrad: Izdatel'stvo Akademii Nauk SSSR, 1950), 7–11.

9. Karamzin, *Istoriya gosudarstva Rossiyskogo. Tom IV,* 240–42.

10. RGIA f. 940, op. 1, d. 296, ll. 29–30.

11. P. I. Gaydenko, "Nasiliye tatar nad metropolitan Maksimom i razgrableniye Kiyeva v 1299 g.: prichinï, obstoyatel'stva i posledstviya sobïtiy, kotorïkh 'ne bïlo,' " *Zoloto-ordïnskoye obozreniye* 9, no. 1 (2021): 76–89.

12. It used to be thought that the khan's promise to leave the metropolitan alone—

not interfere in his affairs—survived, but the document in question is a sixteenth-century forgery. P. P. Sokolov, "Podlozhnïy yarlïk khana Uzbeka mitropolitu Petru," *Rossiyskiy istoricheskiy zhurnal* 5 (1918): 70–85.

13. Syvatitel' Pyotr, mitropolit Moskovskiy i vseya Rusi (Saint Peter, Metropolitan of Moscow and All Russia), Poucheniye igumenam, popam i diakonam (Instructions for abbots, priests, and deacons), *azbuka.ru,* accessed July 24, 2021, https://azbyka .ru/otechnik/Petr_Moskovskij/pouchenie-igumenam-popam-i-diakonam/.

14. John Fennell, *A History of the Russian Church to 1448* (New York: Longman, 1995), 134–36; V. A. Kuchkin, " 'Skazaniye o smerti mitropolita Pyotra,' " in *Trudï Otdela drevnerusskoy literaturï. Tom 18,* ed. Ya. S. Lur'ye (Moscow and Leningrad: Izdatel'stvo Akademii Nauk SSSR, 1962), 59–79.

15. Ivan Zabelin, *Istoriya goroda Moskvï* (Moscow: Tip-litografiya T-va I. N. Kushnerev i Ko., 1905), 76.

16. OPl GIM f. 440, d. 191, l. 1 ob.–2. [I. Ye. Zabelin, "Proizshestviya, sluchivshiesya v Moskve," 1830s–early 1840s]; Zabelin, *Istoriya goroda Moskvï,* 80–81.

17. D. V. Puzanov, "Myortvïye v gorode: o mnogoobrazii interpretatsiy odnogo syuzheta iz Povesti vremennïkh let," *Paleorosiya. Drevnyaya Rus': vo vremeni, v lichnostyakh, v ideyakh,* no. 1 (2023): 20.

18. The Gospel According to Matthew 20:16.

19. B. J. Hinnebusch and D. L. Erickson, "*Yersinia pestis* Biofilm in the Flea Vector and Its Role in the Transmission of Plague," PubMed Central, July 30, 2013, https:// www.ncbi.nlm.nih.gov/pmc/articles/PMC3727414/pdf/nihms489972.pdf.

20. Alina Repina, "Skromnoye obonyaniye stolichnoy burzhuazii: Kak pakhla Moskva v proshlom i chem pakhnet teper'," *gazeta.ru,* July 26, 2015, https://www.gazeta.ru/ social/2015/07/24/7655757.shtml?updated.

21. Medieval European doctors instead advised washing in vinegar and rosewater or, in lieu of bathing, grinding up an emerald and imbibing it with wine. There is no record of this advice making it to Rus. "The Black Death: The Plague, 1331–1770," John Martin Rare Book Room, Hardin Library for Health Sciences, University of Iowa, accessed August 18, 2021, http://hosted.lib.uiowa.edu/histmed/plague/.

22. The statistics are compiled by Lawrence N. Langer, "The Black Death in Russia: Its Effects Upon Urban Labor," *Russian History* 2, no. 1 (1975): 53–67.

23. Mark Wheelis, "Biological Warfare at the 1346 Siege of Caffa," *Emerging Infectious Diseases* 8, no. 9 (September 2002): 971–75; quoting de' Mussi, *Istoria de Morbo sive Mortalitate quae fuit Anno Dni MCCCXLVIII* (History of the Disease, or the Great Dying of the Year of Our Lord 1348). Additional information in this paragraph is from Hannah Barker, *That Most Precious Merchandise: The Mediterranean Trade in Black Sea Slaves, 1260–1500* (Philadelphia: University of Pennsylvania Press, 2019), 129, 131–35; and Uli Schamiloglu, "The Impact of the Black Death on the Golden Horde: Politics, Economy, Society, Civilization," *Golden Horde Review* 5, no. 2 (2017): 329–30.

24. Faye Marie Getz, "Black Death and the Silver Lining: Meaning, Continuity, and Revolutionary Change in Histories of Medieval Plague," *Journal of the History of Biology* 24, no. 2 (Summer 1991): 270–71.

25. The Decameron Web, accessed July 31, 2021, https://www.brown.edu/Depart ments/Italian_Studies/dweb/texts/DecShowText.php?myID=d01intro&expand =empty&lang=eng.

26. Focused on triumph not setbacks, the overlapping chronicles of Rus describe the plague only vaguely, offering meager fodder to historians. Vasiliy Tatishchev, the Russian imperial statesman who during the 1740s produced a five-volume history of Russia, elaborated the Novgorod and Pskov chronicles, as did Karamzin in his twelve-volume *History of the Russian State*. Vasiliy Nikitich Tatishchev, *Istoriya rossiyskaya s samïkh drevneyshikh vremen. Kniga chetvortaya* (St. Petersburg: Tipo-grafiya Veytbrekhta, 1784), 172–75; Karamzin, *Istoriya gosudarstva Rossiyskogo. Tom IV,* 271–74.

27. Tatishchev, *Istoriya rossiyskaya s samïkh drevneyshikh vremen,* 172.

28. Crummey, *Formation of Muscovy,* 42.

29. *Polnoye sobraniye russkikh letopisey. Tom 10. Letoposnïy sbornik, imenuemïy Patri-arsheyu ili Nikonovskoyu letopis'yu,* ed. A. F. Bïchkov (St. Petersburg: Tipografiya Ministerstvo vnutrennikh del, 1885), 228–29. The source dates from the time of Ivan the Terrible and is named after the then patriarch of Moscow, Nikon. It covers the years 859–1520 with supplements moving forward to 1558. As evidence of the complicated histories of these chronicles, the tale of RGADA f. 181, op. 1, d. 15, is worth telling. This is a later variant of the Nikon/Patriarch chronicle, including material taken from printed books, compiled in the eighteenth century by several unnamed people, and ending up in the possession of a German-born Russian states-man, Count Andrey Osterman, in 1727. He received it from the "secret office" of another statesman, Ivan Cherkasov, after the latter was expelled from the court in St. Petersburg to Moscow in a power struggle.

30. Crummey, *Formation of Muscovy,* 43.

31. The Byzantine patriarch, Philotheos, backed Alexei by excommunicating those princes in Rus who rejected an alliance with Moscow in favor of the grand duke of Lithuania, Algirdas (ca. 1296–1377). Philotheos rethought that support in 1371, having learned of Alexei's involvement in nefarious doings in the House of Moscow—the imprisonment of the prince of Tver, for example—and about the metropolitan's neglect of those of his dioceses that fell under Lithuanian control. The "pagan" grand duke recommended appointing a separate metropolitan for the Orthodox believers of Lithuania. Philotheos agreed to do so. He appointed a cler-gyman named Cyprian (ca. 1336–1406) as metropolitan of Kyiv and Lithuania, and left Alexei in place in Moscow. The Rus–Lithuania divide in the Church would be resolved after Alexei's death, when Cyprian became metropolitan both of Rus (Moscow and Kyiv) and the grand duchy. Neither Moscow nor the Golden Horde supported this arrangement, however, and when Alexei died and Cyprian turned up in Moscow, he was arrested as a Lithuanian agent. Dimitri Obolensky, "A 'Philorho-maios Anthropos': Metropolitan Cyprian of Kyiv and All Russia (1375–1406)," *Dumbarton Oaks Papers* 32 (1978): 85–89.

32. Zabelin, *Istoriya goroda Moskvï,* 87; quoting from the *Voskresenskaya letopis'* (Resur-rection Chronicle) of 1542–44.

33. M. D. Priselkov, *Troitskaya letopis': Rekonstruktsiya teksta* (Moscow and Leningrad: Izdatel'stvo Akademii Nauk SSSR, 1950), 381. The source, a prose chronicle in Church Slavonic, belonged to the Trinity Sergius Lavra northeast of Moscow. The lone copy (on parchment) was destroyed in the Moscow fire of 1812 but had earlier been consulted extensively by Karamzin in his *History of the Russian State*. Priselkov reconstructed the chronicle based on Karamzin's quotations and several other sources.

34. Merridale, *Red Fortress*, 34.

35. Crummey, *Formation of Muscovy*, 46.

36. The word for marten, *kunitsa*, is related to the word for coin, *kuna*, and it is assumed that Yevsevka was required to come up with five such coins each year as payment to Donskoi—as opposed to handing over five marten pelts. There was another possible form of payment: *grivnas*, or ingots, which tended to be partitioned into four rubles (from the verb *rubit'*, to separate). Ingots were in much shorter supply than coins. A large swath of time, the twelfth through much of the fourteenth century, was characterized by a shortage of the silver needed to make them. The shortage has been attributed to the struggles against the Golden Horde, and the feudal fragmentation of Rus, which did not allow for the organization of metal production and circulation. The rise of the tsardom of Muscovy also increased the need for silver.

37. RGADA f. 135, op. 1, d. 19. The birchbark letter is dated 1363–74. A second, partially preserved letter, dated 1363–89, concerns the relocation of another resident from Torzhok, Mikula Andreyev and his three children (RGADA f. 135, op. 1, d. 20). On the 1843 discovery of the letters, see T. Panova, "Drevniye gramotï iz mednogo kuvshina," *Nauk i zhizn'*, no. 8 (2001), https://www.nkj.ru/archive/articles/6602/.

38. The heroic Donskoi is a product of later sources, chiefly the *Skazaniy o Mamayovom poboishche* (*Tale of the Rout of Mamai*). Kati Parppei, "Notes of *The Tale of the Rout of Mamai* in the Context of the Collective Imagery Concerning the Battle of Kulikovo," *Russian History* 42, no. 2 (2015): 221.

39. See Kati Parppei, *The Battle of Kulikovo Refought: "The First National Feat"* (Leiden: Brill, 2017), esp. 1–18.

40. It was damaged in battle and scuttled, intentionally sunk in the Russo-Japanese War of 1905. A South Korean treasure-hunting firm falsely claimed that it had found the wreck of the ship with 200 tons of gold on board, bilking shareholders in the process. Rick Spilman, "Claims of Vast Treasure on Dmitrii Donskoi Wreck a Likely Cryptocurrency Scam," *The Old Salt Blog*, August 21, 2018, http://www.oldsaltblog.com/2018/08/claims-of-vast-treasure-on-dmitrii-donskoi-wreck-a-likely-cryptocurrency-scam/.

41. He abolished the elected position of *tïsyachnik* and presided over the first known public executions in Moscow outside of the Kremlin on Kuchkov field (named after Stepan Kuchko, the Suzdal governor killed—in legend—by Yuri Dolgorukiy).

42. Information in this paragraph is from S. Frederick Starr, *Lost Enlightenment: Central Asia's Golden Age from the Arab Conquest to Tamerlane* (Princeton, NJ: Princeton University Press, 2013), 479–514.

43. "Tamerlane Chess," *The Chess Variant Pages,* accessed August 19, 2021, https://www.chessvariants.com/historic.dir/tamerlane.html.

44. "O prikhode Tokhtamïsha-tsarya, i o plenenii im, i o vzyatii Moskvï," sedmitza.ru, accessed August 13, 2021, https://www.sedmitza.ru/lib/text/438533/.

45. She inspired a pair of books, the first by Aleksey Viktorov, *Velikaya knyaginya Yevdokiya, vo inochestve prepodobnaya Yevfrosiniya, osnovatel'nitsa Voznesenskogo devich'yego monastïrya v Moskovskom Kremle* [Grand Princess Eudoxia, Tonsured as Euphrosyne, Founder of the Ascension Maidens' Convent in the Moscow Kremlin] (Moscow: Universitetskaya tipografiya, 1857). The author conducted research in the library and manuscript collection of the patriarchal sacristy. The second book, a discursive, fairytale-like 356 pages, is by amateur historian and television commentator Konstantin Kovalyov-Sluchevskiy, *Yevdokiva Moskovskaya: Zhizneopisan-iye svyatoy Yevfrosinii, velikoy knyagini, zhenï i vdovï Dmitriya Donskogo* [Eudoxia of Moscow: Biography of Saint Euphrosyne, Grand Princess, Wife and Widow of Dmitri Donskoi] (Moscow: Molodaya gvardiya, 2018). It is part of a popular series of biographies dating back to 1890—though "biography" is not a concept easily applied to figures like Eudoxia.

46. The following information is from Lyudmila Morozova, "Rol' velikoy knyagini Yev-dokii Dmitriyevnï v sozdanii Moskovskogo velikoknyazheskogo svoda nachala XV v.," in *Issledovaniya po istochnikovedeniyu istorii Rossii (do 1917 g.). K 80-letiyu chlena-korrespondenta RAN V. I. Buganova. Sbornik statey,* ed. N. M. Rogozhin (Moscow: ROSSPEN, 2012): 140–55.

47. The following information is from "Yevdokiya Dmitriyevna," *Pravoslavnaya Entsik-lopediya,* April 24, 2009, https://www.pravenc.ru/text/187095.html; see also A. S. Usachev, "'V male skazaniye' o Yevdokii-Yevfrosinii v Knige Stepennoy tsarskogo rodosloviya," in *Dukhovnïy put' Moskovskoy Rusi. Materialï nauchnoy konferentsii, posyvyashchyonnoy 600-letiyu so dnya blazhennoy konchinï prepodobnoy Yevdokii-Yevfrosinii, velikoy knyagini moskovskoy* (Moscow: Fond Yevdokii Moskovskoy, 2007), 69–78.

48. David B. Miller, "Legends of the Icon of Our Lady of Vladimir: A Study in the Development of Muscovite National Consciousness," *Speculum* 43, no. 4 (October 1968): 657–70, esp. 661.

49. Ibid., 658.

50. Metropolitan Hilarion (Alfeyev), "Theology of Icon in the Orthodox Church. Lecture at St. Vladimir's Seminary, 5 February 2011," Russian Orthodox Church Department for External Church Relations, accessed July 26, 2021, https://mospat.ru/en/news/56024/.

51. "Icons: Symbolism in Color," *Pravmir.com,* accessed July 26, 2021, http://www.pravmir.com/icons-symbolism-in-color/.

52. Metropolitan Hilarion, "Theology of Icon."

53. "The Martyrdom of St. George: Introduction," in *Saints' Lives in Middle English Collections,* ed. E. Gordon Whatley, Anne B. Thomson, and Robert K. Upchurch (Kalamazoo, MI: Medieval Institute Publications, 2004), https://d.lib.rochester

.edu/teams/text/whatley-saints-lives-in-middle-english-martyrdom-of-st-george -introduction.

54. "Novgorodnaya shkola ikonopisi," *StudFiles,* accessed July 26, 2021, https://studfile .net/preview/5239422/page:10/.

55. "Uchyonïye raskrïli zagadku pervoy chudotvornoy ikonï Rusi," *RIA Novosti,* accessed July 26, 2021, https://ria.ru/20200901/donskaya-1576550495.html.

56. See Priscilla Hunt, "Andrei Rublev's Old Testament Trinity Icon in Cultural Con-text," in *The Trinity-Sergius Lavra in Russian History and Culture. Readings in Russian Religious Culture,* vol. 3, ed. Deacon Vladimir Tsurikov (Jordanville, NY: Holy Trin-ity Seminary Press, 2006), 99–122; and Alexander V. Voroshilov, "*The Old Testa-ment Trinity* of Andrey Rublyov: Geometry and Philosophy," *Leonardo* 32, no. 2 (1999): 103–12.

CHAPTER 4

1. Information in this paragraph is from Mirko Dejic, "Prvi mekhanički sat u Moskvi, delo Srbina Lazara Hilandarca," *Godišnjak Učiteljskog fakulteta u Vranju, knjiga V* (2014): 61–70; and Gerhard Dohrn-van Rossum, *History of the Hour: Clocks and Modern Temporal Orders,* trans. Thomas Dunlap (Chicago: University of Chicago Press, 1996), 110–12. The chronicle describing Lazar's clock, the *Litsevoy letopis-nïy svod* or *Illustrated Chronicle Compilation,* dates from 1568–76. Assembled in or near Moscow by a team of scribes and illustrators on order of Ivan the Terrible, it describes the biblical "creation of the world," "universal" history, and "Russian" his-tory through 1567.

2. Robert O. Crummey, *The Formation of Muscovy, 1304–1613* (Abingdon, UK: Rout-ledge, 2013), 62–66, Kindle.

3. Edward Louis Keenan, Jr., "Muscovy and Kazan: Some Introductory Remarks on the Patterns of Steppe Diplomacy," *Slavic Review* 26, no. 4 (December 1967): 554–55.

4. *Fyodor Andreyevich Koshkin (Koshka),* KHRONOS, accessed May 13, 2025, https:// www.hrono.ru/biograf/bio_k/koshkin_fa.php.

5. The events are almost impossible to summarize without seeming irreverent. Con-sider the account in this anonymous manuscript, describing the start of the civil war: "Grand Prince Vasiliy Vasil'yevich, known as the Dark, that is, the Blind, sat on the throne of Rus at age ten, when his father died. Too young to rule, his rela-tives (other appanage princes) made a habit of attacking him. Vasiliy Vasil'yevich defended himself from them and, under the leadership of Prince Fyodor Davydov-ich Petrov, managed to achieve victory over the Bulgars, a brave and cruel people in battle. He argued with his uncle, Prince Yuri Dmitriyevich Galitskiy, about his succession and then went to the horde to retain his right to rule. Meantime, the aforementioned uncle took Moscow, leaving just Kolomna to his nephew. Seeing that all the boyars and better people followed Grand Prince Vasiliy to Kolomna, Prince Yuri got scared and left Moscow for Galich. When he heard this news, Grand Prince Vasiliy went to Galich and burned it down" ("Kratkoye skazaniye o proizve-

denii i vozreshchenii naroda russkogo po 1696-y god," RGADA f. 181, op. 1, d. 79, ll. 30v.–31r.).

6. Information and quotations in this paragraph are from C. K. Woodworth, "Sophia and the Golden Belt: What Caused Moscow's Civil Wars of 1425–50," *The Russian Review* 68, no. 2 (April 2009): 187–98, esp. 196.

7. Donald Ostrowski, *Muscovy and the Mongols: Cross-Cultural Influences on the Steppe Frontier, 1304–1589* (Cambridge: Cambridge University Press, 1998), 24.

8. Shemyaka, Dmitri's byname in the sources, perhaps derives from *shee-myaga,* neck-presser or strangler.

9. Crummey, *Formation of Muscovy,* 74.

10. Vasiliy Nikitich Tatishchev, *Istoriya rossiyskaya s samïkh drevneyshikh vremen. Kniga chetvortaya* (St. Petersburg: Tipografiya Veytbrekhta, 1784), 560.

11. Ibid., 562–63.

12. Charles J. Halperin, "'Know Thy Enemy': Medieval Russian Familiarity with the Mongols of the Golden Horde," *Jahrbücher Für Geschichte Osteuropas* 30, no. 2 (1982): 172.

13. *Polnoye sobraniye russkikh letopisey. Tom 20. L'vovskaya letopis'. Chast' I,* ed. S. A. Andrianov (St. Petersburg: Tipografiya M. A. Aleksandrova, 1910), 260.

14. A. A. Zimin, *Vityaz' na rasput'ye. Feodal'naya voyna v Rossii XV v.* (Moscow: Mïsl', 1991), 153; *Polnoye sobraniye russkikh letopisey. Tom 20,* 262.

15. Nikolay Mikhaylovich Karamzin, *Istoriya gosudarstva Rossiyskogo. Tom V* (St. Petersburg: Tipografiya N. Grecha, 1819), 344.

16. Crummey, *Formation of Muscovy,* 76.

17. Lithuania allied with Poland against the Teutonic Order, whose grand masters had long menaced the tribes of the Baltic shores and Neman River. To the Knights, Lithuania was the "quintessence of Otherness," a "dangerous place on the very edge of Christendom, where pagans, schismatics, and Tatars abounded" (S. C. Rowell, "Christian Understanding of the Faith Through Contacts with Non-Christians in the Late-Medieval Grand Duchy of Lithuania," *Lietuvių katalikų mokslo akademijos metraštis* 37B [2013]: 9). The brotherhood of the Polish and Lithuanian nobles on the battlefield, in councils, and in the churches was of benefit to both sides. Aristocrats from the two nations intermarried and over time blended into one. There were differences: the language of the Polish court was Latin, whereas Lithuanians spoke Ruthenian. And Polish monarchs were elected, but succession in Lithuania was dynastic. (Fortunately, an acceptable Lithuanian candidate for the Polish throne always appeared, so the election of the king was untroubled.) Poland had a university in Kraków and because Lithuania had none, the sons of nobles went to Kraków to study. Thus, the Lithuanian-Polish union evolved into a commonwealth at once monarchic and republican, with a population contributing to affairs of state.

18. Vasiliy II gained control of Novgorod and Pskov after signing a peace treaty with Casimir IV, one of Vytautas's successors as grand duke of Lithuania who also ruled, from 1447 to his death to 1492, as king of Poland. Casimir IV turned his attention from Rus to the Teutonic Order. In 1466, he brought the Thirteen Years' War against the Order to an end and acquired the Order's former possessions.

19. Demetrios Bathrellos, "Love, Purification, and Forgiveness Versus Justice, Punishment, and Satisfaction: The Debates on Purgatory and the Forgiveness of Sins at the Council of Ferrara-Florence," *Journal of Theological Studies* 65, no. 1 (April 2014): 78–121, esp. 87 and 114.

20. Marios Philippides, "The Fall of Constantinople, 1453: Classical Comparisons and the Circle of Cardinal Isidor," *Viator* 38, no. 1 (2007): 358, 378–82.

21. *Russkiy feodal'nïy arkhiv XIV—a pervoy treti XVI veka*, comp. A. I. Pliguzov, ed. A. V. Kuz'min (Moscow: Yazïki slavyanskikh kul'tur, 2008), 94 (message to Shemyaka's allies dated between December 15, 1448, and April 13, 1449).

22. Ibid., 93 (circular from after December 15, 1448, announcing his consecration as metropolitan of Kyiv and All Rus) and 225 (letter from between December 6, 1449, and December 1550, defending the legality of his consecration to the prince of Kyiv). "Iona," *Pravoslavnaya Entsiklopediya*, May 30, 2011, https://www.pravenc.ru/text/578250.html.

23. Crummey, *Formation of Muscovy*, 81.

24. Ibid., 80.

25. Catherine Merridale, *Red Fortress: History and Illusion in the Kremlin* (New York: Metropolitan Books, 2013), 44.

26. The area was first settled by Bulgars (Bulgurs), a Turkic tribe that roamed the steppe and converted to Islam. A branch of the tribe crossed the Danube and adopted the South Slavic tongue as ancient forebears of modern Bulgarians.

27. The use of the patronymic, a middle name taken from a father, relates to this crucial development. Ivan III is formally Ivan III Vasil'yevich (son of Vasiliy).

28. *Polnoye sobraniye russkikh letopisey. Tom 8. VII. Prodolzheniye letopisi po Voskresenskomu spisku*, ed. A. N. Bïchkov (St. Petersburg: Tipografiya Eduarda Pratsa, 1859), 150.

29. Crummey, *Formation of Muscovy*, 87.

30. Ibid.

31. Ibid., 90.

32. Information in this paragraph is from Gail Lenhoff and Janet Martin, "Marfa Boretskaia, Posadnitsa of Novgorod: A Reconsideration of Her Legend and Her Life," *Slavic Review* 59, no. 2 (Summer 2000): 342–68.

33. *Polnoye sobraniye russkikh letopisey. Tom 25. Moskovskiy letopisnïy svod kontsa XV veka*, ed. M. N. Tikhomirov (Leningrad: Izdatel'stvo Akademii Nauk SSSR, 1949), 285; also Marat Shaikhutdinov, *Between East and West: The Formation of the Moscow State* (Boston: Academic Studies Press, 2021), 153–54.

34. Shaikhutdinov, *Between East and West*, 155.

35. Crummey, *Formation of Muscovy*, 88.

36. Shaikhutdinov, *Between East and West*, 155; quoting Karamzin.

37. Crummey, *Formation of Muscovy*, 89.

38. Shaikhutdinov, *Between East and West*, 146.

39. George P. Majeska, "The Moscow Coronation of 1498 Reconsidered," *Jahrbücher für Geschichte Osteuropas* 26, no. 3 (1978): 354–55.

40. J. R. Howlett, "The Heresy of the Judaizers and the Problem of the Russian Reformation" (PhD diss., Somerville College, University of Oxford, 1976), 1–3; also George Vernadsky, "The Heresy of the Judaizers and the Policies of Ivan III of Moscow," *Speculum* 8, no. 4 (October 1933): 436–54, esp. 439.

41. Information in this paragraph is from Robert M. Croskey, "The Diplomatic Forms of Ivan III's Relationship with the Crimean Khan," *Slavic Review* 43, no. 2 (Summer, 1984): 257–69.

42. M. A. Nesin, "K voprosu o prichine otstupleniya tatarskogo voyska posle stoyaniya na Ugre," *milhist.info*, October 23, 2015, http://www.reenactor.ru/ARH/PDF/Nesin_05.pdf.

43. Luigi Pulci, *Lettere di Luigi Pulci a Lorenzo al Magnifico e ad altri*, ed. Salvatore Bongi (Lucca, Italy: Giusti, 1886), 113–15.

44. Anastasiya Sïropyatova, "Sofiya Paleolog: pravda i kinovïymïsel o velikoy knyagine," *marie claire*, accessed April 11, 2022, https://www.marieclaire.ru/stil-zjizny/sofiya-paleolog-pravda-i-vimisel-o-knjagine/.

45. Paul Pierling, *La Russie et le Saint-Siège: Études diplomatiques* 1 (Paris: E. Plon, Nourritt et Cie, 1896), 160.

46. Ibid., 169–70.

47. Josafa Barbaro and Ambrogio Contarini, *Travels to Tana and Persia*, trans. William Thomas and S. A. Roy (London: Hakluyt Society, 1873), 158–63.

48. Information in this paragraph and the next is from Adriano Ghisetti Giavarina, "Fioravanti, Aristotele," *Dizionario Biografico degli Italiani* 48 (1997), https://www.treccani.it/enciclopedia/aristotele-fioravanti_(Dizionario-Biografico); and Dmitry Shvidkovsky, *Russian Architecture and the West* (New Haven, CT: Yale University Press, 2007), 80–82.

49. Shvidkovsky, *Russian Architecture*, 82; quoting Metropolitan Jonah.

50. Pierro Cazzola, "Pietro Antonio Solari architetto Lombardo in Russia," *Arte Lombarda* 14, no. 1 (1969): 51.

51. Oleg Germanovich Ul'yanov, "Kto avtor programmï rekonstruktsii rezidentsii moskovskogo gosudarya v kontse XV veka: Russkiy pravitel' ili ital'yanskiy zodchiy?," *Mir istorii*, no. 2 (2005), http://www.historia.ru/2005/02/ulyanov.htm.

52. Until the seventeenth century, Russian fighters used harquebuses (matchlock guns with tripod bases). The more familiar flintlock muskets date from later. My thanks to Chester Dunning for this information.

53. Merridale, *Red Fortress*, 59–60.

54. M. I. Pïlyayev, *Staraya Moskva. Razskazï iz bïloy zhizni pervoprestol'noy stolitsï* (St. Petersburg: Izdaniye A. S. Suvorina, 1891), 98.

55. I. Ya. Stelletskiy, *Poiski biblioteki Ivana Groznogo* (Moscow: Sampo, 1999); David Arans, "A Note on the Lost Library of the Moscow Tsars," *Journal of Library History (1974–1987)* 18, no. 3 (1983): 304–16. Photographs of the tunnels are included in Rayn Andrey, "Ignatiy Stelletskiy. V poiskhakh biblioteki Ivana Groznogo," *Istoriya.RF*, July 23, 2021, https://histrf.ru/read/articles/ignatiy-stelleckiy-v-poiskah-biblioteki-ivana-groznogo.

56. These are the Troitskaya and Kutaf'ya towers. The heights of all twenty towers are given in A. Goncharova and A. Khamtsov, *Stenï i bashni Kremlya* (Moscow: Moskovskiy rabochiy, 1960), 69.

57. Maks Fasmer, *Etimologicheskiy slovar' russkogo yazïka. Tom II (Ye-Muzh)*, trans. [from German] O. N. Trubachyov (Moscow: Progress, 1986), 368.

58. Stefan Kozakiewicz, "Aloisio da Carcano," *Dizionario Biografico degli Italiani* 2 (1960), https://www.treccani.it/enciclopedia/aloisio-da-carcano_(Dizionario-Biografico).

59. Boris Kagarlitsky, *Empire of the Periphery: Russia and the World System* (London: Pluto Press, 2008), 65–66.

60. "Gde bïl Alevizov rov moskovskogo Kremlya?," Istoriya Moskvï v voprosakh i otvetakh, August 2, 2015, http://moscow-in-web.blogspot.com/2015/08/blog-post_5.html.

61. Merridale, *Red Fortress*, 64.

62. Information in this paragraph and the next is from Georgy Manaev, "Why Were There Several New Year Days in Russia?," *Russia Beyond*, December 31, 2021, https://www.rbth.com/history/334596-why-were-there-several-new-year-days -russia; and Dimitri Strémooukhoff, "Moscow the Third Rome: Sources of the Doctrine," *Speculum* 28, no. 1 (January 1953): 89–91.

63. The Gospel According to Matthew 24:36.

64. "Poslaniya startsa Filofeya," ed. and trans. V. V. Kolesov, *Institut russkoy literaturï (Pushkinskogo Doma) RAN*, accessed January 9, 2022, http://lib.pushkinskijdom .ru/Default.aspx?tabid=5105. Additional information is from Nikolay Andreyev, "Filofey and His Epistle to Ivan Vasil'yevich," *Slavonic and East European Review* 38, no. 90 (December 1959): 1–31; and Crummey, *Formation of Muscovy*, 136–37.

CHAPTER 5

1. Edmund Spenser highlights the "glorious pourtraict figure" of this "dred Soueraine" in the third book of his epic poem *The Faerie Queene. The Complete Works in Verse and Prose of Edmund Spenser* (Renascence Editions), accessed August 15, 2022, http:// www.luminarium.org/renascence-editions/queene3.html. The "Terrible" nickname dates from the mid-eighteenth century, and was first used in Europe before being accepted, hesitantly, in Russia. Edward L. Keenan, "How Ivan Became 'Terrible,'" *Harvard Ukrainian Studies* 28, no. 1/4 (2006): 521–42.

2. James Meek, "In Fonder Times, the Tsar Scalded and Stabbed to Death a Prince," *London Review of Books* 27, no. 3 (December 1, 2005), https://www.lrb.co.uk/the -paper/v27/n23/james-meek/in-fonder-times-the-tsar-scalded-and-stabbed-to -death-a-prince. The contemporaries are Pomeranian diplomat Albert Schlichting, Livonians Johann Taube and Elert Kruse, and Prince Andrey Kurbsky.

3. Hugh F. Graham, "A Brief Account of the Brutal Rule of Vasil'evich, Tyrant of Muscovy (Albert Schlichting on Ivan Groznyi)," *Canadian-American Slavic Studies* 9, no. 2 (January 1975): 254.

4. Nikolay Andreyev, review of *The Kurbskii-Grozny Apocrypha: The Seventeenth Century Genesis of the "Correspondence" Attributed to Prince A. M. Kurbskii and Tsar*

Ivan IV, by Edward L. Keenan, *Slavonic and East European Review* 53, no. 133 (1975): 582–88; Donald Ostrowski, *Who Wrote That? Authorship Controversies from Moses to Sholokhov* (Ithaca, NY: Cornell University Press, 2020), 160–89.

The letters are written in different styles but might still be authentic. Between the fifteenth and seventeenth centuries, the ancient Russian (*drevnerusskiy*) language of the birchbark *gramotï* morphed into old Russian (*starorusskiy*), which coexisted with the Old Church Slavonic used in ecclesiastical communications. Old Russian was spoken and written in Moscow, and it spread to other cities through population movement and printing. Ivan used biblical cant, sarcasm, folk idioms, and profanity in his efforts to beat down his opponent. Kurbsky absorbed foreign languages during the years of his emigration, including Latin, and his letters to Ivan, though also written in old Russian, are loftier and rhetorically more florid. He writes for the tsar, but also for readers in the "Polish-Lithuanian state" and for himself, for posterity. See D. S. Likhachyov, "Stil' proizvedeniy Groznogo i stil' proizvedeniy Kurbskogo (tsar' i 'gosudarev izmennik')," in *Perepiska Ivana Groznogo s Andreyem Kurbskim,* ed. Ya. S. Lur'ye and Yu. D. Rïkov (Leningrad: Nauka, 1979), 183–213.

5. See Charles J. Halperin, "Ivan the Terrible's Temper, or Ivan IV's Terrible Temper," in *Ivan IV and Muscovy* (Bloomington, IN: Slavica, 2020), 343–58.

6. Meek, "In Fonder Times."

Travelogues like Richard Chancellor's brief *Book of the Great and Mighty Emperor of Russia,* from the mid-1550s, consider Ivan a statesman. Chancellor was the commander of one of three English ships looking for China and the Indonesian Moluccas Spice Island. Two of them sailed north over Russia and ended up locked in ice; the sailors froze to death. Chancellor's ship made it into the White Sea down to Arkhangelsk. Russians brought him and his men to Moscow, where he was received by Ivan and given a letter to present to English authorities proposing a new trade relationship. "I take [Moscow] to be greater than London with the suburbs," Chancellor recalled of his entry into the city, noting that the people were ruder than Londoners, their houses ramshackle and waiting to be burned down, and their religion baffling. He turned his nose up at "the pickle of Herring and other stinking fish." Inside the Kremlin, the tsar sat on a throne wearing "a diadem or crown of gold, appareled with a robe all of goldsmith's work, and in his hand he held a scepter garnished and beset with precious stones; and, besides all other notes and appearances of honor, there was a majesty in his countenance proportionable with the excellency of his estate." His power was "marvelous great," Chancellor added; he "bring[s] into the field two or three hundred thousand men." He inspired devotion in his men and presided over a fair and simple legal system. Clement Adams, Richard Chancellor, Nicholas Casimir, and Richard Hakluyt, *Muscovy in the Sixteenth Century: Containing "The Discovery of Muscovy," "The Booke of the Great and Mighty Emperor of Russia," and "The English in Muscovy During the Sixteenth Century"* (self-pub., Renaissancealive, 2024), loc. 535, 289–90, 587, 702, Kindle.

7. William F. Ryan, "Ivan the Terrible's Malady and Its Magical Cure," *Incantatio* 2 (2012): 24.

Before typesetting, words were reproduced from woodcuts. Chiselers created bas-relief of entire pages of text that were inked and pressed onto paper a few hundred times before wearing out. Whether the Church introduced typesetting operations before the reign of Ivan IV is a matter of dispute. See E. B. Gruznova, "Izvestiya o popïtkakh vvedeniya pechatnogo dela pri Ivane III i ikh izucheniye," *Paleorosiya. Drevnyaya Rus': vo vremeni, v lichnostyakh, v ideyakh,* no. 2 (2021): 102–26.

8. Sergey Bogatyrev, "Ivan IV (1533–1584)," in *The Cambridge History of Russia,* vol. 1, *From Early Rus' to 1689,* ed. Maureen Perrie (Cambridge: Cambridge University Press, 2006), 242; Charles J. Halperin, *Ivan the Terrible: Free to Reward and Free to Punish* (Pittsburgh: University of Pittsburgh Press, 2019), 31–32.

9. *Prince A. M. Kurbsky's History of Ivan IV,* ed. and trans. J. L. I. Fennell (Cambridge: Cambridge University Press, 1965), 10–11; Halperin, *Ivan the Terrible,* 39; Isabel de Madariaga, *Ivan the Terrible: First Tsar of Russia* (New Haven, CT: Yale University Press, 2005), 75, Kindle.

10. *The Correspondence Between Prince Kurbsky and Tsar Ivan IV of Russia 1564–1579,* ed. and trans. J. L. I. Fennell (Cambridge: Cambridge University Press, 1963), 74–77.

11. De Madariaga, *Ivan the Terrible,* 353.

12. Edward Keenan, "Ivan IV and the 'King's Evil': Ni Maka Li To Budet?," *Russian History* 20, no. 1/4 (1993): 5–13.

13. *Correspondence Between Prince Kurbsky and Tsar Ivan IV,* 154–55, 126–27; Vladimir Sharov, "Perepiska Ivana Groznogo (1530–1584) s Andreyem Kurbskim (1528–1583)," in *Perekrestnoye opïleniye (vremya, mesto, lyudi). Sbornik esse* (Moscow: Arsis, 2018), 138.

14. Vladimir Sharov, "Oprichnina Ivana Groznogo: Chto eto takoye?," in *Iskusheniye Revolyutsiyey (Russkaya verkhovnaya vlast')* (Moscow: Arsis, 2009), 191.

15. Two of the hymns survive. The first is dedicated to Metropolitan Peter, who helped establish Moscow as the center of the Russian Orthodox Church. The second is for the feast of the Presentation of the Icon of the Vladimir Mother of God. Ivan based both on an existing hymn, "O divnoye chyudo" (O wondrous wonder) and enriched them with fragments from other musical models and lines of his own. Sung at Great Vespers, the hymns date from around 1572, the year Ivan began his spiritual testament. There he refers to the Icon of the Vladimir Mother of God as the deliverer of Moscow and intercessor of the Russian state. N. V. Parfent'yeva and N. P. Parfent'yev, "Stikhirï 'na podoben' tsarya Ivana Groznogo v chest' Vladimirskoy ikonï Presvyatoy Bogoroditsï," *Vestnik YuUrGU* 15, no. 4 (2015): 83–99.

16. Roman Jakobson, "On Russian Fairy Tales," in Aleksandr Afanas'ev, *Russian Fairy Tales,* trans. Norbert Guterman (New York: Random House, 1973), 635; Alexandre Benoit, "Johann Taube and Elert Kruse: A Broken Window on Ivan IV's Oprichnina," *Canadian-American Slavic Studies* 54, no. 4 (2020): 356.

17. The coronation is described in the Nikon chronicle and elaborated, anachronistically, in a document from 1557–60. Paul Bushkovitch, *Succession to the Throne in Early Modern Russia: The Transfer of Power, 1450–1725* (Cambridge: Cambridge University Press, 2021), 72.

18. Halperin, *Ivan the Terrible,* 46.

19. De Madariaga, *Ivan the Terrible,* 48, 50–51.

20. Sergey Bogatyrev, "Reinventing the Monarchy in the 1550s: Ivan the Terrible, the Dynasty, and the Church," *Slavonic and East European Review* 85, no. 2 (April 2007): 274.

21. "Makariy," *Pravoslavnaya Entsiklopediya,* November 13, 2020, https://www.pravenc .ru/text/2561278.html; De Madariaga, *Ivan the Terrible,* 52.

22. David B. Miller, "The Coronation of Ivan IV of Moscow," *Jahrbücher für Geschichte Osteuropas* 15, no. 4 (December 1967): 564.

23. Joan Neuberger, *This Thing of Darkness: Eisenstein's Ivan the Terrible in Stalin's Russia* (Ithaca, NY: Cornell University Press, 2019), 229–30.

24. De Madariaga, *Ivan the Terrible,* 53.

25. Yuvenaliy [I. G. Voyeykov], *Kratkoye opisaniye o proisshestvii znamenitogo roda Yur'yevïkh-Romanovïkh i zhizni velikogo gosudarya svyateyshego Filareta Nikiticha, patriarkha Moskovskogo i vseya Rossii* (Moscow: Universitetskaya tipografiya Khr. Ridigera i Khr. Klaudiya, 1798), 8–9.

26. Bushkovitch, *Succession,* 75.

27. De Madariaga, *Ivan the Terrible,* 142–43.

28. Nikolay Mikhaylovich Karamzin, *Istoriya gosudarstva Rossiyskogo. Tom IX* (St. Petersburg: Tipografiya N. Grecha, 1821), 17.

29. Ibid., 139–40.

30. Daniil Prints fon-Bukhau [iz Bukhova], *Nachalo i vozvïsheniye Moskovii,* Vostochnaya literatura, accessed May 20, 2022, https://www.vostlit.info/Texts/rus11/ Buchow/text4.phtml?id=4041. This is Iv. A. Tikhomirov's 1877 translation of the 1668 Latin book *Moscoviae ortus et progressus.*

31. Isolde Thyrêt, "The Royal Women of Ivan IV's Family and the Meaning of Forced Tonsure," in *Servants of the Dynasty: Palace Women in World History,* ed. Anne Walthall (Berkeley: University of California Press, 2008), 163.

32. Fon-Bukhau, *Nachalo i vozvïsheniye Moskovii;* A. L. Yuganov, *Kategorii russkoy srednevekovoy kul'turï* (Moscow: MIROS, 1998), 66.

33. Russell E. Martin, *A Bride for the Tsar: Bride-Shows and Marriage Politics in Early Modern Russia* (Ithaca, NY: Cornell University Press, 2012), 156 and 130 (quoting the Polish diplomat Reinhold Heidenstein).

34. Thyrêt, "Royal Women," 161.

35. Information and quotations in this paragraph and the next are from Nikolay Mikhaylovich Karamzin, *Istoriya gosudarstva Rossiyskogo. Tom VIII* (St. Petersburg: Tipografiya N. Grecha, 1819), 96–98; and *Polnoye sobraniye russkikh letopisey. Tom 13. Chast' 1. Letopisnïy sbornik, imenuemïy Patriarsheyu ili Nikonovskoyu letopis'yu,* ed. S. F. Platonov (St. Petersburg: Tipografiya I. N. Skorokhodova, 1904), 152–54.

36. Karamzin, *Istoriya gosudarstva Rossiyskogo. Tom VIII,* 98; R. G. Skrïnnikov, *Ivan Groznïy* (Moscow: Nauka, 1983), 28–29; Catherine Merridale, *Red Fortress: History and Illusion in the Kremlin* (New York: Metropolitan Books, 2013), 76.

37. *Polnoye sobraniye russkikh letopisey. Tom 13. Chast' 1,* 154.

38. Adam Oleyariy, *Podrobnoye opisaniye puteshestviya Golshtinskogo posol'stva v Mos-*

koviyu i Persiyu v 1633, 1636, i 1639 godakh, trans. Pavel Barsov (Moscow: Universitetskaya tipografiya Katkov i Ko., 1870), 107–108.

39. The ranks are listed in A. L. Korzinin, *Gosudarev dvor russkogo gosudarstva v dooprichnïy period, 1550–1565 gg.* (Moscow: Al'yans-Arkheo, 2016), 230–58; see also Ivan Zabelin, *Domashniy bït russkago naroda v XVI i XVII st. T. 1. Domashniy bït tsarey v XVI i XVII st.* (Moscow: Tovarishchestvo tipografii A. I. Mamontova, 1895), 277–307; and Gerkhard Fridrikh Miller, *Izvestiye o dvoryanakh rossiyskikh* (St. Petersburg: Tipografiya Ivana Rakhmaninova, 1790).

40. Giles Fletcher, "Of the Russe Common Wealth," in *Russia at the Close of the Sixteenth Century,* ed. Edward A. Bond (London: Hakluyt Society, 1856), 111.

41. *The Domostroi: Rules for Russian Households in the Time of Ivan the Terrible,* ed. and trans. Carolyn Johnston Pouncy (Ithaca, NY: Cornell University Press, 1994), 21, Kindle.

42. On good-bad characterizations of Ivan's rule, see Sergey Bogatyrev, "Micro-Periodization and Dynasticism: Was There a Divide in the Reign of Ivan the Terrible?," *Slavic Review* 69, no. 2 (Summer 2010): 398–99.

43. Halperin, *Ivan the Terrible,* 167.

44. *Polnoye sobraniye russkikh letopisey. Tom 13. Chast' 2. Dopolneniya k Nikonovskoy letopisi,* ed. S. F. Platonov (St. Petersburg: Tipografiya I. N. Skorokhodova, 1906), 393.

45. Bogatyrev, "Micro-Periodization," 408.

46. Sharov, "Oprichnina Ivana Groznogo," 194.

47. This idea greatly informs Vladimir Sorokin's cyberpunk novel *Den' oprichnika* (Day of the Oprichnik, 2006).

48. Zabelin, *Domashniy bït',* 16.

49. M. N. Tikhomirov, "Maloizvestnïye letopisnïye pamyatniki XVI v.," *Istoricheskiye zapiski 10* (1941), https://www.vostlit.info/Texts/Dokumenty/Russ/XVI/1520–1540/Kratk_otr_opric/text.htm.

50. De Madariaga, *Ivan the Terrible,* 182.

51. *Polnoye sobraniye russkikh letopisey. Tom 13. Chast' 2,* 394–95.

52. Charles J. Halperin, "Sixteenth-Century Foreign Travel Accounts to Muscovy: A Methodological Excursus," *Sixteenth-Century Journal* 6, no. 2 (October 1975): 92.

53. This information is from Benoit, "Johann Taube and Elert Kruse," 360–62.

54. Ibid., 364. The author parses the reasons for Ivan's dissatisfaction with Filipp on p. 363 n. 93: Aleksandr Zimin argued that the metropolitan's resistance to the tsar's centralizing aims was the cause; Ruslan Skrïnnikov suggests that the tsar had been suspicious of the metropolitan from the start, since he came from a boyar clan that had opposed his coronation.

55. *Zhitiya svyatïkh na russkom yazïke, izlozhennïye po rukovodstvu Chet'ikh-Miney, svt. Dimitriya Rostovskogo,* 12 vols. (Moscow: Moskovskaya sinodal'naya tipografiya, 1903–16), 5:281.

56. Ibid., 284–87. Russian president Vladimir Putin has publicly cast doubt on this tale. When the governor of the Tver region proposed relocating the dock that was built on the site of the monastic cell where Skuratov "strangled" the metropolitan, Putin demurred. "That's just one of the versions of what happened. The second version

is simple, that he [Skuratov] didn't kill him and didn't go there, and if he did go there, he was just passing by." "Putin zayavil, chto Malyuta Skuratov mog 'proyez-zhat' mimo' mesta ubiystva mitropolita Filippa," *Novaya gazeta*, September 3, 2021, https://novayagazeta.ru/articles/2021/09/03/putin-zaiavil-chto-maliuta-skuratov-mog-proezzhat-mimo-mesta-ubiistva-mitropolita-filippa-news.

57. Benoit, "Johann Taube and Elert Kruse," 354.

58. Charles J. Halperin, "Did Ivan IV's *Oprichniki* Carry Dogs' Heads on Their Horses?," *Canadian-American Slavic Studies* 46, no. 1 (2012): 40–67.

59. Sharov, "Oprichnina Ivana Groznogo," 197.

60. Information and quotations in this paragraph and the next are from Hugh F. Graham, "How Do We Know What We Know About Ivan the Terrible? (A Paradigm)," *Russian History* 14, no. 1/4 (1987): 179–85, esp. 181–82.

61. Ibid., 180 n. 5; quoting Francis Carr.

62. Ibid., 186.

63. *Prince A. M. Kurbsky's History of Ivan IV*, 188–89.

64. Lloyd E. Berry and Robert O. Crummey, eds., *Rude and Barbarous Kingdom: Russia in the Accounts of Sixteenth-Century English Voyagers* (Madison: University of Wisconsin Press, 1968), loc. 5613–5628, 5921–5936, and 5964, Kindle.

65. Eizo Matsuki, "The Crimean Tatars and Their Russian-Captive Slaves: An Aspect of Muscovite-Crimean Relations in the 16th and 17th Centuries," Mediterranean Studies Group at Hitotsubashi University, March 1, 2006, http://hermes-ir.lib.hit -u.ac.jp/hermes/ir/re/14906/chichukai0001801710.pdf.

66. Fletcher, "Of the Russe Common Wealth," 208.

67. Tikhomirov, "Maloizvestnïye letopisnïye pamyatniki XVI v." For Muscovites, the "universe" was not the stars and galaxies but the "inhabited land" as seen by them or described to them. The Russian word for "universe," *vselennaya*, has *selo*, village, as a root. It derives from *v'selen'* in Old Church Slavonic, which means "in-settlement," "inhabited."

68. Graham, "A Brief Account," 259–62; De Madariaga, *Ivan the Terrible*, 257–59. The location of the massacre is discussed by Yu. D. Rïkov, "Torgovaya ploshchad' za stenami kremlya ili 'Poganaya luzha'? K voprosu o meste soversheniya massovïkh kazney 'gosudarevïkh izmennikov' v Moskve 25 iyulya 1570 g.," in *Epokha Ivana Groznogo i yeyo otrazheniye v istoriografii, pis'mennosti, iskusstve, arkhitekture*, ed. B. N. Morozov, M. K. Rïbakova, and S. I. Smirnova (Moscow: Institut slavyanove-deniya RAN, 2018): 124–54. The author concludes that it happened in a hollowed-out part of the marketplace rather than a foreigner's enclave called Pagan Pond, Poganaya luzha.

69. Tikhomirov, "Maloizvestnïye letopisnïye pamyatniki XVI v."

70. Michael S. Flier, "Filling in the Blanks: The Church of the Intercession and the Architectonics of Medieval Muscovite Ritual," *Harvard Ukrainian Studies* 19 (1995): 122.

71. Natalie Challis and Horace W. Dewey, "Basil the Blessed, Holy Fool of Moscow," *Russian History* 14, no. 1/4 (1987): 47.

72. Flier, "Filling in the Blanks," 124–25.

73. A. M. Panchenko, "Holy Foolishness as Spectacle," in *Holy Foolishness in Russia: New Perspectives,* ed. Priscilla Hunt and Svitlana Kobets (Bloomington, IN: Slavica, 2011), 82.

74. Information in this paragraph and the previous one is from "Vasiliy Blazheniy," *Pravoslavnaya Entsiklopediya,* August 4, 2009, https://www.pravenc.ru/text/150789.html; Challis and Dewey, "Basil the Blessed, Holy Fool of Moscow," 48–55.

75. "Predstavleniye svyatogo i pravednogo Vasiliya Blazhennogo, chudotvortsa Moskovskogo," in *Zhitiya svyatïkh na russkom yazïke, izlozhennïye po rukovodstvu Chet'ikh-Miney, svt. Dimitriya Rostovskogo,* 12:38.

76. Adam Olearius (1599–1671; Oleyariy per the Russian translation of his travelogue referenced here) assisted the ambassador sent by Frederick III, Duke of Holstein-Gottorp, to the shah of Safavid Persia. "Outside the Kremlin in Kitai-gorod," he reports, "on the right side of the large Kremlin gates, stands the skillfully built Church of the Holy Trinity, the architect of which, after its completion, was blinded by the tyrant, so as not to build anything like it in the future" (Oleyariy, *Podrobnoye opisaniye,* 110). Konrad van Klenk was a Dutch merchant sent to Moscow by the Prince of Orange and Stadtholder of Holland; he makes the claim in *Historisch Verhael, of, Beschryving Van de Voyagie, Gedaen onder de Suite van den Heere Koenraad van Klenk* [History or Description of the Voyage Taken Under the Leadership of Koenraad van Klenk] (Amsterdam: Balthasar Coyet, 1677), 158. Bernard Leopold František Tanner (1654–after 1715) traveled with Polish emissaries to Moscow; he makes the claim in *Legatio Polono-Lithuanica in Moscoviam potentissimi Poloniae regis ac reipublicae mandato et consensu anno 1678. feliciter suscepta* [The Polish-Lithuanian Embassy in Moscow by the mandate and consent of the most powerful King of Poland and the Republic in 1678. successfully undertaken] (Nuremberg: Johannes Zieger, 1678), 62.

77. "Barma," *Pravoslavnaya Entsiklopediya,* April 12, 2009, https://www.pravenc.ru/text/77556.html.

78. See Andrey V. Ivanov, "Reformation and the Muscovite Czar: Anti-Protestant Polemic in the Writings of Ivan the Terrible," *Sixteenth Century Journal* 40, no. 4 (2009): 1109–29.

79. Pavllo Oderbornio, *Ioannis Basilidis Magni Moscoviae* (Wittenberg: Haeredes Ioannis Cratonis, 1585), 303, 317, 319. I am grateful to classicist Denis Feeney for the translation. Oderborn borrows from Flavius Josephus's description of King Herod's "distemper" in *Antiquitates Iudaicae* [The Antiquities of the Jews, 1544]. See *The Works of Flavius Josephus,* trans. William Whiston, Christian Classics Ethereal Library, accessed May 20, 2022, https://www.ccel.org/j/josephus/works/ant-17.htm.

80. *The Muscovia of Antonio Possevino, S.J.,* trans. Hugh F. Graham (Pittsburgh: University of Pittsburgh Press, 1977), 12–13; De Madariaga, *Ivan the Terrible,* 352. Karamzin, *Istoriya gosudarstva Rossiyskogo. Tom IX,* 352–53, claims that the murder did not involve Elena, but stemmed from an argument about the leadership of the armed forces. The tsar suspected his son of trying to depose him.

CHAPTER 6

1. Giles Fletcher, "Of the Russe Common Wealth," in *Russia at the Close of the Sixteenth Century,* ed. Edward A. Bond (London: Hakluyt Society, 1856), 61; see also Peter B. Brown, "Muscovy, Poland, and the Seventeenth Century Crisis," *Polish Review* 27, no. 3/4 (1982): 58.

2. Chester Dunning and Norman S. Smith, "Moving Beyond Absolutism: Was Early Modern Russia a 'Fiscal-Military' State?," *Russian History / Histoire Russe* 33, no. 1 (Spring 2006): 19–43.

3. The ruler between the two Ivans, Vasiliy III, "the inadequate," died of an infection.

4. Adam Oleyariy, *Podrobnoye opisaniye puteshestviya Golshtinskogo posol'stva v Moskoviyu i Persiyu v 1633, 1636, i 1639 godakh,* trans. Pavel Barsov (Moscow: Universitetskaya tipografiya Katkov i Ko., 1870), 110–11.

5. Ibid., 112.

6. Nicole Prevost-Logan, "Moscow Reclaims Its Past," *Archeology* 50, no. 4 (July/August 1997): 30.

7. Ibid., 31.

8. "The *Missio Muscovitica* [of Antonio Possevino]," ed. and trans. Hugh F. Graham, *Canadian-American Slavic Studies* 6, no. 3 (Fall 1972): 470.

9. The following information is from Aleksandr Mozhayev, "Prizraki Belogo goroda," Arkhnadzor, October 10, 2013, http://www.archnadzor.ru/2013/10/10/prizraki -belogo-goroda/.

10. N. I. Fal'kovskiy, *Moskva v istorii tekhniki* (Moscow: Moskovskiy rabochiy, 1950), 41, 43.

11. The following information is from V. V. Kostochkin, *Gosudarev master Fyodor Kon'* (Moscow: Nauka, 1964), 34–71.

12. V. N. Prishchepenko, "K biografii F. S. Konya," *Sovetskaya arkheologiya,* no. 4 (1966), https://www.vostlit.info/Texts/Dokumenty/Russ/XVII/1600-1620/Kon_F_S/ text1.htm.

13. Kostochkin, *Gosudarev master,* 46. The author claims that a receipt survives for "36 altïns and 4 dengas from the Trinity estate in the Moscow region for nine barrels of lime mortar delivered from Myachkovo to Moscow, and for limestone, and for a cartload of cherry tree rods for tying timber [for the scaffolding] for the sovereign's stone works." According to information compiled at https://ru.wikipedia .org/wiki/Алтын_(денежная_единица), an altïn was worth six dengas. It was not minted as a real coin during this time but used, like the ruble, as an accounting unit. The word is a portmanteau of *altï tiyen,* Tatar for "six squirrels."

The foundation pit was about six feet deep, filled with gravel, rocks of different sizes, and a leveling layer of crushed limestone. Where the ground was unstable, Kon' strengthened the foundation with oak pilings and stone slabs separated by layers of dirt. Renaissance artist Albrecht Dürer's 1527 *Ars fortificatoria* (*Art of Fortification*) explained how to make the curtain defenses, consisting of a double ring of walls either filled in with rocks and mortar or a dirt balk. Igor' Kondrat'yev, "Belïy

Tsaryov gorod," Arkhnadzor, March 12, 2008, http://www.archnadzor.ru/2008/03/12/bely-j-tsaryov-gorod/.

14. Kostochkin, *Gosudarev master,* 56.

15. vladimirdar, "Arkheologicheskiy park-amfiteatr 'Fragment stenï Belogo goroda na Khokhlovskoy ploshchadi,'" LiveJournal, September 26, 2017, https://vladimirdar .livejournal.com/125979.html.

16. Mozhayev, "Prizraki Belogo goroda." Bulls, like water, are associated with fertility and the source of life in folklore. V. A. Burnakov, "Bïk, kak simvol plodorodiya v traditsionnoy kul'ture khakasov (konets XIX–seredina XX veka)," *Tomskiy zhurnal lingvisticheskikh i antropologicheskikh issledovaniy,* no. 4 (2017): 72.

17. According to Austrian diplomat Sigismund von Herberstein, who traveled to Moscow in 1517 and 1526, "The *Neglima* [*sic*] flows from certain marshes, but is so blocked up before the city around the upper part of the fortress, that it comes out like stagnant water" (*Notes upon Russia: Being a Translation of the Earliest Account of That Country,* ed. and trans. R. H. Major, vol. 2 [London: Hakluyt Society, 1852], 5).

18. Chester Dunning with Caryl Emerson, Sergei Fomichev, Lidiia Lotman, and Antony Wood, *Boris Godunov: The Case for Pushkin's Original Comedy, with Annotated Text and Translation* (Madison: University of Wisconsin Press, 2006), 118.

19. Pushkin modeled this character on Nikolka of Pskov, who died in 1576, during Ivan the Terrible's reign. Ibid., 493–94 n. 195.

20. Sergey Mikhaylovich Solov'yov, *Istoriya Rossii s drevneyshikh vremen. Kniga vtoraya. Tom VI–X* (St. Petersburg: Obshchestvannaya pol'za, 1896), 545.

21. Ibid., 545–46.

22. Jerome Horsey, "The Most Solemne and Magnificent Coronacion of Pheodor Ivanowich, Emperour of Russia," in Bond, ed., *Russia at the Close of the Sixteenth Century,* 270.

23. Ruslan G. Skrynnikov, *Boris Godunov,* ed. and trans. Hugh F. Graham (Gulf Breeze, FL: Academic International Press, 1982), 1.

24. Dunning with Emerson et al., *Boris Godunov,* 459–60 n. 20.

25. "Travels of Sir Jerome Horsey," in Bond, ed., *Russia at the Close of the Sixteenth Century,* 222.

26. Isaac Massa, *A Short History of the Beginnings and Origins of These Present Wars in Moscow: Under the Reign of Various Sovereigns Down to the Year 1610,* trans. G. Edward Orchard (Toronto: University of Toronto Press, 1982), 24.

27. Chester S. L. Dunning, *Russia's First Civil War: The Time of Troubles and the Founding of the Romanov Dynasty* (University Park: Pennsylvania State University Press, 2001), 61.

28. Ibid., 62.

29. Ruslan Skrïnnikov, *Vasiliy Shuyskiy* (Moscow: ACT, 2002), https://www.rulit.me/books/vasilij-shujskij-read-225457-18.html.

30. Fletcher, "Of the Russe Common Wealth," 36.

31. "Travels of Sir Jerome Horsey," 156.

32. Information in this paragraph and the next is from Dunning, *Russia's First Civil War,* 67–69.

33. "Talking tools" is the common translation of "genus vocale instrumenti," from Roman scholar Marcus Terentius Varro's *Res rusticae* (*Farm Topics*). Juan P. Lewis argues that the phrase is benign and mildly tongue-in-cheek. Humans (who can talk) and animals and equipment (which can't) are all instrumental to successful farm operations. "Did Varro Think That Slaves Were Talking Tools?," *Mnemosyne* 66, no. 4/5 (2013): 634–48.

34. *Sobornoye ulozheniye 1649 g.*, KHRONOS, accessed June 22, 2022, http://www .hrono.ru/dokum/1600dok/1649_22.php.

35. Taxes on the land had long been a spoils system known as *kormleniye,* in which unsalaried dignitaries "fed" themselves by keeping a portion of the goods they collected from the peasants growing the grain and making the butter and delivered the rest to the ruler. Little could be done to prevent excess "feeding" (skimming), and ruble exchange rates were nothing if not whimsical. Under Boris Godunov, efforts were made to strengthen and then circumvent the *kormleniye* system. The more fertile the land and the better its location, whether inside or outside of a town or city, the greater the taxes imposed on it. (Taxable land units were called "plows" in the registers.) Breaking the backs of peasants for profit is just part of the picture, however. Part of the revenue that flowed into Moscow came from sales taxes, tolls, and fees for commercial transactions. Collecting taxes was dangerous and fell to a hardened, no-nonsense group of merchants called "toll farmers," responsible for collecting fees on the movements of goods and revenues from taverns. For all the hand-wringing in official documents about the evils of drunkenness, getting people drunk helped with the bottom line. Paul Bushkovitch, "Taxation, Tax Farming, and Merchants in Sixteenth-Century Russia," *Slavic Review* 37, no. 3 (1978): 381–98. The cadaster (plow) register is the subject of a magisterial two-volume publication that appeared just before the ultimate tax reform in Russia: the 1917 Revolution. See S. Veselovskiy, *Soshnoye pis'mo: issledovaniye po istorii kadastra is pososhnogo oblozheniya Moskovskogo gosudarstva* (Moscow: Tipografiya G. Lissnera i D. Sobko, 1915–16).

36. Paul Bushkovitch, *Succession to the Throne in Early Modern Russia: The Transfer of Power, 1450–1725* (Cambridge: Cambridge University Press, 2021), 128.

37. Ibid., 128–29, 133–35.

38. Fletcher, "Of the Russe Common Wealth," 22.

39. A. S. Suvorin, *O Dimitrii Samozvantse: Kriticheskiye ocherki* (St. Petersburg: Izdaniye A. S. Suvorin, 1906), 192–93.

40. Information in this paragraph is from Edward V. Williams, *The Bells of Russia: History and Technology* (Princeton, NJ: Princeton University Press, 1985), 47–50, 207 n. 40. Russia has a rich animist tradition; bells, plants, fireflies, lightning, thunder, and other phenomena are believed to have spirits. None are as powerful as the spirits of animals. A book by American animal rights advocate E. P. Evans, *The Criminal Prosecution and Capital Punishment of Animals* (London: William Heinemann, 1906), 175, adds this detail to the tale of the Uglich bell: "A like sentence was imposed by a Russian tribunal on a butting ram in the latter half of the seventeenth century."

41. Presumably: Historians have gone back and forth about his fate. Chester Dunning has challenged the epileptic seizure explanation to propose that Dmitri might have been the target of an assassination plot masterminded by Boris but somehow survived it only to disappear. Chester Dunning, "Who Was Tsar Dmitrii?," *Slavic Review* 60, no. 4 (Winter 2001): 718–19.

42. *Polnoye sobraniye russkikh letopisey. Tom 34. Piskarevskiy letopisets,* ed. V. I. Buganov and V. I. Koretskiy (Moscow: Nauka, 1978), 202.

43. Williams, *Bells of Russia,* 135–38.

44. Fletcher, "Of the Russe Common Wealth," 47–48.

45. The following information is from L. E. Morozova, "Inostrantsï o Moskve v pravleniye tsarya Borisa Godunova (Dnevnik Akselya Gyul'denstierne)," *Paleorosiya. Drevnyaya Rus': vo vremeni, v lichnostyakh, v ideyakh,* no. 2 (2022): 193–200.

46. The following information is from Vyacheslav Nikolayevich Kozlyakov, "Boris Godunov. Tragediya o dobrom tsare," VikiChteniye, accessed June 23, 2022, https://biography.wikireading.ru/116322.

47. Albert, "The Winter of Huaynaputina," Volcano Café, June 30, 2017, https://www.volcanocafe.org/the-winter-of-huaynaputina/comment-page-1/.

48. *Polnoye sobraniye russkikh letopisey. Tom 34,* 202. A Moscow clerk, Nechay Perfil'yev, and an unidentified churchman were tasked with compiling the chronicle. The older parts are recycled, verbatim in places, from other chronicles; the narrative of the reign of Ivan the Terrible and the Time of Troubles is more eclectic, referencing, according to research by Sof'ya Khazanova ("Piskarevskiy letopisets: proiskhozhdeniye, istochniki, problem avtorstva," PhD thesis, Institut vseobshchey istorii RAN, 2009), Perfil'yev's own notes, oral legends, and recollections.

49. *Polnoye sobraniye russkikh letopisey. Tom 14. Chast' 1. Novïy letopisets,* ed. S. F. Platonov and P. G. Vasenko (St. Petersburg: Tipografiya M. A. Aleksandrova, 1910), 55.

50. Massa, *Short History,* 54.

51. Ibid., 51.

52. Jacques Margeret, *The Russian Empire and Grand Duchy of Moscow: A 17th Century French Account,* trans. Chester S. L. Dunning (Pittsburgh: University of Pittsburgh Press, 1983), 58.

53. Massa, *Short History,* 52.

54. Dunning, *Russia's First Civil War,* 99.

55. The Cossacks, a Slavic group of the southern steppe frontier in Ukraine, fought against the Tatars on the side of the Poles, took on the Turks in the Crimea, and, as their ranks swelled with disaffected Russians, became major actors in the *Smuta.*

56. My thanks to Chester Dunning for this information from his ongoing research into the life of the False Dmitri.

57. Massa, *Short History,* 81.

58. Ibid., 94.

59. *Polnoye sobraniye russkikh letopisey. Tom 34,* 206.

60. Dunning, *Russia's First Civil War,* 191.

61. Margeret, *Russian Empire,* 165 n. 245.

62. Chester S. L. Dunning, "Captain Jacques Margeret: A Remarkable Huguenot Sol-

dier in Russia's Time of Troubles," *Vestnik VolGU. Seriya 4, Istoriya. Regionovedeniye. Mezhdunarodnïye otnosheniya* 24, no. 2 (2019): 83.

63. Catherine Merridale, *Red Fortress: History and Illusion in the Kremlin* (New York: Metropolitan Books, 2013), 121.

64. Bushkovitch, *Succession*, 147.

65. Ivan Zabelin, *Domashniy bït russkago naroda v XVI i XVII st. T. 1. Domashniy bït tsarey v XVI i XVII st.* (Moscow: Tovarishchestvo tipografii A. I. Mamontova, 1895), 51.

66. Dunning, *Russia's First Civil War*, 214, 228.

67. Ruslan G. Skrynnikov, *Time of Troubles: Russia in Crisis*, ed. and trans. Hugh F. Graham (Gulf Breeze, FL: Academic International Press, 1988), 21.

68. L. E. Gorelova, "Pamyatniki russkoy meditsinskoy pis'mennosti," *Russkiy Meditsinskiy Zhurnal* 8, no. 5 (2000): 227.

    The diary ascribed to Marina offers no perspective on her fate, as she didn't write it; one of her servants did, and it focuses on things that a servant would have seen or heard, like the "whimsical buffet" with a strange object on the table. "There stood a large silver container, as tall as a peasant, with a stack of copper bowls beside it. Boiling water splashed into them from above. No one washed their hands, however." The Polish visitor is trying to describe a Russian samovar. *Dnevnik Marinï Mnishek*, trans. V. N. Kozlyakov (St. Petersburg: Dmitriy Bulanin, 1995), 41, 145.

69. Dunning, *Russia's First Civil War*, 206–7.

70. Ibid., 207–8; Margeret, *Russian Empire*, 163–64 n. 240.

71. Dunning, "Captain Jacques Margeret," 84.

72. Dunning, *Russia's First Civil War*, 235.

73. Chester S. L. Dunning, "An Overlooked Anglo-Russian Tale of the Time of Troubles," in *Dubitando: Studies in History and Culture in Honor of Donald Ostrowski*, ed. Brian J. Boeck, Russell E. Martin, and Daniel Rowland (Bloomington, IN: Slavica, 2012), 380. Freese was the son of an English employee of the Muscovy Company. He had a Russian mother, and so grew up bilingual (ibid., 370).

74. Dunning, "Captain Jacques Margeret," 84.

75. Bushkovitch, *Succession*, 147.

76. This and the preceding quotations are from Massa, *Short History*, 159–61.

77. Dunning, "Who Was Tsar Dmitrii?," 723–24.

78. Massa, *Short History*, 145.

79. The account of Saint Dmitri in the semi-official *Pravoslavnaya Entsiklopediya* (*Orthodox Encyclopedia*) is quite different from the one provided here. In 1606, this source claims, the tomb was opened and Dmitri's remains revealed to be in perfect integrity: A letter sent to Moscow claimed that "the hair is black, and the flesh is intact on the bones." The corpse released not a foul stench but a beautiful fragrance. Dmitri was canonized and his remains transferred on July 3 to the Archangel Cathedral in Moscow as miracle-working relics, shown to the public on the *lobnoye mesto* platform on Red Square. After several healings, Tsar Vasiliy (Shuisky) brought the remains into the Archangel Cathedral in the Kremlin, where a pit was dug and lined with stones for the burial. The hole filled itself—a sign that Dmitri did not want his

remains kept underground—so a shrine was built instead. "Dimitriy Ioannovich," *Pravoslavnaya Entsiklopediya,* June 13, 2020, https://www.pravenc.ru/text/178207 .html.

80. Margeret, *Russian Empire,* 79.
81. Dunning, *Russia's First Civil War,* 370. "To this day," Dunning writes, "no one knows for sure" who False Dmitri II was.
82. *Polnoye sobraniye russkikh letopisey. Tom 34,* 211.
83. False Dmitri III is a cipher. His real name might have been Sidor, but the sources also align him with a Moscow deacon named Matvey, who "came to Ivangorod from the part of Moscow on the far side of the Yauza River and called himself Tsar Dmitri" (Skrynnikov, *Time of Troubles,* 177). Before arriving in Ivangorod, a fortress constructed by Ivan III on the Russian-Estonian border, he had peddled knives in Novgorod while also peddling the tale of his being the "fourth manifestation" of "Tsar" Dmitri: he escaped assassination in Uglich; he had risen from the dead in Moscow as the reincarnation of False Dmitri I; he had had his head cut off in Kaluga but somehow reattached it as the reincarnation of False Dmitri II (ibid., 178). That he attracted any supporters at all is proof of the successive crises of succession in Moscow dissolving Russia into total chaos. False Dmitri III established a ragtag base of support in Pskov, but what Dunning calls his "reign of rape and terror" alienated the populace and allowed agents of the Cossack leader Ivan Zarutsky to capture him on May 20, 1612. False Dmitri III was put on exhibit in a cage in Moscow for the "amusement of the soldiers," after which he was hung (Dunning, *Russia's First Civil War,* 432–33).
84. Conrad Bussow, *The Disturbed State of the Russian Realm,* ed. and trans. G. Edward Orchard (Montreal: McGill–Queen's University Press, 1994), xix.
85. Dunning, *Russia's First Civil War,* 402.
86. Dunning, "An Overlooked Anglo-Russian Tale," 380.
87. Bussow, *Disturbed State,* 219 n. 6.
88. Dunning, "Captain Jacques Margeret," 88.
89. Brown, "Muscovy, Poland, and the Seventeenth Century Crisis," 60.
90. Ibid.
91. Jędrzej Moraczewski, *Dzieje Rzeczypospolitej polskiej. Tom 7. Dalszy ciąg siedmnastego wieku* (Poznań: N. Kamieński, 1852), 79–80.
92. Dunning, "Captain Jacques Margeret," 88.
93. Max Harris, *Christ on a Donkey: Palm Sunday, Triumphal Entries, and Blasphemous Pageants* (Croydon, UK: Arc Humanities Press, 2019), 78–80.
94. "Ermogen," *Pravoslavnaya Entsiklopediya,* April 21, 2009, https://www.pravenc.ru/text/190175.html.
95. Bussow, *Disturbed State,* xx–xxiii.
96. Mozhayev, "Prizraki Belogo goroda."
97. "Urochishche Chertol'ye," Places Moscow, accessed July 13, 2022, https://places .moscow/places/chertolie/chertolie.html.
98. Bussow, *Disturbed State,* 163–64; Mozhayev, "Prizraki Belogo goroda."

99. Bussow, *Disturbed State*, 164.

100. Ibid., 164–66.

101. Dunning, "Captain Jacques Margeret," 91.

102. "Putin rasskazal o chuvstve dolga Minina i Pozharskogo," *Izvestiya*, November 4, 2020, https://iz.ru/1082770/2020-11-04/putin-rasskazal-o-chuvstve-dolga-minina -i-pozharskogo.

103. Bussow, *Disturbed State*, xxiii.

104. V. N. Tatishchev, *Istoriya rossiyskaya v semi tomakh. Tom shestoy* (Moscow and Leningrad: Nauka, 1966), 357.

105. *Polnoye sobraniye russkikh letopisey. Tom 34*, 217.

106. Anna Bogolitsyna, Bernhard Pichler, Alfred Vendl, Alexander Mikhailov, and Boris Sizov, "Investigation of the Brass Monument to Minin and Pozharsky, Red Square, Moscow," *Studies in Conservation* 54, no. 1 (2009): 12–13.

107. O. I. Zakharova, "Oratoriya S. A. Degtyareva 'Minin i Pozharskiy ili osvobozhdeniye Moskvï,'" July 25, 2017, https://nasledie.admin-smolensk.ru/personalii/glinka -mihail-ivanovich/novospasskij-sbornik-vypusk-chetvertyj/o-i-zaharova-oratoriya -s-a-degtyareva-minin-i-pozharskij-ili-osvobozhdenie-moskvy/.

    Other musical treatments include Eduard Nápravník's *Nizhegorodtsï (The People of Nizhny Novgorod*, 1868), a grand opera blending Italian and German elements in the style of Giacomo Meyerbeer. It sets a treacherous Russian prince on the side of King Sigismund III against Minin and a handsome and deeply patriotic young boyar named Kuratov. Near the start of the five-act pageant, Minin is set upon by the malfeasant prince's serfs. There's also a romantic complication: the prince's daughter loves the handsome boyar, but the prince imagines her married to a Pole, an idea that horrifies her and almost results in her death after Moscow is liberated by Minin's men. The highlight is the fourth act scene in which the people's militia is formed and unleashed against the heathens in the garrison—though, in the end, the Poles are gently chased out of Moscow rather than slaughtered. The treacherous prince, meantime, is shot.

108. "Zapiski kiyevskago meshchanina Bozhka Balïki o moskovskoy osade 1612 goda (Iz letopisnago sbornika Il'i Koshchakovskago)," *Kiyevskaya starina* 1, no. 7 (1882), http:// iht.univ.kiev.ua/library/ks/1882/pdf/kievskaya-starina-1882-7-A-(1408–1416).pdf.

109. Tomasz Bohun, *Moskwa 1612* (Warsaw: Bellona, 2005), 261–62, reproduces Polish ensign Józef Budziłło's chronicle of the siege.

110. Ibid., 272–73.

111. Dunning, *Russia's First Civil War*, 447. Additional information about Minin and Pozharsky's campaign is from pp. 433–35 and 438–39.

CHAPTER 7

1. Alexander Pushkin, *Ruslan and Ludmila,* trans. Irina Zheleznova (Moscow: Raduga, 1986), 55.

2. The 2018 World Cup was jarring for the influx of intoxicated music-making foot-

ballers and the big increase in the noise level. The police looked on, having been instructed to let the carousers carouse. When the World Cup ended, the police resumed their document checks, and Moscow quieted down.

3. The origin of the name *skomorokh* is ambiguous. It might derive from the verb *morochit'*, to fool around, or from an obsolete Polish adjective, *skomrośny*, meaning shameless, immodest.

4. Claudia R. Jensen, *Musical Cultures in Seventeenth-Century Russia* (Bloomington: Indiana University Press, 2009), 15.

5. There had been other contenders: A Polish ruler remained a possibility. Novgorod had fallen under Swedish control, leading to contemplation of a Swedish prince in the Kremlin. Mikhaíl's relatives had lobbied on his behalf, and his anointing was backed by the Cossacks manning the defenses of Moscow, who had no interest in a Swede depriving them of their hard-won salaries and bread allowances—a foreign ruler who would treat them, ironically, like foreigners. And Mikhaíl could boast a distant connection to Ivan the Terrible. (His grandfather's sister was Ivan IV's first wife.) The boyars endorsed him for selfish reasons: they felt they could easily manipulate him. See Chester S. L. Dunning, *Russia's First Civil War: The Time of Troubles and the Founding of the Romanov Dynasty* (University Park: Pennsylvania State University Press, 2001), 440–42; see also Russell E. Martin, "Choreographing the 'Tsar's Happy Occasion': Tradition, Change, and Dynastic Legitimacy in the Weddings of Tsar Mikhail Romanov," *Slavic Review* 63, no. 4 (2004): 794.

6. Adam Olearius, *The Travels of Olearius in Seventeenth-Century Russia,* ed. and trans. Samuel H. Baron (Stanford, CA: Stanford University Press, 1967), 112.

7. Elio Christoph Brancaforte, *Visions of Persia: Mapping the Travels of Adam Olearius* (Cambridge, MA: Harvard University Press, 2003), 9.

8. Dunning, *Russia's First Civil War,* 465–66.

9. The Dutch cartographer Pieter van der Aa published a copy of the map in 1729.

10. Olearius, *Travels,* 113–14.

11. P. Mel'nikov, "Mariya Ivanovna Khlopova, nevesta tsarya Mikhaíla Fyodorovi-cha," *Pribavleniya k Nizhegorodskim gubernskim vedomostyam,* February 17, 1845, pp. 87–89.

12. Catherine Merridale, *Red Fortress: History and Illusion in the Kremlin* (New York: Metropolitan Books, 2013), 145.

13. Information in this paragraph is from Maureen Perrie, "The Tsaritsa, the Needle-women and the Witches: Magic in Moscow in the 1630s," *Russian History* 40, no. 3/4 (2013): 297–314.

14. Muscovite historians have slowly chipped away at the periodization of Russian history that makes Peter the Great a revolutionary rather than an evolutionary figure. The changes he took credit for, and that Romanov historians extolled him for, had roots as far back as 1450. See Donald Ostrowski, *Russia in the Early Modern World: The Continuity of Change* (Lanham, MD: Lexington Books, 2022), esp. 435–50.

15. See Clare Griffin, "Bureaucracy and Knowledge Creation: The Apothecary Chancery," in *Information and Empire: Mechanisms of Communication in Russia, 1600–*

1854, ed. Simon Franklin and Katherine Bowers (Cambridge, UK: Open Book Publishers, 2017): 255–86.

16. R. G. Skrïnnikov, *Rossiya v nachale XVII v. "Smuta"* (Moscow: Mïsl', 1988), 138.

17. Robert Collis, "Magic, Medicine and Authority in Mid-Seventeenth-Century Muscovy: Andreas Engelhardt (d. 1683) and the Role of the Western Physician at the Court of Tsar Aleksei Mikhailovich, 1656–1666," *Russian History* 40, no. 3/4 (2013): 415.

18. John J. Keevil, *Hamey the Stranger* (London: Geoffrey Bles, 1952), 44; Aleksey Kuznetsov, "Imat' po retseptam lekarstva," *Diletant,* November 26, 2019, https://diletant.media/articles/45273637/.

19. Sergei M. Soloviev, *Michael Romanov: The Last Years, 1634–1645,* ed. and trans. G. Edward Orchard (Gulf Breeze, FL: Academic International Press, 1996), 83–84.

20. Russell Zguta, *Russian Minstrels: A History of the Skomorokhi* (Philadelphia: University of Pennsylvania Press, 1978), 50–51.

21. Sergei V. Lobachev, "Patriarch Nikon's Rise to Power," *Slavonic and East European Review* 79, no. 2 (April 2001): 294.

22. Pavel Aleppskiy, *Puteshestviye Antiokhiyskogo patriarkha Makariya v Rossiyu v polovine XVII veka, opisannoye yego sïnom, arkhidiakonom Pavlom Aleppskim. Vïpusk tretiy* (Moscow: Universitetskaya tipografiya, 1898), 135–39.

23. Merridale, *Red Fortress,* 157–58.

24. *The Domostroi: Rules for Russian Households in the Time of Ivan the Terrible,* ed. and trans. Carolyn Johnston Pouncy (Ithaca, NY: Cornell University Press, 1994), 77, Kindle.

25. "Tsarskaya gramota v Belgorod ob ispravlenii nravov i unichtozhenii suyeveriy," Vikiteka, accessed November 2, 2022, https://ru.wikisource.org/wiki/Царская _грамота_в_Белгород_об_исправлении_нравов_и_уничтожении_суеверий.

26. Jensen, *Musical Cultures,* 79.

27. Peter B. Brown, "Muscovy, Poland, and the Seventeenth Century Crisis," *Polish Review* 27, no. 3/4 (1982): 68.

28. Ibid.

29. He stopped receiving invitations to the tsar's feasts, and the tsar stopped going to his services. Their relationship further soured over a trivial incident on July 6, 1658, when one of Alexei's aides accidentally bopped one of the patriarch's aides on the head with a staff in a crowded room, which Nikon interpreted as a "public desecration of his patriarchal rank." N. F. Kapterev, *Patriarkh Nikon i tsar' Aleksey Mikhaylovich* (Moscow: Izd-vo Spaso-Preobrazhenskogo Valaamskogo monastïrya, 1996), https://www.sedmitza.ru/lib/text/439660/.

30. Ivan Zabelin, *Istoriya goroda Moskvï* (Moscow: Tip-litografiya T-va I. N. Kuchnerev i Ko., 1905), 165–66.

31. Richard Khelli, "Stoimost' stroitel'nïkh materialov v Moskovskom gosudarstve XVII v.," in *Kul'tura srednevekovoy Moskvï: XVII vek,* ed. B. A. Rïbakov (Moscow: Nauka, 1999), 237.

32. Ushakov adhered to tradition in icon-making but with greater precision in the rep-

resentation of light and dark, softer lines, a sense of volume and depth and other natural features. His updating of a miracle-working Greek icon of Mary and Jesus includes details as minute as the lacrimal caruncle, the red flesh in the corner of the eye (David, "The Eyes Have It: The Westernization of Russian Icons in the 17th Century," *Icons and Their Interpretation,* July 4, 2014, https://russianicons .wordpress.com/tag/simon-ushakov/). Ushakov produced a remarkably self-conscious treatise about icon-making that defends his naturalistic approach. The artist should reflect reality as in a mirror. "Many of us, who know the art of painting, create what is more deserving of ridicule than reverence and tenderness, they encourage the wrath of God on themselves and the condemnation of foreigners and great shame from honest people" (Simon Ushakov, "Slovo k lyubotshchatel'nomu ikonnogo pisaniya," krotov.info, accessed November 24, 2022, http://krotov.info/ acts/17/krizhanich/ushakov.html). Ushakov's fear of God is matched by his fear of the government's disapproval.

33. "Dvorets tsarya Alekseya Mikhaylovicha," Gosudarstvennïy vïstavochnïy zal-muzey 'Naslediye,'" accessed November 22, 2022, https://gvzm-nasledie.ru/eto -interesno/dvorets-tsarya-alekseya-mihajlovicha/.

34. Lindsey Hughes, *Sophia, Regent of Russia: 1657–1704* (New Haven, CT: Yale University Press, 1990), 138.

35. Claudia Jensen, Ingrid Maier, and Stepan Shamin, with Daniel C. Waugh, *Russia's Theatrical Past: Court Entertainment in the Seventeenth Century* (Bloomington: Indiana University Press, 2021), 148–49. Preobrazhenskoye means "Transfiguration."

36. M. A. Katritzky, "Stefanelo Botarga and Pickelhering: Fishy Italian and English Stage Clowns in Spain and Germany," in *Theatre Cultures Within Globalising Empires: Looking at Early Modern England and Spain,* ed. Joachim Küpper and Leonie Pawlita (Berlin: De Gruyter: 2018): 15–39.

37. Hughes, *Sophia,* 136.

38. Jensen et al., *Russia's Theatrical Past,* 108–9.

39. Marina Swoboda, "The Furnace Play and the Development of Liturgical Drama in Russia," *Russian Review* 61, no. 2 (April 2002): 232–33.

40. "How strange and frightening it is to hear that a simple peasant in Christ's image is nailed to a cross, a crown of thorns is put on his head, and a bladder with blood is hidden under his armpit so that he bleeds between the ribs when stabbed," an unnamed churchman complained. "Moreover, instead of the image of the Virgin, a foreign damsel with loose hair weeps; and instead of John the Theologian being summoned, the body of Christ is handed over to a young beardless man" (Jensen et al., *Russia's Theatrical Past,* 171).

41. And this Slavophile position—that of "continuity" between the two cities—was itself a myth created by a seventeenth-century German monk and adopted by Moscow rulers. See Mikhail Zygar, *War and Punishment: Putin, Zelensky, and the Path to Russia's Invasion of Ukraine* (New York: Scribner, 2023), 7–27.

42. Paul Bushkovitch, *Peter the Great* (Lanham, MD: Rowman & Littlefield, 2016), 71–72.

43. Hughes, *Sophia,* 222.

44. *Passages from the Diary of General Patrick Gordon of Auchleuchfries. A.D. 1635—A.D. 1699* (Aberdeen, Scotland: Spalding Club, 1859), 166.

45. Ivan Afanas'yevich Zhelyabuzhskiy, *Dnevnïye zapiski,* Vostochnaya literatura, accessed November 12, 2022, https://www.vostlit.info/Texts/rus13/Zeljabuzskij/text1.phtml?id=489.

46. Hughes, *Sophia,* 244.

47. Johann Georg Korb, *Diary of an Austrian Secretary of Legation at the Court of Czar Peter the Great,* ed. and trans. [from Latin] Charles MacDonnell, 2 vols. (London: Bradbury & Evans, 1863), 2:95–96, 111; see also Nancy Shields Kollmann, *Crime and Punishment in Early Modern Russia* (Cambridge: Cambridge University Press, 2012), 407.

48. Ostrowski, *Russia in the Early Modern World,* 444.

49. *Perepisnïye knigi goroda Moskvï 1665–76 gg.* (Moscow: Gorodskaya tipografiya, 1886), 231–38; see also P. M. Luk'yanov, "The First Chemical Laboratories in Russia," *Chymia* 9 (1964): 64.

50. See Kees Boterbloem, *Modernizer of Russia: Andrei Vinius, 1641–1716* (Houndmills, UK: Palgrave Macmillan, 2013), 184–96.

51. "3 December 1701. The first private pharmacies in Russia [were] opened by Decree of Peter I," Boris Yeltsin Presidential Library, accessed October 23, 2022, https://www.prlib.ru/history/619778.

52. Maria Di Salvo, "The 'Italian' Nemetskaia Sloboda," *Slavonic and East European Review* 88, no. 1/2 (January/April 2010): 104.

53. This and the following information and quotations are from Daniel L. Schlafly, "Filippo Balatri in Peter the Great's Russia," *Jahrbücher Für Geschichte Osteuropas* 45, no. 2 (1997): 185, 188, 190, and 197.

54. "U zabroshennïkh palat Annï Mons XVII veka na Baumanskoy obvalilas' stena," *Moskvich,* January 14, 2020, https://moskvichmag.ru/gorod/u-zabroshennyh-palat-anny-mons-xvii-veka-na-baumanskoj-obvalilas-stena/.

55. *Passages from the Diary of General Patrick Gordon,* 169.

56. Lindsey Hughes, *Peter the Great: A Biography* (New Haven, CT: Yale University Press, 2002), 38.

57. Zhelyabuzhskiy, *Dnevnïye zapiski.*

58. Korb, *Diary of an Austrian Secretary,* 81.

59. Kollmann, *Crime and Punishment,* 407.

60. Simon Sebag Montefiore, *The Romanovs, 1613–1918* (New York: Alfred A. Knopf, 2016), 87.

61. Anthony Anemone, "The Monsters of Peter the Great: The Culture of the St. Petersburg Kunstkamera in the Eighteenth Century," *Slavic and East European Journal* 44, no. 4 (2000): 586.

62. Anthony Cross, *Peter the Great Through British Eyes: Perceptions and Representations of the Tsar Since 1698* (Cambridge: Cambridge University Press, 2000), 8.

63. "Peter the Great in England," *Scientific American* 4, no. 23 (1861): 363.

64. Kollmann, *Crime and Punishment,* 409.

65. Andreas Schönle, "Calendar Reform Under Peter the Great: Absolutist Preroga-

tives, Plural Temporalities, and Christian Exceptionalism," *Slavic Review* 80, no. 1 (Spring 2021): 71.

66. Ostrowski, *Russia in the Early Modern World,* 445.
67. Evgenii Akelev, "Is It Possible to Make Money from Beards?," *Cahiers du Monde Russe* 61, no. 1/2 (2020): 86.
68. Ibid., 90, 97, 101.
69. Jensen et al., *Russia's Theatrical Past,* 244.
70. Ibid., 241–42.
71. Lyudmila Starikova, "Panorama teatral'no-zrelishchnoy zhizni russkikh stolits v Petrovskuyu epokhu," *Voprosï teatra / Proscaenium,* nos. 1–2 (2017): 144.
72. Sergey Ignatov, *Nachalo russkogo teatra i teatr petrovskoy epokhi* (Petrograd and Moscow: Izdaniye teatral'nogo otdela narodnogo komissariata po prosveshcheniyu, 1919), 19–20.
73. Starikova, "Panorama," 151.
74. Michael Wachtel, "Russian," in *How Literatures Begin,* ed. Joel B. Lande and Denis Feeney (Princeton, NJ: Princeton University Press, 2021), 286.
75. Starikova, "Panorama," 148.
76. Akelev, "Is It Possible to Make Money from Beards?," 88–89.
77. admin, "Komediynaya khramina (1702)," Petrovskoye barokko, February 2, 2013, http://petro-barocco.ru/archives/1806.
78. Starikova, "Panorama,"151.
79. Richard S. Wortman, *Scenarios of Power: Myth and Ceremony in Russian Monarchy from Peter the Great to the Abdication of Nicholas II* (Princeton, NJ: Princeton University Press, 2006), 28.

CHAPTER 8

1. They were in charge from 1725 to 1796—except for 1727–30, thirteen months in 1740–1741, and seven months in 1761–62. Richard S. Wortman, *Scenarios of Power: Myth and Ceremony in Russian Monarchy from Peter the Great to the Abdication of Nicholas II* (Princeton, NJ: Princeton University Press, 2006), 40.
2. Marina Zavgorodnyaya, "Fridrikh Vil'gel'm: 'nelepïy' konets zhiznennogo puti muzha Annï Ioannovnï," Dzen.ru, August 28, 2021, https://dzen.ru/a/YSoUlwq JmgsEC5Bx.
3. A. A. Kozlova, "Vïstupleniye na prestol russkoy imperatritsï Annï Ioannovnï," *Vestnik Omskogo universiteta,* no. 3 (2013): 70.
4. Ibid., 74. Russia's rulers oversaw "secret" and "investigative" offices of different sizes and regulations, but all were tasked with rooting out political and religious dissidents. The first taynïy prikaz (secret chancellery) dates from the mid-seventeenth century and Tsar Alexei, who sought to keep the boyars' duma in check. During his rule, Peter the Great relied on a prosecutorial office outside of Moscow called the Preobrazhenskiy prikaz. It included the Chancellery of Secret Investigations, Kantselyariya taynïkh i rozïsknïkh del, which in 1717 became its own entity. He also relied on agents called "secret counsellors" in the Table of Ranks. Catherine I disbanded

the Chancellery of Secret Investigations but it was brought back by Empress Anna under the direction of Andrey Ushakov, a figure of "fear and contempt" who kept the torture chamber in the Peter and Paul Fortress full. The chancellery was head-quartered in St. Petersburg with an office in Moscow. David Tarschys, "Secret Institutions in Russian Government: A Note on Rosenfeldt's Knowledge and Power," *Soviet Studies* 37, no. 4 (October 1985): 527–29.

5. Prozhito, "Istoriya bolezni: chto svelo v nebïtiye imperatritsu Annu Ioannovnu," Dzen.ru, July 1, 2018, https://dzen.ru/a/WzeZ6lY2RwCpU3Hn.

6. Denis Olegovich Alyoshin, "Otrazheniye obstoyatel'stv smerti imperatritsï Annï Ioannovnï v Petersburgskom fol'klore—istoriko-istochnikovedcheskiy analiz," in *Nauchnoye soobshchestvo studentov XXI stoleiya. Obshestvennïye nauki,* ed. Natal'ya Vital'yevna Dmitriyeva (Novosibirsk: SibAK, 2020), 5.

7. The more famous storming of the Winter Palace, in 1917, produced numerous casualties.

8. Yevgeniy Anisimov, *Yelizaveta Petrovna* (Moscow: Molodaya gvardiya, 2005), 40.

9. Ivan was kept in Kholmogorï for twelve years, after which he was transferred to a fortress close to St. Petersburg. Four years later he was killed by his guards, foiling an attempt to restore him to power. His body was secretly buried back in Kholmogorï. "Naydyonï ostanki rossiyskogo imperatora Ivana VI," lenta.ru, September 13, 2010, https://lenta.ru/news/2010/09/13/joann/.

10. Wortman, *Scenarios of Power,* 43. The ode was composed by Mikhaíl Lomonosov "on the occasion [in 1742] of a defeat over the Swedes."

11. The governing senate oversaw all departments (collegiums) of the government: the collegiums of commerce, foreign affairs, justice, Ukraine (Little Russia), and so on. Each of these bureaucracies had its own document office. The governing senate was headed by the general prosecutor, who served as liaison between the senate and the sovereign. The power of the governing senate decreased in the eighteenth century as the power of the general prosecutor increased. The governing senate's power was further diminished by what Olga A. Narkiewicz calls "successive cliques of favorites," and ambitious provincial governors. "Alexander I and the Senate Reform," *Slavonic and East European Review* 47, no. 108 (January 1969): 116.

12. Yevgeniy Akel'yev, *Povsednevnaya zhizn' vorovskogo mira Moskvï vo vremena Van'ki Kaina* (Moscow: Molodaya Gvardiya, 2012), 16.

13. Wortman, *Scenarios of Power,* 49.

14. Simon Sebag Montefiore, *The Romanovs, 1613–1918* (New York: Alfred A. Knopf, 2016), 176, 180.

15. Anisimov, *Yelizaveta Petrovna,* 196. Razumovsky rose through the ranks to become the overseer of Elizabeth's court. He sang and played the bandura, a Ukrainian string instrument. Their relationship inspired an example, anachronistically speaking, of revenge porn: a watercolor of the empress and her most dedicated servant "in flagrante delicto." There are four other such images in the early-nineteenth-century series, whose author is unknown. Ernest A. Zitser, "A Full-Frontal History of the Romanov Dynasty: Pictorial 'Political Pornography' in Pre-Reform Russia," *Russian Review* 70, no. 4 (October 2011): 557–83, esp. 558–60.

16. Anisimov, *Yelizaveta Petrovna,* 234.

17. Susan P. McCaffray, *The Winter Palace and the People: Staging and Consuming Russia's Monarchy, 1754–1917* (DeKalb: Northern Illinois University Press, 2018), 27.

18. Ibid., 18.

19. Marcus C. Levitt, " 'The First Russian Ballet': Sumarokov's 'Sanctuary of Virtue' (1759), Defining a New Dance," in *Early Modern Russian Letters: Texts and Contexts* (Boston: Academic Studies Press, 2009), 136.

20. Anna Aronova, "Ognennïye sadï Yelizavetï Petrovnï," *Iskusstvoznaniye,* nos. 3–4 (2012): 253–75; quoted words from Wortman, *Scenarios of Power,* 50.

21. Andrey V. Ivanov, *A Spiritual Revolution: The Impact of Reformation and Enlightenment in Orthodox Russia, 1700–1825* (Madison: University of Wisconsin Press, 2020), 130.

22. The following quotations and information are from "8481. 15 dekabrya 1741. Imennoy, prinyatïy Senatom ukaz 'O milostivom proshchenii prestupnikov i o proshchenii shtrafov, nedoimok i nachetov s 1719 po 1730 god," in *Polnoye sobraniye zakonov Rosskiyskoy imperii s 1649 goda. Tom XI. 1740–1743* (St. Petersburg: Tipografiya II Otdeleniya Sobstvennoy Yego Imperatorskago Velichestva Kantselyarii, 1830), 546–49.

23. Elena Marasinova, "Punishment by Penance in 18th-Century Russia," *Kritika: Explorations in Russian and Eurasian History* 17, no. 2 (Spring 2016): 307–8.

24. Elena Marasinova, "The Death Penalty Moratorium in 18th-C Russia," *Quaestio Rossica* 7, no. 4 (2019): 1089; Cyril Bryner, "The Issue of Capital Punishment in the Reign of Elizabeth Petrovna," *Russian Review* 49, no. 4 (October 1990): 389.

25. Bryner, "The Issue of Capital Punishment," 389–91.

26. Marasinova, "The Death Penalty Moratorium," 1090.

27. Ibid., 1099–1100.

28. Christine D. Worobec, "Late Witchcraft Prosecutions in Imperial Russia Within a Comparative European Context," *Canadian-American Slavic Studies* 57, nos. 3–4 (2023): 491.

29. Marasinova, "The Death Penalty Moratorium," 1087, 1102.

30. RGADA preserves the records of the bureau, everything from visitors' logs to the cost of supplies to the paperwork concerning "the construction of the dungeon near the former Sïsknoy prikaz" (f. 372, op. 1, d. 515) and "the putting of shackles and handcuffs on convicts" (f. 372, op. 1, d. 1623).

31. Yelena Prikazchikova, "Van'ka Kain v kul'turnom prostranstve Rossii: semiotika povedeniya," *Quaestio Rossica* 10, no. 1 (2022): 276, 281; Ronald Vroon, "Aleksey Kruchenykh's 'Razboinik Van'ka-Kain' and the Literary Politics of LEF," *Slavic Review* 50, no. 2 (Summer 1991): 359–70.

32. Mark Galeotti, *The Vory: Russia's Super Mafia* (New Haven, CT: Yale University Press, 2018), 9–10.

33. Anastasia Gordienko, *Outlaw Music in Russia: The Rise of an Unlikely Genre* (Madison: University of Wisconsin Press, 2023), 76. I have slightly modified the author's translation of the lyrics.

34. Akel'yev, *Povsednevnaya zhizn',* 112.

35. The house doesn't survive (it was chiefly made of wood), but another house owned

by the Filatev family in the tranquil surroundings of Ivashevo does. It dates from the second half of the eighteenth century. Oykumena, "Ivashevo. Usad'ba Filat'yevïkh," Dzen.ru, June 27, 2022, https://dzen.ru/a/YrntEh1Emmza5hZi.

36. Akel'yev, *Povsednevnaya zhizn'*, 119.

37. Ibid., 123–24.

38. "Zhizn' i pokhozhdeniye rosskiyskogo Kartusha, imenuemogo Kaina," in Matvey Komarov, *Istoriya moshennika Van'ki Kaina*, ed. V. D. Rak (St. Petersburg: Vita Nova, 2015), 263. In English, the title of this 1777 booklet is *The Life and Adventures of the Russian Cartouche, by Name Cain, a Notorious Thief and Informer on People of That Trade, Who for His Repentance for His Villainy Received a Reprieve from His Death Sentence but Who for His Return to His Former Trade Was Exiled for Life to Hard Labor, First in Rogervik and Then in Siberia, Written by Himself in 1764*. It followed the publication of an anonymous fable titled *O Van'ke-Kaine, slavnom vore i moshennike, About Vanka Cain, Glorious Thief and Swindler,* which appeared in 1775 and was reprinted in 1815 and 1830. Matvey Komarov's novelized biography was published in 1779 and had multiple reprints. Elisabeth Stenbock-Fermor, "The Story of Van'ka Kain," *Journal of American Folklore* 69, no. 273 (July–September 1956): 254–55; Ecatherina Rai-Gonneau, "Van'ka Kain, Le Cartouche Russe: Essai de Biographie Criminelle Dans La Russie de Catherine II," *Revue des Études Slaves* 78, no. 1 (2007): 100; David Gasperetti, "Introduction" to Mikhail Chulkov, Matvei Komarov, and Nikolai Karamzin, *Three Russian Tales of the Eighteenth Century: The Comely Cook, Vanka Kain, and "Poor Liza,"* trans. David Gasperetti (Ithaca, NY: Cornell University Press, 2012), 15.

39. Akel'yev, *Povsednevnaya zhizn'*, 143–46.

40. Matvei Komarov, "The True and Detailed Account of the Good and Wicked Deeds of the Russian Rogue, Thief, Robber, and Former Moscow Police Spy Vanka Kain, and of His Entire Life and Strange Adventures," in *Three Russian Tales*, 117.

41. "Zhizn' i pokhozhdeniye rosskiyskogo Kartusha," 263.

42. Ibid., 264.

43. Ibid. In Cyrillic the passage reads: "Пол да серед сами съели, печь да полати в наем отдаем, а идущим по сему мосту тихую милостыню подаем, и ты будешь брат, нашего сукна епанча! Поживи здесь в нашем доме, в котором всего довольно: наготы и босоты изнавешены шесты, а голоду и холоду анбары стоят. Пыль да копоть, притом нечего и лопать."

44. Worobec, "Late Witchcraft Prosecutions," 490 n 17.

45. Anisimov, *Yeliziveta Petrovna*, 295.

46. Ibid., 297.

47. Mark Vincent, "Cult of the 'Urka': Criminal Subculture in the Gulag, 1924–1953" (PhD thesis, University of East Anglia, 2015), 39, 41.

48. Anisimov, *Yeliziveta Petrovna*, 304.

49. Akel'yev, *Povsednevnaya zhizn'*, 381.

50. M. A. Grachev, "Treka kalach ela, stromïk, sverlyuk straktirila," *Russkaya rech'*, no. 2 (2005): 126–27.

51. I. D. Kostina, "Faktï, sobïtiye, lyudi. Tsar-kolokol i yevo sozdateli," *Voprosï isto-*

rii, no. 5 (1982): 180–83; Georgiy Oltarzhevskiy, "Pozharishche i torzhishche," Moslenta.ru, June 9, 2015, https://moslenta.ru/city/fightfirewithfire.htm.

52. Semyon Saltïkov, *Doneseniye yeya imperatorskomu velichestvu, gosudarïne imperatritse Anne Ioannovne, o moskovskom bol'shom pozhare, sluchivshemsya maya 29 dnya, 1737 goda* (Moscow: Tipografiya S. Selivanovskogo, 1858).

53. N. I. Fal'kovskiy, *Moskva v istorii tekhniki* (Moscow: Moskovskiy rabochiy, 1950), 154–55.

54. Mikail Puşkin, "Kremlin on Fire: 18th-Century Russia Through the Tongues of Flame," *Humanitas* 7 (2019): 467.

55. A. I. Sumkina, *Pamyatniki moskovskoy delovoy pis'mennosti XVIII veka* (Moscow: Nauka, 1981), 150; Puşkin, "Kremlin on Fire," 463.

56. Akel'yev, *Povsednevnaya zhizn'*, 22.

57. Ibid., 339–42.

58. Ibid., 332–34.

59. Ibid., 331–32.

60. Ibid., 24.

61. Daniil Konstantinov, "Nikol'skiy Grecheskiy monastïr'—podvor'ye Zaikonospasskogo stavropigial'nogo monastïrya," *Monastïrskiy vestnik,* accessed December 18, 2023, https://monasterium.ru/monastyri/monastery/nikolskiy-grecheskiy-mon astyr-podvore-zaikonospasskogo-stavropigialnogo-monastyrya/.

62. Akel'yev, *Povsednevnaya zhizn'*, 329.

63. Ibid., 30.

64. Ibid., 27–29.

65. Ibid., 30–32.

66. Andrey Sidorchik, "Van'ka-Kain, otets russkoy korruptsii. Kak vor bïl khozyainom Moskvï," *Argumentï i faktï,* October 13, 2019, https://aif.ru/society/history/vanka -kain_otec_russkoy_korrupcii_kak_vor_byl_hozyainom_moskvy.

67. Ye. V. Akel'yev, "Arkhivnïye materialï sledstvennogo dela o Van'ke Kaine," in *Gishtorii rossiyskiye, ili Opïtï razïskaniya k yubileyu Aleksandra Borisovicha Kamenskogo,* ed. Ye. V. Akel'yev and V. Ye. Borisov (Moscow: Drevlekhranilishche, 2014), 312.

68. Akel'yev, *Povsednevnaya zhizn'*, 39.

69. Ibid., 66–82.

70. RGADA f. 372, op. 1, d. 6210.

71. Akel'yev, *Povsednevnaya zhizn'*, 87–88.

72. Starozhil, "Iz proshlago," *Peterburgskiy listok,* May 29, 1897, p. 5.

73. T. S. Rozhdestvenskiy and M. I. Uspenskiy, eds., *Pesni russkikh sektantov mistikov* (St. Petersburg: Tipografiya P. P. Seykina, 1912), 15.

74. Information in this paragraph is from K. T. Sergazina, "Khristovshchina v XVIII veke: moskovskaya obshchina Andriana Petrova," *Studia Religiosa Rossica,* no. 1 (2019): 31–47, esp. 44; see also Eugene Clay, "The Theological Origins of the Christ-Faith [Khristovshchina]," *Russian History* 15, no. 1 (1988): 21–22.

75. G. V. Yesipov, "Van'ka Kain," in Komarov, *Istoriya moshennika Van'ki Kaina,* 319–20.

76. "9574. Fevralya 13. Imennïy, ob'yavlennïy iz Kabineta Eya Velichesta Politseymeysterskoy Kantselyarii. 'O prekrashchenii v Moskve svoyevol'stv, chinitïkh

dvorovïmi lyud'mi; i ob obyazannosti kazhdago obïtalya lovit' i privodit' v Politsiyu vsekh tekh, kotorïye dnyom ili noch'yu proezzhayushchikh bit' ili grabit' stanut," in *Polnoye sobraniye zakonov Rosskiyskoy imperii s 1649 goda. Tom XIII. 1749–1753* (St. Petersburg: Tipografiya II Otdeleniya Sobstvennoy Yego Imperatorskago Velichestva Kantselyarii, 1830), 10.

77. A. N. Pozhilenkova, "Tatishchev Aleksey Danilovich—nachal'nik Rossiyskoy politsii pri Yelizavete Petrovne," in *Gosudarstvo i pravo: evolyutsiya, sovremennoye sostoyaniye, perspektivï razvitiya (navstrechu 300-letiyu rossiyskoy politsii): Materialï mezhdunarodnoy nauchno-teoreticheskoy konferentsii molodïkh issledovateley. Sankt-Peterburg, 28 aprelya 2017 g.,* ed. N. S. Nizhnik, 2 vols. (St. Petersburg: MVD Rossii, 2017), 2:9–10.

78. Akel'yev, *Povsednevnaya zhizn',* 379–80.

79. "Zhizn' i pokhozhdeniye rosskiyskogo Kartusha," 287.

80. Akel'yev, *Povsednevnaya zhizn',* 389.

81. The engineering challenges are summarized by M. V. Lavrent'yev, "Rogervik—katorga v imperatorskoy Rossii v 1726–1761 gg.," in *Sotsial'no-ekonomicheskiye protsessï sovremennogo obshchestva: materialï Vserossiyskoy nauchno-prakticheskoy konferentsii s mezhdunarodnïm uchastiyem* (Cheboksarï, 26 fevralya 2021 g.), ed. E. V. Fomin (Cheboksarï, Russia: Sreda, 2021), 155–57.

82. Marasinova, "The Death Penalty Moratorium," 1094.

83. "Zhizn' i pokhozhdeniye rosskiyskogo Kartusha," 288.

84. A. T. Bolotov, *Zhizn' i priklyucheniya Andreya Bolotova, opisannïye samim im dlya svoikh potomkov, 1738–1760* (St. Petersburg: Pechatnya V. Golovina, 1871), 341.

85. Ibid., 342; Anisimov, *Yeliziveta Petrovna,* 307.

CHAPTER 9

1. Michael Josselson and Diana Josselson, *The Commander: A Life of Barclay de Tolly* (Oxford: Oxford University Press, 1980), 111.

2. Dominic Lieven, *Russia Against Napoleon: The True Story of the Campaigns of* War and Peace (New York: Viking, 2010), loc. 864, Kindle.

3. Ibid., loc. 847–51.

4. Ibid., loc. 3401.

5. Ibid., loc. 3470–86.

6. "Proiskhozhdeniye familii Kutuzov," Analiz familii, accessed March 12, 2024, https://www.analizfamilii.ru/Kutuzov/proishozhdenie.html.

7. Lieven, *Russia Against Napoleon,* loc. 4298, 4631.

8. Sergey V. Kushchayev et al., "Two Bullets to the Head and an Early Winter: Fate Permits Kutuzov to Defeat Napoleon at Moscow," *Neurosurgical Focus* 39, no. 1 (2015): 1–18. This article caused great offense in Russia.

9. Adam Zamoyski, *Moscow 1812: Napoleon's Fatal March* (New York: HarperCollins, 2004), 229.

10. Alexander M. Martin, *Enlightened Metropolis: Constructing Imperial Moscow, 1762–1855* (Oxford: Oxford University Press, 2013), 185.

11. Ibid., 124.

12. Ibid., 126, 129, 132, 141, 156, 160.

13. A. O. Meshcheryakova, *F. V. Rostopchin: U osnovaniya konservatisma i natsionalizma v Rossii* (Voronezh: Kitezh, 2007), 184.

14. Ibid., 74.

15. *Rostopchinskiye afishi 1812 goda. Bibliograficheskoye izdaniye v 300 ekzemplyarakh* (St. Petersburg: Tipografiya A. S. Suvorina, 1889), 26–28.

16. Nadezhda Aurova, "Vtorzheniye Napoleona v Rossiyu v vospriyatii russkogo obshchestva," *Perspektivï*, no. 3 (2023): 75.

17. Meshcheryakova, *F. V. Rostopchin*, 97.

18. The project was pursued in secret on an estate outside Moscow in the settlement of Vorontsovo. The inventor, Franz Leppich (or, as Rostopchin preferred to call him, "Schmidt"), purchased masses of silk, barrels of acid, boxes of explosives, and light steel for his work. The locals, assuming that he was an agricultural equipment developer, wondered how these materials benefited the harvest. After a while, Rostopchin started complaining about the increasing costs and blasted the "ball" as "a devil's instrument." But Tsar Alexander I allowed the project to continue. Time passed; Napoleon loomed. The flying machine was rolled out for its inaugural flight, rose a few feet into the air and crashed. Leppich blamed everyone but himself for the fiasco, packed up, and left. Alexander Tarsaidze, "The Air Blitz of 1812," *Russian Review* 2, no. 1 (Autumn 1942): 89–101 (information and quotations).

19. Meshcheryakova, *F. V. Rostopchin*, 187–88.

20. Lieven, *Russia Against Napoleon*, loc. 3886–3901.

21. Aleksandr Bayura, "Napoleonovskiye vïpuski fal'shivïkh rossiyskikh assignatsiy," *Bankaŭski vesnik*, no. 19 (2012): 63. One of the printing presses he relied on was hidden in the gatehouse of a cemetery outside Moscow.

22. Zamoyski, *Moscow 1812*, 241.

23. Martin, *Enlightened Metropolis*, 191.

24. Alexander Pushkin, *Eugene Onegin*, trans. James E. Falin (Oxford: Oxford University Press, 1995), 174; Aleksandr Vas'kin, "O besplodnïkh ozhidaniyakh Napoleonom klyuchey ot Moskvï 2 sentyabrya 1812 goda," *Aspirant i soiskatel'*, no. 2 (2000): 8.

25. Information and quotations in this paragraph and the previous one are from Vas'kin, "O besplodnïkh ozhidaniyakh Napoleonom," 8–11.

26. Leo Tolstoy, *War and Peace*, trans. Richard Pevear and Larissa Volokhonsky (New York: Vintage, 2008), 875.

27. V. N. Zemtsov, *Napoleon v Moskve* (Moscow: Media-Kniga, 2014), 23–28.

28. Mariya Nikolayevna Pavlova, "Upravleniye Moskvoy i zhizn' moskvichey v period frantsuzskoy okkupatsii 1812 goda" (PhD thesis, Moscow State Regional University, 2019), 41–42, 109–110.

29. Martin, *Enlightened Metropolis*, 201–2.

30. Letter from Napoleon I to Alexander I About a Fire in Moscow, prlib.ru (Presidential Library of the Russian Federation), accessed March 14, 2024, https://www.prlib.ru/en/node/357502.

31. Martin, *Enlightened Metropolis*, 181.

32. Zemtsov, *Napoleon v Moskve*, 168–70.

33. A. P. Glushkovskiy, *Vospominaniya baletmeystera* (Leningrad and Moscow: Iskusstvo, 1940), 106.

34. Ibid., 108.

35. "Iz Venï," *Moskovskiye vedomosti*, December 25, 1812, p. 8.

36. Martin, *Enlightened Metropolis*, 210.

37. V. N. Zemtsov, "Abbat Syuryug i frantsuzskiy 'mif' o moskovskom pozhare 1812 goda," *Imagines mundi: al'manakh issledovaniy vseobshchei istori XVI-XX vv.* 4, no. 2 (2006): 90.

38. Pavlova, "Upravleniye Moskvoy," 153.

39. Martin, *Enlightened Metropolis*, 201.

40. The case of court councilor Alexei Bestuzhev-Ryumin, who decided against evacuating in August, is instructive. He considered it his duty to guard the archive of his workplace: the patrimonial department of the Moscow Senate. Since he could speak French, he was asked to join Napoleon's occupation government. He refused at first, claiming that he couldn't serve two emperors at once, but then, under duress, his family homeless, hungry, and unwashed, agreed. (The sight of French soldiers "throwing books and bundles of files out of the windows" of his archive also helped change his mind.) After Napoleon's expulsion, Rostopchin had Bestuzhev-Ryumin investigated for embezzlement but ultimately acquitted him. Aleksandr Vas'kin, "Napoleon i moskvichi: O popïtakh frantsuzov organizovat' v Moskve munitsipalitet," *Istoricheskiye nauki*, no. 3 (2012): 6–9.

41. David J. Galloway, "Victim of Circumstance: Rastopchin's Execution of Vereshchagin in Tolstoi's *Voina i mir*," *Carl Beck Papers*, no. 1404 (January 2000): 26; *Rostopchinskiye afishi 1812 goda*, 22–23. In the bulletin, Rostopchin alerts the public to the distribution in Moscow of lurid information about Napoleon's plans to be in both Russian capitals in six months. He adds that Vereshchagin had confessed to writing the document and a provincial secretary, Meshkov, to copying it. The governor-general promises just punishment "for their crime."

42. Pyotr Sheremetevskiy, *Delo o Vereshchagine i Meshkove. Ugolovno-sudebnïy epizod iz istorii Moskvï v 1812 godu* (Moscow: Universitetskaya tipografiya [Katkov i Ko.], 1867), 15.

43. Tolstoy, *War and Peace*, 888.

44. Galloway, "Victim of Circumstance," 17.

45. Tolstoy, *War and Peace*, 892.

46. N. V. Borsuk, *Rostopchinskiye afishi. Tekst s primechaniyami i predisloviyem* (St. Petersburg: Novoye vremya, [1912]), 34; see also Galloway, "Victim of Circumstance," 3.

47. Meshcheryakova, *F. V. Rostopchin*, 213–14.

48. F. V. Rostopchin, *Pravda o pozhare Moskvï*, trans. [from French] Aleksandr Volkov (Moscow: Universitetskaya tipografiya, 1823), 12–14. After these denials, Rostopchin offered two explanations for the fire:

    (1) In Moscow there is a whole street with carriage shops, where only carriage makers live. When Napoleon's army entered the city, many generals and officers rushed to this quarter, and after visiting all the establishments therein, they chose carriages for themselves with their names to be put on them. The owners, by mutual

agreement, agreed not to provide the enemy with carriages, and set fire to all their shops.

One of the merchants left with his family for Yaroslavl, entrusting the care of his house to a nephew. When the police returned to Moscow, this nephew turned up to announce that seventeen dead bodies were in his uncle's cellar. He spoke about the incident thusly: the day after the enemy entered the city, four [French] soldiers came to the house. They went through it and, not finding anything to steal, went into the basement, where they found a hundred bottles of wine. They told the merchant's nephew to look after those bottles. In the evening, they came back with the thirteen other soldiers. They lit candles in the basement, began to drink and sing and then fell asleep. The young Russian merchant, seeing them fully immersed in drunken slumber, decided he should kill them. He locked the cellar, blocked the entrance with stones and ran away down the street. After several hours had passed, and having thought carefully about how these seventeen people might perhaps free themselves from their captivity, catch up with him and kill him, he decided to set the house on fire. This he did with straw. Probably these unfortunate seventeen people suffered from smoke.

(2) Already on the first night after the occupation of Moscow, a large building of shops located opposite the Kremlin was completely in flames. Subsequently, and even continuously, there were fires in many parts of the city; but on the fifth day a terrible whirlwind spread the flames everywhere, and in three days the fire consumed seven thousand six hundred and thirty-two houses. One cannot expect great caution on the part of the soldiers who walked from house to house at night with candle stubs and torches in their hands; many even laid a fire in the middle of their courtyards to warm themselves. The given order, which gave the right to each regiment located in bivouacs near the city to send a designated number of soldiers to plunder the houses of those already burned, was, so to speak, an invitation or permission to increase the number of thieves. What confirms to Russians that Moscow was burned by the enemy was the pointless blowing up of the Kremlin.

That's all I can say about the great Moscow fire, an incident ever more surprising for having no precedent in history (ibid., 21–25).

49. Ekaterina Pravilova, *The Ruble: A Political History* (New York: Oxford University Press, 2023), 387 n 64.

50. P. S. Nikol'skiy, "Finansovaya sostavlyayushchaya voynï Rossii protiv napoleonovskogo nashestviya v 1812–1815 godï," *Gumanitarnïye nauki*, no. 3 (2012): 82.

51. T. A. Molokova, "Vosstanovleniye Moskvï posle pozhara 1812 g.: novïy oblik goroda," *Vestnik MGSU*, no. 6 (2012): 20.

52. In 1816, Bové married a widowed princess, Avdotya Trubetskaya, who surrendered her title to be with him and made him illegitimately (it was gossiped) rich.

53. Alexander Griboedov, *Woe from Wit: A Verse Comedy in Four Acts*, trans. Betsy Hulick (New York: Columbia University Press, 2020), 50–51.

54. S. A. Shcherbakov and M. V. Korolyova, "Rekonstruktsii arkhitekturno-landshaftnogo ansamblya Aleksandrovskogo sada u sten Moskovskogo Kremlya," *Academy*, no. 11 (2019): 59.

55. Molokova, "Vosstanovleniye Moskvï," 19.

56. Ibid.

57. Egor Kholmogorov, "Gagarin Yuriy Alekseyevich," RusKontur, accessed March 30, 2024, https://ruskontur.com/gagarin-yurij-alekseevich/.

58. A. Smirnov, *Moskva—geroyam 1812 goda* (Moscow: Moskovskiy rabochiy, 1981), 16.

CHAPTER 10

1. Alexander M. Martin, *Enlightened Metropolis: Constructing Imperial Moscow, 1762–1855* (Oxford: Oxford University Press, 2013), 17.

2. "Neobïchnïye i udivitel'nïye nazvaniya moskovskikh ulits," Progulki po Moskve, November 9, 2011, http://moscowwalks.ru/2011/11/09/strange-streets/.

3. In a 1790 book allegorizing a trip from St. Petersburg to Moscow, Alexander Radishchev, the foreign-educated head of the St. Petersburg customs house, railed against the evils of serfdom, religious intolerance, the rigged legal system, censorship, sexual assault, people sold at auction to settle their debts, and the plight of anyone seeking redress for abuse. He romanticized peasants, laborers, and pilgrims for their chasteness, moral correctness, and better health compared to the foul-breathed aristocratic class. Life on Lazy Lane wasn't so bad after all.

    Radishchev correctly anticipated a hostile reception for his book, which he published anonymously. The manuscript passed the censors in abbreviated guise, then Radishchev added polemics. The result so infuriated Catherine that, having identified Radischev as the author, she locked him up in the Peter and Paul Fortress in St. Petersburg and had all the copies of the book she could retrieve destroyed. (A total of 650 copies were printed, a lot for the time; Pushkin got his hands on one of the few that survived the stove.) Radishchev begged for forgiveness and escaped the death penalty. The empress instead exiled him in shackles to a tiny town in southeastern Siberia. Her successor, Pavel, recalled him and put him to work on his estate, where Radischev continued to spout subversive ideas. Presumably threatened with another exile, he committed suicide in 1802 by drinking nitrohydrochloric acid (Andrew Kahn and Irina Reyfman, introduction to Alexander Radishchev, *Journey from St. Petersburg to Moscow,* trans. Andrew Kahn and Irina Reyfman [New York: Columbia University Press, 2020], x–xviii).

4. Lurana Donnels O'Malley, *Two Comedies by Catherine the Great, Empress of Russia: Oh, These Times! and The Siberian Shaman* (New York: Routledge, 1998).

5. The following information on Maddox and the Petrovsky Theater is from Rossiyskiy gosudarstvennïy arkhiv literaturï i iskusstva (RGALI) f. 2, op. 1, yed. khr. 329 (A Osipov, "Antreprener proshlogo veka"); Ol'ga Chayanova, *Teatr Maddoksa v Moskve, 1776–1805* (Moscow: Rabotnik prosveshcheniya, 1927); and M. P. Pryashnikova, "Angliyskiy predprinimatel' M. Medoks v Rossii," in *Pamyatniki kul'turï. Novïye otkrïtiya. Pis'mennost'. Iskusstvo. Arkheologiya. Yezhegodnik 2005,* ed. T. B. Knyazevskaya (Moscow: Nauka, 2013), 216–34.

6. Chayanova, *Teatr Maddoksa v Moskve,* 99.

7. RGIA f. 759, op. 94, d. 102, l. 2.

8. Ibid., l. 4.

9. RGIA f. 13, op. 1, d. 92, l. 2.

10. Ibid., l. 3.

11. Ibid.

12. K. Medoks, "Proiskhozhdeniye russkikh dvoryan Medoksov," *Russkiy arkhiv*, no. 10 (1886): 262.

13. Sigizmund Krzhizhanovsky, "Postmark: Moscow," 1925, in *Autobiography of a Corpse*, trans. Joanne Turnbull with Nikolai Formozov (New York: New York Review of Books, 2013), 186.

14. Leo Tolstoy, *War and Peace*, trans. Richard Pevear and Larissa Volokhonsky (New York: Vintage, 2008), 561.

15. Krzhizhanovsky, "Postmark," 186.

16. The following information on the Bolshoi Petrovsky Theater is from A. I. Kuznetsova and V. Ya. Libson, *Bol'shoy teatr: Istoriya sooruzheniya i rekonstruktsii zdaniya* (Moscow: Al'fa-Print, 1995), 35–63, 184–91.

17. *Moskovskiye vedomosti* No. 5, v subboty, yanvarya 17 dnya, 1825 goda [Saturday, January 17, 1825], 141.

18. "Destruction of the Imperial Theatre, Moscow, by Fire," *Illustrated London News*, July 2, 1853, p. 525.

19. *Moskovskiye vedomosti* No. 5, v subbotu, yanvarya 3 dnya, 1825 [Saturday, January 3, 1825], 11. Tickets for the opening performance and masquerade ranged from 50 kopecks for the "second side gallery" to 15 rubles for a "loge in the stalls."

20. Vladimir Gilyarovsky, *Moscow and Muscovites*, trans. Brendan Kiernan (Montpelier, VT: Russian Information Services, 2013), 187–88.

21. "Destruction of the Imperial Theatre, Moscow, by Fire."

22. RGIA f. 497, op. 2, d. 14484.

23. Certainly the fire ended careers, including that of the first great Muscovite ballet dancer, Ekaterina Sankovskaya (1816–78), who called it quits before the ashes had cooled. She had risen to the top of her profession and remained there despite a long list of ailments caused by dancing: frayed nerves, gastrointestinal distress, liver irritation, fever, and back pain. (The details are in her *lichnoye delo* preserved in RGALI f. 659, op. 4, yed. khr. 1298.) Her claque of supporters ensured that she lived better than other dancers employed by the Bolshoi Petrovsky, who worked on the side in laundries, mills, even as supervised street prostitutes, dressed in yellow and carrying a "ticket" documenting their required medical examinations (D. V. Zaslavskiy and L. V. Belova, "Portret neznakomki: k istorii bor'bï s prostitutsiyey v Rossii [XV v.—1917 g.]," *Dermatovenerologiya. Kosmetologiya* 9, no. 2 [2023]: 207, 210).

24. "Simvolika i znacheniye Krïmskoy voynï," Russkaya ideya, October 17, 2007, https://rusidea.org/25101703.

25. Ibid.

26. Tat'yana Belova, *Bol'shoy teatr Rossii: Istoricheskaya stsena* (Moscow: Novosti, 2011), 87.

27. Ibid., 12.

28. [William Howard Russell], "Russia," *The Times,* September 20, 1856, p. 7.

29. S. P., "Moskovskaya zhizn'," *Golos,* March 4, 1969, p. 1.

30. RGIA f. 777, op. 2, d. 12, l. 43.

31. G. A. Laroche, "*The Oprichnik,*" April 17, 1874, in *Russians on Russian Music, 1830–1880: An Anthology,* ed. and trans. Stuart Campbell (Cambridge: Cambridge University Press, 1994), 242.

32. N. G. O. Pereira, "Alexander II and the Decision to Emancipate the Russian Serfs, 1855–61," *Canadian Slavonic Papers* 22, no. 1 (March 1980): 104.

33. Richard Wortman, "The Coronation of Alexander III," in *Tchaikovsky and His World,* ed. Leslie Kearney (Princeton, NJ: Princeton University Press, 1998), 289–90.

34. Richard S. Wortman, *From Alexander II to the Abdication of Nicholas II,* vol. 2 of *Scenarios of Power: Myth and Ceremony in Russian Monarchy* (Princeton, NJ: Princeton University Press, 2000), 350.

35. T. D. Sinitsïna, "Dokumentï GARF o sobïtiyakh Khodïnskoy katastrofi," *Tendentsii razvitiya naukha i obrazovaniya* 79, no. 3 (2021): 158–59.

36. Boris Galenin, "Neizvestnaya Khodïnka," Imperatorskoye Pravoslavnoye Palestinskoye Obshchestvo, accessed December 10, 2024, https://www.ippo.ru/history ippo/article/neizvestnaya-hodynka-bg-galenin-201695.

37. RGIA f. 652, op. 1, d. 523, l. 13 ob.

CHAPTER 11

1. Ivan Belousov, *Ushedshaya Moskva* (Moskovskoye tovarishchestvo pisateley, 1927).

2. Yu. A. Labïntsev and L. L. Shchavinskaya, "Moskovskiy literatur I. A. Belousov—perevodchik i populyarizator poeticheskogo naslediya Tarasa Shchevchenko i Yanki Kupalï," *Slavyanskiy al'manakh,* nos. 1–2 (2016): 183.

3. Maria Nashchokina, "Zaryadye in Modern Age," in *Zaryadye,* ed. Anatoly Belov (Moscow: Arkhsovet Moskvï, 2017), 192–94.

4. Ibid., 183.

5. Yu. V. Koroneva, "Imeni svyatïkh na karte Moskvï," in *Russkiy yazïk v slavyanskoy mezhkul'turnoy kommunikatsii. Sbornik nauchnïkh trudov po itogam Mezhdunarodnoy nauchnoy konferentsii, posvyashchyonnoy pamyati doktora filologicheskiykh nauk, professora Voylovoy K. A. (g. Moskva, 27 fevralya 2020 g.),* ed. O. V. Shatalova (Moscow: Diona 2020), 172.

6. Belousov, *Ushedshaya Moskva,* 11–12.

7. Ivan Belousov, *Literaturnaya Moskva (vospominaniya 1880–1928). Pisateli iz naroda. Pisateli—narodniki* (Moscow: Moskovskoye tovarishchestvo pisateley, 1929), 5; N. Teleshov, *Zapiski pisatelya. Rasskazï o proshlom i vospominaniya* (Moscow: Sovetskiy pisatel', 1950), 173.

8. A. V. Kalinina, "Reformirovaniya sistemï shkol'nogo obrazovaniya v Rossii v 1860-e—1870-e gg." (master's thesis, Ural'skiy federal'nïy universitet imeni pervogo Prezidenta Rossii B. N. Yel'tsina, 2015), 92.

9. Belousov, *Ushedshaya Moskva,* 12–13.

10. Belousov, *Ushedshaya Moskva,* 13. The eighteenth century witnessed the introduction of hierarchical rankings for commercial businessmen based on their self-declared wealth. The first guild included bankers, bigger traders, doctors, jewelers, and icon-makers. The second included smaller merchants, and the third included irregular, itinerant dealers. Taxes and fees were collected according to rank. A. S. Panchenko, "Formirovaniye kupecheskikh gil'diy v Rossiyskoy imperii v 1775–1785 gg.," *Problemï zakonnosti,* no. 121 (2013): 230–37.

11. Belousov, *Ushedshaya Moskva,* 15.

12. Ibid., 43.

13. Ibid., 43–45.

14. "6 noyabrya professional'nïy prazdnik otmechayut sotrudniki sluzhbï deloproizvodstva i arkhiva ugolovno-ispolnitel'noy sistemï Rossiyskoy Federatsii," Federal'naya sluzhba ispolneniya nakazaniy, November 6, 2023, https://fsin.gov.ru/news/index.php.

15. Shaun Walker, "Notorious Moscow Prison, Once Home to Solzhenitsyn, to Close," *Guardian,* December 17, 2018, https://www.theguardian.com/world/2018/dec/17/notorious-moscow-butyrka-prison-once-home-to-solzhenitsyn-to-close; "Notorious Moscow Detention Center to Close Before Its 250th Anniversary," Radio Free Europe, December 17, 2018, https://www.rferl.org/a/russia-butyrka-detention-center-moscow-closing-250th-anniversary/29660808.html.

16. "Tyurmï v Moskve," Progulki po Moskve, October 29, 2010, http://moscowwalks.ru/2010/10/27/tyurmi-moskvi/.

17. "Pis'mo v Sledstvennïy komitet ot Zhiteley Khitrovki (nachalo)," LiveJournal, September 25, 2014, https://ivanovska-gorka.livejournal.com/485961.html.

18. Henri Troyat, *Daily Life in Russia Under the Last Tsar,* trans. [from French] Malcolm Barnes (Stanford, CA: Stanford University Press, 1961), 57–61.

19. Vladimir Gilyarovsky, *Moscow and Muscovites,* trans. Brendan Kiernan (Montpelier, VT: Russian Information Services, 2013), 34–35, 42–43.

20. Belousov, *Ushedshaya Moskva,* 48–49.

21. Ibid., 57.

22. Ibid., 69–70.

23. M. N. Fursov, "Glebovskoye podvor'ye v Zaryad'ye. O yevreyskom voprose v Moskve v pervoy polovine XIX v.," in *Moskoviya: materialï i issledovaniya po istorii i arkheologii,* ed. M. V. Moiseyev (Moscow: Muzey Moskvï, 2015), 49–50.

24. Harold Frederic, *The New Exodus: A Study of Israel in Russia* (London: W. Heinemann, 1892), 199.

25. Fursov, "Glebovskoye podvor'ye v Zaryad'ye," 51–52.

26. Belousov, *Ushedshaya Moskva,* 21–22.

27. Margarita Lobovskaya, "Putevoditel' po yevreyskoy Moskve," in *Moskva yevreyskaya. Sbornik statey i materialov,* ed. K. Yu. Burmistrov (Moscow: Dom yevreskoy knigi, 2003), 26.

28. Belousov, *Ushedshaya Moskva,* 21.

29. Ibid., 67.

30. John T. Alexander, *Bubonic Plague in Early Modern Russia: Public Health and Urban Disaster* (Baltimore: Johns Hopkins University Press, 1980), 42–43.

31. Belousov, *Ushedshaya Moskva,* 99–102.

32. The Mary in question was either the incomparably beautiful wife of a boyar's son or the leader of a band of robbers—no one knows for sure. Ivan the Terrible's musketeers lived there, and noblemen across eras hunted in the woods. In 1646 the central village housed fewer than two hundred people. A century later, in the 1740s, Mar'yina roshcha belonged to the Sheremetyev family, who erected a gilded palace and laid down a stretch of road. A century after that, the construction of the Moscow–St. Petersburg railroad befouled the area. In the 1860s, lots were sold or leased to former serfs and flimsy barracks built, ending the quiet for good. Mar'yina roshcha fell into disrepute, becoming known as much for paupers' houses as paddocks. "Istoriya rayona Mar'yina roshcha," Mar'yina roshcha. Ofitsial'niy sayt Soveta deputatov i Administratsii munitsipal'nogo okruga, accessed November 4, 2023, https://m-roscha.ru/istoriya-rayona-mr/.

33. Gilyarovsky, *Moscow and Muscovites,* 275.

34. L. V. Klimova, "Problemï vzaimodeystviya mestnïkh organov vlasti v Moskve vo vtoroy polovine XIX v.," *Vestnik Moskovskogo gosudarstvennogo oblastnogo univer-siteta,* no. 3 (2015): 117.

35. Belousov, *Ushedshaya Moskva,* 24–26, 51, 88–90, 104–05, 112–13.

36. Ibid., 92–93.

37. Denis Shiryaev, "Moscow, Tverskaya Street in 1896," YouTube video, February 26, 2020, 2:10, https://www.youtube.com/watch?v=6FN06Hf1iFk.

38. Belousov, *Ushedshaya Moskva,* 94–95.

39. A. I. Levitov, *Izbrannoye,* ed. E. M. Zheslova (Moscow: Moskovskiy rabochiy, 1982), 7.

40. ygashae_zvezdu, "Spivshiysya pisatel'," LiveJournal, January 16, 2019, https://ygashae-zvezdu.livejournal.com.

41. His stories are sometimes included in Russian textbooks with a few biographical details. Often cited is a playful novella with the semiliterate title "Moskovskiye 'komnatï snebil'yu,'" meaning "Furnished Rooms in Moscow" but with "furnished" spelled roughly as "funnished." In such rooms, the narrator begins, "timid poverty makes a nest for itself as best it can." The rooms are advertised on a scrap of "gray, dirty paper" whipping and trembling in the wind, "absurdly stuck to the gate post by a few crumbs of black bread." An "unfortunate line of homeless people stretches out before my eyes, condemned, it seems, by fate itself, to an eternal wandering through 'funnished rooms' recommended by a gray patch." Levitov, *Izbrannoye,* 195.

42. Marjorie L. Hilton, *Selling to the Masses: Retailing in Russia, 1880–1930* (Pittsburgh: University of Pittsburgh Press, 2012), 14–15, 27–28.

43. L. P. Lapteva, "Ideya slavyanskoy vzaimnosti i slavyanskiye s'ezydï XIX v.," in *Slav-yanskiye s'ezydï XIX–XX vv.,* ed. M. Yu. Dostal' (Moscow: Institut slavyanovedeniya i balkanistiki RAN, 1994), 19–20.

44. Frederic, *The New Exodus,* 195.

45. Klimova, "Problemï," 122; N. P. Rozanov, *Vospominaniya starogo moskvicha* (Moscow: Russkiy mir, 2004), 248.

46. Frederic, *The New Exodus,* 187.

47. Klimova, "Problemï," 122.

48. Antony Polonsky, *The Jews in Poland and Russia,* vol. 2: *1881 to 1914* (Liverpool: Liverpool University Press, 2019), 13; "Pobedonostev Konstantin," *Elektronnaya yevreyskaya entsiklopediya,* accessed November 4, 2023, https://eleven.co.il/jews-of-russia/government-society-jews/13248/.

49. Samuil Vermel' (Samuel Vermel), "Yevrei v Moskve," in *Moskva yevreyskaya. Sbornik statey i materialov,* 162. Although this source bears a 1936 date, it remained unpublished until after the Soviet period, with the exception of an excerpt about the events of 1891–92 (ibid., 216 n 1).

50. "Otradnoye yavleniye," *Peterburgskiy listok,* March 24, 1891, p. 2.

51. "K yevreyskomu voprosu," *Peterburgskiy listok,* January 1, 1891, p. 2.

52. Vermel', "Yevrei v Moskve," 164.

53. Ibid.; S. M. Dubnov, *Yevrei v Rossii i zapadnoy Yevrope v epokhu antisemitskoy reaktsii* (Moscow and Petrograd: L. D. Frenkel, 1923), 109.

54. Artur Ionovich Klempert, "Yevrei Moskvï v russkoy periodicheskoy pechati 1870–1910-x gg." (PhD thesis, Moskovskiy gosudarstvennïy universitet, 2006), 12, 109. *Sunrise* was published between 1881 and 1906—mostly monthly, with a weekly chronicle as supplement. It covered politics (the fight for equal rights for Jews in Russia), social issues, and culture.

55. E. Khasina [Chaim Zhitlowsky], *Yevrey k yevreyam* (London: Fond Russkoy Vol'noy Pressï, 1892), 36–37.

56. Vermel', "Yevrei v Moskve," 171.

57. Ibid.

58. Inessa Medzhibovskaya, "Tolstoy's Jewish Questions," in *Tolstoy and His Problems: Views from the Twenty-First Century,* ed. Inessa Medzhibovskaya (Evanston, IL: Northwestern University Press, 2019), 98–99.

59. Information in this paragraph is from Halina Bednenko, "Istoriya moskovskoy yevreyskoy obshchinï i Khoral'noy synagogi," *Medium,* June 8, 2018, https://halinabednenko.medium.com/галина-бедненко-история-московской-еврейской-общины-и-хоральной-синагоги-5da24fe177d.

60. "The Report of the United States Commissioners on the Russian Jews," *Jewish Chronicle,* April 1, 1892, p. 9.

61. Vermel', "Yevrei v Moskve," 168.

62. Frederic, *The New Exodus,* 213–14.

63. Vermel', "Yevrei v Moskve," 168.

64. Dubnov, *Yevrei v Rossii,* 111.

65. Vermel', "Yevrei v Moskve," 174.

66. Dmitriy Sof'in and Marina Sof'ina, eds., *Dnevnik moskovskogo general-gubernatora Velikogo knyazya Sergeya Aleksandrovicha. 1892 god* (Perm, Russia: Permskiy gosudarstvennïy national'nïy issledovatel'skiy universitet, 2018), 38.

67. Konstantin Konstantinovich Poleshchuk, "N. A. Alekseyev i yego deyatel'nost' na

postu moskovskogo gorodskogo golovï" (PhD thesis, Moskovskiy gosudarstvennïy universitet, 2017), 97.

68. Ibid.; Vermel', "Yevrei v Moskve," 175.
69. Poleshchuk, "N. A. Alekseyev," 75–77.
70. T. D. Sinitsïna, "Dokumentï GARF o sobïtiyakh Khodïnskoy katastrofï," *Tendentsii razvitiya naukha i obrazovaniya* 79, no. 3 (2021): 159–60.
71. Vermel', "Yevrei v Moskve," 175.
72. Onisim Gol'dovskiy "Yevrei v Moskve (po neopublikovannïm dokumentam)," in *Moskva yevreyskaya. Sbornik statey i materialov*, 394.
73. [Unsigned], "The Jews in Russia," "Darkest Russia" supplement to *The Jewish Chronicle,* June 12, 1891, p. 12.
74. [Unsigned], "The Jews in Russia, "Darkest Russia" supplement to *The Jewish Chronicle,* January 16, 1891, p. 9.
75. Vermel', "Yevrei v Moskve," 175.
76. Ibid., 176.
77. Klempert, "Yevrei Moskvï," 109–10.
78. Allen Spetter, "The United States, the Russian Jews, and the Russian Famine of 1891–1892," *American Jewish Historical Quarterly* 64, no. 3 (March 1975): 236–44, esp. 240–41.
79. Quoted in Howard Markel, "'Knocking Out the Cholera': Cholera, Class, and Quarantines in New York City, 1892," *Bulletin of the History of Medicine* 69, no. 3 (Fall 1995): 422.
80. William Paterson, "Refugees at Leith," "Darkest Russia" supplement to *The Jewish Chronicle,* March 25, 1892, p. 8.
81. Lev Klyachko, "Za chertoyu," in *Moskva yevreyskaya. Sbornik statey i materialov,* 467.
82. Nashchokina, "Zaryadye in Modern Age," 200.
83. Vermel', "Yevrei v Moskve," 180.
84. Frederic, *The New Exodus,* 218.
85. Ibid., 190–92, 205.
86. Pavel Sergeyevich Kupriyanov, "Dva Zaryad'ya: Vizual'nïye obrazï i kul'turnïye smïslï gorodskogo prostranstva," *Kul'turnaya i gumanitarnaya geografiya* 2, no. 1 (2013): 75–77.
87. Nikolay Yerofeyev and Mikhal Muravski, "Politestetika rossiyskogo urbanizma," Syg .ma, June 26, 2022, https://syg.ma/@sygma/poliestietika-rossiiskogho-urbanizma. Additional information in this paragraph is from Mikhal Muravski, "Zaryad'yelogiya," *Gorodskiye issledovaniya i praktiki* 2, no. 4 (November 2018): 71–77.
88. Ellen Barry, "In Big New Museum, Russia Has a Message for Jews: We Like You," *New York Times,* November 8, 2012, p. A14.
89. Jonathan Dekel-Chen, "Between Myth, Memories, History, and Politics: Creating Content for Moscow's Jewish Museum and Tolerance Center," *Public Historian* 40, no. 4 (November 2018): 100.
90. Elissa Bemporad, *Legacy of Blood: Jews, Pogroms, and Ritual Murder in the Lands of the Soviets* (New York: Oxford University Press, 2019), 13.
91. Email communication with the author, November 2, 2023.

CHAPTER 12

1. S. Sergeyev, "Ot Moskvï do samïkh do okhrain," *Izvestiya,* February 2, 1965, p. 1.
2. Anna Val'man, " 'Vïkhodish' na Novïy Arbat i tam mul'tfilmï pokazïvayut.' Kak zhila odna iz samïkh znamenitïkh stolichnïkh ulits polveka nazad," Moslenta.ru, January 14, 2023, https://moslenta.ru/city/proekty/vykhodish-na-novyi-arbat-a-tam -multfilmy-pokazyvayut-kak-zhila-odna-iz-samykh-znamenitykh-stolichnykh-ulic -polveka-nazad.htm.
3. Mikhaíl Timofeyevich, "Poteryannïy Arbat," timofeyich.ru, accessed April 11, 2024, https://timofeyich.ru/content/arh/moscow/arbat.php.
4. Ibid.
5. Anton Razmakhnin, "Arkhitektor peshekhodnogo Arbata vspomnila, kak yego spasali," *MKRU,* November 22, 2018, https://www.mk.ru/moscow/2018/11/22/ akhitektor-peshekhodnogo-arbata-vspomnila-kak-ego-spasali.html.
6. Ibid.
7. " 'Dvor s chelovech'yey dushoy': kakiye taynï khranit Arbat," Moskva24, April 15, 2024, https://www.m24.ru/articles/Arbat/15042014/41908.
8. Timofeyevich, "Poteryannïy Arbat."
9. Cynthia H. Whittaker, "The Women's Movement During the Reign of Alexander II: A Case Study in Russian Liberalism," *Journal of Modern History* 48, no. 2 (June 1976), 35–69, esp. 38–39; Barbara Alpern Engel, "Engendering Russia's History: Women in Post-Emancipation Russia and the Soviet Union," *Slavic Review* 51, no. 2 (Summer 1992): 311–14.
10. Vladislav Khodasevich, "Konets Renatï," in *Nekropol': Vospominaniya* (Moscow: Olimpa, 1991), 7–8.
11. Caryl Emerson, "Philosophy as Novelistic Fiction in the Work of Two Old Friends: Mikhail Epstein and Vladimir Sharov," *Studies in East European Thought* 76, no. 4 (2024): 688.
12. S. S. Lenevskiy, " 'Prozrachnaya nezhnost' kremlya . . .' Andrey Belïy i Aleksandr Blok v Moskve," in M. L. Spivak, Ye. V. Nasedkina, A. E. Rudnik, and M. B. Shaposhnikov, *Andrey Belïy. Aleksandr Blok. Moskva* (Moscow: Moskovskiye uchebniki i Kartolitografiya, 2005), 26.
13. Sigizmund Krzhizhanovsky, "Postmark: Moscow," 1925, in *Autobiography of a Corpse,* trans. Joanne Turnbull with Nikolai Formozov (New York: New York Review of Books, 2013), 190.
14. D. S. Merezhkovskiy, *O prichinakh upadka i o novïkh techeniyakh sovremennoy russkoy literaturï* (St. Petersburg: B. M. Vol'f, 1893), 37, 39, 40, 63, 83.
15. Aleksandr Tregubov, " 'Chelovek-skandal': Andrey Belïy naprorochil sebe sobstvennuyu smert'," *MKRU,* October 25, 2020, https://www.mk.ru/culture/2020/10/25/ chelovekskandal-andrey-belyy-naprorochil-sebe-sobstvennuyu-smert.html.
16. Ibid.
17. Yevgeniya Sergeyevna Buzhor, "Kontseptsiya teurgicheskogo tvorchestva u Vl. Solov'yova i Vyach. Ivanova," *Obshchestvo: Filosofiya, istoriya, kul'tura,* no. 6 (2019): 12.

18. Andrey Bely, *The First Encounter,* trans. Nina Berberova and Gerald Janacek (Princeton, NJ: Princeton University Press, 1979), 23 (lines 299–314).

19. J. D. Elsworth summarizes them in *Andrey Bely: A Critical Study of the Novels* (Cambridge: Cambridge University Press, 1983), 174–219.

20. Andrei Bely, *The Moscow Eccentric,* trans. Brendan Kiernan (Montpelier, VT: Russian Life Books, 2016), 27.

21. A. Belïy, *Moskva pod udarom* (Moscow: T8rugram, 2018), 183.

22. Vakana Kono, "Nauka i okkul'tism. Glaz, vozrozhdayushchiy mir, v romane 'Moskva' A. Belogo," *21st Century COE Program Occasional Papers* 9 (2009): 19, 23–24.

    The plot of *Moscow* (1926–32) centers on a professor who falls into the clutches of a German secret agent named Mandro, embodiment of all things evil, symbol of Belïy's self-loathing. Mandro is responsible for multiple sexual assaults—including that of his own daughter—and several contract killings. In one especially lurid episode he sticks a candle into the professor's eye: "a sticky mess enveloped the pupil, which loudly burst; he felt his brain getting torn; a glassy liquid poured out onto his swollen cheek" (Belïy, *Moskva pod udarom,* 251). Belïy drew a picture of this scene with what appears to be a ghost hovering in the background (Spivak et al., *Andrey Belïy. Aleksandr Blok. Moskva,* 302). He feared being falsely accused of rape and was haunted, at the end of his life, by his cavalier treatment of women and his "monstrous sensual attraction" to the sister of his first wife, Asya (Monika Spivak, " 'Kak sladko s toboyu mne bït' . . . " [avtobiograficheskiy podtekst v romane Andreya Belogo 'Moskva']," *Ruthenia,* September 7, 2003, https://www.ruthenia .ru/document/529333.html).

23. M. K. Morozova, "Moi vospominaninya," *Nashe naslediye,* no. 6 (1991): 100. Additional details in this paragraph are from Aleksey Mitrofanov, "Moskovskaya krasavitsa: Margarita Morozova," *Moskvich,* June 4, 2019, https://moskvichmag.ru/ lyudi/moskovskaya-krasavitsa-margarita-morozova/.

24. Morozova, "Moi vospominaninya," 99.

25. T. I. Luzina, " 'Khristianskoye bratstvo bor'bï' i russkaya intelligentsiya nakanune revolyutsii," *Vestnik Sankt-Peterburgskogo universiteta,* no. 1 (March 2009): 35.

26. For several years, Morozova supported Scriabin with an annual stipend of 2,400 rubles. E. M. Shabshayevich, "Kul'turno-prosvetitel'skiy potentsial moskovskikh muzïkal'nïkh salonov XIX—nachala XX veka," in *Khristianstvo, iskusstvo, obrazovaniye: dialog kul'tur, traditsii i sovremennost',* ed. S. E. Radchenko and M. F. Rudzik (Kursk: Kurskiy gosudarstvennïy universitet, 2023), 62.

27. M. K. Morozova, "Vospominaniya ob A. N. Skryabine," *Nashe naslediye,* no. 41 (1997): 49.

28. L. L. Sabaneyev, *Vospominaniya o Skryabine* (Moscow: Klassika XXI, 2003), 271.

29. Eckart Altenmüller, "Alexander Scriabin: His chronic right-hand pain and its impact on his piano compositions," in *Music, Neurology, and Neuroscience: Historical Connections and Perspectives,* ed. Eckart Altenmüller, Stanley Finger, and François Boller (Amsterdam: Elsevier, 2015), 206. Scriabin recovered full use of the hand, but the "pain syndrome" was a "psychological disaster for his compositions" (ibid., 209).

30. V. L., "Vtoroy russkiy simfonicheskiy kontsert," *Peterburgskiy listok,* November 12, 1900, p. 4.

31. Henry Miller, *The Rosy Crucifixion,* Book 3: *Nexus* (New York: Grove Press, 1965), 307.

32. Vladimir Aleksandrovich Markus, "Vospominaniya," in *A. N. Skryabin glazami sovremennikov,* ed. A. S. Skryabin and V. V. Popkov (Moscow: Nestor-Istoriya, 2022), 113–14.

33. Val'man, "Vïkhodish' na Novïy Arbat."

34. "Muzïka i tsvet," *Sovetskaya kul'tura,* August 12, 1965, p. 1; "Istoriya muzeya," scriabinmuseum.ru, accessed April 14, 2024, https://scriabinmuseum.ru/pages/about-museum/history/.

35. Shaborkina responded as follows to a lecture and article by musicologist Yuriy Keldïsh on "ideological contradictions" in Scriabin's music: "Comrade Keldïsh accuses Scriabin of becoming detached from life, immersing in the fantastic images of his *Mysterium.* In his lecture he didn't seek an understanding of why Scriabin might have removed himself from his time and place. Might it be that the ugliness of capitalist existence failed him as a source of inspiration, that his focus was on the future and its freedom-loving ideals? This is the reason Scriabin remains relevant to us, why his music is close to our hearts. His subject is that of the will and it is the focus of most of his works, beginning with the symphonic poem he composed in his youth and ending with his final prelude op. 74, no. 5, which expresses the will at its most active. It might have been useful to recall that time in Scriabin's life when he refused to perform in a [Romanov] palace (according to the recollections of his aunt, Scriabin's first teacher). Comrade Keldïsh also failed to note the composer's thoughts about the revolution of 1905: 'Finally, life has awakened among us!' As we know, Scriabin loved life passionately, more than anything else: 'Life is action, aspiration, struggle,' he said. For every unprejudiced listener and reader, this is undeniable." A. S. Skryabin, *Zhizn' v Muzeye: Tat'yana Shaborkina i Muzey A. N. Skryabina* (Moscow: Petroglif, 2019), 112.

36. Ibid., 232 (recollection of historian Yelena Berkovskaya, one of Shaborkina's "museum girls" growing up). The archive was ordered evacuated "to somewhere in the east," but the Germans stood close to Moscow in Khimki and the train containing the archive stopped in Zagorsk, one of the Golden Ring of church-filled towns surrounding Moscow. The archive remained there (in the Trinity Lavra of St. Sergius) until 1944, when another train brought it back to the museum.

37. Ibid., 302 (philosopher and Scriabin enthusiast Bulat Galeyev's recollection).

38. S. Rikhter, N. Dorliak, T. Nikolayeva, S. Averintsev, A. Mikhaylov, E. Pasternak, [letter to the editor], *Ogonyok,* June 23, 1987, p. 17.

39. "Sights in Arbat District," rusmania.com, accessed May 4, 2025, https://rusmania.com/central/moscow-federal-city/moscow/arbat.

CHAPTER 13

1. Gosudarstvennïy arkhiv Rossiyskoy Federatsii (GARF) f. r-4042, op. 4, yed. khr. 5, l. 68.

2. Father George Gapon, *The Story of My Life* (New York: E. P. Dutton & Co., 1906), 1–4.

3. Ibid., 18.

4. Stephen Kotkin, *Stalin: Paradoxes of Power, 1878–1928* (New York: Penguin, 2014), 73.

5. Judy M. Westrate, "The 1905 Bloody Sunday Massacre: American Reactions" (master's thesis, University of Nebraska, 1973), 10, 61.

6. "Day of Terror in Czar's Capital," *New York Times,* January 23, 1905, p. 1.

7. Alexei Anisin, "The Russian Bloody Sunday Massacre of 1905: A Discursive Account of Nonviolent Transformation," *Politics, Groups, and Identities* 2, no. 4 (2014): 644.

8. Erast Galumov, "Istoriya izdatel'stva 'Izvestiya,'" *Obozrevatel',* no. 7 (2010): 105–6.

9. Igor' (Zavodfoto), "Iz serii 'Promistoriya Rossii'—tipografiya t-va I. Sïtina (1907)," Dzen.ru, February 10, 2023, https://dzen.ru/a/Y-AeC-BYM3jvZqr-?experiment= 942751.

10. China Miéville, *October: The Story of the Russian Revolution* (London: Verso, 2017), 34, Kindle.

11. Diane Koenker, *Moscow Workers and the 1917 Revolution* (Princeton, NJ: Princeton University Press, 1981), 19.

12. Michael A. Denner, "Tolstoy as Social Theorist," in *Tolstoy and His Problems: Views from the Twenty-First Century,* ed. Inessa Medzhibovskaya (Evanston, IL: Northwestern University Press, 2018), 40.

13. "Moskovskaya khronika," *Novoye vremya,* December 8, 1905, p. 2.

14. M. I. Vasil'yev-Yuzhin, *Moskovskiy sovet rabochikh deputatov v 1905 g. i podgotovka im vooruzhennogo vosstaniya* (Moscow: Nedra, 1925), 103.

15. "Moskovskaya khronika," *Novoye vremya,* December 9, 1905, p. 2.

16. I. V. Bocharnikov and O. A. Ovsyannikova, "Sïtin Ivan Dmitriyevich. Knizhnïy metsenat Rossii," *Chelovecheskiy kapital,* no. 11 (2019): 32.

17. "Moskovskaya khronika," *Novoye vremya,* December 10, 1905, p. 2.

18. Dmitriy Pavlov, Stanislav Tyutyukin, and Igor' Khristoforov, "Dekabr'skaya repetitsiya oktyabrya: krovavaya khronika Moskovskogo vosstaniya 1905 goda," *Vokrug sveta,* no. 12 (December 2005), https://www.vokrugsveta.ru/vs/article/1759/.

19. "O bïtiye l.gv. semyonovskago polka v Moskvu," *Peterburgskiy listok,* December 16, 1905, p. 5.

20. "Moskovskaya khronika," *Novoye vremya,* December 13, 1905, p. 2; see also "Telegrammï," *Peterburgskiy listok,* December 13, 1905, p. 4: "According to some witnesses, the print houses burned because of artillery fire; according to others, the workers themselves torched it."

21. "Moskovskaya khronika," *Novoye vremya,* December 16, 1905, p. 1.

22. Pavlov, Tyutyukin, and Khristoforov, "Dekabr'skaya repetitsiya."

23. Ibid.

24. Yelena Maksimovna Shukhova, "Moskva, 1905-y," *Moskovskiy zhurnal,* no. 11 (November 2020): 104–5; Aleksey Mitrofanov, "Nikolay Shmidt: revolyutsioner, fabrikant, romantic," Mitropost.ru, March 14, 2021, https://mitropost.ru/konec -fabriki-shmidta/.

25. "Moskovskaya khronika," *Novoye vremya,* December 20, 1905, p. 2; Ya shagayu po

Rossii i miru, "Tryokhgornaya manufaktura—serdtse revolyutsii 1905 goda," Dzen .ru, December 20, 2020, https://dzen.ru/a/X9-2Q_Wm9Cn8J1Um?experiment= 942707/.

26. Koenker, *Moscow Workers,* 72–73.

27. Information and quotations in this paragraph are from A. I. Denikin, *Put' russkogo ofitsera* (Moscow: Veche, 2012), 241–44, 252–56, 259–61, 287–89.

28. V. I. Lenin, "Zadachi revolyutsionnoy sotisal-demokratii v yevropeyskoy voyne," September 1914, Revolyutsionnïy arkhiv, accessed January 11, 2024, http://revarchiv .narod.ru/vladimilitch/lenin26/taches.html.

29. Miéville, *October,* 79.

30. "Zlobï dnya," *Moskovskiye vedomosti,* May 11, 1917, https://rapsinews.ru/incident _publication/20170508/278507170.html.

31. Mariya Sapozhnikova, "1917 god v 10 istoriyakh," arzamus.academy, November 7, 2017, https://arzamas.academy/mag/468-revol.

32. According to Timothy J. Colton, *Moscow: Governing the Socialist Metropolis* (Cambridge, MA: Harvard University Press, 1995), 757, the population in February 1917 was about 2,017,000. Mobilization, migration, epidemics, and hunger would reduce the number to 1,027,000 by August 1920.

33. Dar'ya Tyukova, "Povsednevnaya zhizn' moskovichey v 1917 godu: dekol'te ekonomili materiyu," March 10, 2017, *Moskovskiy komsomolets,* https://www.mk.ru/ moscow/2017/03/10/povsednevnaya-zhizn-moskvichey-v-1917-godu-dekolte -ekonomili-materiyu.html.

34. Ye. V. Pashkov, "Antialkogol'naya kampaniya v Rossii v godï Pervoy mirovoy voynï," *Voprosï istorii,* no. 10 (2010), https://www.demoscope.ru/weekly/2010/0443/ana lit01.php.

35. Slava Bogomolov, "Lenin—Shumenskoye—Revolyutsiya 1917," *Medium,* November 7, 2017, https://medium.com/@Bogomolov/революция-ленин-шушенское -фото-6ae61b2ef6b1.

36. Catherine Merridale, *Lenin on the Train* (New York: Henry Holt, 2016), 76, Kindle.

37. Ibid., 256.

38. Ibid.

39. Gabrielle Cornish, "Lenin in the Groove," *Slavic Review* 82, no. 4 (Winter 2023): 888–89.

40. Pyotr Romanov, "Kerenskiy, pro kotorogo vrali i pravïye, i levïye," *Argumentï i fakti,* July 23, 2015, https://aif.ru/society/opinion/kerenskiy_pro_kotorogo_vrali_i _pravye_i_levye.

41. ahvenas, "Lenin's Hut," *Atlas Obscura,* July 31, 1918, https://www.atlasobscura .com/places/lenins-hut.

42. Predsaditel' Soveta Narodnïkh Komissarov Ul'yanov (Lenin), "K naseleniyu," *Pravda,* November 20, 1917, p. 1.

43. Joshua Rubenstein, *Leon Trotsky: A Revolutionary's Life* (New Haven, CT: Yale University Press, 2011), 100.

44. Romanov, "Kerenskiy."

45. N. P. Okunev, *Dnevnik moskvicha, 1917–1920* (Moscow: Voyennoye izdatel'stvo, 1997), 99–100.

46. "Moskva," *Pravda,* November 12, 1917, p. 3.

47. Konstantin Paustovsky, *The Story of a Life,* trans. Douglas Smith (New York: New York Review of Books, 2022), 578, Kindle.

48. Ibid., 614.

49. Okunev, *Dnevnik moskvicha, 1917–1920,* 108, 110.

50. "Russia did not need to conclude the shameful peace treaty which you signed with the external enemy," the Patriarch (Tikhon) of Moscow and All Russia wrote to the Council of People's Commissars on October 25, 1918, "but you needed that peace treaty because you planned to finally destroy the internal peace of the nation" (Hoover Institution 62015, folder 1).

51. Alexander Rabinowitch, *The Bolsheviks in Power: The First Years of Soviet Rule in Petrograd* (Bloomington: Indiana University Press, 2007), 201.

52. Kotkin, *Stalin: Paradoxes of Power,* 261.

53. R. H. Bruce Lockhart, *Memoirs of a British Agent* (London: Pan, 2002), 258.

54. Richard Pipes, *The Russian Revolution* (New York: Vintage Books, 1990), 781. Stephen Kotkin clarifies that there is no "solid, direct evidence" of Lenin's "complicity" in the murder or "reaction" to it. Email communication, November 29, 2015.

55. Sally A. Boniece, "The Spiridonova Case, 1906: Terror, Myth, and Martyrdom," in *Just Assassins: The Culture of Terrorism in Russia,* ed. Anthony Anemone (Evanston, IL: Northwestern University Press, 2010), 128.

56. Kotkin, *Stalin: Paradoxes of Power,* 275.

57. Alexander Rabinowitch, "Maria Spiridonova's 'Last Testament,'" *Russian Review* 54, no. 3 (1995): 424–28.

58. On the arrests and searches of members of the Union for the Defense of the Motherland and Freedom (Soyuz zashchitï Rodinï i Svobodï), see "Raskrïtïye kontrrevolyutsionnago zagovora [Discovery of a counterrevolutionary conspiracy]," *Izvestiya,* June 1, 1918, p. 3; Spiridonova is called a "fiendish demagogue" in "Aleksinskiy i Spiridonova," *Pravda,* July 6, 1918, p. 1.

59. The preceding information is from Vladimir Drobïshev, "O dnevnike moskovskogo obïvatelya N. P. Okuneva," in Okunev, *Dnevnik moskvicha, 1917–1920,* 316–19.

60. The Soviet Union emerged in 1922 from lands conquered by the Red Army. It included Russia, Ukraine, Belarus, Armenia, Azerbaijan, and Georgia. Uzbekistan joined the union in 1924, Turkmenistan in 1925, and Tajikistan in 1929. Kazakhstan and Kirghizstan followed in 1936, Estonia, Latvia, Lithuania, and Moldova, in 1940.

61. GARF f. 393, op. 18a, yed. khr. 59, l. 8.

62. Present-day Moscow is organized along entirely different lines. There are twelve massive administrative districts of 125 regions, each with its own coat of arms. The Arbat neighborhood belongs to the central administrative district. The coat of arms—an open book, a quill, an Ionic order (the top of an ancient Greek or ancient Roman column), and a golden shield—tells us that Moscow's biggest bookstore is there, along with museums dedicated to classic writers and other artists, like the

composer Scriabin. Moscow's first modern suburb, Mar'yina roshcha, belongs to the northeastern administrative district and has a coat of arms of a dancing maiden in a red dress and flowers in her hair.

63. GARF f. 393, op. 18a, yed. khr. 59, l. 33.

64. Yevgeniy Natarov, "'Pervïy sposob bor'bï-rasstrelivat', vtoroy—izolirovat.' Sto let nazad lyudei tïsyachami ubivali radi svetlogo budushchego," Moslenta.ru, May 11, 2018, https://moslenta.ru/istoriya/pervyi-sposob-borby-rasstrelivat-vtoroi-izoli rovat.htm.

65. GARF f. 393, op. 23, yed. khr. 95 (police chief report about fires, thefts, murders, etc., in the city of Moscow and Moscow province), l. 19 (April 22, 1921): "Officer Mark-hovich was on patrol with MUUR [Interregional Criminal Investigation Department] agent Shecter of the third district. At about 3 o'clock in the morning they detained two unidentified persons, and during the search of one of the unidentified persons, with Markhovich standing next to the other, the unidentified person said 'Let me get the documents' but instead took a gun out of his pocket and began to shoot at Markhovich, wounding him in the right shoulder before disappearing. The second unidentified person, hearing the shot, made a run for it but was wounded in the neck by Shecter and taken to the precinct. Because he was badly wounded, he was taken to Old Catherine Hospital. Markhovich was also placed in Old Catherine Hospital."

66. GARF f. R-8419, op. 1, yed. khr. 349, l. 1.

67. GARF f. 393, op. 45, yed. khr. 218, l. 4.

68. S. I. Chernyavskiy, "Velikaya rossiyskaya revolutsiya v perepiske shveytsarskikh dip-lomatov," *Vestnik SPbGU* 63, no. 3 (2018): 790–91.

69. GARF f. R-8419, op. 1, yed. khr. 349, ll. 53.

70. Leonid Mazïra, "Pis'mo v redatskiyu," *Mech i Trost'*, March 29, 2012, http://apologetika.eu.

71. "Vospominaniya kn. T. G. Kurakinoy (urozhd. baronessï Vrangel')," in *Russkaya letopis'. Kniga pyataya* (Paris: Russkiy ochag, 1923), 226.

72. Ibid., 249.

73. Ibid., 230.

74. There are other models. Ivan the Terrible turned a monastic retreat on the far northern Solovetsky Islands into a prison. Centuries later, the retreat, Solovki, became a Cheka hard labor camp with cultural offerings. These are described in Andrea Gullota, *Intellectual Life and Literature at Solovki, 1923–1930* (Cambridge: Legenda, 2018).

75. John P. LeDonne, *Ruling Russia: Politics and Administration in the Age of Absolutism, 1762–1796* (Princeton, NJ: Princeton University Press, 1984), 189.

76. GARF f. R-4042, op. 4, yed. khr. 5, l. 4. The action is set in the spring of 1793 in France. King Louis XVI has been beheaded, and Europe is seething. The nobleman Erneste des Tressailles has joined the Austrian army in opposition to the revolutionaries and risks his neck by returning to France to collect his young bride-to-be, Countess Alaine de l'Estoile. She's less fond of him than he is of her, setting up the melodrama to come (after an episode in which she and her maid dress up like each other for fun). The castle is stormed by the revolutionaries and Erneste is arrested

by Marc-Arron, a handsome, steadfast lieutenant colonel. In the end, Erneste flees, Marc-Arron and Alaine fall in love, and Marc-Arron, dressed in Erneste's clothes, is executed by his comrades for betraying their cause. Sophus Michaëlis, *Revolutions-Bryllup* (1906), Arkiv for Dansk Litteratur, accessed December 28, 2023, https://tekster.kb.dk/text/adl-texts-michs_07-root.

77. Yevgeniy Natarov, "Novopeskovskiy (Novo-Peskovskiy) kontslager'," Eto pryamo zdes', accessed December 29, 2023, https://topos.memo.ru/article/174+2.

78. A February 19, 1927, report on Moscow's detention facilities from "representatives of the prosecutor's office" has a certain "comrade Shkele" interviewing prisoners about their conditions. He rejects their complaints about late mail deliveries ("I've confirmed that the mail received on the date is getting marked and checked, there's no delay"), poor meals ("I found the food/dinner/satisfactory, bread is provided in 600-gram servings and of appropriate quality"), and bad medical care ("the sick rooms are kept clean"). On April 15, 1927, "comrade Demvitsky" reported from a different location (Sokol'niki): "At present 23 prisoners from the armed forces are held in two cells separate from other prisoners in this correctional labor house. The cells to the right are sufficiently clean and the prisoners report getting baths once every two weeks along with fresh sheets and the food is satisfactory. Today's meal was cabbage soup and wheat porridge with vegetable oil. There have been no complaints about the administration." The same Demvitsky returned to this same *ispravtrudom* on August 29: "The total number of imprisoned military personnel today is 51," he informed his superiors. "Copies of sentences are available for all convicted persons, and terms of their imprisonment have been calculated correctly. Prisoned military personnel are kept in separate cells, locked, regime maintained. There were no complaints against the administration. . . . According to the prisoners there are no bedbugs or lice in the cells. . . . The prisoners' cells and corridors of the wings are kept quite clean. The kitchen and bakery are kept quite clean. I tried today's meal: borscht with meat, potatoes, cabbage and herbs and buckwheat porridge with vegetable oil and fried onions. The borscht was cooked quite well, the porridge had boiled enough. The bread was well baked and tasty. The guardhouse suits its purpose; there is a room for the guard commander and a separate stove for food cooking. The guards said nothing about being insulted by the prisoners while on duty." GARF f. R-4042, op. 2, yed. khr. 397, ll. 1, 3, 5.

CHAPTER 14

1. Paul R. Gregory, *Lenin's Brain and Other Tales from the Secret Soviet Archives* (Stanford, CA: Hoover Institution Press, 2008), 24–35, esp. 31 and 33.

2. Rossiyskiy gosudarstvennïy arkhiv noveyshey istorii (RGANI) f. 89, op. 72, d. 8, l. 1. Discussions about securing and storing Lenin's brain, keeping an eye on Vogt (who would run afoul of Hitler owing to his work with the Soviets), providing funding for the brain's preservation and analysis, and propagandizing the results of that analysis lasted from February 1925 to May 1936 (RGANI f. 89, op. 72, d. 1–12).

3. Jan Adam Romer, "My Two Years Spent in Soviet Russia Under Stalin," Hoover Archives Collection 2022C35, box 1, p. 3.

4. GARF f. R-9414, op. 1, yed. khr. 77, ll. 70, 97.

5. Address and phone books couldn't keep up with the reorganization of municipal enterprises, street name changes, and the shuffling of personnel in the commissariats. The 1936 edition of *Vsya Moskva* (*All Moscow*) includes a note from the publisher acknowledging the directory's almost instant obsolescence.

6. Romer, "My Two Years," p. 82.

7. Stephen Kotkin, *Stalin: Waiting for Hitler, 1929–1941* (New York: Penguin, 2017), 448.

8. Information in this paragraph and the next is from Leah Dickerman, Review of David King, *The Commissar Vanishes: The Falsification of Photographs and Art in Stalin's Russia,* in *Art Bulletin* 80, no. 4 (1998): 756; Serguei Alex, Oushakine, Review of Denis Skopin, "Photography and Political Repressions in Stalin's Russia: Defacing the Enemy," in *Nationalities Papers* 52, no. 5 (2024): 1211.

9. *SSSR na stroyke,* no. 9 (1931): 2. The editorial provides specifics: "Industrial fortresses created and being created by the revolution include Elektrozavod [an electric lighting plant], Dinamo [electric motors, trains, cranes, and hoists], the automobile plants AMO [Moscow Automotive Society] and Avtosborochnïy [auto assembly line], the tool and die factories Sharikopodshipnik [ball bearings], Stankostroy [machine tools], Frazer, and Caliber define the face of Moscow today" (ibid.).

10. Gwendolyn Leick, *Tombs of the Great Leaders: A Contemporary Guide* (London: Reaktion Books, 2013), 40.

11. Dmitriy Koshlakov-Krestovskiy, "Khlebnïy pereulok, 19," *Vedomosti,* August 28, 2022, https://www.vedomosti.ru/kp/interior/article/2022/08/08/934968-hlebnii -pereulok-dom-19.

12. Aleksey Mitrofanov, "Dobrïy i besposhchadnïy doktor Gannushkin: pered nim preklonyalas' vsya Moskva," *Miloserdiye,* February 19, 2021, https://www.miloserdie .ru/article/dobryj-i-besposhhadnyj-doktor-gannushkin-pered-nim-preklonyalas -vsya-moskva/; see also O. Yu. Kazakova, "'Revolyutsionnoye bezumiye' v Rossii nachala XX veka: ot figurï rechi k nauchnoy definitsii," *Uchyonïye zapiski Orlovskogo gosudarstvennogo universiteta,* no. 1 (2020): 40.

13. Kazakova, "Revolyutsionnoye bezumiye," 39.

14. Information in this paragraph is from Alena Solntseva, "'Pochemu mne, tonuvshemu, nikto ne protyanul ruku?': zhizn' i smert' Meyerhkhol'da v pis'makh i dokumentakh," Arzamus, February 9, 2024, https://arzamas.academy/mag/1238 -meierhold.

15. Ya. Kornfel'd, "Dlya kogo stroitsya teatr Meyerkhol'da?," *Izvestiya,* August 26, 1937, p. 3.

16. P. Kerzhentsev, "Chuzhoy teatr," *Pravda,* December 17, 1937, p. 4.

17. "Na sobraniye v teatre Meyerkhol'da," *Izvestiya,* December 23, 1937, p. 4.

18. N. Moleva, "Vs. Meyerkhol'd: 'Ya okazalsya v sostoyanii velichayshego odinochestva,'" *Sovetskiy muzey,* no. 2 (March–April 1989), http://museums.artyx.ru/ books/item/f00/s00/z0000002/st019.shtml.

19. Solntseva, "Pochemu mne, tonuvshemu, nikto ne protyanul ruku?"
20. Ibid.
21. Ann Pasternak Slater, "Rereading: Doctor Zhivago," *Guardian,* November 5, 2010, https://www.theguardian.com/books/2010/nov/06/doctor-zhivago-boris-pasternak-translation.
22. Dmitriy Okunev, "Mest' Stalina? Za chto zverski ubili Zinaídu Raykh," *gazeta.ru,* July 15, 2019, https://www.gazeta.ru/science/2019/07/15_a_12500161.shtml?updated.
23. Leonid Maksimenkov, comp., *Muzïka vmesto sumbura. Kompozitorï i muzïkantï v Strane Sovetov, 1917–1991* (Moscow: Demokratiya, 2013), 135–36.
24. Dmitriy Shostakovich, *Pis'ma I.I. Sollertinskomu,* ed. D. I. Sollertinskiy et al. (St. Petersburg: Kompozitor, 2006), 178.
25. Christina Ezrahi, *Swans of the Kremlin: Ballet and Power in Soviet Russia* (Pittsburgh: University of Pittsburgh Press, 2012), 59.
26. Yekaterina Vlasova, *1948 god v sovetskoy muzïke* (Moscow: Klassika XXI, 2010), 160.
27. Shostakovich, *Pis'ma I. I. Sollertinskomu,* 176; letter of October 30–31, 1935.
28. O. G. Digonskaya and G. V. Kopïtova, *Dmitriy Shostakovich. Notagraficheskiy sprav-ochnik. Vïpusk 1* (St. Petersburg: Kompozitor, 2016), 151, 153.
29. A. Alikhanyan, V. Kirillov-Ugryumov, and N. Shostakovich, "O sushchestvovanii nestabil'nïkh zaryazhennïkh chastits s massoy, prevïshayushchey massu protona," *Dokladï Akademii nauk SSSR. Novaya seriya* 92, no. 4 (1953): 719-21; A. I. Alikha-nian, N. V. Shostakovich, A. T. Dadian, V. N. Fedorov, and B. N. Deriagin, "On the Mass Spectrum of Charged Cosmic Ray Particles," *Journal of Experimental and Theoretical Physics* 4, no. 6 (July 1957): 817–30. (This is an English translation of a Russian article published in June 1957).
30. The prohibition of the opera meant that little good could be said about the pro-ductions. The best Pavel Markov could offer of the Nemirovich-Danchenko staging was that "in the aggregate it offered a harsher assessment of the social environ-ment [represented in the opera] than Shostakovich achieved with his ironic and duplicitous music." It was tragic without being especially emotional; Nemirovich-Danchenko labored to drain anything "Romantic" from his production. (P. A. Mar-kov, *Vl. I. Nemirovich-Danchenko i Muzïkal'nïy teatr yego imeni* (Leningrad: Izdaniye Muz. teatr imeni nar. art. SSSR Vl. I. Nemirovich-Danchenko, 1936), 168, 170. A follow-up book by Markov, *Rezhissura Vl. I. Nemirovicha-Danchenko v muzïkal'nom teatre* (Moscow: Vserossiyskoye teatral'noye obshchestvo, 1960), 218–19, modestly expands these points.
31. Laurel E. Fay, "From *Lady Macbeth* to *Katerina:* Shostakovich's versions and revi-sions," in *Shostakovich Studies,* ed. David Fanning (Cambridge: Cambridge Univer-sity Press, 1995), 177.
32. His identity was brought to light by Yevgeniy Yevgenov (*Sumbur vokrug 'sumbura' i odnogo 'malen'kogo zhurnalista.' Stat'ya i materiali* [Moscow: Flinta, 2006]), who dug up the invoice for the *Pravda* articles at RGALI. Zaslavsky used the fee to settle his Party dues.

33. [D. Zaslavskiy], "Sumbur vmesto muzïki. Ob opere 'Ledi Makbet Mtsenskogo Uyezda,'" *Pravda,* January 28, 1936, p. 3.

34. [D. Zaslavskiy], "Baletnaya fal'sh'," *Pravda,* February 6, 1936, p. 3.

35. Leonid Maksimenkov, *Sumbur vmesto muzïki. Stalinskaya kul'turnaya revolyutsiya 1936–1938* (Moscow: Yuridicheskaya kniga, 1997), 112.

36. Shostakovich, *Pis'ma I. I. Sollertinskomu,* 188.

37. Maksimenkov, *Muzïka vmesto sumbura,* 138.

38. Ibid., 139.

39. Ibid.

40. "Velikoye narodnoye iskusstvo. Iz rechi tov. Yu. Oleshi," *Literaturnaya gazeta,* March 20, 1936, p. 3.

41. Aleksey Korolyov, "Rastvorivshiysya geniy: Pochemu Yuriy Olesha stal futbol'nïm reporterom," *izvestiya.ru,* March 3, 2019, https://iz.ru/851771/aleksei-korolev/rastvorivshiisia-genii-pochemu-iurii-olesha-stal-futbolnym-reporterom.

42. Maksimenkov, *Muzïka vmesto sumbura,* 203–4. The ensemble entertained NKVD officers during the 1939–40 Soviet-Finnish Winter War and operated through WWII. Shostakovich contributed to three NKVD revues in the 1940s: *Native Leningrad (Rodnoy Leningrad,* part of *Otchizna,* 1942); *Russian River (Russkaya reka,* 1944); and *Victorious Spring (Vesna pobednaya,* 1946). See Gerard McBurney, "Shostakovich and the Theatre," in *The Cambridge Companion to Shostakovich,* ed. Pauline Fairclough and David Fanning (Cambridge: Cambridge University Press, 2008), 175–77; and Derek C. Hulme, *Dmitri Shostakovich Catalog: The First Hundred Years and Beyond* (Lanham, MD: Scarecrow Press, 2010), 248–50, 262–63, 286–88. On March 15, 1947, the composer signed a collective letter to the NKVD chief, Lavrentiy Beria, indicating his familiarity and involvement with the ensemble "from the day it was founded." He and the other signatories expressed concern that the singers and dancers were not getting the material support they needed (Maksimenkov, *Muzïka vmesto sumbura,* 204).

43. V. P. Konev, *Sovetskaya khudozhestvennaya kul'tura* (Novosibirsk: Novosibirskiy gumanitarnïy institut, 2001), 54.

44. Shostakovich's political embeddedness is the subject of Leonid Maksimenkov's *Shostakovich. Marshal sovetskoy muzïki* (Moscow: Veche, 2025).

45. Shaun Walker, *The Long Hangover: Putin's New Russia and the Ghosts of the Past* (New York: Oxford University Press, 2018), 23.

46. Geoffrey Roberts, "The Soviet Decision for a Pact with Nazi Germany," *Soviet Studies* 44, no. 1 (1992): 65, 70–71.

47. Philip Decker, "Calling on a Tsar and Not on Stalin: How Certain Nazis Contemplated a Soviet Abandonment of World Revolution, 1936–1941" (lecture, Princeton University, Princeton NJ, February 1, 2024).

48. "Directive No. 21 Operation Barbarossa (December 18, 1940)," German History in Documents and Images, accessed May 7, 2024, https://ghdi.ghi-dc.org/pdf/eng/English57_new.pdf. Italics in original.

49. "Predveriye bitvï (22.06-29.09.1941 g.)," in V. P. Filatov et al., *Moskovskaya bitva v khronike faktov i sobïtiye* (Moscow: Voyenizdat, 2004), 23.

50. Ibid., 30.
51. Ibid., 26.
52. Ibid., 34.
53. Ibid., 81–82.
54. Viktor Valer'yevich Maksimov, "Moskva voyennaya v vospominaniyakh sovremennikov (1941–1942 gg.)," in *Istoriya Moskvï: metodologiya, istochnikovedeniye, istoriografiya, populyarizatsiya: sbornik materialov nauchno-prakticheskoy konferentsii,* ed. S. V. Orlov (Moscow: Moskovskaya gorodskaya Duma, 2023), 265.
55. Ibid., 264–65.
56. "Predveriye bitvï (22.06-29.09.1941 g.)," 87, 82.
57. Ibid., 39, 123.
58. Ibid.
59. Ibid., 87–88.
60. "Oborona Moskvï (30.09–4.12.1941 g.)," in Filatov et al., *Moskovskaya bitva v khronike faktov i sobïtiye,* 159.
61. Ibid., 156.
62. "Predveriye bitvï (22.06-29.09.1941 g.)," 73.
63. O. A. Balandina, "Deyatel'nost' Sovinformbyuro za rubezhom v godï Velikoy Otechestvennoy voynï: effektivnost' i ideologicheskiye prioritetï," *Nauchnïy dialog,* no. 3 (2019): 219; V. Yu. Noskov, "Obraz rebyonka-zhertvï v sovetskoy propagande perioda Velikoy Otechestvennoy voynï (po materialam soobshcheniy Sovinformbyuro)," *Zhurnal istoricheskikh, politologicheskikh i mezhdunarodnïkh issledovaniy,* no. 1 (2018): 13.
64. "Predveriye bitvï (22.06-29.09.1941 g.)," 103.
65. "Kontranastupleniye (5.12.1941 g.–7.01.1942 g.)," in Filatov et al., *Moskovskaya bitva v khronike faktov i sobïtiye,* 238.
66. Ibid., 273.
67. Information in this paragraph is from Artem Bol'shakov, Nataliya Volkhonskaya, and Nikolay Lïsenkov, "'Ustanovit', chto telo tovarishcha Stalina dolzhno bït' polozheno v grob v voennoy forme.' Dokumentï komissii po organizatsii pokhoron generalissimusa," *Rodina,* March 5, 2018, https://rodina-history.ru/2018/03/05/rodina-stalin-pohorony.html.
68. Vsevolod Ivanov, "Velikiy prazdnik velikogo goroda," *Ogonyok,* September 14, 1947, pp. 9–10.
69. I. V. Stalin and Ya. Chadayev, "Postanovleniye Soveta Ministrov SSSR 'O stroitel'stve v g. Moskve mnogoetazhnïye zdaniy.' 13 yanvarya 1947 goda," Biblioteka Mikhaïla Grachyova, accessed July 7, 2023, http://grachev62.narod.ru/stalin/t18/t18_199.htm.
70. David Kramer, "K 40-letiyu Olimpiadï—80: kak posledniy triumf SSSR izmenil Moskvu," *Moskvich,* July 8, 2020, https://moskvichmag.ru/gorod/k-40-letiyu-olimpiady-80-kak-poslednij-triumf-sssr-izmenil-moskvu/.
71. Anatoli Rybakov, *Children of the Arbat,* trans. Harold Shukman (Boston: Little, Brown, 1988), 145.
72. This and the following quotations are from Irina Rishina, "Zarubki na serdtse:

Posledneye moskovskoye interv'yu," *Druzhba narodov,* no. 3 (1999), https://magazines.gorky.media/druzhba/1999/3/zarubki-na-serdcze.html.

73. *Fear* (*Strakh*) is also the title of a 1931 play by Alexander Afinogenov, a writer who experienced a great deal of that emotion. The play highlights the presence of fear on the streets of Moscow and lives of Muscovites but insists, earnestly, that it shouldn't.

CHAPTER 15

1. Andrew Osborn, "Moscow's Dostoevsky Station Could be 'Suicide Mecca,'" *The Telegraph,* June 21, 2010, https://www.telegraph.co.uk/news/worldnews/europe/russia/7843557/Moscows-Dostoevsky-station-could-be-suicide-mecca.html. Dostoevsky's fiction is mostly set in St. Petersburg, but he was born and raised in Moscow and so assigning him a station near his parents' apartment on the grounds of a onetime hospital for the poor had some justification. The station is adjacent to the blighted, once beautiful neighborhood of Mar'yina roshcha.

2. Another legend concerns the Mossovet (Moskva) Hotel, built at the same time as the first phase of the Metro. Supposedly, two façades drawn on the same sheet of paper were shown to Stalin for his approval. Stalin put his signature in the middle of the drawing. The architect didn't dare ask for clarification, and instead incorporated both façades in one, with large windows and a more ornate façade on the left and one with smaller windows and clean lines on the right. The tale is poppycock, but the truth of the matter is no less bizarre. The dissonance arises from conflicts among the three architects involved in the project, the constructivists Leonid Savel'yov and Osval'd Stapran and the neoclassicist Dmitri Shchusev, who became the chief architect of the project after the denunciation of the other two in 1938. Reconciling the hotel with the surrounding historical buildings was a challenge, so too was the incorporation of a smaller grand hotel (a splendid place with Dutch ovens and a French restaurant) in an imperial style. E. V. Druzhinina-Georgiyevskaya and Ya. A. Kornfel'd, *Zodchiy A. V. Shchusev* (Moscow: Izdatel'stvo Akademii Nauk SSSR, 1955), 62–66; Il'ya Varlamov, "Gostinitsa Moskva," varlamov.ru, May 21, 2013, https://varlamov.ru/780468.html.

3. "Obshchestvennïy transport Moskvï," ru.wikipedia.org, accessed May 17, 2025, https://ru.wikipedia.org/wiki/Общественный_транспорт_Москвы.

4. Tony Dunnell, "Compassion," AtlasObscura, May 20, 2019, https://www.atlasobscura.com/places/compassion-malchik-monument.

5. "Moskovskoye metro 'pereimenovalo' dve stantsii iz-za koronavirusa," RIA Novosti, March 29, 2020, https://ria.ru/20200329/1569300492.html.

6. Anna Kanevskaya, "Dmitriya Prigova pominali v vagone metro," *gazeta.ua,* August 27, 2007, https://gazeta.ua/ru/articles/world-newspaper/_dmitriya-prigova-pominali-v-vagone-metro/179244.

7. The killer, Leonid Nikolayev, had lain in wait for Kirov near his office at the Smolny Institute (the Leningrad Party headquarters) and put a bullet in his head. Nikolayev was arrested at the scene of the crime and, during his interrogation, hysterically claimed estrangement from the Communist Party as his motive. Other theories have

Nikolayev seeking revenge after finding out that Kirov was sleeping with his wife (the "jealous husband" theory), and Nikolayev acting on Stalin's instigation. Stephen Kotkin, *Stalin: Waiting for Hitler, 1929–1941* (New York: Penguin, 2017), 201–13.

8. Aleksandr Zinov'yev, *Stalinskoye metro. Istoricheskiy putevoditel'*, 2011, https://royallib .com/read/zinovev_aleksandr/stalinskoe_metro_istoricheskiy_putevoditel.html#0.

9. Ibid.

10. S. M. Kravets, "Arkhtektura stantsiy i vestibyuley," in *Arkhitektura Moskovskogo metropolitena* (Gosudarstvennoye arkhitekturnoye izdatel'stvo Akademii akhitekturï SSSR, 1941), 39–41.

11. Ibid., 28.

12. Yelena Slobodyan, "Kakiye stantsii Moskovskogo metro bïli pereimenovanï i pochemu?," *Argumentï i faktï,* October 4, 2014, https://aif.ru/dontknows/file/kakie _stancii_moskovskogo_metro_byli_pereimenovany_i_pochemu; "Stantsiya 'Aleksandrovskiy sad,'" Mir metro, accessed August 5, 2023, https://www.mirmetro.net /moscow/cruise/04/10_aleksandrovskiy_sad.

13. Dietmar Neutatz, *Die Moskauer Metro. Von den ersten Plänen bis zur Grossbaustelle des Stalinismus (1897–1935)* (Cologne: Böhlau Verlag, 2001), 26.

14. A. A. Romanov, "Moskovskoye metro—nachalo istorii," *Vestnik universiteta,* no. 4 (2012): 295.

15. "Pervïye proyektï moskovskogo metro," mokvax.ru, accessed August 8, 2023, http://moskvax.ru/metro_34565.html.

16. "Opening of the Metropolitan Railway to the Public," *Guardian,* January 11, 1863, https://www.theguardian.com/world/1863/jan/11/transport.uk.

17. Aleksey Sochnev, "'Grekhovnoy mechtoy yavlyaetsya popïtka proniknut' v podzemnïy mir.' Pochemu v 1900-x godakh ne udalos' realizovat' proyekt podzemki Balinskogo—Knorre," lenta.ru, May 31, 2015, https://lenta.ru/articles/2015/05/ 31/metro1902/.

18. Romanov, "Moskovskoye metro."

19. Neutatz, *Moskauer Metro,* 32–33.

20. The official website of the current Moscow mayor, Sergey Sobyanin, includes the document in a posting titled "The Metro System Moscow Might Have Had. From the Main Archives. The Knorre-Balinsky Proposal," mos.ru, September 22, 2020, https://www.mos.ru/en/news/item/79821073/.

21. Neutatz, *Moskauer Metro,* 36.

22. Ibid.; Sochnev, "Grekhovnoy mechtoy."

23. Neutatz, *Moskauer Metro,* 38–39.

24. Konstantin Georgiyevich Paustovskiy, *Meshchorskaya storona* (Moscow: OLMA Media Grupp, 2014), 9.

25. M. S. Lavrent'yeva and V. A. Davïdov, "Istoriya sozdaniya i razvitiya organov vnutrennikh del na Moskovskom metropolitene," *Vestnik Moskovskogo universiteta MVD Rossii* 3 (2010): 129.

26. Neutatz, *Moskauer Metro,* 59–60.

27. Francis X. Clines, "L. M. Kaganovich, Stalwart of Stalin, Dies at 97," *New York Times,* July 27, 1991, sec. 1, p. 11.

28. N. Osinskiy, "Nuzhen li Moskve Metropoliten?," *Izvestiya*, May 14, 1931, pp. 2–3; G. Puzis, "K voprosu o Metropolitene," *Izvestiya*, June 4, 1931, pp. 2–3.

29. Neutatz, *Moskauer Metro*, 89–91.

30. Vladimir Goraychuk, "Kak sozdavali metro: vzglyad inzhenera," arzamas.academy, accessed July 28, 2023, https://arzamas.academy/materials/1941.

31. Ibid., 144–45; Mikhail Ryklin, " 'The Best in the World': The Discourse of the Moscow Metro in the 1930s," in *The Landscape of Stalinism: The Art and Ideology of Soviet Space*, ed. Evgeny Dobrenko and Eric Naiman (Seattle: University of Washington Press, 2003), 264.

32. L. A. Ostrovskiy, "Zhivaya lestnitsa," in *Kak mï stroili metro*, ed. A. Kosarev (Moscow: Istoriya fabrik i zavodov, 1935), https://www.metro.ru/library/kak_my_stroili_metro/298/; E. Tarakhovskaya, "Lestnitsa-chudesnitsa," in *Gotov! Rasskazï i stikhi o metro*, ed. M. Gershenzon and K. Piskunov (Moscow: Izdatel'stvo detskoy literaturï, 1935), 49–50.

33. *Moskovskiy metropoliten. Zaklyucheniye pravitel'stvennoy ekspertizï po proyektu. 1933*, ed. P. P. Rotert and V. Ya. Volïnskiy (Moscow: Izdaniye upravleniya Moskovskogo metropolitena, 1933), esp. 18–19, 62, 70.

34. Yelena Osokina, *Alikhimiya sovetskoy industrializatsii: vremya Torgsina* (Moscow: Novoye literaturnoye obozreniye, 2024).

35. Neutatz, *Moskauer Metro*, 534–39.

36. Ibid., 118.

37. "Front i tïl mramornïkh rabot," *Udarnik metrostroya*, April 1, 1938, p. 1.

38. Irina Sergeyevna Bogatïreva, "Taynïy, poleznïy, opasnïy: Moskovskiy metropoliten v gorodskikh legendakh," *Fol'klor i antropologiya goroda* 1, no. 1 (2018): 177.

39. Neutatz, *Moskauer Metro*, 231–33.

40. *Istoriya metro Moskvï. Rasskazï stroiteley metro*, ed. A. Kosarev (Moscow: Istoriya fabrik i zavodov, 1935), 164.

41. The dauntlessness of the Komsomol is the subject of an experimental novel by Andrey Platonov called *Happy Moscow* (*Schastlivaya Moskva*). Dating from 1932 to 36, it remained buried in Platonov's papers until its rediscovery in 1991. The heroine is a loveable *komsomolka* surrounded by men obsessed with Esperanto, Frankensteinian experiments on the flesh, and eternal life. Her (mis)adventures include descending from heaven into the underworld and laboring in the Metro after her parachute burns up. When her work is done, she wants to go home but doesn't have one. Her barracks have disappeared, leaving her drifting through time and space and several bad romances.

42. Neutatz, *Moskauer Metro*, 331.

43. Yuri Slezkine, *The House of Government: A Saga of the Russian Revolution* (Princeton, NJ: Princeton University Press, 2017), 814.

44. *Istoriya metro*, 232.

45. Ryklin, "The Best in the World," 269.

46. Goraychuk, "Kak sozdavali metro."

47. Karen L. Kettering, "An Introduction to the Design of the Moscow Metro in the Sta-

lin Period: 'The Happiness of Life Underground,' " *Studies in the Decorative Arts* 7, no. 2 (Spring–Summer 2000): 7.

48. "Yest' metro. Polnometrazhnïy fil'm, 1935 god," #MuzeyTsSDF, accessed July 10, 2023, https://csdfmuseum.ru/films/27-есть-метро.

49. E. Reznichenko, *Dni i godï metrostroya* (Moscow: Moskovskiy rabochiy, 1981), 100.

50. "A Lightness of Flight with Labas at New Tretyakov," *Moscow Times,* March 15, 2011, https://www.themoscowtimes.com/2011/03/15/a-lightness-of-flight-with-labas -at-new-tretyakov-a5646.

51. Unfortunately, the plane subsequently crashed. See Dmitriy Okunev, " 'Razrushil-sya v vozdukhe': kak pogib samolyot 'Maksim Gor'kiy,' " *gazeta.ru,* May 18, 2020, https://www.gazeta.ru/science/2020/05/17_a_13086853.shtml.

52. Neutatz, *Moskauer Metro,* 124–25.

53. Goraychuk, "Kak sozdavali metro."

54. Neutatz, *Moskauer Metro,* 123.

55. Yu. G. Murin, *Iosif Stalin v ob'yatiyakh sem'i. Iz lichnogo arkhiva* (Moscow: Rodina, 1993), 174 (diary of Mariya Svanidze).

56. Ibid., 175; see also Kotkin, *Stalin: Waiting for Hitler,* 234–35.

57. Goraychuk, "Kak sozdavali metro."

58. Bogatïreva, "Taynïy, poleznïy, opasnïy," 159.

59. *Stalinskiye rasstrel'nïye spiski. Spisok ot 20.08.1938,* accessed August 1, 2023, https:// stalin.memo.ru/lists/list186/ (reproducing Rossiyskiy gosudarstvennïy arkhiv sotsial'no-politicheskoy istorii f. 17, op. 171, d. 417, ll. 221–35); L. G. Eremina and A. B. Robinskiy, *Rasstrel'nïye spiski: Moskva, 1937–1941: "Kommunarka," Butovo: Kniga pamyati zhertv politicheskikh repressiy* (Moscow: Memorial, 2000), 318.

60. "Stalin dostayet i iz-pod zemli," *Novaya gazeta,* December 21, 2009, https://novaya gazeta.ru/articles/2009/12/21/39875-stalin-dostaet-i-iz-pod-zemli.

61. Yuriy Gor'kov, *Gosudarstvennïy komitet oboronï postanovlyaet (1941–1945)* (Moscow: OLMA-Press, 2002), 506.

62. Rodric Braithwaite, *Moscow 1941: A City and Its People at War* (New York: Vintage, 2009), 290, Kindle.

63. yapet, "Moskovskiy metropoliten v godï Velikoy Otechestvennoy Voynï," LiveJournal, October 13, 2014, https://yapet.livejournal.com/313688.html; Braithwaite, *Moscow 1941,* 291–94.

64. yapet, "Moskovskiy metropoliten."

65. Bogatïreva, "Taynïy, poleznïy, opasnïy," 168–70.

66. De-Stalinization has recently become re-Stalinization: "Moscow Metro Installs Replica of Stalin Monument," *Moscow Times,* May 15, 2025, https://www .themoscowtimes.com/2025/05/15/moscow-metro-installs-replica-of-stalin -monument-a89089.

67. [Aleksandr Strelkov], "V dushe cheloveka dolzhna zazvuchat' muzïka," 1988, http://www.metro.ru/library/architecture/88/.

68. A. S. Georgiyevskiy, "Korin," *Pravoslavnaya Entsiklopediya,* August 17, 2019, https:// www.pravenc.ru/text/2057286.html.

69. E. A. Rees, *Iron Lazar: A Political Biography of Lazar Kaganovich* (New York: Anthem Press, 2012), 256.

70. Ibid., 253.

71. Ibid., 258–59, 261.

72. Oleg Torchinskiy, "Taynï Moskovskogo metropolitena," *Moskovskaya pravda*, March 29, 2013, p. 21.

73. "Prizraki metro Sokol," moskva-x.ru, accessed August 8, 2023, https://moskva-x.ru/prizrak_metro_sokol.

74. Mark Griffiths, "Moscow After the Apocalypse," *Slavic Review* 72, no. 3 (Fall 2013): 500.

CHAPTER 16

1. I make reference to D. K. Zelenin's typology of those who died unnatural deaths and cannot rest (*Izbrannïye trudï. Ocherki russkoy mifologii: Umershiye neyestestvennoyu smert'yu i rusalki*, ed. E. E. Levkiyevskaya [Moscow: Indrik, 1995], 39–73).

2. Marina Mikhaylovna Valentsova, "Slavyanskaya demonologiya," *Bol'shaya rossiyskaya entsiklopediya*, September 12, 2023, https://bigenc.ru/c/slavianskaia-demonologiia-595bf7.

3. "25296. Dekabrya 25. Manifest'—O postroyenii v Moskve tserkvi vo imya Khrista Spasitelya, v oznamenovaniye blagodarnosti k promsïlu Bozhiyu za spaseniye Rossii ot vragov," in *Polnoye sobraniye zakonov Rosskiyskoy imperii s 1649 goda. Tom XXXII. 1812–1815* (St. Petersburg: Tipografiya II Otdeleniya Sobstvennoy Yego Imperatorskago Velichestva Kantselyarii, 1830), 487–88:

   It is proclaimed to all the people:

   The salvation of Russia from the enemy—so mighty in its plans and ferocity—accomplished in six months by their total destruction, such that only a miserable remnant escaped our borders during their final flight, is a clear manifestation of God's grace and a truly memorable event, never to be erased from our national history.

   To preserve the eternal memory of this unparalleled zeal, faithfulness, and love for the Faith and Fatherland shown by our people during these trying times, and to express our gratitude to Divine Providence for saving Russia from imminent ruin, we have resolved to build in our first capital, the city of Moscow, a church in the name of Christ the Savior.

   A detailed decree will be announced in due course.

   May the Most High bless our undertaking! May it be completed! May this church stand for centuries, and may the prayers of future generations, filled with love and emulation of their ancestors' deeds, rise within its walls in gratitude before the holy altar of God.

4. Konstantin Akinsha, Grigorij Kozlov, and Sylvia Hochfield, *The Holy Place: Architecture, Ideology, and History in Russia* (New Haven, CT: Yale University Press, 2007), 14–15; A. L. Vitberg, "Zapiski akademika Vitberga, stroitelya khrama Khrista Spasitelya v Moskve," *Russkaya starina* 5, no. 1 (January 1872): 19.

5. A. L. Vitberg, "Zapiski akademika Vitberga, stroitelya khrama Khrista Spasitelya v Moskve," *Russkaya starina* 5, no. 2 (February 1872): 175–77.

6. Andrei Zorin, *By Fables Alone: Literature and State Ideology in Late-Eighteenth–Early-Nineteenth-Century Russia,* trans. Marcus C. Levitt with Nicole Monnier and Daniel Schlaffy (Brighton, MA: Academic Studies Press, 2014), 306–11.

7. M. Mostovskiy, *Istoriya Khrama Khrista Spasitelya v Moskve* (Moscow: Tipografiya M. N. Lavrova i Ko., 1884), 219–20.

8. Ibid., 221.

9. Ibid., 227–29.

10. Akinsha, Kozlov, and Hochfield, *Holy Place,* 40.

11. Aleksandr Ivanovich Gertsen, *Bïloye i dumï. Chast' vtoraya. Tyurma i ssïlka (1834–1838),* gertsen.lit-info.ru, accessed July 3, 2023, http://gertsen.lit-info.ru/gertsen/proza/byloe-i-dumy/2-glava-xvi.htm.

12. Mostovskiy, *Istoriya Khrama,* 229–36; see also the chapter on "the unfortunate Vitberg" in Vladimir Rezvin, *Arkhitektorï i vlast'* (Moscow: Iskusstvo-XXI vek, 2013), 145–60.

13. Rezvin, *Arkhitektorï i vlast',* 176.

14. Akinsha, Kozlov, and Hochfield, *Holy Place,* 53; Vladlen Sirotkin, *Napoleon i Rossiya* (Moscow: OMLA-Press, 2000), 250; "Alekseyevskiy monastïr'," Moscow.org, accessed July 3, 2023, http://moscow.org/moscow_encyclopedia/27_alekeevsky_monastery.htm.

15. Irina Sergiyevskaya, "Strashnïye taynï Prechistenki," *Moskovskiy komsomolets,* February 1, 2008, https://www.mk.ru/old/article/2008/02/01/57274-strashnyie-taynyi-prechistenki.html.

16. Catherine Merridale, *Red Fortress: History and Illusion in the Kremlin* (New York: Metropolitan Books, 2013), 228.

17. Dmitri Sidorov, "National Monumentalization and the Politics of Scale: The Resurrections of the Cathedral of Christ the Savior in Moscow," *Annals of the Association of American Geographers* 90, no. 3 (September 2000): 557; Mostovskiy, *Istoriya Khrama,* 188.

18. Andrew Gentes, "The Life, Death and Resurrection of the Cathedral of Christ the Savior, Moscow," *History Workshop Journal* 46, no. 1 (1998): 72.

19. Polina Dimova, "Polar Fantasies: Valery Bryusov and the Russian Symbolist Electric Aesthetic," in *Russian Energy Culture: Work, Power, and Waste in Russia and the Soviet Union,* ed. Jillian Porter and Maya Vinokur (London: Palgrave Macmillan, 2023), 91.

20. Akinsha, Kozlov, and Hochfield, *Holy Place,* 90; I. A. Slonov, *Iz zhizni torgovoy Moskvï (Polveka nazad)* (Moscow: Tipografiya Russkago T-va Pechatnago i Izdatel'skago Dela, 1914), 56–57.

21. Ivan Belousov, *Ushedshaya Moskva. Zapiski po lichnïm vospominaniyam. S nachala 1870 godov* (Moscow: Moskovskoye tovarichestvo pisateley, 1927), 29–30; Akinsha, Kozlov, and Hochfield, *Holy Place,* 89–90.

22. Alexei V. Makarkin, "Orthodoxy and the Soviet Regime: From Conflict to Adaptation," *Russian Studies in Philosophy* 60, no. 5 (2022): 400.

23. RGANI f. 89, op. 49, d. 8, l. 3.
24. Ibid. The patriarchate had been restored by Patriarch Tikhon in 1917. He opposed the confiscation of Church assets during the 1921–22 famine and was imprisoned until he declared the legitimacy of the revolution and denounced the counter-revolutionary activities of the faithful. Meantime, the regime stoked internal conflict in the Church—left against right against center—in hopes that it would decentralize of its own accord to become, "ideally," impotent. RGANI f. 89, op. 49, d. 17, l. 2.
25. RGANI f. 89, op. 49, d. 21, ll. 2–3.
26. A. L. Beglov, "Mol'bï o pomoshchi. Pis'ma pravoslavnïkh veruyushchikh Pape Rimskomu 1931 g.: novïye dokumentï iz arkhivov Vatikana," *Vestnik Pravoslavnogo Svyato-Tikhonovskogo gumanitarnogo universiteta* 91 (2019): 137, 140–42.
27. Vladislav Mikosha, *Ya ostanavlivayu vremya* (Moscow: Algoritm, 2005), 72–76.
28. Yuri Slezkine, *The House of Government: A Saga of the Russian Revolution* (Princeton, NJ: Princeton University Press, 2017), 390.
29. Mikosha, *Ya ostanavlivayu vremya*, 77.
30. Akinsha, Kozlov, and Hochfield, *Holy Place*, 149.
31. B. Iofan, V. Shchukho, and V. Gel'freykh, "Dvorets Sovetov," *Izvestiya*, June 18, 1937, p. 2.
32. Karl Schlögel, *Moscow 1937*, trans. Rodney Livingstone (Cambridge: Polity Press, 2012), 549.
33. Korney Chukhovskiy, *Dnevnik 1901–1963. Tom 2. 1930–1969* (Moscow: OLMA-Press, 2001), 63. Lazar Kaganovich, a member of the Council for the Construction of the Palace of Soviets, didn't want the cathedral demolished and blanched at the idea of replacing it with a monument to communism. Stalin participated in a meeting of the council on June 2, 1931, and "asked simple business questions. He was worried about whether the Palace of Soviets would fit on the site of the demolished temple; discussed how to distribute the flow of people; proposed adjoining the main entrance to the Kremlin." Different sites were assessed before "sacred horror" was overcome and a consensus reached regarding the vanished cathedral grounds (S. O. Kuznetsov, "Rol' Stalina v organizatsii konkursa na proyektirovaniye Dvortsa Sovetov [1931–1932 gg.]," *Arkhitektura i sovremennïye informatsionnïye tekhnologii,* no. 3 [2019]: 58).
34. William J. R. Curtis, *Modern Architecture Since 1900* (Upper Saddle River, NJ: Prentice Hall, 1996), 212–14.
35. Christopher Gray, "For the Car, and Far from Pedestrian," *New York Times,* September 12, 2010, p. RE5. Hamilton was replaced in the design competition by Vladimir Shchuko, architect of the Lenin (Russian State) Library.
36. Slezkine, *House of Government,* 408.
37. Kuznetsov, "Rol' Stalina," 54.
38. "Panteon dlya Stalina i Lenin vïshe statui Svobodï: arkhitekturnïye planï SSSR, kotorïye mogli stat' realnost'yu," *Komsomol'skaya pravda,* March 31, 2020, ttps://www.kp.ru/russia/zametki-o-puteshestviyah/panteon-dlya-stalina-i-lenin-vyshe-statui-svobody/.

39. R. Khiger, "Dvorets Sovetov (na vïstavke predvaritel'nïkh proyektov)," *Izvestiya*, August 22, 1931, p. 4.

40. The Metro station in question ended up being called Kropotkinskaya, after the anarchist socialist Pyotr Kropotkin. It primarily serves the Museum of Fine Arts.

41. Tat'yana Anatol'yevna Platonova, "Kinofikatsiya Dvortsa Sovetov (1933–1941)," *Mir tekhniki kino* 13, no. 3 (2019): 40.

42. A. Shchusev, "Moskva blizhayshego budushego," *Izvestiya*, May 4, 1934, p. 3.

43. Boris Bazhanov, "Pobeg iz nochi. Iz vozpominaniy bïvshego sekretarya Stalina," *Kontinent*, no. 151 (2012), https://magazines.gorky.media/continent/2012/151/pobeg-iz-nochi.html.

44. "Arkhitektura Dvortsa Sovetov. Doklad tov. B. M. Iofana," *Pravda*, June 20, 1937, p. 4.

45. Maria Tumarkin, *Traumascapes: The Power and Fate of Places Transformed by Tragedy* (Melbourne, Australia: Penguin, 2005), loc. 47, Kindle.

46. The palace also appears in the movie *New Moscow* (*Novaya Moskva*, 1938), which was banned for its bittersweet recollection—in a time-traveling episode—of Old Moscow. See Hanin Hannouch, "The Trouble with Alexander Medvedkin: Ideological Errors in *New Moscow* (1938)," *Slovo* 28, no. 1 (Winter 2016): 21–38.

47. Danilo Udovički-Selb, "Between Modernism and Socialist Realism: Soviet Architectural Culture Under Stalin's Revolution from Above, 1928–1938," *Journal of the Society of Architectural Historians* 68, no. 4 (2009): 486.

48. Akinsha, Kozlov, and Hochfield, *Holy Place*, 139–41.

49. I. V. Stalin and Ya. Chadayev, "Postanovleniye Soveta Ministrov SSSR 'O stroitel'stve novogo zdaniya dlya Moskovskogo gosudarstvennogo universiteta.' 15 marta 1948 goda," Biblioteka Mikhaíla Grachyova, accessed June 11, 2024, https://grachev62.narod.ru/stalin/t18/t18_210.htm.

50. Tat'yana Tess, "Pod svetlïm nebom," *Izvestiya*, May 1, 1950, p. 2.

51. GARF f. R-9414, op. 1, d. 1363, ll. 5–7. The prosecutor general of the USSR authorized the "release" of 2,000 low-risk Gulag prisoners as "volunteer" construction workers. A total of 1,774 ended up being transferred from the camps to the Moscow State University construction site, where they worked "either until the end of their unserved sentence or the university was finished." The Construction Directorate used prisoners for the other Stalinist skyscraper projects.

52. Aleksandr Dobrovol'skiy, "Vïsotka na vïsote," *MKRU*, September 1, 2003, https://www.mk.ru/editions/daily/article/2003/09/01/127942-vyisotka-na-vyisote.html. Historian Anna Tsepkalova clarifies that the prison camp located inside the building had 368 people, of which 208 were women, all occupying the 23rd floor. They attended to the "interior decoration" of floors 24–30. Another 7,105 prisoners worked at lower levels of the construction site and lived in makeshift barracks (A. A. Tsepkalova, "Prinuditel'nïy trud v kontekste mobilizatsionnoy politiki: trudovoye ispol'zovaniye zaklyuchyonnïkh GULAGa na ob'yektakh kapstroitel'stva Glavpromstroya," 2009, hist.msu.ru, accessed June 28, 2024, https://www.hist.msu.ru/Departments/Inf/Asp/Cepkalova-Mbl.pdf). For a complete—as much as the accessible archival documents will allow—accounting of the use of Gulag

prisoners in postwar construction projects, see Tsepkalova, "Glavpromstroy v sisteme GULAGa: ekonomika prinuditel'nogo truda na 'Velikikh stroykakh kommunizma,'" 2008, hist.msu.ru, accessed June 20, 2024, https://www.hist.msu.ru/gulag/Articles/statya-ejegodnik-tsepkalova.htm.

53. Katherine Zubovich, *Moscow Monumental* (Princeton, NJ: Princeton University Press, 2021), 192, 204, 212–14.

54. D. Chechulin, "Krupneyshiy v Moskve otkrïtïy plavatel'nïy basseyn," *Arkhitektura i stroitel'stvo Moskvï,* no. 10 (1958): 24, 26.

55. Pilip Pilipich, "Iztoriya Dvortsa Sovetov v Moskve," LiveJournal, September 7, 2013, https://pilip-pilipich.livejournal.com/4932917.html.

56. Valeriy Burt, "Moskovskoye more ot Khrushchyova," Moslenta.ru, July 15, 2015, https://moslenta.ru/city/bassein.htm.

57. "Pochti po Chekhovu," *Krokodil,* no. 23 (August 29, 1960), p. 14. These lines are recited at the end of act 2 of Chekhov's play *Three Sisters* by Irina, the youngest of the three sisters, who is desperate to escape her provincial life for the big city. (Though, as Anne Lounsbery notes, Moscow is less an actual place than a symbol of a plush, plentiful life that the sisters could never attain. "'To Moscow, I Beg You!': Chekhov's Vision of the Russian Provinces," *Toronto Slavic Quarterly* 9 [Summer 2004], http://sites.utoronto.ca/tsq/09/lounsbery09.shtml.)

58. "Basseyn 'Moskva.' Korotkometrazhnïy fil'm, 1960 god," #MuzeyTsSDF, accessed July 9, 2023, https://csdfmuseum.ru/films/98-бассейн-москва.

59. O. Oparin, "Plyazhi v tsentre Moskvï," *Izvestiya,* July 16, 1960, p. 8.

60. My thanks to historian Jane Howlett for this detail.

61. Zelenin, *Izbrannïye trudï. Ocherki russkoy mifologii,* 141–48.

62. Mgsupgs, "Basseyn Moskva," LiveJournal, August 29, 1913, https://moya-moskva.livejournal.com/4125216.html.

63. Email communication with the author, August 13, 2023.

64. [Mariya Survillo], "Moskva iz babushkinskogo sunduka is at Metro Kropotkinskaya," Facebook, June 21, 2023, https://www.facebook.com/p/Москва-из-бабушкиного-сундука-100063868933254/.

65. Ol'ga Negnevitskaya, "Promïvka shpaler v GMII im. A. S. Pushkina," *Khronika muzeynïkh sobïtiy,* 2018, https://pushkinmuseum.art/data/epublication/chronic/11692_file_pdf.pdf.

66. Boris Sitko et al., "Khram vostannem, basseyn vzorvem," *Izvestiya,* January 29, 1994, p. 8.

67. Akinsha, Kozlov, and Hochfield, *Holy Place,* 158; Dmitriy Butkevich and Maksim Shevchenko, "Podrobnosti o glavnom khrame stranï," *Nezavisimaya gazeta,* December 20, 1999, https://www.ng.ru/art/1999-12-22/6_cathedral.html.

68. I make reference to Avery F. Gordon, *Ghostly Matters: Haunting and the Sociological Imagination* (Minneapolis: University of Minnesota Press, 1997), 23–24.

69. "Istoriya khrama Khrista Spasitelya: proyekt Drovtsa Sovetov i basseyn 'Moskva,'" stroi.mos.ru, accessed May 16, 2024, https://web.archive.org/web/2018022521 0332/.

70. Sergiyevskaya, "Strashnïye taynï."

71. Akinsha, Kozlov, and Hochfield, *Holy Place,* 159.

72. Tumarkin, *Traumascapes,* loc. 249.

73. Carol Rumens, "Pussy Riot's Punk Prayer Is Pure Protest Poetry," *Guardian,* August 20, 2012, https://www.theguardian.com/books/2012/aug/20/pussy-riot -punk-prayer-lyrics.

74. Yury Senin, "Moskva-ta! Basseyn 'Moskva,' 1976 god.," Facebook, July 11, 2021, https://www.facebook.com/groups/moskva.ta/.

75. Ibid.

CONCLUSION

1. Alexei Yurchak, *Everything Was Forever, Until It Was No More: The Last Soviet Generation* (Princeton, NJ: Princeton University Press, 2005).

2. See Roman Szporluk, *Russia, Ukraine, and the Breakup of the Soviet Union* (Stanford, CA: Hoover Institution Press, 2000).

3. He spent the night before the coup attempt drinking with friends. Nikita Petrov, "Kooperativ 'Lebedinoye ozero,'" *Novaya gazeta,* August 18, 2021, p. 2.

4. M. Berger, "Naruchniki dlya naroda," *Izvestiya,* August 26, 1991, p. 4. "Promising a happy life, frozen prices, ever increasing prosperity, the State Committee for the State of Emergency had prepared another, not as widely advertised gift for the people," the author writes about the order for handcuffs.

5. The coup plotters, aka the State Emergency Committee, ordered the chairman of the State Committee of Television and Radio Broadcasting, Leonid Kravchenko, to run the ballet on a loop. "Interv'yu Leonida Kravchenko 'Komsomol'skoy pravde,'" *Novoye russkoye slovo,* September 21–22, 1991, p. 1. It inadvertently became the swan song of the USSR.

6. Paul Gilbert, "How Yeltsin Justified the Demolition of the Ipatiev House," tsarnicholas.org, February 25, 2020, https://tsarnicholas.org/2020/02/25/how -yeltsin-justified-the-demolition-of-the-ipatiev-house/.

7. Louise Shelley, "Privatization and Crime: The Post-Soviet Experience," National Council for Soviet and East European Research, August 10, 1995, https://journals .sagepub.com/doi/epdf/10.1177/104398629501100405.

8. Sciences Po, "Inside Russia with Ekaterina Schulmann," YouTube video, 28:33, May 8, 2023, https://www.youtube.com/watch?v=9_0E9IzXT34.

9. Andrew Osborn and Andrey Ostroukh, "Putin Rues Soviet Collapse as Demise of 'Historical Russia,'" Reuters, December 12, 2021, https://www.reuters.com/world/ europe/putin-rues-soviet-collapse-demise-historical-russia-2021-12-12/.

10. Steven Lee Myers, *The New Tsar: The Rise and Reign of Vladimir Putin* (New York: Alfred A. Knopf, 2015), 49–50.

11. Leon Aron, "Putin Decides That Stalin's Victims Were Guilty After All," *Atlantic,* December 5, 2024, https://www.theatlantic.com/international/archive/2024/ 12/putin-stalin-prisoners-ukraine/680874/.

12. December 2, 2016, and November 16, 2018, at the Mariinsky Theater in St. Petersburg.

13. Elizaveta Antonova, "Hacked Emails Reveal Intelligence Agent's Harassment of Theater Luminaries and Infiltration of Russia's Performing Arts Industry," Meduza .io, April 12, 2024, https://meduza.io/en/feature/2024/04/12/hacked-emails -reveal-intelligence-agent-s-harassment-of-theater-luminaries-and-infiltration-of -russia-s-performing-arts-industry; "Russia's Sber confirms list of over 250 books removed from online marketplace due to 'LGBT propaganda' law, including works by Dostoevsky and Stephen King," Meduza.io, February 21, 2024, https:// meduza.io/en/news/2024/02/21/russia-s-sber-confirms-list-of-over-250-books -removed-from-online-marketplace-due-to-lgbt-propaganda-law-including-works -by-dostoevsky-and-stephen-king.

14. Sciences Po, "Inside Russia," 29:00.

15. Tat'yana Grigor'yeva, "Pochemu Patriarshiye prudï tak nazïvayutsya?," kul'tura.rf, accessed April 29, 2024, https://www.culture.ru/s/vopros/patriarshie-prudy/.

16. Dmitriy Sokolov, "Patriarshiye prudï: roskosh' staroy Moskvï," snob.ru, June 20, 2022, https://snob.ru/how-to-live/patriarshie-prudy-roskosh-staroj-moskvy/.

17. Aleksey Shchukin, "Moskva po sobyaninski: aziatskiy gorod s arkhitekturnïmi dominantami i fasadami," Monokl', May 20, 2024, https://monocle.ru/monocle/2024/ 21/moskva-po-sobyaninski-aziatskiy-gorod-s-arkhitekturnymi-dominantami -i-fasadami/.

18. "V Moskve startuyet kompleksnaya rekonstruktsiya parka Gorkogo," Moskovskaya perspektiva, April 17, 2024, https://mperspektiva.ru/topics/v-moskve-startuet -kompleksnaya-rekonstruktsiya-parka-gorkogo-/; Igor' Karev, "TsPKiO ne khvatayet belok i drugikh posetiteley," *gazeta.ru*, May 23, 2011, https://www.gazeta.ru/ culture/2011/05/23/a_3626277.shtml; Fyodor Kiryukhin, "Otdïkhayem. Yesli voskresnet Gerbert Uells," *Moskovskaya pravda,* August, 7, 2000, p. 5.

19. "Imperskaya formula prinyata ofitsial'no: Rossiya nigde ne zakanchivayetsya," February 24, 2023, Meduza.io, https://meduza.io/feature/2023/02/24/imperskaya -formula-prinyata-ofitsialno-rossiya-nigde-ne-zakanchivaetsya.

20. Shaun Walker, "From One Vladimir to Another: Putin Unveils Huge Statue in Moscow," *Guardian,* November 4, 2016, https://www.theguardian.com/world/2016/ nov/04/vladimir-great-statue-unveiled-putin-moscow.

21. "Pochemu Bïkov i Akunin kupilis' za rozïgrïsh?," stringer, December 16, 2023, https://stringer-news.com/publication.mhtml?Part=46&PubID=46722.

22. Boris Akunin, *Auto-Graph: Russian Political Prisoners Answer 13 Questions from Boris Akunin,* vol. 2, trans. Joanne Turnbull with Nikolai Formozov (self-pub., Best Authors Bookshop, 2024), 47, 49.

23. Information in this paragraph is from Caryl Emerson, "Philosophy as Novelistic Fiction in the Work of Two Old Friends: Mikhail Epstein and Vladimir Sharov," *Studies in East European Thought* 76, no. 4 (2024): 686–87.

24. Vladimir Sharov, *Staraya devochka* (Moscow: AST, 2013).

25. Or, as the devil says in Mikhaíl Bulgakov's novel *The Master and Margarita,* unfinished at the time of the writer's death in 1940 and first published in 1967: "Manuscripts don't burn."

INDEX

small-circulation journals of, 275
as visionaries, 272

Tale of Batu's Capture of Ryazan, 42–43
Tale of the Invasion of Tokhtamïsh, 64
Tanya (guide), 5–6, 390
Tarasov, Lev (Henri Troyat), *Daily Life in Russia Under the Last Tsar*, 247
Tarkovsky, Andrey, 69–70
  Andrey Rublyov (film), 333
Tatars, 36, 53, 140
  Ivan III and Crimean khan, 81–82
  Ivan IV's campaigns against, 104–5
  Mongol Empire and, 72
  plague and, 58–59
  raids on Moscow, 72, 75, 97
  Russian war with the Crimean Tatars, 162
Tatarstan, 36–37
Tatishchev, Afanasiy, 183
Tatishchev, Alexei, 183, 194–95
Tatishchev, Vasiliy, 31–32, 60, 141, 409n77
  History of the Russian State, 417n26
Taube, Johann, 106
Tchaikovsky, Anatole, 272
Tchaikovsky, Peter
  Bolshoi Theater and, 237–38
  death of, 263
  1812 Overture, 156, 372
  The Oprichnik, 238
  portends the end of the Romanovs, 242
  The Queen of Spades, 242
  The Sleeping Beauty, 152
  Swan Lake, 391, 479n5
  The Voyevoda, 237–38
Theophanes the Greek, 68–69
Thevet, André, 36
Thon, Konstantin, 370–71
Timur the Lame, 63
Tisyatskaya kniga (Thousand Book), 101
Titov, Vasiliy, 347
Tokhtamïsh, 63–64, 65, 77

Tolbuzin, Semyon, 85, 86
Tolstoy, Leo, 218
  "On the Census in Moscow," 287
  granddaughter Tanya's diary (1917), 295
  Khamovniki home, now a museum, 287
  Resurrection, 267
  War and Peace, 200, 215–16, 229–30, 278
Trinity Chronicle, 65–66
  "Legend of the Grand Princess Eudoxia," 66
Trinity Sunday fire (1737), 187–88
Trotsky, Leon, 300, 308, 321, 373
Truth About the Moscow Fire, The (Rostopchin), 217, 449–50n48
Tsoi, Viktor, 267
Tsvetayeva, Marina, 272
Tuchman, Barbara W., 405n25
Turgenev, Ivan, 324
  Home of the Gentry, 267
Tutolmin, Ivan, 215
Tver (city), 49–50, 54, 62, 99
  strife with Moscow, 51, 54, 56, 78, 86
Twelve, The (Blok), 272
Tyutchev, Fyodor, 235, 271

Uglich (town), 126
  death of Dmitri and investigation, 126–27
  Dmitri's tomb and exhumation, 135
  pardon of the bell, 127, 433n40
  rebellion and hanging of the mayor, 127
Ukraine
  national symbol of, 28
  as original Soviet republic, 19
  part of the Russian Empire, 19
  pogroms of 1881–84 and 1903–06, 265
  Polish-Lithuanian Commonwealth domination and Tsar Alexei's war, 156–57

ILLUSTRATION CREDITS